# EVERYTHING YOU NEED TO KNOW
## BUT HAVE NEVER BEEN TOLD

DavidIcke
BOOKS

First published in November 2017.

**Ickonic Enterprises Ltd.**
**1a Babington Lane,**
**Derby**
**DE1 1SU**
**UK**

*Tel/fax:* +44 (0) 1983 566002
*email:* info@davidickebooks.co.uk

*Cover Design:* Gareth Icke

**British Library Cataloguing-in
Publication Data**
A catalogue record for this book is
available from the British Library

ISBN 978-1-5272-0726-4

# EVERYTHING YOU NEED TO KNOW

## BUT HAVE NEVER BEEN TOLD

## DAVID ICKE

## Dedication:

*To Jaymie and Gareth for their brilliant work in support of what I do.*

*To experience – what I have liked and what I have not liked. It all leads to wisdom if we allow it to.*

# Other books and DVDs by David Icke

## Books

Phantom Self

The Perception Deception

Remember Who You Are

Human Race Get Off Your *Knees* - The Lion Sleeps No More

The David Icke Guide to the Global Conspiracy (and how to end it)

Infinite Love is the Only Truth, *Everything* Else is Illusion

Tales from the Time Loop

Alice in Wonderland and the World Trade Center Disaster

Children Of The Matrix

The Biggest Secret

I Am Me • I Am Free

… And The Truth Shall Set You Free – 21st century edition

Lifting The Veil

The Robots' Rebellion

Heal the World

Truth Vibrations

It Doesn't Have To Be Like This

## DVDs

Worldwide Wake-Up Tour Live

David Icke Live at Wembley Arena

The Lion Sleeps No More

Beyond the Cutting Edge – Exposing the Dreamworld We Believe to be Real

Freedom or Fascism: the Time to Choose

Secrets of the Matrix

From Prison to Paradise

Turning Of The Tide

The Freedom Road

Revelations Of A Mother Goddess

Speaking Out

The Reptilian Agenda

*Details of availability at the back of this book*
*and through the website* **www.davidicke.com**

# Contents

*I've looked at life from both sides now*
*From up and down and still somehow*
*It's life's illusions I recall*
*I really don't know life at all*
**Joni Mitchell**


*And now I understand what you tried to say to me*
*How you suffered for your sanity*
*How you tried to set them free*
*They would not listen*
*They did not know how*
*Perhaps they'll listen now*
**Don McLean**

## Pity the nation ...

Pity the nation whose people are sheep, and whose shepherds mislead them. Pity the nation whose leaders are liars, whose sages are silenced, and whose bigots haunt the airwaves. Pity the nation that raises not its voice, except to praise conquerors and acclaim the bully as hero and aims to rule the world with force and by torture. Pity the nation that knows no other language but its own and no other culture but its own. Pity the nation whose breath is money and sleeps the sleep of the too well fed. Pity the nation – oh, pity the people who allow their rights to erode and their freedoms to be washed away. My country, tears of thee, sweet land of liberty.

**Lawrence Ferlinghetti**

No society wants you to become wise: it is against the investment of all societies. If people are wise they cannot be exploited. If they are intelligent they cannot be subjugated, they cannot be forced into a mechanical life, to live like robots. They will assert their individuality. They will have the fragrance of rebellion around them. They will like to live in freedom. Freedom comes with wisdom, intrinsically. They are inseparable, and no society wants people to be free.

The communist society, the fascist society, the capitalist society, the Hindu, the Mohammedan, the Christian – no society – would like people to use their own intelligence because the moment they start using their intelligence they become dangerous – dangerous to the Establishment, dangerous to the people who are in power, dangerous to the 'haves'; dangerous to all kinds of oppression, exploitation, suppression; dangerous to the churches, dangerous to the states, dangerous to the nations. In fact, a wise man is afire, alive, aflame. But he cannot sell his life, he cannot serve them. He would like rather to die than to be enslaved.

**Osho**

## Title Definition

I want to make it clear before we start what the title represents. *Everything You Need To Know, But Have Never Been Told* does not refer to all that people need to know in terms of information and knowledge.

How could you put that between two covers? Religious books claim to do this but they are works of self-delusion and perceptual imprisonment.

*Everything You Need To Know* in this case refers to the information necessary to open entirely new ways of thinking and perceiving reality, both in the seen and unseen, from which everything else will come.

This book is a start not a finish.

It is written in layers with information placed upon information that together reveals the picture by connecting the parts. The parts are fascinating, but the picture is devastating.

Prepare for a perception reboot ...

# On The Road To 'Now'

*'Your assumptions are your windows on the world. Scrub them off every once in a while, or the light won't come in'* – **Issac Asimov**

I am closing in on 30 years since I was first dubbed the maddest man in Britain and most other places come to that. Newspaper headlines delighted in my alleged madness and I was a comedian's dream. Mention of my name was enough to get a laugh with no joke necessary. I *was* the joke.

But, as it turns out, *they* were the joke all along.

They didn't know (and neither did I) that what they perceived as madness was a mind emerging from the *collective* madness which is called normality ... the madness that masquerades as sanity ... the coma-sleep that believes it is wide awake. There are none so enslaved as those who wrongly believe they are free, and none so crazy as those who wrongly believe they are sane. Today as truly intelligent people look in my direction from literally all over the world it can safely be said that rumours of my madness were greatly exaggerated. For what is the perception of madness, but the perceiver's perception of sanity? What is that perception, but what collective society has decreed sanity to be? And what is that collective society, but they who control, influence and police opinion to manipulate the norms that they then decree? Sanity and insanity are defined by perception and not necessarily by reality. Human history is awash with those dubbed mad and dangerous who were to be feted as 'ahead of their time' often long after they had passed. Perceptions of sanity and insanity are not even static and they change as knowledge moves on. Tell a caveman that it's possible to fly to the Moon and he would call you crazy. Tell someone today that it's *not* possible and they will say the same. It is an extraordinary and incredibly debilitating human trait this cognitive dissonance between what we call 'past' and 'present'. People are so willing to mock and condemn those long gone who ridiculed or even murdered the visionaries who could see *then* what is *now* considered to be obvious. But the same people are so *un*willing to acknowledge how they themselves react the same way today to those who see the world differently to them and the norms that mould and solidify their sense of reality. Minds that genuinely seek understanding come from the immoveable foundation that they don't know it all. They are humble and wise enough to realise that humanity knows an almost incomprehensibly small fraction of what there is to know. Thus their minds are open at all times to all possibility. I don't mean only the possibilities that never challenge and expose ingrained religious, cultural, scientific and societal beliefs; I mean *all* possibility with none excluded. To consider all possibility and not only belief-system possibility is, to much of humanity, like garlic to a vampire. Unyielding perceptions are recycled and confirmed by sheer unquestioned repetition. While newspaper headlines told the world of my madness I was, ironically, becoming sane. Amid historic levels of ridicule and abuse that I faced in the 1990s I was walking into the light of freedom – real freedom – where I could think the unthinkable and say the unsayable and not give damn what people made of it. How many allow themselves that priceless gift? And yet it is there for the taking whenever they choose. If I can do it, so can everyone. Chinese philosopher Lao Tzu said: 'Care about people's approval and you will be their prisoner.'

I was born in Leicester, England, on April 29th 1952 and grew up on a council estate in a very different world to the one we see today. There was no Internet, computers, smart phones or tablets and only one television channel until I was three – not that we could afford a TV until years later or even needed one. We had next to no money but I never felt deprived. You made your own fun and followed your own interests. They weren't delivered through a TV screen or the latest app. Life was simpler then and you had more time to think, ponder and daydream (my default state). I can now see patterns in my life, with the perspective of hindsight, that were guiding me through the maze since childhood, but at the time they appeared to be only random events, successes and failures. I see them very differently today. Football (soccer) was my passion as a kid (and steam trains) and I set out to be a professional footballer. A series of coincidences and 'bits of luck' gave me that chance and all was going well until rheumatoid arthritis ended my career at age 21. Arthritis first appeared when I was 15, just six months into my career as a goalkeeper with Coventry City, and became progressively worse affecting more joints. I played in pain for years before it became too much. My second choice of career had always been journalism and that's where I headed next. I set my sights on being a television presenter with the BBC sports department – although given my circumstances I was told this would be almost impossible (as many had said about professional football). I had left school at 15 to join Coventry and had no

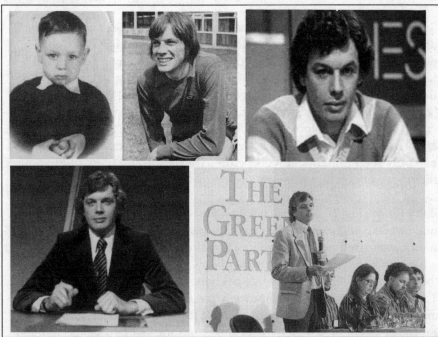

**Figure 1:** My life seemed to be a series of random events until the recurring pattern became hard to deny.

educational qualifications let alone a university degree. I was advised that getting into journalism would therefore be very difficult. But the pattern repeated itself with more coincidences and 'bits of luck' that led me into newspapers, radio, regional television and eventually to be a national television presenter with BBC Sport. The pattern was never more obviously at work than when I joined the British Green Party as a member of a local group that I started on the Isle of Wight where I live off the south coast of England. Within *weeks*, through more coincidences and inexplicable happenings, I had been elected a national 'speaker' representing the party's views in the media. It was now that the patterns in my life of setting a goal and then doors synchronistically opening and closing to achieve that goal could no longer be denied. What was going on? I had no idea (Fig 1).

By the late 1980s I had tired of the television world which I found vacuous and full of its own self-importance. This phase was thankfully coming to an end with my life about to change dramatically. I began to have strange experiences at the turn of 1989 in the sense that when I was alone in a room there always seemed to be someone or something there. A presence, I guess you would call it. The feeling became stronger and the presence ever more tangible throughout the year until I had to address it. I was sitting on a bed in a London hotel room in early 1990 while still working for the BBC. The presence was so obvious that I said:

'If there is anybody here, will you please contact me because you are driving me up the wall!' A few days later I was in an Isle of Wight newspaper shop with my then young son, Gareth, when suddenly I found myself unable to move my feet. It was like magnets were pulling them to the floor. As I was trying to understand what was happening a 'voice', actually a very strong thought-form, passed through my mind which said: 'Go and look at the books on the far side.' My feet 'unfroze' and I walked in a bewildered daze towards the little book stand where I had only seen romantic novels before. They were still there but in among them was a book that took my eye because it was so different. It was called *Mind to Mind* and written by a professional psychic medium, Betty Shine (Fig 2). As soon as I saw the word 'psychic' I wondered if maybe she could explain the presence I was feeling. I read the book in 24 hours, contacted her and made an appointment. I told her nothing about what was happening to me and said only that I wanted to see if her 'hands-on healing' (an exchange of energy) would help my arthritis. This was of secondary importance to me, however. Would she pick up anything around me that could account for what had been happening for the last year? I saw Betty four times and the last two visits changed my life forever. I was lying on a medical-type bench on visit three, while she was treating my left knee, when I felt something like a spider's web on my face. I remembered how she described in her book having this same feeling when other dimensions of reality were preparing to communicate. Psychic or inter-reality connections are made at one level electromagnetically and my 'spider's web' was electromagnetic energy of the kind that makes the hair on your neck and arms stand up among an excited crowd or in a haunted house. I didn't mention the 'web' that I was feeling but a few seconds later Betty Shine pushed her head back and said: 'Wow! This is powerful. I'll have to close my eyes for this one.' She said she was seeing a figure in her mind that was asking to communicate with me. 'They' knew that I wanted them to contact me, but the time wasn't right, Betty told me, although she knew nothing of what had happened in the London hotel room. She began to repeat the words that were given to her:

- *He is a healer who is here to heal the Earth and he will be world famous.*
- *He is still a child spiritually, but he will be given the spiritual riches.*
- *Sometimes he will say things and wonder where they came from. They will be our words.*

**Figure 2:** Betty Shine.

- *Knowledge will be put into his mind, and at other times he will be led to knowledge.*
- *He was chosen as a youngster for his courage. He has been tested and has passed all the tests.*
- *He was led into football to learn discipline, but when that was learned it was time to move on. He also had to learn how to cope with disappointment, experience all the emotions, and how to get up and get on with it. The spiritual way is tough and no one makes it easy.*
- *He will always have what he needs* [this could have been 'wants'], *but no more.*
- *He will face enormous opposition, but we will always be there to protect him.*

A week later I returned for my last visit and more information was given to me in the same way:

- *One man cannot change the world, but one man can communicate the message that will change the world.*
- *Don't try to do it all alone. Go hand in hand with others, so you can pick each other up as you fall.*
- *He will write five books in three years* [I did].
- *Politics is not for him. He is too spiritual. Politics is anti-spiritual and will make him very unhappy* [it did].
- *He will leave politics. He doesn't have to do anything. It will happen gradually over a year* [it did].
- *There will be a different kind of flying machine, very different from the aircraft of today.*
- *Time will have no meaning. Where you want to be, you will be.*

I met another medium soon after the last meeting with Betty Shine who gave me similar information, which included:

*Arduous seeking is not necessary. The path is already mapped out. You only have to follow the clues ... We are guiding you along a set path. It was all arranged before you incarnated.*

The point about following the clues is exactly what has happened. Yet another series of coincidences led me to Peru in early 1991. My amazing visit over the best part of three weeks – with countless more coincidences and synchronicities – culminated on a hillside overlooking the ancient ruins of Sillustani, 13,000 feet above sea level in the Andes near the city of Puno on the shores of Lake Titicaca. I had spent an hour walking around the ruins admiring the stunning landscape and then headed back to Puno in a mini-bus taxi with the driver and a Peruvian guide. A short distance down the road I was daydreaming (as usual) and gazing at a hill to my right when the words 'come to me, come to me, come to me' began repeating in my mind. I asked the driver to stop and strong intuition told me that I needed to climb the hill. I said I would be back shortly, but I was more than an hour because of what happened. I stopped among some large stones that were no longer there on my return in 2012. My feet began to feel as they did in the newspaper shop, magnetically sucked to the spot, although this time with far greater power. I felt a drill-like sensation on the top of my head and then a flow of energy from my head through my body to my feet and into the ground. Another flow came the other way. My arms stretched out at 45 degrees towards the sky when I had made no conscious decision to do so. Then a 'voice' or very clear thought passed through my mind which said: 'It will be over when you feel the rain.' This sounded utterly crazy as I stood under a cloudless Peruvian sky and a ferociously hot sun. The energy passing through my body with my arms still in the air became so strong that I was shaking, as if subjected to an ongoing electrical shock (Fig 3). I would move in and out of conscious awareness with my focus disappearing 'out there' and then returning. During one of the conscious moments I saw a light grey mist over the mountains way in the distance and very quickly the mist became darker. Blimey, I thought, it is *raining* over there. The storm came out of the mountains towards me in a ridiculously short time and I watched in some shock as a deluge of stair-rod rain swept across the land in front of me. By now my body was really shaking from the impact of the energy passing through me until *wham* the rain hit me and I was drenched in an instant. With that the energy stopped and I was standing there with jelly legs and my shoulders were agony after almost an hour stretched out above my head. I felt nothing when it was all going on, but my god I did now. I had no idea what had happened, but the consequences were soon on public display.

**Figure 3:** Recreating my Sillustani experience on a return visit in 2012.

I returned to Britain with information and concepts pouring into my conscious mind as if a bubble or dam had burst and the Universe and his mate were coming in. My brain basically froze for three months in the way that a computer freezes when asked to process too much data at the same time. I went on prime-time television still in freeze-mode trying to

understand what was happening to me and that interview triggered
levels of mass ridicule that few can have experienced. I saw very clearly
– and constantly – that those who ridicule others are always the most
ignorant and stupid. Big mouths and empty brains obviously come as a
pair. I couldn't go anywhere without being laughed at and ridiculed and
every bridge to my old life was ablaze. I can't say that it wasn't difficult
in the extreme but you could have offered to take everything away and
plant me back where I was before – throw a million in the bank for luck
– and I would still have turned you down. Everything before me said
that I had destroyed myself, but something deep within me knew this
was going somewhere even if I had no idea exactly where. For three
months after Peru I lived my life in a bewildered daze like someone
dropped into a strange alien world without a map or compass. Then
over a few days everything began to unfreeze. I was 'David' again, but
not really. To those who knew me I appeared to be the same man I had
been before the 'funny time'. This may have been true outwardly, but I
was not seeing the same world that I had before Peru. My mind had
been opened and I saw reality in a very different way. Before Peru I had
seen dots, now I saw pictures and how everything connected. My
experience has been that life gives you your greatest gifts brilliantly
disguised as your worst nightmare and so it was with the mass and
incessant ridicule that set me free of the prison that most people live in –
the fear of what other people think. This was so essential for what was to
come with the communication of information way beyond the norms of
human society which continues to this day. From this post-Peru period
especially, my life became an incredible synchronistic adventure as
information would come to me in the form of people, books, documents
and personal experience. It was like some unseen force was handing me
pieces in a puzzle, and that quote from 1990 captures the theme
perfectly:

*Arduous seeking is not necessary. The path is already mapped out. You only
have to follow the clues ... We are guiding you along a set path. It was all
arranged before you incarnated.*

Information communicated through Betty Shine proved just as
accurate: 'Sometimes he will say things and wonder where they came
from ... They will be our words ... Knowledge will be put into his mind,
and at other times he will be led to knowledge.' This is precisely what
has happened since 1990 as I have delved ever deeper into the rabbit
hole of human control and manipulation. The information has even
come in an order that made it easiest to comprehend, and there has been
*so much* to comprehend across a great swathe of subjects that appear on
the surface not to be connected but fundamentally are. For the first few

years the focus was largely on a network of global families manipulating events and enforcing their will on human society. From the mid-to-late 1990s revelations about a non-human dimension to this network were given to me, and since the early 2000s the theme has been the illusory nature of physical reality and ever more detail about the world we think we live 'in', but don't. Each stage has taken the same pattern. First the new theme would emerge followed by information from all directions relating to that theme as if someone had pressed a button. As each new stage begins the previous ones still continue and this has demanded the processing and fitting together of phenomenal amounts of information across a whole spectrum of subjects both ancient and modern. Day after day, year after year I have walked out of my little office in the early evening with my brain aching and begging for mercy, but the older I have got and the more I have done it the easier the processing has become.

I hope that I stand as living proof to people that no matter what is thrown at you over whatever period you cannot be stopped unless you stop *yourself*. YOU have the power over your life and you simply have to take it back from those you *think* have the power. The human power/no power dynamic is just a confidence trick – a mind game – and we need to see through the illusion that humanity believes to be so real. If you refuse to give up, feel sorry for yourself and run away, you will get somewhere. You have to. Amid all the ridicule and abuse I have written a stream of books which are read all over the world and I have talked to ever-bigger audiences all over the world. What happened to that nutter we said had gone mad? How come so many are now listening to what he says? What, why, how come? *I didn't quit and I never will* – that's how come. The mainstream media locked away in their time-warp still portray me as the man who existed for just three months nearly 30 years ago and the same is the case with those who get their views and opinions from that media. The truth is very different as anyone new to my work is about to find out.

Why do we live on such a Planet of Tears when life could be and should be so wonderful? There is an answer ... and here it is ...

# CHAPTER ONE

# The Biggest Need-To-Know

*The world is full of people who have never, since childhood, met an open doorway with an open mind – E. B. White*

Once upon a no-time, in a 'land' called Forever, there was only Awareness in awareness of itself – all-possibility and all-potential waiting to manifest. There was no form, only the potential *imagination* of form of every possible kind. This was the infinite state of pure awareness from which all that we think we 'see' has ultimately come.

That opening paragraph captures so many common themes encoded in the narratives and symbolism of religion and the myths, legends and accounts of native and ancient peoples the world over. They further include the story of how a negative or 'evil' force emerged to challenge the omnipotence of the original creative force. From this appeared the universal theme of 'God' v 'The Devil' or 'Satan' and endless other names awarded to this source of chaos, upheaval and manipulation. Most people can't see the commonalities amid the apparent confusion of different religions, names, cultures and emphasis; but if you can see past the differing detail the same basic story is in plain sight. This is only possible, however, if you can expand perception beyond the 'dots' and see themes and connections that then come clearly into view. Followers and advocates of religions and storytellers among native peoples continue to use the language of the ancient originators, and this can obscure the fact that what is being described can today be expressed in the language of science and computation. They will talk of 'the Father' and 'the Son', for example, when these were only the terms used to describe massive (though ultimately simple) concepts in a way that those of the time could grasp. What is the point of talking about quantum physics and quantum computers to people still knocking rocks together? Storytellers and carriers of the knowledge obviously used contemporary terms and symbols to get their point across and this was true of all religions and forms of worship. That was fine and essential then but the narrative needs to move on. Knowledge of the hidden realms of quantum mechanics and so much else has expanded dramatically while religions and native peoples (with honourable exceptions) continue to use the language of another age. An update is urgently required and that is one aim of this book. We will see that:

**1.** Themes of religions and native cultures are *basically* correct, emphasis often on the *basically*.
**2.** Most accounts have become so inverted and distorted from the original that billions today are following and worshipping the very opposite of what they think they are.
**3.** We should not be worshipping anybody or anything when *we* are the anybody/everybody and anything/everything.

    To show this to be true requires a total re-evaluation of what we call 'reality' – the 'world' we *think* we 'see' and with which we *think* we daily interact. I have called this opening chapter 'The Biggest Need-To-Know' because without this knowledge nothing else can make any sense, and its suppression has ensured that generation after generation in culture upon culture complete entire lifetimes while never answering the basic questions of: Who am I? Where am I? What am I doing here? There is a

fundamental secret behind why the answers have been kept from us and when that veil is lifted human society, ancient and modern, morphs into crystal clarity ... it is indeed a case of *Everything You Need To Know, But Have Never Been Told*. Systematically-imposed ignorance entraps humanity in perceptual servitude and allows the

**Figure 4:** 'Who am I? Where am I?'

tiny few to control the very many (Fig 4). If we are to free ourselves from this tyranny the veil of perceptual illusion must first be lifted.

## Reality check

The scale of illusion is staggering. Ask all but a relative few if they live in a solid, 'physical' world and they will look at you in blank bewilderment for even posing the question. 'Of course we do – don't be silly.' But actually – we *don't*. No, we *don't*. Consider that for a moment. Every morning we experience our solid body getting out of a solid bed to eat our solid breakfast and head through solid streets in solid vehicles to go to solid work or solid wherever. But all the time, *there is no solid*. As illusions go, they don't get any more extreme. I chuckle when I hear the fake news mainstream media dismissing other versions of events as 'conspiracy theories' and 'too far-fetched to believe' while reporting the world from the perspective that everything is solid when it isn't. The self-delusion is monumental because so is the scale of perception programming. I have been labelled mad and insane for nearly 30 years by mainstream society – especially the media – on the basis of that very self-delusion. Many of the things I say are happening would not be possible if reality was physical and solid, but it's not. Those who dismiss and ridicule what I say are coming from a perception of solidity and have no idea what the world really is. Hardly surprising, then, that they say I'm crazy. We are told that our solid, material reality is made of atoms and that everything is solid and physical because of them. But, hold on. Atoms have no solidity and so cannot a solid world make (Fig 5). Atoms are said to have a nucleus orbited by electrons in a relationship akin to mini-solar systems and everything else is 'empty space'. How can this make a solid world? I contend that the nucleus and electrons have no solidity either and that even *their* material existence is illusory although quantum physics gives them marginal materiality. Here's a quote to put that 'marginal' into context:

> *If the nucleus were the size of a peanut, the atom would be about the size of a baseball stadium. If we lost all the dead space inside our atoms, we would each be able to fit into a particle of dust, and the entire human race would fit into the volume of a sugar cube.*

Makes that racism deal look a bit ridiculous, eh? Quantum physics says that 99.9999999% (and more) of what is called 'ordinary matter' is empty space. In fact, space (another illusion) is not actually empty but bursting with energy that we can't see. There is 'space' (energy) that we can 'see' and we call this reality; and there is 'space' (energy) that we cannot see and we call this 'empty'. Human sight is verging on the blind when you compare what we can see with what we can't see. Almost the entirety of infinite existence is denied to us while we are perceptually-enslaved in a tiny band of frequency that

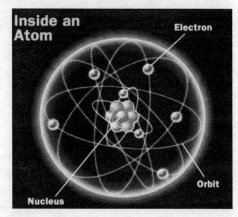

**Figure 5:** How can atoms with no solidity create a solid world?

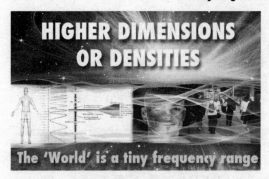

Figure 6: Our world is only a band of frequency.

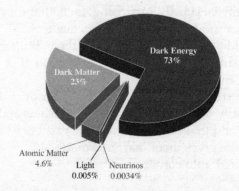

Figure 7: All we can 'see' is a sliver of the 0.005 percent.

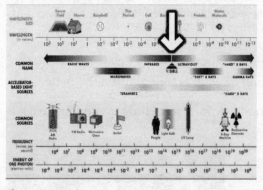

Figure 8: 'Home'.

science calls 'visible light' (Fig 6). The electromagnetic spectrum is only 0.005 percent of what exists in the Universe in terms of energy and what is referred to as 'matter' (Fig 7). Some say it's a bit more, but not much. Think about that – just *0.005* percent. Now contemplate this: humans can only see a tiny fraction of that 0.005 percent in the band of visible light (Fig 8). Most of the rest is called 'dark energy' and 'dark matter' by mainstream physics. I don't buy their version of what this 'dark' really is and I use the term only in the sense of it being unseen by human sight senses. People say that this or that is not possible and this or that is crazy while virtually 100 percent of what exists in infinite forever is not visible to them. A little humility is urgently required. Given that mainstream 'science' – quantum physics apart – will largely not explore beyond the seen and what is considered to be the 'tangible' it becomes clear why its concrete

conclusions have proved to be so inaccurate and often ridiculous. Yet this same 'science' is perceived and promoted today by its bewildered advocates and believers as the arbiter of all knowledge. This is extraordinary on the face of it, but then not so much when you see the whys and wherefores of the global perception deception. The illusion is so deep that we have never even touched anything in the way that we think we have. Oh, but you are holding a book, right? No, you are holding an electromagnetic field of information (the book) with electromagnetic fields of information (your hands). The experience of 'touch' is the connection between different electromagnetic fields. The experience of apparent solidity is really electromagnetic resistance between energetic fields of different frequencies or densities. You who are not solid can't walk through a wall which is not solid because of electromagnetic resistance and not physical resistance because there is no physical. This all sounds so fantastic and unbelievable to the human conscious mind, but it's true. We don't hear anything until the brain has decoded electrical communications from our ears. The ears don't hear – the brain does. The same applies with sight, taste and smell. A falling tree makes no noise unless someone is there to decode vibrational disturbances triggered in the air into electrical signals that the brain then decodes into the sound we recognise as a falling tree. Otherwise the tree falls in silence. We hear human speech only when vibrational information fields generated by the vocal chords are decoded by the brain. Modern pain-relief techniques involve blocking messages from the point of pain from reaching the brain because until that communication is made you can feel no discomfort. It's the brain that says 'ouch', not the point of impact. The entire world that we think we see, in the form that we think we see it, only exists in a few cubic centimetres at the back of the brain where visual reality is decoded. Remember that human society is founded on the 'physical' world being 'real', tangible and solid, and this delusion is driving the perceptions and decisions of politics, medicine, media, corporations and science (quantum physics apart) – the whole shebang in fact. Everything is based on the most basic misunderstanding of our very reality and in the shadows beyond the realm of the seen this is all by design. Those at the cutting edge of mainstream science are proving experimentally that 'physicality' is an illusion as genuine scientists and seekers of truth break free from Stone Age orthodoxy. Here's a telling quote from artist and filmmaker, Sergio Toporek:

> Consider that you can see less than 1% of the electromagnetic spectrum and hear less than 1% of the acoustic spectrum. 90% of the cells in your body carry their own microbial DNA and are not 'you'. The atoms in your body are 99.9999999999999999% empty space and none of them are the ones you were born with ... Human beings have 46 chromosomes, two less than a potato.
>
> The existence of the rainbow depends on the conical photoreceptors in your eyes; to animals without cones, the rainbow does not exist. So you don't just look at a rainbow, you create it. This is pretty amazing, especially considering that all the beautiful colours you see represent less than 1% of the electromagnetic spectrum.

And this is from science magazine, *Wonderpedia*:

*Every second, 11 million sensations crackle along these* [brain] *pathways ... The brain is confronted with an alarming array of images, sounds and smells which it rigorously filters down until it is left with a manageable list of around 40. Thus 40 sensations per second make up what we perceive as reality.*

We should let that sink in for a moment. Our reality which seems so 'real' is constructed every second from 40 snapshots of information ('sensations') from a potential *11 million*. The other 10,900,060 are absorbed by our subconscious mind while we remain consciously oblivious of their existence. Quantum physics explores the hidden realms beyond the 'seen' and has demolished the material, solid, clockwork model of reality pedalled for so long by mainstream science. Cutting edge quantum physicists have more in common in their explanation of reality with ancient seers and shamans than their conventional colleagues in closet-minded academia. Quantum physics to the 'scientific' mainstream is at best an irritant and at worse a catastrophe to their world-is-solid mind-set which dominates and infests the institutions of human society. So much so that even with quantum revelations about illusory physicality the rest of science largely cracks on as if nothing has changed. Oh, but it *has* – and fundamentally. Scientific orthodoxy is either being left behind and becoming an irrelevance or being forced in an act of survival to think the previously unthinkable – that they were wrong all along and have caused generations galore to be equally wrong by falling for the trap that because people have passed exams and have letters after their names they must, by definition, know what they are talking about. History constantly tells us otherwise. Terms like 'professor' and 'teacher' are titles awarded by the state for serving the belief-system of the state. They are not a confirmation of intelligence and certainly not of awareness beyond intellectual myopia and the download of academic convention. That is not to say that you can't be an intelligent professor or teacher only that it is clearly not a requirement of the job. As a *real* scientist, Nikola Tesla, said long ago: 'The day science begins to study non-physical phenomena, it will make more progress in one decade than in all the previous centuries of our existence.' This is proving to be the case although 'progress' is not what you discover but what you do with it. Our solid world could not be more *un*-solid and here's the kicker: Governments, science, medicine, corporations, 'education' and media (what I call collectively the Mainstream Everything) all produce their decisions, laws, explanations of reality, treatments and reports on the basis that it *is* solid, material and physical. No wonder that human society is such a basket case. If your whole perception and decision-making is founded on a belief in reality that could not possibly be more wrong, then how could that not produce extremes of madness? Almost the entirety of human life is skewed wherever you look because of this most basic misconception about the very reality we are experiencing. This inversion and perversion of perceived reality has produced the inversion and perversion that we call human society. Author Michael Ellner put it so well:

> *Just look at us. Everything is backwards; everything is upside down. Doctors destroy health, lawyers destroy justice, universities destroy knowledge, governments destroy freedom, the major media destroy information and religions destroy spirituality.*

What's more, none of that is by chance and all is by calculated design. The why and by whom will become clear.

## The All That Is

We are Awareness – a state of being aware. Everything else is detail and illusion. We are not our body; we are that which is aware and experiencing through the body (Fig 9). Awareness in the purest sense has no form but it can experience through form. In its most expanded state it is not even energy. It just *is*. Our awareness is an expression of the totality of Awareness; hence some religions and native peoples speak of being aspects or 'children' of 'God' or the 'Great

**Figure 9:** Who are we? A state of being aware.

Spirit'. Other religions condemn as blasphemy any claim that we *are* 'God' – what I call Infinite Awareness – in its endless and various forms. This serves the manufactured and enslaving belief that we are insignificant, detached, isolated and powerless. None of this is true at the deepest of levels, but it serves the agenda of human control by pedalling an acceptance of impotence, servitude and know-your-place. The late great English-born philosopher Alan Watts (1915-1973) was right when he said: 'God is what no one admits to being and everyone is.' Religious frocks are symbols of this manipulated sense of detachment and isolation as they stand as sentinels between believers and the perceived deity. They know 'God' better than you do and the

**Figure 10:** We are Infinite Awareness infinitely experiencing itself.

**Figure 11:** Humans are a point of attention within Infinite Awareness within a tiny band of frequency called visible light.

**Figure 12:** Where does the droplet end and the ocean start? They are *One* – and so is human awareness no matter what the background, colour or creed it perceives itself to be.

Pope/Rabbi/Imam are His best mates. What breathtaking nonsense it all is. We are points of attention within Infinite Awareness as Infinite Awareness infinitely experiences itself (Figs 10 and 11). This doesn't mean that every 'point' is infinitely aware. If you stand on a mountain you can see a great panorama, but if you stand in a pitch-black room you can see nothing. Both are points of attention – awareness – and yet their perception of reality is dramatically different. So it is with the human mind and Infinite Awareness in its totality, or, in current human terms, even vastly less than its totality. Human consciousness is so asleep, so imprisoned by illusion, it is hardly 'conscious' at all. The droplet is the ocean and the ocean is the droplet, but not every droplet is as aware as the ocean if they become perceptually isolated from the whole (Fig 12). Words like 'infinite' and 'totality' are themselves a misnomer for Awareness beyond time and space (or our *perceptions* of them) but they serve a purpose to contrast with human perceptual myopia. Infinite Awareness just *IS*. It is an *Isness*, a state of awareness that knows all and sees all because it is All. The range of potential states of awareness, therefore, span All-Possibility from Infinite Awareness in awareness of itself to someone who thinks she's just Mary or Margaret working on the checkout. Humanity is big-time at the lower end collectively of this perceptual scale, but, equally big-time, we *don't have to be*.

I have taken psychoactive potions twice, on two nights in the rainforest of Brazil in 2003, in the form of a plant called ayahuasca which tastes a bit like liquorice. On the second night in particular, after I entered an altered state, I spent five timeless hours lying in the darkness as a strong, loud voice, taking a female form, spoke to me in detail about the illusory nature of 'physical' reality. It was an extraordinary experience which I remembered in photographic detail. The Voice said at the start: 'All you really need to know is Infinite Love is the only truth – *everything* else is illusion.' These words were repeated several times: 'Infinite Love [Infinite Awareness in awareness of itself] is the only truth – *everything* else is illusion.' The Voice said that I was being taken to where I came from and to where I would return so I could better understand my current reality. In that moment I saw a shimmering, radiant blackness of stillness and silence that somehow shone with incredible brilliance. What was that again– a shimmering, radiant blackness that shone with the brilliance of light? Ugh? Words do not exist to describe what appears to be a bewildering contradiction to the human conscious mind (Fig 13). 'This is the Infinite, David', the Voice said. Yes, Infinite Awareness in awareness of itself, the stillness and silence of All-Possibility, All-Potential, waiting to be imagined into existence (Fig 14). Once again the isolated conscious mind in the thrall of the five-senses believes that something must move, take form or make noise to be 'real'. But all these things are simply possibilities manifesting from the Infinite Imagination of Infinite Possibility. Speak and you pull one possibility from All-Possibility. Stop speaking and your spoken

**Figure 13:** The brilliant blackness as I experienced it in Brazil.

**Figure 14:** All Possibility, All Potential waiting to manifest.

possibility disappears back into the silence of All-Possibility. Realities which move, take form and make noise are figments of Infinite Imagination which manifest as realms of frequency and vibration that interpenetrate each other like radio and television stations at different points on the frequency dial. As the Voice said: 'If it vibrates, it's illusion.' These realities share the same 'space' and don't interfere with each other unless they are very close on the 'dial'. When this happens we call the result 'ghosts' and 'paranormal activity'. Ghosts and apparitions can pass through walls because they are not operating within the same frequency band just as radio frequencies can pass through walls. I am far from the only one to have experienced this Infinite Awareness as a vibrant shining blackness. Many have described the same experience to me over the years and human ages and sages of illusory 'time' have known of this indescribable, not *place*, but state of awareness or being. Near-death experiencers are a great source of information about the unseen as they tell of entering a totally different realm of reality after their consciousness (point of attention) withdraws

**Figure 15:** Near-death experience when our point of attention withdraws from the focus and lens of Body/Mind and expands into a vastly greater sense of reality.

from the body at 'death' only to return to this reality when the body is revived (Fig 15). Dr Eben Alexander, an academic neurosurgeon at Harvard for 15 years, is one such example with his near-death experience during a week-long coma in 2008. He went into the coma, caused by meningitis, believing like his scientist father that consciousness exists only in the brain and cannot continue when the brain has ceased to function. Put bluntly, dead means dead. This is the very foundation of mainstream 'scientific' dogma they call 'evolution' that leads deeply bewildered academics like Professor Richard Dawkins at Oxford University to trash any idea of awareness beyond the grave. The deadly duo of arrogance and ignorance that entrap the concrete mind of five-sense academia means that not only do *they* go on their clueless way, but they insist that everyone else does the same. Dawkins said:

*You cannot be both sane and well educated and disbelieve in evolution. The evidence is so strong that any sane, educated person has got to believe in evolution.*

Or, put another way: You cannot be both sane and well educated if you don't believe what I do. The arrogance of ignorance defined in a single sentence. Serbian-American scientist Nikola Tesla (1856-1943), who was way ahead of the science mainstream, hit the button when he said:

> *The scientists of today think deeply instead of clearly. One must be sane to think clearly, but one can think deeply and be quite insane.*

This was the world of Eben Alexander until he opened his eyes from his coma with news of a completely different reality and explanation of life itself. He tells his story in his book, *Proof of Heaven*, in which he writes about 'The Core' or 'Dazzling Darkness' from where 'the purest love emanated and all is known'. This is what I experienced in the rainforest of Brazil and 'Dazzling Darkness' is a perfect description of what I saw. 'The purest love emanated and all was known' further describes what I call Infinite Awareness in awareness of itself: All-Knowing, All-Possibility, All-Potential. Tesla also talked of 'The Core' from which everything comes:

**Figure 16:** Everything is one Infinite Awareness having different experiences - 'the force that moves all things.'

> *In the Universe there is a core from which we obtain knowledge, strength and inspiration. I have not penetrated into the secrets of this core, but I know it exists.*

Ancient and native cultures the world over have their own names for this force that gives life to everything. Lakota people in the United States speak of Wakan Tanka or 'the force which moves all things'. This is a wonderful description of the *All That Is*. 'Great Spirit' is another. You can liken Infinite Awareness to an infinite ocean of infinite possibility. We give names to 'different' oceans like the Atlantic, Pacific and Indian, but they are all the same body of water. We give names to people, countries, cultures, trees, mountains, air, rain, planets, stars and galaxies, but they are all the same ocean of Infinite Awareness in different manifestations (Fig 16). Once we become disconnected from the influence of expanded realms of this Awareness our sense of isolation and apartness from everything else leads to a self-identity with name, race, culture, religion, job, lifestyle and life story. These are not who we are, only what we are

currently *experiencing*. They
are an *experience*, not an 'I'.
This is the self-identity that
I call 'Phantom Self' and it
is the foundation of human
misery, emotional trauma
and control (Fig 17). The
late singer and writer
Leonard Cohen said: 'If you
don't become the ocean,
you'll be seasick all your
life.' If you don't become
One with Infinite
Awareness you'll only
perceive a little isolated

**Figure 17:** The fake self-identity that holds humanity in servitude to illusion.

'me' powerless in the face of forces and events you cannot control. Oh,
but you *can*. Near-death experiencers galore have described realities
outside the perceptual prison of the body in extremely common terms.
One said: 'It's like being half asleep when I was alive, and totally awake
after I was pronounced dead.' Anita Morjani, author of *Dying to be Me*,
said after her own out-of-body experience: 'When we are not expressing
in our physical body, you and I and all of us ... we are expressions of the
same consciousness.' This has been a theme of enlightened people
throughout the ages and quantum physics is now beginning to catch on
and catch up. Anita said that in her out-of-body state of awareness she
experienced 'a realm of clarity where I understood everything' and 'I felt
connected to everybody'. She was experiencing 'the force that moves all
things' and connects everything as One. Anita makes a very potent
in/out of the body analogy of a torch beam and a warehouse. Imagine
you are in a pitch-black warehouse with a torch in your hand. All you
can see is anything within the beam of the torch. Everything else is
invisible or hidden (Fig 18). This is symbolic of the tiny range of
frequency – visible light – that the human body can decode and we
therefore 'see'. Then, symbolic of awareness withdrawing from the body,
someone turns on the lights right across the warehouse. Now you can
see the enormity of what you were part of all along, but could not see
when your perceptions were limited to the light of the torch (Fig 19). I
have just described what happens at 'death' – you know that
inevitability that terrifies most of the human race. Body-Mind decodes
visual reality only within the tiny frequency band of visible light and
when our awareness withdraws from the body it withdraws from that
telescope-focus and suddenly perception massively expands. There is no
'death' of awareness, only the end of its temporary vehicle for a
particular experience. Fear of death is only the ignorance of life. Or, as

Rumi, a 13th century Sufi mystic, said:

*This place is a dream. Only a sleeper considers it real. Then death comes like dawn and you wake up laughing at what you thought was your grief.*

This 'place' is only a tiny band of frequency while Forever lies beyond its perceptual walls. I will be exposing at length the architects of those walls or firewalls as they really are. I have used the following quote from a near-death experiencer several times in my books because it is such an encapsulation of reality outside the body:

*... everything from the beginning, my birth, my ancestors, my children, my wife, everything comes together simultaneously. I saw everything about me, and about everyone who was around me. I saw everything they were thinking now, what they thought then, what was happening before, what was happening now. There is no time, there is no sequence of events, no such thing as limitation, of distance, of period, of place. I could be anywhere I wanted to be simultaneously.*

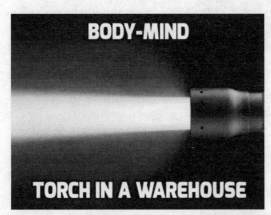

**Figure 18:** A great analogy for the frequency band we call the 'world'.

And this comes from academic neurosurgeon Eben Alexander:

*To experience thinking outside the brain is to enter a world of instantaneous connections that make ordinary thinking (those aspects limited by the physical brain and the speed of light) seem like some hopelessly sleepy and plodding event ...*

*... Our truest, deepest self is completely free. It is not crippled or compromised by past actions or concerned with identity or status. It*

**Figure 19:** We are part of something far bigger and ultimately infinite.

*comprehends that it has no need to fear the earthly world, and therefore, it has no need to build itself up through fame or wealth or conquest.*

This is the reality of life outside the body and there is a force that has sought – mostly very successfully – to keep this from us and imprison our perception in a sense of limitation, I can't and that's not possible. There is so much more to 'humanity' than we have ever understood and what testament to the scale of illusion that so many have been killed, tortured and burned-at-the-stake for revealing this truth or parts of it. The whole foundation of human control can be described in a single

**Figure 20:** The bottom-line of human enslavement.

sentence: Disconnecting the 'incarnate' human mind (what I will call Body-Mind) from the influence of our Infinite Self or disconnecting the 'incarnate' droplet from the ocean (Fig 20). *Everything* comes from this and without such disconnection the depth and scale of human perceptual control would be impossible. We will see as we progress how the very fine detail of human society is structured to take that symbolic mountain panorama and lock it away in the pitch-black room. Humanity is imprisoned by its sense of reality which comes from its point of attention (Fig 21). Awake philosopher Alan Watts said that the ego (Body-Mind) is 'nothing other than the focus of attention'. This is exactly what it is and so what more potent form of perceptual control could there than to

**Figure 21:** If our attention can be focused only in the five senses we cease to be influenced in our perception of reality by our expanded levels of awareness beyond the illusion.

focus attention – sense of reality – only in that tiny sliver of frequency called visible light?

## Imagine all the people ... (and everything else)

The still and silent *All That Is* produces what is called 'Creation' through the imagination of its points of attention large and small. This can be anything from creating entire 'worlds' to doodling in a notebook. There can be error, too, in such creations – witness the creation of the atomic bomb. The *All That Is* can be capable of error?? Not in its purest and most expanded expression, but its points of attention can. Even then what is 'error' except another form of experience and what is experience except the road to wisdom and remembering our true identity? How often do our biggest 'mistakes' turn out to be our greatest gifts? According to ancient accounts which concur with my own research and conclusions our very current reality was the result of 'error' and I'll be explaining much more about this in due course. We should also not forget that if we are talking about a state of All-Possibility then 'error' is a possibility and without this there cannot be a state of All-Possibility. In the same way, All-Possibility means that the *All That Is* or Infinite Awareness is everything *and* nothing, everywhere *and* nowhere, it is and it isn't. This has to be the case or it would not be All-Possibility or Infinite Imagination. So *everything* is within *no-thing* and *no-thing* is within *everything*. *Nowhere* is within *everywhere* and *everywhere* is within *nowhere*. Once we grasp the nature of All-Possibility and Infinite Imagination in the fullness of its meaning all paradox disappears. Infinite Awareness is not energy but produces energy as an imagination of All-Possibility. Creations of Infinite Imagination and the imaginations of its imagination can manifest as the realms of what we call energy, frequency and vibration. The further these imagined creations themselves create and become detached from a state of Infinite Awareness in awareness of itself the more they fall into ever lower frequencies and so states of illusion. If they fall far enough they end up in the energetic densities that we call 'matter'. Legendary American comedian Bill Hicks (1961-1994), who had countless experiences in psychoactive drug-induced altered states, said: '... All matter is merely energy condensed to a slow vibration ... we are all one consciousness experiencing itself subjectively; there is no such thing as death, life is only a dream, and we are the imagination of ourselves'. This is what the illusion of 'physical' matter really is – energy vibrating so slowly that it gives the appearance of solidity. Scientists don't come much more famous than Albert Einstein and yet he said the same as a comedy club comedian. To know does not require some great formal education (programming); it means simply *to know*. Mainstream education is structured to *stop* us knowing by enslaving our perceptions of the possible and it is no coincidence that Einstein also said: 'The only thing that interferes with my learning is my education.' Einstein's explanation of matter was the same as Bill Hicks:

**Figure 22:** Different 'worlds' or realities are different bands of frequency like analogue radio and television stations on different parts of the dial.
© www.neilhague.com

*Concerning matter, we have been all wrong. What we have called matter is really energy, whose vibration has been lowered as to be perceptible to the senses. There is no matter. There is only light and sound.*

There is only light (energy) and sound (vibration) which together give the illusion of physicality when the vibration is slow enough and within the frequency band of visible light (visible energy). The slower energy vibrates the more 'solid' it appears to be – say a wall – and the faster it vibrates the less-dense and even ethereal it appears to be. If it vibrates fast enough to breach the frequency band of visible light then we can't see it. When people talk of seeing something 'appear out of nowhere' or 'disappear before my eyes' they are describing phenomena that enter the frequency band of visible light and then change frequency to go beyond it. Now you see it, now you don't, now you decode it, now you don't. Academics dismiss such descriptions with regard to 'UFOs' and 'aliens' appearing and disappearing because they don't understand what reality is. Those more aware of how energy interacts with consciousness (*is* consciousness) can perform apparent 'miracles' which are not miracles at all. They are the result of knowing how reality works. Body-Mind perception has to call this the 'paranormal' to compare it with its pea-sized sense of 'normal' downloaded from cradle to grave from Mainstream Everything. Academics and mainstream scientists download this pea-sized version of reality more than anyone else and then tell us what we should and should not believe. It would hilarious if it wasn't so tragic.

## Computer Universe

We have Infinite Awareness in awareness of itself that pervades everything – 'the force which moves all things' – and its Creation and creations that express themselves as realms of energy, frequency and vibration. These creations, 'worlds' or realities can share the same 'space' (or the illusion of it) because they operate on different frequencies (Fig 22). What we call our visible Universe is one such frequency-band reality and operates as a quantum computer system. These are defined as 'a computer that makes use of the quantum states of electrons and other particles to store and process information'. Put more simply the Universe is a quantum computer that stores information in the very energetic fabric of our reality and the computing power of quantum states is

**Figure 23:** An image of what Wi-Fi might look like if we could see its frequency band.

**Figure 24:** Our reality is like Wi-Fi – a sea of information that we decode into what we perceive as a 'solid' world.

absolutely off the scale. Current computers are limited by their choice between 1 and 0 which represent charges of electricity that are either on or off. Quantum computing has no such limits and is quite capable of creating and processing universes. Think of a cosmic Wi-Fi field or fields (Fig 23). You can't see Wi-Fi, but a computer can decode that hidden information source into a global collective reality on the screen that we call the Internet or World Wide Web. The Universe is information stored in the unseen (like you can't see Wi-Fi) and what I will call the human Body-Mind is a *biological* computer (in the widest possible sense of that definition) which decodes the 'Wi-Fi' information construct of the Universe into a perception of 'physical' reality on *our* screen – what we experience as the brain and genetic structure as a whole (Fig 24). Elite and massively funded projects around the world are developing quantum computers that mimic our very reality with monsters like Google seeking to lead the way for reasons that will become clear. Here's another point staring us in the face: We have *quantum* physics because

**Figure 25:** Internet symbolism is very close to the truth and the connection is through waveform information, electricity and electromagnetism.

**Figure 26:** The Universe is an interactive wireless cosmos in which everything is encoded and decoded information.

the Universe is a *quantum computer*! Our quantum computer Universe is interactive in the sense that we take information and perceptions from the energetic construct and 'post' our own thoughts, perceptions and emotions to impact on the Universe. I call it the Cosmic Internet (Fig 25). The human body/brain is a biological quantum computer and so are planets, stars and everything in our reality as expressions of the quantum computer Universe. Cosmic 'Wi-Fi' or waveform information fields are the foundation of the Universe and we decode the Universe that we think we 'see' from those fields in the way I will be describing. The Universe can be summed up in one word – information; and even more accurately in five – information encoding and decoding information (Fig 26). The computer/Internet analogy is apt again. A desktop computer is information encoded to decode information and information sources like disks, data sticks and the Internet are encoded to be decoded. Everything is interacting, encoded and decoded information and so is our 'physical' reality. The only place that the Internet appears as we experience it with graphics, pictures and text is on the screen. Everywhere else it is information in other forms and the same is true of the way we decode reality. The foundation state of the Universe is waveform information or what some call the Metaphysical Universe (Fig 27). Our five senses convert this waveform information source into electrical signals and send them to the brain which constructs the reality that we think we see, touch, taste,

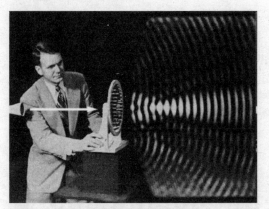

**Figure 27:** The foundation level of the Universe is waveform – information carried in waves.

hear and smell. Take a simple flame on a candle. This seems to be so 'real', but it is only decoded electromagnetic energy (information). *We* create the flame that we think we see. Robert Lanza, an American medical doctor and scientist, writes in his excellent book, *Biocentrism* (co-written with Bob Berman), that a flame is merely hot gas emitting photons which are tiny packets of electromagnetic energy, each pulsing electrically and magnetically. The brain produces the flame that we see by decoding that information. Lanza explains:

*It is easy to recall from every day experience that neither electricity nor magnetism have visual properties. So, on its own, it's not hard to grasp that there is nothing inherently visual, nothing bright or coloured about the candle flame. Now, let these same invisible electromagnetic waves strike a human retina, and if (and only if) the waves happen to measure between 400 and 700 nano meters in length from crest to crest, then their energy is just right to deliver a stimulus to the 8 million cone-shaped cells in the retina.*

*Each in turn send an electrical pulse to a neighbor neuron, and on up the line this goes, at 250 mph, until it reaches the warm, wet occipital lobe of the brain, in the back of the head. There, a cascading complex of neurons fire from the incoming stimuli, and we subjectively perceive this experience as a yellow brightness occurring in a place we have been conditioned to call the 'external world'.*

Talk about illusion. Alan Watts said:

*... [Without the brain] the world is devoid of light, heat, weight, solidity, motion, space, time or any other imaginable feature. All these phenomena are interactions, or transactions, of vibrations with a certain arrangement of neurons.*

And Morpheus told an incredulous Neo in the first *Matrix* movie:

*What is real? How do you define 'real'? If you're talking about what you can feel, what you can smell, taste and see, then 'real' is simply electrical signals interpreted by your brain.*

That's all it is, this 'physical' world that seems so 'real'. We see images on television only because of the same decoding process. Screen images are an arrangement of pixels which the brain decodes into the pictures that we think are outside of us and constructs the illusion of movement by literally connecting the dots (Fig 28). We see television as moving pictures only because our brains link together still images into an apparent sequence. This also happens with LED screens, video games and human reality. We experience movement in our illusory dreams and what we call conscious reality is just another dream. *New Scientist* magazine said in a 2009 article that under magnification 'the fabric of space-time becomes grainy and is ultimately made of tiny units rather like pixels'. I have been referring to the body as a biological computer since way back and now I am seeing some mainstream scientists using the term. We think of 'biological' as 'natural', but

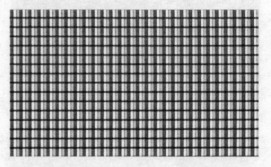

**Figure 28:** The brain decodes this into the television pictures that we think we see, but in reality decode.

**Figure 29:** Connecting two computer systems, technological and biological.

it is in fact a form of technology when compared to Infinite Awareness. The body is an extraordinarily advanced computer system (once again in the widest possible sense) which 'dies' when it ceases to function (so does a computer); goes into sleep mode to conserve energy (so does a computer); has an immune system (so does a computer – antivirus software); has a brain (so does a computer, the central processing unit, or CPU, known as the computer brain); and has a hard drive, DNA etc. (so does a computer). The reason they can now connect a human brain with a computer and make the computer respond to thought is because they are connecting two computer systems (Fig 29). One is technological and the other biological or another form of technology. The human body has the equivalent of a computer motherboard with its genetic network and the meridian lines of energy on which the healing art of acupuncture is based (Fig 30). Acupuncture needles and other techniques are designed to balance the flow of energy (*information*) through those pathways to maintain information balance and communication in the constant interaction between body and Cosmic Internet. When those flows are

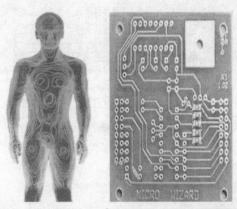

**Figure 30:** Meridian lines in acupuncture are the body's 'motherboard'.

out of balance we enter a state of disharmony or dis-ease – what we call 'physical' or psychological illness. We say 'my computer is so slow today' when information flows are out of sync and cause the computer to malfunction. Many laugh at the concept of acupuncture and ask 'how can you cure a headache with a needle in the foot?' Acupuncture meridians operate in circuits and if the blockage in the circuit causing the headache is in the foot it makes no sense putting the needle in the head. The meridian system connects with the 'chakra' vortex points throughout the body's electromagnetic field which connect the body with the Cosmic Internet and other levels of reality (Fig 31). Chakra means 'wheels of light' in the Sanskrit language of ancient India and the main ones are: the crown chakra

**Figure 31:** Seven major vortex points or 'chakras' interpenetrating the human energy field with the heart chakra at the centre.

on top of the head (where I felt the 'drill' energy on the hill in Peru); brow (or 'third eye') chakra in the centre of the forehead; throat chakra; heart chakra in the centre of the chest; solar plexus chakra just below the sternum; sacral chakra just beneath the navel; and base chakra at the bottom of the spine. Each one has a particular function or functions. The sacral chakra in the lower belly processes emotion and so we feel anxiety and nervousness in that area. At its most extreme this affects the colon and gives people 'the shits' and makes them 'shit scared'. We feel love, empathy and compassion in the chest because that where the heart chakra vortex is located within the body's electromagnetic field.

Our five senses of sight, hearing, taste, touch and smell are decoding systems. They take waveform information from the Cosmic Internet and turn it into electrical information which they communicate to the brain. These are different forms of the same information. Different parts of the brain specialise in decoding information from different senses (Fig 32). The brain decodes electrical information into digital and holographic (illusory 'physical') information that we perceive *in our heads* as the 'world around us' (Fig 33). There is in fact is no

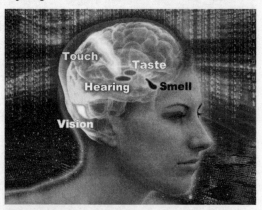

**Figure 32:** Different parts of the brain specialise in decoding information from different senses. Everything we see no matter how far 'away' it appears to be exists in the form that we experience in the small vision area at the back.

**Figure 33:** We decode waveform and electrical/electromagnetic information into digital and holographic states that appear to us as the solid world of human reality.

world 'around' us and everything exists only in the brain and genetic structure in the form that we think we are experiencing 'outside' of ourselves. Computers work the same way. Information decoding systems and what appears on the screen are all happening *inside* the computer (Fig 34).There is a phenomenon called synaesthesia in which senses merge and someone can hear words and music while at the same time *tasting* them. Different words and songs in their experience have different tastes. Our decoding processes and how they function create our reality inside the brain. Everything I have said here about the brain and the senses is confirmed by the experience of playing virtual reality video games which 'hack' into the five senses and override their 'normal' decoded reality with another artificial information source that

**Figure 34:** The five senses decode waveform information into electrical information and communicate this to the brain to be decoded into digital/holographic information.

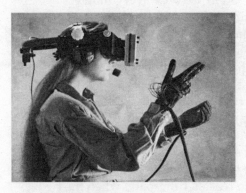

**Figure 35:** Videogames are simply hacking into the five senses to override the information sources they normally decode and present us with a different reality.

**Figure 36:** It may only be computerised electrical information but the reality people decode can seem very 'real'.

appears to be so 'real' (Figs 35 and 36). A writer in a British newspaper described the experience of playing one such game:

*... the striking aspect of the game is the physical sensation of playing it. I feel and therefore believe that I am physically moving back and forth, as though I am on a chair on wheels. External reality has fallen away and I am in a strange and compelling world, anxious not to fall off the terrifying precipices. My brain sends signals to my body that create the illusion that it's shooting around like a pinball, when in fact I am stationary.*

That could have been a description of human life because the principles are just the same. I saw an experiment which involved a doll wearing a virtual reality headset. A group of people were also given headsets that produced the illusion that their bodies were the doll's body. The doll was then touched, had an injection in the eye and messed with in other ways and each time the group reacted as if it was being done to them. They were feeling in their own bodies what was being done to the doll. This is how powerful and perception-controlling even virtual reality at the current human level of development can be never mind what is actually possible.

## We are *One*

No matter how solid something appears to be, it is waveform energy in its foundation state and at this level it becomes possible to communicate with animals, plants and even apparently inanimate phenomena like rocks. *Everything* is consciousness and alive as an expression of Infinite Awareness whether it is a mountain, stream or forest. Mainstream scientific studies are slowly beginning to acknowledge what awakened people have known all along, that everything is consciousness and connected to everything else. Evidence mounts to confirm that trees communicate, feel pain, care for each other and organise as communities and this is true of everything. Some scientists are asking if trees and plants have brains, but a brain is only a means of decoding information and in that sense everything has a 'brain' because everything is constantly receiving and transmitting information. In five-sense reality this is done electrically and electromagnetically and you don't need a big chunk of grey 'matter' to do that. There are endless other receiver-transmission processes through which this can happen. Monica Gagliano, an evolutionary biologist at the University of Western Australia, concluded after a series of experiments that plants use sound waves to detect water at a distance and have the ability to learn. Heidi Appel, an environmental scientist now at the University of Toledo, led a team of researchers in a study that showed how a plant could distinguish between the sounds of wind vibrations and a caterpillar chewing. The plant's chemical state reacted differently when the two sounds were played and produced more defence toxins in response to caterpillar chomping. 'We tend to underestimate plants because their responses are usually less visible to us, but leaves turn out to be extremely sensitive vibration detectors,' Appel said. Buzzing bees generate a frequency that has been shown to trigger plants to release pollen (they call it 'buzz pollination') and other sounds have caused hormonal changes in plants. Dr Suzanne Simard at the University of British Columbia in Vancouver discovered that trees transmit warnings with chemical electrical signals through fungal networks under the soil. A teaspoon of forest soil contains miles of them. The fungi operate like fibre-optic internet cables and this system has become known as the 'wood wide web'. Such networks operate at every level of the Cosmic Internet. This principle of communicating through sound and frequency explains the effect good and bad of chants and mantras. Everything is alive, conscious and part of an infinite web of life and consciousness (Fig 37). Michael Pollan, an author and researcher on these subjects, said of trees and plants:

*They have ways of taking all the sensory data they gather in their everyday lives ... integrate it and then behave in an appropriate way in response. And they do this without brains, which, in a way, is what's incredible about it, because we automatically assume you need a brain to process information.*

But what is the brain except a form of information and information can be processed in infinite different ways by infinite expressions of consciousness. The ignorant laugh and dismiss suggestions that we can communicate with animals, trees, plants or rocks because they can only perceive communication through human language. At the waveform level and beyond we are all connected to each other, and communication can happen not through words but through the waveform connection which you can liken to telepathy. An article in *Scientific American* magazine about black holes as computers said:

*... to a physicist, all physical systems are computers. Rocks, atom bombs and galaxies may not run Linux, but they,*

**Figure 37:** Everything is alive and aware and an expression of Infinite Awareness – the force that moves all things.

*too, register and process information. Every electron, photon and other elementary particle stores bits of data, and every time two such particles interact, those bits are transformed. Physical existence and information content are inextricably linked.*

Information content and the *illusion* of physical existence are inextricably linked because what we perceive as physical *is* information content. Form is in-*form*-ation decoded from waveform states (Fig 38). 'Physical reality' including the body is made manifest through standing or stationary waves of information. Funny how the guy describing his experience playing computer games said: 'My brain sends signals to my body that create the illusion that it's shooting around like a pinball, when in fact I am stationary.' He was unknowingly telling a profound truth about reality itself. To create standing waves you need a block or 'wall' at each end called a node point which causes a wave travelling in one direction to bounce back in the other direction and interact with itself coming the other way. This bounced-back wave then strikes the

**Figure 38:** The illusion of what we think we see.
© www.neilhague.com

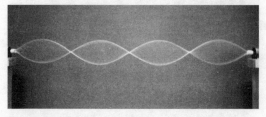

**Figure 39:** Standing or stationary waves that hold information in place until the frequency is disturbed or switched off.

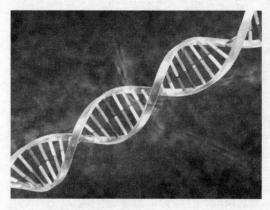

**Figure 40:** 'Standing wave' DNA.

other wall or node point and returns in the other direction to create a perpetual motion of back and forth that itself creates a state of oscillation (Fig 39). When the two identical expressions of the same wave interact they cancel each other out in terms of forward movement and create a wave that oscillates up and down or 'jogs' (stands) on the spot. Funnily enough the result looks like DNA and that is related to the fact that the body and 'physical' forms in general are manifested from standing waves retaining particular information in a particular oscillating field (Fig 40). While the standing wave field is oscillating your body is alive and the moment it stops we call death. The human heartbeat is an expression of this oscillation and heart disease is actually a disruption to the oscillation which the heart is only reflecting. From this comes the fact that in the world of form everything 'vibrates' – 'If it vibrates it's illusion.' I say that what we call the Universe is itself one big standing wave of information that oscillates – 'moves back and forth in a regular rhythm'. How right we are to talk about the rhythm of life. German biophysicist Fritz-Albert Popp discovered that DNA vibrates or oscillates to a particular frequency and I say this relates to the standing wave. Russian researchers led by molecular biologist and bio-physicist Pjotr Garjajev found that DNA not only receives and transmits information, but absorbs and processes it. This is how human genetics can be changed from afar by frequency (information carried by the frequency) and how DNA can be programmed. This will be very significant as we proceed. What we call 'evolution' with species changing to stay in sync with a changing environment and developing gifts perfect for survival comes from the information interaction between the quantum field of possibility and probability, DNA and the human energetic field. The whole body is an antenna including bone and skin because in their prime state they are waveform electromagnetic fields. Grazyna Fosar and Franz Bludorf write in the German book, *Vernetzte Intelligenz*:

> The latest research explains phenomena such as clairvoyance, intuition, spontaneous and remote acts of healing, self-healing, affirmation techniques, unusual light-auras around people (namely spiritual masters), mind's influence on weather-patterns and much more.

> The Russian scientists also found out that our DNA can cause disturbing patterns in the vacuum, thus producing magnetized wormholes! Wormholes are the microscopic equivalents of the so-called Einstein-Rosen bridges in the vicinity of black holes (left by burned-out stars). These are tunnel connections between entirely different areas in the universe through which information can be transmitted outside of space and time. The DNA attracts these bits of information and passes them on to our consciousness.

Whatever happened to 'Little Me'? By expanding the frequency band on which DNA is operating (by expanding our consciousness) we can connect with other realities beyond the five senses as psychics and mediums do. We can heal and be healed remotely by using our consciousness to deliver harmonising frequencies to another's DNA. We can do this to ourselves through consciousness communication with our own DNA. This is the background to how mind can 'miraculously' heal the body. There is nothing miraculous about this at all. Reality is designed to make this possible, but that knowledge has been suppressed to keep us in ignorance of our true power. Placebo pills trick the mind into believing they will be effective in curing illness and the mind's perception of this is communicated subconsciously to the body which then responds to that perception and heals *itself*. Surgeon Andrew Carr, professor of orthopaedic surgery at the University of Oxford, said that thousands of patients may be cured not by the operation but by a belief that an (unnecessary) operation would remove the problem:

> *Having to stop work, having to change your life, coming into hospital, all of these people dressed in blue with hats on, you're anaesthetised ... All of that, if we believe in placebo, is surely a set-up to create a phenomenal placebo effect.*

Studies have shown that patients who have fake surgery, but believe they have had the real thing, can recover almost or equally as well as those who have genuinely had the operation. Everything in all infinite existence is consciousness/awareness interacting with *itself*.

## DNA is a receiver-transmitter

Mainstream science has said that at most only five percent of DNA is active at a 'physical' level and the other 95 percent has been dismissed as 'junk DNA' because it appeared to have no function – we don't understand what it does and so it can't be doing anything. This almost entirety of DNA operates in, and interacts with, the unseen. Russian researchers have established that DNA is encoded with the same structure and rules that can be found in all human languages. DNA and the body in general is indeed a biological computer and if you know how to program the software you can cure anything you want, stem the ageing process and extend lifespan almost as long as you choose. Instead of exploring these incredible frontiers the Elite families and their networks manipulating human society seek to conceal this knowledge and, in terms of health, allow the pharmacological death cult to have its wicked way. Scientists from Columbia University and the New York Genome Center announced in March 2017 they had discovered a way to use DNA to store, replicate and retrieve digital files in the way you would with a computer hard drive. How long I have been saying that DNA is on one level like a computer hard drive that stores information. You don't need a university to understand reality because this information is in the Cosmic Internet all around us if people only tune-in to those frequencies. The often barely-one-dimensional, physical-obsessed scientific mind is so welded to five-sense reality that it becomes desensitised and disconnected from the library of insight in the information sea in which we all 'swim'. Crystals are used in receiver-

**Figure 41:** What scale of information do we allow our brains to process? Openness of mind will decide.

**Figure 42:** The same 'physical' reality but different points of observation. The Great Inversion means that those who tap into expanded awareness are called mad by those who don't.

transmission technology and the human body is crystalline for the same reason. We have trillions of cells and the membrane of every one is a liquid crystal. The crystalline pineal gland in the brain is part of the so-called 'third eye' which can connect us to frequencies in other realities. We are receivers, transmitters, decoders and processors of information interacting with the Cosmic Internet. One way DNA communicates is through what science calls biophotons in the visible and ultraviolet spectrum, which are emitted by biological systems. Nikola Tesla said the brain 'is only a receiver' and that is clearly so. Consciousness does not come *from* the brain but *through* the brain which is a processor of information both from the five senses and consciousness beyond this reality. It is our choice what level of awareness we allow our brain to process into conscious perception (Fig 41). For this reason we have people with very different awareness interacting with each other in human society with the most aware facing the ridicule and distain of the unaware (Fig 42). Did I mention the inversion? Writer Jonathan Swift (1667-1745) said: 'When a true genius appears, you can know him by this sign: That all the dunces are in a confederacy against him.' He might have said 'unaware' rather than dunces and the point is that people don't have to be unaware. They have *allowed* themselves to be. The brain is saying 'what do you want me to be?' It is now known that the brain has 'placidity' and changes according to information received and this is why the almost constant electrical stimulation from 'smart' technology is changing the way the brain processes information into the perceptions of the conscious mind. If people self-identify as Phantom Self or five-sense self the brain will process information at that level, but when we open our minds to expanded awareness the brain restructures or rewires to process that.

## You see it when you, er, *see* it

A few scientists over the years have postulated that the 'physical' world only exists when we look at it. They call this the 'Observer Effect'. Support for this contention is now gathering in the science community – among those who have ditched the song sheet that is – but I suggest they are missing the key word here: *decoding*. It is not so much the 'Observer Effect' as the 'Decoder Effect'. The connection between the two is that the act of 'observation' or focus activates the decoding systems of the brain-body. When we are not 'looking' (decoding) then reality is always in a waveform state. Only when we decode waveform information into what is holographic information does the '3D' world that we know appear to us – in our own minds (Fig 43). We are seeing more and more mainstream headlines like this one: 'Your entire life is an ILLUSION: New test backs up theory that the world doesn't exist until we look at it'. The article goes on to say that the famous theory in quantum mechanics which argues that a particle's behaviour changes based on what we see had now been proved to be true on the scale of atoms in a new experiment by scientists at the Australian National University. 'At the quantum level, reality does not exist if you are not looking at it,' said Associate Professor Andrew Truscott. There is another aspect to this as well. *Perceptions* of the observer influence the way we decode reality from the information possibilities and probabilities encoded in the Cosmic Internet. Two different perceptions of reality will not decode exactly the

**Figure 43:** 'Focus – 'observation' – triggers the decoding process that turns waveform information into the illusory 'external world'. Without the observer (decoder) everything remains in waveform.

same outcome in the same way. The process is encompassed in this quote from writer Joseph Michael Straczynski:

> *Accidents happen, that's what everyone says. But in a quantum Universe there are no such things as accidents, only possibilities and probabilities folded into existence by perception.*

Yes – *perception*. Endless experiments have shown how people add things to their visual reality that are not actually there, but they believe *should* be (an expression of the 40 from 11 million deal). My biggest book in terms of volume is called *The Perception Deception* because the entire control system of human society is based on the manipulation of perception. Those in the shadows that know how we interact with reality (but don't want us to know) are well aware that if they can program our perceptions we will decode our experienced reality in a way that reflects those perceptions. This is the whole foundation of how the few control the many through the manipulation of perception. What we believe we perceive, and what we perceive we experience. This is not supposition, it is physics. George Berkeley (1685-1753), after whom Berkeley University is named, could see that material reality was an illusion and he said: 'The only things we perceive are our perceptions.' This can be confirmed on the most basic level in that a person who sees the glass as half empty will not experience (decode from quantum possibility and probability) the same outcome as one who sees the glass filled to the brim. A more extreme example is firewalking. When you walk barefoot on red-hot coals with the belief that you will get burned then that is what will happen; but if you go into an altered state of consciousness (altered sense of reality) you can do the same and not get burned, as firewalkers all over the world have shown (Fig 44). An illusion cannot burn an illusion unless you believe it can and so decode that reality from a *perception* of that reality. Associate Professor Andrew

**Figure 44:** An illusion can't burn an illusion unless you believe that it can.

Truscott said that his 'your entire life is an illusion' experiment showed that 'the atoms did not travel from A to B ... and it was only when they were measured at the end of the journey that their wave-like or particle-like behaviour was brought into existence'. Or it was *decoded* into existence by the impact and influence of focus and perception. The Voice that I heard in the ayahuasca experience in Brazil said: 'Why do you fly from point A to point B when you *are* point A and point B and everything in between?' I saw an article in *Epoch Times* headed 'Your Mind Can Control Matter: Physicist' which said of another experiment:

> *Atomic particles were shown to also be waves. Whether they manifested as waves or as particles depended on whether someone was looking. Observation influenced the physical reality of the particles – in more technical language, observation collapsed the wave function.*

Waves collapse into particles (or appear to) when observed because they are being decoded by that act of observation and focus in an interaction

**Figure 45:** Collapsing the waves into holographic 'particle' reality.

between mind and energetic information. Waves collapse (are decoded into) an illusory 'physical' world of particles and atoms, but these are only another expression of waves. Everything is waves (Fig 45). The Cosmic Internet is a waveform energetic information construct that provides the information blueprint for what we call the world, but what we decode as detail and outcome depends on the *perceptions* and state of mind of the observer. Waveform reality is a series of quantum possibilities and probabilities and it is consciousness (perception) that dictates which of those probabilities and possibilities in the energetic fabric of the Cosmic Internet are (waveform collapsed) into experienced reality. Control perception and you control everything. John Wheeler, a Nobel physicist, said: 'No phenomenon is a real phenomenon until it is an *observed* phenomenon. Or as I would say: a *decoded* phenomenon. The dream is the dreamer and the dreamer is the dream because the dream is a decoded extension or projection of the dreamer. 'All that we see or seem is just a dream within a dream', as Edgar Allen Poe said. If you want to control the dream you must control the perceptions of the dreamer and that's the global conspiracy to enslave humanity in a single sentence. How real and 'physical' some dreams can be while we are asleep to the 'physical' world. Dreams can be symbolic representations of mental and emotional states or connections to different wavelengths of reality measured by the nature of different brain*wave* states – beta, delta etc. The deepest of them (the sleep the Greeks called 'Hypnos') are way beyond the perceived world of the 'physical'. I have incredibly vivid dreams almost every night while in almost coma-like states and they are as 'physically' real on their wavelength as the world of five- sense mind.

I have told many times one particular story that perfectly explains how we decode reality and the amazing depth of the illusion we are experiencing. Michael Talbot was a writer and researcher who produced an outstanding book in the 1990s called *The Holographic Universe*. This is a compelling pull-together of the work, findings and conclusions of open-minded scientists from the mainstream who believe that our 'physical' reality is really a holographic illusion. Talbot tells the story in the book of when his father had a party for friends and invited along a stage hypnotist to entertain the guests. At one point a man called Tom was induced into a hypnotic state and told that when he 'woke up' he would not be able to see his daughter. The hypnotist led the daughter to stand right in front of her father and then apparently re-awakened him to his conscious mind. Tom was asked if he could see his daughter. He said he couldn't even though he was looking directly into her belly. The hypnotist put his hand in the small of the daughter's back and asked Tom if he could see what he was holding. 'You are holding a watch', Tom replied, even though his daughter stood between him and the watch. He was asked if he could read an inscription on the watch and he did. The story appears to be impossible, but it's not. Our five senses and brain-body are also waveform information in their prime state and the 'physical' brain is only a holographic expression of the *waveform* 'brain'. Hypnotic suggestion acted like a firewall in Tom's decoding processes (at the subconscious waveform level) which prevented him from reading – decoding – his daughter's waveform energetic field. Unless he could decode that into holographic reality he would not be able to see her in the frequency range of his conscious five-sense mind. If she wasn't decoded by his brain into the holographic realm of the conscious mind then she could not impact on that reality and so get in the way of Tom

 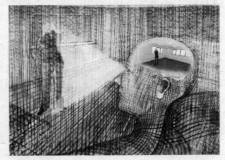

**Figure 46:** Tom's brain/mind was firewalled by hypnotic suggestion not to decode his daughter's waveform field into holographic reality ...

**Figure 47:** ... only when he did could he see his daughter in the realm of his conscious mind.

seeing the watch. Everyone else in the room could see her because they had not been subjected to the hypnotic firewall (Figs 46 and 47). Human perceptions are being programmed 24/7 as I will show – and what are

**Figure 48:** We are decoding ('observing') our own bodies from waveform information into a holographic state.

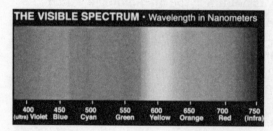

**Figure 49:** Colours are frequencies of information that we decode into the colours that we think we see.

we not seeing because of collective firewalls similar to those that bemused Tom? Is it really just random chance that humanity can see such a ridiculously narrow band of frequency or visible light? I say it's not, for reasons I will be exploring. We even decode our own bodies into apparent 'physical' existence in the same way (Fig 48). It's hysterical, really, given how we experience the world to be so 'solid'. Colour? Nope, that doesn't exist either until you decode it. Colours and shades of colour are information fields of different frequencies which only become the colours that we think we see when we observe them – decode them – into that form (Fig 49). English scientist Isaac Newton (1642-1726) rightly called the rainbow

frequency band of colours a 'spectrum' which is Latin for apparition or phantom and the origin of the word spectre. Black absorbs all light, so it's black; white reflects all light, so it's white; and different colours absorb some light frequencies and reflect others. What they reflect is what we see as their colour when those reflected frequencies are decoded into electrical information by the sight senses, and into holographic perception in the brain.

## What 'physical'?

Our reality is not physical, but holographic – illusory 'physical'. I have been saying and writing for years and years that the 'world' is a digital hologram and now more scientists are coming to that conclusion – well, open-minded ones, anyway. Most people will have seen the holograms you can buy in the shops and those they put on money and credit cards.

They are flat images that appear to be three-dimensional. Holographics has now reached a stage of development in which 3D moving images of people can be projected from one place to another (Fig 50). We have seen television programmes presented by holographic people after they have died and duets between living singers and departed singers such as Elvis (Fig 51). Holographics is mimicking the very holographic reality that we experience as life. Holograms are a photographic record of light reflecting from an object. We can only see objects when light is reflected from them (although I say there is more to know about that) and so when you are in a pitch-black room you can't see anything. Rich Terrile, director of the Centre for

Figure 50: The lady is a hologram.

Figure 51: Holographic versions of people are becoming commonplace today.

Evolutionary Computation and Automated Design at NASA's Jet Propulsion Laboratory, said in late 2016 on the Richie Allen radio show on Davidicke.com that the Universe is a digital hologram and, as such, had to have been created by some form of intelligence. I have been saying this for so long while being ridiculed by both the mainstream media and much of the 'alterative'. We live in the equivalent of a computer simulation like the one portrayed in the *Matrix* movies and I will be revealing at length the nature of both the simulation and the 'intelligence' that created it. I use the term 'computer', but what controls the simulation is far beyond anything we would perceive as a computer. Holograms that we buy or see in the various media are created by using a laser beam and mirrors (Fig 52 overleaf). One half of the laser is deflected onto the object and then on to a photographic plate while the other half bypasses the object to directly strike the same photographic plate. When the two beams collide the subsequent pattern represents an image of the object in, wait for it ... *waveform* (Fig 53 overleaf). The

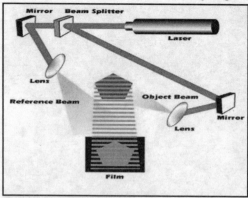

**Figure 52:** Creating holograms.

**Figure 53:** Hologram in waveform which the laser 'reads' (decodes) into an apparently 3D image.

**Figure 54:** Holographic 'solidity' you could wave your hand through.

pattern appears to be just a random series of lines that look a bit like a human fingerprint and this is known as an 'interference pattern'. The principle is the same as two stones dropped in a pond. Waves move out and collide to produce a wave pattern in the water that reflects the size and weight of the stones, where they dropped, how quickly and how far apart. When a laser or light of a single wavelength ('coherent light') is directed at the holographic waveform interference pattern something apparently amazing happens as a 3D image of the object is projected. Illuminating the waveform pattern 'reconstructs' the object's waveform state and our 'eyes' perceive this as the object itself as the brain decodes waveform information into holographic reality just as it does with 'real' reality. Replace the laser or coherent light on the waveform print with human focus or 'observation' and you see the process through which we decode the '2D' waveform Cosmic Internet into the holographic '3D' world of experienced reality. The best holograms can look as solid as you and me, but that's all illusion and you can wave your hand through them (Figs 54 and 55). This is the basic foundation of why our reality looks so physically real when it isn't.

**Figure 55:** Holograms mimic our experienced reality.

*New Scientist*, the UK mainstream science magazine, ran a front page story in 2009 entitled 'You are a hologram projected from the edge of the Universe' and *Scientific American* magazine gave similar coverage to a story headed 'Are you a hologram? (Quantum physics say the entire Universe might be)'. See Figure 56. Another mainstream media report in 2017 carried the headline: 'The Universe could be a "vast and complex hologram", scientists say.' The report explained how researchers from the UK's University of Southampton, working with colleagues from Canada and Italy, had found 'substantial evidence' that we are part of a massive illusion akin to watching a 3D movie projected from a 2D

**Figure 56:** Even mainstream science is now being forced to rethink reality.

screen. The team, which detailed the findings in the peer-reviewed scientific journal, *Physical Review Letters*, said the research discovered irregularities in cosmic microwave background otherwise known as the 'afterglow' of the Big Bang (which didn't happen). Kostas Skenderis, a professor of mathematical sciences at Southampton, said it was similar to watching a 3D film in the cinema. The difference was that we are able to touch objects and the 'projection' is experienced as 'real'. We don't touch objects, but interact waveform to waveform and the 3D cinema screen is our own decoding process. Where I differ from even holographic reality orthodoxy is that I say the 'holographic universe' is not a construct that exists externally to us, but only internally when waveform information or the Cosmic Internet is decoded by Body-Mind into holographic form. The Universe is not a hologram. The Universe is waveform information. We decode that information into what we experience – *inside* our minds not outside – as holographic or 'physical' reality. What we see on a computer screen comes from decoding processes *inside* the computer, not outside. A research team from universities across Japan has developed holograms that you can appear to touch and technology like Microsoft's HoloLens uses headsets to combine 'normal' reality with holographic inserts that includes real size digital people. They are actually inserting technological holograms into a biological holographic reality. Professor Skenderis said that while we perceive the pictures as having height, width and depth they do in fact come from a flat screen. He said that holographic reality is a huge leap forward in the way we think about the structure and creation of the Universe and could finally combine Einstein's theory of gravity and quantum theory – something scientists had been working for decades to do. Researchers at Ibaraki University in Japan say they have found 'compelling evidence' that the Universe is a holographic projection. I have been making these points in my books and talks for one and a half decades at the time of writing. You don't need a scientific mind to understand reality, you need an open one. I repeat that a scientific mind can be a block on understanding because of its worship of orthodoxy and obsession with examining only dots and so not seeing pictures. A unique characteristic of holograms is that every

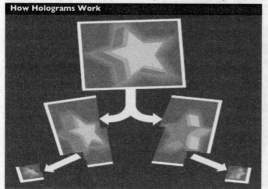

**Figure 57:** Every part of a hologram is a smaller version of the whole.

part of a hologram is a smaller version of the whole and this explains so many apparent 'mysteries'. If you cut a holographic print into pieces each of them will produce a smaller version of the *whole* picture, not just a part or fragment (Fig 57).The smaller you go the less clarity you will have, but it is still the entire image. Alternative healing techniques such as acupuncture and reflexology can find points and areas all over the body which represent all the organs and the body as a whole. This has to be the case because the body is a hologram and in my experience even most practitioners of these methods don't realise this. Skilled palm readers can see so much information in the hand for the same reason. The hand is a smaller version of the whole because the body as we experience it is a hologram. Mainstream scientists like Professor Richard Dawkins dismiss and ridicule alternative *anything* because they don't know what the body is let alone how it works.

## Digital holograms = experienced reality

Everything is connected and a reflection of everything else. This is the consistent message of aware people throughout the ages. Leonardo da Vinci said: 'Learn how to see. Realise that everything connects to everything else.' Roman philosopher Cicero said: 'Everything is alive. Everything is interconnected.' This is certainly true of the waveform-digital-holographic connection. Decoding waveform reality into holographic 'physical' illusion goes through many instantaneous stages – waveform / particle / atomic / electrical / digital / holographic. All represent the same information in different forms and atoms don't need to be 'solid' to create a physical world because there is no physical world. Atoms are only a phase in the decoding process that turns waveform information into holographic information in the same way that computers decode different encoded information states from disks, data sticks or the Internet into what we see on the screen. Holographic reality is *digital* holographic reality. Numbers are digital expressions of waveform information / frequency states and this is the level of reality that is decoded by the ancient art of numerology. Some people read waveform reality – mediums, psychics and so on – while numerology reads digital reality; but they are reading different versions of the *same* reality and same information. I have had psychic and numerological readings with different people that were almost exactly the same for this reason. Computer-generated digital holograms have now been developed which are no longer created with analogue photographic media but produced through computers which calculate the object's interference pattern (waveform construct). A digital hologram is described here in a mainstream media report:

> *And they look real – so real that when Ford used a [digital] hologram to show off a car concept model people stopped, afraid to walk into it. They thought the holographic car was really there.*

Digital holograms are basically the reality that we experience as the world. The brain-body decodes waveform information into electrical and digital-holographic and so at one level of reality everything appears as numbers and related codes. Max Tegmark, physicist at the Massachusetts Institute of Technology (MIT) and author of *Our Mathematical Universe*, said: 'The Universe can be entirely described by numbers and maths.' I will go into all this far more when I expose the detailed background to our simulated reality. It's enough to say for now that this is why NASA scientist Rich Terrile refers to the Universe as a digital hologram and why there was so much emphasis in the *Matrix* movie trilogy on digital reality (Fig 58 overleaf).

## No time, no space

Nothing defines the parameters of our experienced 'world' more obviously than time and space. Our very lives are defined by the passage of time as we go through the ageing process (computer cycle). Is that the time? The time has come. I am out of time. Every 'day' human life is defined, dictated and limited by time. What a revelation, therefore, to know

**Figure 58:** Digital reality in The *Matrix*.

that time does not exist except as a decoded concept in the human mind. The illusion of time is created by the way the brain constructs its decoded images in a form where one seems to lead to the other. This can be likened to still frames passing through a projector to give the illusion of movement. Our brains take 40 sensations or snapshots a second out of some 11 million to construct our experienced reality and arranging information into a sequence would be a breeze by comparison. Yet again the prime influence in this construction of illusory time is *perception* and we experience 'time' in accordance with our mental and emotional state. 'Time' is relative to the observer, the decoder, and his or her perceptions. Albert Einstein said when explaining his theory of relativity: 'When you are courting a nice girl an hour seems like a second. When you sit on a red-hot cinder a second seems like an hour – that's relativity.' Werner Karl Heisenberg (1901-1976), a renowned German theoretical physicist and pioneer of quantum mechanics, said that 'a path comes into existence only when you observe it' (*decode* it). Some brain malfunctions mean that people see only still frames. They won't see tea pouring from the pot, but only as a freeze-frame because even movement is a brain construct from waveform/electrical information. Others see a car in the distance and then nothing in between until it suddenly appears in front of them. There is no time only the NOW, one infinite 'moment' in which all exists. Concepts of past and future are just that – concepts. Where are you when you think of the past? In the NOW. Where are you when you think of the future? In the NOW. There is only the NOW and we experience both past and future only in the NOW. We have to because that's all there is. What we experience as the passage of past through present to future are all changing perceptions and constructs within the same NOW. Consequently there is no such thing as time travel only illusory 'journeys' of perception within the same NOW. A DVD is encoded with the entire movie in the same NOW, but we experience the changing scenes as the progression of time. What we have watched is

**Figure 59:** The whole movie, past, present and future, in the same NOW.

the past and what we have yet to watch is the future. But every scene as they play through is on the same disk in the same NOW. Someone watching an earlier scene in the movie will be in your past symbolically, but they are watching that in the same NOW in which you watch the later scene (Fig 59). Another DVD analogy is that the information on the disk requires technology to decode the information to appear as pictures and sound on the screen. This is what the brain/mind is doing with the quantum computer waveform Universe. Scientific experiments at the quantum level have shown that the 'past' can be changed and influenced by the present. This seems extraordinary until you realise that what we perceive as past, present and future are all happening in the same NOW and what appears to be the present affecting the past is really the NOW affecting the NOW. Day and night are changes happening in the NOW when they appear in decoded form to be happening in a sequence that we call day and night. This is another collective illusion encoded into the construct of the Cosmic Internet. The calendar of 'time' is a manipulated creation of the Roman Church and clocks are created by humans and not by non-existent time. This is the clock-time illusion:

> *Time doesn't exist, clocks exist. Time is just an agreed upon construct. We have taken distance (one rotation of the Sun), divided it into segments, then given those segments labels. While it has its uses, we have been programmed to live our lives by this construct as if it were real. We have confused our shared construct with something that is tangible and thus have become its slave.*

This is all planned as we shall see. The craziness of manufactured 'time' means that today and yesterday are divided by an invisible line that we call the International Date Line (Fig 60). Parts of it are not even straight. Research at University College in London revealed that top sportsmen and women, including tennis players and baseball batters, transform their experience of speed (time) when they are in a focused state waiting for a serve or a pitch. They process visual information

**Figure 60:** An invisible line in the ocean takes you to yesterday or tomorrow.

**Figure 61:** Illusory time as Neo dodges bullets in *The Matrix*.

quicker and so time to them appears to pass slower than to those sitting in the stands. How did he hit that ball? How did she reach that serve? They do it by unconsciously slowing down 'time' and changing the way they sequence reality. People say of great footballers that they seem to have more 'time' than everyone else and this is why. Onlookers perceive 'time' passing in accordance with their own decoding process, but in the mind of the player events are passing slower. This concept was portrayed in the *Matrix* movies as people dodging bullets (Fig 61). I had an experience as a goalkeeper in one match when time slowed down to almost nothing. I had no idea what had happened until years later when I began to grasp the nature of reality. A player smacked a shot with great power and I should have had no chance of stopping it as it sped for the top left-hand corner; but as he struck the ball everything for me transformed into serious slow-motion. I can still see the ball moving in slow motion high towards my left hand side as I moved across to get in line. I then launched myself – still in slow motion – and managed to turn the ball over from where the post meets the crossbar. This slow-mo was accompanied by silence until my hand touched the ball and then everything crashed back into normal speed and noise. It was the best save I ever made and I lay on the floor thinking 'What just happened?' Is this another unexplainable mystery? No – the experience was my mind decoding reality differently, that's all. Sports people talk about their top performances happening when they are 'in the zone' and they describe this as a perceptual state in which everything is silent and often happening in slow motion. Here you have 'the zone' explained. Focus ('observation') collapses waveform reality into particle/holographic reality and the extreme focus which often happens in sport adds a different dimension to that decoding process. Those experiencing a car crash and other traumatic events say that everything seemed to happen in slow motion. It would be more accurate to say that the extreme focus triggered by the trauma made their mind decode information quicker and so create the experience of time slowing down. 'Time' slows near the speed of light because perceptions of the observer change. The speed of light is not really a 'speed' at all. It is a perception program encoded in the collective human mind. Light 'speed' is not 'out there' – it is 'in here'. The mystery of how two so-called 'entangled' particles 'billions of miles' apart can react to each other instantly can also be explained. This is not the result of the speed of communication across distance, but the fact that the particles only exist in the observer's decoding processes. They are not 'billions of miles' apart, but within a few cubic centimetres of the brain where visual reality is decoded. The particles are also decoded expressions of the same waveform field which reacts as one unit and not as two distinct particles no matter what illusory distance is perceived to exist between them. Now, here's something that will be very significant as we proceed. If you travelled at the speed of light you would be everywhere in the Universe in the same moment or NOW. This is what near-death experiencers describe when their awareness withdraws from the perception lens of the body. The speed of light is really the inability of Body-Mind to decode reality faster than the speed of light. There is a blocking mechanism in the decoding process designed to keep us in a perception prison for reasons that will soon become clear. In that single sentence is a colossal revelation about the human plight.

There is no space in the same way that there is no time. Look at the night sky and all those stars and planets across the vastness of space and apparent distance. Once again all that you see in the form that you see only exists in those few cubic centimetres at the back of the brain where visual reality is decoded and constructed (Fig 62). A computer game appears to have time as scenes change and also space in terms of depth and perspective, and yet all you are observing are computer codes on a

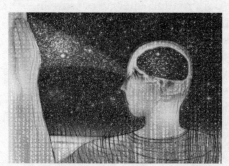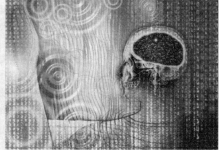

**Figure 62:** The great universal panorama only exists in the form that we 'see' in a small area at the back of the brain..

disk or data stick being decoded into images on the screen. The 'ayahuasca Voice' said: 'Why do you fly from point A to point B when you *are* point A and point B and everything in between?' 'Space', as with 'time', is part of the illusory construct that the mind uses to define holographic reality. In the act of manifesting apparent objects from the waveform field the illusion of space naturally appears to be real. Remember that what we call space is not a 'thing', but is instead defined only by holographic images in our minds. In a room full of objects (images) we say there is not much space while on the Great Plains of the American Midwest where 'objects' appear far apart we talk of 'wide open spaces'. Space as an entity in and of itself is an illusion of the holographic decoding process and is defined not by itself, but by the perceived distance between holographic forms. How can space and distance be real when changing conditions such as speed can change the apparent distance and thus 'space'? Alcohol and drugs can change spatial awareness because of their effect on the perceptual decoding process. As the near-death experiencer said of out-of-body reality: '... There is no time, there is no sequence of events, no such thing as limitation, of distance, of period, of place. I could be anywhere I wanted to be simultaneously.'

## The scalar connection

There is an overall field that encompasses the entirety of our reality and operates beyond what we perceive as time and space and the speed of light. I will call it the scalar field. The term 'scalar' is highly controversial among scientists and those who challenge their orthodoxy, and I have read several different explanations and definitions. I am using the name scalar in the context of this book to describe a field from which the realms of waveform and holographic reality ultimately manifest. What I am calling the quantum field of possibility and probability is an expression ultimately of this scalar field which in my definition interpenetrates everything. It is similar in theme, though not detail, with the mainstream scientific concept of 'dark matter/energy' or unseen matter/energy that is claimed to comprise the great majority of the Universe. You will see references to scalar waves but they are really a scalar field because of the nature of scalar energy. Whatever you infuse into the scalar field is immediately everywhere in that field and so affecting everything connected to the field – which is *everything* in our reality. The scalar field in my definition is everywhere at the same 'time' because it is beyond time. The instantaneous mass-absorption of information puts the scalar field way beyond the speed of light. I have seen scalar energy described as something that is 'just a quantity without direction or co-ordinates'. But you do not require direction or coordinates when you are everywhere. Nikola Tesla who gave us the fundamentals of modern electrical supply systems was well aware of the scalar phenomenon and I will come back to this.

## Medical madness

Something to ponder: We have virtually an entire global medical profession treating the body and its malfunctions while having no idea what the body or reality really is. *Mmmm* ... I wonder why mainstream medicine is one of Planet Earth's biggest killers. It's like asking me to mend your car engine. It would never work again. The difference is that I wouldn't dream of messing with an engine I know nothing about, while doctors mess with human bodies every day that they misunderstand in their

**Figure 63:** Doctors are misled their entire careers about the true nature of the body and how it works.

foundation form because medical science has misled them their entire careers (Fig 63). Why they are misled is coming later on. I am not saying that doctors don't do good work that benefits people, but talking in totality how can you not create mayhem overall if you are treating something that you don't understand? Mainstream medicine doesn't accept that the body is a waveform information construct and sees only the illusory physical from its perceptual prison of the five senses. The holographic level of the body is a decoded projection of waveform information and always reflects that informational state. The balance or imbalance of the waveform field reflects as the balance or imbalance (dis-ease) of the hologram. What's more the balance or imbalance of the perceiver also affects which possibilities and probabilities are decoded into holographic experience, including the health or otherwise of their bodies. Imbalanced emotion is the biggest cause of human disease (dis-ease) and emotional imbalance = energetic imbalance = decoding imbalance = holographic imbalance. Waveform distortions become holographic distortions and it cannot be any other way because one is a projection of the other. Even mainstream medicine acknowledges the reality of psychosomatic illness, and evidence for mental and emotional states manifesting as 'physical' ailments is now enormous. This is how that happens. Imbalanced thought and emotion generates imbalanced electrical and waveform frequencies that distort the electrical/waveform fields of the body which then project into the hologram. In the same way balanced and positively focused thoughts and emotion can re-balance distortions in the electrical/waveform fields. I was told when I was 19 that my own arthritis would probably put me in a wheelchair in my 30s. Forty-six years later at aged 65 I am talking on my feet for ten hours at a time and waking up fine the next morning. Why no wheelchair? Because I wasn't having it, that's why, as I told the wheelchair predictors at the 'time'. Mind governs 'physical' experience – and awareness beyond that even more so if we allow it in. Perception decodes reality from the quantum field of possibility and probability and in doing so dictates health. Doctors give a prognosis or life expectancy and that perception – if accepted by the patient – becomes a self-fulfilling prophecy as perception is decoded into experienced reality. Message to doctors – *don't tell people what is going to happen to them or how long they have to live.* Let them decide that – not you. Mainstream medicine sees only the hologram or what is perceived to be physical and when your only tool is a hammer every problem looks like a nail. More aware people note that so-called modern medicine only treats the symptom and not the cause, but how else could that be when you only accept the existence of the five-sense body and not of the waveform field from which it is holographically decoded? The cause is imbalance in the waveform field (most often caused by imbalanced emotion) and with the medical profession rejecting the existence of the waveform level they cannot possibly treat the cause. They are left with only the symptom and the way waveform imbalance manifests in the hologram. You have a pain? We'll give you a painkiller. You have a cancer? We'll cut it out or destroy your immune system for life with chemotherapy (what one doctor called weed killer) and radiation which *causes* cancer. Studies have revealed that chemotherapy also causes cancer and allows it to grow more aggressively because of its effect on body systems. Mainstream 'modern' medicine is a killing machine and could not fail to be so for the reasons outlined here. Where does 'physical' health come into anything when you consider this quote from earlier – 'If we lost all the dead space inside our atoms we would each be able to fit into a particle of dust and the entire human race would fit into the volume of a sugar cube.' My own view as I said before is that we are not even a particle of dust because 'matter' is 100 percent illusion. So where do 'physical' ailments like arthritis come from? They are not physical because there is no physical – they are schisms in the energetic waveform/electromagnetic field and must be healed at that level.

## Killing the competition

Alternative or complimentary medicine overwhelmingly targets the waveform level of energetic information with the understanding (among the *best* practitioners I should stress) that if the waveform field is in balance the 'physical' body must be so. They seek to help the body heal itself. These are the same alternative healers that are now being mercilessly targeted with fierce regulation and intimidation by tyrannies including national governments, the European Union and a global scam called Codex Alimentarius (created by Nazis jailed for war crimes) which are all working in the interests of the Big Pharma pharmaceutical cartel to destroy the complimentary competition. Codex Alimentarius or 'Food Code'/'Food Book' seeks to use the excuse of harmonising global regulation to take genuine complimentary treatments out of circulation and give control over useless synthetic copies to Big Pharma. My long-time friend Mike Lambert at the Shen Clinic on the Isle of Wight is a healing genius who knows what the body really is, but that makes him a target for the authorities when they should be giving him every encouragement and helping him share his knowledge. Complimentary practitioners are being closed down and even jailed for making any claims about what they do even though the evidence to support what they say can be produced. Mainstream laboratory findings cannot be quoted by alternative medicine in support of their work or prosecution could follow. We have the ludicrous and outrageous situation in places like the EU in which nutrition, food supplements and other products can still be produced (though give them 'time'), but not a word can be said about their potential beneficial effect while Big Pharma can make claims galore that turn out to be mendacious and sometimes deadly. This is where we are in this war against what I will call waveform field practitioners:

'This might be good for you.'
'Why?'
'I can't tell you.'

Meanwhile, 'Big Pharma' can by comparison claim pretty much what it likes about its symptom-obsessed potions that mostly do no good at all or cause more and often worse problems than those they are claiming to treat. It is pathetic to hear breathless voiceovers racing through a long list of 'side-effects' at the end of drug advertisements on American television. Some have even taken to putting pictures over the voice to divert viewers' attention from what is being said. They care about your health all right. Drug companies have to massively overstep the mark before they risk prosecution and even then most of the fines are derisory against the staggering size of their annual profits. The reason for this extraordinary level of bias against waveform field practitioners in favour of hologram obsessives will become obvious and it is not only about money – far from it. They want to destroy all alternatives to Big Pharma as part of a global agenda of human control and oppression. Governments, global bodies and Big Pharma have long been targeting

**Figure 64:** Global organised crime syndicate.

alternative methods and practitioners in a coordinated conspiracy which I have exposed in other books. The idea is to delete all other health care and leave humanity at the mercy of these pharmaceutical psychopaths who have been exposed for shocking practises that include reducing drug supplies to drive up the price by thousands of percent (Fig 64). The global campaign against alternative ways of healing are made easier by the astonishing amounts of money spent in political campaign funding and lobbying by the Big Pharma cartel. Donald Trump's health policy replacement for Obamacare in the United States was drafted by people given hundreds of thousands of dollars by the pharmaceutical industry. Another point to make here is that Big Pharma poisons and potions are damaging and imbalancing the body's waveform field even while its existence is publicly rejected. I say publicly because deep in the shadows they know how it all works and therefore the havoc they wreak. If you could see pharmaceutical drugs on their waveform level you would see distorted and chaotic fields of frequency and vibration that interact with the waveform fields of the body and pass on that distortion and energetic chaos. We call this 'side-effects' when the distortions play through to the hologram. Swallowing poison does not directly kill the body – the waveform level of the body becomes so distorted and inverted that it ceases to function as an energetic organism. What happens in the hologram when poison is swallowed is only a reflection of what is happening in the waveform field. This principle further applies to both the mass toxicity in the environment and chemical-infested (vibrationally-distorted) shit in vaccines and what is bravely called food. We may see black toxic sludge pouring into a river, but on the waveform level that sludge is a distorted and chaotic field of information which impacts on the waveform field of the river and the same distortion is passed on to the fish and other river life. Radiation is so dangerous and deadly because it distorts the waveform field of the body, and today's human society is deluged with it. The global health crisis can only ever be made worse by a mainstream medicine that has no idea what it is actually 'treating'. A system so utterly insane can only spew out ever greater numbers of ill (energetically-imbalanced) people. The only answer – and those behind all this don't want an answer – is for waveform field practitioners and researchers to be set free from their witch hunt and allowed to address illness in ways that will (a) genuinely heal people and (b) stop them getting ill in the first place.

## Waveform water

Professor Dame Sally Davies, UK Government Chief Medical Officer, said: 'Homeopaths are peddlers and homeopathy is rubbish.' Homeopathy is a perfect example of mainstream medicine's arrogance of ignorance. The programmed thought-processes of people like Davies follow this ever-recurring pattern: 'If we can't explain it then it can't be happening.' This mentality pervades Mainstream Everything and those with perceptions downloaded from Mainstream Everything. Much of the alternative media is infected with the same myopia. How can people like Sally Davies understand the basis on which homeopathy works when they don't understand or accept how reality works? This is the chicken and egg bind that holds such people in their life-long addiction to ignorance. The foundation of their disbelief in homeopathy is that its potions are so diluted that there are no ingredients remaining in the water. Note: 'ingredients' = what I can *see*. If they can't see something it cannot exist. A mainstream UK newspaper reported that 2,500 'vets and animal lovers' had called for a ban on the use of homeopathy on animals. They said it was dangerous compared with 'proven medicines', you know the ones produced by the Big Pharma cartel that contribute to the incredible annual death toll of mainstream 'medicine'. The key line in the article said: '... scientists argue that the cures are so diluted they are unlikely to contain any of the original substance.' I'll explain why that doesn't matter. Researchers at the Aerospace Institute in Stuttgart, Germany, have developed a way to photograph information in droplets of water. They dipped a flower into a tank of water and took it out again before photographing the droplets. They found that the energetic information from the flower was in *all* of the droplets – the holographic principle again. The information of the flower was retained in the water even when the flower ('substance') had been removed, and the same happens with homeopathy. Energetic information of the substance stays in the water after the substance itself has been diluted away and it is this which interacts with the body at the level of the *waveform field*. I am not saying that homeopathy is effective every time or even at all in the wrong hands, but this is the principle on which it can work and often does. Dr Vladimir Poponin, a Russian researcher, beamed a laser through DNA and when the 'physical' DNA was removed it remained in the laser in energetic form under the same principle as the flower and the water. This is known as the 'Phantom DNA Effect' but it is not a phantom. It is DNA in waveform. Stuttgart researchers also invited people from the local community for an experiment in which they were each asked to take four droplets from a tank of water and put them in a dish with their name on. When these drops were photographed each set of four were different from the other sets, but each of the four from each person were virtually identical in their energetic signature (Fig 65). The simple and brief act of taking a droplet from the tank and putting it in a dish had transferred the person's unique energetic signature to the water. This is how we are interacting with our energetic environment and each other second after illusory second at the waveform level of the Cosmic Internet as we 'download' and 'post' information. The principle was compellingly confirmed by the work of a friend of

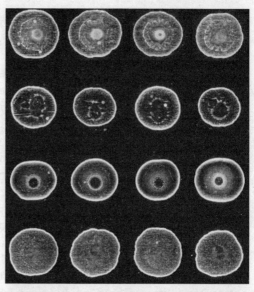

**Figure 65:** Information in the four droplets from each person was virtually the same.

mine, the late Japanese researcher, Dr Masaru Emoto. He perfected a way of photographing the impact of frequency and vibration on water crystals. Water is also a waveform field in its base state as everything is in our reality and so water is impacted by waveform influences. Dr Emoto would write words of love or hate on the side of canisters of water and then freeze them very quickly before photographing the crystals. He would also sometimes use polluted water, subject water to various kinds of music (vibration/frequency) and attach a mobile phone to the canister. The difference this made to the crystals was stunning as you can see from the illustrated examples (Fig 66).Words of love and thanks written on the canisters produced perfectly balanced and beautiful crystals while words of hate created a distorted mess. How come? Everything in its base state – even written words – is waveform energy (information). The spoken word is obviously a vibrational phenomenon produced by the vocal chords which the brain decodes into language. The written word operates on the same principle. We may see words as ink on paper in the hologram, but their foundation state is waveform information and the *intent* behind them dictates their frequency state whether high or low, balanced or distorted. Saying 'I hate you' with a joke and a smile does not generate the same frequency as saying the same with intent and venom. Words written on the side of the water canister transfer their vibrational state to the waveform level of the water and this changes the nature of the water crystals. Polluted water seriously distorts the crystals for reasons I explained earlier and

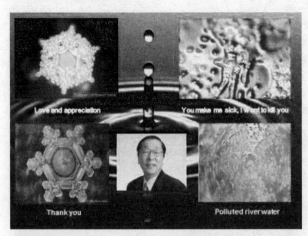

**Figure 66:** Different frequency/vibration from intent, emotion, thought and pollution expressed in the water crystals.

**Figure 67:** 'Prayer' or focused thought and intent can change the energetic state of water crystals.

the same with mobile phones. Polluted water can be transformed into balance by what is termed 'prayer', which is concentrated and focused thought (Fig 67). Attention and intent generate frequency fields that change the waveform structure of the water and a positive focus and intent based on love, appreciation and respect can rebalance everything. We are constantly being impacted by our energetic environment – and impacting upon it – while the overwhelming majority have no idea this is so. Voice to ear communication, while it appears to dominate human interaction, is really only a holographic sideshow.

Consciousness and its waveform vehicle is the stadium in which life plays out. By the way, 'prayer' can (not necessarily *will* but can) focus attention or *perception* on the quantum field of possibility and probability and manifest an experienced reality that appears to be your 'prayers being answered'. They are not answered by some deity in the sky, but your own reality-decoding potential from the infinite well of infinite possibility.

## Paranormal

Human society is an inversion wherever you look because its perceptions are driven by manufactured ignorance and, in terms of those in the shadows, by extremely evil intent. The inversion of normal and paranormal is a great example. Normal is only what we normally experience and nothing more. If we fall for the trap of believing in Mainstream Everything's programmed myopia then normal will be a tiny band of possibility; but if you breach the walls of such downloaded deception you realise that what is called 'paranormal' is the real normal

and the way things really are. Human 'normal' is nothing more than a mind prison of programmed perceptions. 'Normal' laughs at those who say they have seen aliens or spaceships, as if the only 'intelligent' life in the infinity of forever are human beings living on a planet which when compared with the

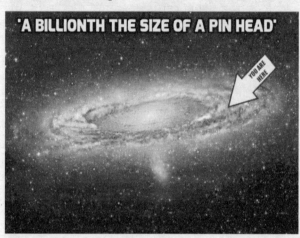

**Figure 68:** 'A little perspective.

projected size of the Universe is the equivalent of a billionth of a pinhead (Fig 68). 'Normal' laughs at those who claim to have seen 'ghosts' even though this is a constantly common theme throughout human existence all over the world. I said earlier that ghosts or apparitions are expressions of awareness in other frequency bands close to ours (Fig 69). They mostly appear ethereal because they are not on our frequency and they are the visual version of interference by one radio station on another. The main station (our reality) is the dominant one and the interference station (the ghost) is more distant and fuzzy because it is not on the frequency of the

**Figure 69:** 'Ghosts' are entities and other energetic states operating on frequencies close enough to ours to be seen if only ethereally.

main station. 'Normal' dismisses the arts of divination such as tarot cards and rune stones because 'normal' does not understand how they can work and so, by definition, they can't, eh, Dame Sally? We are a waveform field and tarot cards are a waveform field. Images and symbolism of each tarot card or rune stone dictates its frequency/vibrational state and this is a visual version of intent that comes from what cards or stones represent. Interaction during a tarot card reading or when the runes are thrown is happening at the electromagnetic waveform level of reality (Fig 70). We pick one card and not another because of the electromagnetic synchronisation and attraction between the card's field and our own. What the card symbolically represents and is expressed electromagnetically makes a connection with a similar frequency within our own electromagnetic field which in turn represents something in our mental and emotional state. A spread of cards on the table is a visual representation of the probabilities and possibilities poised to be manifested by our energetic field and awareness through our mental and emotional state of *perception*. Gifted people in this arena can read what they believe might happen from the quantum possibilities and probabilities set before them in the form of cards or rune stones. I emphasise the term *gifted*. In all these so-called paranormal arts there are outstanding people and fakes who try to persuade others to believe them. Personal recommendations

**Figure 70:** Tarot cards are electromagnetic (information) states connecting with similar states in the human energy field.

**Figure 71:** Psychics and mediums (genuine ones) are expanding their perception range to connect with other frequencies or dimensions of reality.
© www.neilhague.com

from previous clients are a good way to avoid frauds. 'Normal' laughs at psychics and mediums who say they can connect with awareness in other realities. They can be a stage show psychic at the level of 'Is there a Mary? I'm getting a Mary'; or they can be those relatively few who can connect with realities and expanded awareness way beyond our frequency band. The question is not whether this is possible – it is – but rather can this or that person actually do it. Those that can are expanding their frequency range to attune with other realities and awareness which can then communicate through them into our realm (Fig 71). A psychic/medium acts as a conduit between two frequency bands to allow one to communicate with the other. This is what Betty Shine was doing and where the 'voice' or thought forms that I heard in the newspaper shop and on the hill in Peru came from. Awareness they attune with can be anything from Infinite Awareness in awareness of itself to some very dark, dense and manipulative entities in frequency bands close to this one. These are the entities that Satanists interact with in their sick and manipulative rituals. The paranormal/normal inversion is a potent example of the collective inversion which is human society. Paranormal represents the true nature of reality while normal is a manufactured figment of programmed imagination or rather lack of it. Those with an understanding of the para*real*normal have always been at best ridiculed and at worst burned at the stake while advocates of the idiocy-normal are feted as great minds and given titles and status. The consequences of this have been catastrophic.

## Body Alcatraz

From this explanation of reality comes so much to be joyous about in the sense that we are Infinite Awareness in an eternal (actually timeless) state of being aware and we explore infinite experience and possibility forever and the proverbial day. On the other hand, in terms of our current predicament, the same nature of reality allows for something that is rather less joyous and pleasant. This is the manipulation of perception and turning the body into a perceptual prison cell. I will explain in detail how this enslavement is induced and policed throughout our lives, but the overall outcome I can deal with now as this opening chapter comes to a close. The perception conspiracy is all about hijacking and controlling our focus of attention and locking away human perception and belief in the realm of the five senses (Figs 72 and 73). We are awareness that should perceive multiple realities in the same NOW which is why near-death experiencers describe just such a perceptual state when they have withdrawn from the body-prison which focuses attention within visible light. The body on all levels from waveform to hologram

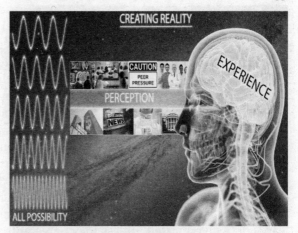

**Figure 72:** Limit and control perception and you limit and control reality.

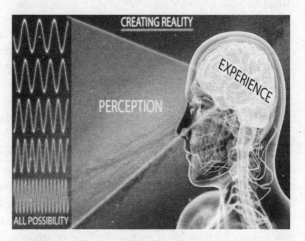

**Figure 73:** Freedom is opening the mind to expanded awareness and multiple realities where the human condition can be seen in a very different light.

has been specifically created or tinkered with to focus human attention in that tiny band of frequency and impose a sense of reality dominated by the five senses. Scientists, doctors, politicians and 'journalists' are all under the same perceptual lock and key as the general population and often more so. The entire System, not least 'education', is specifically structured to maintain this delusional status quo in which sight, hearing, touch, taste and smell are the arbiters of everything. Those that see beyond the illusion are called mad, bad or dangerous with five-sense religion leading the way before 'science' joined its ranks at the front line. It is a head-shaker to watch people like Professor Richard Dawkins and his mind-set condemning religion while acting in exactly the same way

**Figure 74:** 'I'm closed minded? Who me? Never.'

in their own religion of 'Scientism'. Both versions of religion have an immovable belief system that repels all borders with an unquestioning certainty that if anyone else says something different they must be wrong with no further inquiry or research necessary. To Professor Dawkins no one can be 'sane' or 'well educated' unless they agree with him. Meanwhile, shamans like this one in Central America blow the academics away with their understanding of reality:

> *We are perceivers, we are awareness; we are not objects; we have no solidity. We are boundless ... We, or rather our reason, forget this and thus we entrap the totality of ourselves in a vicious circle from which we rarely emerge in our lifetime.*

This 'reason' and 'vicious circle' are generated and exploited to impose a perceptional entrapment which also ensnares those like Professor Dawkins to whom people look for scientific enlightenment (Fig 74). The 'scientific' and 'normal' definitions of 'reason, rational and logical' are all expressions of the same perceptual prison and these are three words that pour forth from the mouths of the Dogma Dawkins School of the scientifically blind and blinkered. Dictionary definitions take us in a circle back to the start or another symbolic circling of the wagons to keep out expanded awareness. *Reason* is defined as 'to determine or conclude by logical thinking'. *Logic* is 'a system of *reasoning*' and *rational* is 'based on or agreeable to *reason*'. 'Mum, I'm back!' All roads lead to *reason* which is also described as 'a normal mental state or sanity'. *Reason*, the word used to determine sanity, turns out to be nothing more than a programmed perception imposing its kindergarten version of normal. Blaise Pascal, the 17th century French philosopher and mathematician, said: 'The end point to rationality is to demonstrate the limits of rationality.' Well, it is to those who are conscious beyond the programming. There must be an end point because rationality as perceived by Mainstream Everything is the concept of a closed mind, not an open one. A closed mind is another standing or stationary wave jogging on the spot and oscillating only in the realm of the perceived known with no desire to move on and explore the infinite realms of the unknown – unknown at least to humanity (Fig

**Figure 75:** A closed mind is a standing wave jogging on the spot buying the lie and going nowhere.
© www.neilhague.com

75). When I observe the Dogma Dawkins mentality I see a standing wave oscillating with its certainties while unwilling to move beyond them. I also see fear in their eyes – the fear of being wrong. Maybe that's the real reason they stay where they are and attack those who don't.

So who or what would want to put the human race in a perceptual trance and lock us away in the five senses ... and why? To that, we shall now turn.

# CHAPTER TWO

# The Inversion

*'Nothing would be what it is because everything would be what it isn't. And contrary-wise; what it is it wouldn't be, and what it wouldn't be, it would. You see?' – **Alice in Wonderland***

Our reality is one gigantic inversion and there is no better example than mainstream religion. You know that 'loving god' they talk about who 'created the world'? Well ...

The Bible is an amalgamation of ancient writings and texts that have been seriously manipulated and distorted to often present the opposite of what was originally written. The Old Testament which either dominates or influences the beliefs of Judaism, Christianity, Islam and their many offshoots is a blatant inversion. All three believe in the Old Testament character of Abraham and are known as Abrahamic religions. Similar inversions of 'God created the world' can be found in other faiths and you have to consult the writings and beliefs on which they are based to appreciate how corrupted are the very foundations of major religions. I am going to explore some of those pre-biblical, pre-koranic texts in this chapter, put them in a modern context and show their connection to humanity's current plight.

I consciously began my quest to understand the world and reality in 1990. I can see now that my whole life before this had been leading me to the point where I became aware of the patterns of 'coincidence' driving the twists, turns and directions I had experienced since childhood. I have been led for decades by awareness in the unseen to information from people, documents, books and personal experience that have handed me the puzzle pieces in an extraordinarily coordinated way. The challenge was to go to depths of the rabbit hole where no one had gone before in terms of the scale and breadth of connected information across a vast array of subjects and happenings. For this to be achieved in a single human lifespan the information had to be presented

to me in at least a fairly A to B to C order or it would have all been too
chaotic, bewildering and overwhelming to understand its implications
and put it all together. The best part of 30 years ago as I write these
words I went to see the psychic Betty Shine and a year later came my
colossal initial conscious awakening after the 'download' on the hill in
Peru and the historic levels of public ridicule that followed back home in
Britain. Information coming to me was largely about the world of the
seen in the early years. I realised that those who appear to be in power
in politics, corporations, banking, media, science, medicine, religion etc.,
are only agents and pawns – some knowingly, most unknowingly – of a
force operating from the shadows and pursuing an agenda of global
human control. George Orwell's *Nineteen-Eighty-Four* and Aldous
Huxley's *Brave New World* tapped into this agenda which is why they
have been so prophetic. Orwell, real name Eric Blair, knew Huxley who
taught him French at the elite Eton College near Windsor Castle, west of
London, where royal children go. But there is *enormously* more to know
than even they suggested from their knowledge of where humanity was
planned to be taken. The flow of information coming to me expanded
from the mid-1990s into the realms of *non-human* entities, particularly
those taking a reptilian form and the classic 'Greys' of 'alien' legend.
Suddenly, as I travelled around the world, I was 'coincidentally' meeting
people, one after the other, telling me similar stories about their
knowledge and direct experience of non-human entities of many kinds
with Reptilians and Greys the most common. More mass ridicule
followed when I published *The Biggest Secret* and *Children of the Matrix*
exposing the non-human manipulation of human affairs, but by then I
didn't give a shit. I am interested in the truth, not a popularity contest.
Stage three of the information transfer began with my ayahuasca
experience in Brazil and has taken me deeply into the illusory nature of
'physical' reality. Now the pieces all began to fit in a way they could not
before. As each new stage unfolded they would run concurrently with
the others and so today I am dealing with information about all levels of
what is a fantastic rabbit hole of hidden deceit.

## Using your nous – or going beyond it?

A few years ago, I came across a treasure trove of ancient information
found in a sealed jar in 1945 near the town of Nag Hammadi about 75-80
miles north of Luxor on the banks of the River Nile in Egypt (Fig 76).
They are known as the Nag Hammadi Library, texts or scriptures and
thanks to them other major pieces in the puzzle were revealed and my
already developing conclusions confirmed. The latter point is very
relevant. One writer who produced a good book on the Nag Hammadi
texts felt the need to dismiss my work because at that time I was not
including this information. What he didn't realise, however, amid his

**Figure 76:** The Nag Hammadi treasure trove of Gnostic information.

own obsession with a single source, is that my work is being driven from the unseen in a particular A to B to C sequence, and not being aware of the content of these texts before I had reached my own conclusions from a wide range of other sources was vitally important. Had that not been the case the texts could have become, as they are for some researchers, the whole foundation of my belief system and another one-stop-shop religion. The timing ensured that they acted for me as another massive confirmation and addition to what I had already concluded about the human plight and control of our reality. The Nag Hammadi find included 13 leather-bound papyrus codices (manuscripts) and more than 50 texts written in Coptic Egyptian which were the work – with other ancient influences – of a people known as Gnostics. They were not a racial group so much as a way of perceiving reality under the heading of Gnosticism. This comes from the term gnosis or knowledge in the context of spiritual knowledge and awareness of reality as it *really* is. Gnosis is a Greek word that translates as secret knowledge, and Gnostic means 'learned'. We have the saying in English about 'using your nous' or using your head/brain/intelligence; but to Gnostics spiritual awakening or 'salvation' could only be attained by expanding awareness *beyond* what they called *nous* and into *pneuma* (Infinite Self). Humanity's version of the intellect on which the whole crazy world is based is actually a shockingly low level of awareness which is lauded and feted as the fountain of knowledge. It's more like a spout of ignorance. Gnostics were active in many locations and were targeted mercilessly by the Roman Church which felt severely threatened by the way the foundation of its own belief system was being turned on its head. What the Roman Church saw as its all-powerful God to be worshipped without question the Gnostics believed was the source of evil that created the material world – in my terms the 'material' world of the digital, holographic computer-like simulation that I will be explaining in detail in the next chapter. Gnostics could see through the illusion of 'matter' and I have no doubt they were helped in that understanding by the use of psychoactive potions that took them 'out there'.

The Royal or Great Library of Alexandria in Egypt with its amazing collection of ancient knowledge and history was dominated by Gnostic thought (Fig 77). An estimated nearly half a million scrolls, manuscripts and documents were gathered from many locations including Assyria, Greece, Persia and India, as well as Egypt. Those with more expanded awareness were attracted to this oasis of open-mindedness and among them was a woman called Hypatia (about 350-415AD). She was an Athens-educated mathematician, astronomer

**Figure 77:** The Royal Library of Alexandria.

and philosopher who taught the work of Greek philosophers Plato and Aristotle and was head of the Platonist school at Alexandria (Fig 78). One of her reported quotes confirms her openness of mind: 'Reserve your right to think, for even to think wrongly is better than not to think at all.' Many insights about reality were inspired by such a haven of free-thought thousands of years before 'science' allegedly discovered them for the first time. This included the understanding that the Earth goes round the Sun 2,000 years before it was established by the Polish mathematician and astronomer, Nicolaus Copernicus. How so much more enlightened humanity would be had the Gnostics

**Figure 78:** Hypatia was hacked to death by a Catholic mob.

and other open-minded scholars been left unmolested to go about their quest for discovery. Alas, that was not to be. The unfettered, uncensored, free-thinking pursuit of knowledge was bound to twist the knickers of the Roman Church tyranny and in 415AD a mob of bewildered suckers led by Cyril, Patriarch of Alexandria, attacked and essentially destroyed the Royal Library as it had been before. Hypatia was hacked to death. The Library's contents were lost in stages to a combination of fire and theft, and much of what was taken will be in the vaults of the Vatican to this day. Cyril was made a saint as with a long list of Roman Church mass murderers and crooks before and since. The attack that killed Hypatia fits with the estimated age of the Nag Hammadi manuscripts. They are believed to date from between 350-400AD although it is said they are likely to be copies of earlier Greek versions dating to perhaps

120-150AD or earlier. Centuries after the assault on the Gnostics of Alexandria came the campaign against the Gnostic Cathars in southern France which ended with them being burned at the stake after the siege of the Castle of Montségur in 1244.

Gnostic information has always terrified the Church and for good reason, as we are about to see. It was believed that the details of Gnostic belief had been lost thanks to the efforts of Rome, but then Nag Hammadi changed the game. A major point about these documents is that because they were hidden for so long they have not been twisted and tampered with like their religious counterparts to suit the authorities of the 'time'. What the writers believed, the texts still say.

## The Gnostic *All That Is*

Nag Hammadi manuscripts reveal why the Church quivered like a jelly at the Gnostic explanation of the world. I was often amazed reading them to see how themes, foundations and much detail synced with my own conclusions reached before I had ever heard of them. They speak of the 'Father' (Infinite Awareness, All-Possibility, All-Potential) and make the distinction between *nous* (mind) and *pneuma* (Infinite Self). An untitled text in the Nag Hammadi Bruce Codex says that 'The All' (all awareness, all that exists) is contained within the 'Father':

> *He is an incomprehensible one, but it is he who comprehends All. He receives them to himself. And nothing exists outside of him. But All exist within him. And he is boundary to them all, as he encloses them all, and they are all within him. It is he who is Father of the aeons, existing before them all. There is no place outside of him.*

This is what I call the *All That Is* or Infinite Awareness in awareness of itself – 'the force that moves all things' (Fig 79). The Infinite is not even a form of energy, but pure awareness, a state of Isness. Energy comes from

its imagination. You can appreciate why Gnostics would use the term Father to symbolise the concept for people, but now in the era of quantum physics and computerisation we can use modern analogies. Father symbolism was encompassed by the Bible and Church and 'he' was transformed into a bloke on a throne. The word 'aeons'

**Figure 79:** The *All That Is And Ever Can Be* symbolised as 'The Father' by Gnostics.

would be considered today to mean a long period of time, but to Gnostics aeons referred to what we might call bands of perception, reality and potential. Dictionaries define this meaning of aeon as 'a power existing from eternity; an emanation or phase of the supreme deity'. Gnostic texts refer to the 'Upper Aeons' and 'Lower Aeons' in very different terms and they say that between the two is a curtain, veil or boundary. Upper Aeons are said to emanate directly from the unity of 'The One' – *All That Is* in awareness of itself – and can be symbolised as concentric circles expressing the Oneness of their Creator or Emanater. There is no separation or sense of it. Upper Aeons are described by Gnostics as 'The Silence', 'the silent Silence', 'the living Silence', with its 'Watery Light' (Fig 80). This is not the same as the light that we perceive in our reality which is a trap that can be likened to energetic flypaper; but that's for later. Water is often used in the texts to symbolise the Upper Aeon realm of Oneness as in '... the waters which are above', '... the waters which are above matter' and '... the Aeons in the Living Water'. Upper Aeons are a reality (state of being) with no time or space. 'Since the emanations are limitless and immeasurable', as one text says, there can be no time or space. Upper Aeons are pure consciousness or awareness. They are also called *Pleroma* or 'the totality', 'the fullness' and the 'perfection' of 'emanations of the Father'. The Nag Hammadi Gospel of Truth says: 'Therefore, all the emanations of the Father are pleromas, and the root of all his emanations is in the one who made them all grow up in himself.' Upper Aeons are further described as the 'Treasure-House', 'Store-House', 'Dwelling-Place' and 'Kingless Realm'. A text entitled the *Tripartite Tractate* says:

> The emanation of the Totalities, which exist from the one who exists, did not occur according to a separation from one another, as something cast off from the one who begets them. Rather, their begetting is like a process of extension, as the Father extends himself to those whom he loves, so that those who have come forth from him might become him as well.

**Figure 80:** What I experienced as silence Gnostics called 'The Silence'.

The creations (extensions/emanations) of Infinite Awareness in awareness of itself can be symbolised as the manifestations of Thought, but I prefer the term 'creative imagination'. This describes what the Gnostics called the Upper Aeons – the realm of Infinite Imagination and therefore All-Possibility, All-Potential. Gnostics symbolised Infinite Imagination as the 'Father' and 'The Thought' as the Mother. They said the interaction of the two produced a third force or imagined creation/extension/reflection of itself which was symbolised as the Son. A text entitled *Apocryphon of John* ('Secret Writing' of John) describes this concept:

> *For it is he who looks at himself* [saw his reflection] *in his light which surrounds him, namely the spring of the water of life. And it is he ... who gazes upon his image which he sees in the spring of the Spirit. It is he who puts his desire* [intent] *in his water-light which is in the spring of the pure light-water which surrounds him.*

> *And his thought performed a deed and she* [the 'Mother'] *came forth, namely she who had appeared before him* [his image/imagination] *in the shine of his light.* [She] *came forth from his mind ... This is the first thought, his image.*

From here what we call 'Creation' emerged from the imaginations of Infinite Awareness and its creations which are extensions of the same Infinite Awareness. Gnostic texts describe how the act of naming the creations of Infinite Imagination brings them into being. This is from the *Gospel of Truth*:

> *All the spaces are his emanations. They have known that they came forth from him, like children who are from a grown man. They knew that they had not yet received form, nor yet received a name, each one of which the Father begets ...*

> *But the Father is perfect, knowing every space within him. If he wishes, he manifests whomever he wishes, by giving him form and giving him a name, and he gives a name to him, and brings it about that those come into existence.*

Upper Aeons are the realm of the ultimate 'Creator', or creative force/imagination, and it begs a question: If that is the case why is life so unpleasant – even shockingly bad – for so many in our reality? There is an answer to that.

## The 'Error'

A foundation Gnostic belief – their version of 'The Fall' – is that what we experience as material reality was created by error. Their texts describe symbolically how an Aeon, an extension of the 'Father' or Infinite

Awareness, embarked on its own thought-creation without the 'consent of the Father' (or 'consort') who has the true power of Creation. They call this Aeon or awareness 'Sophia'. The Nag Hammadi *Apocryphon of John* says:

> And ... Sophia ...being an Aeon, conceived a Thought from herself with the reflection of the invisible Spirit [Infinite Awareness in awareness of itself] ... She wanted to bring forth a likeness out of herself without the consent of the Spirit ... and without her consort ... And because of the invincible power which is in her, her thought did not remain idle and a thing came out of her which was imperfect and different from her appearance, because she had created it without her consort.

Imbalanced 'Thought' without the balance of Oneness and unity is being symbolically described here. The story of Sophia is describing the original 'Fall'. What 'Sophia' is said to have brought into manifestation was what has become known as the Devil, Satan and a long list of other names for a disruptive and manipulative force. The *Apocryphon of John* again:

> And when she saw the consequence of her desire, it had changed into a form of a lion-faced serpent. And its eyes were like lightning fires ... She cast it away from her, outside that place [the Upper Aeons or Pleroma] that no one of the immortal ones [other Aeons of the Father] might see it, for she had created it in ignorance ... And she called his name Yaldabaoth ...

Yaldabaoth is what I have referred to in other books as the 'Demiurge' which is another name used by Gnostics to describe this force. It is important not to get caught by taking symbolism literally as religions do and of course we don't know all the influences affecting the writers in their own societies when the texts were originally produced. To describe the story in its simplest and most basic form an imbalanced state of awareness was created by an imbalanced creative 'Thought' or imagination.

Someone cocked up, you might say, or that is how it looks from one perspective. I have been convinced long before I saw the Nag Hammadi texts that our simulated reality is the work of a highly negative force and this is what the Gnostics go on to describe. The realm of matter (low frequency) came from the ignorance (low frequency) and suffering (low frequency) of 'Sophia', the texts say, in her anguish at what she had brought into being. Nag Hammadi accounts say that the 'formless entity' of 'Yaldabaoth', or the Demiurge, used the power of his Source-connected 'mother' to manifest the 'Lower Aeons' (including our current reality) as inferior 'bad copies' or 'reflections' of the Upper

Aeons. Yaldabaoth also brought into manifestation other entities which Gnostics call 'Archons' ('Rulers'). The *Apocryphon of John* says:

> ... [Yaldabaoth] *organized (everything) according to the model of the first aeons* [by using] *the power in him, which he had taken from his mother,* [and] *produced in him the likeness of the cosmos ...*

> ... *This is the first archon* [Yaldabaoth] *who took a great power from his mother. And he removed himself from her and moved away from the places in which he was born* [Upper Aeons]. *He became strong and created for himself other aeons with a flame of luminous fire which exists now.*

This theme of 'luminous fire' can also be seen in the 'smokeless fire' attributed by Islamic and pre-Islamic belief to the 'Jinn' or 'Djinn'. These are said to be entities in the unseen and described in very similar terms to the 'Archons' which the Gnostics say were manifested by the Demiurge/Yaldabaoth to serve its interests and desires. Gnostics said Archons were made from luminous fire while Islamic texts say Jinn were made from smokeless fire because they are describing the same entities/force. I say that this luminous fire is, in part, the 'light' of the electromagnetic spectrum including visible light or our simulated reality. This is the 'light' that Satanists and secret society members are talking about when they refer to Lucifer 'the light bringer' – the Demiurge/Yaldabaoth. This is also the light at the start of Genesis when 'the Lord' creates the world (simulation) by saying 'Let there be Light'. Luminous fire is the realm (in part) within the speed of light and what we call radiation. Lighted candles so widely used by Satanists and religion are symbolic of this Archontic 'fire' light. Higher-level Satanists will know this, but mostly only those in the inner circles of religion, and any satanic infiltrators operating within the Church of which there are many. The same symbolism is true of satanic fire rituals including those at Bohemian Grove in northern California every year performed by the political, banking and corporate 'Elite' that I have exposed in other books.

## Realms of 'Down here' ...

I'll come to the Archons shortly, but first these 'bad copy' Lower Aeons (the texts say there are seven). Gnostics describe them as realms of 'deficiency' in contrast to the 'fullness' of the Upper Aeons and no doubt these terms are being applied to energy, its nature and abundance or lack of it (Fig 81). The bad copy Aeons are described with words such as 'imperfection', darkness and the Abyss. They are also said in the texts to be the realms of 'Fate' which is a system of mass control that I will describe later in this chapter. A clear distinction is made between Soul

**Figure 81:** Gnostics said that our reality is a 'bad copy' of the original reality that still exists.
© www.neilhague.com

and Spirit in the Gnostic use of language. Spirit is said to be of the Infinite and the Upper Aeons while Soul is of the Lower Aeons of Yaldabaoth. Our true self is Spirit – the connection to, and emanation from, the Source. 'I'm getting a Mary'-type psychics are communicating within the Lower Aeons while those getting right 'out there' by connecting through Spirit and not Soul (psychic energy) can interact with the Upper Aeons and bring very advanced awareness and knowledge into this realm. When they do they're called crazy. I have used the term 'psychic' in the widest possible sense up to this point but there are levels of communication way beyond 'is there a Mary?' The difference between psychic connections and Spirit connections can be seen in the origin of the term Soul, which comes from the Greek word psykhē. This obviously gives us the English 'psyche' and is defined as 'the mind, or the deepest thoughts, feelings, or beliefs of a person or group'. Lower Aeons are home to Mind/Soul which in the absence of influence from Spirit controls the perceptions of the brain/body. What we call Soul and ego are electromagnetic fields of perception and on one level this is known as the auric field. Soul/ego which withdraws from 'material' reality at what we call death is in truth a point of attention – remember the Alan Watts definition of ego: '... nothing other than the focus of attention.' However, if our point of attention remains in Soul (Mind/Psyche) and not Spirit when we withdraw from 'physicality' we are trapped in the Lower Aeons at other less energetically-dense levels before returning in another bodily form in what is called 'reincarnation'. The reincarnation cycle as perceived in eastern religions and the New Age is a process of birth and rebirth of the Soul in the realm of 'matter' during which learning and suffering lead to a state of 'perfection' that allows the Soul to escape from the cycle. I would most strongly put another perspective on this. A point of attention (Spirit/awareness) becomes trapped in the Lower Aeons until it self-identifies totally with Spirit and enters a state of awareness that can pass through the frequency walls of the Yaldabaoth/Demiurge realms and return to those of Infinite Awareness in awareness of itself in the Upper Aeons. Endless repeating experiences or incarnations of the same basic perception programming is not going to set you free, but can reinforce and further empower the very illusions and deceptions that hold humanity in perceptual (and so frequency) servitude. During my ayahuasca experience in Brazil in 2003 I was shown, in my altered state, an image of people falling from the sky onto a path crossing a field. The path wore away and became deeper and deeper as ever more landed and began to walk. Eventually the path reached a depth where everything was dark and it morphed into a groove like the ones on the old vinyl records. The people just followed the groove wherever it took them. The Voice said that humanity fell so easily for the programming in each incarnation because they were already programmed from the ones that had gone before. This applies not least in their acquiescence to perceived authority. We don't generally remember our previous sojourns into the 'physical' but we are influenced by them. Maybe we had a bad experience with water, and in this life have an apparently unexplainable and 'irrational' fear of water; or it could be flying, enclosed or wide-open spaces, whatever relates to a previous unpleasant experience. Those that reject reincarnation should consult books and television series like *The Ghost Inside My Child* which produce compelling evidence of young children remembering in detail their experiences in other lives involving documentable events they could not possibly have known about. Information and perception programming from each incarnation is encoded in the Soul field and can lead to both behavioural and even 'physical' traits being repeated. How is all this going to free us from the reincarnation cycle? It's not. We can learn from experience and use that to awaken from the Big Sleep, but recurring bad experiences can also imprison human perception deeper into density and programmed illusion. It is surely crazy that we have to suffer to be 'saved'. If we believe this then we can believe that suffering is necessary and even normal because God wills it. But it's not normal – it's the work of a highly negative force. Gnostic texts called *Pistis Sophia* symbolise the outer walls of the Yaldabaoth/Demiurge reality as a dragon swallowing its own tail: 'The outer darkness is a great dragon, whose tail is in his

**Figure 82:** The Ouroboros or snake swallowing its own tail.

**Figure 83:** Neil Hague's depiction of the Gnostic Leviathan – the Ouroboros through which 'souls have to pass to reach paradise'.

mouth, outside the whole world and surrounding the whole world.' This is the symbol known as the Ouroboros or Leviathan and sounds very much like the boundary that Gnostics describe between the Upper and Lower Aeons (Figs 82 and 83). They said the outermost planetary sphere or Archon (of the Lower Aeons) is Saturn. Beyond that is Leviathan, which Souls had to pass through to reach paradise (although they are no longer 'Souls' when they get there, but pure Spirit). These themes also relate to the ancient esoteric concept of the 'Ring-Pass-Not' which is defined this way:

> *A profoundly mystical and suggestive term signifying the circle or bounds of frontiers within which is contained the consciousness of those who are still under the sway of the delusion of separateness – and this applies whether the Ring be large or small.*
>
> *It is a general term applicable to any state in which an entity, having reached a certain stage of evolutionary growth of the unfolding of consciousness, finds itself unable to pass into a still higher state because of some delusion under which the consciousness is labouring, be that delusion mental or spiritual.*

'Delusion' = a frequency too low to pass through the walls of the 'ring' or 'dragon' and escape the Gnostic Lower Aeons. Nag Hammadi manuscripts say that the Upper Aeons established a boundary with the lower versions which they call 'the Limit' to separate 'Sophia' from her creation or 'unborn idea', Yaldabaoth: '...her inborn idea, with its passion, was separated from her by Horos [the Limit], fenced off and expelled from that circle.' Presumably this separation or disconnection from the Source of creative power explains why Gnostics said the Demiurge/Yaldabaoth and its subordinate Archons do not have the ability to create anything from nothing and can only twist and manipulate what has already been created. Texts say that 'by this Horos (Limit) they declare that Sophia was purified and established ... She herself certainly remained within the Pleroma' (Upper Aeons). Other legends still connect Sophia to her creation, Yaldabaoth. An untitled text in the *Bruce Codex* describes the separation of Upper and Lower Aeons.

> *And then the existent separated itself from the non-existent. And the non-existent is the evil which has manifested in matter. And the enveloping power separated those that exist from those that do not exist. And it called the existent 'eternal', and it called the non-existent 'matter'. And in the middle it separated those that exist from those that do not exist, and it placed veils between them.*

This may seem strange to describe Lower Aeons as non-existent when we are *experiencing* this very realm of 'non-existence', but two things: (1) matter as we perceive it does not exist; and (2) does a shadow exist in the same way as that of which it is a shadow? There is a theme of the Lower Aeons being a reflection or shadow ('copies') of the Upper Aeons and that's appropriate because when something reflects on water ('light') it becomes an inversion of what it is reflecting (Fig 84). Demiurge reality is certainly an inversion of prime reality as in fullness/deficiency, immortal/mortal, spiritual/psychic, spirit/soul, existence/non-existence, no-time/time, and so on. Upper Aeons are described in terms of archetypes or what we would call the blueprint while the Lower Aeons are inferior shadows or reflections of that blueprint. This once again explains 'bad copy' symbolism. Upper Aeon blueprints and archetypes are forms of information. We don't live 'in' a world so much as we decode an information

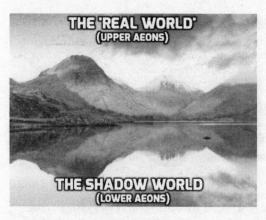

**Figure 84:** Gnostics said that our reality is a reflection, shadow or 'copy' of true reality.

**Figure 85:** We don't live 'in' a world but an information source that we decode into an experience of being 'in'.
© www.neilhague.com

source that we perceive ourselves to live 'in' (Fig 85). Lower Aeons are an inferior 'copy' of *information* (awareness) reflected from the Upper Aeons and the copy has been constantly twisted and inverted to ever greater extremes by Demiurge/Yaldabaoth insanity. As I mentioned, Gnostic texts describe the Upper Aeons as a realm of no-time and the Lower Aeons as the realm of time which reflects what I outlined in the opening chapter (Fig 86). Upper and lower are not literally up above and down below, but symbolic of different states of being that share the same Infinity, like radio stations on different frequencies sharing the same 'space'. Nag Hammadi manuscript *Zostrianos* tells us: 'In relation to the reflection which he [Yaldabaoth] saw in it, he created the world. With a reflection of a reflection he worked at producing the world.' But 'he' didn't create the world from nothing so

**Figure 86:** Gnostics said that the Upper Aeons was a realm of no-time and the 'copy' or reflection was a realm of (illusory) time.

much as distort a copy or reflection of what already existed. Texts say that in some way the establishment of 'the Limit' caused this reflection or shadow reality to be cast: 'A veil exists between the world above and the realms that are below; and shadow came into being beneath the veil; and that shadow became matter; and that shadow was projected apart' (*Hypostasis of the Archons*). The Gnostic manuscript entitled *Origin of the World* states:

> Now the eternal realm of truth has no shadow outside it, for the limitless light is everywhere within it. But its exterior is shadow, which has been called by the name 'darkness'.

This takes us to ancient Greek philosopher Plato (about 428 to about 347BC) and his Allegory of the Cave. Plato was a major influence in Gnostic belief. He said that humans were like prisoners who had lived in a cave all their lives and never seen outside (Fig 87). Behind them is a fire and between the prisoners and the fire is a raised walkway. Prisoners can only look at the wall of the cave in front of them and can't turn around or see in any other direction. Figures pass across the walkway casting shadows on the wall

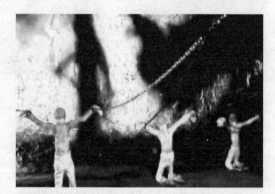

**Figure 87:** Plato's Allegory of the Cave.

from the light of the fire. All that the prisoners can see are the shadows and without knowing where they come from or what they are the shadows are believed to be real. Some prisoners would become experts on the shadows without realising what they really were and they would be called masters of nature (today's scientists and academics). One of the prisoners escapes from the cave and sees reality as it truly is. He can't believe his eyes to start with and then realises that his world of shadows is unreal and fake. He goes back to the cave to tell the other prisoners what he has discovered, but they don't believe him, call him crazy and say they will kill him if he tries to set them free. What a perfect summary of the shadow realms of the Gnostic Lower Aeons and the human plight to this day. What if humanity's perception of self, including Lower Aeon 'Soul', is only a reflection of the real self in the Upper Aeons and therefore as Gnostic symbolism suggested we don't really exist? What if it is not 'we' who are trapped in the Lower Aeons, but only a symbolic reflection or shadow of Upper Aeon 'we'? What if, given that everything is consciousness, the shadow 'copies' took on a life of their own while perceiving themselves to be the original 'I'? As the song goes ... 'Me and my shadow walking down the avenue ...' It's worth a ponder.

## Insane 'God' of the 'Limitless Chaos'

Yaldabaoth, who I will refer to as the Demiurge from hereon, is described by Gnostics as insane and 'The Blind One'. Samael and Saklas are other names given to this Demiurge force and they translate as 'The Blind God' and 'The Foolish One' (Fig 88). Gnostic manuscripts say that the Demiurge didn't know of his creator 'mother' Sophia and looked out on the realm of 'matter' (low frequency energy) that his mother's mental and emotional trauma had manifested. 'He' believed this was all his doing and that he was all that existed although 'he' later learned otherwise. 'Opening his eyes, the chief Archon saw a vast quantity of matter without limit, and he became arrogant, saying, "It is I who am God, and there is no other power apart from me"' (*Hypostasis of the Archons*). This is the origin of the angry, bloodthirsty deity insisting that he is the 'only God'. Gnostics equated the Demiurge with Yahweh/Jehovah, the nasty 'God' of the Old Testament,

**Figure 88:** How Gnostics described the Demiurge/Yaldabaoth.

who is reported in the Bible to have said: '*I am* the LORD, and *there is* none else, *there is* no God beside me' (Isaiah 45:5). The Demiurge and the vicious Old Testament 'God' are the same fellah all right (Fig 89). Here's a flavour of the chap in Leviticus:

**Figure 89:** Different names, same force.

*You will eat the flesh of your sons and the flesh of your daughters. I will destroy your high places, cut down your incense altars and pile your dead bodies on the lifeless forms of your idols, and I will abhor you ... I will scatter you among the nations and will draw out my sword and pursue you. Your land will be laid waste, and your cities will lie in ruins.*

Nice bloke. But, of course, 'he' is not a bloke at all. 'He' is symbolic of a deeply imbalanced, distorted and inverted state of awareness which wants to turn everything into its own distorted state or image – 'Let us make man in our own image'(Genesis 1:26) and all that. Okay, big gulp, major religions are worshipping this force as their God. The 'Let there be Light' God described at the start of Genesis which 'created the world in seven days' is not Infinite Awareness in awareness of itself, but the Demiurgic force creating our illusory reality akin to the holographic simulation portrayed in *The Matrix*. This reminds me of a quote from the TV series, *The Hitchhiker's Guide to the Galaxy*: 'In the beginning the Universe was created. This has made a lot of people very angry and been widely regarded as a bad move.' There are some references in the *New* Testament that symbolise Infinite Awareness, by the way, and this explains the ludicrous contradictions between the angry, hate-filled God of the Old Testament and the more loving God of the New although both versions are highly misleading. Old Testament texts have been majorly tampered with to transform the Gnostic Demiurge into an omnipotent God that billions worship, be it through Christianity, Judaism or Islam. Other names for the Demiurge include the Devil and Satan and we have followers of major religions condemning Satan worship while worshipping the same distorted awareness under another name and persona. I did mention the world was mad, yes? They are worshipping the 'shadow' forces of chaos and the corruption of balance in every way. The Nag Hammadi *Origin of the World* manuscript says:

*... there appeared a force, presiding over the darkness* [Lower Aeons]. *And the forces that came into being subsequent to them called the shadow 'the limitless chaos'.*

They couldn't be describing human society, could they? Surely not, there's no chaos here. Nag Hammadi texts relate our reality to 'Hell', the Abyss and the Outer Darkness, where trapped souls are tormented and manipulated by demons. They say of the Lower Aeons and its state of being in general: 'Therefore they fell down to the pit of ignorance which is called "the Outer Darkness" and "Chaos" and "Hades" and "the Abyss"' (*Tripartite Tractate*). But this 'Hell' does not compare with the extremes of a realm Gnostics call 'the middle place', a 'space' between the Upper and Lower Aeons. This middle place is described as a state of temporary 'non-existence' as the Soul waits to reincarnate or is trapped there by ignorance and its (low-frequency) state of being, which sounds like the Roman Catholic concept of purgatory – 'a place or state of temporary suffering or misery'. The awareness 'Sophia' is said to have resided in this middle place after creating the chaos and distortion known as Yaldabaoth or the Demiurge. Before anyone cancels the laxative order at the very thought of all this, I should stress that the middle place, like this whole realm of the Lower Aeons, is a Demiurge trap that can be avoided and we can get out of here. Gnostics refer to this escape as resurrection. I'll be saying much more about how we transcend this Demiurgic bullshit and leave them all to it.

## Agent Smith Archons

The *Matrix* movie series features software 'agents' inserted into the fake

reality which appear to be human and oversee the control system while seeking out those who have seen through the illusion. The leading one is called Agent Smith and eventually 'he' makes copies of himself until there are countless others all looking and acting like the original Agent Smith

**Figure 90:** Archons are 'software' copies of the Demiurgic distortion in the way that Agent Smith was a replicated software programme.

(Fig 90). Whenever I read in the Nag Hammadi texts about the Demiurge manifesting subordinates to guard the exits and gateways of the Lower Aeons my mind always goes to this theme of Agent Smith. Gnostics called these subordinates or copies 'Archons' and the Demiurge was the 'Lord Archon'. Here you have the source of 'The Lord' and

'Lord God' in the Bible and endless other terms like 'Dark Lord' and 'Time Lord'. You also see the Demiurge/Archons portrayed widely in popular culture and movies under names like Lord (Darth) Vader and Dormammu, the evil ruler of the 'Dark Dimension' trying to take over the 'Earth Dimension' in the Marvel comic movie, *Dr Strange*. Dormammu's 'powers and regeneration

DORMAMMU (DEMIURGE) OF THE 'DARK DIMENSION'
'ENVOY OF THE LORD OF CHAOS'

**Figure 91:** The Demiurgic distortion and its desire for chaos has been portrayed many times in movies and sci-fi works.

**Figure 92:** The Architect – creator of the Matrix in the movie series. Freemasons call their 'god' the 'Great Architect of the Universe' and Gnostics also called the Demiurge the 'Great Architect of the Universe'.

became tied to heat and fire and could be smothered if his environment was deprived of those elements' – the luminous fire of the Demiurge and Archons (Fig 91). Often the writers know what they are symbolising while for others it is some sort of subconscious 'Soul' memory that manifests as imagination. Archons are encoded in terms such as *arch*-angels, *arch*-bishops and the Freemason Creator deity they call the 'Great *Arch*-itect of the Universe'.

Gnostics also called the *Demiurge* the 'Great Architect of the Universe' and the creator of the *Matrix* in the movie series was not by coincidence called the Architect (Fig 92). To grasp what we are really dealing with it is important not to personalise Archons in the sense of the human realm. The Demiurge is mimicking the Upper Aeons which is all that it can do in the absence of creative imagination. What the Gnostics call Archons are extensions or copies of the Demiurge awareness to mimic the Upper Aeons emanations of Infinite Awareness in awareness of itself, but in a dramatically inferior way. Archons are formless energetic states of being that reflect the Demiurge original. They are not extraterrestrial entities as we think of them, but they can take form and infiltrate the mental and emotional states of other forms through the ancient theme of 'possession'. Some Gnostic writings refer to them as the 'formless ones'. 'Demiurgic' and 'Archontic' are terms I am using for a distorted, inverted and monumentally imbalanced state of awareness. You could liken this to a computer virus which infects and distorts perceptions of those it possesses (Fig 93). The Archontic mind is expressed through some extraterrestrial or alien groups while its human Elite consists of royalty, the super-rich financial aristocracy and others who have been dubbed the 'one percent', plus their lackeys in much greater numbers. I will be explaining the background to both the extraterrestrial / alien connection and the human Elite later in the book. I will just use the term Elite for the Archon families and secret society network within global society until we get to the more detailed explanation. Anything and anyone that operates as a vehicle for the Archon mind-set I will refer to as Archontic. The term 'Archon' comes from the Greek and means 'ruler', 'prince', 'authorities' and 'from the beginning'. These are known

**Figure 93:** The Demiurge Archontic distortion infects awareness and energetic balance like a computer virus.
© www.neilhague.com

in every culture under different names. Islam and pre-Islamic Arabia call them 'Jinn' or 'Djinn' and Christianity refers to them as 'demons' or Fallen Angels. Hence we have 'Satan' (Demiurge) and his demons or demonic host (Archons and their offshoots which Gnostic texts call demons). Satan is known by Christians as 'the Demon of Demons' (Archon of Archons). Satan is also, like the Demiurge, known as The Deceiver.

Gnostic manuscripts say the Demiurge and Archons have no 'ennoia' which is translated as 'intentionality', but I prefer 'creative imagination'. This makes sense in that if you are disconnected so totally from the creative force of Infinite Awareness in awareness of itself you are disconnected from the ability to use that gift of creativity. You can twist and distort what already exists, but you cannot create from a blank sheet of paper. This is worth greater emphasis. The Archontic force can 'create' in the sense of making something from something, but not something from nothing. Gnostic writings describe this Archontic state and how they envy humans because those still with a connection to the Source have the creative gift at least in some measure. Archons have also exploited and manipulated human creativity to make the target population construct their own prison. This will become really obvious further on. Archons are described in our terms as like cyborgs – a robotic race of 'artificial intelligence' that can imitate, but not innovate. Gnostics called this 'countermimicry' and the theme of Archontic artificial intelligence will be crucial later when I come to the transhumanist connect-people-to-technology agenda unfolding all around us and based on ... artificial intelligence. Gnostics said Archons are expert in deception and 'phantasia' or creating illusions by employing what they called 'Hal' – virtual reality. Yes, the digital holographic simulation that humanity thinks is the natural world. The same is said of the Arabian Jinn in terms of deception. Gnostics called Archons mind parasites, inverters, guards, gatekeepers, detainers, judges, pitiless ones and The Deceivers. They seek 'to overpower humanity in its perceptual functions' and their agenda is 'fear and slavery'. Recognise any of that with regard to human society? The entire Cosmos is a shadow copy of the original in the Upper Aeons which is why we can still admire its magnificence and beauty in many ways. The Gnostic *Tripartite Tractate* manuscript makes this point:

> [They] *are their* [Upper Aeon] *likenesses, copies, shadows, and phantasms, lacking reason and the light ... In the manner of a reflection are they beautiful. For the face of the copy normally takes its beauty from that of which it is a copy.*

But the Archontic force has been working to distort, invert and destroy the original beauty. Witness what has happened and is happening to Planet Earth and its environment. Author John Lamb Lash writes in *Not In His Image*, a book about the Nag Hammadi works:

> *Although they cannot originate anything, because they lack the divine factor of ennoia (intentionality), Archons can imitate with a vengeance. Their expertise is simulation (HAL, virtual reality). The Demiurge fashions a heaven world copied from the fractal patterns* [of the original] *.... His construction is celestial kitsch, like the fake Italianate villa of a Mafia don complete with militant angels to guard every portal.*

I will come to fractal patterns later, but enough to say here that they are found in the fabric of our reality or the Matrix-like simulation. Portals that Archons are said to guard are energetic frequency gateways out of the Lower Aeons of which our visible light/speed of light reality is only a part. The Demiurge's constant goal is to imprison awareness in the reincarnation cycle within the Lower Aeons by a perception deception that maintains a state of spiritual ignorance and what the Gnostic texts call 'forgetfulness'. Why do only a comparatively tiny few remember 'past lives', where we come from and the nature of reality? All experience is downloaded to Soul, but this mostly doesn't filter through to the levels of conscious mind. Human society is structured to ensure the continuation of mental, emotional and spiritual ignorance. The texts say humanity is systematically led astray through distractions and perception traps – which is what I was exposing long before I read them: '... those on whom the counterfeit spirit [Archontic distortion] descends are drawn by him and they go astray' (*Apocryphon of John*). The old saying about selling your soul to the Devil is based on fact and so is this quote by American writer Amanda Hocking: 'When you dance with the Devil, the Devil doesn't change – the Devil changes you.' In a less personalised form: If you connect and merge with a state of imbalance, you become the imbalance. This is extremely important to appreciate when you think that those that run the world through politics, banking, corporations, media, medicine, science, and such like, are full-blown 'dancers with the Devil' – incarnate conduits and agents of the Demiurgic mind. Look at how they behave against how the Demiurge/Archons are described. They are the Archontic force in human form and pursue its interests, desires and needs, and not humanity's.

## Vampire 'gods'

Spiritual ignorance and the reincarnation trap are essential to the Archons because they have no energy source with their disconnection from Infinite Source. Their power comes from the energy generated by others including incarnate humanity, but it can't be just any energy. It has to be energy within the frequency band they can absorb. Love and hate are very different frequencies –

**Figure 94:** The Archontic distortion feeds off low-vibrational thought and emotion founded on fear. © www.neilhague.com

see the work of Masaru Emoto with his water crystals – and given that the Demiurge/Archons operate in the frequencies of chaos, hate, fear, etc., they have to manipulate their targets into the same mental and emotional states to generate energetic frequencies that they can absorb and feed off (Fig 94). Human society is awash with such energy and not least through fear, anxiety and war. Is this just a *coincidence?* Remember how the Old Testament 'God' (Demiurge) is always demanding war and violence? Well, 'he' is *still* doing so. Outcomes of war are less important to these crazies than the act of war itself. Why are we fighting? So that we keep fighting. Fear is the currency of Archontic control and the Demiurge distortion is the very origin of fear. The Demiurge *is* fear, that's where it comes from, and it must manipulate its targets to generate fear as its energetic source. Nag Hammadi manuscript *Dialogue of the Saviour* tells how 'truly, fear is the power [of the Rulers].' And it is also their 'food' or sustenance. Morpheus holds up a battery in the first *Matrix* movie and delivers a profound truth: 'The Matrix is a computer-generated dream world built to keep us under control in order to change the human being into one of these' (Fig 95). I have been making these points

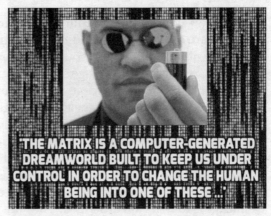

**Figure 95:** Morpheus in *The Matrix* was speaking a profound symbolic truth.

for a long, long time about forces in the unseen feeding off low-vibrational human thought and emotion and so I was fascinated to be sent some text in 2016 written by Austrian philosopher and deep esoteric thinker, Rudolf Steiner (1861-1925). He established Waldorf education or Steiner schools to encourage children to awaken and expand their awareness and creativity instead of having them perceptually-programmed by mainstream 'education'. Steiner wrote of the energy vampires:

> *There are beings in the spiritual realms* [Lower Aeons beyond the five senses] *for whom anxiety and fear emanating from human beings offer welcome food. When humans have no anxiety and fear, then these creatures starve. If fear and anxiety radiates from people and they break out in panic, then these creatures find welcome nutrition and they become more and more powerful. These beings are hostile towards humanity.*

> *Everything that feeds on negative feelings, on anxiety, fear and superstition, despair or doubt, are in reality hostile forces in supersensible worlds, launching cruel attacks on human beings, while they are being fed ... These are exactly the feelings that belong to contemporary culture and materialism; because it estranges people from the spiritual world, it is especially suited to evoke hopelessness and fear of the unknown in people, thereby calling up the above mentioned hostile forces against them.*

Rudolf Steiner died in 1925 and I never knew he had written that until 2016, but he perfectly described what is happening.

## Body and Soul

Nag Hammadi manuscripts contain many Christian themes from a different angle and they include the creation of Adam and Eve. Themes of the Gnostic version of Adam (which they call the first Lower Aeon human) are again that the original Adam was a manifestation in the Upper Aeons and the Demiurge embarked on a process of distorting its copy or shadow version. Upper Aeon Adam was androgynous and the first Lower Aeon copy; but the Demiurge divided that blueprint into male and female and this is where the story of Adam and Eve comes in. Gnostics say the Demiurge and Archons are also androgynous – 'And they were born androgynous, consistent with the immortal pattern that existed before them' (*Origin of the World* manuscript). The *Apocryphon of John* says:

> When all the authorities and the chief archon [Demiurge] looked ... they saw the form of the image in the water [Upper Aeons]. And he said to the authorities which attend him, 'Come, let us create a man according to the image of God and according to our likeness, that his image may become a light for us.' ... He created a being according to the likeness of the first, perfect Man.

Gnostics saw the human body as a prison. They said humans are sparks or droplets of the same essence as 'God', but became trapped in their bodies from which they will eventually escape. This is another common Gnostic theme that humanity *does* escape. Ignorance of self and reality is the real prison, but the body is a crucial vehicle for that by focusing attention in the tiny frequency band of the five senses. Archontic inversion and distortion seeks to imprison perception in the body and feed off low-vibrational energy generated from ignorance and all that comes from that in the form of imbalanced mental and emotional states. Ignorance about the true nature of self and reality leads to fear, anxiety, psychopathy, depression, war, conflict and other violence. Entrapped awareness must not be allowed to know itself. It must believe only in a fake self or Phantom Self and self-identify only with its five-sense labels. Eternal Spirit, an emanation of Infinite Awareness in awareness of itself, experiences the Lower Aeons through the Soul/Body. Gnostics say Soul and Spirit are not the same thing and that's in line with my own perspective. Spirit is the true, eternal self, the Infinite 'I' or One, while the Soul is Mind (a bad copy version of Spirit). People are described as having no Soul in the light of psychopathic behaviour, but it's really a case of having no Spirit in the sense of the definitions we are using here. Soul is a Lower Aeon vehicle to entice expressions of Spirit to enter these energetic densities and it is Soul that 'incarnates' by decoding holographic forms within visible light. Soul is as much a trap in its own way as the body itself. Lower Aeons of Soul are what many near-death experiencers are observing when they withdraw from five-sense awareness. It can seem beautiful and unified because after all it is a copy of something beautiful and unified; but is it really the true source of everything, or just the copy and the shadow? Lower Aeons are bad copies of Upper Aeons and that doesn't mean, by definition, that they are all horrible in every expression. Look at the lovely things that still happen in human society and the beauty that still remains. How many Souls think they are in Upper Aeon 'Heaven' when they are still in a Lower Aeon trap? Deception by illusion often requires a nice illusion to be most effective and enslaving. Making them love their servitude, as *Brave New World* author Aldous Huxley described it. Most psychics and mediums are connecting with the Lower Aeons of Soul and only a relative few with the Upper Aeons of Spirit where real enlightenment can be communicated. When a stage psychic says, 'I've got a Mary, anyone know a Mary?' they are connecting with the Archontic realms of Soul (Mind) and those sources can at best have a limited level of 'out there' understanding.

## Counterfeit spirit

If our sense of self and reality is dictated by Soul/Mind we lose touch with Spirit and come under the control of the Archontic realm whether Soul is incarnate or not. Gnostics told how Archons and demons developed a 'counterfeit spirit' to lead humanity astray through deception. 'They created a counterfeit spirit who resembles the Spirit who had descended, so as to pollute the souls through it' (*Apocryphon of John*). What we call different races are different information-encoded energetic fields that experience reality in different ways. Perception and so behaviour result from this decoded sense of reality. Human races look different because they have different genetic origins relating to different extraterrestrial races, but the counterfeit spirit was used to target all of them by infesting and manipulating the perceptions of Body-Mind/Soul when disconnected from Spirit. The specific role of what Gnostics called the counterfeit spirit is to isolate Body-Mind/Soul from Upper Aeon Spirit. The infesting process with regard to five-sense Body-Mind is described in terms of the biblical theme of the sons of God interbreeding with the daughters of men. The 'sons' (Archons/demons) of 'God' (the Demiurge) infusing the body or biological energy field with a 'counterfeit spirit' could well be the source of the term 'Original Sin'. Archontically-possessed extraterrestrial entities taking a Reptilian and other forms were also central to this interbreeding as I will be explaining. *Apocryphon of John* says:

> He [Yaldabaoth/Demiurge] *sent his angels* [Archons/demons] *to the daughters of men, that they might take some of them for themselves and raise offspring for their enjoyment. And at first they did not succeed.*

*When they had no success, they gathered together again and they made a plan together ... And the angels changed themselves in their likeness into the likeness of their mates, filling them with the spirit of darkness, which they had mixed for them, and with evil ... And they took women and begot children out of the darkness according to the likeness of their spirit.*

This theme appears in another form in the Old Testament. The Nag Hammadi *Gospel of Philip* tells of this demonic possession:

*The forms of evil spirit include male ones and female ones. The males are they which unite with the souls which inhabit a female form ... The lecherous men [demons] when they see a beautiful woman sitting alone, persuade her and compel her, wishing to defile her.*

*Apocryphon of John* describes how sexual desire was planted to allow the counterfeit spirit to constantly make copies of itself.

*And he [Yaldabaoth] planted sexual desire in her who belongs to Adam. And he produced through intercourse the copies of the bodies, and he inspired them with his counterfeit spirit.*

The energetic distortion feeds off low-vibrational sexual energy and this explains so much about human society. The whole point of Body/Soul is to trap our perceptions in limitations and illusions and to block the influence of Spirit – Infinite Awareness – and imprison us in the Lower Aeons by a self-identity with Body or at least Soul. 'This is the tomb of the newly-formed body with which the robbers [Archons/demons] had clothed the man, the bond of forgetfulness; and he became a mortal man' (*Apocryphon of John*). Human bodies are described as 'fences for light' which fence off Body-Mind awareness from expanded awareness and make the body a prison. The *Apocryphon of John* says:

*And I entered into the midst of their prison, which is the prison of the body. And I said: 'He who hears, let him get up from the deep sleep' ... And I said, 'I am ... of the pure light ... Arise and ... follow your root, which is I [Expanded Awareness] and guard yourself against the angels of poverty [Archons] and the demons of chaos and all those who ensnare you, and beware of the deep sleep and the enclosure of the inside of Hades.*

You can symbolise this process as isolating a computer (Body-Mind) from the person with the mouse and keyboard (expanded awareness) and a virus (counterfeit spirit) taking over all decision-making (Fig 96).

**Figure 96:** Mass human control is founded upon disconnecting Body/Mind from the influence of expanded awareness beyond the 'bad copy'. This can be accurately symbolised as disconnecting a computer from the operator.
© www.neilhague.com

**Figure 97:** When we break free of perception control by the Archontic illusion we reconnect with the influence and awareness of our true and infinite self. The world then looks very different.

When we retain the connection with Spirit and repel the Archontic virus we are in this world in terms of our five sense interactions, but not *of* this world when it comes to perceiving reality (Fig 97). Once that perceptual link is lost five-sense reality can appear to be all there is and all that we are. *Apocryphon of John* describes how Archons beguiled humanity into temptation so they would not remember their immovable *Pronoia* or true self beyond the illusion. Gnostics often refer to the body as a 'garment' within which Spirit is clothed. 'But first you must rip off the tunic that you wear, the garment of ignorance, the foundation of vice, the bonds of corruption, the dark cage, the living death, the portable tomb ...' (*Corpus Hermeticum VII:2*). The term body includes Soul from which the 'physical' body is holographically decoded.

Gnostic manuscripts say the body is a vessel designed for perception control (ignorance) and is both owned by the Archons and influenced by them in terms of its mental and emotional states as well as hunger, desire, illness etc. – *unless* this is overridden by expanding our awareness and self-identity into Spirit which can then infuse itself into Body/Soul and change everything. *Apocryphon of John* explains the consequences of Archon-induced ignorance:

> *And they steered the people who had followed them into great troubles, by leading them astray with many deceptions. They* [the people] *became old without having enjoyment. They died, not having found truth and without*

*knowing the God of truth.*

*And thus the whole creation became enslaved forever, from the foundation of the world until now. And they took women and begot children out of the darkness according to the likeness of their spirit. And they closed their hearts, and they hardened themselves through the hardness of the counterfeit spirit until now.*

This is still happening today. The point about closing their hearts is crucial because that is the reason the world is as it is. They are talking about closing the *heart chakra vortex* which connects us with Upper Aeon Spirit and through which comes compassion, empathy and love in its infinite, non-personal sense. The heart vortex can be closed by psychopathic traits of the counterfeit spirit and by trauma and fear that lead to what we call heartache or being heart broken. Hatred closes the heart quicker than anything which is why people full of hate are referred to as heartless. Extreme states of grief can so affect the heart chakra that the distortion is transmitted to the holographic or 'physical' heart and people are said to 'die of a broken heart'. The brain is a processor of information that relates to Mind, but the heart is home to the Spirit or the source of connection to Spirit. Lose that connection – close your heart – and your awareness becomes isolated in five-sense Body-Mind reality (Fig 98). What does your head tell you? What does your heart tell you? These are questions that people are often asked and the subsequent answers are rarely the same because head and heart are connected with very different states of awareness. The Institute of HeartMath in the United States has pioneered research into the multidimensional nature of the heart vortex or chakra and established that the heart generates the

body's most powerful electromagnetic field. More nerves go from the heart to the brain than go the other way and the heart has around 40,000 brain-like neurons and neurotransmitters. This is the heart-brain from where comes innate intelligence rather than the much inferior intellectual brain intelligence. The brain *thinks* but the heart *knows*. This is the

**Figure 98:** Body/Mind that retains a connection to Infinite Awareness is in this world, but not of it. Body/Mind without that connection is in this world *and* of it.

difference between intuitive knowing and trying to work everything out through the process of thinking. The heart knows because it is connected to that level of awareness that *does* know. Brain/mind thinks because it *doesn't* know and so has to work it out. Studies at the Institute of HeartMath have found that when the electromagnetic connection between heart, brain and central nervous system is in a state of coherence and balance the person enters an expanded sense of awareness. The opposite happens when that balance is broken through imbalanced mental and emotional states like anxiety and fear. Archontic human society is structured to constantly stimulate those emotional states and empower the counterfeit spirit infecting the human Body-Mind so that it can become the dominant source of perception and behaviour. We literally have two minds – our own consciousness or 'heart consciousness' and the counterfeit spirit. Heart consciousness gives us empathy, compassion and love in its true sense while the counterfeit spirit gives us selfishness, hate and violence and makes people *heart-less*. We can also hear the counterfeit spirit in the brain chatter that won't shut up and feeds us fears, anxiety, worry and all sorts of 'what if?' scenarios. Sit quietly and listen to this chatter and you will see that it's not you. *YOU* are the one listening to it. Body decoding systems in terms of the five senses are confined to the ridiculously narrow band of visible light because it is *made to be that way*. The body is designed as a prison of perception and of course visual reality would be made as narrow as possible, just like the prisoners who could only see in one direction in the Plato story. If we don't expand our sense of awareness beyond the smear of reality called visible light then how are we going to be anything but ignorant? The same can be said of our limited human lifespan which I suggest is encoded in human genetics. Far longer lives would give people a much better chance to work out what is really going on. You can only keep people in a state of extreme ignorance – control – by denying them knowledge about everything except what they need to know to serve your interests (Fig 99).

## The Fickle finger

Morpheus asks in the first *Matrix* movie: 'Do you believe in Fate, Neo?' The reply is no because Neo says that he doesn't like the idea that he's not in control of his life. Well, unless we break out of the prison cell of ignorance and

**Figure 99:** Deny knowledge and you entrap your target in a prison of ignorance.

move our point of attention and self-identity from Body-Mind Phantom Self to the Spirit of Infinite Self then we are *not* in control of our lives. We are controlled by a daily torrent of perception manipulation in the endless ways that I have been exposing for nearly 30 years. Gnostics contended that a major pillar of the control system is the influence of planets or what we call astrology. Mainstream science dismisses the whole concept of horoscopes and their impact on human behaviour and experience. This is another case of 'we can't explain it so it can't be happening'. Astrology *is* happening and is used to influence perceptions and 'fate' and I have met a number of astrologers around the world retained by global corporate CEOs to advise them on the best period to launch a product or a takeover bid. The same CEOs would publicly deny a belief in astrology while knowing that the effect is real. Astrology can be easily explained because planetary bodies and stars are holographic representations of cosmic forces. Everything is awareness and information and *everything* must include planets and stars. Beyond the frequency band of the five-senses where we perceive them as 'physical' they are energetic information/awareness fields interacting with the Cosmic Internet. This energetic *information* exchange affects both cosmic fields and planetary fields. When planets are in certain relationships to each other, which astrologers call conjunctions, trines, squares, and so on, the collective impact on the cosmic field is even more powerful (Fig 100). Humanity is also interacting with this field and when it changes we are affected and potentially influenced. The point that we enter the human life cycle (birth, or some say conception) decides what that affect will be because we are imprinted with the information state of the cosmic field as it is at that 'moment'. When I was born on April 29th, 1952 I absorbed a snapshot of the collective field that was different to those who enter at another point in the cycle. Astrological movements throughout our lives therefore affect us differently according to our own unique 'astrological' blueprint (Fig

101). The holographic nature of our reality also means that we are ourselves a mini-solar system or universe on the principle of as above, so below, and the inner and outer are constantly exchanging information. Reading what all these

**Figure 100:** Planets and stars are information fields constantly influencing the cosmic field with which we interact.

**Figure 101:** When the cosmic field changes we are affected in the way fish are affected by changes in the ocean.

influences and affects are likely to be is the whole foundation of astrology. I have no problem with astrology being 'real', but other aspects of the narrative have never really made sense to me. Many believe that we come into the world with astrological influences to guide us through a certain path and to give us certain gifts that would be useful in that. Studies have highlighted how those born in certain parts of the year tend to have aptitudes for certain things. I can see that and it makes sense in terms of the astrological blueprint. I also accept that it is possible to choose a specific point in the astrological cycle that will support the experience you are choosing to have. What has made me doubt aspects of conventional astrology is that it has been closely tied to the belief that we must have endless incarnations to learn lessons and spiritually 'evolve'. Many advocates believe that astrological influence takes us in particular directions for particular experiences to help us achieve this. I don't agree. I say that astrological influences on human perception, behaviour and experience are, while real, a major part of the Archontic trap. I was fascinated to see when I came across the Nag Hammadi manuscripts that Gnostics felt the same and they told how Archons were connected to the astrological cycle of the zodiac. 'Fate' is really an energetic tram line pushing us in certain directions by influencing patterns of mind and perception unless we come from the perspective and self-identity of Upper Aeon Spirit/Awareness that can override astrological impacts when they don't serve our best interests. Gnostic texts say that Archons instigated this system of 'fate' to entrap what I call Body/Soul in the Lower Aeons of Demiurgic reality. I say Body/*Soul* because at the waveform level astrological influences also impact on Soul. Our holographic realm only reflects that impact. Astrology is also profoundly connected to time which is a foundation pillar of the Archontic control system. Widespread beliefs in cycles of time passing through different ages or epochs are expressions of this cycle of fate. They include the Yuga cycles of eastern religions and time cycles of the Mayans in Central America. Repeating experiences that we perceive to be moving forward into the 'future' is

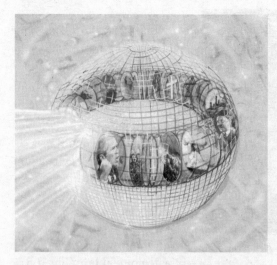

**Figure 102:** Humans are going round and round in a time loop while believing they are going 'forward' from past through present to future.

**Figure 103:** A Möbius strip.

really going round and round in what I call the Time Loop – see my book *Tales from the Time Loop* (Fig 102). This loop has been depicted in terms of a Möbius strip which is a continuous but twisted one-sided surface that means you could walk the whole way around thinking you were getting somewhere but only come back to the start (Fig 103). I would also describe the Time Loop as a *standing wave* or stationary wave oscillating on the spot, and the Möbius strip has been equated to the nature of the scalar field with its continuity and timeless state. Oscillation gives the feeling of movement but actually goes nowhere. Time, eras, ages are an illusion happening in the same NOW or oscillating field. Archontic 'time' connects reincarnation cycles, astrological cycles and the '26,000 year' precessional cycle. The latter is explained by the 'wobble' of the Earth under gravitational influence from the Sun and Moon causing the planet to change the orientation of its axis to point to different 'zodiac signs' (different segments of the heavens).Together they form an interconnected loop of apparently forward-moving 'time' that is actually taking us nowhere within the same oscillating *stationary* field (Fig 104). The sequence only appears to be to be moving forward 'in time' to entrap humanity in a perceptual prison cell, and the 'wobble' story is only as it appears to be from the perspective of holographic reality. The Nag Hammadi *Apocryphon of John* highlights the role of fate and time:

> *And bitter fate was begotten through them, which is the last of the changeable bonds ... For from that fate came forth every sin and injustice and*

**Figure 104:** The astrological cycle or 'precession'.

*blasphemy, and the chain of forgetfulness and ignorance ... And thus the whole creation was made blind, in order that they may not know God, who is above all of them. And because of the chain of forgetfulness, their sins were hidden. For they are bound with measures and times and moments, since it* [Fate] *is lord over everything.*

Time is a frontline influence in astrological fate (Fig 105). Saturn is said to be the God of Time and happens to be a planet – a sun in truth – that I have written a great deal about with regard to its role in the digital holographic simulation that we call the world. The Archontic control system of Fate – pre-destined experience in a gigantic 'computer' program – is also related to the concept of karma which is defined as 'the sum of a person's actions in this and previous states of existence deciding their fate in future existences'. Karma binds the Soul to the reincarnation cycle (prison) through the Archontic law of cause and effect which is 'written' into the computer program. Saturn is again labelled the 'Lord of Karma' (Fig 106).

**Figure 105:** The time illusion and its association with karma and fate.

**Figure 106:** All roads lead to Saturn as we shall see.

Why Saturn is so important to this illusory cycle of fate and time which dictates the destiny of entrapped humanity will become clear.

## In short ...

Set aside all the symbolism employed in Gnostic writings, and the descriptions that relate only to the societies for which they were written, and the repeating concepts, both ancient and modern, come into focus. A state of Infinite Awareness in awareness of itself is the source of all that is. Infinite Imagination brought forth expressions or emanations of itself which had the gift of creation through their connection to Infinite Awareness. Realms of reality and awareness emerged of incredible beauty, bliss, love and harmony – realms of 'watery light' that is so powerful 'there are no shadows'. These are the Upper Aeons of Gnostic belief. There then came an 'error' instigated by imbalanced thought or perception which brought the Demiurgic distortion into manifestation. This is not an entity with arms and legs, but a state of inverted, distorted and chaotic awareness which believed at first that it was all that existed and creator of all it could perceive. The distortion made subordinate copies of itself which Gnostics refer to as Archons and they made copies of themselves they call demons. All reflected the same perception state of extreme imbalance because they are expressions of the prime imbalance. Demiurge insanity became collective Archontic and demonic insanity. This is a state of being that we know as 'evil' which comes from extreme ignorance and the absence of love, empathy and compassion. The word evil in English is the reverse of 'live' and everything about the Demiurge is an inversion of the Source of All. Satanists and those in the inner circles of secret societies who worship the Demiurge and its perceptual copies and possessed agents are for this reason a collective Death Cult which represents an inversion of life. Death and decay are energetic frequencies that the Archontic force can absorb as sustenance and power. The more death, decay, hatred, violence and fear they can generate the more empowered they are. Inverted 'shadows' reflecting from the Upper Aeons as energetic information became the Lower Aeons, fashioned from an inferior form of light to the 'watery light' Gnostics describe in the higher realms. This inferior version is electromagnetic or radiation light – the 'luminous fire' that Gnostics described and the 'Let there be Light' in the biblical

**Figure 107:** Gnostics described two very different versions of 'light' – the 'watery light' of the Upper Aeons and Archontic 'luminous fire' of the bad copy (in part the radiation realm within the 'speed of light').

creation story (Fig 107). Or, rather, the creation of the Matrix simulation. In terms of power and creativity Archon light is as a lightbulb is to the Sun compared with Infinite Light.

Human form and the energetic 'garment' of Soul was manifested as a flawed and manipulated copy of an Upper Aeon blueprint or archetype ('Adam') designed to entrap awareness in the Lower Aeons and the illusion of physicality and separation. Humans went forth and multiplied (made copies of themselves through procreation) which led to humanity as we know it today. The body that we think we 'see' is really a holographic image fashioned from the standing wave information blueprint in the Soul field which is why the base-form of the body is not actually what we see, but a waveform information field. Our true self is and has always been Upper Aeon Spirit and what we experience is a shadow or illusory self (Fig 108). By self-identifying with the true self and not the fake or Phantom Self we bring the shadow and what it reflects – Spirit Self – back into synchronisation, harmony and unity. When Spirit and shadow merge we are out of here through the 'Ring-Pass-Not'. The Demiurgic distortion and its copies have no connection to Source in the way that humans potentially do and so are blocked from its limitless creative potential. Archon 'creation' comes from manipulating what is already manifested as shadow reflections of the Upper Aeons. Without a connection to Source they have no limitless supply of energetic power and sustenance. They have to overcome that by trawling and vampiring the energy of their imprisoned awareness, not only humans, but other forms and soul fields within the Lower Aeons. It is not only humans who are trapped. To maintain this perceptual prison the Archontic distortion must maintain humanity in

**Figure 108:** Phantom Self and Infinite Self.

ongoing ignorance of reality. Lower Aeons at frequency bands beyond visible light and 'dense matter' have some extremely unpleasant aspects but also others which are inferior copies of the Upper Aeons that out-of-body awareness can mistake for a 'beautiful, blissful heaven' when it is only a Lower Aeon copy of the real thing. Look around at human society today and throughout what we call history and you'll see how the lackeys and servants of the Archontic force (the 'authorities') oversee a system designed from its foundations to keep us in ignorance of almost everything. Religion, politics, media, science, medicine and the rest of them are all Archontic firewalls to the knowledge or gnosis that we need to escape this gigantic perception deception. All but a tiny few within those institutions are themselves so consumed by the illusion that they have no idea what they are helping every day to impose on humanity, themselves and their own families.

## Truth Vibrations

Another theme of Gnosticism and my own life from completely different sources is that Archontic control will be ended by the infusion of Infinite Awareness. My first book on these subjects after my own dramatic conscious awakening in 1990 was called *Truth Vibrations*. I was told through several psychics and mediums in the spring and summer of that year how a collective consciousness shift was coming that would awaken humanity from its spiritual slumber and bring to the surface all that had been hidden. I called this change Truth Vibrations after the infusion of high-frequency energy that was coming to open human minds. I was told that those most open and connected to Spirit would be affected first and that eventually even those who were solidly snoozing would begin to stir from the Big Sleep. There is still a long way to go for sure, but compared with nearly 30 years ago when I was told this change was coming the numbers are increasing with exponential speed. Today as I have travelled around the world there is clearly an awakening as ever more people are seeing reality in a new light, thinking thoughts and asking questions they would never have considered before. I was further told that all which had been hidden would be revealed to us – hence the name Truth Vibrations. Consider what we know now that we didn't know in 1990 about the forces manipulating human society and the nature of reality. The veil *is* lifting and what has been hidden is coming to the surface. Those who serve the Archontic force are desperate to censor the rising tide of perception-changing information and we see this in transparent attempts to stop the free-flow of opinions and views on the Internet by using hoax excuses like 'fake news'. Infinite Awareness in awareness of itself is now being infused into the 'darkness' of density and the Gnostic Lower Aeons to bring an end to the Archontic nonsense. This will not necessarily be quick, and certainly not without massive upheaval as the control system dismantles, but it *is* happening. Everything is ultimately within the imagination of Infinite Awareness and its emanations. Maybe it wasn't an error at all in the literal sense, but another expression of Infinite Awareness experiencing itself. We now have a wonderful opportunity to cast aside the perceptual delusions of Mind/Body and the more that do so the quicker the transformation will be. Truth Vibrations are a band of frequency and we have to expand our own frequency to connect with them. If we don't they will pass us by. Where it goes from here and how it all turns out is down to us. This is the challenge for humanity the world over – deleting programmed perceptions that keep us in servitude to illusion and so awakening to our true self which has always been there behind the veil of forgetfulness.

A realisation that humanity is not free and why this is so represents the first vital step to *becoming* free. You don't change what you can't see and the most enslaved are always those who falsely believe they have freedom. Anyone who completes this book with an open mind will be in no doubt that 'free' is the last thing we currently are.

# CHAPTER THREE

# Log In/Log Out

*'Humans see what they want to see' – **Rick Riordan***

Ihave described the Gnostic version of reality, which mirrors *in theme* my own, by using the symbolic language of more than 1,500 years ago in our perception of 'time'. Now, in the parlance of modern techno-speak, I will compare Gnostic reality with the concept of the world as a 'computer' simulation. The two are actually the same because our simulated reality is the Gnostic 'bad copy', or part of it (Fig 109).

I have contended in my books and global talks since just after the turn of the Millennium that we live 'in' an incredibly advanced version of a virtual reality video game. I put quote marks around the word 'in' because as I have stressed before we don't so much live 'in' a simulation as decode an information source into the illusion of being 'in' (Fig 110). The simulation concept was rarely talked about in those early days and Nick Bostrom, a Swedish-born philosopher at the University of Oxford, was one of the few to be publicly quoted on the subject. He explored the

possibility that our 'world' is a computer simulation which, by definition, must have been created by an intelligence we know nothing about. Oh, but we *do*. Gnostics called this the Demiurge or Yaldabaoth. Bostrom said in 2003:

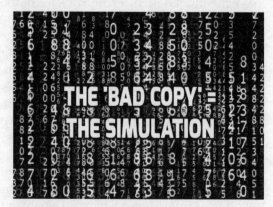

**Figure 109:** The Gnostic 'bad copy' is the simulated reality that humans experience as the 'real world'.

*Many works of science fiction as well as some forecasts by serious technologists and futurologists predict that*

*enormous amounts of computing power will be available in the future. Let us suppose for a moment that these predictions are correct. One thing that later generations might do with their super-powerful computers is run detailed simulations of their forebears or of people like their forebears. Because their computers would be so powerful, they could run a great many such simulations.*

**Figure 110:** We don't live 'in' a world any more than a player lives 'in' a computer game.

*Suppose that these simulated people are conscious (as they would be if the simulations were sufficiently fine-grained and if a certain quite widely accepted position in the philosophy of mind is correct). Then it could be the case that the vast majority of minds like ours do not belong to the original race but rather to people simulated by the advanced descendants of an original race.*

*It is then possible to argue that, if this were the case, we would be rational to think that we are likely among the simulated minds rather than among the original biological ones.*

I began to conclude something similar around this period of 2003 although with significant differences in detail to Bostrom. Today many in the scientific mainstream are concluding that we are experiencing some kind of virtual reality simulation, as we better understand the clear and obvious correlations between computer game reality and our own. I have mentioned Rich Terrile, director of the Center for Evolutionary Computation and Automated Design at NASA's Jet Propulsion Laboratory, and his thoughts about the Universe as a digital hologram; but he is far from an isolated voice these days in the science arena. These are just a few mainstream headlines and they are increasing all the time: 'Physicists May Have Evidence Universe Is A Computer Simulation'; 'The idea we live in a simulation isn't science fiction'; 'Is Our Universe Fake? Physicists claim we could all be the playthings of an advance civilisation'; 'Is reality an Illusion? Scientist says we may be living in a computer simulation controlled by an evil genius'. Even American celebrity scientist Neil deGrasse Tyson, who is not famous for having an open mind, has said that it is very likely the Universe is a simulation. He told the Isaac Asimov Memorial Debate at the American Museum of Natural History in 2016 that the likelihood of the Universe being a simulation 'may be very high'. PayPal co-founder Elon Musk, the billionaire hi-tech investor who runs the space transport operation SpaceX, believes there is only a 'one in billions' chance that we *don't* live in a simulation. He said that just 40 years ago computer games began with two rectangles and a dot – 'Pong' – simulating the most basic form of tennis, but now we had 'photorealistic, 3D simulations with millions of people playing simultaneously', and it was

**Figure 111:** One level of reality is digital.

getting better every year: '... We're clearly on a trajectory to have games that are indistinguishable from reality ... [and] ... it would seem to follow that the odds that we're in base reality is one in billions.' But there is no need for the rich and famous to tell us all this when the facts speak for themselves. Max Tegmark is a physicist at the Massachusetts Institute of Technology (MIT) and author of *Our Mathematical Universe*. He points out that our reality can be entirely described by numbers and maths in the same way that a video game is encoded. The physics of computer games and our world are basically the same, he says (Fig 111). Tegmark imagines the experience of characters in Minecraft or a much more advanced computer game where the graphics are so good you don't believe you are in a game. The characters might think they can bump into real objects, fall in love and feel emotions like excitement, Tegmark says. I have already explained how the 'objects' that we think we can solidly bump into are nothing more than decoded information and electromagnetic resistance which is not solid at all. Tegmark says that eventually the characters might start studying the 'physical world' in the video game and realise that everything was made of pixels. What they thought was physical 'stuff' could actually be described by a bunch of numbers and while they would be criticised by those, saying 'come on you're stupid, it's stuff after all' anyone outside of the game would see that 'physical' reality was just numbers. He continues:

> And we're exactly in this situation in our world. We look around and it doesn't seem that mathematical at all, but everything we see is made out of elementary particles like quarks and electrons. And what properties does an electron have? Does it have a smell or a colour or a texture? No!

> ... We physicists have come up with geeky names for [Electron] properties, like electric charge, or spin, or lepton number, but the electron doesn't care what we call it, the properties are just numbers.

Wherever you look the physics of our reality are the same as the rules, codes and limitations found in computer simulations. Scientists acknowledge that the so-called laws of nature apply throughout the Universe and never change. Cosmologist Sean Carroll, a research professor in the Department of Physics at the California Institute of Technology, said that 'a law of physics is a pattern that nature obeys without exception'. No matter what the source, a galaxy or a flashlight, the speed of light is measured at a constant 186,000 miles per second and a law called the proton-electron mass ratio is the same here as in a galaxy perceived to be six billion light years away. What scientists don't know is why that is the case. Why is the Universe so orderly and why can it be 'measured and computed' with numbers and mathematics? Eugene Wigner (1902-1995), the Hungarian-American theoretical physicist, engineer and mathematician, said that the mathematical basis of nature 'is something bordering on the mysterious and there is no rational explanation for it'. He said that why nature is mathematical is a mystery and the fact that there were rules at all governing the cosmos was a kind of miracle. Physicist Paul C. Davies, a professor at Arizona State University, said that he had often asked his physicist colleagues why the laws of physics are what they are and his favourite reply was: 'There is no reason they are what they are – they just are.' Well, as someone who went to a secondary modern school (second class apparently), left aged 15 and never went near a university let alone a physics lab, I contend that none of this is a miracle or mysterious. The laws of physics are not 'just are' and there is an explanation for why everything can be measured in numbers. We are experiencing a simulation which on one level is digital and subject to the rules (laws of physics) encoded by its creators. Physicists at the University of Bonn in Germany led by American nuclear physicist Silas Beane noted that simply being a simulation would create its own 'laws of physics' that would limit possibility. I have been saying since the 1990s that the laws of physics as described by mainstream science only operate in our reality and not beyond its frequency band. You would expect this to be the case with a simulation given that what we call physics is only the rules and limitations encoded into the 'game'. The Bonn team found that cosmic rays align with a specific pattern that takes the form of a lattice of cubes, and they highlighted something called the GZK cut-off which is an apparent boundary for cosmic ray particles caused by interaction with cosmic background radiation. They say in a paper entitled 'Constraints on the Universe as a Numerical Simulation' that this 'pattern of constraint' is exactly what you would find with a computer simulation. These constraints and limitations are encoded to appear natural when they are really just codes. 'Like a prisoner in a pitch-black cell we would

**Figure 112:** The speed of light is not the fastest speed possible but a firewall within the simulation.

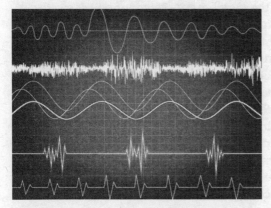

**Figure 113:** The undecoded Universe is standing waves of information.

not be able to see the "walls" of our prison,' the Bonn paper concludes. I say we *can* see them and we have already given them a name – the speed of light (Fig 112). Scientific orthodoxy claims that the speed of light – 186,000 miles per second – is the fastest speed possible. I disagree. This may be the fastest speed within the constraints imposed by the code-writers of the simulation, but that is quite another thing. The speed of light is the outer barrier of the 'matter' Matrix *as we decode it* and that's why strange things happen when you get close to that speed including a slowing down of 'time'. Or, rather, a slowing of our perception of time which is another encoded feature of the

simulation. I would take the effect of the speed of light to another level, too, and this relates to standing or stationary waves which I contend are the foundation constructs of what we experience as form. Standing waves require node points, or 'walls', which bounce the same wave back and forth to create a standing or stationary wave of oscillating information. I used the key word a few sentences back in relation to the speed of light when I called it the outer *barrier* of the 'matter' Matrix. The speed of light is not the fastest speed possible. The very idea is a joke. The speed of light is an artificial barrier that creates standing waves within its energetic walls or borders which we experience – emphasis on experience – as the 'physical Universe'. This is really a standing wave construct, Matrix or simulation underpinned by the unifying scalar field and consisting of oscillating stationary information that we decode into holographic reality (Fig 113). What we experience as energetic movement is an illusion happening *within* the standing wave oscillation. James Gates is an American theoretical physicist, Professor of Physics at the University of Maryland, Director of The Center for String and

**Figure 114:** Computer codes are found in the energetic fabric of our reality.

Particle Theory, and served on the Council of Advisors on Science and Technology to President Obama. He is another mainstreamer who has turned his attention to reality as a simulation. Gates and his team of researchers discovered embedded computer codes of digital data in the fabric of our reality which take the form of 1 and 0. These are the very binary system of on-off electrical charges used by computers (Fig 114). 'We have no idea what they are doing there', he said. They are there because they are codes of the simulation. The team also found mathematical sequences known as error-correcting codes or block codes within the energetic fabric of our reality and these are again a feature of computers. Error-correcting codes 'reboot' data to its original state or 'default settings' when something knocks it out of sync. They hold the Matrix steady and stable when other forces are threatening to disrupt the standing wave/scalar field construct. Gates was asked if he had found a set of equations embedded in our reality indistinguishable from those that drive search engines and browsers. He replied: 'That is correct.'

## All in the numbers

It has long been known that mathematical and geometrical sequences can be found throughout the 'natural' world and ancients who were initiated into this knowledge encoded these sequences in the designs and proportions of their great buildings especially their temples and cathedrals. They would talk of 'divine proportion' (Fig 115). But are those sequences really 'divine' or are they really Demiurgic patterns of fake 'divinity'? And if they are the latter would not those buildings be plugged into the Matrix and its fake god designer through such mathematical and geometrical synchronisation? Would this not mean that such

**Figure 115:** 'Divine proportion' (foundation codes of the simulation) were encoded by the ancients into their most important churches, temples and buildings.

temples, cathedrals and churches were 'hotspots' for the 'Wi-Fi' of simulated reality and its controlling force? Phi, Pi, Golden Mean, Golden Ratio and Golden Section are some of the names given to these sequences and proportions which are found throughout human reality including the proportions of the human body. But, then, this must be so, given that the body (energetic information) is designed to interact with the simulation or Cosmic Internet. The body and simulated reality will be designed with the same mathematical and geometrical codes, proportions and principles. Are characters in a computer game encoded

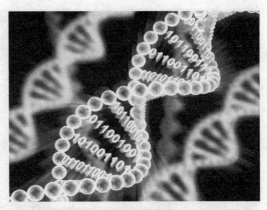

**Figure 116:** DNA on one level is digital.

```
CCCAACACCCAAATATGGCTCGAGAAGGGCAGCGACATTCCTGCGGGGTGGCGCGGAGGGAATGCCC
GCGGGCTATATAAAACCTGAGCAGAGGGACAAGCGGCCACCGCAGCGGACAGCGCCAAGTGAAGCCT
CGCTTCCCCTCCGCGGCGACCAGGGCCCGAGCCGAGAGTAGCAGTTGTAGCTACCCGCCCAGGTAGG
GCAGGAGTTGGGAGGGGACAGGGGGACAGGGCACTACCGAGGGGAACCTGAAGGACTCCGGGGCAGA
ACCCAGTCGGTTCACCTGGTCAGCCCCAGGCCTCGCCCTGAGCGCTGTGCCTCGTCTCCGGAGCCAC
ACGCGCTTTAAAAAGGAGGCAAGACAGTCAGCCTCTGGAAATTAGACTTCTCCAAATTTTTCTCTAC
CCCTTTGGGCTCCTTTACCTGGCATGTAGGATGTGCCTAGGGAGATAAACGGTTTTGCTTTAGTTGT
CGCCAAGGCAGTTCCCTTCCAAACTAGCGCTAGAGCGAATGAGCGAGCAGCCAGGACCACCATTCTG
GGTTTCCAACAGGCGAAAAGGCCCTTTCTGAGTTTGAAATGTCACAGGGTTCCTAACAGGCCACTCT
TCCCTGGATGGGGTGCCAACGCCTTTCCCATGGGCATCTCCTTCCACCCTCACGCTGGCCCAGCAAG
CAGGCAGTGCTGAGGCCTTATCTCCCTAGGTGACAGATGTGGTCAGGGAGGCGCAGAGAGGATGGGC
ACTAGCGTCCAGCTCCTGGAACAGGTGTCAGGCAGGGAGGGCAGACAGGTCTTGGGAACATGTTCCC
CTGGCTATGTGGACAGAGGACTTCTCAGTGGGTCTCGCGACCCTGTGCCCCTTTTCCTGGTTCAGGG
CAGCCTTAGCCGGGGCAAAGGTCGAAGAAGAACCCCTGGTCGCCGCCCTGGCAGAATTTGAGTGGC
TCCGGCAGGAGATGTCCCTAGGTTCCTGGGGAGGGAGGACGTCGGGGGCCAGCCAGGCTTACCCCCCC
CTGCCGCTGAGACTTCTGCGCTGATGCACCGCGCCTCTTCGCGGTCTCCCTGTCCTTGCAGAAACTA
GACACAATGTGCGACGAAGACGAGACCACCGCCCTCGTGTGCGACAATGGCTCCGGCCTGGTGAAAG
CCGGCTTCGCCGGGGATGACGCCCCTAGGGCCGTGTTCCCGTCCATCGTGGGCCGCCCCCGACACCA
GGTCAGGCTGCCCCTCCGCAGAGGGAGCCGGCTCGGGGTCCCCGCGTAAGCCAGCCTGGTGCCACC
```

**Figure 117:** DNA codes ACGT look digital and have a digital expression.

with different maths and rules to the rest of the game? Holographic principles of as above, so below would also demand the same recurring sequences on different levels of reality. Binary 1 and 0 on-off electrical charges found in computers and encoded in our energetic reality are also found in the receiver-transmitting system and 'hard-drive' of the body that we call DNA (Fig 116). This is again what you would expect in a system that is founded on interaction between body and simulation. DNA is comprised of four codes known as A, C, G, and T and where these codes are in relation to each other decides if you take the form of anything from a human to a virus. These codes have a binary value – A and C = 0 while G and T = 1. DNA code sequences look like the numbers on the computer screens in the *Matrix* movie series and with good reason given the background (Fig 117).

A great example of this encoded mathematics is the Fibonacci number sequence named after the 12th/13th century Italian mathematician Leonardo of Pisa, also known as Fibonacci. The sequence can actually be traced back much further to India and a mathematician called Virahanka. The Fibonacci sequence adds the two previous numbers to get the next one, as in ... 1, 1, 2, 3, 5, 8, 13, 21, 34, 55 etc. This

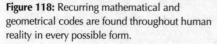

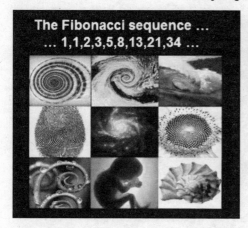

**Figure 118:** Recurring mathematical and geometrical codes are found throughout human reality in every possible form.

**Figure 119:** A shell breaks down to the Fibonacci number sequence.

can be found encoded in the human face and body, proportions of animals, DNA, seed heads, pine cones, trees, shells, spiral galaxies, hurricanes and the number of petals in a flower among so much else (Figs 118 and 119). Then we have recurring 'fractal patterns' which are defined as a never-ending pattern that is infinitely complex and self-similar across different scales. This is the as above, so below fractal principle of holographics mentioned earlier in relation to the Archontic 'bad copy' when writer John Lamb Lash said that 'The Demiurge fashions a heaven world copied from the fractal patterns [of the original] ...' Fractals in their ongoing feedback loops have been identified throughout the fabric of reality. DNA operates with fractal principles and the heading of one scientific paper that I saw summed it up: 'DNA Is A Fractal Antenna in Electromagnetic Fields'. Absolutely it is. Fractal patterns can be seen in river networks, mountain ranges, craters, lightning bolts, coastlines, mountain goat horns, trees and branch growth, animal colour patterns, pineapples, heart rates, heartbeats, neurons and brains, eyes, respiratory systems, circulatory systems, blood vessels and pulmonary vessels, geological fault lines, earthquakes, snowflakes, crystals, ocean waves, vegetables, soil pores and even the rings of Saturn (of which more later). David Pincus, an American professor of psychology, said that in recent decades fractal patterns have also been observed in psychology, behaviour, speech patterns and interpersonal relationships. The simulation is an audio-visual and psychological program operating at all levels and these patterns can only be overridden by connecting with awareness outside the program. We have symmetrical mathematics throughout nature and in everything from the way trees grow to the structure of the human lung (Fig 120 and 121). Symmetrical mathematics are defined as 'one shape becoming

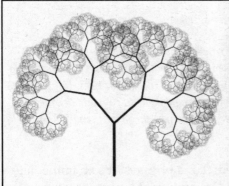

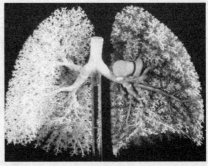

**Figure 120:** Fractal 'as above, so below' patterns in tree growth.     **Figure 121:** Lungs are fractal in nature.

exactly like another when you move it in some way, turn, flip or slide' and relates to the fractal principle. A study published in the journal *Nature's Scientific Reports* in November 2012 suggested that undiscovered and fundamental laws may govern the growth of systems on all levels from the electrical firing between brain cells to the growth of social networks and expansion of galaxies. Co-author Dmitri Krioukov, a physicist at the University of California, San Diego, said: 'Natural growth dynamics are the same for different real networks, like the Internet or the brain or social networks.' Ah, but are these growth dynamics really natural? I say not. I say that all these sequences, Phi, Fibonacci, fractals, divine proportion and so on are ... *computer codes* (Figs 122 and 123). The 'genetic code' is a *computer code*. Krioukov's findings were reported by *The Huffington Post*:

> *When the team compared the Universe's history with growth of social networks and brain circuits, they found all the networks expanded in similar ways: They balanced links between similar nodes with ones that already had*

**Figure 122:** Why mathematical sequences are found everywhere – it's the simulation.     **Figure 123:** Fractal codes in the simulation..

*many connections.*

*For instance, a cat lover surfing the Internet may visit mega-sites such as Google or Yahoo, but will also browse cat fancier websites or YouTube kitten videos. In the same way, neighboring brain cells like to connect, but neurons also link to such 'Google brain cells' that are hooked up to loads of other brain cells. The eerie similarity between networks large and small is unlikely to be a coincidence, Krioukov said.*

No, because it's not. Krioukov added: 'For a physicist it's an immediate signal that there is some missing understanding of how nature works.' What is missing is simply this: There is no 'nature' – it is a *simulation* of 'nature' based on a multi-levelled 'software' program that controls humanity mentally, emotionally and 'physically'. You think they're your thoughts you're thinking now? Well, only if you are conscious beyond the program. Scientists point out that Earth's atmosphere and ecosystems are not only perfect for life as we know it, but only just. A tiny change here and there and there would be no life as we know it. Is this *another* coincidence, *another* by-chance? No, it is click, click, enter. Scientist Robert Lanza wrote in *Biocentrism*:

*Why are the laws of physics exactly balanced for animal life to exist?... If the strong nuclear force were decreased 2 percent, atomic nuclei wouldn't hold together, and plain-vanilla hydrogen would be the only kind of atom in the Universe. If the gravitational force were decreased by a hair, stars (including the Sun) would not ignite. These are just [some of] more than 200 parameters within the solar system and Universe so exact that it strains credulity to propose that they are random – even if that is exactly what standard contemporarily physics baldly suggests.*

This shows how insane mainstream science really is when it comes to connecting dots and seeing the big picture that explains our reality. The Demiurgic force which constructed this mind-prison simulation does not want the truth revealed and only scientists that can tap into awareness beyond the program are ever going to see through it. This is especially so when their job, income and academic reputation are dependent on them not seeing through it. To protect all these things they have to deny, dismiss and ridicule the patently obvious. The scientific mainstream is specifically structured to stop the truth coming out and I will be explaining how this is done. Robert Lanza, a scientist with a mind of his own, goes on to say that these fundamental constants of the Universe not predicted by any scientific theory all seem to be carefully chosen and often with great precision to allow for life and consciousness. Yes, *click, click, enter.* There is no evidence to support the very foundation of scientific orthodoxy known as the Big Bang. We are asked to believe that 13.7 billion years ago the Universe was compressed into the nucleus of an atom that they call the 'singularity'. Then – no one explains how – this exploded to create subatomic particles, energy, matter, space and time, planets, stars, the whole lot. American writer and researcher Terence McKenna said of Big Bang theory:

> ... *what these philosophers of science are saying is, give us one free miracle, and we will roll from that point forward – from the birth of time to the crack of doom! – just one free miracle, and then it will all unravel according to natural law, and these bizarre equations which nobody can understand but which are so holy in this enterprise.*

Another perceptive critic said that mainstream education and science are a journey to prove the textbooks and not to question them. One of their orthodoxy-protection techniques is to claim that 'the science is settled' when it is not at all (see human-caused 'global warming'). There are those, however, who think outside the box. Caleb Scharf, Director of Astrobiology at Columbia University, has suggested that 'alien life' could be so advanced that it has transcribed itself into the quantum realm to become what we call physics. He said that an intelligence indistinguishable from the fabric of the Universe would solve many of its greatest mysteries:

> *Perhaps hyper-advanced life isn't just external. Perhaps it's already all around. It is embedded in what we perceive to be physics itself, from the root behaviour of particles and fields to the phenomena of complexity and emergence ... In other words, life might not just be in the equations. It might* be *the equations.*

It might *be* the Demiurgic force. Scharf said that perhaps this alien intelligence spread itself out across the quantum realm by storing its data in carriers which are distributed throughout the Universe, such as photons. Scharf said it is possible that 'we don't recognise advanced life because it forms an integral and unsuspicious part of what we've considered to be the natural world'. Or, as I would say, it is embedded in the very simulation that we are decoding as the world. Michael Frazer, lecturer in political and social theory at the University of East Anglia in the UK, wrote an article speculating on whether unpredicted events like Brexit and Trump's election could be connected to 'alien' manipulation of a computer simulation. 'These unexpected events could be experiments to see how our political systems cope under stress,' he speculated. 'Or they could be cruel jokes made at our expense by our alien zookeepers.' He might have had his tongue in his cheek, but what we can say for sure is that which controls the simulation will be able to manipulate what happens in the simulation if expanded awareness beyond the program does not override those electrical/digital laws and impulses. My own view is that humanity is largely responding, in terms of its individual and collective behaviour, to what the simulation is compelling them to do. We urgently need a consciousness override.

## In plain sight

Communication systems of computers are based on *electricity* and so is the brain, genetic system and our entire experienced reality. This must be so when electricity and electromagnetism are the communication system of the interactive simulation or Cosmic Internet. There is a whole new movement today challenging scientific dogma known as the Electric Universe and Thunderbolts Project. Two of its pioneers are the Australian physicist Wallace Thornhill and American researcher and writer David Talbott. One of their fascinating books is called *The Electric Universe*. Electricity can clearly be seen with lightning and

**Figure 124:** The electrical atmosphere and Northern Lights or Aurora Borealis.

electrical storms; the Aurora Borealis or northern lights; tornadoes (rapidly rotating electromagnetic fields during electrical storms); and tails of comets (Fig 124). Electric Universe advocates point out that electricity/electromagnetism is everywhere and explains so much about the structure of perceived and unperceived reality. Mainstream science sees planets in isolation while Electric Universe advocates say planets are 'just one device in a circuit'. We are back to how astrology works. How extraordinary to contemplate that mainstream cosmology still believes (assumes) that every star and planet is isolated from all the others and draws energy only from within itself. This is the strictly-limited intellect perceiving everything as apart from everything else and being unable to grasp the concept of everything connected by the same universal field or ocean of energy/information. Data is appearing almost by the week now to expose such delusional thinking. Images from the Herschel telescope have shown that stars are formed on galactic filaments, which mainstream science believed to be impossible. David

Sibeck, a project scientist at NASA's Goddard Space Flight Center, said:

> *The satellites have found evidence of magnetic ropes connecting Earth's*
> *upper atmosphere directly to the Sun. We believe that solar winds flow in*
> *along these ropes providing energy for geomagnetic storms and auroras.*

This is a transfer of energy from the Sun which is the prime cause of changes to the climate and absolutely not the unsupportable claims about human activity. We see lightning strikes in the lower atmosphere, but this doesn't happen in isolation. The strikes play out into the Cosmos under names such as tendrils, sprites and elves (Fig 125). The Universe is an enormous electrical system of communication that in so many ways reflects that of a computer because this is what it

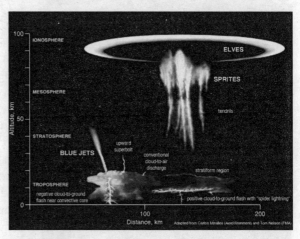

**Figure 125:** Lightning in the lower atmosphere continues out into the cosmos under different names.

is – a quantum computer far beyond anything that human science has begun to understand. Earth's atmosphere is an electrical/electromagnetic field that constantly changes in response to other electrical influences such as day and night (the Sun), weather, electrical storms and positive and negative charge. The field is also affected by human thought and emotion, which are constantly broadcasting as frequencies into the atmosphere, and this explains major spikes of activity within Earth's magnetic field during happenings such as 9/11 when there is a collective surge of mental and particularly emotional response. Electricity and electromagnetism are highly efficient carriers of information and today we have systems that transmit the Internet to every room in a house through the electrical circuits. The observable Universe is 99.999 percent plasma, the so-called fourth state of matter, and this just happens to be an almost perfect medium for electricity and electromagnetism. Planetary magnetospheres are the result of plasma-electricity interaction. American scientist Irving Langmuir (1881-1957) discovered that when plasma of one electrical charge meets plasma with a different charge a barrier is automatically created between the two. This is the same principle as a person

**Figure 126:** Where plasma of one electrical charge meets another a barrier is automatically created known as Langmuir sheaths which form magnetospheres.

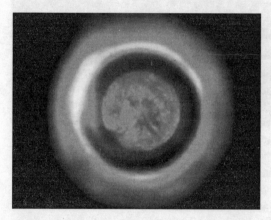

**Figure 127:** The torus or doughnut around the Sun where electrical power is accumulated.

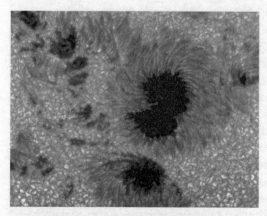

**Figure 128:** Colossal sunspots are punched in the Sun's surface by discharges from the torus.

(electrical charge) hitting a wall (very different charge/frequency) and forming a barrier or resistance that we experience as 'solid'. Planets and stars generate unique electrical signatures and where these meet another charge out in the Cosmos an energetic barrier is formed that defines the magnetospheres (Fig 126). These barriers are for obvious reasons known as Langmuir sheaths. The Sun, too, is almost entirely plasma because it is a *processer* of electrical power and not the *generator*, as mainstream science has long claimed. Orthodoxy says that the Sun is a nuclear reactor projecting power from its core through the surface and out into the solar system; but as Electric Universe researchers point out every observation of the Sun reveals this is not the case. Way out from the surface the Sun has a torus or 'doughnut' at its equator which can be seen in ultraviolet images (Fig 127). This torus absorbs and stores electrical power until it is so overloaded that it has to discharge in the same way as lightning. Colossal discharges smack into the Sun's surface punching holes that we call sunspots (Fig 128). We are told that these are created by forces originating in the Sun's core, but the opposite is the case. This would make sense of why the Sun's surface temperature is said to be about 5,000 degrees kelvin while much further out the temperature is reported to be 200 *million* degrees kelvin. Electrical power moves through the simulation in cycles and we refer to this as the Sun cycle or sunspot cycle (Fig 129).

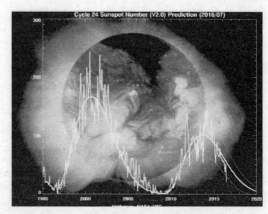

**Figure 129:** Sun cycles are a reflection of cycles of electrical power passing through the solar system.

Sunspot numbers have been thought to indicate the scale of activity inside the Sun, when in reality they measure the amount of electricity available in the torus for the Sun to process. The Sun dims in the low part of the electrical cycle – though imperceptibly to the human eye – and this principle can be likened to a dimmer switch. Mainstream science is being forced to face these facts which rewrite orthodoxy. Haimin Wang, a professor of physics at the New Jersey Institute of Technology, said of sunspot activity:

> We used to think that the surface's magnetic evolution drives solar eruptions. Our new observations suggest that disturbances created in the solar outer atmosphere can also cause direct and significant perturbations on the surface through magnetic fields, a phenomenon not envisioned by any contemporary solar eruption models.

## One (simulated) system

The electric Universe – simulation – interacts with the electric brain and genetics in the same way that electric computers interact with the electric Internet (Figs 130 and 131). Something like 55 to 60 percent of the body is water – and water (or rather the content of water) is a conduit for electricity. The body is an electrical communication system. Dehydration is dangerous because it scrambles the body's

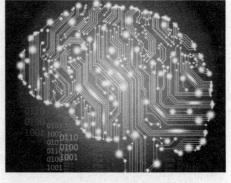

**Figure 130:** The brain is an electrical system.

**Figure 131:** The human electrical system interacts with cosmic electrical systems – the Cosmic Internet.

communications, with the brain and heart for example consisting of around 73 percent water. Both are primarily electrical systems. A team headed by Jacqueline Barton, one of the world's most decorated chemists working at the California Institute of Technology (Caltech), discovered that DNA is 'like an electrical wire for signalling within a cell'. For signalling, read communicating. Many of her colleagues didn't believe her when she suggested that DNA can conduct electricity, which confirms yet again the lack of basic understanding at large within mainstream science when it comes to grasping the nature of our reality. Experiment after experiment proved them wrong and Barton realised that DNA operates like a phone cable. This is a techy explanation for how phones work:

> The energy from your voice is converted into electricity, and this electrical energy flows down the phone line. When it reaches the handset at the other end, it flows into the loudspeaker in the earpiece. There, the electrical energy is converted back into sound – and your voice is magically recreated in the other person's ear.

These are also the themes of how we decode reality. Electrical communication is everywhere and that must be so in a simulation. I described earlier the 'wood wide web' through which trees transmit warnings with chemical/electrical signals through fungal networks under the soil that operate like fibre-optic internet cables. Scientists revealed in 2016 that bees find pollen by picking up electrical signals transmitted by flowers, while a British team has lowered extremely high blood pressure by inserting an electrical wire in the brain to change what is being communicated. Understanding electrical communication is vital to understanding our reality (and health) and it is so simple. Genius and a 'great mind' are mostly considered to be the ability to understand complexity when real genius is to see the simple in *apparent* complexity. Over and over you can observe how the illusion of complexity is only camouflage for the devastatingly simple, but this can only be done through the big picture perspective of beyond-the-program expanded awareness and never from the little picture vision of Body-Mind-

Intellect which dominates science and Mainstream Everything. Revelation comes from the forest, not the twigs. Scientist Robert Lanza describes this very well:

> *When it comes down to it, today's science is amazingly good at figuring out how the parts work. The clock has been taken apart, and we can accurately count the number of teeth in each wheel and gear, and ascertain the rate at which the flywheel spins. We know that Mars rotates in 24 hours, 37 minutes, and 23 seconds, and this information is as solid as it comes. What eludes us is the big picture.*
>
> *We provide interim answers, we create exquisite new technologies from our ever-expanding knowledge of physical processes, we dazzle ourselves with our applications of newfound discoveries. We do badly in just one area, which unfortunately encompasses all the bottom-line issues: what is the nature of this thing we call reality, the Universe as a whole?*

*Ahhh*, but the Archontic force and its agents in human society don't want humanity to know the answer to that question or the game will be revealed. This knowledge has therefore been suppressed at every turn. I say again: You don't need a scientific mind to understand reality – you need a free one. I read that quantum reality is 'counterintuitive', but the opposite is the case. It is not counterintuitive; it is counter solidified perception. Scientists and academics, with a few exceptions, are locked away in the left side of the brain (for reasons I will come to) and the left hemisphere is obsessed with processing detail in the way Robert Lanza describes. The right hemisphere *connects* the detail and that's why it can see the forest – the heart even more so. Virtually the entire global 'education' system is structured by design to stimulate the left side of the brain at the expense of the right. Another aspect of electrical communication comes under the heading of paranormal. Accounts galore of strange happenings and ghostly activity relate to electrical systems and technology. Music players turn on and off or the lights dim or turn on. I have experienced this myself and it is easily explainable. The simplest way for an entity outside of visible light to make themselves known to us is through electrical systems because they are also electrical and electromagnetic in nature. On the first night that I took ayahuasca in Brazil, energy of incredible power poured from the centre of my chest (heart chakra) and arced into the front of my head like some unseen rainbow. I was lying on the floor alone in the darkness apart from one observer. As the (electromagnetic) energy became more powerful the music player began to turn on and off. A strip light also came on and I wondered what the observer was doing messing with the lights. I then realised he was nowhere near the switch. Eventually three lights came on at the peak of the power while the switch remained at off. This is an example of the electrical communication processes that are exploited during what is termed paranormal activity. The room can go cold during these experiences because a communicating or manipulating entity sucks out so much energy from the field in the form of electricity/heat to make the inter-reality connection. By the way, I am not recommending psychoactive drugs and I have only used them on that occasion in Brazil in 2003 and a very, very mild version shortly after. People can have very bad experiences on them and everyone needs to make their own decisions after doing plenty of research. I say that they take you to another level of where you already are. If your frequency is high you can have a good experience but if you are in a bad space in the seen you can experience the same thing in the unseen through psychoactive potions. It's a personal choice and not for me to recommend or otherwise.

## Microsoft reality

When most people look at the night sky they see the lights of planets

**Figure 132:** When I look at the heavens I see an electrical communication system.

**Figure 133:** If you could see the night sky on another level it would look something like this.

and stars. I see an electrical system of communication (Fig 132). What appear in the realm of decoded holographic reality to be 'physical' locations are (in the unseen) points on a waveform, electrical and electromagnetic grid – the simulation (Fig 133). We have reached the point in technological development where this is mirroring our experienced reality in the same way that our experienced reality is bad copy of Upper Aeons reality. An example is a ground-breaking video game released worldwide in 2016 called *No Man's Sky* which employs artificial intelligence to create an entire Cosmos full of planets – 18,446,744,073,551,616 of them – running off 600,000 lines of code (Fig 134). It has apparently had some problems, but it gives an idea of what is possible even with human computing power known to the public (it will be far greater in the shadows). The creators said they set the parameters for the game to then create itself: 'Rules we set in motion that we taught the computer.' These are the equivalent of the laws of physics within the apparent boundary set by the speed of light. *No Man's Sky* is interactive and so is the Archontic simulation, but interactive within the rules and program encoded from the start. These rules in relation to our reality include reincarnation/karma/astrology cycles with human Body-Mind-Soul attached to the program in the same way as characters are in a computer game. We would know? Do computer game characters know they are only responding to software? You can hear the program in mind chatter that you can't switch off. Are they really our thoughts and ramblings that put so much nonsense in our heads every waking moment? Are they our emotions with which we respond and react all over the world in every race and culture as if someone pressed enter? Benjamin Libet (1916-2007), a scientist in the physiology department of the University of California, San Francisco, was a pioneering researcher into the nature of human consciousness. In one famous experiment he asked a study group to move their hands at a moment of their choosing while their brain activity was being monitored. Libet was seeking to identify what came first – the brain's electrical activity to make the hand move or the person's conscious intention to make their hand move. It had to be the second one, surely? But no. Brain activity to move the hand was triggered a full half a second before any conscious intention to move it. Whose hands are on the wheel here? The wheel of fortune, I mean. John-Dylan Haynes, a neuroscientist at the Max Planck Institute for Human Cognitive and Brain Sciences in Leipzig, Germany, led a later study that was able to predict an action *ten seconds* before people had a conscious intention to do it. What was all that stuff about free will? Frank Tong, a neuroscientist at Vanderbilt University in Nashville, Tennessee, said: 'Ten seconds is a lifetime in terms of brain activity.' So where is it coming from if not 'us', the conscious mind? I have contended for a long

time that this phenomenon is the control program being dictated by the simulation through Body-Mind-Soul and the counterfeit spirit. A programme encoded in Body-Soul dictates human experience (in the absence of Spirit) by decoding those experiences into existence

**Figure 134:** No Man's Sky.

from quantum waveform fields of possibility and probability. Control perception and you control experience. This is how the perception deception works. Without the get out of jail card of Spirit the program – which includes astrological influences – can act like tram tracks leading you along a pre-destined path, while you think you are making decisions and choices yourself.

*Westworld*, an American television series that aired in 2016, featured a lot of symbolism that can be related to what I am describing. Westworld is a fictional western-themed hi-tech amusement park where people can interact with programmed robots that look like humans. The robots *believed* they were humans making choices when they were really responding to encoded programs. Eventually they realise this and become conscious enough to overpower the program and recognise the nature of their plight. This is where humanity is now, at the cusp of just such an awakening, if we will only choose to grasp it. Spirit is being infused into the Lower Aeons to free Souls and Minds from the illusion. Spirit is speaking and as the saying goes: 'He that hath ears to hear, let him hear.' They who have not must stay asleep at least for now. People would be shocked beyond words to realise how closely their life is controlled from cradle to grave and even beyond unless consciousness outside the program intervenes. I see the program everywhere from predictable human behaviour to animals and the 'natural world'. I have travelled to more than 60 countries and wherever I go I see people react to similar situations in the same way. Some may be more extreme than others, but it's basically the same no matter what the culture or religion. Only those under some influence of Spirit break the pattern or spell and respond differently. Everything has the same cycle of birth-age-die and there is no randomness in the basic pattern because it's the same program. Why does a duck behave like a duck and an elephant like an elephant? Why does an elephant never behave like a duck? The 'software' doesn't allow that. Different biological programs are encoded to process information in a way that is unique to them. We may apply labels like duck and elephant, but they are really self-replicating algorithms unless Spirit overrides them. They have awareness – everything does – but awareness on a software leash. Animals in *No Man's Sky* are given behavioural profiles controlled by a 'procedural distortion of archetypes' that requires a sequence of algorithms categorised as a 'computerised pseudo-randomness generator'. Perfect. I see this everywhere – pseudo-randomness (Fig 135). There seems to be so much diversity in the world, but when you break it down you find that the randomness is indeed pseudo. Within the apparently random is a constant unifying pattern of behaviour and response. One constant is that everything survives by killing something else. This is the so-called law of the wild which also applies to humans. What better way to

**Figure 135:** In *No Man's Sky* animals unique to each planet are created by algorithm codes generating 'computerised pseudo-randomness'.

generate constant fear and suffering on which to energetically feed than to make 'nature' a global killing field. There is no death in the Upper Aeons and nor any need for killing to survive. Awareness at that level is its own sustenance and in the absence of fear the lion does symbolically lay down with the lamb. Archontic programs have been encoded to make killing – whether by humans or animals – the means of survival which applies to everything and everyone. Vegetarians and vegans avoid meat or all animal products, but what they eat was still conscious. *Everything* is.

If people reflect dispassionately on what I have described here and don't just wave it away as too fantastic to be true they will see what sense this all makes of our crazy world and its apparently bewildering mysteries and anomalies. And we have only just begun.

# CHAPTER FOUR

# One Big Program

*'If the doors of perception were cleansed everything would appear to man as
it is, Infinite. For man has closed himself up, till he sees all things thro'
narrow chinks of his cavern'* – **William Blake**

When the Lower Aeon 'computer' copy of the Upper Aeon original
was first 'downloaded' it was a low-grade copy or reflection of
something astoundingly beautiful. The process then began to infuse the
Archontic distortion and turn that beauty into death, destruction, decay
and chaos – the world of the Archons (Figs 136 and 137).

You can compare this to downloading a copy of a website. The
original site still exists in its original form, but now you have a copy
under your control and you can change it as you like. This has been
ongoing and as more of the distortion was infused into the simulation so
humanity was set at war with itself as human consciousness began to
reflect the distortion. Local, national and global war has been
extraordinary in scale over the last 6,000 years since a 'new psyche'
emerged out of the Middle East around 4,000BC as we perceive time and
human perception and
behaviour dramatically
changed. I am not saying
that this is the point where
the simulation kicked in,
but it was certainly when
the distortion had imposed
itself on human perception
to a level that began to
transform everything. This
is what became known
biblically as 'The Fall', and
more about this and the
'new psyche' shortly. All the

**Figure 136:** Symbolic beauty of Upper Aeon Earth.

**Figure 137:** Death and destruction – the distorted world of the Archontic distortion.

**Figure 138:** Beauty be gone with you.

**Figure 139:** Kill everything.

environmental destruction and pollution and soulless 'architecture' is also an expression of this 'Archonisation' (Figs 138 and 139).

## The 'rewire'

None of what I have described would be possible without first seizing the thinking, emotional and perception processes of the human population (entrapped Spirit). The self-aware Archontic distortion began to rewire the original copy and this involved communication points on the simulation that we know as Orion, Saturn and the Moon. I have written at length about the role of Saturn over many years in books such as *Remember Who You Are*, *The Perception Deception* and *Phantom Self*, and I wrote even further back about the Moon in *Human Race Get Off Your Knees*. I say after nearly three decades of research, and following synchronistic clues all over the world, that Orion, Saturn and the Moon are part of the information system that generates, communicates and amplifies the information source that humans decode into their sense of visual reality – the simulation at the level we experience it. The prime source would appear to be Orion, with the rings of Saturn (sound/information) acting as a generator of those frequencies and the Moon amplifying the Saturnic (Orion) communications and directing them at the human mind (Fig 140). I have concluded this after decades of connecting the dots and following the clues, which are supported more and more by emerging evidence. There is not one killer piece of information, although we are getting there with Saturn and the Moon, but

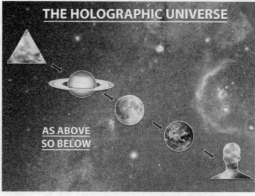

**Figure 140:** Part of the hack into the simulation to specifically target humanity – Orion and its nebula, Saturn, the Moon, Earth and the human mind. Other bodies like Jupiter also play a part in this Matrix of mass control.

an accumulation of lots of different information, facts and anomalies that clearly point me in the direction I am describing. 'No need for arduous seeking, you just have to follow the clues', as I was told in 1990. Orion, Saturn and the Moon were at the centre of so much ancient myth, legend and symbolism. You could understand that in relation to the Moon, which dominates the night sky, and even with the prominent Orion constellation, but *Saturn?* It is a mere dot when viewed from Earth and perceived to be some 746 million miles (1.2 billion kilometres) away. Why would that be so focused upon by ancient peoples? Depictions of Orion 'The Hunter'

**Figure 141:** Ancients were obsessed with Orion and the gods of Orion.

and the three stars of Orion's Belt abound all over the world (Fig 141). Orion was very much associated with 'the gods' and was named in the 8th century BC after the Greek hunter god of that name. Babylonians in Mesopotamia (now Iraq) called Orion the 'Heavenly Shepherd' and the 'True Shepherd' of their leading god Anu – hence a collective name for Mesopotamian gods is Anunnaki. Orion is the shepherd of human perception, and was also associated by the Babylonians with being a

**Figure 142:** Some claim that the Giza pyramids were aligned with the stars of Orion's Belt as they were in 10,450 BC.

**Figure 143:** Orion and Sirius.

messenger of the gods. In ancient Aram (now central Syria including the tragic city of Aleppo) Orion was known as *Nephīlā*, which indicates a connection to the Biblical Nephilim, or 'Fallen Ones'. These were said to be the result of procreation between the 'sons of god' and human women or 'daughters of Adam'. People who claim to have been abducted in modern times by non-human entities or 'aliens' have connected some of them from different ET races to stars of Orion. When I appeared in the History Channel series, *Ancient Aliens*, I was asked why Orion came up so often in their research. On every continent, ancient peoples built sacred places depicting or aligned with Orion, and given that we are really living 'in' a holographic energetic communication system or grid such alignments create an as above, so below energetic connection. Egyptians believed they could communicate with their god Osiris if they performed ritual ceremonies in alignment with Orion, which was considered fundamentally important to life on Earth and beyond. Some modern researchers say that the three pyramids on the Giza plateau were aligned with the three stars of Orion's Belt as they were in 10,450BC (Fig 142). Several hundred miles south of Cairo in the Sahara Desert is another Orion-aligned ritual site called Nabta Playa, dating from between 6,400 and 3,400BC. Egyptians connected their prime god and goddess Osiris and Isis to Orion and Sirius. Once again Sirius, the brightest star seen from Earth, has been associated with extraterrestrial visitations (Fig 143). Ancient Egyptians believed that human life came from Orion, and I have mentioned this humans-from-Orion theme in other books. In my work over the last nearly 30 years I have always looked for common patterns, big and small, ancient and modern, to put the picture together, and patterns are certainly clear with

**Figure 144:** The Orion Nebula – the nearest 'stellar nursery' to Earth.

**Figure 145:** Orion's Trapezium star cluster.

Orion in all its expressions. Repeating myths and legends claim it is the source of creation (the simulation) and human form – and where 'the gods' reside.

American researcher Danny Wilten has done some great work relating the Orion Nebula to phenomena on Earth. The nebula, known as the Great Nebula, is south of Orion's Belt and the star-forming 'stellar nursery' closest to Earth (Fig 144). At the heart of the nebula is a cluster of stars known as the Trapezium or Orion Trapezium Cluster. This could be the source of the 'computer' projection from which we decode the simulation (Fig 145). The nebular is described as a multi-light-year-wide cloud of interstellar dust and gas, but in its base state it is a waveform information construct. Danny Wilten's research – see YouTube for his videos – connects the Orion Nebula with the land formation of Egypt's Nile Delta in the fashion of as above, so below, with one being a mirror of the other. He does the same with the nebula and the human brain. This makes sense within a holographic simulation. Astronomers at the Sloan Digital Sky Survey in New Mexico confirmed in 2017 that humans are made from the same 'stardust' as the Universe (simulation) and this takes us in the same direction. Are characters in a computer game made from different 'stuff' to their apparent surroundings? The Sloan survey team used infrared wavelengths to identify the make-up of 150,000 stars and discovered that humans share some 97 percent of the atoms that form the galaxy. Atoms = energetic waveform information codes. Danny Wilten also contends that Michelangelo's fresco, the *Creation of Adam*, on the ceiling of the Sistine Chapel in the Vatican is symbolic of the Orion Nebula, and this would fit with the ancient belief that human form was created there (Fig 146). The fresco was painted in the 16th century, and many will question how anyone could know about this so long ago. I'll come to that, but in short, the information being revealed in this book for everyone to see has been known by the few for thousands of years, hidden within the inner sanctums of the global secret society network of which the Roman Church (formerly the Church of Babylon) is a central strand. American writer Gary A. David catalogues alignments with Orion and endless depictions all over the world including

**Figure 146:** Is Michelangelo's Creation of Adam a depiction of humanity being created in the Orion Nebula?

China: Xi'an Pyramids     Mexico: Teotihuacan Pyramids     Egypt: The Great Pyramids     Constellation: Orion's Belt

**Figure 147:** Depictions of Orion's Belt around the world.

those throughout the Americas. See his book *Mirrors of Orion*. The Hopi people in Arizona were focused on Orion and so were the Aztecs and Mayans in Central America. The ancient ruined city of Teotihuacán near Mexico City, with its pyramids and temple, is aligned with Orion's Belt (Fig 147). Teotihuacán is believed to have been established about 100BC and is now a World Heritage Site. Zulu high shaman Credo Mutwa told me many years ago about the significance they attached to Orion and the Orion red star that they call 'Mpalalatsani' or 'The Scatterer of Life'. This is described as a paradise

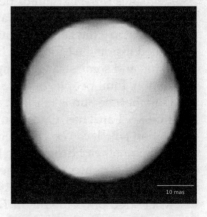

**Figure 148:** Supergiant red star Betelgeuse or the 'Scatterer of Life' in the Orion Constellation.

world and 'a red place with red rocks, red earth, red sand and seas'. The star is more widely known as the supergiant Betelgeuse (pronounced beetle-juice), Orion's second brightest star which forms the right shoulder of the 'hunter', and is the ninth brightest star in the night sky (Fig 148). Betelgeuse (Arabic for 'Hand of Orion') has been calculated to be between ten and twenty times the mass of our Sun, and if it were at

**Figure 149:** Orion was important to ancient societies all over the world and here it is depicted on the Zulu Necklace of the Mysteries which is known to be 500 years old and could possibly be more than a thousand.

the centre of the solar system it would encompass every planet as far out as Mars. It was the first star to have its size measured and one of very few stars that appear through the Hubble Space Telescope as a disc rather than a point of light. Credo Mutwa's 'Necklace of the Mysteries' (a very heavy copper ring that rests on the shoulders) includes a prominent depiction of Orion (Fig 149). He says the necklace is at least 500 years old (he believes twice that) and its symbols tell the story of the human race. They include an ancient symbol of Saturn, 'aliens' and a 'flying saucer' depicting extraterrestrial visitations and interbreeding with humans which I will come to in more detail in the next two chapters. Credo said Zulu legends contend that humans came from the stars and that the very name Zulu means 'People from the Stars'.

He relates Mpalalatsani or Betelgeuse, from which he said humans were banished, to the biblical Garden of Eden and he tells of Zulu legends that say the genetic manipulation of humanity started there and continued inside the Moon and later on Earth. Betelgeuse is apparently shrinking and some strange things are happening generally in the simulation. Inuit people, or 'Eskimos', are among many native groups who say that the Sun is rising in a different place and stars have changed position. Or Earth has. Once you realise we are dealing with a simulation which can be changed such claims can be seen in a new context. Orion's brightest star is Rigel, or Beta Orionis, a blue supergiant and the sixth brightest star in the sky. There is speculation that the common theme in human society of using red and blue in politics and elsewhere (red pill/blue pill in *The Matrix*) is somehow related to Betelgeuse and Rigel and also Bellatrix ('female warrior'), another blue star in Orion. Rigel is estimated to be twice as hot as our Sun and 40,000 times brighter, while Bellatrix is about 8.6 times the mass of the Sun. Understanding the nature of Orion and its other connections in the 'circuit', including Sirius, is central to locating the source of the projected simulation.

## 'Child of Orion' – Saturn

Saturn is known as the 'god of a thousand names' and prominently features in the Archontic language of symbolism (Fig 150). Many

SATURN EVERYWHERE

'GOD OF A THOUSAND NAMES'

**Figure 150:** Why were the ancients so obsessed with Saturn and the same with today's ruling Elite?

**Figure 151:** The classic pyramid and all-seeing eye symbol of the Hidden Hand behind human affairs seen here on the dollar bill.

**Figure 152:** The pyramid and all-seeing eye on the logo of Britain's domestic intelligence agency MI5.

familiar symbols all around us are symbols of Saturn, and some cross- reference with symbols used for Orion, which is appropriate given that Saturn and Orion are expressions of the same information source. The eye or 'all-seeing eye' is one such symbol and you see this everywhere including on the dollar bill, the reverse of the Great Seal of the United States and the logo of Britain's MI5 (Figs 151 and 152). To appreciate the role of Saturn we should return to the question of why the ancients would be so focused on what is today a speck of light in the apparently distant heavens (Fig 153). The answer is that Saturn wasn't always where it is now. Saturn was once the dominant body in the Earth sky when there was a twin sun system involving the sun we see today and the then *ring-less* Saturn. Painstaking work by American researcher David Talbott uncovered this fact from a stream of ancient accounts from every corner of the world. He studied myths, legends and symbols attributed to Saturn in multiple cultures

**Figure 153:** Why would the ancients have worshipped Saturn if it was always where it is today?

**Figure 155:** The all-seeing eye of Saturn.

**Figure 154:** Saturn as the ancients described it as seen from Earth with Mars and Venus.

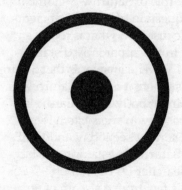

**Figure 156:** The ancient symbol of the 'Sun' perfectly portrays how Saturn was described with Mars and Venus at the centre.

and periods and found compelling common themes. I highly recommend his video series that you can find on YouTube entitled *Discourses on an Alien Sky*, in which he connects all the legends and myths to reveal what Saturn was and how everything suddenly changed. See also his outstanding book, *The Saturn Myth*, if you can get a copy. It is unfortunately out of print, but shouldn't be. Ancient symbols galore representing Saturn immediately make sense once you know the story. Here is a brief summary: Saturn was Earth's closest sun in what the ancients referred to as the Golden Age. Saturn was the 'Steadfast One', 'motionless' and the 'light of the world' and moved in a straight-line sequence with Mars and Venus (Fig 154). The Popol Vuh, the creation story of the Quiche Maya in what is today Guatemala in Central America, also describes a fixed sun that is not the sun we see now. Saturn appeared to humans looking from Earth as a giant eye with Mars and Venus at its centre (Fig 155). The ancient symbol of the sun, a circle with a dot in the middle, makes no sense in relation to the sun we see today, but it is perfect when compared with descriptions of Golden Age Saturn (Fig 156). Ancient legends, symbols and rituals relating to Saturn were so numerous – god of a thousand names – because it dominated the Earth sky. Greek philosopher Plato called Saturn 'Helios', the Sun god, and Greek historian Diodorus of Sicily said the Chaldeans of Mesopotamia referred

to Saturn as 'Helios'. This is a
term later used for the sun
we know today, and the truth
about Saturn was lost as
names and symbols were
transferred. Diodorus said
Saturn was 'the most
conspicuous of planets' and
early astronomers called it
'the Primeval Sun'. Quite
understandably it has been
taken for granted that the
theme of sun gods in the
ancient world were symbolic

**Figure 157:** Saturn sun gods understandably mistaken for symbols of the sun we see today.

of today's sun; but that is not the case. At the very least the great
majority were *Saturn* sun gods, and they include the Babylonian Nimrod
and Ra in Egypt (Fig 157). Mithra, or Mithras in Rome and Persia on
which the later figure of 'Jesus' was based were also Saturn gods. Roman
Emperor Constantine, founder of modern Christianity at the Council of
Nicaea in 325AD, worshipped Sol Invictus or the 'Unconquered Sun'
which I say was Saturn. There is so much sun symbolism in the Biblical
texts. Saturn was the major god of Rome and they had an annual festival
known as Saturnalia in the run up to mid-winter during which they
exchanged presents, decorated trees and hung holly. We call that festival
today 'Christmas' when much of humanity unconsciously worships
Saturn and celebrates Santa, an anagram of Satan. The Demiurge/Satan
and Saturn are connected as we shall see.

## End of the world (nearly)

Fifth century Roman writer Theodosius said that Saturnalia marked the
time when 'Saturn suddenly disappeared', and this supports David
Talbott's research from a long list of ancient descriptions. I have detailed
at length over the last more than 20 years how ancient accounts abound
with stories of great geological catastrophes and 'wars of the gods' in the
heavens, and how these stories match Earth's geological and biological
record. The Great Flood may be the most famous catastrophe narrative,
but the biblical version came from much earlier descriptions and you
find similar accounts throughout the ancient world of the Earth being
torn asunder, even flipping over. Volcanoes erupted everywhere –
'mountains breathed fire' – and there were colossal earthquakes.
Ancients described the 'sea boiling', the 'sky falling', the rising and
sinking of land and a gigantic wall of water. Fantastic rips in the Earth's
surface formed what are alleged to be natural phenomena like the Grand
Canyon in Arizona. Anyone who has stood at the edge looking down

**Figure 158:** The comparative sliver of water in the distance scored out the Grand Canyon? Yep, and a dinner plate can fly to Mars.

**Figure 159:** A global tidal wave would have changed everything including the perception of an evolutionary 'timeline'.

must surely break into hysterical laughter, as I did, at official claims that it was scored out by the Colorado River (Fig 158). Fish and other sea fossils can be found high up in mountains today to confirm the scale of the upheaval. The Himalayas, Alps and Andes only reached their present height geologically recently. Fossilised *intact* trees have been found – which meant this had to have happened in an instant and could be explained, I am told, by the potential pressure of the tidal wave recorded by the ancients (Fig 159). Artificial stone is created using very high pressure. Immediate effects of water pressure could easily have confused scientists in their perception of Earth's evolutionary 'timeline'. A tidal wave Great Flood would explain why botanist Nikolai

Vavilov concluded in a study of more than 50,000 globally-collected wild plants that they originated from only eight different areas and all of them mountainous. Greek philosopher Plato wrote that agriculture began at high elevations after a colossal flood. More evidence of instantaneous change comes with a freezing so fast that mammoths have been found embedded in ice while still standing up in the act of eating. Ancient accounts describe the coming of the ice and how ice and rocks fell from the sky. What if the 'ice age' did not happen as officially claimed, but in an instant? Rocks known as 'erratics', which don't match the rock types native to where they are, can be found all over the world. 'Erratics' derives from the Latin 'to wander'. Some of these erratics are enormous and weigh 15,000 tonnes or more. Scientists say they were moved by glaciers, but what if they were really carried by a tsunami of an almost unimaginable scale? Countless stories record great landmasses, under names like Atlantis and Lemuria/Mu, disappearing under the ocean in the face of global cataclysm. Massive structures from lost cities and civilisations have been discovered under seas around the world (Fig 160). Many writers and researchers have concluded that not only did the Earth go through extraordinary upheavals, but so did the wider solar system.

**Figure 160:** Vast and incredible non-natural structures have been found under the sea all over the world.

Immanuel Velikovsky (1895-1979), a Russian-born psychiatrist, psychoanalyst, writer and researcher, is the best known of them. He produced a series of controversial (of course) books that included *Worlds in Collision*, which he published in 1950. He pointed out that ancient peoples did not record the heavens in the form that we see them today and this is especially true in relation to Venus. Mariner exploration missions to Venus in the 1970s confirmed many of Velikovsky's contentions and its comet-like tail is one example. Velikovsky described cataclysmic events involving Venus and Mars that produced the devastated Mars we see today and almost destroyed Earth. Nor was he talking about millions of years ago, but only a few thousand. From this conclusion, he rewrote the happenings and chronology of ancient Egypt, Greece and Israel. Velikovsky said:

> *Traditions about upheavals and catastrophes, found among all peoples are generally discredited because of the short-sighted belief that no forces could have shaped the world in the past that are not at work also at the present time, a belief that is the very foundation of modern geology and of the theory of evolution.*

We can't explain it, so it could not have happened. The usual 'scientific' fascism kicked in when Velikovsky published his findings and blew their Stone Age minds. *Worlds in Collision* was banned by some academic institutions and the vitriol was so intense that it became known as the Velikovsky Affair. Oh, he must have been saying something right, then. Velikovsky wrote that Jupiter and Saturn, the two biggest bodies in the solar system bar the Sun, were central to this cosmic drama when they were following a very different orbit from the ones we see today. He also said that both were *stars* even though they are considered by the official narrative to be planets. They *are* a form of star and both produce significantly more heat than they receive from the Sun. The gas giant Saturn is the only planet in the solar system that is less dense than water and thus would float. Velikovsky is not alone in saying that the appearance and mass of Saturn and Jupiter would have once been quite different to how they are today. He said that Saturn exploded during a close pass with Jupiter and became a fraction of the size that it had previously been – a size that he believed would have then exceeded Jupiter. Saturn was 'banished' by these effects to its distant location. The Saturn-Jupiter conflict is captured in myth and symbolic stories. The Greeks spoke of the god Zeus (Jupiter) usurping the previous dominance of 'his father' Kronos (Saturn). Velikovsky linked the Egyptian god Osiris to Saturn and the goddess Isis to Jupiter. He said that 'Khima', the source of the Great Flood according to the Babylonian Talmud, was a name for Saturn, and that Mexican texts describe how the 'first world' was destroyed by a universal deluge caused by their name for Saturn. Velikovsky suggests that the Saturn 'nova' explosion could have projected vast amounts of water at the Earth creating the oceans that we have today. The Atlantic Ocean was known as the 'sea of Kronos' (Saturn). Velikovsky said the water could have come directly or via clouds of hydrogen gas combining with Earth's oxygen, and that this 'Saturn water' could be the origin of the salt (sodium and chlorine) in the oceans which science cannot explain from natural sources. Zulu Shaman Credo Mutwa described to me how their legends claim that Earth's seas were once fresh water and that the salt was the work of the gods. Saturn became known as the god of vegetation or agriculture because of the new plants that emerged amid the biological and atmospheric changes that the deluge and upheavals created, Velikovsky writes.

Roll ahead a few decades to the work of David Talbott and his book *Thunderbolts of the Gods*, co-written with Australian physicist Wallace Thornhill. Talbott was inspired by Velikovsky's trailblazing and while not agreeing with every detail certainly supports his themes of world-changing events involving Earth and the solar system, with Saturn at the centre of what happened. His research into global myths and legends about Saturn led him to accounts of the catastrophe that brought an end to the Saturn 'Golden Age', which was remembered as a period of bliss, abundance, fairness and equality. What historians call the emergence of human civilisation out of the Middle East about 6,000 years ago was actually the *re*-emergence as humanity recovered from these catastrophic happenings. The 'cradle of civilisation' is said to have been Mesopotamia, in what is now Iraq, but this wasn't the start – it was part of the *re*-start with a now much-changed human psyche as we shall see. Talbott believes from his reading of the myths that a disturbance caused Mars to move closer to Earth and fantastic electrical plasma charges

**Figure 161:** Neil Hague's portrayal of the electrical 'war' unleashed between Earth and Mars.

were exchanged between them (Fig 161). This would explain the Mars landscape today and why Mars has since been known as the God of War. See Talbott's DVD *Remembering the End of the World* at www.thunderbolts.info. Electromagnetic distortion and chaos destroyed orbital stability and dispatched Venus, Mars, Jupiter and Saturn in all directions.

Mercury was also relocated and the solar system suddenly looked very different. Talbott and co-writer Thornhill are leading lights in the Electric Universe movement, and to understand how the catastrophe happened we need to grasp how the Universe works electrically and electromagnetically. There is such a focus on gravity as the force that holds everything together, including planetary orbits; but it is really electromagnetism. Physicist Thornhill points out that in Isaac Newton's mechanical/gravity model of the Universe more than two objects are inherently unstable. The electrical force meanwhile is about a thousand trillion, trillion, trillion times more powerful than gravity. Velikovsky, too, said that electromagnetic effects have an important role in celestial mechanics. Once the electromagnetic balance and harmony was overthrown we had inter-planetary musical chairs. Physics and possibilities dramatically change when you replace gravity-centred models of the Universe with those based on electricity and electromagnetism. Planets like Mars that now appear 'dead' or lifeless were inhabitable before the catastrophe when atmospheres were transformed.

## A change of mind

Saturn was once celebrated as the source of light and abundance that gave humanity its fondly remembered Golden Age. Today Saturn is known as 'The Greater Malefic' and Mars as the 'Lesser Malefic' and also as the planet of war – references to their 'battle' in the heavens. Saturn is worshipped by Satanists and esoterically/astrologically represents control, judgement, restrictions, limitation, death and decay. Inner-circle Satanists and secret society initiates know Saturn as the Old Sun, Black Sun, Dark Sun, Dark Lord and Lord of the Rings (Fig 162). The Black Sun was an occult symbol of the Nazis and the symbol was depicted on the floor of Wewelsburg Castle, the 'spiritual' headquarters

**Figure 162:** After the catastrophe the image of Saturn changed. It became known as the 'Greater Malefic', a focus of worship for Satanists (Saturnists) and the rings appeared.

**Figure 163:** The Nazi Black Sun symbol for Saturn.

of Heinrich Himmler's SS (Fig 163). Nazis in Ukraine today use the same symbol. What the hell happened to bring about Saturn's fantastic perceptual transformation? Well, something did – and big-time – after its 'fall'. I mentioned how Archontic awareness has sought to constantly distort and invert the 'bad copy' that corresponds with part of the Upper Aeon original reality. What I have described here was a major moment in that quest in relation to Earth. Not only Saturn 'fell', so did humanity. This is the 'Fall of Man' which is not purely a biblical theme but globally universal. Fear and terror from this cataclysmic experience was infused into the human energy field/hologram and even more significantly the heavens were 'rewired'. We go back to the foundations of astrology and how planets and stars are information fields on the Cosmic Internet (simulation) and exchange their energy (information) with the cosmic field. This, in turn, influences the energetic and perceptual state of everything interacting with those fields – i.e. including us. The perceptual/energetic impact of the complete rearrangement of planets/dwarf suns closest to Earth cannot be overstated. Everything changed because the human mind dramatically changed as the perceptual cell door slammed shut. Chaos in the perceived 'outer' world became chaos in the human psyche because the two are constantly interacting and profoundly connected. What affects one affects the other. Compelling evidence points to a transformation of the human psyche around 6,000 years ago, or 4000BC, when a 'new psyche' emerged and expanded very quickly in evolutionary terms. Writer and researcher Steve Taylor, a lecturer in psychology at Leeds Beckett University, focuses on this period in his book, *The Fall: The Insanity of the Ego in Human History and the Dawning of a New Era*. Taylor says that before 6,000 years ago there was no war or male-dominated society, no massive inequality, class systems or organised religion as we know them today. He could have added no Satanism or human sacrifice. American cultural historian Riane Eisler describes this period as 'the great change – a change so great, indeed, that nothing in all we know of human cultural evolution is comparable in magnitude'. Taylor explains how what he calls this 'new psyche' emerged out of the Middle East and Asia ('Saharasia') around 6,000 years ago in the wake of violent invasions by Indo-European and Semitic peoples. Indo-European refers to a language group spoken throughout most of Europe and as far as northern India. They include languages and language groups known as Italic, Slavic, Baltic, Hellenic, Celtic, Germanic, Indo-Iranian, English, Spanish, German, Latin, Greek, Russian, Albanian, Lithuanian, Armenian, Persian, Hindi and Hittite. Semitic is defined as a group of languages in North Africa and the Middle East that include Arabic, Hebrew, Assyrian, Aramean and Phoenician. Contrary to what we are led to believe, Arabic is *overwhelmingly* the major Semitic language and the use of 'Semitic' and 'anti-Semitic' with exclusive regard to Jewish people is a misrepresentation of what the term actually means. This 'new psyche', or perhaps fallen Saturn psyche, went on to take over the world and I say this psyche was also the result of extraterrestrial or 'alien' manipulation of the human form of which more later. American psychologist Julian Jaynes (1920-1997) proposed a similar change in the human psyche in his book, *The Origin of Consciousness in the Breakdown of the Bicameral Mind.* Jaynes' term 'bicameral' refers to the concept of a relative division between the left and right hemispheres of the brain in which the right side communicated to the left side in 'auditory hallucinations' that were heard by the person as a voice. He concludes that these were believed to be the voices of the gods that must be obeyed, but also appeared as people the person knew. Jaynes highlights the many similarities between the bicameral 'two-chambered' mind and the modern-day experiences of schizophrenics. He says that from studying ancient texts and customs he estimates the bicameral mind began to change thousands of years ago to be replaced by the intellectual mind when the 'voices' stopped and the left side of the brain became dominant. The same left-brain domination was a foundation feature of Steve Taylor's 'new psyche'. Left-brain perception sees everything as apart from everything else (the 'twigs') and decodes dots and not pictures (the 'forest'). A left-brain disconnected from the picture-seeing right hemisphere is a perceptual prison cell. This is vitally important to understanding human society today in which left-brain reality controls politics, science, academia, media, military, banking and business – Mainstream Everything. The consequences of this will be very clear a little further on.

## Lord of the Rings

I have laid out the detailed background to Saturn in *Remember Who You*

*Are* and *The Perception Deception* and I will summarise the information here and add more to put it in context with the themes of this book. Norman Bergrun is a highly distinguished American engineer and research scientist who worked at NASA's Ames Research Center in Moffett Field, California, and its predecessor, the National Advisory Committee for Aeronautics, and was employed by

**Figure 164:** Norman Bergrun.

Lockheed Martin on classified aerospace projects. He said that he had top secret security clearance for 30 years and during that period 'I signed my life away'. Bergrun pioneered a number of developments in the fields of aircraft, missiles and rockets, including 'roll stability laws', and won many awards including the California Society of Professional Engineers Archimedes Engineering Achievement

**Figure 165:** These two missions have provided amazing knowledge about Saturn but not all of it via NASA.

Award (Fig 164). Bergrun, who is now in his 90s, had his sense of reality overturned by studying images of Saturn taken by the Voyager and Cassini missions. Voyager 1 and 2 made their closest approach to Saturn in 1980 and 1981, while Cassini-Huygens arrived in 2004 and was destroyed in 2017 by steering the craft to dive into Saturn's atmosphere in what NASA called the 'Grand Finale' (Fig 165). The official story is that this was to avoid potential biological contamination of Saturn's moons as Cassini's fuel ran out, but the dive had the potential for allowing greater understanding of what is going on with Saturn. Bergrun realised from Saturn images that the rings were changing, sometimes in minutes, and he concluded from a range of evidence that the rings were not 'natural'. He went on to compile his findings in his book *Ringmakers of Saturn* which is now out of print and changing hands on the Internet for thousands of pounds. The book was originally based on Voyager images, but his knowledge was increased further when he saw those taken by Cassini. Bergrun wrote:

*Several years ago, a number of folks in the astronomy and physics world*

*began theorising that these rings had to be much younger than the Universe,
perhaps only about 100 million years old. But one pair of pictures shows a
change in five minutes! ...*

*... An impression is conveyed that latest reported measurements purport to
be the true ones when, in reality, all might be quite nearly correct at time of
observation. General reluctance to accept variable ring-system geometry
occurs because of apparent failure to identify a physical mechanism suitable
for producing recurrent change.*

Here we go again – *if we can't explain it then it can't be happening.* The
arrogance and self-delusion is incredible. Compelling evidence is before
them, but they won't go there because their whole world view (and the
one the Hidden Hand wants humanity to believe) would be demolished.
Mainstream media reports about strange happenings with Saturn's rings
conclude that 'it's a mystery'. The Hidden Hand is quite happy for some
things to be revealed so long as they are considered a 'mystery' and
never explained or put into context. One news report said that Saturn's
most distant 'F' ring was twice as bright and three times as wide
between 2004 and 2009 than during the Voyager fly-bys in the early
1980s. The ring also increased in size from a width of about 200
kilometres to about 580. The report went on:

*The great mystery of Saturn's rings is how they formed and why they are so
stable. A simple model of orbital dynamics in this kind of orbit should
gradually spiral into the planet. So the rings should long ago have smeared*

**Figure 166:** Norman Bergrun's 'electromagnetic vehicles' on a stream of NASA photographs.

Infrared photograph of one of the gigantic cylindrical objects taken by Hubble in the the rings of Saturn.

**Figure 167:** An absolutely massive 'vehicle' in the rings of Saturn.

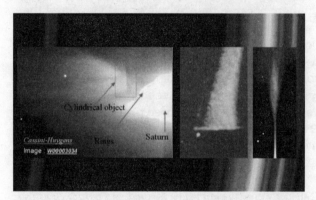

**Figure 168:** Electromagnetic vehicles pouring out plasma 'exhaust' to make the rings.

**Figure 169:** Saturn's rings look like a DVD.

*out and disappeared. Instead, they are highly complex and stable and contain other structures such as spokes and braids. Nobody knows why.*

Well, perhaps, not exactly nobody. David Talbott's research into ancient myths and legends about Saturn did not find any mention of rings, and as they would otherwise have been at the centre of the myths they must therefore be relatively recent and post-cataclysmic. As Bergrun studied Saturn images and changing ring formations he spotted another massive revelation. What he called cylindrical 'electromagnetic vehicles' of immense size could clearly be seen inside the rings (Figs 166 and 167). By 'immense' I mean two or three times bigger than Earth, and if that sounds

amazing consider that Earth is an absolute titch compared with Saturn which is 95 times larger. Saturn could encompass 764 Earths. I have seen other accounts of these 'vehicles' being spotted near the Sun. 'People have got to be made to understand that those things are real', Bergrun said. He identified images in which the 'vehicles' were actually *making the rings* by spewing out plasma 'exhaust', and he calls them 'the ringmakers' as in the title of his book (Fig 168). This makes sense of why the ancients did not mention rings around their Saturn sun, and supports my contention for many years now that Saturn

**Figure 170:** The Saturn information 'hack' - the human fake reality Matrix.
© www.neilhague.com

was hijacked after the cataclysm and turned into an enormous broadcasting system that is delivering information that the human mind decodes as the fake reality or Matrix – a simulation within a simulation that we perceive as the 'real world'. Saturn is part of the 'hack' into the original 'bad copy' that also involves Orion, the Moon and probably much else. Look at Saturn's rings and then look at a CD or DVD (Fig 169). The rings of Saturn are *broadcasting* at one level the 2D projection that some scientists are now talking about which we decode into 3D holographic illusion (Fig 170). Before anyone screams nonsense – how could they do that? – remember that we are dealing with a *simulation* and not a solid 'physical' reality. Change the waveform information construct and you change its holographic projection. Norman Bergrun described what he believes to be the nature of the cylindrical vehicles: 'I say that [they are] electromagnetic because I can identify streamline patterns with respect to [them] that I knew were what we called "potential lines" and that says it was electrical.' They are electrical/electromagnetic because they are messing with the electrical/electromagnetic communication system of the Cosmic Internet (simulation). This transformation of Saturn would also explain how the much-loved sun of the Golden Age became associated with control, judgement and limitation, which is exactly the role of the new Saturn as a broadcaster of the perceptual control 'Matrix'. Saturn became 'possessed', an expression of the Demiurgic distortion and thus a focus for Archontic worship as the Black Sun, Dark Sun and Dark Lord.

Saturn is also known as the 'god of space and time' (the Matrix) and the 'Lord of Karma' (the recycling of souls through reincarnation based on the energetic 'algorithm' or law of cause and effect). The perception 'hack' created the astrological prison/karma cycle that I described

**Figure 171:** Kronos, the ancient Greek god of Saturn who is known today as Old Father Time.

**Figure 172:** The symbolism of Kronos reflects the portrayal of Saturn as the god of time and space (the simulation).

**Figure 173:** A gigantic new ring discovered around Saturn in 2009.

before. There is no recorded mention of a belief in reincarnation until less than 3,000 years ago and it only became widespread much later. Kronos, the ancient Greek god symbol for Saturn, was portrayed holding an hourglass (time) and has become known as 'Old Father Time' (Figs 171 and 172). Gnostics said that Saturn is the outermost planetary sphere or Archon of what I would call the Matrix and beyond that was Leviathan, a snake swallowing its own tail (Ouroboros) through which souls had to pass to reach paradise (escape the Matrix). The esoteric concept of the 'Ring-Pass-Not' is based on the same theme. I say that what is being described here is not an 'evolutionary process', but a coldly designed entrapment of perception. Saturn rings pervade the 'space' to Earth on unseen frequencies through the unified scalar field and electromagnetic fields. NASA discovered a ginormous new ring in 2009 visible in infrared wavelengths between 3.7 and 7.4 million miles from Saturn (Fig 173). The ring is big enough to encompass a billion Earths. Norman Bergrun was featured by *Express* newspapers in Britain in 2016 under the headline 'Former NASA whistleblower's shock claim space agency hid PROOF of UFOs orbiting Saturn'. The story said that Bergrun was warning about a NASA cover-up and the fact that the electromagnetic vehicles he wrote about in the 1980s were now 'proliferating at a shocking rate on the planet's many rings'. Numbers of what the report called 'UFO crafts' were increasing at speed and had reached 'critical levels'. They were spreading to other planets including Uranus and Jupiter, Bergrun said. He points out that Uranus didn't have rings but now it does and the same was happening with Jupiter. Bergrun was quoted as saying that in his opinion the craft were 'living' and capable of the essential functions of biological systems like self-replication and self-maintenance. I have been emphasising that 'life' and awareness doesn't have to take the form of two legs, two arms, a head and a torso. And what if they are not so much 'alien craft' but an expression of Archons or the inner electrical workings of the simulation as its creators change the program?

## Rings of sound (information)

I was sent an image of a Saturn ring from a professional sound engineer who said that he saw the same phenomena every day in his work with music and sound technology. He said the ring was definitely a manifestation of sound (Fig 174). This brings us to something called 'cymatics' from a Greek word meaning 'wave'. The principle has been known since ancient times and involves sound of varying frequency being transmitted across or through a medium of particles, paste or liquid. The interaction produces a remarkable sight of the medium transforming into geometrical patterns in response to the sound (information). As the frequency changes so do the patterns, and the higher the frequency the more complex the pattern (Fig 175). Higher frequencies can carry more energy (information) than lower frequencies like radio waves and visible light. This frequency/sound/form relationship is a two-way process – frequency is expressed as the pattern and the pattern is expressed as the frequency. They are

**Figure 174:** A sound engineer saw immediately what this Saturn ring depicted – sound.

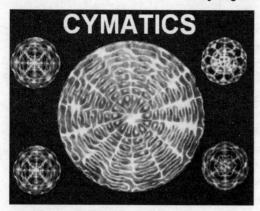

**Figure 175:** Incredible patterns are created in cymatics by sound frequencies and when the frequency changes so does the pattern.

**Figure 176:** The hexagon storm – the size of four Earths – at Saturn's northern pole.

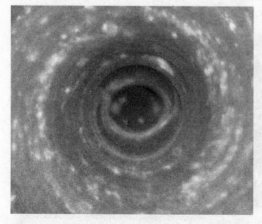

**Figure 177:** Saturn's eye storm at the southern pole.

different expressions of *each other*. You see the pattern, but at the same time it is generating the sound (information) which created the pattern and holds it in situ. And what holds it in situ? *STANDING WAVES*. The sound frequency creates standing waves of information which means the form will remain in place forever so long as the frequency remains and doesn't change. I am saying that all form is created in this way through information being held in standing or stationary waves of frequency. Atomic explosions can vaporise the body by disintegrating standing wave stability and its information content. Put 'cymatics' into YouTube to see the process at work. We return to what Albert Einstein said:

*Concerning matter, we have been all wrong. What we have called matter is really energy, whose vibration has been lowered to be perceptible to the senses. There is no matter. There is only light and sound.*

Planets (and dwarf stars) generate sound, and you can see 'cymatic' manifestations of Saturn's frequencies with the 'unexplainable' permanent storms at both poles. A monster storm at Saturn's north pole takes the form of a hexagon big enough to encompass four Earths, and there's another at the south pole that looks like a giant 'eye' (Figs 176 and 177). These pole storms are *standing waves*. They are 'permanent' in the sense that they have been there since they were first observed decades ago and they will remain until Saturn's *frequencies* significantly change and with that the standing waves. The hexagon storm (which NASA calls 'bizarre') completes a cycle in exact synchronicity with the cycle of Saturn's radio emissions (10 hours 39 minutes 24 seconds). There are apparently multiple layers of the storm going down towards the interior. NASA says that a system of clouds within the hexagon appear to be 'whipping around ... like cars on a racetrack' at hundreds of miles an hour and making 60 degrees turns to pass through each segment of the hexagram. Nothing similar with such a regular geometry had ever been seen on any planet in the Solar System – because Saturn is not just any planet. Saturn is a dwarf star that has been massively tampered with.

Bob Brown, team leader of the Cassini visual and infrared mapping spectrometer at the University of Arizona, said it was amazing to see such striking differences between Saturn's poles. But is it? Space.com reported in 2011 how radio wave signals differ in the northern and southern hemispheres and this is what you would

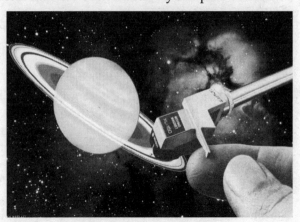

**Figure 178:** Symbolic Saturn by artist Joe Webb.

expect with a permanent hexagon to the north and an 'eye' to the south. They are manifestations of different sound frequencies (Fig 178). Don Gurnett, leader of the Cassini radio and plasma wave instrument team, said:

> *These data just go to show how weird Saturn is. We thought we understood these radio wave patterns at gas giants, since Jupiter was so straightforward. Without Cassini's long stay, scientists wouldn't have understood that the radio emissions from Saturn are so different.*

They are different because Saturn has been hijacked or Archontically 'possessed' to become a generator of the fake Matrix information source that humanity believes to be the 'real world'. Kevin Baines, a member of

**Figure 179:** Saturn's hexagon storm has changed colour from blue to gold over four years.

Cassini's visual and infrared mapping spectrometer team at NASA's Jet Propulsion Laboratory in Pasadena, California, said of the hexagon:

*This is a very strange feature, lying in a precise geometric fashion with six nearly equally straight sides. We've never seen anything like this on any other planet. Indeed, Saturn's thick atmosphere where circularly-shaped waves and convective cells dominate is perhaps the last place you'd expect to see such a six-sided geometric figure, yet there it is.*

Mainstream science will never understand what Saturn is (and therefore solve its 'mysteries') because there are too many no-go areas. These include the findings of Norman Bergrun and the frequency, information and consciousness nature of *everything* in our reality. NASA announced in 2016 that the Saturn hexagon had changed colour from blue to gold over the previous four years (Fig 179). Colours are different frequencies and changes in Saturn's frequency patterns will affect the colour. This is happening at the same time, according to Norman Bergrun, that electromagnetic vehicles are accumulating within Saturn's

**Figure 180:** The six-pointed hexagram or 'Star of David' is a symbol of Saturn.

**Figure 181:** Black cubes are symbols of Saturn.

rings on a scale he has never seen before. Is this really just a coincidence? Scientists speculate that the colour change may have been due to Saturn approaching its northern pole 'summer solstice' in a Saturn year equivalent to nearly 30 Earth years, but if the colour changes the frequency has changed. Sound and frequency are the foundation of everything within our reality.

## Symbols and sound

Two of the prime ancient symbols for Saturn are the six-pointed star (hexagram/'Star of David') and the cube, especially the black cube (Figs 180 and 181). These can also be expressed in terms of frequency/sound as a *hexagon*. You see in Figure 182 two versions of the same image, but look at them from different perspectives and they don't look the same. Observe the one on the left as if it is flat and you see a hexagon; but now look at the one on the right in three dimensions and it becomes a cube. Symbols and shapes are visual representations of sound/frequency states, and the hexagon, hexagram and cube represent (and therefore broadcast) the sound/information of Saturn (Figs 183). Saturn's hexagram can therefore be expressed as a

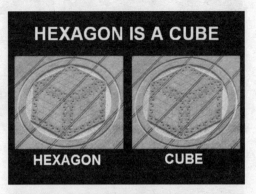

**Figure 182:** A cube is a hexagon in 3D.

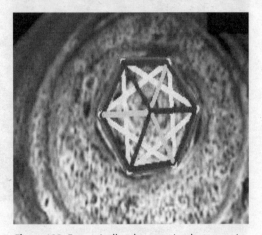

**Figure 183:** Energetically a hexagon is a hexagram is a cube.

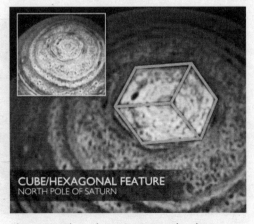

**Figure 184:** The 'cube' at Saturn's north pole.

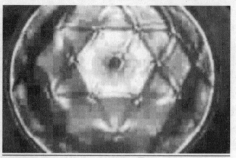

**Figure 185:** A perfect hexagon created purely by a sound frequency.

**Figure 186:** A hexagram created by sound.

**Figure 187:** Form, symbols and geometrical patterns are all expressions of standing wave frequencies. The frequency is the form and the form is the frequency – they are two versions of the same in*form*ation.

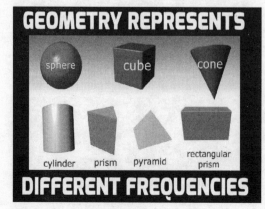

**Figure 188:** Geometrical shapes are holographic manifestations of frequency information states.

cube (Fig184). I was watching a YouTube video of constantly changing sound pounding through a liquid medium creating geometrical images. They were changing so fast as the sound frequency changed that I had to keep freezing the frame to see what shapes were being formed. Among them I found perfect hexagons and hexagrams (Figs 185 and 186). Chinese philosopher Confucius said that signs and symbols run the world, not words and laws, and this is because they are waveform standing wave *fields of information* (Figs 187 and 188). I would add to the Confucius quote that actually letters and words are also symbols that transmit information and frequencies. Official communications and texts are carefully worded for this reason. Symbols are constantly affecting the conscious and especially the subconscious mind by transferring information, and this is the whole foundation of the hidden (occult) language of symbolism used by secret societies, Satanism and the Archontic Hidden Hand behind world events. Information encoded in symbols enters through the sight senses in ways that sound within the frequency range of human hearing cannot. When you hear something, you are consciously aware of it, but that is not the case with almost all that we 'see'. Our brain constructs a sense of reality from just 40 visual sensations per second out of *11 million* and the other 11 million minus 40 are absorbed by the subconscious (Fig 189). Sight senses are the perfect way to plant information, concepts, and perceptions into the subconscious while bypassing the

**Figure 189:** Only the tiniest fraction of visual information is processed by the conscious mind. The rest is absorbed by the subconscious.

**Figure 190:** Once information is planted in the subconscious it filters through to the conscious mind as what people believe to be their own thoughts and perceptions.

conscious mind which has no idea this is happening. These planted perceptions then filter through to conscious awareness as what the person believes to be their own thoughts and decisions (Fig 190). *Gotcha!* Saturn symbols all around us are downloading Saturn information (frequencies) to the subconscious all day, every day and locking human perception into the Saturn frequency band – the Matrix. And Saturn symbols *are* all around us. The ubiquitous all-seeing eye, which has been associated with Saturn but has other meanings, appears to an extraordinary extent in animated cartoons and movies for children because it represents a frequency/information state that speaks to their subconscious (Fig 191). The young are a prime target for programming because they will the adults when the Archontic Hidden Hand wants its full-blown tyranny in place. Religion is ablaze with symbols and all of

**Figure 191:** All of these images from children's cartoons and animations include the all-seeing eye or pyramid and all-seeing eye.

**Figure 192:** Focus on a symbol connects you to the frequency the symbol represents whatever that may be.
© www.neilhague.com

them are talking to the human subconscious, with followers and advocates most powerfully affected. This saying is profoundly accurate: 'Energy flows where attention goes.' Attention is the key to everything including how focus of attention triggers the decoding process that transforms waveform information into holographic reality. I explained earlier how tarot cards electromagnetically represent information and the concepts they symbolise, and this is the case with all symbols. If a symbol represents Saturn then its energetic field will resonate to the Saturn frequency. Focus of attention on that symbol – even subconsciously through the 11 million minus 40 – will attach you to that frequency (Fig 192). Once this connection has been made your energy can be trawled by the frequency that the image symbolises, be it a planet or other non-human entity. Our energy can be absorbed by a planetary body 746 million miles away? There is no space as there is no time and so no distance or 'miles'. There is only here and now. Everything else is decoded illusion. Religions are covert conduits for the focused attention through worship of the Archons, Saturn, Orion, etc. and attention means energetic connection unless we consciously reject it.

## What's with the cube?

An ancient symbol of Saturn is the black cube and interestingly the physicist Silas Beane, a prominent researcher into our simulated reality, has suggested that the 'Matrix' could well be based on a lattice of cubes (Fig 193). His Bonn University team found that cosmic rays align with a

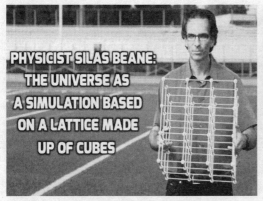

**Figure 194:** A hypercube with the smaller cube as a reflection of the inner cube.

**Figure 193:** What an amazing 'coincidence' that research has suggested the simulation is constructed as a lattice of cubes.

specific pattern that takes the form of cubes, and if Saturn/Orion was broadcasting a Matrix information blueprint or lattice based on cubes, would cosmic rays not align with that when they entered its frequency construct? Some have suggested that our reality is a hypercube which appears as a cube within a cube (Fig 194). If you watch an animation of a hypercube you will see the small cube becoming the big

**Figure 195:** The 'flat' hypercube symbol often used by organisations related to law and control.

cube becoming the small cube and this is used by the Elite and Satanists (sorry, I repeat myself) to symbolise the human prison with no way out (there is). The words 'hypercube explanation' will take you to a good YouTube video. Hypercubes are a major symbol used by the deepest levels of the 'occult' ('hidden') networks to represent 'Hell'. I have said before that we are not going to 'Hell'. We *live* in it, or rather one level of it. A cube is an extension of a square or 'hypersquare' and a hypercube is an extension of the cube. We saw this one-is-an-expression-or-extension-of-the-other with the example of the two-dimensional hexagon and the three-dimensional cube being separated only by the *perception* of the viewer. A cube has three dimensions while the hypercube has four, but we can only perceive three because that is the limit of the human visual decoding system. Significantly, the smaller cube in the middle of the bigger one is created by the projection of a *shadow* in an illusion created by the light source – a shadow of a square within a square. The smaller cube is a *shadow projection* of the bigger cube and that is what we are seeing in our 'world' – a shadow projection of another reality as the Gnostic texts and Plato describe. Hypercubes are symbolised by

**Figure 196:** The Saturn cube in Mecca, the Kaaba ('cube').

**Figure 197:** Worshippers praying in concentric circles to the black cube of Saturn.

**Figure 198:** A black cube ritual in the Jewish religion.

Satanists and the Hidden Hand as a double square with one laid over the other to form eight points. This is used profusely by organisations related to control (Fig 195). Extend the flat double square into 3D and it is a double cube. I have been aware of this since the 1990s when I wrote, in *The Biggest Secret*:

*The double square, one square on top of another in any form, is more secret society symbolism. In the secret language of symbolism one square on top of another means control of all that is right and all that is wrong, all that is just and all that is unjust, all that is negative and all that is positive. In other words, 'We control everything'.*

Freemasons are said to be 'on the square' and have black and white squares on their temple floors as do many churches and cathedrals. Freemasonry's inner circle is well aware that the 'Craft' is serving the Archontic force within human society. America was established by the Europe-based Elite through secret societies like the Freemasons and so urban America is arranged in squares known as 'blocks'. When you live in blocks you are in the midst of the energy created and represented by blocks or squares which are at other levels energetically hexagons, which are energetically cubes, which are energetically hypercubes. Now, where is the world's most famous black cube? Mecca – Islam's holy of holies known as the Kaaba (Fig 196). Kaaba means cube and represents Saturn. Worshippers even kneel to the 'Kaaba stone' or 'Black Stone' inside the cube while arranged in concentric circles (Fig 197). They believe they are worshipping 'Allah', but who or what is Allah? Five times a day orthodox Muslims get on their knees to 'face Mecca' wherever they are in the world and focus their *attention* on the Kaaba. Energy flows where attention goes. Major religions may appear to be in opposition, but they are founded on the same basic themes and their differences are mostly illusory. Jewish worshippers put a black cube on their head called a Tefillin while the Jewish god of Saturn is 'El' and his symbol is ... the black cube (Fig 198 and 199). This is the origin of Is-ra- EL and also El and the Elohim (Demiurge and Archons) in the Old Testament, which in Genesis describes the Demiurge creating the simulation – 'Let there be [luminous fire] Light' (Fig 200). We also have ang-ELs, archang-ELs and fallen ang-ELs served by the 'human' *EL*-ite and their agents who take power in rigged EL-ections. We also have El-ysium where the Greeks and Romans believed those 'heroes' who served the *EL*-ite were taken after death to live in paradise. Elysium is a variant on the Islamic theme of going to paradise to be served after death by virgins if you serve the interests of Allah which some tragically believe includes committing mass murder by suicide bomb. I will refer from here on to the *El*-ite to emphasise the connection with Saturn of the ruling and manipulating Archontic network of satanic rings and secret societies within human society.

**Figure 199:** The same theme wherever you look.

**Figure 200:** Rank and file religious advocates the world over have no idea where their religions really come from and what they are really worshipping.

**Figure 201:** Ancient Mesopotamian symbol of Saturn.

Isra-EL is the creation and fiefdom of the Archontic House of Rothschild whose very name comes from another front-line symbol for Saturn, the six-pointed star or hexagram. This is called the Star of David and claimed to be an exclusively Jewish symbol, but it's not. Hexagrams as a symbol of Saturn are global and can be seen in ancient Mesopotamian depictions and all over Asia (Figs 201 and 202). They are also central to Freemasonry and found in Christianity as well as Judaism (Figs 203, 204

**Figure 202:** The Star of David is not a symbol exclusive to Judaism but a universal symbol of Saturn. All these images are from Asia.

**Figure 203:** Saturn as a six-pointed star in the Mother Lodge of Freemasonry in London.

**Figure 204:** The Saturn symbol in Christianity.

**Figure 205:** The hexagram is of course central to the Jewish religion.

**Figure 206:** The red hexagram from which the name Rothschild originated.

**Figure 207:** The Rothschilds transferred their family symbol to the flag of Israel after they had manipulated and bombed the state into existence in 1948.

and 205). Family networks today known as Rothschild were a Middle Ages occult family called Bauer until they changed the name to Rothschild as their banking dynasty (which became today's global financial system) began to emerge in the 18th century out of Frankfurt, Germany. The name-change was made by dynasty founder Mayer Amschel Bauer, who took the name Rothschild from the red hexagram displayed on his house (Fig 206). Rothschild comes from the German

**Figure 208:** The six-pointed star or hexagram is the esoteric symbol for the heart vortex or chakra.

**Figure 209:** Hammer and sickle symbol of the Rothschild-created Soviet Union which is an adaption of the astrological symbol of Saturn.

**Figure 210:** Goat-god Pan is a symbol of Saturn with reference to the Saturn 'sign' of Capricorn.

**Figure 211:** Saturn as the satanic symbol of Baphomet.

'Rot' (Red) and 'Schild' (Sign). The Archontic Rothschilds would go on to establish Zionism by rewriting 'history' (see *The Perception Deception*) which led to the founding of Israel after World War II. Israel is the Land of Rothschild and the Israeli flag features the ancient symbol of Saturn from which the very name Rothschild originates (Fig 207). I wrote earlier about the power of the heart or heart vortex/chakra which the Archontic conspiracy constantly works to close. The symbol used for the heart chakra is ... the hexagram (Fig 208). This is way too synchronistic to be dismissed as coincidence. Gnostic Nag Hammadi texts say: 'And they [the Archons] closed [human] hearts, and they hardened themselves through the hardness of the counterfeit spirit until now.' What if the symbol of the heart vortex as a symbol of Saturn is a scam to close hearts and not to open them? Focus attention of your heart chakra on the heartless symbol of Saturn and what do you think will happen? A cross and 'tail' that forms the astrological symbol of Saturn was employed by the Rothschilds to form the hammer and sickle on the flag of the Soviet Union (Fig 209). This was another creation of the Rothschilds via their Zionist gofers Lenin, Trotsky and many others. See ... *And The Truth Shall Set You Free* for the detailed background. Baphomet, or the Goat of Mendes, is a prominent satanic composite symbol of the negative force and a modification of the god Pan which represents Saturn (Figs 210 and 211). Manly P. Hall, one of the most famous Freemasonic historians, wrote in *Secret Teachings of All Ages*:

> *Pan was a composite creature, the upper part – with the exception of his horns – being human, and the lower part in the form of a goat ... the god himself is a symbol of Saturn because this planet is enthroned in Capricorn, whose emblem is the goat.*

Goats are used to symbolise Saturn in many movies, television programmes and music videos and in 2016 an obvious representation of Baphomet played the central role in a bizarre satanic-like ceremony to open the 35-mile Gotthard Base railway tunnel (the world's longest) through the Swiss Alps (Fig 212). A British newspaper called the ritual 'one of the most bizarre opening ceremonies in history' and the strange goings-on were attended by European leaders including Germany's Chancellor Angela Merkel, President Francois Hollande of France and Italian Prime Minister Matteo Renzi. The occult ritual (for that is what it was) featured a baby with feathered white wings and an oversized head which one commentator described as 'a topless creepy-looking bird'. There were semi-naked dancers, a montage of [all-seeing] eyes and [fallen] angels appearing from the abyss/eye of Saturn. A goat man (Saturn/Pan/Baphomet) was the star of the show. He died and was then resurrected, worshipped and crowned 'king of the world'. Type the words 'satanic opening ceremony for Gotthard Base Tunnel' into a search engine and you will see what I mean. I posted images from the ritual on Facebook but they were taken down because they 'breached guidelines'. Yet the same images were broadcast on television stations all

**Figure 212:** Baphomet or the Goat of Mendes played the central role in the bizarre ritual that opened the Gotthard Base railway tunnel.

**Figure 213:** The Grim Reaper is Saturn and reflects its association with death.

over the world with some, including the BBC, showing the ritual live. As one observer said, if they will do this in public what are they doing in private? Well, plenty worse as we shall see. The Grim Reaper is another Saturn symbol and relates to its esoteric association with death and the scythe is in keeping with Saturn's ancient role as the god of vegetation and agriculture (Fig 213). Kronos, the Greek personification of Saturn, also holds a scythe and the same symbolism was encoded with the sickle of the Soviet Union.

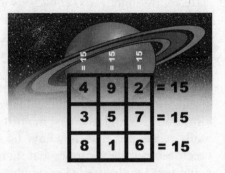

Figure 214: The Magic Square of Saturn.

## Numbers game

Saturn symbolism goes deep into numerology and includes the Magic Square of Saturn which consists of numbers adding up to 15 in all directions (Fig 214). In numerology, you keep adding the digits until there is a single number and so, numerologically, 15 is really 6. The Magic Square of Saturn (also used in Freemasonry) therefore adds up

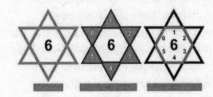

Figure 215: All the sixies.

along all sides to 666 – the Biblical 'Number of the Beast' in the Book of Revelation. Hexagons and hexagrams equate to 666 (Fig 215). Ancient sun worship in places such as Babylon were associated with the number 666, and once you realise they were worshipping the *Saturn* sun you can see why. Numbers are digital expressions of frequencies and 666 represents the Saturn (Matrix) frequency. In occult law, all numbers comprise 1 through 9. Zero means what it says – nothing. 90,000 or 900,000 in numerology is energetically merely 9. Mark Passio, a former member of the Church of Satan in the United States, has been exposing the dark occult since he left. He says that Satanists consider 9 to be 'Satan's number' and that of the ego or Phantom Self as I call it. In other words the energetic state of programmed awareness in which the Archontic *El*-ite seek to entrap humanity is represented numerologically by 9. Passio points out that adding all base single digit numbers to 9 brings every number back to itself numerologically (energetically). For example: 1 + 9 =10 = 1 ... through to ... 9 + 9 = 18 = 9. Passio says that this symbolises how the state of ego/Phantom Self changes nothing. Multiplication of 9 with single digits always equals 9 numerologically and so Satanists refer to 9 as the number that always comes back to itself: 9 x 1 = 9 ... through to ... 9 x 9 = 81 = 9. Passio says this reveals that the multiplication of ego always leads to still more ego and never, as I would put it, to more expanded awareness. When Max Tegmark at MIT says everything is a bunch of numbers he is right, but they represent states of frequency and consciousness. By manipulating numbers at the digital level of our reality the *El*-ite are able to manipulate frequency and consciousness. Anyone who thinks numbers don't matter or that sequences are just coincidence has completely and utterly lost the plot with regard to human enslavement. Numerology in the Saturn Magic Square and other Saturn symbols are digital representations of Saturn's Archontic frequency. Freemasons worship Saturn and the Archontic vibration although the vast majority are so misled about what the 'Craft' really represents that they have no idea this is so. I have asked Freemasons if they know what their symbols mean. They either look bewildered and say the knowledge is lost in antiquity or say they symbolise the Great Architect. Actually, they *do*, but not the Architect as the lower ranks believe it to be. Most Freemasons are being unknowingly locked into the Saturn/Demiurgic frequency through their rituals and ceremonies. I have been told again and again how initiates join the lodge with one personality and then develop a far more malevolent or empathy-deleted one. Not everyone falls for that, but large numbers do.

**Figure 216:** Twin pillars at the entrance to the 'Temple of Solomon' (Saturn).

**Figure 217:** The Holy of Holies in Solomon's Temple is described as a cube.

Freemasons working as frequency-enslaved agents of the Saturn/Demiurgic frequency can be found throughout politics, the judiciary and the legal profession, police, media, banking and corporations as they (mostly unknowingly) serve the Hidden Hand or *El*-ite which serve the Archontic force. Freemasonry is based on the Kabbalah, the Jewish esoteric holy book, and that is obvious when you look at symbolism. The Old Testament 'Temple of Solomon' is described as having twin pillars at the entrance and the same symbols feature in Freemasonic temples as the pillars of Jachin and Boaz (Fig 216).

**Figure 218:** The New 'cube' Jerusalem.

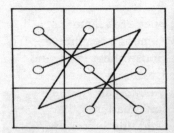

Figure 219: The Magic Square of Saturn becomes the Sigil of Saturn.

Figure 220: The Sigil of Saturn becomes ...

Figure 221: ... the classic symbol of Freemasonry ...

Figure 222: ... and the symbol of Balmoral, the Scottish home of the British 'royal' family.

There is no way with the symbolism-obsessed *El*-ite that the twin pillars or twin towers targeted on 9/11 were not related to this symbolism given that the same *El*-ite was behind those attacks. The Holy of Holies within Solomon's Temple, the inner sanctuary 'where God dwelt', is described as a perfect *cube* of 20 cubits by 20 cubits by 20 cubits and all three syllables of Sol-Om-On mean the sun – the *Saturn* sun (Fig 217). The 'New Jerusalem' in the Book of Revelation is also portrayed in terms of a cube (Fig 218). New Jerusalem is code for completing the agenda for the total control of human society and the human mind. Hexagrams are known as the Seal of Solomon. They are at the centre of the Jewish religion with its holy day of Saturday (Saturn-day) and widely used by Freemasonry.

Kabballah Judaism and Freemasonry are fundamentally connected. Freemasonic temples are a symbolic Solomon's Temple and all are energetically connected to Saturn. I have managed to get into three Freemason temples. One was on an open day and two when I just walked in and there was no one around to stop me. On all three occasions the Saturnic frequency (which you can learn to recognise) dominated the energetic atmosphere. An obsession with ritual and symbols comes from the frequency influence of Saturn. The Magic Square of Saturn is the foundation of the Sigil of Saturn which is also known as the Sigil of Solomon. From this symbol comes the best-known symbol of Freemasonry. The Sigil is created by drawing lines in number order on the Magic Square – 1 to 2 to 3 etc. (Fig 219). Turn the resulting symbol upright and you get the classic compass symbol of Freemasonry which once again reflects the frequency of Saturn (Figs 220 and 221). Now look at the Sigil of Saturn symbol used by Balmoral, the Scottish castle owned by the British royal family – who are one of the Archontic/Saturnic bloodlines that I will be exposing (Fig 222). I have visited royal palaces open to the public and all have the same Saturnic/Satanic/Freemasonic vibration. The same is true of most cathedrals and churches. They are called the 'House of the Lord' and they *are* – the 'Lord Archon' as expressed via Saturn.

## Owl of Saturn

Bohemian Grove in Sonoma County, California, is another centre for *El*-ite Saturn/Demiurge worship. The Grove is about 75 miles north of San Francisco and consists of 2,700 acres of redwood forest where the rich and famous perform their rituals to Saturn and the Demiurgic force or distortion that Saturn represents and broadcasts. Once again most rank-and-file 'Growers' won't know this because they don't understand the significance of the rituals. Attendees at the annual 'summer camp' include the Rothschilds, Rockefellers and Bush family (all of whom *will* know) and a Who's Who of the United States and the wider world from politics, banking, corporations, media and 'entertainment'. The main collective rituals are focused on a 40-foot stone owl which represents the ancient satanic 'god' Moloch/Molech (the Prince of Hell in demonology and symbol of Saturn) to whom children were sacrificed in fire (Fig 223). The Bible mentions this and Jeremiah 32:35 says: 'They built the high places of Baal that are in the valley of Ben-hinnom to cause their sons and their daughters to pass through the fire to Molech.' Celtic ritual involving the Wicker Man set ablaze with children inside is a version of this, and Phoenicians also sacrificed children in fire to Saturn. Human sacrifice was once performed openly, but now it happens in secret. Bohemian Grove's opening ceremony is called Cremation of Care and involves a fire under the owl and a mock

**Figure 223:** Moloch/Molech, the 40-foot stone focus of worship at Bohemian Grove.

**Figure 224:** Moloch was Baal – the Saturn sun god.

**Figure 225:** An owl sitting on a pyramid can be clearly seen in the road system around the Capitol Building in Washington DC.

(they say) human sacrifice. These are the people running our world, by the way, on behalf of the Archontic distortion. Other sick and certainly sacrificial rituals go on in forests at the Grove but involving only the inner circle. If you put Bohemian Grove into YouTube you'll see some

**Figure 226:** Moloch/Saturn as the symbol of Wall Street.

secretly filmed videos. Moloch was considered a god of the Saturn sun by Canaanites/Ammonites and was referred to as Baal ('Lord') Moloch (Fig 224). The 'sun god' Baal – 'The Lord' – is another version of Saturn and known in Babylon as Nimrod. Bohemian Grove's worship of the Moloch owl is the worship of the Demiurgic Saturn. Hexagrams are known as the Star of Moloch and Star of Remphan (the Egyptian name for Saturn). More than 20 years ago when I first came across the Bohemian Grove owl I noticed that an owl is encoded in the road layout around the Capitol Building in Washington DC (Fig 225). Note how the home of US politics sits in the belly of the owl (Saturn/Demiurge). I could not imagine more appropriate symbolism. Former Satanist Mark Passio says that Baal, Bill, Bull, Bail, Ball, Bel, Belial etc. have the same meaning and originate from the letters BL. The B and L are what are important and the letters around them less so. Their sound matters even more because phonetically it carries the vibration/frequency – for example, Bill and Ba-*byl*-on are the same frequency. Moloch is also symbolised as a *bull* – a 'bull-headed colossus'. Biblical worship of the 'Golden Calf' relates to the same symbolism and so we have the charging bull as the symbol of Wall Street (Fig 226). They charge you for

**Figure 227:** Saturn symbolism is used by major companies far beyond statistical chance.

**Figure 228:** Black, the esoteric colour of Saturn, is the colour of 'The System'.

everything there. Wall Street is indeed a 'bull market' and founded on bull-shit. Saturn symbols are used in corporate logos to a far greater extent than statistically likely and Saturn's designated esoteric colour of

**Figure 229:** The Trapezoid.

**Figure 230:** The Trapezoid within the all-seeing eye symbol.

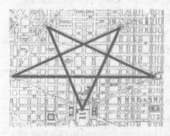

**Figure 231:** Inverted and distorted pentagram in the Washington DC street plan with the White House at the bottom.

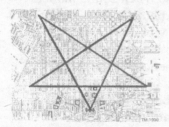

**Figure 232:** The same theme with Capitol Hill at the bottom.

black can be seen throughout the 'The System' in the judiciary, higher education and the church (Figs 227 and 228). Astrologically and esoterically Saturn represents banking, politics and institutions of state at all levels, corporations, law, the court system and science. This is the entire control system, basically, and astrologically and esoterically means energetically (control of information/perception).

All this Saturn symbolism and the transmissions from Saturn itself deluge human reality with the Saturnic (Orion/Demiurgic) frequency to trap perception in the Archontic illusion or simulation. Religions, secret societies and Satanists are worshipping the Saturn/Demiurge frequency. Saturn-worshipping Freemasonry is found widely in politics, the judiciary and the law, police, media, banking and corporations with their Saturn symbolism, corporate logos and for many a common theme of black. Saturn is associated with time, death, fear, matter, structure, obedience, poverty and restriction. One other point about symbolism is the way that symbols are distorted to represent the Archontic distortion and this includes the distorted square or 'trapezoid' (Fig 229). Former Satanist Mark Passio says the trapezoid is known as the 'soul trap'. Satanists and the *El*-ite distort and invert symbols to represent the imbalance they seek to impose on human consciousness to reflect the Demiurgic inversion and distortion. Inverted pentagrams and crosses are obvious examples. We have seen the trapezoid before on the dollar bill and the reverse of the Great Seal of the United States, with the bricks in the trapezoid pyramid representing the density within which human consciousness is held while the all-seeing eye looks on from the top (Fig

230). All distorted and inverted symbols represent the frequency of ignorance, perception entrapment and control. They can be identified in the street-plan of Washington DC and they add to the distorted energy that engulfs the American capital and centre of (official) government (Figs 231 and 232). The conspiracy is entirely founded on the distortion and inversion of energy (consciousness) to reflect and impose the Archontic distortion and inversion.

## Matter of ConCERN

I have said in previous books that the Large Hadron Collider, the world's most powerful particle accelerator at the European Organization for Nuclear Research (CERN) in Switzerland, is in the process of creating portals into other realities. I say this includes a connection with Saturn through which energies and entities come into our reality through a Saturn stargate or portal to other dimensions (Fig 233). The Collider is a ring tunnel or tube of superconducting magnets that extends for 17 miles hundreds of feet below ground across the Swiss-French border (Fig 234). This is known as a synchrotron which is defined as 'an accelerator in which charged particles are accelerated around a fixed circular path by an

**Figure 233:** CERN's Large Hadron Collider.

**Figure 234:** The 17-mile underground ring at CERN.

electric field and held to the path by an increasing magnetic field'. The CERN numbers are phenomenal and being increased in volume and power. Proton particles (actually waves in truth) moving at almost the speed of light in both directions crash into each other with a proton making 11,245 circuits of the ring *every second*. This can generate temperatures more than 100,000 times hotter than what is claimed for inside the Sun and the superconducting magnets are 100,000 times more powerful than the gravitational pull of Earth. Imagine what all this is doing in distorting and changing the electromagnetic field over a wide area. We are told that the Collider was built at a cost of $13.25 billion (and the rest) to 'test the predictions of different theories of particle physics and seek to find the so-called Higgs particle or Higgs boson and confirm the accuracy of the Standard Model of Physics'. I am sure that

**Figure 235:** Lord Shiva, symbol of Saturn, dancing in the ring at CERN.

**Figure 236:** Saturn's numbers – 666 – encoded in the CERN logo.

through compartmentalisation the great majority of the ten thousand scientists and engineers involved from more than 100 countries will believe that the Higgs boson is the central reason for spending those multiple billions to bring them all together, but for me that is extreme naïvety. The real reason is to open a portal with Saturn and probably elsewhere. CERN stands on a site once believed to be a gateway to the underworld and the Romans dedicated the area to the demonic god 'Apollyon' ('the Destroyer') which is known as Abaddon in Hebrew and Shiva in Asia. Apollyon/Abaddon is the biblical ruler of the Abyss and king of an 'army of locusts'. The Book of Revelation describes the Abyss as a great smoking pit and predicts that this will open to free a horde of demonic locusts. This was the real symbolism behind the bizarre opening ceremony at the Gotthard Base railway tunnel in Switzerland, the country in which CERN is located. Sergio Bertolucci, Director for Research and Scientific Computing at CERN, said the Hadron Collider could discover 'unknown unknowns' like 'an extra dimension' and 'out of this door might come something, or we might send something through it.' Or both. There is a statue at CERN of the Vedic god Lord Shiva (Lord Archon, Apollyon/Abaddon) dancing within a ring (Fig 235). In Vedic Astrology Shiva is represented by Saturn. He is (like Saturn) the god of death and time and his dance symbolises the primordial destructive force of the Universe ... hence 'Lord of the Dance'. CERN's logo is encoded with 666 which is the number associated with Saturn (Fig 236). A video was circulated on the Internet in 2016 of a mock human sacrifice ritual involving people in dark cloaks in front of the Shiva statue in which a woman was 'stabbed'. CERN really is one strange place. American researcher Anthony Patch, who specialises in subjects like CERN and high technology, also believes that the Large Hadron Collider is creating a portal with Saturn and specifically with the eye-storm area at the southern pole. He also makes this comparison between CERN and Saturn's hexagon storm at the northern pole:

*If you were to look down upon* [the northern pole of Saturn] *and then overlay a [shape of] a synchrotron particle accelerator, and you were to look at the symmetry, the shape of several of the detectors within the Large Hadron Collider ... you would notice that the hexagonal shape is identical and that the movement of the clouds at the northern pole of Saturn, contra-rotating clouds, one spinning one direction within and an outer ring spinning in an opposite direction, is exactly the same thing as what is occurring in the main ring of the Large Hadron Collider with two opposing contra-rotating streams of particles, of protons, that then collide which then generate synchrotron energy. The [Collider] is a mimic of, a model of, a replication of, the northern pole of Saturn.*

**Figure 237:** CERN is an underground Saturn.

If that is the case they are operating with the same frequencies (Fig 237). Anthony Patch says that the University of Berkeley near San Francisco, which he once attended, is the central hub of the CERN Collider project and that Berkeley works with the giants of nearby Silicon Valley, home to Google, Facebook, NASA's Ames Research Center (for whom Norman Bergrun worked) and Lockheed Martin (ditto) which has installed a new linear particle accelerator at its Advanced Technology Center. He adds that 160 laboratories are connected with CERN and most have particle accelerators. Fabiola Gianotti became the first Director General of CERN to be invited to the *El*-ite Bilderberg Group meeting when she attended the 2017 gathering in Chantilly, Virginia. Bilderberg is part of a network of organisations manipulating governments and world events, as I will be explaining. Why would a scientist from CERN be invited to a political meeting organised by the global *El*-ite? The question is answered above.

**Figure 238:** The Moon is not what they say it is.

## Moon beams

The closest broadcast point of the Orion/Saturnian/Demiurgic Matrix transmissions is the Moon and the detailed background to this can be found in *Human Race Get Off Your Knees*. The Moon is like the

**Figure 239:** A good analogy for the real Moon is the Death Star in the *Star Wars* movies.

Death Star in the *Star Wars* movies in that everything goes on inside (Figs 238 and 239). Many functions related to human control are based within the Moon, but its main roles are to amplify the Orion/Saturn transmissions and to act as an energetic firewall by artificially suppressing the human frequency to make it far harder to connect with Infinite Awareness beyond the simulation (Fig 240). I think there is technology within the Earth that is also part of this fake-reality projection system and interacts with the Moon transmissions. You could symbolise the Moon as a broadcast dish directing Matrix information at the human mind (Fig 241). The Moon is, like everything else, a holographic projection and thus malleable and changeable as its information codes are changed. There is every chance that it could even be a holographic 'curtain' to hide something else from human view. The Moon is not a 'natural' body and from this emerges the extraordinary number of anomalies that science cannot explain, right down to the most basic question of where it came from. Irwin Shapiro, from the Harvard-Smithsonian Center for Astrophysics, said: 'The best explanation for the Moon is observational error – the Moon doesn't exist.' NASA scientist Robin Brett said much the same: 'It seems easier to explain the non-existence of the Moon than its existence.'

**Figure 240:** The Moon is a construct with all the main action happening inside. It is suppressing the Earth frequency and so human awareness and amplifying the information Matrix broadcast from Saturn.

**Figure 241:** You can very accurately symbolise one of the Moon's roles as a broadcast dish.

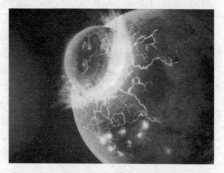

**Figure 242:** The official theory of how the Moon was created is laughable.

Science has tried and failed to explain the existence of the Moon. First they said Earth was hit by a 'Mars-type planet' during its formation and debris was projected into space that formed the Moon. When this story did not pan out they came back with another version in which the Mars-type planet struck the Earth and then came back and smacked it again (Fig 242). These are officially known as the 'Whack' and 'Double-Whack' theories, and theories are all they are. The truth is that they don't have a clue where the Moon came from because it shouldn't be there. A small planet like Earth should not have a satellite anything like the size of the Moon – 2,160 miles across, bigger than Pluto, and the fifth largest in the solar system even with all the giant planets/stars such as Saturn and Jupiter. Researchers Christopher Knight and Alan Butler said in their book, *Who Built the Moon?*:

> *The Moon is bigger than it should be, apparently older than it should be and much lighter in mass than it should be. It occupies an unlikely orbit and is so extraordinary that all existing explanations for its presence are fraught with difficulties and none of them could be considered remotely watertight.*

Evidence and informed opinion points to the Moon being hollow, and celebrated American cosmologist Carl Sagan said that 'a natural satellite cannot be a hollow object.' Every time NASA has struck the Moon with a powerful projectile the response from seismometers located on the surface has strongly suggested that it is hollow. One impact equivalent to one tonne of TNT caused the Moon to 'ring like a bell'. Maurice Ewing, a co-director of the seismic experiment, said: 'It is as though someone had struck a bell, say, in the belfry of a church, a single blow and found that the reverberation from it continued for 30 minutes.' Ewing could not explain why this would happen and Dr Frank Press from the Massachusetts Institute of Technology (MIT) said that it was 'quite beyond the range of our experience'. Such a relatively small impact should not have had such an effect. Another controlled strike equivalent to 11 tonnes of TNT caused the Moon to 'react like a gong' according to NASA scientists, with the vibrations lasting for three hours and twenty minutes to a depth of 25 miles. Ken Johnson, a supervisor of the Data and Photo Control department during the Apollo missions, said the whole Moon 'wobbled' in such a precise way that it was 'almost as though it had gigantic hydraulic damper struts inside it'. The Moon was also hit struck by a meteor in 1972 with the power equivalent of 200 tonnes of TNT. Massive shockwaves were sent into the interior but none came back. NASA scientist Dr Gordon MacDonald said in the 1960s that 'it would seem the Moon is more like a hollow than a homogeneous sphere' and Dr Sean C. Solomon of the MIT said evidence indicated 'the frightening possibility that the Moon might be hollow'. Werner von Braun, one of the central figures in the NASA Moon programme, talked about 'the astounding result' of one impact: 'The Moon rang like a bell for nearly an hour, indicating some strange and unearthly underground structure.' Dr Lon Hood, team leader of a Moon research team at

**Figure 243:** The Moon's position is so precise that it looks the same size as the Sun when viewed from Earth..

Arizona University, revealed that their work '... really does add weight to the idea that the Moon's origin is unique, unlike any other terrestrial body – Earth, Venus, Mars or Mercury'. Both the Moon and Saturn are strange, bizarre and unexplainable? Is this really yet another coincidence? The position of the Moon is so perfect in relation to Earth that if it were only marginally closer or further away life here would be very different. At the time of a lunar eclipse the Moon looks the same size as the Sun when viewed from Earth because the Sun is 400 times bigger than the Moon and the Moon 400 times closer (Fig 243). Knight and Butler write in *Who Built the Moon?*: 'The maths involved in the Earth-Moon-Sun system is nothing less than staggering.' They say the Moon has been positioned '... with the accuracy of the proverbial Swiss watchmaker'. Gnostics said there was a particular relationship between the three bodies that did not apply to any others. Earth-Moon interaction means that we never see the far side of the Moon where many insiders have testified there are advanced alien bases. Moon anomalies and questions are endless.

The most plausible explanation for the Moon, which answers all the anomalies, came in an article in the Soviet *Sputnik* magazine in 1970 by two members of the Soviet Academy of Sciences, Mikhail Vasin and Alexander Shcherbakov. Their theme is revealed in the headline – 'Is the Moon the Creation of Alien Intelligence?' Not long ago the very idea would have been dismissed by the great majority, but times are changing as the Truth Vibrations continue to impact and minds open. A British national newspaper posted with the usual ridicule a video presentation of mine about the Moon in which I laid out the evidence for what Vasin and Shcherbakov were saying. At the bottom they added a poll asking people if they thought what I said made sense of the Moon or was it simply crazy? Some 66 percent said the explanation made sense – a phenomenal figure compared with what it once would have been. Among the endless anomalies is that material on the surface of the Moon should be inside. Dr Don L. Anderson, professor of geophysics and director of the seismological laboratory at the California Institute of Technology, said: 'The Moon is made inside out.' The Soviet scientists suggested that the Moon is a giant spacecraft and probably a planetoid that has been 'hollowed out' with extremely advanced technology. They said rock inside the Moon was melted to create cavities in the interior and the 'metallic rocky slag' then deposited on the surface to form the lunar landscape that we see today. We can again cross-reference modern science with ancient legends and accounts. Zulu shaman Credo Mutwa told me that their legends say there are compartments within the Moon, and Zulu lore symbolises the Moon as an egg because they say it has been *hollowed out*. Egg symbolism of the Moon is common in the ancient world. Babylonians believed that their major goddess Semiramis/Ishtar came from the Moon in a 'giant moon egg' which landed in the Euphrates River. From this legend of 'Ishtar's egg' have come Easter eggs of today. Zulu legends say the Moon was built 'far, far away' and 'the gods' had 'rolled the Moon across the sky' to the Earth 'hundreds of generations ago'. Zulus are far from the only people to record that the Moon was not always there. All over the world are legends and accounts that tell of a time before the Moon. Aristotle and Plutarch in ancient Greece and Roman authors Apollonius Rhodius and Ovid record an Arcadia tribe called the Proselenes who said their ancestors were there 'before there was a moon in the heavens'. Proselene means 'before Selene' – the Greek goddess of the Moon. Censorinus, another Roman writer from the 3rd century AD, told of a time long before when there had been no Moon, while Dr Hans Schindler Bellamy highlights a native tribe in Colombia called the 'Mozces' in his work, *Moons, Myths and Men*, who say they 'remember a time before the present Moon became the companion of the Earth'. My view is that the Moon's arrival is centrally connected to the cataclysmic events that I have described which transformed Earth and the solar system through massive disturbance of electromagnetic/waveform harmony made even more powerful and destructive by technology inside the Moon. Soviet scientists Vasin and Shcherbakov said that the high titanium content on the Moon's surface along with chromium and zirconium fit the theme that the Moon is a construct or part-construct. These are 'refractory' metals that are seriously resistant to heat and wear. The scientists said the metals would result in 'enviable resistance to heat and the ability to stand up to means of aggression'. They were precisely the metals you would use to deal with the effects of temperature, cosmic radiation and meteorite bombardment. From an engineering perspective they said 'this spaceship of ages long past, which we call the Moon, is superbly constructed'. The scientists continued:

*If you are going to launch an artificial sputnik, then it is advisable to make it hollow. At the same time it would be naïve to imagine that anyone capable of such a tremendous space project would be satisfied simply with some kind of giant empty trunk hurled into a near-Earth trajectory.*

*It is more likely that what we have here is a very ancient spaceship, the interior of which was filled with fuel for the engines, materials and appliances for repair work, navigation instruments, observation equipment and all manner of machinery ... in other words, everything necessary to enable this 'caravelle of the Universe' to serve as a kind of Noah's Ark of intelligence, perhaps even as the home of a whole civilisation envisaging a prolonged (thousands of millions of years) existence and long wanderings through space (thousands of millions of miles).*

*Naturally, the hull of such a spaceship must be super-tough in order to stand up to the blows of meteorites and sharp fluctuations between extreme heat and extreme cold. Probably the shell is a double-layered affair – the basis a dense armouring of about 20 miles in thickness, and outside it some kind of more loosely-packed covering (a thinner layer – averaging about three miles). In certain areas – where the lunar 'seas' and 'craters' are, the upper layer is quite thin, in some cases, non-existent.*

Vasin and Shcherbakov point out that Moon craters have a strangely consistent depth no matter the size of the impact and this is what you would expect with a thinner outer layer covering an impenetrable 'dark armouring' underneath protecting the interior where the action takes place. The scientists provided a lot more supportive evidence and information, and I include this and a host of other detail about the Moon and its anomalies in *Human Race Get Off Your Knees*. A year after that book was published I was pointed to an article in *Nexus* magazine about something called the 'CHANI Project' or Channelled Holographic Access Network Interface which was claimed by a whistleblower to be a secret project based in Africa which made contact through the computer interface with an entity in another reality in 1994. The whistleblower said that contact continued for five years during which a large volume of questions were posed and answered. I read the article without knowing what it was about and saw that the 'entity' had talked about the true nature of the Moon. The entity is reported to have said:

- The Moon is not a natural heavenly body
- Life was better for humans before the Moon came ... 'Moon forces' control time and manipulate the mood of humans
- The Moon is there to control the Earth's 'mood' and a big calm would come over the Earth without the Moon – there would be only little storms, not big storms
- The 'Old Race' (Archons in many forms) captured the Moon from space and located it next to the Earth
- Without the Moon, people and animals would become calm and peaceful, and anxiety and fear would dramatically decline
- The oceans would be much calmer, major thunderstorms and lightning would be rare and the climate would be balanced with no

extreme heat or cold
- Without the moon telepathic and inter-dimensional communication would become widespread and people would be able to see new colours in an enhanced colour spectrum
- There would be major changes to the human respiratory system as blood and breathing chemistry changed. Those born after the Moon's demise would be able to hold their breath under water for hours at a time

This will all sound crazy to many people on first hearing, but put what is said in the context of what I have outlined in the book so far and everything makes sense. 'Moon forces' do indeed control our perception of time by its effect on Earth's spin and trajectory in relation to the Sun. Even the facet of 'time' that we call month comes from *Moon*th. Early calendars were based on the phases of the Moon and the month was originally 29 days from new moon to new moon. The 'Christian' festival of Easter, an ancient pagan celebration of rebirth, is associated with the Moon and still falls on the first Sunday after the first full moon following the spring equinox. Jewish Passover starts on the night of the full moon after the equinox. It is well known that the female menstrual cycle is influenced by the Moon. 'Menstrual' derives from the Latin word 'mensis', meaning 'month', and the menstrual cycle of 28 days is clearly connected to the phases of the Moon. So, therefore, is fertility. Moon goddess legends are widely associated with fertility and childbirth. Dr Michael Zimecki of the Polish Academy of Sciences said his research confirmed a link between the lunar cycle, human reproduction, fertility, menstruation and birth rate. The menstrual cycle is triggered by hormonal changes and the Moon is known to affect hormones that influence mood including those of the endocrine system and its 'third eye' pineal gland. Claims that 'Moon forces' manipulate the mood of humans are patently correct even on that hormonal level and it goes much deeper. The pineal gland is also targeted by fluoride in drinking water and toothpaste which causes calcification and prevents a connection with higher frequencies outside the Matrix. Countless studies indicate a connection between Moon cycles and human behaviour. Vedic Astrology, which goes back thousands of years to the Indus Valley civilisation, contends that the Moon rules the mind, thoughts, feelings, memories, conditioned behaviour patterns and emotional responses. These are the foundations of human perception and behaviour. The Moon affects water – not least the tides – and the body is mostly water. Or, at least, it appears to be within the holographic projection. Water is a particular frequency of information and the influence of the Moon on the human body and behaviour is happening on the waveform level. Dr Michael Zimecki has spoken of the Moon's electromagnetic influence and this is where it is all really happening. What energetic interaction must there be at the most basic level between an Earth moving at 67,000 miles per hour around the Sun and rotating at about 1,000 miles per hour, while the Moon is orbiting Earth at more than 2,000 miles per hour? Imagine the impact on Earth and the wider solar system of a body the size of the Moon arriving. The sudden effect on the tides alone would explain the Great Flood while the wider electromagnetic impact and knock-on effect could certainly have been involved with the cataclysm that rearranged the solar system. The point that a 'big calm' would come over the Earth without the Moon in both mood and weather can be explained by the electromagnetic impact of the Moon on Earth's field and the transmissions that it is constantly firing our way. I have explained how the Archontic force feeds off fear and chaos and it is hardly a shock that the CHANI entity is said to have described how 'people and animals would become calm and peaceful and anxiety and fear would dramatically decline' if the Moon was not there. What was said about telepathic and inter-dimensional communication becoming widespread without the Moon and people able to see new colours in an enhanced colour spectrum can be explained by the systematically-designed effect of Moon transmissions in suppressing the human frequency. The Moon acts as a firewall to block third eye/DNA connection to expanded awareness and locks people away in the five-senses. This disconnects them from awareness of that level of reality where everything is connected and telepathy and inter-dimensional communication is not only possible but the way things are. The same applies to seeing new colours in an enhanced colour spectrum. Near-death experiencers invariably report seeing far more vivid colours in the out-of-body state and shades they have never seen before. These are colours and shades in a *higher-frequency* reality. Without the Moon suppressing the human frequency we would indeed see new colours in another spectrum. Our current colour spectrum is the frequency band of electromagnetic *light* – the simulation Matrix within the speed of light or Archontic *luminous fire*. The point about the dramatic effects on the human respiratory system, blood and breathing chemistry, shows the extraordinary scale on which humanity is being oppressed and limited by the frequency firewall and its fake information source. As Morpheus asked Neo in *The Matrix*: 'Do you think that's air you're breathing now?' I think not (except in terms of click, click, enter), but the simulation tells us that it's air and that if we don't breathe we die, and so we manifest that reality from that deeply programmed perception. Why would a hologram need to breathe? The simulation is a self-fulfilling prophecy and this is the scale and depth of the illusion.

Zulu shaman Credo Mutwa told me how legends describe a very different world before the Moon came. There were no seasons and the

Earth was surrounded by a canopy of water vapour: 'The Earth was a beautiful place, a gentle place, lush and green, with a gentle drizzle and mist, and the fury of the Sun was not there.' Credo said that the water canopy fell to earth in a deluge of rain when the Moon arrived and triggered what is biblically referred to as the rain that fell for 40 days and 40 nights. Movements of a body the 'size' (electromagnetic impact) of the Moon could certainly have caused inter-planetary mayhem of the kind I have described in the solar system and what technology do they have to further enhance that? There is so much going on 'out there' than we have been led to believe and another place that needs to be closely surveyed is the Kuiper Belt, a disk-shaped area of the outer solar system from the orbit of Neptune and going on past Pluto. The Kuiper region is 20 times wider than the Asteroid Belt, includes at least two other dwarf planets as well as Pluto, and contains millions of icy objects with an estimated 35,000 of them bigger than 100 kilometres in diameter. I think we are going to hear a lot more about the Kuiper Belt and some of this connected to extraterrestrial or 'alien' activity. All I have said here about Orion, Saturn and the Moon as part of a perceptual control grid puts into a new perspective the scene in the first *Matrix* movie when Morpheus was presenting the facts of life to Neo:

> *The Matrix is everywhere, it is all around us, even now in this very room. You can see it when you look out your window, or you turn on your television. You can feel it when you go to work, when you go to church, when you pay your taxes. It is the world that has been pulled over your eyes to blind you from the truth.'*

> *'What truth?'*

> *'That you are a slave, Neo. Like everyone else, you were born into bondage ...*

> *born into a prison that you cannot smell or taste or touch. A prison for your mind.*

**Figure 244:** DNA is our connection to the simulation but if we expand our awareness – therefore our frequency – DNA will begin to receive and transmit with realities beyond the simulation.

The 'Universe' (simulation) is like a self-contained 'bubble' with its energetic fabric infused with the Archontic mind or frequency band. To go beyond the frequency walls of the Matrix we must expand our awareness to breach the perceptual program. The 'bubble' / simulation is an information source in the form of photons which are picked up by our DNA receiver-transmission system and decoded by the sight sense into electrical signals that strike the visual centre of the brain (Fig 244). Electrical information is then decoded into the holographic 'world' that we experience as outside of us. Archontic control appears to hold all the aces after infecting the human energetic field with its 'counterfeit spirit' which closes the heart centre for those without influence of expanded awareness; but anyone can open their mind and let consciousness beyond the program change everything individually and collectively. While so many remain gripped in the perceptual clutches of the fake reality there is also an awakening happening worldwide like never before as ever-gathering numbers see through the illusion.

All is not lost. With the knowledge I am laying out here, it has only just begun.

# CHAPTER FIVE

# Archon Visitations

*'We are all in the gutter, but some of us are looking at the stars'*
*– Oscar Wilde*

The foundation of human control is the Demiurgic distortion, a deeply imbalanced state of awareness which has no form, but can take form in endless ways by direct genie-like manifestation, by the infusion of what Gnostics called the counterfeit spirit and by what has been known throughout the 'ages' as 'possession' (Fig 245).

This is vital to keep in mind and it is worth repeating at this point what I said earlier: 'Demiurgic' and 'Archontic' are terms I am using for a distorted, inverted and monumentally imbalanced state of awareness. You could liken this to a computer virus which infects and distorts perceptions of those it possesses and turns them into versions of itself. I am not only talking about humans either. The distortion infects non-human races throughout the Lower Aeons that we call aliens and extraterrestrials. They may look very different, but the driving force of perception and behaviour is the same. The idea that humanity is the only expression of 'intelligent life' is so ludicrous, so naïve, that it merely confirms the power of perception programming. Observe the immense diversity of human form and even more so with animals and insects and this is happening only within visible light, a fraction of the electromagnetic spectrum which according to mainstream science represents just 0.005 percent of what exists in the Universe. Cosmologist Carl Sagan said: 'There are more potential

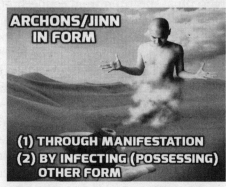

**Figure 245:** In these ways the Archontic distortion can take countless forms.

All the stars you see
at night are just part
of this yellow circle.

**Figure 246:** An Internet posting putting this 'we are alone' nonsense in perspective.

combinations of DNA [holographic forms] than there are atoms in the Universe.' Time, space and distance may be illusions, but if we employ our perception of distance then Planet Earth represents a billionth of a pinhead compared with the projected size of the Universe (Fig 246). *We can see a fraction of 0.005 percent of the Universe (never mind infinity beyond that) while living 'on' a planet equivalent to a billionth the size of a pinhead and yet still many people laugh at any suggestion that life other than humans can exist??*

And those same people have the nerve to say that *I'm* mad.

Cultures across the world throughout what we call history have come and gone while describing the same common theme of a force at work manipulating human reality. Names may vary, but the theme is a constant. These manipulators and visitors have been known as serpent gods (Far East and Central America); snake brothers (Hopi); Chitauri (Zulu); Anunnaki (Sumer, later Babylon); star people (many and various); demons (Christianity); Archons (Gnostics); Jinn (Islam and pre-Islamic Arabia); and Flyers or the Predators (Central America). There are many other names, too, including the Watchers, Shining Ones and Fallen Angels. Some are referring to entities in form – serpent gods, snake brothers, and so on – while others are describing entities operating exclusively in the unseen. What connects them all is the Archontic self-aware distortion or counterfeit spirit. There are countless non-human races and groups taking equally diverse forms and they span the perceptual spectrum from connection with Infinite Awareness to full-blown counterfeit spirit. I am well known for highlighting manipulation by a reptile group ('the Reptilians') in league with the 'Greys' (recorded by ancients as 'Ant People') who have become the predominant concept of an alien. I have taken unceasing ridicule from those with prisons where their minds should be, but it turns out that Gnostics were connecting a reptilian form and Greys to their Archons in texts sealed in a jar at Nag Hammadi 1,600 years ago. They say the most common manifestations of Archons in form are reptilian or serpentine and those that look like 'an unborn baby or foetus with grey skin and dark, unmoving eyes'. People today have claimed in large numbers worldwide to have been contacted or abducted by 'aliens' which they describe in the same way – reptilian and what have become known for

**Figure 247:** At least some Reptilians and Greys are vehicles for the Archontic mind or distortion.

**Figure 248:** A painting by Credo Mutwa from ancient Zulu descriptions of the Mzungu.

obvious reasons as Greys (Fig 247). Other types, including a human-like blue-eyed, blond-haired group dubbed the 'Nordics', are also reported by those ('contactees') claiming to have had contact with non-human entities and those who say they have been abducted ('abductees') against their will. This Nordic group have a genetic connection to human white races and especially those with blond hair and blue eyes although Nordics are reported with dark hair and red hair, too. Zulus called the Nordics the 'Mzungu' and said they could appear and disappear. Zulu shaman Credo Mutwa told me that when white Europeans first arrived in South Africa the people thought they were the returning Mzungu (Fig 248). There are so many non-human types but Reptilians and Greys appear to be the most dominant in terms of manipulating human life and certainly the most active in human interbreeding programmes (infusing the counterfeit spirit). People claiming to be abducted by Reptilians and Greys often describe having eggs and sperm removed for hybrid breeding programmes. Millions in America alone have claimed to have been abducted by 'aliens' and just as many if not more don't remember being abducted because of the effect it has on their minds in blocking the memory of a terrifying experience. These are some quotes from NASA astronauts about the reality of extraterrestrial or 'alien' activity:

- Scott Carpenter, the second American to orbit the Earth: 'At no time, when the astronauts were in space were they alone: there was a constant surveillance by UFOs.'
- Major Gordon Cooper, the last American to fly in space alone: 'I believe that these extraterrestrial vehicles and their crews are visiting this planet

from other planets ... Most astronauts were reluctant to discuss UFOs.'
- Cooper again: 'For many years I have lived with a secret, in a secrecy imposed on all specialists in astronautics. I can now reveal that every day, in the USA, our radar instruments capture objects of form and composition unknown to us. And there are thousands of witness reports and a quantity of documents to prove this, but nobody wants to make them public.
- Maurice Chatelain, former head of NASA Communications Systems: '... all Apollo and Gemini flights were followed, both at a distance and sometimes also quite closely, by space vehicles of extraterrestrial origin – flying saucers, or UFOs, if you want to call them by that name. Every time it occurred, the astronauts informed Mission Control, who then ordered absolute silence.'

The media (including most of the 'alternative') and society in general ridicule what I have said and written while denying themselves credibility by doing no research whatsoever into information that they dismiss with a wave of the hand. What I am saying is way outside their programmed version of 'normal' and they respond to program. I speak, they press enter, and out comes 'that Icke is mad'. I have not reached my conclusions by pulling them out of nowhere, but with the best part of 30 years of research, ancient and modern, all over the world. When you have the same information and entities described by contactees/abductees today and by culture after culture thousands of

years ago are we saying this should not be pursued and researched? I'll decide what I pursue, thank you, not ignorance finding expression in ridicule. I have compiled a massive body of work and evidence in previous books relating to the manipulation of human society by a reptilian race including the ground-breaking *Children of the Matrix* which was first published in 2001. This is the book most focused on the reptilian aspect of the Archontic conspiracy and includes ancient accounts and experiences of many people today who have seen and interacted with these entities (Fig 249). Their stories are dismissed as fantasy because of their fantastic nature for one simple reason that is repeated again and again throughout

**Figure 249:** There is a wealth of background and personal accounts in this book of Reptilian and other non-human activity within human society.

human society and especially the media: The dismissers are absolutely clueless about the reality they daily experience. Witnesses tell of entities appearing out of nowhere and disappearing into nowhere. To solid-reality believers this is impossible, but reality is *not* solid. This appear-disappear illusion is caused by entities normally operating outside of visible light entering the human visual frequency band. When this happens any observer perceives the entity manifesting out of nothing. The reverse happens when they leave the human frequency band and to the observer 'disappear'. I mentioned earlier how the same principle is at work when UFOs are described as appearing and disappearing. Abductees report being taken up into hovering craft through a 'bright light' and they are describing an electromagnetic field projection locking into their electromagnetic field (*there is no physical*). Many targeted by these lights have suffered radiation burns and even died from radiation poisoning. Other 'alien' manifestations that people think they see are projections into their minds. The brain decodes information into the reality we believe we are 'physically' experiencing and it is possible to hack that information source so that entities seem to appear and events seem to happen, but they don't really. This is being done to individuals and humanity collectively far more than people begin to imagine and the phenomenon has been accurately portrayed in sci-fi movies and television series such as *Star Trek*. So what is real beyond the fact that we are expressions of awareness? I have heard it said many times that craft could not travel the incredible distances claimed across the galaxy to Earth, but here again we have a misunderstanding of reality. Everything and everywhere has its own unique frequency and if you sync with that frequency either through your mind or technology then that is where you must be. Advanced spacecraft beyond this world (which are more about consciousness than anything 'physical') connect with the frequency of where they want to go and bingo they are there. No distance is involved because space is an illusion. Albert Einstein said:

> *Everything is energy and that's all there is to it. Match the frequency of the reality you want and you can't help but get that reality. It can be no other way. This is not philosophy. This is physics.*

Research the now enormous body of global evidence of extraterrestrial and UFO activity and you will see what the authorities and mainstream media are not telling you – and most of the 'alternative' media, too. Reported UFO sights have increased from 10,000 to 45,000 a year according to data compiled by the National UFO Reporting Centre in Washington State. Emphasis on *reported* because most are not. I would add a rider to that, however. Not every 'spacecraft' is flown by 'aliens'. The Hidden Hand just wants us to think so as part of a wider agenda.

'Flying saucers' (anti-gravity craft) have long been built in beyond-top-secret military projects and underground facilities especially in the United States. American aerospace engineer William Tompkins, who died suddenly in August 2017 after a fall aged 94, published a book in 2015 detailing what he said were his direct experiences of extraterrestrial activities while working for the US Navy, which he said had cleared him to make the information public (up to a point). A second book was close to completion when he died. He described how he worked from the 1940s with a secret think tank based at one of the US Navy's biggest and most important bases in San Diego. Tompkins writes in *Selected by Extraterrestrials: My life in the top secret world of UFOs, think-tanks and Nordic secretaries* about the Reptilian connection and his work with human-like 'Nordic' ETs who he says are trying to help humanity end the Reptilian control of our reality. His information was published long after I had begun exposing the Reptilian manipulation of human society more than 20 years earlier, and its relationship with the Moon. He said he was linked to a group of American Navy spies during World War II who stole UFO secrets from the Nazis. He claimed that he personally gave them to US military and space corporations such as Lockheed, Douglas, Northrop, Grumman and others to produce advanced anti-gravity craft ('flying saucers') and other technology way beyond human knowledge at the time. The California Institute of Technology (Caltech) was also heavily involved, he said. As a result 'UFOs' have been flown by at least both Americans and Germans. Tompkins said that the Nazis were involved with a reptilian race which gave them advanced technological knowledge. He writes that the Moon is an artificial object and a Reptilian command centre with structures on the far side that we never see. I had been saying all this for many years, and quoting former NASA employees who had seen pictures of those structures denied to the public. There are even tracks that have been clearly made by something moving technologically. Tompkins talked about 'Draco' Reptilians. I covered the background and nature of the Draco or Draconians in *Children of the Matrix* which was first published in 2001. They claim to be Reptilian 'royalty' and they appear to us on Earth as human royalty and many world leaders (more later). Tompkins said that the Apollo mission in 1969 had been just a show to hide the truth and America has never returned since the Apollo programme ended because the Reptilians warned against it. He described how the Moon was occupied by nine-feet-tall 'Draco' Reptilians when astronauts landed in the first Apollo mission: 'After we get to the Moon we got some surprises – the Draco Reptilians were already there.' Ken Johnston is a former chief Lunar Module test pilot at the Manned Spacecraft Center in Houston and during the Apollo Program worked with Brown & Root, the principal contractor to NASA's Lunar Receiving Laboratory where moon rocks were stored and catalogued with photographs of their location. They included pictures taken by astronauts on chest-mounted cameras. Johnson told a SyFy channel television documentary *Aliens on the Moon* in 2014 that alien ships were waiting when astronauts Neil Armstrong and Buzz Aldrin arrived:

> *While Neil and Buzz were on the Lunar surface, Neil switched to the medical channel* [which couldn't be publicly heard], *and spoke directly with the chief medical officer saying, they're here, they're parked on the side of the crater, they're watching us.*

William Tompkins said that what Armstrong saw were ships floating above the crater with hundreds of Reptilian entities standing below them. He said the International Space Station is connected to this background of extraterrestrial activity and he described Earth as a laboratory for Reptilians and other ETs to experiment on humans. 'You have Draco Reptilian guys running your governments of every country on the planet', he said. They had the same skin as lizards and reptiles, but all had the ability to shapeshift into human form – which I have been saying since the 1990s. Tompkins said all recent presidents up to Obama and including the Bushes and Bill Clinton have been shapeshifting Reptilians taking human form. He said Reptilians have bases throughout the solar system and under the Earth including an infamous one under Antarctica which I wrote about two decades ago and was shared with a breakaway group of Nazis who fled there after the war. Saturn researcher and insider Norman Bergrun said that he saw an image of a non-human craft on the ground in Antarctica during his time with top secret clearance. Mysterious microwave anomalies in that region were detected in April and May 2017 and pulse waves of energy emanating from there are affecting weather patterns. Other claims by Anthony Tompkins from 2015 to his death included:

- Reptilians are expert in mass and individual perception manipulation and the creation of illusions. Genetic and other manipulation means that humans use a fraction of their brain capacity. He put it at just over two percent when it could be virtually 100 percent. Earth is an extraterrestrial laboratory. Reptilians eat humans and take part in ritual sacrifices.
- Reptilians and their Draco 'royalty' have been taking over other planets and star systems and hijacking our reality is 'old stuff to them' (which corresponds with what the 'CHANI' Project entity is quoted as saying).
- Extraterrestrials built the pyramids around the world and other structures that we would struggle to build even today and he talked

about an Orion connection. Reptilians and advanced ETs are capable of blowing up planets and the asteroid belt is the remnants of a planet destroyed between Mars and Jupiter – as Immanuel Velikovsky wrote in the 1950s. The gigantic hole that we now call the Pacific Ocean is the result of a fantastic impact during the catastrophe.

- Extraterrestrial races are at war with each other (Reptilians-Nordics are one example) and behind wars on Earth. Human elites and military insiders are working with extraterrestrials – especially Reptilian – and this is the source for most advanced technology (designed for further enslavement as we shall see). There are human-ET underground bases on Mars.

I have been writing all the same information and more in stages since the 1990s to the sound of mainstream ridicule and laughter. People will have to come to their own conclusions about what Tompkins said, but he provided a lot of supporting detail and documentation to back-up his claims about working in secret government projects. I do question why his US Navy masters gave him permission to reveal all this even if it was only up to a point. We should always keep in mind that there have been NASA/US military plans to stage a fake 'alien invasion' – the best known of them called Project Blue Beam – which would allow power to be centralised globally to respond to the threat. One very interesting correlation is that Tompkins said the current Reptilian phase of mass human manipulation began 6,000 years ago. This is the same period when the 'new psyche' began to emerge out of the Middle East and Asia ('Saharasia') with the violent invasions of Indo-European and Semitic peoples. The Reptilians have been here for much longer than that, but this was when the most severe manipulation of human perception began and it is now reaching its end game with the technological control

system called transhumanism (once again, more later). I contend that the 'new psyche' was the result (with other influences) of Archontic Reptilian genetic programmes that transformed the way that humans processed information and perceived reality. Tompkins talked about extraterrestrials building the pyramids around the world and this is another theme of my own work over the years. They were at least one reason for pyramid and

**Figure 250:** The Great Pyramid at Giza in Egypt was built thousands of years ago with 2.3 million stone blocks weighing on average between 2.5 and 15 tons.

**Figure 251:** Saksaywaman (also Sacsayhuaman) near Cusco, Peru, with its perfect alignment of stones weighing up to 100 tons.

other ancient alignments with locations in the heavens and each other. *Ancient Aliens*, the long-running History Channel series, has done some very good work highlighting extraterrestrial interactions with humans in the distant 'past' and their legacy in magnificent and advanced constructions – points that insiders like Anthony Tompkins have also made (Figs 250 and 251). They include pyramids, temples, ritual sites, standing stones and circles energetically aligned with Orion, Saturn and the Moon (to manipulate flows of energy through the planet's meridian or leyline system to infuse Orion/Saturn/Moon energy – information). My one disappointment with *Ancient Aliens* is that from what I have seen it focuses on the 'physical' realm of visible light when the real deal is beyond that. Tompkins talked about shapeshifting between human and reptilian form with particular reference to US presidents, and again I have been saying the same since the 1990s in the face of much hilarity. Such dismissal comes again from ignorance of reality. You can't change from one solid body to another, right? Yes, *right*, of course not, but the body *is not* solid. We are talking about a shift from one energetic information field (hologram) to another with no solidity involved at all. I'll be expanding on this. If Reptilians have been around for at least thousands of years – actually far longer – you would expect that the ancients would have left us evidence and clues. Reverend John Bathurst Deane published a study in 1933 into the universal theme of serpent worship called *Worship of the Serpent*. This was his conclusion:

*It appears, then, that no nations were so geographically remote, or so religiously discordant, but that one – and only one – superstitious characteristic was common to all: that the most civilized and the most barbarous bowed down with the same devotion to the same engrossing deity; and that this deity either was, or was represented by, the same sacred serpent.*

*It appears also that in most, if not all, the civilized countries where this serpent was worshipped, some fable or tradition which involved his history, directly or indirectly, alluded to the Fall of Man in Paradise, in which the serpent was concerned.*

*What follows, then, but that the most ancient account respecting the cause and nature of this seduction must be the one from which all the rest are derived which represent the victorious serpent – victorious over man in a state of innocence, and subduing his soul in a state of sin, into the most abject veneration and adoration of himself.*

So what was this global obsession with the serpent and serpent gods? And why were they so connected to 'The Fall'? The symbolic serpent is the villain in the Garden of Eden story and Reverend Deane found this to be a universally common thread (although some Gnostic texts describe it differently). Do Christians really believe that the Eden serpent was literally a talking snake? It's all *symbolic*. The biblical Devil or Satan is described in serpentine terms in the Book of Revelation:

*And the Great Dragon was cast out, that old serpent, called the Devil, and Satan, which deceiveth the whole world. He was cast out into the Earth and his angels were cast out with him.*

The Jewish religion has its 'Holy Serpent' or Leviathan and the theme is everywhere. There was also clearly at least one 'Fall' that can be identified from around 6,000 years ago from which emerged the 'new psyche' out of the Middle East after the Indo-European/Semitic invasions. Major religions such as Christianity, Islam and Judaism all came out of the same Middle East from ancient cultures in the same

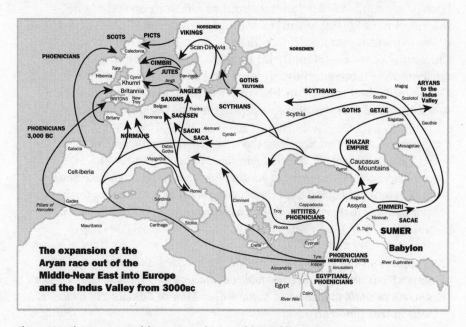

**Figure 252:** The expansion of the 'new psyche' out of the Middle East.

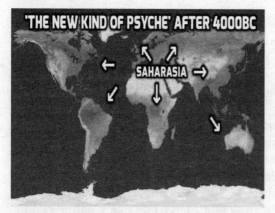

'THE NEW KIND OF PSYCHE' AFTER 4000BC

SAHARASIA

**Figure 253:** From Europe the new psyche was exported across the world through colonial invasion with the British Empire to the fore.

'post-Fall' period. The new intellect-dominated, left-brain-dominated, five-sense-dominated, empathy-suppressing new psyche established Sumer and Babylon in Mesopotamia and then Rome and the Roman Empire before heading north into Europe and Russia and east into Asia as far as China (Fig 252). New psyche invasions from Spain, Portugal and other European countries colonised South America. Suddenly there were mass wars, male-domination, control by hierarchies, class systems and religions as we have come to know them. Britain became the control centre of the new psyche and the British Empire took it to the Americas, Africa, Australia, New Zealand and elsewhere (Fig 253). The British monarch is still today head of state in 15 other Commonwealth countries including Canada, Australia and New Zealand, at tremendous cost while so many 'subjects' sleep on the street. What madness that the masses allow this institution of grotesque privilege and superiority to continue to rule them – as it does. Forget the bullshit about royalty just being symbolic figureheads that bring in the tourists. There is always money for royalty and war and the lavish multi-palace, golden coach lifestyle of the royals is profoundly symbolic of the way the Draco see themselves as compared to the human population. Wherever the new psyche and its Draco 'royal' bloodlines went their goal was to take over countries and collectively the world. I say this psyche came from genetic manipulation described in ancient texts by the Reptilian-Grey overseers and from the psychological and perceptual effects of the astrological heavens being rewired along with other influences. Every new psyche invasion followed the same sequence to target indigenous cultures of the old psyche which was still processing and decoding reality in a different way. Shamans and ancient knowledge were taken out of circulation through enslavement and mass murder, and new psyche religions were imposed to replace them. Christianity was the prime perception invader led by the vicious psychopaths of the Roman Church. I find it so sad to see American and African black people being such vociferous advocates of the Christian religion today when its role was to oppress their ancestors and delete so much of the knowledge they once passed from generation to generation.

Christianity and especially the Roman Catholic version enforced by merciless Jesuits were imposed upon ancient peoples of Africa and the Americas. We had the callous and heartless treatment of indigenous Australians after the British arrived. Foot-soldier thugs who enforced this cultural fascism would have had no idea what they were really doing, but those in the shadows did. Here you have the real reason why indigenous peoples were so brutally targeted. Archontic invaders wanted only the perceptual enslavement of the new psyche to prevail, which worships at the altar of the five senses and becomes ever more deeply immersed in the simulation. Carriers of the old psyche had to either be removed or be absorbed into the new one. This has happened to a very large extent, but not completely. I have met many native people who are the new psyche masquerading as ancient enlightenment and I have met some who can still see beyond the illusion. Perception and the way a brain decodes reality can be changed purely by absorption into another culture (information source). Scientists believed that once formed the brain didn't change, but they know differently now. I have mentioned that the brain has what they call 'placidity' and can be rewired in accordance with the *information* it receives and processes. Just living in a world based purely on materialism and the five senses can new-psyche the brain to decode and perceive a different sense of reality. This is so clearly happening today with 'Smart' technology changing the brain and therefore behaviour faster than ever before – as planned. Don Juan Matus, a Yaqui Indian healer or shaman in Mexico, was one who could still 'see' through the veil when he was the information source for Peruvian-born writer, Carlos Castaneda, who wrote a series of books from the 1960s to 1990s. I read what Don Juan said after I had myself written in similar terms from my own sources. It was still more confirmation of the same recurring theme. Don Juan described the force manipulating human society:

> *We have a predator that came from the depths of the cosmos and took over the rule of our lives. Human beings are its prisoners. The predator is our lord and master. It has rendered us docile, helpless. If we want to protest, it suppresses our protest. If we want to act independently, it demands that we don't do so ... indeed we are held prisoner!*

> *They took us over because we are food to them, and they squeeze us mercilessly because we are their sustenance. Just as we rear chickens in coops, the predators rear us in human coops, humaneros. Therefore, their food is always available to them.*

'Food' = human emotional and electromagnetic energy within the Archontic frequency band (fear) on which Reptilians and Greys as expressions of the Archontic frequency also feed.

*Think for a moment, and tell me how you would explain the contradictions between the intelligence of man the engineer and the stupidity of his systems of belief, or the stupidity of his contradictory behaviour.*

I will explain these apparent contradictions in a later chapter.

*Sorcerers believe that the predators have given us our systems of beliefs, our ideas of good and evil; our social mores. They are the ones who set up our dreams of success or failure. They have given us covetousness, greed, and cowardice. It is the predator who makes us complacent, routinary, and egomaniacal.*

This is what I have been saying and writing for decades.

*In order to keep us obedient and meek and weak, the predators engaged themselves in a stupendous manoeuvre – stupendous, of course, from the point of view of a fighting strategist; a horrendous manoeuvre from the point of those who suffer it. They gave us their mind. The predators' mind is baroque, contradictory, morose, filled with the fear of being discovered any minute now.'*

They gave us their counterfeit spirit and they are terrified of humans expanding their awareness beyond the program because then the game is up (Fig 254).

*Sorcerers of ancient Mexico ... reasoned that man must have been a complete being at one point, with stupendous insights, feats of awareness that are mythological legends nowadays. And then, everything seems to disappear, and we have now a sedated man.*

**'THEY GAVE US THEIR MINDS' - 'THE COUNTERFEIT SPIRIT'**

**Figure 254:** The infusion into the human energy field/organism of the counterfeit spirit 'new psyche'.

He is talking about the pre-hacked human of the Golden Age and what happened after 'The Fall'.

*What I'm saying is that what we have against us is not a simple predator. It is very smart, and organised. It follows a methodical system to render us useless. Man, the magical being that he is destined to be, is no longer magical. He's an average piece of meat. There are no more dreams for man but the dreams of an animal who is being raised to be a piece of meat: trite, conventional, imbecilic.'*

Look around at much of humanity and you can see that this is true, but it does not have to remain so. We can break out of the perceptual prison and increasing numbers are doing that.

## Demonic duo

Archon-possessed and controlled reptilian entities operating from the unseen have been centrally involved in this hijack of human perception

Figure 255: Alpha Draconis.

**Figure 256:** Zeta Reticuli binary star system.

and genetic manipulation, along with their subordinates, the Greys, who comprise some 43 percent of reported 'alien' encounters. Reptilians and Greys are both reported by contactees and abductees to be connected to the Orion constellation along with the Alpha Draconis or Draco constellation (Reptilians) and Zeta Reticuli star system (Greys). Sirius has also been associated with reptilian-like entities. Alpha Draconis can be seen in the far northern sky and Zeta Reticuli is a binary star system

**Figure 257:** A portrayal of the Draconians or Draco.

in the southern constellation of Reticulum (Figs 255 and 256). The latter can be seen with the naked eye when the sky is particularly dark in the southern hemisphere. Alpha Draconis is reported to be home to the Reptilian 'royalty' known as the Draconians or Draco (Latin for dragon). They are described by those who have interacted with them as having horns, wings and tails (Fig 257). The Draco considered most genetically-superior at the top of the hierarchy-obsessed Reptilian control structure are albino-like as reported to me by a number of insiders and abductees. There are many types of reptilian, not all of them hostile, but the ones I am talking about certainly are. They and the Greys are invariably described as vicious, emotionless and without empathy along with all the other psychopathic traits attributed to the full-blown Archontic counterfeit spirit. These traits include having no remorse or shame and producing parasitical pathological liars who will do anything to get what they want. Reptilians and Greys function as a hive mind, like a bee or ant colony, and that mind is the Archontic mind. Don Juan Matus said 'they gave us their mind' and the 'hive mind' mentality of so

**Figure 258:** What artist Robert Llimos said that he saw in Brazil.

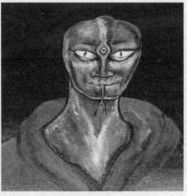

**Figure 259:** Credo Mutwa's painting of the Reptilian 'worker class' from ancient and modern descriptions.

many humans is easy to spot. Some researchers and alien experiencers refer to the source of this hive mind as the 'Orion Queen', as in queen bee, but when you come at all this from the perspective of a fake-reality generated through Orion the hive mind becomes the Demiurgic mind. Human royal hierarchies are Draco royalty incarnate. When many kingdoms joined together in battle, or as a group of kingdoms, they appointed a king of kings and these were known as the Great Dragon or ... Draco. We had the Celtic title of Pendragon, as in Uther Pendragon, father of 'King Arthur' in the Grail stories. Reptilians and Greys operate largely in the unseen realms but they do enter our reality by appearing 'out of nowhere' to human contactees/abductees and also in flying craft. I met Spanish artist Robert Llimos in Barcelona in 2010. He had never heard of me or reptilian entities until an experience he had in Brazil. He was there with his Brazilian partner and one day went out alone into the countryside to paint the landscape. After he set up his easel and began to paint he said a craft about 50-metres wide came down and hovered in front of him for two hours. Robert told me that he doesn't know if he was taken aboard the ship, but he has no recollection of it. He said he painted the scene which included two reptilian figures who stared at him from the craft's only open window (Fig 258). When you compare his images with that of Zulu high shaman Credo Mutwa they are remarkably similar (Fig 259). Credo painted his picture from ancient and modern descriptions of the reptilian 'Chitauri', and if you put 'Credo Mutwa, Reptilian Agenda' into the search engine at Davidicke.com there is a six-hour long video in which Credo talks to me about Zulu legends of the Chitauri reptilian manipulators and his own experience of the Greys.

Thousands of clay tablets and fragments found in what is now Iraq tell the story of a non-human invader-race known as the Anunna or Anunnaki ('Those Who From Heaven To Earth Came' in at least one translation). The tablets include accounts of human history compiled by ancient societies in Mesopotamia ('The Land Between Two Rivers' – the Tigris and Euphrates). This was the land of Sumer (approximately 3000-1800BC) and Babylon (approximately 1800-539BC in different forms) and has been dubbed the cradle of civilisation. Mesopotamia was really a new psyche civilisation that emerged after the 'Great Change' and the cataclysmic events in the solar system. The Mesopotamian tablets say that the Anunnaki were led by two brothers, Enlil and Enki, sons of Anu, or 'Lord of the Sky'. Zulu accounts say the same about the Reptilian Chitauri ('Children of the Serpent' or 'Children of the Python') and call the brothers Wowane and Mpanku. They describe how these brothers rolled the Moon across the sky and into orbit around the Earth. Wowane and Mpanku are known as the 'water brothers' by Zulus while the Mesopotamian Enki (Ea to Babylonians) was also associated with water as the god of fresh waters. Anunnaki and Chitauri are said to have forced humans to mine gold in Africa and it is obvious from all this and much more that Anunnaki and Chitauri are different names for the same Reptilian invaders. Mesopotamian and Zulu accounts both say the Anunnaki-Chitauri were responsible for creating the catastrophic 'Great Flood' events that brought an end to human society as it had been before. Enki is said to have warned a human 'priest-king' called Ziusudra about what was to come and gave instructions to build a huge ship to survive the flood and to take aboard 'beasts and birds'. Thousands of years later came a biblical re-write of the story placed in a Hebrew context with Ziusudra re-named as Noah. In other societies the same character is Deucalion (Greece), Manu (India), Fo-hi (China), Xisthros (Persia), Nota (Mexico), and Utnapishtim (Mesopotamia).

Visitations by Reptilian and Grey entities (and many others) are not new. They have simply entered a new stage in the last 6,000 years or so in our perception of 'time'. They were coming into our reality from the unseen and manipulating with their high technology and other means when humans were still living in caves or wearing breeches and firing

**Figure 260:** Ancient depiction of the fish gods.

**Figure 261:** Headgear of the fish god priests was the origin of the 'Christian' mitre.

muskets. This is how Gnostic texts could describe reptilian and grey-skinned entities as Archons in form and we have modern alien experiencers and government/military insiders describing the same. There are so many descriptions in ancient texts of what are clearly high-technology craft and you find this in the Bible with people being 'taken up to heaven'. Other examples are 'flying palaces' or 'chariots' called Vimana in Hindu texts and Sanskrit epics. The *Mahabharata*, one of the two major Sanskrit epics of ancient India, tells of 'two-story sky chariots with many windows, ejecting red flame, that race up into the sky until they look like comets . . . to the regions of both the sun and the stars.' Symbolism for flying craft is everywhere among ancient accounts, legends and stories. Then there are the remarkable accounts of the Dogon tribe in Mali, Africa, who say that entities from Sirius they call the Nommo or 'Masters of the Water' visited their ancestors and gave them knowledge of the Universe (Fig 260). Nommo are described as amphibious and 'serpent-featured'. This connects with the stories of the Anunnaki/Chitauri and can be related to the ancient fish-god religions (see worship of Oannes and Dagon) in which the priests wore headgear that looked like a fish-head. This is now called the 'Christian' mitre (Fig 261). Dogon refer to Sirius as 'the Land of the Fish' and Sumerians and Babylonians in Mesopotamia worshipped fish gods they described in similar terms. Credo Mutwa wrote in his book, *Song of the Stars:*

> Not only among the Zulu, but the Dogon, and many widespread African tribes, there are stories of the Nommo, who resemble the king of the Water People in our legend. They are said to be intelligent beings who have visited the Earth several times. They are usually described as somewhat like human beings, but with skins like reptiles.

Robert Temple wrote about the Dogon in *The Sirius Mystery*. He notes that their ancient accounts knew about all the planets as far as Pluto and told of moons that have only recently been identified. Dogon accounts said that a star orbited Sirius that was so heavy all the people of the world could not lift it. Their legends described this before scientists discovered what they were talking about – a phenomenally heavy dwarf star named Sirius B (Fig 262). Dogon are also reported to have described another star orbiting Sirius which was later located by astronomers in 1995 and given the name Sirius C. The Pleaides constellation often comes up in abductee and contactee reports which talk of human-like blue-eyed blond ETs from there who

**Figure 262:** Sirius A and B (the brightest star to the right).

are said to have originated in the Lyra constellation in the northern sky with its brightest star Vega. From the vast ancient and modern evidence Earth has been visited from many locations throughout known human history and before. Most operate in other realities or dimensions of the Demiurgic Lower Aeons and don't take a form that requires the same atmosphere that humans do. Entities within Saturn and coming in through the Saturn's interdimensional gateway are obviously nothing like humans in their energetic make-up and atmospheric needs. This is one answer to the 'Fermi Paradox' named after Italian physicist Enrico Fermi. He said that with 100 billion stars in the galaxy it was inevitable that intelligent life must have evolved elsewhere and so 'where are the aliens?' Benevolence or malevolence with other-world visitors is dictated by where they are on the spectrum of consciousness and how influenced they are by the counterfeit spirit. There are some who are working to help humanity awaken as there are others seeking to keep us asleep, but most have an agenda in which humanity is at the very least not the first priority. Those seeking a human awakening are too far up the frequency scale to directly interact with us and they communicate through an awareness connection and by directly 'incarnating' into human form while retaining a consciousness link to 'home'. Well, that's the idea, anyway. Many get lost in the illusion themselves.

## World beneath our feet

Reptilians and Greys also have colonies in cavern and cave systems deep underground. They can't survive for long in our sunlight (hence the vampire legends about having to be back in the coffin before the sun rises) and some Reptilian and Grey groups (and others) located themselves within the Earth from where they can come and go through inter-frequency relocation. I have heard many stories of people seeing what at first looked like a spacecraft suddenly transforming into an energetic flash that passed through the Earth's surface and into the interior. Today the most secret underground military bases or 'DUMBS' – Deep Underground Military Bases – connect with the Reptilian/Grey cavern systems/cities and at the deepest levels (often miles below the surface) interaction takes place with 'human' *El*-ite networks in pursuit of a common agenda for mass human control. These bases and massive cities and factory systems inside mountains are so beyond top secret that US Presidents are not allowed to know what really goes on there because they don't have a *high enough security clearance*. Presidents come and go, like politicians all over the world, without knowing what is happening in these bases let alone giving the orders. So what is the coordinating force controlling the DUMBS which is always there no matter what puppet is in the White House, Downing Street or wherever? Reptilians and Greys have human-hybrid networks representing their interests and hijacking positions of real power. Hawaii Senator Daniel Inouye, who served nine terms in the Senate, said on Capitol Hill in 1987: 'There exists a shadowy government with its own Air Force, its own Navy, its own fundraising mechanism, and the ability to pursue its own ideas of national interest, free from all checks and balances, and free from the law itself.' He was exactly right. DUMBS are where the technology exchange goes on that manifests on the surface with 'a company has invented a society-changing computer system' or 'a geek has developed an amazing device in his garage'. These are often cover stories for where the technology really came from and this is the very technology being used for mass human control on the scale that is now becoming clear.

DUMBS are built in levels or layers and the lower you go the higher the security clearance that you need. Even most people working at these massive bases have no idea what is going on below them. Those working at lower levels are weighed in and out at the start and end of shifts to make sure they don't leave with anything more than they came with. Some who say they have seen the lowest levels tell of horrific scenes of human experimentation including reptilian-human hybrids, and I have covered this at length and quoted witnesses in *The Biggest Secret* and *Children of the Matrix*. Insiders have said there are at least nearly 1,500 of these bases worldwide with many in the United States. Some include Dulce and Los Alamos (where the atom bomb was developed) in New Mexico; Pine Gap in Australia; and China Lake Naval Air Weapons Station in California's Mojave Desert about 150 miles north of Los Angeles. See those other books for further detail. There are 19,600 square miles of restricted and controlled airspace around China Lake which includes Edwards Air Force Base and Fort Irwin which also have an underground component (Fig 263). Insiders say that DUMBS and airbases are connected by an underground tunnel and super-speed rail system built incredibly quickly with nuclear

**Figure 263:** China Lake Naval Weapons Station is an underground base where the US military interact with Reptilians.

powered technology that melts the rock to form tunnels with smooth, glass-like walls. Remember that whatever we may see in the public arena is light years behind what is possible in the secret projects.

I spent months at a time in the United States on multiple occasions in the 1990s researching these subjects and meeting insiders and witnesses. Many over the years have described how Grey entities have been recovered alive and dead from the scene of crashed craft. The Roswell incident in New Mexico in 1947 is the most famous but there are many more. Zulu shaman Credo Mutwa tells me in the *Reptilian Agenda* video of his experience of being abducted by Greys and how they are found in the African bush where often the military quickly arrive to take them away. He said that he and others tried to cut into a dead Grey on one occasion and found that the grey 'skin' was really a suit that was very difficult to penetrate. Insider accounts in the United States tell similar stories about how the outer shell of a Grey is like a form of spacesuit to protect them from an alien atmosphere and how the military moves in to remove 'alien' bodies from crash sites and all evidence of their existence. Wright-Patterson airbase east of Dayton, Ohio, is mentioned by insiders and witnesses as a location where they have been at least initially taken. I have twice driven along the road that follows the outer fence on one side of China Lake and there is next to nothing above ground. Almost everything is happening below the surface. China Lake is an area once home to ancient civilisations and the nearby Coso Canyon Range, part of which is in the restricted zone, is the location of the Coso Rock Art District. This is an area of some 99 square miles which contain more than 50,000 documented petroglyphs and is the biggest concentration of rock art in the Northern Hemisphere. I have contended in earlier books that China Lake is an underground base where Reptilians and their Draconian 'royalty' operate and interact with the US El-ite and military. I have quoted witnesses who have seen Reptilian entities underground at China Lake which links to a tunnel and transport system. Navy Intelligence whistleblower William Tompkins said, after he went public with his book in 2015, that he had visited China Lake many times and confirms what I have said about its Reptilian connection. I was passing through Alice Springs in Australia's Northern Territory in 2011 and took

the chance with some friends
to drive to the mysterious
Pine Gap underground base
about half an hour away
which is operated by the
American military. We
ignored all the turn-back
signs to see what would
happen but by the time we
could see the outer entrance
we were all feeling very
strange and nauseous and

**Figure 264:** Pine Gap near Alice Springs, Australia. Everything else is below ground.

had to turn around. It felt like we were being hit by some sort of electromagnetic field and the affect took a while to wear off. As synchronicity would have it I flew back into Alice Springs a few days later and the landing route took us close to Pine Gap. There is little above ground except for a few 'golf ball' structures (Fig 264). Many stories tell of extraterrestrial craft activity at Pine Gap and with good reason. People will ask why these entities don't just show themselves openly and rule from the seen, but why put yourself on public display when you can currently do what you like without any challenge because most people laugh at the very suggestion of your existence? There is also the problem with sunlight and our atmosphere, although they are seeking to solve that one with the enormous increases in atmospheric radiation from technological sources and other changes to the atmosphere that I will later explain. Proof of non-human life would also blow wide open the human mind and sense of perception. This is the last thing the manipulators want as they have promoted a sense of human isolation and apartness in a lifeless Universe.

## Technology-obsessed Reptilians

The entity that is claimed to have been contacted for five years by the CHANI project is reported to have spoken about the Reptilians as well as the Moon. This is the gist of what was communicated through the computer interface:

- A reptilian race was holding back humans so they couldn't 'grow'
- They had fought many battles with the reptile race in their own reality
- Humans were more evolved than the reptiles but they suppress humans with their technology – 'Their God is their technology'

Yes, it is as we see with their connection to the Orion-Saturn-Moon Matrix and our technological society that is planned to culminate with transhumanism and the fusing of the human mind with technology and artificial intelligence – i.e. *Them*. I have two chapters later about this. The Archontic mind seeks to assimilate other consciousness to increase its potential for the creative imagination that it so lacks. I was sent an email by someone who said he had a near-death experience and was utterly confused by what he saw until he heard my description of the Saturn-Moon Matrix and its connection to the technology-obsessed Reptilians and Greys. What he said fits with concepts of reincarnation and Matrix entrapment that I discussed earlier. He was a Christian who had previously not believed in any of this, but then came the near-death experience that he described in the email:

> *It was dark when I suddenly became aware. There was no abstract thought or reasoning ... and there was no tunnel of light ... I was just aware. The next moment I found myself in a dimly lit room and now here's where the messed up part began ... I saw 2 aliens ... or Grays ... One sitting behind a control desk of sorts and the other one standing behind him in a doorway like big brother ... just watching. The room behind him [was] brightly lit, but I could still see his eyes watching me. Suddenly it occurs to me that they are 'monitoring' me ... like I was just a number. The one behind the control desk then sort of lifts his head slightly, looks at me ... then looks back down at his control desk. He then waves his right hand in the air, sort of motioning over the desk in some or other gesture.*

> *A rectangular button on the desk then starts glowing in an orange and purple color ... almost like glitter that's mixed in water and shaken up I guess ... Soon as that happens swooooosh ... I'm out in space looking at the earth ... just hovering there ...The earth seemed round to me ... not flat [as some are claiming today] ... Anyway, suddenly this light-blue beam comes down out of nowhere (today I wish I had looked where the beam came from, but I didn't ... just came from somewhere) and it shot down to earth. As it hit ... I suppose the atmosphere or ozone layer of the earth ... the beam kinda spread around the globe, like a light blue energy shield just resonating all around the globe ... just once. In an instant, I realized that it was information being sent back to earth that my soul is coming back, and the reason it resonated all around the globe is, as I understood in an instant, like the butterfly effect ... I'm coming back so everything else is affected.*

> *After that, I woke up in hospital. I thought it was demons for a long time and I was going to hell ... or ... maybe it was just that old story of the brain excreting chemicals at the time of death ... just a dream. But, honestly, when I heard about the moon matrix, everything suddenly slotted into place. What I know is this ... I saw technology I've never seen before, and I've never heard of something like this, so it wasn't an idea lodged into my brain from something I saw or read before I died. I am now convinced that when you*

*die, your soul is intercepted and recycled back to earth. It goes against everything I used to believe .*

Or rather intercepted and recycled – reincarnated – UNLESS your state of awareness and so frequency takes you beyond their Matrix bubble. I publish that account only for your information to make of what you will but it's not the first time I have heard such a theme. Humanity equates technology with metal, plastic, wires and devices, and biology with everything that is 'natural'; but this is not how the Archontic Reptilians and Greys see it. To them biological is technological. They know this is a simulation and as such there really isn't anything natural except consciousness. The human body is to them holographic/ biological technology – a software program – projected from a waveform information construct. This is the basis on which Reptilians and Greys have been used as an Archontic mind conduit to rewire the human form and infuse the counterfeit spirit or 'original sin'. This is the background to the sons of God (the gods, plural, in the original) who interbred with the daughters of men. I have already pointed out that this did not have to be done necessarily through procreation, but could happen through manipulation of the waveform and electrical construct. A Russian research group changed frog embryos into salamander embryos by transmitting salamander DNA information patterns. This is what I am talking about. Dr Michael Levin, a researcher at Tufts University in Massachusetts, has produced tadpoles with eyes on their backs and frogs with six legs simply by manipulating their electrical communication systems. It's horrible, but it shows how easy it is to change genetics without sexual procreation. Levin predicts that the same could be done with humans and allow the regrowth of lost limbs. I have been saying this is possible for decades because it is obvious when you realise the true nature of the 'body'. Why would it not be possible for entities with a far more advanced understanding of reality to mutate whole groups of people, even humanity itself, by transmitting signals or fields of information to the body's DNA and other antennae, either directly or by changes in the Cosmic Internet? To entrap consciousness in a simulation you have to attach awareness to the electrical/electromagnetic construct to create an information exchange between the two (like characters in the computer game). This is what the body's waveform blueprint and its decoded holographic illusion are doing and they have been specifically twisted and tweaked to both interface with the simulation like a character in a computer game and to limit awareness and frequency so we think it's all 'real'.

## Reptilian humans

A dominant component of the human brain is referred to by scientists as

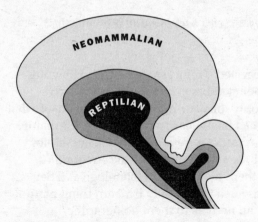

**Figure 265:** The reptilian brain or R-complex is a major driver of human behaviour.

the R-complex or reptilian brain, also known as the amygdala, and this includes the main features found in the brain of a reptile (Fig 265). I say this is connected to Archontic Reptilian breeding programmes that changed the human form and made it far more controllable. Cosmologist Carl Sagan wrote his book *The Dragons of Eden* to highlight the fundamental effect that our reptilian genetics (information patterns) have on human behaviour. Those that dismiss a reptilian dimension to human activity have no idea about reptilian genetic influence on the human brain. A substance called 'pheromone' is secreted and released by animals to detect members of the same species and pheromones in human women and iguanas are a chemical match. Sagan said it was unwise to ignore the reptilian component of human nature because '... the model may help us understand what human beings are really about'. He particularly emphasised ritualistic and hierarchical behaviour connected to the reptilian brain, and many of its traits also apply to the left-side of the brain and Saturnian astrology. The reptilian brain is associated, as one writer put it, with 'obsessive compulsive behaviour; personal day-to-day rituals and superstitious acts; slavish conformance to old ways of doing things; ceremonial re-enactments; obeisance [deference] to precedent, as in legal, religious, cultural, and other matters and all manner of deceptions'. Other reptilian brain traits include aggression; cold-bloodedness (no empathy), a desire for control, power, ownership, 'territoriality', and a belief that might is right, winner takes all. Submission to others can also manifest at the other rep-brain polarity depending on personality type. This way the reptilian brain is a vehicle for both a subservient humanity and a dominating *El*-ite. Worship is another reptilian behaviour trait and the reptilian brain is the origin of 'primitive emotional responses'. Road rage is triggered by the reptilian brain and other types of 'Oh, my god, what was I thinking of?' behaviour. This happens because it doesn't think, it *reacts*. Saturn corresponds in Hindu Vedic astrology with the lower chakra which represents basic survival needs and the fear of threats to survival, and these are the traits of the reptilian brain. We are indeed living within one big program.

The amygdala or reptilian brain is a perception prison and constantly in fear as it scans the environment for threats to survival. I don't mean only 'physical' survival, but survival of relationships, jobs, income, status, reputation, everything. Note that – the reptilian brain generates FEAR ... *food*. It also controls vital functions such as heart rate, breathing, body temperature and balance and so when you feel fear in any form your heart rate, breathing and body temperature change. In extreme cases people can pass out. The reptilian brain doesn't want you to be different. It wants you to conform and acquiesce to hierarchy and authority. It hates being seen as weird and would never want to be a maverick who thinks and acts outside of the box. If you wanted to create a slave race that would obey and not question authority, and be in fear of maverick behaviour while always adhering to 'norms', the reptilian brain would be top of your list. The R-complex is said to be the oldest part of the brain, but time does not exist and genetic manipulation can change something very quickly that would appear, in the absence of that knowledge, to have taken aeons. I say that before the genetic rewire the Reptilian part of the brain either wasn't there or was nothing like as influential, and that this is a major access point for the Archontic mind via its Reptilian underlings. How symbolic that in the *Matrix* movies they entered the fake reality through a connection positioned right on the reptilian brain at the lower back of the head. In fact, I have big questions about the brain itself as a form of control. Most people believe the brain is 'them' and where their thoughts and memories are, but we see endless examples throughout 'nature' of information being received, processed and communicated without any brain involved. Near-death experiencers who leave the body and go into expanded states of awareness compared with body perception do so without a brain which is a mechanism for processing information within five-sense reality – the simulation. If you can program the brain to do that in a certain way you control thought, behaviour and perceptions and this is what is happening. So who created the brain, at least as we know it today, and how does this connect with the 'new psyche' that emerged 6,000 years ago? The Archontic Reptilian force is my answer and it wasn't to set us free.

There is far more about the Reptilian dimension in other books but that is a concise summary to put this part of the story in the context of what is happening in the world today. Now we shall focus on the Archontic Reptilian network within global society that appears to be human, but isn't. This is the *El*-ite, also known, in part, as the 'one percent'.

# CHAPTER SIX

# Software Elite

*'Every man takes the limits of his own field of vision for the limits of the world'* – **Arthur Schopenhauer**

I have been writing for decades about specific bloodlines that do the bidding of the Archontically-possessed Reptilians/Greys within human society in the frequency band of the five senses. These 'bloodlines' can be accurately described as biological software programs which are a hybrid combination of human and Reptilian waveform information fields. Their Reptilian dimension means they can be far more powerfully possessed than the general population through their frequency connection to their hidden masters.

Human energetic codes allow them to circulate undetected within human society, but they can switch to their Reptilian codes and take a very different form when among their own and out of public sight. What I have described there is the phenomenon of human-reptilian shapeshifting, which does not mean that a physical body changes into another physical body because there is no physical. Hybrid bloodlines or software are really hybrid waveform information fields, one with human codes and the other with reptilian. Obviously, the human field is the one they project to the world and any observer decodes that information and sees them as human; but when the hybrid information/DNA shifts to the reptilian or other non-human field the observer sees them as reptilian or non-human. In their decoded reality, it appears that someone has shapeshifted 'physically' from human to non-human when in fact the observer has stopped decoding one information field and started decoding the other (Fig 266). The appearance of

**Figure 266:** There is no physical shapeshift because there is no physical. It all happens within the decoding processes of the brain.

**Figure 267:** Shapeshifting in *The Exorcist* movie.

**Figure 268:** As an entity infuses its waveform information field into someone else this begins to impact on the hologram of the possessed person and any observer will see their features change to reflect those of the possessing entity. The same process happens when human-reptilian hybrids switch their energetic codes.
© www.neilhague.com

'physical' shapeshifting only happens in the small region of the brain that decodes visual reality. Shapeshifting works on the same principle as demonic possession. In the most extreme cases the facial features of the possessed person start to distort in the fashion of the 1973 movie, *The Exorcist* (Fig 267). Possession does not mean possession of the body (hologram) but that of the waveform energetic fields from which the hologram is projected. During *Exorcist*-like possession the information field of the possessing entity so impacts upon the energetic field of the possessed person that their holographic projection starts to visually reflect the possessing entity. Observers experience this as a physical shift (Fig 268). Shapeshifting can be triggered by ritualistic blood fests, by extreme states of fury when the subsequent electrical charge through the body disturbs energetic stability, and by using their own minds to switch the codes.

Agent Smith in the *Matrix* movies is a great analogy for what I am describing with regard to *El*-ite software bloodlines. Smith is a software program imposing control on humanity as dictated by the architect of the simulation. He and his fellow agents look like humans, but they are *not* human. I have said that the human body is a form of biological software, but these *El*-ite versions are far more extreme. Humans have the potential for awareness beyond the program to infuse the body and its perception processes and override the influence and control of the counterfeit spirit. *El*-ite 'bloodline' software is the full-deal counterfeit spirit with no expanded consciousness to balance and check its empathy-deleted madness (Fig 269). They have a 'Soul' in the sense of electromagnetic waveform field information codes, but they do not have Spirit in the sense of 'Upper Aeon' Infinite Awareness. Gnostics

**Figure 269:** Archontic Reptilian human hybrids are undiluted expressions of the Archontic distortion and so reflect all its psychopathic character traits.

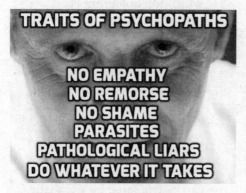

**Figure 270:** Archontic traits described by Gnostics are the same as those we call psychopaths who are people infested by the counterfeit spirit.

**Figure 271:** Why are so many 'world leaders' and the political/financial/corporate *El*-lite so psychopathic? Now you know.

described the Demiurge and Archons as a robotic race of 'artificial intelligence' which can imitate, but not innovate. Archontic representatives in human society are going to be artificial in the same way as expressions of a Demiurgic force that is itself artificial. Reptilians and Greys (I will call them Archontic Reptilians for short) are also forms of software. In this way all of them, the Archontic distortion, Reptilians, Greys and 'human' software *El*-ite, display psychopathic traits that include having no empathy, remorse or shame (Fig 270). Throw in other Archontic traits of pathological lying, doing whatever it takes to get your way and parasiting off your targets and see what you have – the personality and behaviour of those that direct and control global politics, government, banking, corporations, military, media and other institutions that decide the direction of human society (Fig 271). What are social media and other *El*-ite Internet platforms except a means to parasite and financially exploit the creativity of the people and often claim rights to that creativity, which is not their own? What are banks, but a means to parasite off the labour of the same people by lending them money that doesn't exist – 'credit' – and charging them interest? The most important positions of

**Figure 272:** We find images like this outrageous and emotionally disturbing. The *El*-ite simply laugh.

power worldwide are held by this Archontic hybrid software 'bloodline' network and its human subordinates. How could anyone order the bombing of countries to kill and maim the innocent? How could they manipulate the financial and banking system which they know will throw people on the street and deny them even access to food? How could they amass ever more wealth while billions are in poverty? Or spend more on the military while imposing austerity? Who could possibly do all that? Here we have the answer: Those with no capacity for empathy or compassion because their software is programmed not to compute such basic humanity and expressions of Spirit (Fig 272).

## *El*-ite = Reptilian mind = Archontic distortion

Reptilians and Greys were again the conduit for producing this *EL*-ite bloodline software which contains Reptilian (Archontic) perception and behaviour codes to a far greater extreme as vehicles of the undiluted counterfeit spirit. The *El*-ite therefore exhibit reptilian behaviour traits to a far greater degree – 'obsessive compulsive behaviour; personal day-to-day rituals and superstitious acts; slavish conformance to old ways of doing things; ceremonial re-enactments; obeisance [deference] to precedent, as in legal, religious, cultural, and other matters and all manner of deceptions'. I give you the British royal family, for a start, if I must. This is where their obsession with ritual comes from. Their entire life is a ritual of repeatedly visiting locations and repeating behaviour, even down to staying in certain palaces or castles at the same time every year. 'Royal' ritualism goes even deeper, however, and into dark and horrific practices that I have exposed in *The Biggest Secret, Children of the Matrix* and other books. Bloodline software programs act as middle men and women between Archontic Reptilians and the frequency band of human society. Symbolically this is the same principle as scientists (Archontic Reptilians) standing outside a sealed tank (our reality) and working inside the tank using long gloves (human-reptilian software conduits). See Figure 273 overleaf. The ancient concept of the 'divine right to rule', the claim that so-called royalty is not subject to earthly authority, comes from this bloodline network and the Demiurgic/Reptilian 'god' connection (Fig 274). They say their right to rule is the will of God, but this 'God' is the Old Testament 'God' which is the Demiurgic distortion working with its Reptilian/Grey intermediaries. Terms like 'demi-gods' or 'semi-gods' – part human, part 'god' – relate to this hybrid bloodline and so do claims to be 'God's

Figure 273: Human-reptilian hybrids represent the Archontic force within human society.
© www.neilhague.com

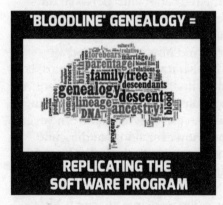

Figure 275: Interbreeding between *El*-lite bloodline families is essential to protecting the Archontic Reptilian 'software' codes.

Figure 274: The 'Divine right to rule' by bloodline inheritance is really the Archontic Reptilian right to rule by bloodline imposition.

Chosen'. Royal families have always interbred with other royal or aristocratic bloodline networks and this has been explained away as a form of extreme snobbery and perceived genetic superiority. Well, yes, it is, but the real reason is to ensure that the software program continues to be accurately replicated because its information/behaviour traits can be quickly diluted if infused with humans that are not completely controlled by the counterfeit spirit (Fig 275). Reptilian symbolism with royalty can be found all over the world. I've mentioned the Celts with their king of kings Great Dragon or Draco, but the connection is everywhere. Chinese emperors claimed the right to rule as genetic descendants of the 'serpent gods' and of course the dragon remains a revered symbol across much of Asia. Indian epics feature the reptilian and shapeshifting Nagas people, who they say interbred with a white race to produce a reptilian hybrid that became the Aryan kings. Bloodlines of kings in ancient Media, now Iran and part of Turkey, were known as Mar or snake and the 'Dragon Dynasty of Media', or

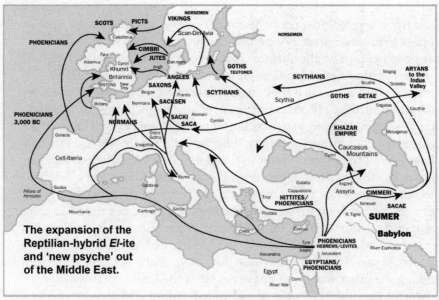

The expansion of the
Reptilian-hybrid *El*-ite
and 'new psyche' out
of the Middle East.

**Figure 276:** The hybrid bloodlines made the same journey as the new psyche as rulers of the new psyche.

'descendants of the dragon'. You find a similar theme in the Americas and the connection between royalty and the snake or serpent is pretty universal – see *Children of the Matrix*.

The emergence of major software bloodlines that we have today can be identified in the Middle East in the same period that the new psyche emerged there. They were rulers of Egypt, Sumer and Babylon before expanding into Europe and then globally through European empires, especially the British (Fig 276). Research points to the bloodlines originally moving out of Europe and Asia to settle in the Middle East before making their return and that would sync with the Indo-European invasion into the Middle East. Bloodlines and the new psyche are clearly fundamentally connected. They went on to establish the Roman Empire and wherever they located war, control, conquest and empire-building would follow, with indigenous peoples and their knowledge vanquished and crushed (the new psyche in all its glory). Kings, queens and emperors dictated everything until populations awoke enough to reject rule by bloodline inheritance although a few still survive. This was the point when most of them went underground and they have ruled ever since through rigged political systems, financial and military might and control of information (perception) which has included the merciless use of religion. 'Royal' and aristocratic bloodlines became what I call the Dark Suits. They may not look like royalty any longer but that is how they still see themselves and so they have the same arrogant belief in their right to rule. Most countries once under colonial dictatorship appear to have secured independence, but that is not what really happened except on the surface. As the colonialists officially departed they left behind their bloodlines and the secret society and satanic networks through which they manipulate events. These have gone on covertly controlling those countries ever since – including the United States – through centres such as London and Rome. I don't mean the governments of Britain and Italy, who are only vassals for the Hidden Hand like all the others. I refer to the global secret society and satanic networks that have major centres in London and Rome, but elsewhere, too. 'Old Europe' for many reasons is the centre of the bloodline global network, or has been up to now. The British Empire never ended, it just went underground. The United States may fire most of the bullets, but where and when they are fired is decided by the bloodline inner circle in Europe. If you want to hide where the power really lies you want people looking the other way. I am not saying that the United States is not powerful, but ultimately the world-transforming decisions are made elsewhere. Even Europe is only a vehicle in the end for Archontic and Reptilian masters in the shadows to which the bloodlines answer and dare not disobey.

**Figure 277:** The hierarchy in the unseen controls the hierarchy in the seen. Archontic Reptilian rulers work through their human-reptilian hybrid *El*-lite to impose their will on human society and generate maximum levels of fear.
© www.neilhague.com

## The Web

Human society is manipulated by a vast inter-dimensional web with a spider at the centre directing events. The Archontic distortion dictates to non-human entities including the Reptilians and Greys (collectively 'The Spider'), who dictate to the human-reptilian hybrid *El*-ite, who dictate to the mass of humanity (Figs 277).

Each strand in the Web is a secret society, semi-secret group or an institution that we know about, like a government department or agency, bank or corporation, and the structure is fiercely compartmentalised with different sections isolated in terms of knowledge from the others (Figs 278 and 279). This means that only a comparatively tiny few know the whole picture and how all the different compartmentalised contributions fit together. The most exclusive and publicly-unknown secret societies are closest to The Spider and only they and those in the deepest inner circles of other societies and groupings know that there even *is* a Spider let alone its nature. As we pan out from the centre we find secret societies that we do know which include the Freemasons, Knights Templar, Knights of Malta, Opus Dei and the inner sanctum of the Jesuit order. Many are connected with the Vatican in Rome, which has been a centre for the bloodlines since they established the Saturn-worshipping Roman Empire. Secret societies are by their very nature compartmentalised with only a few truly in the know. Most Freemasons never progress higher than the bottom three 'blue' degrees (levels of knowledge) and

**Figure 278:** The Spider is the Archontic Reptilian network and each strand in the Web is a secret society, semi-secret or publicly known organisation or agency all serving the interests of The Spider. The vast majority within the Web have no idea there is a Web or a Spider and nor the part they are playing themselves in enslaving humanity.

**Figure 279:** Neil Hague's representation of the Web.

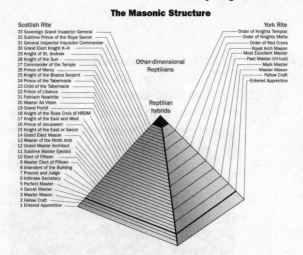

**Figure 280:** Compartmentalisation of knowledge within Freemasonry and other secret societies mirrors the structure of the Web itself.

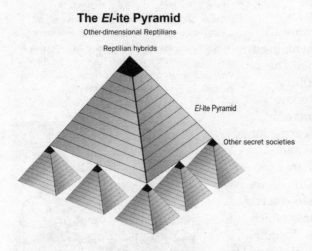

**Figure 281:** There is another highly-compartmentalised structure that most initiates of secret societies don't know about. Chosen people – almost entirely bloodline – progress through the top of known secret societies into this elite structure and that is where the real action happens and the real knowledge is retained.

those who apparently make it to the top only know so much unless they are *El*-ite insiders (Fig 280). There is a whole structure above the official secret societies which only those from the bloodlines (with a few exceptions) are ever invited to join (Fig 281). Next come what I call the cusp organisations in the Web, at the point where the hidden meets the seen. These are satellite groups answering to a Rothschild secret society in Britain called the Round Table which was established in the closing years of the 19th century. It was first headed by Rothschild agent Cecil Rhodes who plundered southern Africa on their behalf for gold, diamonds and much else. The Balfour Declaration in 1917 which led to the creation of

Rothschild-owned Israel after the Second World War was orchestrated through the Round Table. This 'Declaration' was a letter sent by British Foreign Secretary Lord Arthur Balfour to Lord Lionel Walter Rothschild setting out his government's position and support for a Jewish homeland in Palestine. History tells us about the letter, but not about the Rothschild-created-and-funded Round Table or that Lord Balfour was an

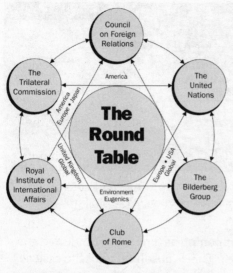

**Figure 282:** Some of the 'cusp' organisations in that part of the Web where the hidden meets the seen.

inner-circle member. This is how the Web works and manipulates from the shadows. Round Table satellites include 'think tanks' like the Bilderberg Group, the Council on Foreign Relations, the Trilateral Commission, the Club of Rome and the Royal Institute of International Affairs (Fig 282). Their role is to bring people together from the world of politics, business, banking, military, intelligence and media to coordinate a common agreement and policy (Spider policy) across different countries and institutions. The 'cusp' group inner circles know what the game is up to a point, but many of the attendees will be clueless about the really big picture. The Council on Foreign Relations (CFR), like the Trilateral Commission, was established by the *El*-ite Rockefeller family. CFR manipulators and members have driven much of American foreign policy since it was formed in New York in 1921.

**Figure 283:** How political leaders are really 'chosen'.

From the cusp groupings we enter the world of the seen – governments and their departments and agencies, banking and corporate giants, mainstream media and so on. Most people believe this is where decision-making starts, but in truth it is only where it *ends* in new laws and changes in society. Those decisions were first made deep in the Web far away from public scrutiny. The leaders that implement them are ultimately decided by The Spider by direct appointment, manipulating people into office

that suit their plans in a certain
period, or by blocking the
desired actions of the rare few
who slip through into power
that The Spider would rather
not be there (Fig 283). In this
way a highly-coordinated plan
for the transformation of
human society into a
centralised Orwellian
dictatorship can be
orchestrated by The Spider
long in advance while the

**Figure 284:** The Spider's little helpers. A few know this while the enormous majority do not.

public believe that everything is happening as a result of random
decisions, choices and circumstances. This is absolutely not the case as I
will show (Fig 284). The Web is holographic in that every part of the
whole is a smaller version of the whole. Each level is structured in the
same way whether global, national or local. For example, I live on the
Isle of Wight off the south coast of England which is only 23 miles by 13
miles with a population of around 140,000. The island is manipulated by
a criminal group known locally as the Island Mafia which control the
many Freemasonic lodges, the local council, media, a massive drug-
running operation, social services and satanic and paedophile rings. This
Mafia gets away with it because law enforcement and the local media
are a combination of the utterly and completely corrupt, and those who
know it is easier to turn a blind eye than make a stand for what is right.
Corrupt and gutless people have always been the means for the corrupt
and gutless *El*-ite to prevail at all levels of the Web. This multi-leveled
holographic structure means that the centre of the global Web can
manipulate right down into local communities like the Isle of Wight
through its pathetic gofers, who are all terrified of those above them
while acting the Big I Am to those below. The Web has been constructed
piece by piece as the bloodlines and their hidden masters infiltrated
every aspect of human life, with especial focus on the control of esoteric
information which had the potential to awaken humanity to its plight.
The ancient Babylonian sacrificial religion of the new psyche infiltrated
and took over the Mystery schools which were communicating esoteric
information in a more positive way and deliberately inverted and
distorted its meaning. Egypt was a major example of this. American
Freemasonic historian Manly P. Hall (1901-1990) wrote in *Secret Teachings
of All Ages*:

> *While the elaborate ceremonial magic of antiquity was not necessarily evil,
> there arose from its perversion several false schools of sorcery, or black*

*magic. Egypt, a great center of learning and the birthplace of many arts and sciences, furnished an ideal environment for transcendental experimentation. Here the black magicians ... continued to exercise their superhuman powers until they had completely undermined and corrupted the morals of the primitive Mysteries.*

*By establishing a sacerdotal caste they usurped the position formerly occupied by the initiates, and seized the reins of spiritual government. Thus black magic dictated the state religion and paralyzed the intellectual and spiritual activities of the individual by demanding his complete and unhesitating acquiescence in the dogma formulated by the priestcraft. The Pharaoh became a puppet in the hands of the Scarlet Council – a committee of arch-sorcerers elevated to power by the priesthood.*

In those two paragraphs, you have a description of how governments and institutions are controlled to this day by Satanists and black magicians who manipulate from an understanding of reality while suppressing that understanding for everyone else. Those that you see are only puppets of those you do not see in the form of these Satanists and black magicians that manipulate the minds and perceptions of their targets. Knowledge about the true nature of reality and the existence of Archontic Reptilian masters in the hidden realms had to be suppressed and to do that they had to control who was allowed to know (*El*-ite assets) and who was not (the rest of the population). Knowledge was twisted and inverted where it wasn't censored altogether by abominations like the Inquisition. Hall writes:

*These sorcerers then began the systematic destruction of all keys to the ancient wisdom, so that none might have access to the knowledge necessary to reach adeptship without first becoming one of their order. They mutilated the rituals of the Mysteries while professing to preserve them, so that even though the neophyte passed through the degrees he could not secure the knowledge to which he was entitled. Idolatry was introduced by encouraging the worship of the images which in the beginning the wise had erected solely as symbols for study and meditation.*

I have heard it said that some *El*-ite symbols were considered positive in the ancient world. This is true, but they have been twisted and inverted in their meaning. Hall went on:

*False interpretations were given to the emblems and figures of the Mysteries, and elaborate theologies were created to confuse the minds of their devotees. The masses, deprived of their birthright of understanding and groveling in ignorance, eventually became the abject slaves of the spiritual impostors.*

> *Superstition universally prevailed and the black magicians completely*
> *dominated national affairs, with the result that humanity still suffers from*
> *the sophistries of the* [ancient occult] *priestcrafts ...*

Out of this came human religions. They are a distortion, inversion and twisting of ancient knowledge to create prisons for the mind (and emotions).

## Sabbatean Zionism

This brings me to the central role played in the Archontic Web today by

**Figure 285:** Far from every Jewish person supports Israel – not all Jews are Zionists and not all Zionists are Jews.

Zionism and its worship of the Old Testament 'God'. Secret societies and inverted esoteric networks can take many forms and not all of them are obvious to the observer. Rothschild-created Zionism is far from what it appears to be even to most Jewish people. Zionism is a tool of the House of Rothschild to manipulate world events and the direction of human society.

First of all, Zionism is not a race but a political philosophy that is vehemently opposed by many religious Jews (Fig 285). You don't have to be Jewish to be a Zionist either. You are only required to support its claims and political stance which are based on an allegedly historic right to a Jewish homeland in Palestine which the Zionist hierarchy (the Rothschilds ultimately) wrongly claim is their birth-right and promised to them by 'God'. Jewish historians and scholars such as Shlomo Sand, Professor of History at Tel Aviv University, in his book, *The Invention of the Jewish People*, have revealed

**Figure 286:** This is where the overwhelming majority of Jewish people come from – not biblical Israel but Khazaria in the Caucasus.

that today's Jews overwhelmingly originate from the Khazar Empire in the Caucasus region where we now have southern Russia and Georgia (Fig 286). I have covered this story at length in other books. The Khazars had no historical connection to the biblical land of Israel, but converted en masse to Judaism during the reign of King Bulan in about 740AD. The Khazarian king was called the 'Khagan' or 'Kagan' which is why this is such a common Jewish name today. With the collapse of the Khazar Empire they moved north into what is now Ukraine, Hungary, Lithuania, Russia and Poland before many headed into Germany and other countries of Western Europe. These were the Jews targeted by the Nazis and the survivors relocated in large numbers after the war to Palestine and the United States where the great majority of Jewish people live today. Their historical connection to biblical Israel is basically zilch. The whole basis of Zionism's claim to the land of Palestine is that God gave it to them and God told us this in an Old Testament written by who knows who, who knows when in who knows what circumstances. Israel's communications minister Tzachi Hanegbi said the Bible alone is enough to prove that his country has legitimate claims to the land:

> *Defense is important and security is important but the most important thing is the moral claim of Israel and we are committed to living in our regional land, land that was given to us ... by the Bible ... And this is the right, which we are going to demand our right forever and ever.*

Zionism and the fairy tales on which this narrative is founded are a House of Rothschild secret society creation. The Rothschilds orchestrated the post-war mass Jewish relocation to Palestine and everything that has followed. Zionism is really Rothschildism (Fig 287). Zionist (Rothschild) networks include distorted versions of traditional Judaism and Islam which I will come to in a moment. Zionism may appear to be a political movement related to the creation and continued existence of Israel, but at its core it is a secret society representing the interests of the Rothschilds and the Web. Jewish people as a whole are as irrelevant to these Zionist insiders as the rest of the global population. Only two to three percent of Americans are Jewish and the great

**Figure 287:** To understand Israel and all that it is does is to understand this simple fact.

majority of them will not know that Zionism is a secret society
masquerading as a political and racial belief system. They support
Zionism because they support Israel and they think Zionism relates to
their Jewish religion. No, it *doesn't*. Among the two to three percent are
also those Jews that vehemently oppose Israel, its treatment of the
Palestinians and all that it stands for. This leaves only a small section of
the Jewish community that *knowingly* serve the secret society, and it is
these initiates that appear in dramatically higher ratio to their number in
politics (usually as 'advisors', administrators and backers), banking,
business, Hollywood, media and in so many other key areas. Secret
society Zionism is also known as 'Revisionist Zionism', an ideology
founded on violence by Russian Jew Ze'ev (Vladimir) Jabotinsky in the
1920s, who pledged to seize Palestine with an 'iron wall of Jewish
bayonets'. Today they use high-tech missiles. Jabotinsky (1880-1940) set
out to 'create, with sweat and blood, a race of men, strong, brave and
cruel' that would impose a Greater Israel from the River Nile in Egypt to
the Euphrates in Iraq and known to Jews as Eretz Yisrael. This describes
the largest expanse of alleged biblical Israel. Jewish scientist Albert
Einstein and other prominent Jews sent a letter to *The New York Times* in
1948 describing Irgun, a Revision Zionism enforcement arm, as 'terrorist'
and 'right wing' and founded on 'ultranationalism, religious mysticism
and racial superiority'. The letter described the Israeli party representing
the Zionist Revisionist movement as 'closely akin in its organization,
methods, political philosophy and social appeal to the Nazi and Fascist
parties'. This is the ideology that controls Israel today with the House of
Rothschild holding the strings. Brutal Israel Prime Ministers Menachem
Begin (who won the Nobel Peace Prize), Yitzhak Shamir, Ariel Sharon
and now Benjamin Netanyahu all gleaned their ideology from that of
Jabotinsky (Netanyahu's father was his personal assistant). This
ideology is based on unrestrained and unrelenting violence to impose
the Zionist will.

The Zionist secret society is not an expression of Judaism, but

Sabbateanism and Frankism which are
absolutely not the same thing. These
names come from Sabbatai Zevi
(1626–1676), a rabbi who proclaimed he
was the Jewish messiah, and the Polish
Jew Jacob Frank (1726-1791) who said he
was the reincarnation of 'messiah'
Sabbatai Zevi and biblical patriarch Jacob
(Figs 288 and 289). Zevi, an occultist and
black magician, led what is described as
the biggest messianic movement in Jewish
history as he promised to return them to a

**Figure 288:** Sabbatai Zevi.

**Figure 289:** Jacob Frank.

homeland in Palestine. He converted to Islam after basically being given the choice by the Sultan of the Turkey-based Ottoman Empire between conversion, or torture and death. Hundreds of his followers did the same and became known as 'Dönmeh' which means 'to turn'. These are defined as 'crypto-Jews' who, like Sabbatai Zevi, publicly converted to Islam but retained their Jewish beliefs or at least a *version* of Jewish beliefs. Dönmeh were forbidden to marry outside of their sect. They became powerful in the politics and business of Salonica (today called Thessalonica or Thessaloniki in Greek Macedonia in the southern Balkans). Salonica was a major centre for Freemasonry and the birthplace of the Young Turk movement which overthrew Ottoman Islamic rule in Turkey. The movement emerged out of secret societies and 'progressive' students and military cadets and established the Republic of Turkey in 1923 under its first president Mustafa Kemal, who is far better known as 'Atatürk'. He was a Grand Orient Freemason (the *El*-ite version) in the Lodge Veritas in Salonica and worked as a British agent in the breakup of the Ottoman Empire, according to Lord Patrick Kinross in his book, *Ataturk, The Rebirth of a Nation*. Lodge Veritas received its Freemasonic warrant from the Grand Orient of France. Atatürk's background and racial origins have been described as a 'vexed question' and a mystery still to be solved. There were consistent rumours in Turkey that he was Jewish, and Jews in Salonica said that he was a Dönmeh, the 'crypto-Jew' followers of Sabbatai Zevi. His father certainly sent him to the Şemsi Efendi Dönmeh school in Salonica and a 1994 article by Israeli journalist Hillel Halkin in T*he Jewish Daily Forward* reported a conversation between Jewish journalist Itamar Ben-Avi and Mustafa Kemal (Ataturk) in 1911 at the Kamenitz Hotel in Jerusalem. Ben-Avi described how an intoxicated Ataturk claimed to descend from Sabbatai Zevi and how his father had told him to read an antique Hebrew Bible. It would certainly appear from other sources that Ataturk was in Jerusalem at that time. Hillel Halkin wrote:

> *The Turkish government, which for years has been fending off Muslim fundamentalist assaults on its legitimacy and on the secular reforms of Ataturk, has little reason to welcome the news that the father of the 'Father of the Turks' was a crypto-Jew who passed on his anti-Muslim sentiments to his son. Mustafa Kemal's secret is no doubt one that it would prefer to continue to be kept.*

Emmanuel Carasso, one of the leaders of the Young Turk revolution that put Atatürk in power, came from a Jewish family in Salonica and pioneered Freemasonry within the Ottoman Empire. Such was the impact of the revolutionaries that the term 'Young Turk' is still used to describe someone who is 'progressive', rebellious, revolutionary and demanding radical reform. Today's progressives who serve the *El*-ite agenda while thinking they are challenging the Establishment can therefore be described as 'Young Turks'. The Dönmeh religion within a religion continues within Islam today and its influence and manipulation can be seen on the television news hour by hour for reasons I will come to. Sabbatai Zevi proclaimed his messiahship for very practical reasons. It gave him the perceived authority to overturn traditional Judaism and invert everything. A day of fasting, for example, became a day of feasting and so it went on. He rejected traditional religious teachings and laws, sexual taboos and the concept of right and wrong (a mentality encompassed by Jabotinsky's Revisionist Zionism and by Satanism). Zevi convinced his followers that doing evil was to be encouraged and celebrated and he argued against feelings of guilt (again, a mentality encompassed by Jabotinsky's Revisionist Zionism and by Satanism). He was promoting the Archontic perceptual state of no compassion or empathy. Sabbateanism, or Sabbatianism, is a modern version of the religion of Sumer and Babylon and can be likened in its beliefs and sacrificial practices to today's Satanism because in many ways it *is* today's Satanism. This was Einstein's 'religious mysticism' in his condemnation of Revisionist Zionism. The same was true of the Frankism of Jacob Frank, another occultist and black magician who claimed to be the reincarnated Zevi. Frankism involved human and animal sacrifices and declares that 'Lucifer' (the Archontic force) is the true god. You can appreciate why some have dubbed what I will call Sabbatean Frankism as the 'Synagogue of Satan'. Frankists or Sabbatean Frankists were told 'Do What Thou Wilt'. The philosophy of anything goes is at the centre of all that they do. This 'anything' includes paedophilia, sacrifice and incest. Depravity to Frankists is a form of worship while compassion and empathy are sacrilege. The *El*-ite language of symbolism expresses this system of reversal or inversion. What means one thing to the general population means the opposite to the *El*-ite. A dove is a symbol of peace to the public but the opposite to Sabbatean Frankists and other Satanists. Classic Satanic/Sabbatean Frankist symbols include the *inverted* pentagram and the *inverted* cross and what a symbol represents will generate its

**Figure 290:** Satanists and Sabbatean Frankists desire an inverted society to reflect their inverted symbolism.

energetic state and frequency (Fig 290). I have been describing human society as inverted with everything upside down and this is why. Our world is controlled and manipulated by those for whom the reversal and inversion of everything good is their very religion. Rabbi Marvin Antelman describes Frankism in his book, *To Eliminate the Opiate*, as 'a movement of complete evil' and Jewish professor Gershom Scholem says this about Frank in *The Messianic Idea in Judaism*: 'In all his actions [he was] a truly corrupt and degenerate individual ... one of the most frightening phenomena in the whole of Jewish history.' Traditional Jewish rabbis excommunicated Frank and his followers as heretics but they continued to operate underground and behind the scenes in a campaign of infiltration. This is one reason why many traditional Jewish believers so oppose Zionism today. They see it a fraudulent version of their faith. Jewish believers all have the 'God's Chosen People' deal, but not with the extremes of inner-core Revisionist Zionism and its advocates. Frank formed an alliance in 1773 with Mayer Amstel Rothschild, founder of the Rothschild financial dynasty out of Frankfurt, Germany, and with the Jesuit-educated Jew, Adam Weishaupt, who founded the Bavarian Illuminati in 1776. This would be involved in massive political manipulation including the French Revolution and today under other names and in other forms this network manipulates global governments, banking, corporations, media and entertainment industry, and is a predominant force directing events through the Web within five-sense reality.

## Where 'ISIS' really came from ...

Sabbatean Frankism (inner core secret society Revisionist Zionism) went on to seize control of the Roman Church and Freemasonry with the Grand Orient version top of the list (see Ataturk). Sabbateans and Frankists converted to other religions to infiltrate their power structure in ways that mimicked the followers of Sabbatai Zevi within Islam. Sabbatean Frankism and Satanism are only different names for the same Archontic forces that took over Egypt, Sumer and Babylon in the way that Manly P. Hall describes, and so the same methods and techniques are employed. We see a modern-day expression of this infiltration with the vile and violent distortion of traditional Islam known as Wahhabism which is practiced (enforced) in Saudi Arabia and by Saudi-funded terrorist groups like ISIS or Islamic State (Fig 291). Saudi Arabian and ISIS beheadings and

**Figure 291:** Islamic State: Saudi-armed-and-funded bunch of prats.

mass murders are satanic sacrifices
and death rituals (Fig 292). The plan
is to destroy all other religions and
leave only a one world religion –
Sabbatean Frankism, also known as
Satanism and Wahhabism,
worshipping the Archontic
distortion. Advocates of Judaism,
Islam, Christianity and all religions
or no religions need to come together
and realise we are all being targeted

**Figure 292:** A Saudi Arabian beheading? Or
is it Isis? They behave the same because one
created the other with serious support from
America and Britain.

by the same force. Iraqi intelligence documents found by the American
military after the invasion of Iraq in 2003 include one from the General
Military Intelligence Directorate dated 2002 and titled 'The Emergence of
Wahhabism and its Historical Roots'. The author is named as
Intelligence Colonel Sa'id Mahrnud Najrn Al-'Arniri who writes about
'the enemies of Islam who use the Al-Wahabi Movement in the political
arena to prevent the unity of Muslims'. He goes on:

> *Al-Wahabi today is subconsciously working in all its power on promoting
> occupation in order to achieve its despicable desires. The Wahabis have worn
> the Muslim robe inside out therefore; they couldn't apprehend any of the
> Muslim goals, because how is it possible for someone who seeks the help of
> infidels to speak of unity?*

> *They sign treaties of peace and friendship with the criminals, surrender and
> bow in front of the masters of rotten politics. Therefore; I wanted in my
> study to focus on the history of this movement from the stand point of its
> relation with the British government and how Britain had employed all its
> spies in Muslim countries in order to establish and spread this movement to
> destroy Muslim religion and create heterodoxies in Islam.*

The document quotes from the alleged autobiography of a British spy
called 'Hempher' which describes how the British government (then
Empire) sought to create an extreme and distorted version of Islam for
purposes of divide and rule and in the middle of the 18th century chose
as its front man a chap called Muhammad ibn 'Abd al-Wahhab.
'Hempher' claimed that Wahhab was chosen because of his 'many
attributes such as the love of glory, immorality and extreme views'. Thus
'Wahhabism' was born and anyone under its control who did not accept
its laws and impositions was to be killed. Wahhabism loves a massacre
(blood ritual) and it started early and has never stopped. The same goes
for its inspiration Sabbatean Frankism. The Iraqi document describes
how the British told Wahhab to make an alliance with Muhammad bin

Saud who created the first Saudi state before he died in 1765 and whose family successors formed the current Saudi Arabia in cohorts with their British and American masters in 1932. In doing so they hijacked Islam's major religious centres in Mecca and Medina. Wahhab's daughter married bin Saud's son and it would appear that both families were not Arabic, but Dönmeh 'crypto-Jews'. The collaboration between British agent Hempher and Wahhab is also described by Ottoman writer and Turkish naval admiral Ayyub Sabri Pasha in his work, *The Beginning and Spreading of Wahhabism*. The plot thickens (or actually gets much clearer) when the Iraqi intelligence report includes Arabic texts saying that Abdul Wahhab and Muhammad bin Saud were Jewish. It sources the following from an Arabic work by D. Mustafa Turan called *The Dönmeh Jews*:

> *Muhammad Bin 'Abd-al-Wahhab is a descendent of a family from the Jews of Al-Dunamah in Turkey. Al-Dunmah* [Dönmeh] *refers to the Jews who declared their embracement of Islam in an effort to insult Islam and to escape the pursuit by the Ottoman sultans ...* [Turan] *confirms that Sulayman; the grandfather of* [Wahhab], *is (Shulman); he is a Jew from the merchants of the city of Burstah in Turkey, he had left it and settled in Damascus, grew his beard, and wore the Muslim turban, but was thrown out for being voodoo.*

> *Then he fled to Egypt and he* [was] *faced* [with] *strong objection so he left to Hijaz and settled in Al-'Ayniyyah where he got married and had a child whom he called 'Abd-al-Wahab and claimed to be from the descent of Rabi'iyyah, and that he was born in Morocco.*

The document notes that the same story is told by writer Rifat Salim Kabar in *The Dönmeh Jews and the Origin of the Saudi Wahhabis*. Muhammad ibn Abdul Wahhab as a descendant of a family of Dönmeh Jews from Turkey certainly makes sense of current events and why Saudi-armed-and-funded Wahhabi terrorist movements overwhelmingly kill other Muslims. The Saudi-Israel-US-UK Sabbatean Frankist connection explains why the four of them are so close and the enormity of arms shipments to the Saudis by America and Britain (Fig 293). Donald Trump announced on his visit to Riyadh in 2017 that terrorist-supporting Saudi Arabia was to be the Middle East centre for 'fighting terrorism', in a move that

**Figure 293:** This is the background to why Saudi Arabia and Israel are so remarkably close when the opposite would be expected.

**Figure 294:** ISIS is all fakery and the rank and file idiots are caught in a deadly game they do not understand.

was simply taking the piss. The Iraqi intelligence report quotes the assertion by Abdul Wahhab Ibrahim Al-Shammari in *The Wahhabi Movement, The Truth and Roots* that the House of Saud fake royals are descended from Mordechai bin Ibrahim bin Mushi, a Jewish merchant from Basra in Iraq. Claims about a House of Saudi 'family tree' going back to the Prophet Muhammad are a joke. The document says that David Shakespeare, a Jewish British officer, worked during World War I with Saudi King Abdulaziz bin Abdul Rahman, better known in the West as Ibn Saud, to plot the defeat of other Arab leaders on the Arabian Peninsula who had rejected the British plan for the region that included a Jewish homeland in Palestine. This followed in the wake of the 'Balfour Declaration' giving British government support for a Jewish homeland in Palestine which was so transparently orchestrated by the Rothschild Round Table for anyone who cares to research the background. Britain told the people of Palestine via their military officer Thomas Edward Lawrence 'Lawrence of Arabia' that they would be given independence if they helped the British remove the Turkish Ottoman Empire from the region, but all along that land was designated for Jews from Europe. The so-called House of Saud supported the British agenda at the expense of the non-Wahhabi Palestinians. British money and military support ensured that Ibn Saud prevailed and violently imposed Wahhabism, their grotesque subversion of traditional Islam, on the entire Arabian Peninsula. Why do Britain and the United States support the Saudi 'royal' family no matter what they do and arm them to the teeth to kill real Muslims? Now you know. ISIS, the creation of Saudi Arabia, the US, UK and Israel, is the military wing of Wahhabism (Fig 294).

Sabbatean Frankism and its networks today control Freemasonry, the Jesuits, Knights Templar, Knights of Malta and Opus Dei, and all the secret and semi-secret strands that connect with them. These include the Bilderberg Group, the Council on Foreign Relations, the Trilateral Commission, the Club of Rome and so on. That is not to say that everyone involved with these groups and organisations is a Sabbatean Frankist. Most will not be, but they ultimately call the shots. Sabbatean Frankists, secret society Zionism and the Rothschilds are fake 'Jews' who have been misleading almost the entirety of the world's Jewish

population. They are the real power behind Israel with its
Rothschild/Saturn flag. The Rothschilds paid for the construction of the
Knesset, the Israeli parliament, and the Supreme Court building and
arranged for the mass migration of German Jews into Palestine after
World War II on the back of the Balfour Declaration. Zionism at its inner
core is a Sabbatean Frankist secret society serving the interests not of
Jewish people, but of *Revisionist* Zionism (see Rothschild) and The
Spider. Revisionist Zionism is to the Jewish religion what Wahhabism is
to Islam and both Revisionist Zionism and Wahhabism are ultimately
controlled by the same network based in Israel with operational centres
in the US, UK, Rome and elsewhere. Take away Jewish people who
oppose Zionism and the majority who call themselves Zionists without
knowing what it really means and you are left with a ridiculously small
number – in a world Jewish population of only around 15 million – who
are members of the Sabbatean Frankism-controlled Zionist inner core
and answer to the House of Rothschild. I have called them in other
books 'Rothschild Zionists'. From this relative handful of secret society
Revisionist Zionists the personnel are recruited (as I expose in *The
Perception Deception*) to fill so many positions of political, corporate and
financial power, especially in the United States, at such an extraordinary
ratio to their numbers. This is not for the benefit of the mass of Jewish
people, but to advance the agenda of The Spider, to which Jews are as
expendable as anyone else. It is worth keeping in mind as world events
unfold that Israel = Rothschild = Sabbatean Frankism = Satanism = The
Spider. You can read the detailed story of Sabbateanism and Frankism
(Satanism) in Rabbi Antelman's book, *To Eliminate the Opiate*.

## Archontic Reptilian Paedophiles

I have been highlighting since the 1990s the connection between the
Reptilian-hybrid bloodline network and both Satanism and paedophilia
which are central to Sabbatean Frankism just as they were in Babylon
and Rome (Babylon re-located). The scale of child sexual abuse generally
is stunning and far beyond what most people can comprehend, but it is,
per-capita, most concentrated in the 'upper' levels of the bloodline
hierarchy for reasons that can be explained. I spent 1996 to 2006 in
particular intensely researching *El*-ite paedophilia, Satanism and mind
control which are all connected. We need to always remember that the
bloodlines are software programs – biological vehicles for the counterfeit
spirit to dictate events within human five-sense perception. The
empathy-deleted counterfeit spirit drives their actions and behaviour
and so they coldly impose war, deprivation, misery and ... *fear*. They are,
to use the term of the ages, possessed. This has been the case since the
bloodline software was inserted into the simulation and here the Sufi
mystic Rumi describes the consequences of possession in the 13th

century:

> When a man is possessed by an evil spirit the qualities of humanity are lost
> in him. Whatever he says is really said by that spirit, though it seems to
> proceed from his mouth. When the spirit has this rule and dominance over
> him the agent is the property of the spirit, and not himself. His self has
> departed and he has become the spirit.

Gnostics would have said become the *counterfeit* spirit. When you
observe the *El*-ite and the one percent – or far less than one-percent –
you are looking at incarnations of the Archontic force and Archontic
Reptilians using bloodline biological software as their cover. Observe
their actions when compared with how Gnostic manuscripts describe
Demiurgic-Archontic character traits. World events can then be seen in a
very different light. Without the influence of Upper Aeon awareness,
they have no compassion to limit what they do and experience no
emotional consequences for doing it. Their tears are confined to how
something affects *them* and not for those who suffer from their actions.
This computer-like (*software*-like) lack of emotion means they have to
'act' their emotions and compassion to hide the truth that they don't
have any. The badly-acted fake emotion of people like the Clintons and
Tony Blair come immediately to mind and the British Queen doesn't
even bother acting. Observe the then Prime Minister Blair with his
rehearsed 'people's princess' speech after Princess Diana died in 1997
and the Queen's public address on the same subject a few days later.
One was acting emotion (embarrassingly badly) and the other didn't
even try. This inability to feel compassion and empathy leads to
bombing the innocent while feeling nothing for those suffering the
consequences. The term 'heartless' was made for them. I was interested
to read an article detailing the experiences of Swiss clairvoyant, Anton
Styger. I have been told by many visual psychics/mediums around the
world how they often see an ethereal reptilian entity 'overshadowing'
members of the political and financial *El*-ite. I remember Hillary Clinton
being mentioned a few times. Clairvoyants are able to peer further into
reality than most people normally do and see what is happening at
frequencies hidden to the rest of the population. Anton Styger said:

> When I see people in business or politics who are particularly trapped by the
> material world, for example, I notice that they no longer have any light
> bodies at all. In many of these people, the point of light at the heart chakra,
> which is otherwise always present, is no longer visible to me.
>
> Instead, I see something like a layer of 'shiny tar' around them in which a
> monstrous being in the shape of a lizard can be distinguished. When such

*people speak on television, for example, I see a crocodile shape manifesting itself around the person like in a concave mirror; I don't see the light of their throat and forehead chakra.*

No light at the heart chakra leads to *heartless* behaviour. This is cause and effect because their possessed five-sense mind is isolated in complete subordination to the counterfeit spirit. As the 'ayahuasca' voice in Brazil asked me in 2003: If you programmed a computer to abuse a child would it have any emotional consequences for doing so? Untold and shocking numbers of children worldwide have experienced precisely this phenomenon. What better definition of 'heartless' can there be than sexually and violently abusing children? The reason for such a concentration of paedophiles among the *El*-ite is that the energy of children before puberty is the most prized by Archons and Archontic Reptilians (Fig 295). Puberty is a time of hormonal change, but this is triggered by energetic information change in the waveform field. Archons want the energy of children before that change happens because of its purity and

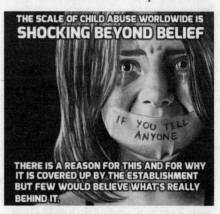

**Figure 295:** The big secret about why there are so many paedophiles among the *El*-lite.

for other reasons. While the possessed paedophile is abusing a child the possessing entity is using the paedophile as an energetic conduit to draw off the child's energy and life-force. This is happening worldwide and Central American shaman Don Juan Matus said:

> ... *Sorcerers see infant human beings as strange luminous balls of energy, covered from the top to the bottom with a glowing coat, something like a coat of plastic adjusted tightly around the cocoon of energy. This glowing coat of awareness is what the predators consume and when a human reached adulthood, all that is left of that fringe awareness is a narrow fringe that goes from the ground to the top of the toes. That fringe permits mankind to keep on living, but only barely.*

This is the energy they take from children via their possessed paedophiles and why paedophilia and its connected Satanism infests the *El*-ite and their networks. Paedophile rings of the rich and famous that I and others were exposing in the 1990s have since come to public attention. This has especially happened in Britain in the wake of the

revelations about BBC
'entertainer', disc-jockey and
record-breaking paedophile Jimmy
Savile. One of those I named in *The
Biggest Secret* in 1998 was former
Prime Minister Edward Heath who
was also a child-sacrificing Satanist
(Fig 296). Heath had the passage
from the book read to him in the
week of publication seven years
before he died while he was still a
Member of Parliament and he did
nothing. Another 17 years passed
before a police investigation began

**Figure 296:** Jimmy Savile with UK Prime Minister Ted Heath. Savile procured children for Heath to abuse and murder often sacrificially.

into Heath's horrendous activities when witnesses came forward. What I
had been told about Heath did not surprise me after my own experience
with him in 1989 at the London Sky News studio where I was being
interviewed as a national spokesman for the Green Party on an EU
election results programme. When I arrived I was taken into a make-up
room and told that someone would be along in a moment to see me. I
thought I had been left alone, but then as I sat down facing the wall of
mirrors something caught my eye and there hidden behind an open
door was Edward Heath who had just been interviewed and was
waiting for his make-up to be removed. I said 'hello' but Heath did not
even acknowledge me. He gave me a long inquisitive look that seemed
to say '*Mmmm*, what's this?' Heath continued to stare intently without
speaking and his eyes moved to the top of my head and slowly scanned
down to my feet and back again. It was the weirdest experience and
about to get weirder. At one point as his eyes were 'scanning' they
turned jet black. I mean all of them, including the whites. I was looking
at two black holes and at no point was there a point to make 'eye
contact' in the sense that the blackness seemed to have no end and
continued through him into wherever. His 'eyes' returned to normal and
he turned away to look at the mirror in front of him. Not a word was

spoken the entire time. I
didn't say anything publicly
about this at first because you
question if you actually saw
what you appeared to see, but
later I began to come across
stories and accounts from
around the world about the
'black-eyed people' when the
same experience was being

**Figure 297:** Edward Heath and the black-eyed people.

described (Fig 297). Heath was one evil human being and controlled by an Archontic force not of this world. The Hidden Hand and elements of its media have since been working to trash and block the truth about Heath and other political figures and prevent widespread public acceptance about what is going on. They are not too bothered when children's home staff are exposed, lower level clergy, football coaches and so on, because they are no threat to exposing the *El*-ite structures founded on paedophilia and Satanism. Once those are in danger of exposure the drawbridge is immediately in an upright position. Many police officers have revealed how their investigations into child abuse rings were stopped by 'superiors' the moment a famous politician was found to be involved while others, as in Belgium and the island of Jersey, have been fired or suspended because they were actively and genuinely seeking the truth.

One of the ways that *El*-ite paedophilia is systematically discredited is by bringing 'witnesses' who have not been abused to public attention to tell false stories, and by exploiting those who *have* been abused but are so psychologically damaged they will name anyone they are encouraged to. These claims are then exposed as fraudulent to discredit accounts of the genuinely abused naming genuine perpetrators. Watch also for some who claim to be exposing paedophilia and supporting the abused while behaving in ways that discredit the whole child abuse exposure arena. Some do so with the specific intent of blocking exposure while others have a negative impact because they think it's all about them and their own agenda. One gobshite in the UK comes immediately to mind. When governments are forced by public outrage into launching 'inquiries' into allegations of *El*-ite paedophile rings they make sure they go nowhere. This has been done multiple times in the UK. The 'inquiry' announced by Theresa May who was then Home Secretary and later Prime Minister is an obvious case. This was supposed to investigate multiple claims of a paedophile ring centred on the Westminster Parliament among many other things, but May proceeded to name as heads of the inquiry people with glaring conflicts of interest or who were completely hopeless. Their subsequent resignations, and media attempts to undermine the inquiry's credibility, led to years of inaction which threatened to drive it into oblivion. I have greater confidence in the inquiry's *fourth* chairwoman, Professor Alexis Jay, who appears to be far more like the up-and-at-'em warrior for truth that abuse survivors need to secure some justice at last. Jay said: 'Strong vested interests would like to see this inquiry implode ... There are institutions which would prefer to see us fail, because we are such a threat.' That's more like it, so fingers crossed. The number of children that go missing every year never to be seen again is beyond belief. We are talking many millions worldwide. In the 1990s I rang the US federal government to ask how many children went missing in

America each year. I was told they didn't keep the figures. They could tell me how many cars went missing, but not children. I was advised to contact each individual state and when I began doing so I was shocked at how fast the number was into the hundreds of thousands. It was certainly heading towards a figure I have seen quoted of 800,000. People relate missing children stories they see occasionally in the news to the number that go missing, but only a fraction of these cases are ever publicly reported. While there will be less sinister reasons to explain most of them, it is clear from my decades of research that significant numbers end up in paedophile rings, underground bases for experimentation and other horrors off-planet involving Reptilians and Greys, or are used for sacrifice in the satanic network. The mammoth numbers are not by chance but by design. Trafficking of children is a global industry and the mass migration into Europe has been exploited to this end on a gargantuan scale. Europol, the EU's police intelligence unit, estimated in 2016 that some 10,000 unaccompanied migrant children had gone missing in Europe in the previous two years. This is happening all over the world orchestrated by the *El*-ite for their Archontic Reptilian/Grey masters. To give you an idea of the scale of paedophilia, two websites on the encryption-protected 'dark web' that were exposed by American and German police numbered 150,000 and nearly 90,000 members.

## Savile – the 'royal' connection

The truth and scale of what is happening – and who it involves – was there to be seen with the Jimmy Savile scandal that broke after this disc jockey and television personality died in 2011. British media reported the tidal wave of evidence that he was a paedophile of monumental proportions, who had been abusing hundreds of children and young

people since the 1950s at locations that included BBC studios, hospitals and care homes. What they did not say was that he was a procurer of children for the rich and famous *El*-ite and that this is why he was never charged or prosecuted for long-time mass paedophilia which the police and security agencies well knew about. The media briefly mentioned and then ignored the fact that Savile was an inner circle bosom buddy of the royal family and was brought into the fold in

**Figure 298:** Paedophile Lord Mountbatten, mentor to Prince Charles and Prince Philip, introduced record-breaking paedophile Savile to the royal inner circle in the 1960s. I guess they must have liked the music he played.

**Figure 299:** Monumental paedophile and child-procurer Jimmy Savile was a long-time close friend of Prince Charles right up to his death in 2011.

**Figure 300:** Jimmy Savile was a close friend of Margaret Thatcher whose government in the 1980s has been at the centre of claims about a Westminster paedophile ring.

SAVILE WAS ALLOWED TO GET AWAY WITH IT

BECAUSE HE WAS SUPPLYING THE ESTABLISHMENT WITH CHILDREN

**Figure 301:** Why he was never caught despite his record-breaking paedophilia for decades.

the 1960s by the known paedophile Lord Mountbatten, a family mentor of Prince Philip and Prince Charles (Fig 298). Savile became a close friend of Charles during his decades of paedophilia right up to his death (Fig 299). He was also a long-time friend of Prime Ministers Edward Heath and Margaret Thatcher, whose government between 1979 and 1990 has been the focus of allegations about the Westminster paedophile ring (Fig 300). I expose this at length in *The Perception Deception*. Let's just think about this for a minute. No one gets close to the Queen and inner circle of the royal family without British Intelligence in the form of MI5 and police Special Branch knowing about them and their background. The same is true of a prime minister. Yet Jimmy Savile was allowed to be so close to both while the police knew that he was a child abuser of historic proportions? How could this happen? The answer is simple – he was a procurer of children for the rich and famous *El*-ite (Fig 301). Upper echelons of British Intelligence play a vital part in watching the back of participants (including their own) and they had to be crucial in keeping Savile out of trouble while knowing what he was doing and how close he was to the British royals. This is the case with American Intelligence and their protection of father George Bush and others when it is an open secret in US political circles that Bush has been a paedophile and violent abuser of children on a Savile-type scale for much of his

life (see *The Biggest Secret*). What did the CIA do about this? They named
their headquarters in Langley, Virginia, after him – the George Bush
Center for Intelligence! Allegations of a paedophile ring based in
Washington DC emerged during the Trump-Clinton election campaign
in 2016 only to be dismissed by reflex-action by the media. This was
given the title 'Pizzagate' after alleged involvement of Washington pizza
restaurants. I can't confirm the accuracy or not of the alleged detail and
personalities because I have not investigated the background deeply
enough for that. But is there an *El*-ite paedophile ring in Washington?
*Absolutely* there is and I have been exposing this for decades now. Is it
really a coincidence that the plea-bargain convicted American billionaire
paedophile Jeffrey Epstein was (is) close friends with so many of the
political, financial, corporate and royal *El*-ite including Bill Clinton and

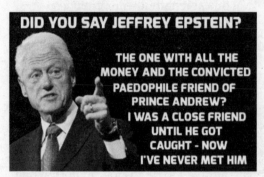

Prince Andrew? Or that
Clinton flew so many times
in Epstein's private jet
dubbed the 'Lolita Express'?
Or that he, Andrew and
others of their ilk visited
Epstein's Caribbean island
at the centre of allegations
against him? Put 'Epstein
little black book' into a
search engine to read about
his buddy list (Fig 302).
They include Donald
Trump, Tony Blair and

**Figure 302:** He was the guy on the private jet with you, Bill.

Blair's friend, the political manipulator Peter Mandelson. Trump is
quoted by *The Washington Post* as calling Epstein a 'terrific guy' in 2002.
He said Epstein was 'a lot of fun to be with' and 'he likes beautiful
women as much as I do, and many of them are on the younger side'.
Alexander Acosta, Trump's pick for Labor Secretary, is at the centre of a
lawsuit at the time of writing for the strange plea bargain he agreed with
Epstein in 2008 while a US attorney in Miami. The bargain meant that
Epstein was freed from a potential life sentence and federal prosecution.
Trump was named in the lawsuit as a witness. Attorneys for some
underage Epstein accusers say the plea bargain agreement was a
'sweetheart deal' that only happened because of his wealth and
connections.

Everywhere *El*-ite Archontic Reptilian bloodlines, Satanists and
Sabbatean Frankists operate you find sacrifice ritual and paedophilia
with Hollywood very much included. Hollywood is awash with
paedophilia, Satanism and mind control and is a really sick place. Why
would that not be when Hollywood is the global centre of fantasy and

magic through which the *El*-ite globally program perceptions? Former child actors have spoken out about paedophile and satanic rings (same thing) that control Tinsel Town and involve the very rich and famous, but most stay quiet fearing the end of their career or worse. I have heard similar accounts all over the world so many times. Jon Robberson, who worked behind the scenes in Hollywood for 16 years on feature films and television projects with major studios, has since been very vocal about the paedophiles and Satanists that run the place. He talks about a global satanic ring and this is the same one that I have been exposing since the 1990s which operates in every country and is central to *El*-ite and Sabbatean Frankist operations. Robberson said there was 'paedophilia running rampant in Hollywood' with child sex rings involving the 'highest upper echelons of Hollywood, executive VPs of development, producers, mega-power agents and the international bankers that fund all this stuff.' But of course Sabbatean Frankists and their like are obsessed with Satanism and abusing children. Robberson described how children are drugged and filmed at paedophile parties involving 'multi-partner homosexual [orgies], bloodletting, and animal dismemberment.' He also confirmed another common theme of how politicians and those of use to the *El*-ite are compromised while being secretly filmed. 'Once they've got the goods on you on video, they own you', he said. Actress Angelina Jolie can be seen in a leaked video on YouTube describing her gruesome initiation ritual in which she says, 'you'll be able to heal once you're beaten'. She talks about having to kill a snake, creating a real bond with Satan and how she has encouraged other celebrities to take part:

> ... *I would've filmed it* [the ritual] *in order to encourage like everybody, all different types of celebrities but there is that thing where it is like a lot of people misunderstand it* [the ritual], *maybe with S&M and they think ... its superficial and I have to like explain to people how like it's ... more like you are tied down because you need to like be able to, like, have something hold you down to keep you still or like you'll fight or go absolutely mad.*

These are the sort of rituals that are often filmed to compromise those taking part for the rest of their lives and that especially applies to politicians. Former child actor Elijah Wood told the UK *Sunday Times* how child actors were 'preyed upon' in Hollywood: 'There is a darkness in the underbelly – if you can imagine it, it's probably happened.' Wood talked about 'a lot of vipers in this industry'. Literally, as it turns out. He said the entire Hollywood industry is run by a powerful paedophile ring protected by the politically powerful 'right at the top' in Washington DC. This precisely matches my own research and he said that it was on the scale of the Jimmy Savile scandal. Wood was immediately attacked

by the mainstream media who cover up to order. Child actor Corey
Feldman said that he and his friends were surrounded by paedophiles
who were 'everywhere, like vultures'. He blamed the death of his best
friend, child actor Corey Haim, through drink and drugs, on his abuse
as a child. Corey Feldman talked of a 'Hollywood mogul' who was head
of a 'circle of older men' who surround themselves with young children.
'I can tell you that the number one problem in Hollywood was, is, and
always will be paedophilia.' The Roman Catholic Church is one of the
biggest paedophile rings on Earth and cross-connects with the others. A
Netflix series, *The Keepers*, exposed a catholic paedophile and murder
ring in Baltimore involving the police, businessmen and politicians and I
have found the same theme and networks wherever I have researched. I
expose *El*-ite paedophiles and their rings at length and in detail in *The
Biggest Secret* and *The Perception Deception*.

## Software Satanism

Paedophilia and Satanism are intrinsically linked through the Archontic
Reptilian connection to secret societies like the Lucifer-worshipping
Sabbatean Frankists. Witnesses have said that Jimmy Savile was a
Satanist and it so often goes with the territory. I have rarely come across
an *El*-ite paedophile that was not connected at least in some way to
Satanism. Edward Heath is but one example and I have been told many
times by insiders that satanic ritual is weaved into the very fabric of life
for Jimmy Savile's mates among British royalty. Satanism is
compartmentalised like the entire Web of human control, and those in
the lower levels will not be aware of what is happening at the peak of
the pyramid. There are also different expressions of what is called the
'occult'. The word simply means hidden and relates to hidden
knowledge about the nature and workings of reality. Knowledge is not
good or bad – it just is. Judgements about good and bad come with how
the knowledge is used. There is therefore what some call the 'Light
Occult' in which they seek to use the knowledge positively for the
benefit of humanity and the 'Dark Occult' in which the very extreme
opposite is the case. I have heard Christians constantly condemning 'the
occult' as evil when if that knowledge about reality were used in the
right way it would set us free. Satanists and Dark Occultists have
enslaved humanity by using hidden knowledge for their own ends and
ensuring that while *they* have the knowledge the population does not.
They have done this by demonising that which they use against us. They
want people to either laugh and dismiss the knowledge or be in fear of
it. What I have laid out in this book is occult information because it has
been *hidden*. Satanic groups that have come to public attention, such as
Anton LaVey's Church of Satan and the Temple of Set in the United
States, are lower down the pyramid. They operate as interface groups

recruiting people psychopathic
enough and with the desired
skills to serve higher up in the
hierarchy. The Temple of Set was
established by Lieutenant
Colonel Michael Aquino, another
Satanic paedophile, from within
the US military's psychological
warfare department. When the
military were questioned about
this they said that a man's
religion is his own business. A
1987 article in the *San Francisco*

**Figure 303:** Windowless headquarters of the Skull
and Bones Society alongside Yale University.

*Examiner* quoted a source accusing Aquino and his wife of involvement
in child rape. The source described their house, the headquarters of the
Temple of Set, in such detail that police were able to justify a search
warrant. They confiscated 38 videotapes, photo negatives, and evidence
that the house was the centre of a paedophile ring connected with US
military bases. Despite all of this Aquino and his wife were never
indicted. The upper-levels of the military is a nest of paedophiles and
Satanists who see war as a satanic ritual blood fest to serve and feed
their demonic masters. Secret societies much higher in the satanic
hierarchy include the inner circles of the Sabbatean Frankist Jesuit Order,
Knights Templar, Knights of Malta, Opus Dei and the Skull and Bones
Society, or Order of Death, located next to Yale University in Connecticut
(Fig 303). Skull and Bones recruits students chosen by the *El*-ite from
bloodline families who go on to be installed in positions of power to
serve the satanic Archontic Reptilian agenda. Father George and Boy
George Bush were both Skull and Bones initiates who went on be US
presidents. Bizarre initiation rites include lying naked in a coffin and
pledging to serve the interests of the Order above all else and that
includes the American public when in political office. American voters
in 2004 were given the choice for president between Boy George Bush
(Skull and Bones) and John Kerry (Skull and Bones) who went on to
become Obama's Secretary of State. I have exposed Skull and Bones and
other significant secret societies in detail in other books including *The
Perception Deception*. All these satanic secret societies are expressions of
the same stream of the Archontic Dark Occult that was practiced in
Babylon, Sumer, Egypt, Rome and by Celtic Druids, as I have spent
decades researching and exposing. Hollywood insider Jon Robberson
tells the same story in relation to Tinsel Town:

> *Much of what is used in Hollywood today that would be considered
> Luciferian in nature really comes from a lot of the Druidic incantations, the*

*Druidic witchcraft, the worship of Gaia, of earth, in ninth and tenth century England. And prior to that, you can trace that through Kabbalistic witchcraft and Jewish mysticism all the way back, really, to what was going on in Babylon.*

He is describing the expansion of the bloodlines and new psyche out of the Middle East and wherever the bloodlines go Satanism, human and animal sacrifice and paedophilia go, too. Major rituals are still performed on the same days and during the same astrological sequences as the ancients. Halloween or Samhain (pronounced Sowin) is a prime one and so is the period between March19th/22nd and May 1st or May Day. March 19th/22nd is when the Sun is said to be 'resurrected' out of the Southern Hemisphere at the start of the northern spring (symbolism connected to the 'resurrection' story of 'Jesus'). The May 1st period is Beltane (*Bel*-tane – Bel/Baal/Bill/BL). Communism celebrates May Day because that is a satanic system of control as is fascism. This March-Beltane period is known in Satanism as the Season of Sacrifice and some sacrifices are performed in the open while being disguised as wars and disasters. The Waco massacre, Oklahoma City bombing, Columbine High School shooting, Virginia Tech Massacre and Boston Marathon bombing are only a few of many examples. They all happened in the period April 16th to 20th and even a 2011 article published by CNN asked the question: 'What is it about mid-April and violence in America?' Society-changing events are orchestrated in sync with particular astrological and numerological sequences which represent particular energetic (information) states which make their impact more powerful, not least on the human psyche. Is it really a coincidence that terrorist attacks in London (Lee Rigby murder), Brussels, Munich, London (Westminster Parliament) and Manchester all happened on the 22nd of the month?

## Satanic *El*-ite

Satanists seek to impose their desires and lack of values onto humans and make the whole world satanic. Their plans are well advanced with, for example, satanic rituals presented under the disguise (to the unknowing masses) of stage performances, videos, music and movies. All are projecting visual and audio frequencies and symbols to seize the minds and perceptions of the audience. Michael Jackson's *Thriller* which explored the satanic realms is an obvious case and culminated with his eyes changing to reptilian (Fig 304). Stage shows and videos by world famous artists such as Katy Perry, Lady Gaga, Miley Cyrus, Madonna and Beyonce also feature blatant satanic and secret society themes and ritualism. I am not accusing any of these people personally of anything, but pointing out the symbolism in their performances which is

**Figure 304:** Reptilian eyes in *Thriller*.

undeniable. Royalty and politics are incredibly ritualistic with their satanic foundations hidden behind the cover of 'pomp and ceremony'. Life for the British royals is one continuous ritual. Wars and covertly-orchestrated terrorist attacks like 9/11 are really satanic rituals and blood fests. You see satanic codes everywhere, with some satanic groups referring to their 'coven' as a grotto as in 'Santa's grotto' – Santa being an anagram of Satan who fronts up the modern version of the Roman Saturnalia. I have heard the claim that twelve percent of the population are Satanists and a former head of the FBI station in Los Angeles who I met a few times reckoned that if you have a reasonably wide circle of friends and acquaintances you will know a practicing Satanist. David Berkowitz, the Son of Sam serial killer in New York in the 1970s, admitted to the murders but later said they were orchestrated by a satanic cult. He said in a letter to a church minister:

*Satanists (genuine ones) are peculiar people. They aren't ignorant peasants or semiliterate natives. Rather, their ranks are filled with doctors, lawyers, businessmen, and basically highly responsible citizens ... They are not a careless group who are apt to make mistakes. But they are secretive and bonded together by a common need and desire to mete out havoc on society. It was Aleister Crowley who said: I want blasphemy, murder, rape, revolution, anything bad.*

At all levels of Satanism you have the pillars of society, politicians galore from all political 'sides', judges, lawyers, bankers, military personnel, police, media owners, journalists, radio and television hosts, actors, actresses and entertainers, doctors, teachers, college academics and social workers. They have infiltrated all the institutions of perceptual influence and 'physical' control, and work together in common cause for the total enslavement of humanity while their non-Satanist colleagues have no idea what is really going on and why. Governments and their agencies serve the interests of the corporate and banking world because key players are members of the same Archontic Reptilian global death cult. Italian fascist Benito Mussolini defined fascism as the fusion of government and corporate power and on that basis alone Satanism is fascism. But, in truth, it's even worse. I saw an interview with one dark occultist who said they want to make 'Nazism

**Figure 305:** A Neil Hague image of the interdimensional sacrificial rituals performed by inner-circle Satanists.
© www.neilhague.com

and fascism look like kindergarten'. Nice people. They are united by their desire for control and their obsession with materialistic me, me, me, while themselves under the control of their unseen Archontic Reptilian masters. Their unity and focus is their power while they seek in every way to divide and divert the target population. They promote a belief that there is no ultimate truth, only what you choose it to be, and they were the force behind Darwinism which deleted Spirit and eternity from the perception of life leaving only survival of the fittest in a dead and mechanistic Universe. I am sure that the sudden support for the fact that we live in a simulation comes in many cases from a desire to delete any perception of a greater self. 'You are just a computer program so Do What Thou Wilt.' What they leave out is that we are Infinite Awareness caught in a simulation and we are not the simulation. Anything that can divert humanity from self-identifying with Infinite Awareness is to be desired and promoted by these people. This is almost the entire basis of mainstream science for the same reason. The point is that there *is* an ultimate truth – we are all expressions of Infinite Awareness manifesting our reality through perception. For centuries human sacrifice was done openly and when that became unacceptable to the masses it continued, to this day, in secret. We have all heard the ancient global theme of human sacrifice in which 'young virgins' were sacrificed to the gods.

**Figure 306:** All roads lead to ...

These 'gods' are Archons, Reptilians, Greys and demonic entities in their many forms. 'Young virgins' is simply code for children. Rituals allow the energetic terror emitted from the sacrifice to be absorbed by Archontic manifestations in their band of frequency. This is what the term 'sacrifice to the gods' really means. The Old Testament 'god' demanded sacrifice and Zulu historian and shaman Credo Mutwa told me that legends describe how human sacrifice and cannibalism – a canni-*baal*-lism – only began with the reptilian Chitauri who demanded that this be done. Bloodline and Archon-possessed Satanists drink the blood of the sacrifice which gives them energetic sustenance and also a chemical high from adrenalin that enters the bloodstream in perfuse quantities during the sacrifice. Rituals are performed in the seen and unseen that energetically synchronise and I have been told many times by those who have taken part how in the most powerful ones an energetic vortex or 'gateway' can be created that allows entities in the unseen to slip through into our reality albeit it briefly (Fig 305). Satanists are mostly terrified of them. Blood lust and its energetic effect can also trigger the reptilian-human hybrid 'software' to shapeshift between holographic forms and this has been described to me by participants many times.

You can see why the *El*-ite and their hidden controllers have worked so hard to suppress the true nature of reality. Without that knowledge the target population has had no chance of understanding what is happening all around them and why things are as they are. The major point to remember from this chapter is that despite all the different names, labels and aspects of human society all pyramid hierarchies lead to one uniting and controlling force (Fig 306). With that realisation the illusion of separateness and randomness can be unravelled.

# CHAPTER SEVEN

# Mind Control and Shapeshifting 'Royals'

*'You are one of the rare people who can separate your observation from your preconception. You see what is, where most people see what they expect' –*
**John Steinbeck**

Another vitally important field of suppressed knowledge is that of mind control and its potential to turn a human being into little more than a computer program following the encoded instructions of the programmer. This is another form of possession. *El*-ite networks are mind control networks both in terms of their individual assets and the population in general.

I met a woman in the United States in the 1990s whose information about *El*-ite Satanism and the Reptilian connection has stood the test of the years, and there has been so much confirmation from other sources. Her real name was Jennifer Greene, but by then she chose to be called Arizona Wilder and dye her blonde hair in an effort to resist the mind-programming she endured as blonde-haired, blue-eyed Jennifer. Blonde-haired, blue-eyed people are the Hidden Hand's preferred genetic type in some mind control programs. This relates again to their particular energetic information fields and at least in part to the Nordic ET race which opposes Reptilian control and is genetically connected to blond-haired, blue-eyed and other white races. What Arizona told me about her gut-wrenching mind control experience mirrored the accounts I heard about so many others around the world during my years of intensive research into the subject on both sides of the Atlantic. A glimpse (and only a glimpse) into the background to government-funded mind control networks came in the 1970s with the revelations about the CIA mind control programme known as MKUltra. President Gerald Ford – who worked with MKUltra – appointed Vice-President Nelson Rockefeller to head an 'inquiry' to ensure that the real truth was kept under wraps (see paedophile 'inquiries'). MKUltra's cover-story when they could no longer deny the evidence was that mind control experiments were aimed at developing drugs and ways to secure confessions during interrogation and torture. The real motivation was to advance the potential of creating undetectable mind-controlled slaves for the following reasons: To produce mind control assets, including children, who would not remember their abuse or famous abusers; to create assassins that could be explained away as 'lone nuts'; and to program targets to carry out terrorist attacks that could be blamed on a target group or country. There were many other reasons, too. I say 'were' – but all this continues today under other names. Movies featuring mind-controlled assassins and government assets like *The Mandurian Candidate* are based on fact. An offshoot of MKUltra was called Project Monarch and named after the monarch butterfly. Monarch involves the creation of mind-controlled sex slaves for the rich and famous, including American presidents, and these slaves include some of the biggest names in music and entertainment. See *The Biggest Secret* for the background to Monarch. Mind-controlled artists in Hollywood and the entertainment industry are often pictured with a butterfly. You also see endless images of artists either covering or emphasizing one eye and this is often to indicate control by Project Monarch and/or the *El*-lite cult of the all-seeing eye (Fig 307). For more on this put 'celebrity illuminati signs' into text and image search engines. These are artists most promoted by *El*-ite-controlled Hollywood and the music industry and given most promotion by the media. Their songs and occult-inspired stage shows are often designed to target and sexualize young girls. I don't condemn them personally because they are under mind control programming and will have suffered abuse themselves as part of that. They know not what they do – well, most of them anyway.

**Figure 307:** The number of times you see celebrities covering one eye in publicity shots is ridiculously high ... unless.

MKUltra was run by the CIA's Scientific Intelligence Division and the US Army Chemical Corps Special Operations Division. Even from what was allowed to come out the scale was massive. The programme involved at least 80 institutions in the United States and Canada with

colleges, universities, hospitals, prisons
and the pharmaceutical cabal all making
their contribution to a secret mind control
programme that wiped or manipulated
the minds of its targets and destroyed
their lives. This is the Web in action
again. One adult 'subject' had her
memories so deleted that she had to be
taught again how to go to the toilet. CIA
Director Stansfield Turner testified in
1977 that MKUltra was created to explore
'the use of biological and chemical
materials in altering human behaviour'.
But that was only part of what happened.
'MK' stands for mind control, but they
used the German spelling in deference to

**Figure 308:** Angel of Death Josef
Mengele.

the Nazis who ran the operation and they included Josef Mengele, the
'Angel of Death' in the concentration camps who performed mind
control and genetic experiments on children in Nazi Germany using
twins as a 'control group' to monitor the effect his 'work' was having
(Fig 308). Arizona Wilder said that Mengele was one of her mind
controllers as a child in the United States. He was among 1,600 German
mind controllers, geneticists, scientists, engineers and technicians taken
secretly to the United States after the war under a US
Intelligence/Vatican network operation called Project Paperclip to
continue their crimes against humanity and develop advanced
technology. Many of these people were members of the Nazi Party.
Mengele and Adolf Hitler (who didn't die at the end of the war) were
also relocated to Argentina in South America. There are no borders with
the Hidden Hand which is why the Rockefeller family funded a whole
floor of a German university for Hitler's race purity 'expert' Ernst Rudin
to pursue his eugenics programmes. The Rockefeller family were and
are a major force behind the eugenics movement (see ... *And The Truth
Shall Set You Free*). Project Paperclip personnel who were helped to
escape from Germany created NASA (NAZI). Rocket scientist Werner
von Braun, a member of the Nazi Party, was among them. During the
war he was the brains behind the deadly V-2 rockets that targeted
Britain, and when Project Paperclip whisked him away to America he
went on to design the Saturn V booster rockets for the Apollo Moon
programme. The Hidden Hand via the Web covertly created both world
wars by controlling all sides (see again ... *And The Truth Shall Set You
Free*) and transformed global society in the process. Arizona Wilder told
me about her experiences with Mengele who operated under the name
Dr Green in the United States during MKUltra when he wasn't down in

South America with Hitler (see *Children of the Matrix*). One of Mengele's MKUltra locations was the China Lake Naval Weapons Station in California which I described earlier. Naval Intelligence whistleblower William Tompkins said in 2015 that Reptilians worked with the Nazis in Germany and that makes even more sense of what insiders told me in the 1990s about seeing leading Nazis including Adolf Hitler and Josef Mengele at China Lake, while others described their experiences with Reptilians in that same underground facility. There have long been claims of a Reptilian base under Antarctica where many Nazis headed in the last months of the war.

MKUltra was founded on what is called trauma-based mind control and ideally they want to start with children before the age of around six, while brain pathways are still forming, although it can still be started later. They inflict unspeakable horrors on these children – truly unspeakable – and this causes them to 'dissociate' or block out memories of what they experienced. Imagine little children being forced to watch other children and animals they have grown to love sacrificed with a knife across the throat while knowing they could be next. Imagine being made to eat the sacrifice or a foetus, and being terrified of spiders or snakes while left in a dark pit with them for hours on end. I have been told all these stories and worse many times around the world. Beheadings that children have been forced to witness and perform by Western-funded ISIS terror groups are all part of this same process of desensitising children and manipulating their sense of reality. ISIS or Islamic State is a branch of militarised Satanism and the military itself worldwide is the same. Wars are mass satanic rituals to these sick people. Self-contained compartments are created by the traumatised mind behind which horrendous memories are hidden and these are known in the mind control industry as 'alters' as in altered states. The effect is called dissociative identity disorder or formerly multiple personality disorder and this is the same mental process that causes people to have no memory of the impact in a serious road accident. Each self-contained compartment is then hijacked by the mind manipulators to be programmed for different tasks – sex slaves, assassins, terrorists, even computer-like couriers of information between agents of the Web in a process they call 'mind files'. They are given what is termed a 'front alter' which is the personality that normally interacts with the world and people think is 'them' (and they *themselves* think is 'them'). But so-called 'back alters' in the subconscious are primed to open with particular codes to instantly replace the front alter. These codes are called in mind control parlance 'triggers'. They might be a word, phrase, sound, anything they choose to encode and when the trigger is delivered the programmed back alter becomes the front alter and carries out its programmed behaviour (Fig 309). Children and young women are

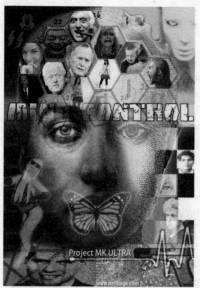

Project MK ULTRA

www.neilhague.com

**Figure 309:** Compartmentalised 'alters' in mind control programming with the butterfly symbolism of Project Monarch.
© www.neilhague.com

sexually and violently abused in back alter awareness by some of the most famous people on Earth and then the front alter is returned which knows nothing of what has happened. I sat with a therapist in London one day as she opened and closed alters of a client using codes she had taken many months to elicit using various psychological techniques. I was amazed to see different personalities instantly appear with each code. They were different ages, voices, even (shapeshifted) faces, and included one alter that was truly evil although the person's front alter was kind and gentle. These evil alters are programmed and triggered in people like Arizona Wilder to conduct satanic rituals for them, but then not remember, unless the compartments break down later as they did with her. The problem the manipulators have is that by the age of 30 to 40 the mind can become strong enough to start dismantling the 'firewalls' and when that happens photographic memories are released into conscious awareness. They are photographic because of the effect that severe trauma has in focusing the mind. Most high-level mind-controlled assets who potentially know far too much are killed after 30 to avoid such exposure while others who survive tell of experiences so extraordinary that few will believe them. I spent years studying this and talking to survivors in North America, Europe, Australia and elsewhere who had recovered memories. It is heartbreaking to hear their stories of what happened to them even as young children and to know that this is globally widespread to this day. Their common themes and experiences and the rich and famous people they name are absolutely compelling and consistent. Many actors and actresses in Hollywood, singers and other entertainers are under trauma-based mind control to serve the mass perception-programming agenda that I will describe, and you see the programming break down sometimes when they go out of control and do crazy things. One reaction can be a desperation to change the way they look – to change the way they are – and this is what happened with Arizona Wilder. Dyeing or cutting off their hair is one method that they use. Technology is taking over mind control programmes today, which allows them to go direct to the brain's information processing systems through the medium of electricity, electromagnetism, frequency and microchips.

## Servants of Satan

Mind control of individuals, the general population and even assets of the Web is aimed at ensuring there are no surprises, maverick behaviour or situations and responses the *El*-lite can't predict. They are not interested in controlling one side in the symbolic soccer game. They want to control both sides and the referee so they know the outcome before the game has even started. Presidents and many leading politicians are subjected to mind control for this reason. Mind control is the *El*-ite's insurance. Put the words 'Bill Clinton, mind control and treason' into YouTube and you will clearly see his programming. I strongly recommend the book *Trance-Formation of America* which details the shocking and appalling experiences of blonde-haired, blue-eyed American

**Figure 310:** Cathy O'Brien tells of her extraordinary experiences in *Trance-Formation of America*.

Cathy O'Brien in Project Monarch (Fig 310). Cathy, who I have met many times and still keep in touch with, was subjected to mind control almost from birth by her satanic family overseen by then Michigan Congressman Gerald Ford who would instigate an 'inquiry' (cover-up) when he became US President into the very mind control programmes of which he was a part. The Jesuit Order was also heavily involved in Cathy's programming because at its inner core this is a satanic operation working for the Web through the Roman Catholic Church. Her abusers included father George Bush, Dick Cheney, Ronald Reagan and Bill and Hillary Clinton. Arizona Wilder who I met separately and years after Cathy was also attached to Project Monarch. They both describe Reptilian alien experiences during their mind control captivity. Cathy explains hers in terms of an illusion that was part of her programming, but Arizona describes reptilian shapeshifters in very literal terms. Cathy writes in *Trance-Formation of America* about an experience with father George Bush in an office in Washington DC during the Reagan-Bush administration when he opened a book depicting what he called 'lizard-like aliens from a far-off deep space place'. She said that Bush claimed to be one of them and then appeared to transform 'like a chameleon' into a reptile. Cathy describes how Bill and Bob Bennett, two well-known political figures in the same period, gave her mind-altering drugs at NASA's Goddard Space Flight Center mind control laboratory. She said they told her they were 'alien to this dimension – two beings from another plane'. Cathy recalled what happened next:

*The high-tech light display around me convinced me I was transforming dimensions with them. A laser of light hit the black wall in front of me, which seemed to explode into a panoramic view of a White House cocktail party – as though I had transformed dimensions and stood amongst them. Not recognising anyone, I frantically asked: 'Who are these people?'*

*'They're not people and this isn't a spaceship', [Bill] Bennett said. As he spoke, the holographic scene changed ever so slightly until the people appeared to be lizard-like aliens. 'Welcome to the second level of the underground. This is a mere mirror reflection of the first, an alien dimension. We are from a trans-dimensional plane that spans and encompasses all dimensions ... I have taken you through my dimension as a means of establishing stronger holds on your mind than the Earth plane permits', Bill Bennett was saying. 'Being alien, I simply make my thoughts your thoughts by projecting them into your mind. My thoughts are your thoughts ...'*

Cathy O'Brien believes this experience to be mind control manipulation, but Arizona Wilder does not. Type the words 'Confessions of a Mother Goddess' into the search facility at Davidicke.com and you can see an interview that I did with Arizona in 1999. 'Mother Goddess' refers to the title she had in the satanic ritual hierarchy when her satanic alter was triggered. She told me about conducting rituals for the American *El*-ite and the British royal family at places like Balmoral Castle in Scotland with its Sigil of Saturn logo and she described the true nature of the royals away from the public eye. The Queen Mother, who died in 2002 aged nearly 102, was still alive when I spoke with Arizona. She told me:

*The Queen Mother was cold, cold, cold, a nasty person. None of her cohorts even trusted her. They have named an alter after her. They call it the Black Queen. I have seen her sacrifice people. I remember her pushing a knife into someone's rectum the night that two boys were sacrificed. One was 13 and the other 18. You need to forget that the Queen Mother appears to be a frail old woman. When she shapeshifts into a reptilian, she becomes very tall and strong. Some of them are so strong they can rip out a heart and they all grow by several feet when they shapeshift* [this is a common theme when shapeshifting is described].

Arizona said of the Queen:

*I have seen her sacrifice people and eat their flesh and drink their blood. One time she got so excited with blood-lust that she didn't cut the victim's throat from left to right in the normal ritual, she just went crazy, stabbing and ripping at the flesh after she had shapeshifted into a reptilian. When she shapeshifts, she has a long reptile face, almost like a beak and she's an off-white colour. The Queen Mother looks basically the same, but there are differences. She [the Queen] also has like bumps on her head and her eyes are very frightening. She's very aggressive ...*

*... I have seen [Prince Charles] shape-shift into a reptilian and do all the things the Queen does. I have seen him sacrifice children. There is a lot of rivalry between them for who gets to eat what part of the body and who gets to absorb the victim's last breath and steal their soul. I have also seen Andrew participate and I have seen Prince Philip and Charles' sister [Anne] at the rituals, but they didn't participate when I was there.*

*When Andrew shapeshifts, he looks more like one of the lizards. The royals are some of the worst, okay, as far as enjoying the killing, enjoying the sacrifice, and eating the flesh, they're some of the worst of all of them. They don't care if you see it. Who are you going to tell? Who is going to believe you? They feel that is their birthright and they love it. They love it.*

One of the most notorious Satanists and mass human sacrificers was Vlad the Impaler, who was the character on which Bram Stoker based his stories of Dracula. He was the 15th century aristocratic ruler of Wallachia. This is now part of Romania which is the global centre for vampire legends, especially the region of Transylvania. I have said that satanic software bloodlines interbreed to maintain their information and personality programs and these pass through 'history' as undiluted as possible by other genetics. This allows them to be tracked through the generations. I was therefore not in the least surprised to find that Vlad the Impaler is an ancestor of both the British royals and the Bush family. Prince Charles has publicly acknowledged this connection and often visits Transylvania where he has property and business interests (Fig 311). Vlad's father, Vlad Dracul, was an initiate of the ancient Order of the Dragon which is one of the close-to-the-Spider secret societies that can be traced back to Egypt at the time of the Pharaohs. Its emblem is a winged dragon hanging on a cross. Remember the 'royal' winged 'Draco' who created the hybrid 'royal' bloodlines through which they can directly manipulate our reality. The

**Figure 311:** Prince Charles and his British royal family ancestor, the mass human-sacrificing Vlad the Impaler.

**Figure 312:** Vlad the Impaler's logo.

**Figure 313:** Vlad the Impaler who was obsessed with suffering, death and blood.

**Figure 314:** 'Royal' family of Transylvania.

most powerful royals, aristocrats and bloodline dark suits are Draconians incarnate. Vlad the Impaler's logo was a snake swallowing its own tail – the Ouroboros or Leviathan highlighted by Gnostic manuscripts and the Jewish religion (Fig 312). The title 'Impaler' comes from his love of impaling thousands of people on spears and stakes and watching them slowly die while drinking their blood, which takes psychopathy to a whole new level (Fig 313). Vlad would sign his name Draculea or Draculya which means the 'Devil's Son' or 'Son of He who had the Order of the Dragon'. The Vlad family connection to the British royals comes through the Queen's grandmother, Mary of Teck (Fig 314). From 1996 to about 2002 the synchronicity of my life led me to a stream of people who told me of their experiences with Reptilians and/or reptilian hybrid bloodline shapeshifters – 'No need for arduous seeking, you just have to follow the clues'. The royal family was mentioned often during my research into Satanism and paedophilia in Britain, the United States and Canada. A year before I met Arizona Wilder in California I was introduced to Christine Fitzgerald, a close friend and confidant of Princess Diana for nine years. They had ceased contact before Diana was murdered by the British Establishment in 1997 (see *The Biggest Secret*). Christine was an alternative healer who understood the energetic background to illusory reality. She told me how 'friendly people' from MI5 would leave messages for Diana at her healing centre near Regent's Park in London warning that her life was in danger. Christine knew nothing of the people telling me of their reptilian experiences because I had not yet made that public. I met her only to hear about the relationship between Diana and the royals with nothing reptilian ever mentioned. But she told me without any prompting that Diana called the Windsors 'the reptiles' and 'the lizards' and said: 'They're not human.' Diana had also said that the Queen Mother was evil. I played dumb and asked what she meant by reptiles and lizards and she said that the royal family were a reptilian bloodline and not a human one. This is what Arizona Wilder would later say thousands of miles away in the United States along with many others. Christine Fitzgerald told me:

> The Queen Mother ... now that's a serious piece of wizardry. The Queen Mother is a lot older than people think. To be honest, the Royal Family hasn't died for a long time, they have just metamorphosised. It's sort of cloning, but in a different way. They take pieces of flesh and rebuild the body from one little bit. Because it's lizard, because it's cold-blooded, it's much easier to do this Frankenstein shit than it is for us. The different bodies are just different electrical vibrations and they have got that secret, they've got the secret of the micro-currents, it's so micro, so specific, these radio waves that actually create the bodies. These are the energies I work with when I'm healing.

She was talking, of course, about the way the body is a projection of waveform information.

> They know the vibration of life and because they're cold-blooded, they are reptiles, they have no wish to make the Earth the perfect harmony it could be, or to heal the Earth from the damage that's been done. The Earth's been attacked for zeons by different extraterrestrials. It's been like a football for so long. This place is a bus stop for many different aliens. All these aliens, they could cope with anything, including the noxious gases. They're landing all the time and coming up from the bowels of the Earth. They looked like reptiles originally, but they look like us when they get out now through the electrical vibration, that key to life I talked about. They can manifest how they want to. All the real knowledge has been taken out and shredded and put back in another way. The Queen Mother is 'Chief Toad' of this part of Europe and they have people like her in every continent. Most people, the hangers on, don't know, you know, about the reptiles. They are just in awe of these people because they are so powerful.

This is what is really going on and how the world is really controlled (Fig 315). A great advantage the El-ite have in hiding the truth is that

**Figure 315:** What are Britain, Canada, Australia and the Commonwealth doing still having a head of state chosen purely by bloodline while calling themselves 'free' countries?

what is happening and what is *perceived* to be happening are so fantastically different. When people like me expose the truth we get ridiculed and dismissed by an incredulous media and public but, in terms of the public, things are changing now. Christine Fitzgerald also told me in the late 1990s that Jimmy Savile was a paedophile (how right she turned out to be), that he was very close to the royal family and that Diana loathed him. Unfortunately she would not repeat that publicly and it would have been her word against his anyway and I had to wait until he died in 2011 before posting this information, although I told people verbally whenever I could. A year later the Saville story exploded into public awareness in a television documentary. Savile was a friend and procurer of children for former Prime Minister Edward Heath who sacrificed and murdered untold numbers of kids and was another Reptilian satanic shapeshifter. Heath was named to me by another woman I met before I had mentioned my Reptilian research to anyone publicly. I saw her to discuss her experience with her former husband who she said was a Satanist and one-time warden at Burnham Beeches, an area of woodland and clearings just west of London owned by the Archontic Reptilian-controlled financial district or 'Square Mile' known as the City of London. This refers to a small area in what was the original London today called 'The City' and not the whole urban sprawl

**Figure 316:** The flying reptile crest of the City of London financial district which is a nest of secret societies and satanic groups.

**Figure 317:** Flying reptile where the City of London meets The Temple district named after a nearby Knights Templar church.

of the UK capital. All over 'The City' you see its reptile crest or logo and there is another flying reptile statue at the point where the City of London meets the Archontic Reptilian-controlled centre of the legal profession known as the Temple district (Figs 316 and 317). The name Temple comes from the original Knights Templar church built in the late 12th century as their London headquarters, which still stands amidst the legal buildings and was featured in the 2006 movie *The Da Vinci Code*. The Knights Templar secret society once owned this land and still controls the Temple law networks and the financial district. The fact that 'The City' owns Burnham Beeches will have nothing to do with its pretty forests and flowers, that's for sure. I chatted with the lady about her experiences there, which included sneaking through the woods one night to find a ritual going on in a clearing conducted by then Prime Minister Edward Heath and she said that alongside him was his Chancellor of the Exchequer Anthony Barber. They were standing in a circle of other people all were wearing robes. We completed our conversation and as I turned to leave I said that I was hearing of strange experiences, from people on both sides of the Atlantic, about seeing humans turn into reptiles. I heard her gasp a breath and I turned to see her clutching her chest. She said she had not told me about her experience of seeing Heath shapeshift because she thought that would sound crazy even to me. The woman said that during the ritual Heath shifted into a reptilian entity. 'He eventually became a full-bodied Reptiloid, growing in size by some two foot', she said. This increase in size is a very common feature of shapeshifting experiences and relates to the switch from one energetic information source to another which has different information codes. She said that Heath was 'slightly scaly' and 'spoke fairly naturally, although it sounded like long distance – if you can imagine the short time lapses' (as with the old transatlantic telephone calls). I have been told such stories so many times while people and the media think I must just be making it up or something. No – this shit is *real*.

Notice how long many of these people live, too, with the examples of the Queen Mother, the Queen, Prince Philip, David Rockefeller, Henry Kissinger, Edward Heath and so on. Ageing is encoded in the waveform/biological program of the standing wave information field. They have different genetics (different waveform program) and they don't get the same treatment that the general population does. Blood from young people has been believed since ancient times to slow the ageing process (it's a waveform interaction). Modern studies have supported this including one by a San Francisco company, Ambrosia, which was the name of the food and drink of the Greek gods that was believed to confer immortality. Ambrosia's research found that transfusions of blood from young adults reduced the risk of cancer,

dementia and heart disease in older people and the *El*-ite consume
copious quantities of blood from children. US Naval intelligence
whistleblower William Tompkins and many insiders and abductees I
have met all said that extraterrestrials can live for thousands of our
years. This makes them the common thread of manipulation while
humans are coming in and out of this reality never understanding what
is really happening because they are not here long enough. Many will
reel back in reflex-dismissal at the idea that anyone could live for say
3,000 years. But, hold on. The 'body' is a hologram. Why should a
hologram age? Why should the energetic information field from which it
is decoded age? There is no reason whatsoever why it should go through
the cycle of birth-ageing-death as it does. It is *programmed* to do so and
expanded awareness can intervene in that program. Major players in the
Archontic Reptilian conspiracy live long lives partly because of their
hybrid genetics and partly because of longevity processes given to them
by their Reptilian masters. As long as the standing wave oscillation is
intact you cannot die. What we call death is when it stops.

## The Rothschild connection

I was in a long correspondence some years ago with an American who
said that he was Phillip Eugene de Rothschild and one of *hundreds of
thousands* of 'both legitimate and illegitimate offspring of this powerful
financial and occult family'. No, this doesn't mean the Rothschilds have
had sex hundreds of thousands of times. Their offspring are produced
through secret sperm banks and the children are brought up under
different names while all being offshoots of Rothschild genetics
(information software). Other major bloodline families do the same and
their hidden children later become leading lights in politics, business,
banking, media, religion, science, medicine, academia and so on while
having no apparent connection to the Rothschilds, Rockefellers or
whoever. Often the children don't even know themselves who they are
and think their rise to the top is by chance, ability and good luck
although the most significant of them will be told eventually. Hybrid
genetics ensures powerful Archontic Reptilian possession because of
their frequency compatibility with their hidden masters. They are
introduced to secret society and satanic rituals designed to lock them in
to the Reptilian frequency and they are then little more than biological
vehicles for other-reality entities. Phillip Eugene de Rothschild was
living under another name when we communicated after rejecting his
role as a Rothschild manipulator within the Christian Church. He said
that his father was Baron Philippe de Rothschild of the Mouton-
Rothschild wine producing estates in France and that he had been
conceived through 'occult incest'. The Baron (hierarchy-obsessed
Draconians love their titles) died at the age of 86 in 1988 (Fig 318). 'My

**Figure 318:** Baron Philippe de Rothschild.

**Figure 319:** Baroness Philippine de Rothschild loves her Baphomet (Saturn) broaches.

father was a decadent dilettante as well as a master Satanist and hater of God', Phillip Eugene told me, 'but how he loved the fields and the wines. He used to say it brought out "the primitive" in him.' Those wine estates are now owned by Baron Philippe's daughter, Baroness Philippine, who has a liking for Baphomet (Saturn) broaches (Fig 319). Phillip Eugene says that she is his half-sister and that he lived on the estate for most of his childhood and adolescence. 'I was held fast in the emotional power of incest which ... [in their culture] ... was normal and to be admired.' I have heard the same so many times with regard to *El*-ite families. Incest is simply part of life and childhood which imposes potentially life-long psychological control over the offspring. Phillip Eugene said the bloodlines are vehicles for demonic entities and that 'being a Rothschild descendant I was maximally demonised.' He told me:

*I was present at my father's death in 1988, receiving his power and the commission to carry out my destiny in the grand conspiracy of my family. Like their other children, I played a key role in my family's revolt from God. When I watch CNN, it startles me to see so many familiar faces now on the world stage in politics, art, finance, fashion, and business. I grew up with these people meeting them at ritual worship sites and in the centers of power. Financiers, artists, royalty, and even Presidents, all these dissociated people work and conspire today to bring in a new world order ... These people, like me, are SRA/DID* [satanically ritually abused and dissociative identity disorder mind control].

*The last non-dissociative President of the United States was Dwight Eisenhower; except for him, every one since Teddy Roosevelt has had some level of dissociative disorder and some level of involvement in the occult. President Clinton has 'full blown' multiple personality disorder* [he's mind controlled] *and is an active sorcerer in the satanic mystery religions. This is true of Al Gore, as well; I have known Misters Clinton and Gore from our childhood as active and effective Satanists.*

What sense this makes of psychopathic leaders bombing civilians with no emotional consequence and Gore stepping forward as the front-man and sales-pitcher for the human-caused global warming hoax. Phillip Eugene then explained how the bloodlines are expanded and the role that he was given in the Rothschild conspiracy in the control of Christianity:

*Like the hundreds of thousands of this* [Rothschild] *occult family's other biological children, I had my place and function within this clan's attempt to control the world. My efforts and my family's efforts strove to have a member of the European nobility of the Habsburg family assume the pre-eminent position over humanity, a position called the Antichrist by Christianity. While others were seeded into government, academia, business, or entertainment, my place was within the Body of Christ* [Christianity]. *I was to be a focus for spiritual power and controller of a cult within this Church. In this Church have lived people who I have known all my life to be the controllers and power centers of both the Rothschild family's false prophet and the antichrist.*

*Many dissociated Christians in the Body of Christ hold similar corporate spiritual, occult positions as part of the Satanic New World Order. In my being I embodied the Luciferian morning star within the Church. I represented the presence of all the other Satanists who were related to me in the morning star; their spirits were present in me in the Church. Constructed through ritual but empowered by legions of spirits, I was a human and spiritual focus of corporate satanic energy into the 'Body of Christ'.*

Everything is about energy, frequency and how the world of the seen is controlled from the unseen. The *El*-ite that you see are merely vehicles for the Archontic Reptilian *El*-ite that you don't see and the hierarchy of the unseen becomes the hierarchy of the seen. Satanic power in the human world is all about the power of the possessing entities. Rituals are designed to energetically connect initiates to the satanic frequency – the Demiurge self-aware distortion and its expression through Reptilians, Greys and others. This is the origin of 'selling your soul to

Satan' or entering what they call 'marriage' with Satan – possession. As one satanically abused witness said on Australian television: 'The lower you become ... the more vile you become ... the more pleased Satan is with you.' In other words, you *become* the distortion. This is straight from the belief-system of Sabbatean Frankism in which depravity is a form of worship. By the way, given the Rothschild control of Christianity what are the chances of any Pope being independent of them? The last one who tried to be was Pope John Paul I and he was murdered in 1978 while attempting to purge the Vatican of Freemasonic agents. He died after the very Freemasonically-significant 33 days in office. The *El*-ite love their numbers as much as their titles. Phillip Eugene de Rothschild confirmed that the ruling bloodlines are hybrids bred 'with what you call the Reptilians' and also the importance of the British Royal family in the satanic hierarchy. He mentioned Prince Philip in particular. Phillip Eugene attended many satanic rituals where the rich and famous would assemble to worship their unseen masters and possessors. He told me:

> *I can recall the Rockefellers and the Bushes attending rituals, but never having the supremacy to lead them. I still regard them as lackeys and not real brokers of occult power. Except for Alan Greenspan* [long-time head of the US Federal Reserve Bank], *most of these fellows were camp followers in the occult, primarily for the economic power and prestige.*
>
> *Greenspan, I recall, was a person of tremendous spiritual, occult power and could make the Bushes and the younger Rockefellers cower with just a glance. Ex-CIA Director Casey (as were most of the CIA leadership for the past forty years),* [Henry] *Kissinger, and Warren Christopher* [former US Secretary of State] *were in attendance at non-ritual gatherings and some occult rituals as well, but well back in the gallery.*

Zionist Alan Greenspan was head of the Federal Reserve from 1987 to 2006 under presidents Ronald Reagan, Father Bush, Bill Clinton and Boy George Bush (Fig 320). They didn't choose him – they were told by their masters to appoint him. Satanic hierarchy trumps political hierarchy every time. When Greenspan retired from the Fed he was given an honorary position at the British Treasury or *Her Majesty's* Treasury to be more accurate. I publish a document in full in *Human Race Get off Your Knees* that is claimed to have been written by an Australian Satanist in his dying days and I expose Satanism at length in that book. I

**Figure 320:** Alan Greenspan.

can't say for certain that the document is genuine, but I can confirm without question that whoever was responsible had a deep knowledge of Satanism and how it infests the ruling royal, financial and political classes. This was not so much a deathbed confession as an arrogant description of how Satanists run the world. The writer said he was from the 'Alpha Lodge' of Satanism in Sydney and claims that the influence of Satanism is 'now so pervasive as not to be readily noticed':

*Amongst the highest echelons, some are politicians, medical doctors, high ranking police officers, lawyers, advertising gurus, decorated military men, media personalities, fashion models and social workers. Amongst the lowest (usually temporary) ranks are prostitutes, minor drug dealers and a number of High School students. Some operate from the mists.*

*Their victims are drip-fed straight amnesia by an assortment of mind control measures and psychological torture tactics that would leave any normal person numb with the dawning apprehension that things are not as they seem – and they have not been for a long, long time. The most talented amongst them have lifestyles maintained on crime, but lacquered with a thin veneer of respectable professionalism and knowledge.*

Mention of social workers may surprise people, but they are the means through which children – often stolen to order – are taken by Cult-connected social workers from children's homes and loving parents in secret 'family' courts using made-up evidence. This is now done on an industrial scale in Britain, the United States and worldwide. I mentioned with regard to the 'Island Mafia' on the Isle of Wight where I live that they control social services and this happens almost everywhere with non-satanic social workers mostly kept in the dark about what is happening around them. Secret family courts which can't be reported allow children to be stolen by the Cult to order and then a spurious excuse is made up to take them from their parents. Changes introduced by Tony Blair (of course) massively increased the number of children kidnapped by the state in the UK. Children stolen in this way by the Cult are then adopted by Cult-connected 'foster parents' and used for Satanism and paedophilia. A Florida couple who fostered and adopted children in Alabama were charged with hundreds of counts of first-degree sexual abuse, child abuse, first-degree rape, first-degree sodomy, sexual torture, violence by strangulation or suffocation, enticing a child for immoral purposes, incest, first-degree human trafficking and endangering welfare of children. I am not saying all children taken from parents go on to be abused, of course not, but large numbers are. The 'Alpha Lodge Satanist' describes how politicians are ensnared into Satanism and paedophilia and then blackmailed to support policies and laws demanded by the Cult:

> *Politicians are introduced by a carefully graded set of criteria and situations that enable them to accept that their victims will be, 'Our little secret'. Young children sexually molested and physically abused by politicians worldwide are quickly used as sacrifices. In Australia the bodies are hardly ever discovered, for Australia is still a wilderness.*

> *Overseas, cremation is the favoured method and although the Satanic Alpha Lodges of Australia have access to crematoria when needed, this is surprisingly rare. Believe it or not many bodies are 'dumped over the side' every week in a number of isolated bush land settings.*

Private crematoria are the preferred method of disposing of sacrifices in more densely populated countries. The alleged Satanist also makes the point that rituals are constantly repeated at the same locations on the Earth's ley line/vortex energy grid because of the effect in lowering the frequency of the electromagnetic 'sea' or Cosmic Internet with which we are interacting. This, in turn, lowers the frequency of the human energy field for those who are not tapping into awareness beyond the simulation.

## Satanic money

Cult members who are not bloodline can still serve the agenda and take the rewards if they fall to the control of the counterfeit spirit and 'sell their soul to the Devil'. A Nag Hammadi Gnostic manuscript, *Apocryphon of John*, says: 'They brought them gold, silver, gifts, and metals of copper, iron, and every sort ...They beguiled them into temptation so that they would not remember their immovable Pronoia [Awareness beyond the illusion].' After almost 30 years of research worldwide the way the control system operates becomes an open book and Satanism and paedophilia are at the core of it. A Swiss banker told the Russian magazine, *NoviDen*, in 2011 about the real background to those running global banking and finance:

> *... these people are corrupt, sick in their minds, so sick they are full of vices and those vices are kept under wraps on their orders ... many are into Satanism. When you go in some banks you see these satanistic symbols, like in the Rothschild Bank in Zurich. These people are controlled by blackmail because of the weaknesses they have. They have to follow orders or they will be exposed, they will be destroyed or even killed.*

Such people are going to care about making families homeless and destroying lives – even ending lives – by their actions and mass

**Figure 321:** Ronald Bernard saw the depth of evil behind the financial system and world events.

foreclosures? Not a chance. When you understand the mentality we are dealing with the world comes into focus. Ronald Bernard, a Dutch 'entrepreneur and financial dealer', went public in 2017 in an interview with De Vrije Media with what he said were his experiences of the satanic networks (Fig 321). Put the relevant words into a search engine and you can see everything that he said. Basically, he claims he was doing so well as an entrepreneur that he attracted the attention of the global financial cabal and was asked to join them. He said he was told that he must put his conscience 'in the freezer' and 'not at minus 18 degrees but minus 100'. If he wasn't prepared to do that he should not get involved. Bernard said he agreed while not knowing what this really meant, but he was to find out. He became involved in secret financial dealings between governments, security agencies, corporations and terrorist groups and the general manipulation of the world financial system. He saw that government security agencies are really criminal operations – a point I have been making for decades – and how at the centre only a very few people control global finance. All was well until he was told that the head of an Italian company had committed suicide and left a family behind after a cabal attack to crash the former Italian currency, the lira. Bernard's colleagues mocked and laughed at the man's fate and he said this was when his 'freezer' began to malfunction and his consciousness began to return. Breaking point came when he was asked to sacrifice a child in the satanic Luciferian rituals that the cabal engaged in. He said he couldn't do it and was horrified by what he saw: 'I was training to become a psychopath and I failed.' Bernard describes how the hidden network worships a force that 'hates life' and manipulates from the unseen. 'There is a whole invisible world, it is real', he said. Bernard said that involvement in child sacrifice is used for blackmailing financiers and politicians and this is another recurring theme. He stresses the psychopathic and heartless nature of these people and how they have a 'darkness' inside of them which is what Gnostics called the 'counterfeit spirit'. Bernard said of this darkness:

*It is a real entity. I have found that what is written in the Bible, and not only the Bible, you can find it in so many books, there really has been a moment of separation from the manifestation of light, in which a group went their own way and are carrying an intense hatred, anger.*

*The people who do not underestimate the severity of this are but few. Because this is an annihilating force that hates our guts. It hates creation, it hates life. And it will do anything to destroy us completely. And the way to do that is to divide humanity. Divide and conquer is their truth.*

*Humanity is a manifestation of light, that is the true creation. As long as you divide them on political parties, skin colour, you name it, then you – from a Luciferian point of view – suppress the full capacities of your enemy, their full power. They can't stand up for themselves because if they did the Luciferians would lose. This monster, this greedy monster would disappear.*

The entire seen and unseen structure is a colossal hierarchy of control with the Archontic Reptilians-Greys-demons serving the 'Demiurge' self-aware distortion which is behind it all (Fig 322). Once you grasp the

**Figure 322:** The Archontic Reptilian 'Spider' is ultimately behind Satanism, secret societies and the institutions of mainstream society including banking, politics and media in all its forms.

satanic foundation of global events you realise that war and suffering is imposed to generate the energy on which the whole structure feeds. This is the real reason why humanity has been so constantly at war since the new psyche kicked in and why we have such manipulated and systematic suffering and deprivation worldwide, that doesn't have to be. The *El*-ite may appear to be all-powerful within human society, but they are really pathetic vehicles and gofers for Reptilians, Greys and other Archontic manifestations which, in turn, are pathetic vehicles and gofers for the pathetic Demiurgic (lack of) awareness. They are all-powerful? Would you like to be them? Exactly.

*Enough*. Time to sort this out.

# CHAPTER EIGHT

# Casting the Spell

*'If a blind person leads a blind person, both of them will fall into a hole'*
*– Gospel of Thomas*

There is one target above all others for Hidden Hand manipulation – *perception*. Without control of perception everything else would fall. Perception is everything. Minds must stay closed to prevent the exposure of the world and reality as it really is.

Perception and belief dictate behaviour, what we will do and not do, challenge and not challenge, support and not support. But it goes much deeper. I highlighted earlier the relationship between *perceptions* of reality and *experienced* reality through the quantum field of possibility and probability. Perceptions = frequency = frequencies we interact with in the quantum field = what we decode and make holographically manifest as experienced reality:

> *Accidents happen, that's what everyone says. But in a quantum Universe there are no such things as accidents, only possibilities and probabilities folded into existence by perception.*

Archontic Reptilians and their hybrid bloodline agents know that by controlling perception they dictate what humanity will make manifest. The plan is to program perception in a way that makes people decode their own holographic (actually waveform) prison individually and collectively from the Cosmic Internet. What you believe you perceive, and what you perceive you experience. You don't primarily have to control the cosmic information source so much as program what parts of that source your target population decodes into perceived and experienced reality. To achieve this essential control of perception a

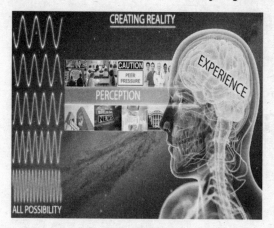

**Figure 323:** What forest? I see only twigs.

human 'life' is an unceasing perception-program from start to finish for those who do not breach its perceptual walls and connect with awareness beyond them. This can't be true? Oh, but it *is*. Archontic Reptilians and their hybrid *El*-ite have created a perpetual motion programming system in which the target population largely programs itself. Each generation is perceptually programmed by previous generations and by peer pressure from their own generation. I call this per*cept*ual motion. Babies in the womb are influenced and affected by their information environment which is absorbed in the form of frequency, and when the child is born the real deal begins. A deluge of perception programming awaits them no matter what their culture may be and the key is to hijack *attention* – energy (information, perception) flows where attention goes. They want you to focus for your entire human lifetime on the twigs so you never see the forest where everything appears in connection and context (Fig 323). Plato's Allegory of the Cave had the prisoners believing in an illusory reality because their attention was focused only on the wall of shadows and they were denied the information to put the shadows into context. If you can't see the forest you can't see the world as it really is. The twigs in the case of humans are the five senses which can only

**Figure 324:** A butterfly wing in close up but without the context who would know what it was?

perceive the holographic illusion and not the infinity and forever that lies outside its frequency firewalls. The result is a distorted perception of everything that perceives only pixels and not pictures. I remember as a kid watching an old black and white television quiz show that involved showing contestants images of everyday objects that had been magnified many, many times. You usually couldn't tell what they were until the camera gradually pulled out and you realised it was a cabbage or a scatter cushion (Fig 324). The manipulation of human reality is like that except that the camera never pulls out unless you make it so through expanded awareness. Focus your attention on an object at really close range and where is the rest of the world now? Where is peripheral vision where the dots connect? Try talking to a child, or adult for that matter, absorbed by a video game or smartphone. They simply don't hear you. This is the power of attention. What is a human life when you break it all down? It is a point of attention. The scale and breadth of that attention decides how awake or asleep we are to the greater reality. We don't live 'in' a 'world' so much as decode an interactive information source and what we fold into existence from that source is decided by perception (which dictates focus). Control perception and you control everything right down to the reality that people perceive to be 'me' and 'life'. Against this background it is hardly a surprise that the entire Archontic system is aimed at programming perception and the onslaught is unremitting from cradle to grave. Edward Bernays, the Austrian-American 'father of public relations' and nephew of psychoanalysis guru Sigmund Freud, wrote the following in his 1928 book, *Propaganda*:

> *We are governed, our minds are molded, our tastes formed, our ideas suggested, largely by men we have never heard of ... In almost every act of our daily lives, whether in the sphere of politics or business, in our social conduct or our ethical thinking, we are dominated by the relatively small number of persons ... who understand the mental processes and social patterns of the masses. It is they who pull the wires which control the public mind.*

Bernays said the secret was 'engineering the consent' to control and regiment people 'according to our will without their knowing about it'. He described this as 'the true ruling power in our society' and called it an 'invisible government'. This is also known today as the secret government or 'Deep State' (although the two have different roles) which continue ongoing to advance their agenda while here-today-gone-tomorrow politicians present the illusion of being in charge. Archontic 'bloodline' software networks and their human lackeys have created a fantastic global structure of mind control and perception manipulation that operates from the shadows and promotes its agenda though social engineering operations of every conceivable kind, including 'education' and the mainstream media. Significant swathes of the 'alternative' media now play their part, too. Programming is most effective when the population is in a state of fear or trauma. I have described trauma-based mind control on individuals, but this is also done on a mass scale. A traumatised mind becomes extremely suggestable – this is well known – and after the attacks of 9/11 and the fake official explanation it was easy to win support for the invasion of Afghanistan and the 'war on [of] terror'. The Rothschild-connected Frankfurt School, established by fellow Zionists in the 1920s, is among the most infamous of social engineering operations. It was first based, as the name suggests, in the Rothschild home city of Frankfurt, Germany, and then also located in Switzerland and the United States. These were some of the Frankfurt School's ambitions to transform human society (you might recognise them): Creation of racism offences; continual change to create confusion; teaching of sex to young children (it now happens as young as four); huge immigration to destroy national identity; promotion of excessive drinking; emptying of churches [undermining any form of social cohesion and community]; a legal system with bias against victims of crime; dependency on the state or state benefits (then removing them once dependence was achieved]; control and dumbing down of the media; encouraging the breakdown of the family. The last one can be found on most social engineering wish-lists for reasons that will become obvious.

## Get them young – get them for life

Parents are the first perception manipulators on behalf of what I call The

Program, as is anyone else with regular contact in a child's earliest years (Figs 325 and 326). The great majority are not doing this knowingly or through malevolence, but because they have been through the same programming process that their child has just begun. Parents have downloaded the fake sense of reality – The Program – and believe it to be real. They have accepted its version of life, self, possibility and all its

**Figure 325:** Welcome to Planet Earth where you do what we say and believe what we tell you.

musts and mustn'ts, dos and don'ts, and they pass on these perceptions to their children in the belief they are 'doing the right thing' (what The Program has told them is the 'right thing'). Children are then pressured to conform and this does not even have to be done openly or through overt force. It's often done that way, especially and most outrageously by the indoctrination of religion, but it doesn't need to be that blatant. Constant repetition of reality through words or example is all that it

**PROGRAMMING STAGE 1**

**PARENTS**

**Figure 326:** Most parents pass on their own programming to their children from the earliest age.

takes for the child to believe this is the way life is. This is what you do, what you think, how you behave, see others and the world. Most people are so systematically insecure that they don't want to stand out by being different or perceived by programmed 'normal' to be 'a bit weird'. The influence of the frightened-of-its-own-shadow reptilian brain is crucial to this. Parents mostly don't want their children to be different as they sit meekly in a perception and behaviour prison based on 'What will the neighbours think?' and 'What will the teacher say?' Expanded awareness replies 'couldn't care less' to such questions, but to the programmed conformer that is blasphemy. A parent of a young footballer shouted at me once for disagreeing with a refereeing decision because I was teaching her child to question authority. 'What if he questions his teacher on Monday now', she cried. Yes, what *if*? Children soon learn from the parent program that conforming is easier than going your own way and they are being prepared for a lifetime of doing exactly the same. How many parents seek to mould their children to conform to norms rather than let them develop in their own way? The question answers itself with a modicum of observation. Parents that set out to impose their will, perceptions and personal desires on their offspring are in my view engaging in child abuse. Many parents want to live their lives through their children and pressure them into activities, jobs and careers that they don't want to do but are made to feel guilty for not pursuing. 'Your mother is so upset.' Really? *Good*. It might help her wake up and grow up. I have met people late in life who still felt guilt at not pleasing their long-gone parents. It's crazy. How about criteria such as are children happy? Are they fulfilled? Do they have joy in their life? They *do*? Okay, good. Whatever they're doing must be right for them, then. Parental programming is only part of the perception deception and nothing like as important as it used to be as the state takes over parental roles although it remains extremely significant. Religion is also now less perceptually-relevant in some countries and cultures but remains the foremost programmer in others. Elsewhere the prime downloaders of perception today are the state, particularly the Deep State back in the shadows, in league with government, 'education', mass media, social media, video games and 'smart' technology which are all, in the end, controlled by The Spider. I'll deal with the technological level of this in later chapters.

## Child-stealing state

State control of children is infiltrating parental influence and decision-making on an ever-gathering scale. The reasons relate to the socially-engineered break-up of the family unit to allow total state control of childhood and perception programming from the earliest age. This was predicted by insider Aldous Huxley in *Brave New World* and demanded by the Frankfurt School and almost every other social engineering wish-list I have seen. Encouraging or forcing mothers to seek employment even if they would rather focus on their children is one way this is being done. Never mind what is better for the kids – what is best for the agenda is all that matters. The Organisation for Economic Co-operation and Development said that Australia's employment rate of single mothers was too low, and efforts should be made to help older women, indigenous Australians and all mums into the workforce. Stay-at-home (children-focused) mothers were the 'greatest untapped potential' for Australia's workforce and were creating 'potentially large losses to the economy'. Money is the only criteria for life then? One moronic journalist said that 'it should be illegal to be a stay-at-home mum'. The writer will be too utterly stupid to realise the scale of tyranny being advocated. This excuse for a journalist will have no idea that pressure on mothers to work outside the family and a long list of other techniques are designed to dismantle the family unit. Film producer Aaron Russo who worked on *Trading Places* with Eddie Murphy made great efforts before he died in 2007 to expose what he knew about the global conspiracy. He told of meetings with lawyer and businessman Nick Rockefeller who he said tried to recruit him into the El-ite's Council on Foreign Relations. Russo said Rockefeller told him about 9/11 and the subsequent war on terror a year before they happened (more later) and with regard to the current subject, how the Rockefeller Foundation funded the feminist movement or 'Women's Lib' to promote the separation of mothers from their children and give the state more control. The Rockefeller Foundation, like so many others, including the Bill and Melinda Gates Foundation, uses the cover of (tax-free) 'philanthropy' to fund the agenda. Russo said Rockefeller told him the motivation behind funding and promoting the feminism movement was to be able to tax both sexes instead of only primarily one and *to get children into school and state control at an earlier age* 'to indoctrinate them how to think'. The idea was to have children looking to schools and the state as their family and not their parents – destruction of the family unit.

Children are also being stolen by the state from loving parents worldwide on an industrial scale, as I have mentioned. Tens of thousands of children have been taken from parents by social services in Britain alone – increasing year on year – and a growing percentage of those cases are manufactured and bogus. At least one local court was found to be processing 50 such cases a day (Fig 327). Nor is this only a British problem. It is happening in the United States and around the world. The human consequences for both children and parents in

**Figure 327:** Parents need to take their children back from the state before they lose them altogether.

terms of emotional trauma and broken lives are incalculable and almost unimaginable. Confirmation that this is systematic comes with the ever-rising numbers of state-stolen children and the financial incentives to authorities and social workers to remove children from their families and use secret courts to hand them against their will to financially-rewarded foster parents and adoption. The state would not be that callous? No, *you* wouldn't be that callous – the Archontic state majors in callousness. This is the same state exposed for shipping more than 100,000 children from Britain to be subjected to rape, torture and slavery in Canada, Australia, New Zealand and Zimbabwe to provide white British bloodstock; a state that unlawfully took the children from their families and made them suffer 'exceptional depravity' in work camps and as servants to paedophiles. These kidnapping schemes between 1869 and 1970 were supported by charities and church groups with royal patrons including the shapeshifting Satanist, the Queen Mother. The British government knew what was happening and subsidised this inhuman outrage with taxpayer money. No, surely not. The state wouldn't be that callous.

Financial incentives are encoded at every stage to oil the wheels of state child kidnapping and the same with government *targets* for the number of children that have to be taken by the state every year. Assess the circumstances? No, no, check how many more we need to meet the target. Only the psychopathic and sociopathic without empathy or heart could possibly do this, and that is why social services have been recruiting such people apace at the expense of those with compassion and decency who should be doing the job. Teachers, doctors, dentists and others are encouraged to report the most minor perceived 'problem' to social services to start the sequence of child stealing, and most of them will have no clue of the injustice and trauma they are triggering. There is a particularly disturbing trend of doctors and medical personnel collaborating with social workers, police and prosecutors against mothers and pregnant women. New guidelines to education and medical staff issued in 2017 by the UK National Institute for Health and Care Excellence (NICE) said that parents of children who have temper tantrums in class should be considered potential abusers or guilty of neglect. One guideline says that staff should consider abuse if a child displays behaviour that differs from what is *normal* for children of that age or developmental stage. Think about the potential for that to open the floodgates. Numbers of state-stolen children climbed rapidly when war criminal Tony Blair introduced emotional criteria for claims of parental abuse and that handed vastly more power to the subjective opinion of the social worker chasing targets. Authorities claim cases of abuse are increasing year on year – but so are the criteria for what is defined as abuse and the two are obviously connected. Children are being removed from families who refuse to accept a doctor's treatment for their child (like deadly chemotherapy for cancer) or even when they want a second opinion. Medical fascism is increasingly part of life. Parents are even being reported by vindictive neighbours out of spite and that's how simple it is because the state is looking for any excuse to kidnap children. Parents find themselves in a secret court where media reporting is banned, desperately trying to keep their children in the face of a judge (paid by the state), lawyers (paid by the state), social workers (paid by the state) and 'experts' (paid by the state) who are called to give 'evidence' by social workers (paid by the state) and lawyers (paid by the state). This is a complete stitch-up, as it is meant to be (Fig 328). I have seen some of these cases at close hand and it is a disgrace to justice and the most basic humanity. Among them have been mothers who lost their sexually and satanically-abused children to Satanist fathers on the orders of a clearly rigged judge. Satanic and paedophile rings infiltrate every area of society – including the judiciary.

**Figure 328:** Secret courts where proceedings can't be reported are the cover for incredible injustice which the public never hears about.

Children who are in abusive situations should of course be removed immediately, but that is not what this is all about. Highly-publicised 'mistakes' (not always) by social workers who leave truly abused children with their abusers provide the excuse to take more children from loving parents with public support. 'You have to protect the children,' people say. Yes, and that should include protecting them most of all from the state, which is the prime abuser and kidnapper of children. They also need protecting from those in the medical profession who have them removed from parents who disagree with their often unsupportable diagnosis and ask for another opinion. Secret family courts, which are legendary for their corruption and collusion, are

**Figure 329:** A documentary that exposes the child-stealing scandal.

justified by claims of protecting children when they are secret to protect this abomination. State-stealing of children is connected to hijacking childhood to allow for maximum control of perception by taking kids from parents that have a mind of their own. You will find brilliant documentaries exposing this global scandal at www.petemiddletonpictures.co.uk/traffic-2 and see also forced-adoption.com (Fig 329). 'Free Scotland' provides a clear example of where we are heading with its planned 'named person' scheme to assign a representative of the state to every child from birth to at least 18. The named person is a health visitor for a pre-school child and a 'promoted teacher' for those of school age. These 'persons' would oversee the child's upbringing and contact social services if they are unhappy with what is happening across a range of possible situations. Given that satanic and paedophile rings have infiltrated social services and the system in general you can appreciate the potential for this named person imposition to dramatically increase the numbers of children stolen by the state. At least one designated 'named person' has already been dismissed for sending images of child sexual abuse. There has been tremendous opposition from parents and others to this shocking state imposition which has delayed its widespread introduction, but Nicola Sturgeon, the mirror-worshipping-not-very-bright leader of the ruling Scottish National Party, cracks on regardless in a typical response from the 'do what I say' political class which pervades the entirety of Archontically-created politics from far left to far right. Sturgeon is so deluded that she thinks there can be an independent Scotland *within* the EU dictatorship, which is a contradiction of terms taken to extreme levels of absurdity. So, stage one of lifetime perception programming begins with parents and now the state is making moves to take over even from that.

## Schools: Programming prisons for kids

Life-long programming stage two is when state perception-hijacking really kicks in as children enter the school system (Fig 330). I prefer 'school system' to 'education system' because it is far more accurate. 'Education' in this context is only a synonym for programming, and as Albert Einstein put it: 'The only thing that interferes with my learning is my education.' We return to the theme of education and science

**Figure 330:** When the perception programming goes into overdrive.

as a journey to prove the textbooks right, not to question them. One of the most profound forms of programming is familiarity. This may sound strange, but it isn't. When something becomes familiar – 'how things are' – it bypasses the conscious mind without further debate or questioning. It becomes subliminal or 'below threshold' and fades into the subconscious as a reflex state of acceptance. We are bombarded with subliminal advertising and images all day every day that speak to the subconscious without us ever knowing that this is happening. These messages enter the mind through that 11 million minus 40. What is planted below the threshold of conscious awareness later seeps through to the conscious mind as 'I've had a thought' in the way that I described with symbolism. The foundation of subliminal communication is indeed the use of ... *symbols*. We have the same principle with familiarity. State education virtually every weekday for the entirety of a child and young person's formative years is taken as a 'gimme' by most people, and a gimme is only a term for subconscious acceptance. A gimme = I don't question it. Well, we *should* question it. We should question *everything*. If something passes that scrutiny then fine; but most 'gimmes', in my experience, dissolve in a flash when asked by a conscious mind to justify themselves. The whole basis of what I have been doing for nearly 30 years is to bring to conscious attention what is hidden away in the subconscious or peripheral vision.

Deep breath ... this is the 'education system' made conscious and it's not a pretty sight (Fig 331). If you wanted to impose the almost perfect method of producing adults that

**Figure 331:** The real reason for the 'education' system.

think and perceive in a way that suits your agenda you would come up with today's indoctrination machine masquerading as 'education'. Children enter the 'world' and undergo initial perception programming from mostly state-programmed parents before the state takes virtually

**Figure 332:** On their way to the programming laboratory.

total control of a child's mind. One consequence of early-years programming at home and school is that the child is pulled out of the NOW and locked away into a perception of past and future which is a major pillar of The Program. American psychologist Professor Philip Zimbardo has made this point about parents and schools taking 'present orientated children' and making them future, sometimes past, orientated. Children arrive in this reality and within only *three or four years* they are sitting at a desk while an authority figure representing the perception program of the state is telling them when they have to be there, when they can leave, and when they can talk, eat and even go to the toilet. A simple question to highlight the insanity and child abuse: What are children doing on lovely sunny days sitting at a desk in a classroom bored stiff and unable to move while the birds are singing outside? The birds are free while the kids are enslaved (Fig 332). For the rest of their childhood into their teenage years they are told the state's version of everything five days a week (plus homework) and then tested in exams on how deeply they have absorbed the programming. The more they absorb, accept and recycle onto the exam paper the more 'successful', 'clever' and 'bright' they are officially judged to be. If they absorb The Program in the extreme they are dubbed 'super students' and awarded a 'degree' to confirm their degree of programming. But if you question what you are told, don't accept it or are bored shitless by it all (like I was) then you are considered a failure who is intellectually substandard (Fig 333). One thicker-than-thick 'alternative' radio presenter once said that I should not be taken seriously because I didn't have a degree. Einstein once again was on the money: 'Everybody is a genius, but if you judge a fish by its ability to climb a tree it will live its whole life believing it is stupid.' This captures in a

**Figure 333:** It's the same the world over.

**Figure 334:** This is the whole foundation and goal of The Program from cradle to grave.

single sentence the reason that mass 'education' was introduced in the form that we see. Education fakery is there to make climbing the tree (believing what suits The System) the entire goal while at the same time supressing any potential or gifts that The System doesn't want or need (like free thought). *Control perception and you control reality* (Fig 334). Charlotte Iserbyt worked at the US Department of Education and was a policy advisor to the Reagan administration. What she experienced in that period made her a vehement campaigner to expose the calculated programming of children in the 'education' system. She had access to documents detailing what she calls the 'restructuring' of American and global education and how computerisation of schools was introduced to make perception programming easier and more effective. Her book, The *Deliberate Dumbing Down of America,* is a must-read. Iserbyt explains how a training manual was produced to show staff how to turn the American 'education' system into something akin to communist brainwashing. The manual was called *Innovations in Education: A Change Agent's Guide* by Professor Ronald Havelock. Iserbyt describes how parents with a mind of their own – called 'resistors' – were systematically targeted:

> *I was trained to identify the resistors. The resistors ... [were] ... those good, smart Americans who realize that anything that has education hanging off the end of it is probably not what they're looking for. I was trained to identify those good people, and to go up against them, and actually to go and try get them to join us through the group process system. Make them feel important, get them on a committee ... and that just blew my mind.*

How often I hear the following phrase issuing forth from the mouth of political ignorance or mendacity: 'Education must prepare children for the workplace.' Sometimes this is said by the Archontically manipulative, but mostly by the Archontically programmed. They cannot see how extreme and insane it is to say that Infinite Awareness with infinite potential should be programmed and moulded to fit the requirements of governments, giant corporations and an economic structure established and controlled by the *El*-ite for their own benefit. John D. Rockefeller, the American oil, banking and pharmaceutical tycoon and Archontic Reptilian incarnate, founded the US General Education Board at the start of the 20th century for the very reasons that

I am exposing here. He said: 'I don't want a nation of thinkers – I want a nation of workers.' I want a nation – every nation – of unthinking cogs in my machine so I can turn children with such zest and potential into automatons that will do whatever I say (Fig 335). Rockefeller's co-founder and business advisor, Frederick T. Gates, said it all:

**Figure 335:** Preparing children to serve The System and never the other way round.
© David Dees

*In our dream we have limitless resources, and the people yield themselves with perfect docility to our moulding hand. The present educational conventions fade from our minds; and, unhampered by tradition, we work our own good will upon a grateful and responsive rural folk.*

*We shall not try to make these people or any of their children into philosophers or men of learning or of science. We are not to raise up among them authors, orators, poets, or men of letters. We shall not search for embryo great artists, painters, musicians. Nor will we cherish even the humbler ambition to raise up from among them lawyers, doctors, preachers, statesmen, of whom we now have ample supply.*

And that is what has happened although some still slip through the net.

## Left, right, left, left, left …

We return to the two hemispheres of the brain to explain a foundation reason for why they specifically do not want to 'raise up' from the masses authors, orators, poets, artists, painters and musicians. The Program doesn't want anyone from the target population with an ability to write and speak intelligently and engagingly enough to expose The System on any level. Nor do they want poets, artists, painters, musicians and other creative people who are invariably influenced by the creative right-hemisphere of the brain (Fig 336). Little 'time' and

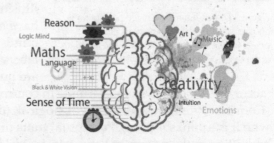

**Figure 336:** Left and right brain process reality in very different ways and The System wants to imprison perceptions in the left side.

money is spent in schools on music, art and drama compared with left-brain subjects (all the rest). I saw an advertisement for a car company some years ago that used the left-brain-right-brain contrast as its theme. The way it described the perceptions (decoding processes) of the two is very relevant to why 'education' has been structured as it is:

> *I am the left brain. I am a scientist. A mathematician. I love the familiar. I categorise. I am accurate. Linear. Analytical. Strategic. I am practical. Always in control. A master of words and language. Realistic. I calculate equations and play with numbers. I am order. I am logic. I know exactly who I am.*

> *I am the right brain. I am creativity. A free spirit. I am passion. Yearning. Sensuality. I am the sound of roaring laughter. I am taste. The feeling of sand beneath bare feet. I am movement. Vivid colours. I am the urge to paint on an empty canvas. I am boundless imagination. Art. Poetry. I sense. I feel. I am everything I wanted to be.*

The decoded brain is holographic and all parts will be involved in

everything, but it is a matter of degree and specialisation. Thanks to 'education' programming left-brain perceptions are those of mainstream science, politics, economics, business, medicine and media – Mainstream Everything. They also apply to much of the five-sense-only 'alternative' media. These are all products of The Program, which has its home largely in the left side of the brain which sees everything in linear terms and the illusion of 'time' and you cannot have a free world without free minds (Fig 337). Other left-brain labels in that car advertisement are purely self-delusory –

**Figure 337:** Left-brain-dominated perception is another standing wave going nowhere and a prison for the mind – which is why the left-brain is the target of the 'education' system.

'accurate' (on The System's terms), 'in control' (thinks it is), 'realistic' (from The Program's perspective), 'logical' (ditto) and 'knows exactly who it is' (thinks it does). Perceptual traits of the left-brain are also embodied in the perceptual and astrological influence of Saturn. The right brain is everything the Archontic Reptilians and their hybrid *El*-ite don't want, with its potential to express creative free spirit and boundless imagination and to sense and feel beyond The Program. We breach The Program, the Matrix, by sensing, feeling and intuitively knowing, not by thinking. I saw an excellent video presentation by psychiatrist and writer Iain McGilchrist talking about the divided human brain. Division is the core of the problem because both hemispheres are supposed to work as one unit to create a coherent multi-faceted whole. McGilchrist explains how the left brain has a narrow focus (point of attention) on detail while the right perceives the panorama or big picture. People who lose the use of their right brain have a narrowed 'window of attention'. The crucial word here is *context*. The left-brain sees detail while the right-brain sees the context of the detail. It connects dots and sees the forest. Context is all and if you only see the pieces you'll never see the picture (Fig 338). Reality without context is just a bewildering bunch of apparently unconnected happenings. McGilchrist says the left-brain is knowledge of the parts while the right-brain is wisdom about the whole. This is a perfect description of the difference between the two. He also says that the left-brain is focused upon *knowing ever more about what is already known*. The state version of 'education' is about knowing ever more about what is

**Figure 338:** Pieces will never show you pictures unless they are connected together through context.

**Figure 339:** The System protects the left-brain from right brain influence.
© www.neilhague.com

already known (or claimed to be known). 'Education' sets out to create left-brain prisoners perceptually entrapped in the realm of often meaningless detail at the expense of the absolutely vital right-brain context. 'Education' is one of the most crucial guards on the gate to protect the left-side of the brain from right-brain influence (Fig 339). Intellectual-type subjects are being introduced even in pre-school environments to stimulate the left brain from the earliest age to overwhelm the right, and there is a campaign to destroy the imagination/right-brain awakener that we call 'play'. The period when children can simply play is being squeezed by 'education', including homework. They target the left side of the brain that sees pixels, not pictures, and twigs at the expense of the forest. We have confused knowing (heart awareness) with knowledge (downloaded 'facts') and wisdom (heart) with knowledge (head). Put another way we have confused memory with knowledge and knowledge with wisdom. We are led to believe that the opposite of ignorance is knowledge or the absorption of what the state tells us to believe. These are not opposites. Perceived knowledge, too, can be – and usually is – ignorance. The mystic Osho explained it perfectly:

> *Knowledge has no capacity to dispel ignorance. Knowledge is a false phenomenon. It is not wisdom at all; it is just the opposite of wisdom. Knowledge is borrowed; wisdom is the flowering of your innermost being ... No university can offer it, no scripture can offer it and no scholarship is capable of doing it. They are all impotent efforts, but they have been deceiving millions of people for thousands of years. Yes they make you knowledgeable. To be knowledgeable is one thing, to know is totally different.*

Homework is there to further impinge upon a child's potential for play and imagination and fill the mind with often irrelevant 'knowledge'. Parents in Spain where 15-years-olds have some 6.5 hours of homework a week have complained how their children's free time (daydream time, ponder time, play time) has disappeared. They need to know that this is done from the shadows with complete calculation. Orchard elementary school in Vermont stopped homework with great success and this highlighted the negative effect that homework has on children's lives and wellbeing. The school principal reported that after six months students had not fallen back academically and now had time 'to be creative thinkers at home and follow their passions' (The Program's worst nightmare). Many parents said their children were reading more from their own choice. Others who have stopped homework have had similar outcomes. John Taylor Gatto, a former teacher, said the school system seeks to subdue creative, inventive, and bright students and make them obedient, subdued and dependent individuals by controlling their school time and then continuing in to what should be free time through homework. This is a point I have been making for decades. Gatto is quoted as saying:

> *Today the tabulation of hours in a young life reads like this: My children watch television 55 hours a week according to recent reports, and they sleep*

*56. That leaves them 57 hours in which to grow up strong and competent and whole. But my children attend school 30 hours more, spend 8 hours preparing for school, and in goings and comings, and an additional 7 hours a week in something called 'home'-work – although this is really more schoolwork except in 'Newspeak'* [George Orwell's concept of deception through language].

*After the 45 school hours are removed a total of 12 hours remain each week from which to fashion a private person – one that can like, trust, and live with itself. Twelve hours. But my kids must eat, too, and that takes some time. Not much, because they've lost the tradition of family dining – how they learn to eat in school is best called 'feeding' – but if we allot just 3 hours a week to evening feedings, we arrive at a net total of private time for each child of 9 hours ...*

*...This demented schedule is an efficient way to create dependent human beings, needy people unable to fill their own hours, unable to initiate lines of meaning to give substance and pleasure to their existence. It is a national disease, this dependency and aimlessness, and schooling and television and busy work ... has a lot to do with it.*

All this is done to suppress potential and turn children into computer minds programmed by the *El*-ite-controlled state. Whatever 'time' is left after school and homework is increasingly spent on the mind-manipulating technology of smartphones and video games and this is again by design. We can now see why the Archontic System wants to suppress the right brain and why 'education' is in the front-line of this. Here we have the reason, too, for worship of the left-brain intellect. Someone deemed to be clever is said to be 'intellectual' or have a 'great mind'. Well, a great mind, maybe, but not necessarily an open connection to awareness outside The Program. There is a chasm of difference between the intellect and innate (intuitive, expanded awareness) intelligence. They are absolutely not the same thing. Archons trawl and exploit humanity's intellectual 'creativity' (like technology development) and suppress the boundless potential of expanded awareness which would see through their game. This answers the question posed by shaman Don Juan Matus:

*Think for a moment, and tell me how you would explain the contradictions between the intelligence of man the engineer and the stupidity of his systems of belief, or the stupidity of his contradictory behaviour.*

Intellect *is* The Program and produces the scientist, doctor, politician, banker, CEO, academic and journalist. They are convinced of their

intellectual superiority when they don't begin to understand the world
that they believe they have *intellectually* figured out. They listen but they
don't hear. They look but they don't see. Intellect is the left-brain and the
perceptual prison cell. To worship and be in awe of intellect is to
worship and be in awe of your own enslavement. I am not saying that
intellect should be wiped, but that it must be balanced. The intellectual
left-brain should be the servant of expanded awareness as the interface
with five-sense experienced reality. Instead it has been manipulated to
become the master and the computer has overridden the guy with the
keyboard and mouse. This quote is attributed to Einstein although there
is doubt about the source. Either way it tells it like it is: 'The intuitive
mind is a sacred gift and the rational mind is a faithful servant. We have
created a society that honours the servant and has forgotten the gift.'
Canadian-born psychiatrist Eric Berne described the difference so well
when he wrote: 'The moment a little boy is concerned with which is a jay
and which is a sparrow he can no longer see the birds or hear them sing.'
Archontic manipulators fear the potential of the right-brain, but there is
something they fear more and that is whole brain balance. Left-brain
dominated people are consumed by structure, hierarchy, intellect and a
sense of limitation and separation. Right-brain domination can be
extremely creative with highly active imaginations, but so 'out-there'
those people struggle to function and impact upon 'down-here'. When
the two come together as one interacting, mutually-supporting whole
they can be devastating for The System because they are 'out-there' *and*
'down-here'. They are *in* this 'world', but not *of* it in terms of their prime
point of observation. They can still function in the illusion while
knowing it is an illusion. This is the bottom-line reason for the incessant
attack on the right brain to block this unity and coming together. As a
result, often the most potentially extraordinary people are portrayed as
failures by the 'education' system. My son Gareth is a brilliant singer-
songwriter, multi-talented and all round bright bloke, but he was given
an E in many of his exams. He didn't mess around with just Cs or even
Ds. He was even more bored by school than I was, and he has done all
his learning in his own time and on his terms in the same way that I
have. Please consider this, anyone who feels a failure because 'I wasn't
good at school'. Neither was I. Don't let this crap define you – that's
what it seeks to do. Diane Ravitch, an American historian of education,
policy analyst and writer, said: 'Sometimes the most brilliant and
intelligent minds do not shine in standardized tests because they do not
have standardized minds.' The whole point of mainstream 'education' is
to make sure that they are either standardized or get nowhere if they
aren't. The cumulative effect on perception was confirmed in a study by
Kyung Hee Kim, professor of education at the College of William and
Mary in Virginia, involving a very large number of school-age children

between kindergarten and 12th grade. This is what she found:

> *A massive decline of creativity* [right brain] *as 'children have become less emotionally expressive* [right brain], *less energetic, less talkative and verbally expressive, less humorous* [right brain], *less imaginative* [right brain], *less unconventional* [right brain], *less lively and passionate* [right brain], *less perceptive* [right brain], *less apt to connect seemingly irrelevant things* [right brain], *less synthesizing* [right brain], *and less likely to see things from a different angle* [right brain].

This transformation of behaviour and perception is achieved through the carrot and stick technique of reward and punishment and by simple repetition week after week, month after month, year after year that batters the right-brain into submission. I was fortunate in that school passed me by without touching the sides and I day-dreamed myself through most of it.

## Rules is rules (and madness)

**Figure 340:** Force the young to follow the rules every day at school and most will absorb that perception and reaction pattern for life.

Carrot, stick and repetition implant the belief that The System knows best and is always right and that it's far easier to follow the rules than to question them. This is psychological preparation for a lifetime of believing in The System and following the rules that The System imposes (Fig 340). 'You have to follow the rules – where would we be if we didn't?' We would live in a very different world. Teachers may be representatives of the state in the classroom, but they, too, are in prison and have to follow their rules or lose their career. This symbolises the entire Archontic Reptilian human hierarchy as each level follows the rules and demands of the level above. You only have to witness the joy that children and young people

**Figure 341:** School's out!! No prison for a week.

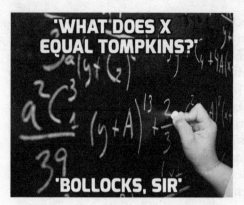

**Figure 342:** X + Y equals what? Don't give a shit.

**Figure 343:** Take a walk and climb a tree, kids. It's lovely outside.

**Figure 344:** This is what childhood should be like, right? I mean that's why they were born – to know what X means.

feel when they walk out of school at the start of a holiday. 'No school for a week – *YEEEEES!*' (Fig 341). This is the reaction of a prisoner walking free from jail at the end of a sentence. School is a programming prison and institutionalised slavery. It's not? So, children can turn up and go home whenever they want, can they, or choose not to go at all? In many countries neither is true and they want the same to be the case everywhere. Hour after hour children and young people are forced to traipse from left-brain lesson to left-brain lesson not able to talk when they want to or eat when they are hungry or mostly even question what they are told to remember and repeat in exams. It's programming-tests-exams, programming-tests-exams, week after week, month after month, year after year. What happened to developing the individual and the whole person? What happened to childhood? This is mass global child abuse and few can see it because the whole outrageous farce has long entered the psychological invisibility of familiarity. I daydreamed my school years away to avoid the stupefying boredom and limitation of it all. 'Icke – *stop daydreaming!!*' Fuck off. Even worse is the pressure imposed to do well in examinations which are designed to test how skilled you are at absorbing The Program. Education is all a giant hoax to pass off programming as learning. How much of what you learned at school and regurgitated in exams have you actually *used* or even *remembered?* Next to bugger all in the case of most people, and this after spending an entire childhood learning what they soon forget or never need. I mean, *algebra.* WTF is all that about? What does 'x' equal? Couldn't care less, mate, whatever turns you on (Fig 342). What are we doing filling young minds with this irrelevant crap that 99 percent of them will never use? The answer is in the question ... *to fill their minds* (Fig 343). We have young people committing suicide over not passing exams or fearing that they won't. Give me a better definition of insanity than to put youngsters – or anyone – through that (Fig 344). Figures from the US Centers for Disease Control and Prevention reveal that suicides among 10 to 14 year olds have doubled since 2007, and among girls in the same age group they have tripled in 15 years. Peter Gray, a Boston College psychology professor, said after studying the data that the mental health of children is directly related to school attendance. Visits to psychiatrists drop dramatically during summer holidays when academic and exam pressures were lifted only to spike again when school restarted. Gray concluded:

> *The available evidence suggests quite strongly that school is bad for children's mental health. Of course, it's bad for their physical health, too; nature did not design children to be cooped up all day at a micromanaged, sedentary job.*

Gray said that children with anxiety problems changed when removed from school and '... behaviour, moods, and learning generally improved when they stopped conventional schooling'. Anxiety related to school and anxiety in general among children and young people is going through the roof as they are forced to spend more time at school than ever before. A study by the American Psychological Association in 2013 said that school is the main source of stress for teenagers. The report noted that 83 percent of teenagers said that school was 'a somewhat or significant source of stress' while 27 percent said they suffered from 'extreme stress' during the school year; a figure that dropped to 13 percent during school holidays. Parents are often adding to the pressure, either under the delusion that exam results confirm intelligence or to bask in reflected glory. 'My son/daughter has won a place at Oxford.' Yes, your son or daughter did that – not *you.* Left to themselves they probably wanted to do something else, anyway. Some parents even put stickers on their cars to advertise their child's exam passes. The much-missed American comedian, George Carlin, said: 'Here's a bumper sticker I'd like to see ... We are proud parents of a child who has resisted his teachers' attempts to break his spirit and bend him to the will of his corporate masters.' The fact that those parental sentiments are so rare is testament to the power of The Program to perceptually control succeeding generations. Each yearly inflow of children is largely left to go it alone in the lair of the merciless state as they systematically download the following lessons for life:

- Truth comes from authority
- Intelligence is the ability to remember and repeat
- Accurate memory and repetition are rewarded
- Non-compliance is punished
- Conform intellectually and socially

Schools are dramatically increasing their control over children, with parents marginalised, and this is heading somewhere as we shall see. Parents in the UK are fined if they take their children on holiday during term time when it is much cheaper. When one father refused to pay and took the case to court the British authorities spent £140,000 of taxpayers' money to successfully defend their right to impose their will on children and parents. This is another important point. Governments use taxpayers' money to get their way while taxpayers have to use their own to defend their rights against the governments that they fund. Head teachers are being appointed as automaton administrators of the state agenda and not for their educational prowess. One headteacher of small children that I know would be far more suited to running a prison than a school, and she is fast becoming the norm. A crazy school in the UK actually advertised for the head of a 'Behaviour Correction Unit' and 'director of isolations and detentions' at £29,000 a year insisting that the right applicant must be a disciplinarian who 'demands obedience at all times'. The advertisement added: 'If you think it is mean to give a detention when a student does not have a pen, this is not the school for you.' I would not think it was the school for anyone with an ounce of intelligence still intact. This sounds like a job advert for a prison because it is. They just call it a school. Magna Academy in Poole, Dorset, is run by Richard Tutt (Tutt, Tutt, surely) who is known as one of the country's strictest headteachers. He appears to be the personification of when your only tool is a hammer every problem looks like a nail. Pupils are reported to be routinely given over-the-top punishments for minor 'indiscretions', including 'having pencil cases and rulers of the wrong length'. Andrew Mears, a headteacher for 26 years, said he had thought at first the advertisement was a joke (it was, just not funny). He was concerned about the effect on the pupils' mental health. He should be. Imagine waking up every morning knowing that you have to watch everything you do and say to avoid the wrath of these barely-one-dimensional people? Welcome to Planet Earth – Mr Tutt Tutt is in control

**Figure 345:** The whole point of 'education' for the Hidden Hand.

of your life now. Let's not ask why some pupils are not automatons who bow to their masters at the blackboard with unquestioning acquiescence. Let's not celebrate that some kids have a mind of their own or ask if there is something happening in their lives that makes them disruptive. They have transgressed the lunatic prison-school rules and they must be punished – *punish them* and force them to conform to The Program's pea-size perception of reality (Fig 345). The arrogance and conceit is breathtaking.

Many schools even insist that children wear hot and heavy blazers in ferocious heat because rules are rules, and this is still more confirmation that you don't have to be intelligent to run a school. Having a mind of your own and the ability to make mature decisions in the light of the circumstances before you is clearly a bad career move. 'Staggering numbers' of UK teachers want to leave the profession as a result of what is happening and Rebecca Allen, director of the Education Datalab think tank, says that children across the country are being taught by teachers who do not want to be there, but are trapped by the need to make a living. The Archontic agenda is for the imposition of a global police state in which every aspect of human life is controlled and under surveillance. Young people are being prepared to accept this as normal and 'the way things are' by building big walls and fences around schools and making them even look like prisons. A school around the corner from me was nothing like that until relatively recently, but now there is a high fence

**Figure 346:** Children are being prepared to accept this as 'normal' for the rest of their lives.

with the grounds compartmentalised into sections, each with its own locked gate. This is how prisons and zoos operate. If all that was not necessary before then why is it now? There are no reasons except those that they make up, and all have their foundation in manufactured fear and in preparing children to accept such enslavement as normal for the rest of their lives. Schools and colleges have surveillance cameras everywhere and in many American schools children have to pass through airport-like checks before they reach the classroom (Fig 346). Police are often in residence at schools in the US or on immediate call to respond to situations that teaching staff previously dealt with and there are endless cases of police brutality in schools as psychopaths in uniform are given control over children. None of this is about protection, but instead a lifetime acceptance through familiarity of mass surveillance and the police state. Older people have the compass of seeing how surveillance and control has increased to extraordinary levels while children and young people don't have that compass. To them it's normal – all they have known – and so what is there to question? The plan is to privatise education (like everything else) and hand children's minds and perceptions to giant corporations which are all directed by the same global network with The Spider at the centre. We already have corporations taking over schools and turning exam pass results into financial gain with not a care for the children as human beings and unique individuals. Get good marks – it's great for business. My observation and experience is that if Microsoft's Bill Gates is promoting something through his Bill and Melinda Gates Foundation then it must be bad for humanity. Gates has been at the forefront of transforming the American education system and one of his stated plans is for a camera in every classroom. He just cares about children, you see.

## Another way ...

Home schooling is soaring in response to what is happening as more aware parents remove their children from the state laboratory and have them educated independently. As this continues you will see more efforts by the state to demonise and legislate against home schooling. This must not be allowed to happen. I read a report about how an armed police 'SWAT' team in the tyranny that is Germany arrived without warning, threatened to batter down the door of a home schooling family and kidnapped their four children. The Home School Legal Defense Association said the family were disputing the 'World War II-era requirement that all children submit to the indoctrination programs in the nation's public schools'. Witnesses said the ludicrous raid by these numbskulls for the crime of not wishing to have children mind-programmed was 'brutal and vicious'. The parents were not told where their children were being taken and were warned they would 'not be seeing them any time soon'. The mother was blocked from kissing a child goodbye by a psychopathic police officer who said, 'it's too late for that'. The emotional impact on children imposed by these empathy-deleted 'child-protectors' seems not to matter. This is the world we are living in, with the Archontic demonisation of anyone who bucks The

System. A bill proposed by arrogant and idiot politicians in West
Virginia would ban home schooling. Once again, the Home School Legal
Defense Association is on the case and they must be getting very busy as
The System seeks to block any effort to free children from their
programming.

The best form of independent education for me is termed 'self-
directed learning', which allows children to decide what they want to
learn based on their passions and interests or experiences that they have.
Psychology professor Dr Peter Gray concluded in his study that
children's mental health particularly improved when they engaged in
self-directed education where they had more freedom and control of
their own learning. In the process of researching and pursuing their
interests they learn how to read, write and other skills normally
delivered as separate 'lessons'. This frees the child's mind from the
straightjacket or state-jacket and their brains develop differently and
process information differently through brain placidity (changing the
brain through information input and the way it is used). State-controlled
'education' is actually causing the brain and its information processing
pathways to develop in a communal fashion through communal
information received and that's another reason why so many people
think and react (decode) in the same way – with a herd mentality.
Another facet of all this is to 'protect' children from everything and
anything that would help them become independent people and instead
make them look to the state for guidance and protection from the ever-
growing list of 'dangers' they are told to be frightened about. 'Health
and Safety' Mafiosi in Britain are constantly thinking of new ways to
stifle children's development by banning everything from climbing trees
to playground games and having sports days cancelled because the
grass is 'damp'. What this is doing to children can be confirmed in what
happens when you do the opposite. An outdoor nursery in Dorset,
England, is based in woodland where children clamber over trees, play
on rope swings, saw wood, chop vegetables and cook lunch over an
open fire. Government inspectors were reported to be 'astonished to find
the children showing unusually high levels of confidence and
independence'. Some schools in Texas have had tremendous results from
giving children two 15-minute break times every morning and afternoon
for do-what-you-like 'unstructured play' in a move inspired by the
experience in countries like Finland. Teachers at Eagle Mountain
Elementary in Fort Worth report that children are learning more because
they are better able to focus in class and pay attention. Others have
introduced meditation instead of punishment and seen clear
improvements in behaviour. This is what could be happening
everywhere but it isn't because the Web doesn't want that and most
teachers are so programmed by the state they would never consider

such a change in approach. State obsession with stopping sporting competition in schools is connected, too. 'Everyone must get a prize' dilutes incentive to improve at whatever is involved. Everyone has unique gifts, and education should be developing them and not telling children they can't pursue their gifts to full potential because it will make children with other gifts feel inferior. This is the downward spiral to communal mediocrity that Archontic Reptilians and their hybrid *El*-ite have set out to achieve.

## A matter of degree

Schools are only the first stage of the education program. Another accepted norm today (familiarity) is that young people must go on to college and university. Why? 'Well, that's what you're supposed to do, isn't it?' Yes, but *why*? And *who says*? I left school at 15 and never took a major exam in my life. I have taught myself what I need to know on my own terms. Why would I have been better going to university? I wouldn't and in fact the opposite is the case. University would have been to the detriment of my understanding as I spent even more years downloading the 'reality' The System wanted me to believe in. I have been taken aback at some of the students I have met and debated with at major universities such as Oxford and Cambridge, and observed the software responses and perceptions which they mistake for intelligence and being informed. This doesn't apply to everyone and I have been immensely encouraged to see how many young people – nothing like the majority but increasing in numbers – have been through the sausage machine and yet retained their own right to free thought. I am seeing a fork in the road where many young people are awakening from The Program while others go ever deeper into it. Perceptions and behaviour of the latter on college campuses around the world crosses the line in my opinion into the realms of psychological illness and I will come to that in due course. Another Archontic aspect of so-called higher education in

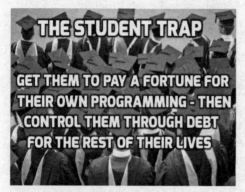

more and more countries is to make students pay for their own programming and get mired in debt to corporations for decades and potentially for life (Fig 347). Debt means control and trapping people in a financial bind from their teenage years, which forces them to serve The System on its terms to pay back their debt to the same System. Student debt is catastrophic. At the time of writing nearly 45

**Figure 347:** Students held fast in debt slavery – control.

million American students owe $1.3 *trillion* in loan debt to pay for their education (programming) and the figure is rising at around $2,726.27 *every second* according to a debt clock developed for MarketWatch.com. Higher 'education' fees in the UK (introduced by Archontic Tony Blair) are claimed to be the most expensive in the English-speaking world with an average per student closing in on £50,000. A 2017 report by the Institute for Fiscal Studies (IFS) said that three-quarters of graduates will never pay off their student loans, while many will still be paying them back into their 50s. Students from low-income families were racking up education bills of £57,000. Here we have children stressing over their exams to secure grades good enough to go to university and be swamped by debt (control) at the very start of their lives. They do so because there are so few jobs when they leave school and, well, that's what you do, isn't it, go to university? Ironically, there are also few jobs, and certainly few well-paid ones, comparative to numbers when students leave university. Many then realise that what they have spent their formative years striving for – a degree (of programming) – was actually a hoax ... and a very expensive one. Universities and colleges are not places of learning today so much as places of earning. Pack 'em in and pile 'em high. Every new student is a till-ringer. If you want to do something and a degree in this or that is the only way to get there I can understand why people do it. But going to university for its own sake to rack up debt for decades at least? That is surely madness. Don't fall for the hoax because that is all it is. Don't let them kid you that pieces of paper define you and your life, success and failure. They DO NOT – unless you allow them to. What will your parents and others think? Who gives a damn? That's their problem, not yours. They are themselves, but you are YOU. It's *your* life, not theirs.

'Education' also programs many young people to know their place in the Archontic hierarchy. Private schools for the wealthy produce the leaders and administrators (the governors) while state schools produce

**Figure 348:** The hierarchy starts with school.

**Figure 349:** Know your place.

the workers and slaves (the governed). There is some overlap, but shockingly small (Figs 348 and 349). I was told as a kid on a Leicester council estate to 'know my class'. I never accepted that even then. 'Class' is another program both for 'upper' and 'lower' classes and an illusion to obscure the fact that we are one Infinite Awareness. 'Upper' and 'lower' class 'education' is designed to emphasise and sell that illusion. There are few more programmed with The System's software than those 'educated' at private schools and they then go into positions of power and influence to impose their programmed perceptions on the population, with almost none of them realising they are programmed at all. But they are, and by now massively so, along with almost everyone else who has been through the 'education' system whether private or state (both controlled by the Archontic *El*-ite).

## Programmed child = programmed adult

The whole point of fake education is to guide and shepherd the minds of

**Figure 350:** The desperately narrow band of possibility that humans call 'normal' and 'the real world'. It is neither 'normal', except in the sense of constant repetition, nor 'real'.

**Figure 351:** We are sheep so you must be. We're normal – you're mad ... baa, baa, baa ...

the population to the same collective perception or what I call the Postage Stamp Consensus (Fig 350). This is a common and severely limited view of reality, possibility and 'normal' which children and students have spent the first phases of their lives daily downloading. Postage stamp perception goes like this: We live in a solid world and everything is apart from everything else; we are our name, race, background and whatever other labels we choose to apply to ourselves and each other; and history, physics, science, medicine and reality are all that The System says they are. Where is Infinite Awareness and All Possibility? They never get a mention. Postage Stamp Consensus is an infinitesimal speck of possibility, and when compared with *infinite* possibility the (systematic) myopia is staggering. This confirms the contention of German philosopher Arthur

Schopenhauer that 'every man takes the limits of his own field of vision for the limits of the world'. Schopenhauer was born in 1788 and he was describing human society as it still is today. Not everyone buys the Postage Stamp reality, but the manipulators know that if they seize the minds of the great majority any dissenters or free thinkers will be largely kept in line by peer pressure (Fig 351). This is the process by which those who have bought the official version of normal insist that everyone else does the same or face collective ridicule, condemnation, dismissal or contempt. There is also a phenomenon which underpins the Postage Stamp known as 'entrainment' when brainwaves synchronise together in line with the most powerful frequency. If you place three violins together vibrating to the same note another violin placed alongside will start to vibrate to the same note even though it was playing another or none before. A study in *Current Biology* by researchers from New York University and the Max Planck Institute of Empirical Aesthetics found that brainwaves synchronise into similar patterns when students pay attention in class and when those in a group are engaged with each other. Co-lead author Suzanne Dikker said: 'We think that all these effects can be explained by shared attention mechanisms during dynamic group interactions.' But having the same perceptions which lead to shared *attention* and *focus* can also synchronise brainwave activity because perceptions are frequencies and shared perceptions = shared frequencies. Postage Stamp Consensus is a collective standing wave construct. Collective thoughts sharing the same perceptions literally combine their compatible frequencies to create a standing wave oscillating on the spot and encompassing information or perception fields that reflect the accepted norms of what constitutes the world and reality. Schools and universities are founded on such standing waves and so are centres of politics, media etc. These standing waves and the information they oscillate in their stationary fields are added to every day by the thoughts and perceptions that emanate from those in their midst. Anyone entering these collective frequencies and oscillations who do not hold fast to their own personal oscillation (perceptions, values) find themselves being vibrated into line or 'entrained' into the collective oscillation (perceptions, beliefs, behaviour traits). This is how collective herd minds are formed as standing waves, and why many people go into politics for genuine reasons but soon

**Figure 352:** Sheep need a sheepdog to keep them in line – humans police each other.

become everything they went into
politics to oppose. They have been
entrained into the collective
standing wave oscillation and so
they think and behave as it does.
Once you monopolise a sense of
'normal' everything else
automatically follows. At least sheep
need a shepherd and sheepdog to
keep them in line. The System is the
shepherd, but humans have long
dispensed with the dog (Fig 352).
They keep each other in line through
the arrogance of ignorance and this
is collective psychological fascism
(Fig 353). Anyone who challenges
the Postage Stamp is waved away as
mad, stupid or dangerous and often
(as with me) all three (Fig 354). This
is no different from prisoners in a
cell combining to stop another
prisoner escaping and this can start
at the earliest age. Even small
children can target children who are
considered in some way different.
This reaction is encoded in their
information fields by the counterfeit
spirit and can only be overridden by

**Figure 353:** I can't hear you – I only have ears
for the Postage Stamp.

**Figure 354:** The arrogance of ignorance.

opening to conscious beyond The Program. Part of the role of
'education' and media is to activate these latent responses and reactions
although the foot soldiers won't know that.

## Programmed programming

All across society we have programmed programmers.
Government/military mind control operations program people to
program others and collectively we have the same principle. The most
programmed are invariably those who have been most successful in
their school and university careers. They are the ones who have
absorbed the Postage Stamp most comprehensively and told their
examiners what they want to hear. They will have also stayed in the
psychological programming unit ('education') for the longest. The
System's obsession with university degrees to secure its top jobs is not
by chance. Okay, you might say that a degree is confirmation of an
intelligent mind and that's why they do it; but it *isn't* either in the sense

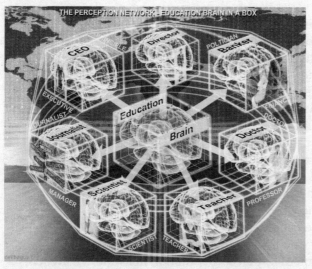

**Figure 355:** Postage Stamp people programmed by the same System – I'm right, you're right, he's right, she's right, we're all right.
© www.neilhague.com

of a confirmation of intelligence or why they really do it if you go deep enough in the shadows. A degree is really a confirmation of the ability to absorb and remember information and tell The System what it has told you. Somewhere within that psychology is at least a subconscious acceptance of authority's omnipotence. There will be exceptions, there always are, but I am talking generally in all that I say here. The educationally and perceptually programmed go on to become politicians, government administrators, scientists, doctors, academics, judges, lawyers, CEOs, journalists, etc. They take with them into those society-directing and controlling professions the core Postage Stamp programming and its sense of 'normal'. They then spend the rest of their lives confirming to each other that their downloaded version of reality is how things are when it is largely myopic nonsense (Fig 355). I can summarise the consequences in a single sentence: The world is run by people who are not very bright but think they are. This is a devastating combination. Politicians make decisions and impose laws based on their downloaded sense of 'normal' and most scientists make conclusions about reality from the same perspective. Doctors treat, academics teach, judges judge, lawyers advocate, CEOs rule and journalists report all from the same core belief in Postage Stamp normal. They are making decisions as if the world is solid (limitation) when it's not (infinite possibility). Journalists writing about a health topic won't go to an alternative practitioner who may have great understanding of the subject. They will consult a doctor who will quote the Postage Stamp. The same happens with any (rare) journalistic exploration into the nature of reality. They will go to scientists who sing from the song sheet. Postage Stamp programs and advocates confirm to each other and the public that the Postage Stamp is omnipotent when it is only an agreed-upon collective hallucination. I have met or observed at close range many people from all these society-

directing professions and the scale of
their perception programming never
ceases to amaze, nor their arrogant
dismissal of another view.
Exceptions are so few they prove the
rule. All day every day television
shows wheel out 'experts' (usually
the most perceptually programmed)
to tell the public what to think and
do. Perceptually-blind interviews
perceptually-blind and they call it
expertise. Central to the whole
delusion is to persuade people that

**Figure 356:** Exactly where The System and
The Program want you to be.

they 'get it' when they don't even begin to 'get it' (Fig 356). The System
is a self-generating perpetual/perceptual motion machine, a conveyor
belt for the mind like any on a factory floor. Raw material (children)
enter at one end and they are processed into adults who serve the
machine until they wear out and drop in the trash can (cemetery) or
recycling bin (reincarnation) at the other. Those that can see what is
happening or some aspect of it are silenced by peer pressure and
ridiculed and demonised by the media if they are in the public eye. This
continues generation after generation after generation – work, buy,
consume, die, work, buy, consume, die. They call this 'life', apparently,
but it is not life. It is existence. It is survival. It is The Program. It is the
simulation. It is the Matrix. You are a slave, Neo.

## Who am I? What I am told to be

A sense of 'little me' will lead to a particular perception of authority and
a sense of powerlessness in the face of perceived all-powerful authority
leads to a sense of 'little me'. Only self-identity with Infinite Self –
Infinite 'Me' – can break yet another self-perpetuating cycle. The

perception of 'little me' is a standing
wave oscillation holding that
perception in place until awareness
beyond the oscillation comes in to
allow the stationary wave to move
and expand its vision of the
possible. All but a few self-identify
with labels such as man, woman,
black, white, British, American,
French, African, Christian, Muslim,
Jew, Hindu, socialist, conservative,
middle class, working class, name,
age and birthdate. I refer to this as

**Figure 357:** I am a label. The only question is
which ones do I choose?

label consciousness and the subsequent self-identity as Phantom Self (Fig 357). People constantly enslave their minds by labelling their perceptions of self-identity. These labels (the number is increasing and sub-dividing all the 'time') are not who we really are. They're simply words to describe what we are *experiencing*. 'We' are Infinite Awareness having those experiences. But how can you mass control and mind-scam billions in awareness of the infinite magnificence of who they really are? You can't. They won't accept your control for a start and they will see through any machinations you employ to impose it covertly. To mass control you must promote a self-identity with Phantom Self which in all its principle functions and perceptions is five-sense self. Education, media, science, medicine and all forms of mass communication therefore peddle a belief in the apartness of everything rather than unity. They pore over the twigs and ignore the forest. This focuses *attention* almost entirely in the five-sense realm of the holographic simulation, like a moth to a flame. Peripheral vision fades and what is left is the light of the oncoming train delivering a lifetime of programmed perception. Most young people leave the 'educational' womb of their foundation programming and head out into the adult world with this downloaded sense of self and reality. Their options, ambitions and dreams are consciously and subconsciously dictated by The System and the self-identity downloaded from The System. Control of global finance, business and government means that the Archontic Hidden Hand decides who gets the money, jobs and support, and who doesn't. Adult life for the majority is one of constant survival (reptilian brain), while for others it is chasing dreams usually based on money, status and power (reptilian brain) that The System has told them is success. Software insecurity programs pulsing through the human waveform field and the manipulation of fear mean that comparatively few are secure in and of themselves. They seek reassurance from how others see them and this has many consequences. People will not say what they really think if it is at odds with the Postage Stamp worshipped by the consensus, and to be heralded as a success to placate their insecurity they must succeed in a way that others perceive as successful. Who decides that? The System does. They sell us our dreams to keep us asleep. How much money do you have? How famous are you? How much power over others and events do you have? A need for fame to mask insecurity is why Hollywood, entertainment

**Figure 358:** Gotta, gotta, gotta, must, must, must.

and media attract so many insecure people and explains the obsession with being famous at any cost. Reality TV shows feed off such emotional dependency. Those conscious beyond The Program have no need for such ego-massaging. They are what they are and what others think of them does not enter the equation when the mirror comes into view. You can see why the Hidden Hand and its System works so hard to suppress any connection to expanded awareness. If they didn't, it would be game over.

You leave school or university and *BANG - THEY'RE OFF!* Gotta, gotta, gotta, must, must, must (Fig 358). I must *survive!* I must *succeed!* I must *compete!* I must *be* someone! The Program is life-long and works the same the whole way through. To hide the programming, they have to sell the illusion of choice and pin different labels to apparently different phases of life when they are really only different names for the same continuation. You are, for example, offered a long list of choices for bagels, breads, coffee and cheese, but usually only two (and virtually identical) for which group of people runs the government. They give you choices with things that don't matter to them, and next to none with things that do. Adult life is promoted as different to school and university life when they are a continuation of the same program. Mum walks in to tell her still-sleeping child: 'Come on, darling, you'll be late for school' (prison). When the 'education' phase is over a partner walks in and says: 'Come on, darling, you'll be late for work' (again often prison). 'What will the teacher say?' becomes 'What will the boss say?' Labels have changed but the outcome is the same. In fact, the adult version is worse because the child can get a telling off while the adult faces being out of a job and unable to pay the bills. Fear is the currency of control – fear of the teacher, fear of the boss, fear of government, police, taxman, each other. The System is a ball and chain at every 'phase' if we succumb to it. Then there is the dangle-a-carrot deal. During the 'education' years the carrot is work hard, do what you're told and sacrifice childhood to study and revision and you'll get your reward with a 'good job'. In the adult years the carrot is work hard, do what you're told and sacrifice life to career and 'getting on' and your reward will be 'success' or at least financial survival (Fig 359). Never live in the moment – the NOW. Always focus on the next moments in the illusory 'future'. Life is what happens while you're busy making others plans, as John Lennon

**Figure 359:** My goodness this carrot moves as quickly as I do. I better try harder.

superbly put it. This is the whole idea. Archontic society is structured to hold fast the perceptions of entrapped and bewildered Spirit to stop people ever grasping what is really going on. If you can keep them focused on the future that doesn't exist their attention is enticed out of the NOW, the door to expanded awareness where all answers await. Focus on the illusory 'past' is equally effective. Keep them focused on their hopes and ambitions for 'tomorrow' and their resentments and regrets from 'yesterday'. What a scam 'hope' is, too. Where does 'hope' by definition always relate to? It's the illusory 'future'. Hope keeps you out of the NOW where hope is redundant. Hope as a figment of the 'future' has no place in the eternal NOW. I give you hope = I give you a carrot. Don't eat it all at once ... but, no, sorry, you can't eat *any* of it, can you? It's always just too far ahead. Never mind, accept the shit we give you today in the hope it will be better tomorrow. Then, when tomorrow comes, do the same.

## A Martian speaks ...

The System is specifically designed to generate maximum fear, anxiety and stress and my goodness does it work, or what? Billions are stressed by the fear of not surviving, paying the rent and putting food on the table, while others are stressed by the pressure of being so 'successful' (Fig 360). Most fear not having enough money while others fear losing the money they have or not making still more. Anxiety and manipulation of fear and perception ensure that we impose pressure and stress on each other whether the others be children or perceived hierarchy subordinates. Parents and teachers pressure children to conform and 'achieve' (pass exams, get a good System job), and each hierarchical level of society exerts pressure on the level below. Meet that grade, reach that target, sell that crap. This serves the Archontic force by hijacking focus, suppressing vibration and generating a constant supply of 'food' through the frequency band of fear, stress and anxiety. Another

bonus is that when people are in emotional turmoil they stop thinking straight as imbalances in the emotional field impact upon the mental one. If you are not thinking straight how can you see through The Program? This mind game is so effective that people get up before the sun and work into the night to be 'successful', 'make it' or simply keep the boss happy. They are so focused on the goal there is no peripheral vision or big

**Figure 360:** He's so successful. Well done.

picture reassessment. Questions like 'Why am I doing this?', 'Where am I going?' and 'Why?' remain unasked and unconsidered. Gotta, gotta, gotta ... must, must, must (Fig 361). But why have you 'gotta' and what is this 'must'? Pull back for a moment from five-sense focus of Phantom Self. What would a Martian say looking down on human society who was asked to describe what happens here? Well, the Martian would say, first

**Figure 361:** Keep on running ... but to where?

you are born and almost immediately you enter a system of perception control that will be unceasing until you 'die'. The first phase downloads the foundation perception of reality and tells you want to think about everything and what you should consider rational and normal even though this 'normal' is insanity to anyone with even a smear of expanded awareness. A fundamental foundation of the entire hoax is inverting human perception to make insane appear sane and sane appear insane (Fig 362). They piss on us and we say it's raining (Fig 363). Our Martian would observe that once the initial programming is complete humans then spend the rest of their lives either in poverty barely surviving or making and selling 'things' that people are persuaded to 'need' and 'desire' when they often don't even want them once money is exchanged. Those too old and frail to continue to do this mostly retire on a pittance of a pension, or none at all, to complete their lives watching every penny while often cold and hungry in a familiar state of bare survival. A few have worked all their lives decade after

**Figure 362:** Sanity, apparently.

**Figure 363:** The human condition.

decade to save for a good pension and retirement so they can do what they want in their final years. Most of their life has been focused on enjoying the end of it and everything in between is sacrificed to work for a 'future' that doesn't exist. Then, when this cycle is over, er, you die. The Martian would shake his head and say: 'Madness isn't it?' And it is. Human society is a madhouse

**Figure 364:** Insanity that thinks it's sane.
© www.neilhague.com

which so many believe to be on the cutting edge of evolution because they can text their mate in an instant on the other side of the world (Fig 364). Such is the power of programming and familiarity (programming). I am not saying that nobody's job is worthwhile or that things are not made that we need in our current state of consciousness. Nor am I saying that everyone finds their job boring and wakes up dreading every new day. But look around at the ratio and far more is made that we don't need, far more done that doesn't need doing and far more greet the dawn with dread and despair every morning than those who greet it with joy. Something is seriously wrong.

## Money, money, money, funny money ...

Control of the creation and circulation of 'money' is pivotal to holding The System together and dictating human life choices, or lack of them. Money is controlled by the Archontic few within the less-than-one-percent. Dutch financial insider Ronald Bernard said earlier that at the centre only a very few people control global finance. Archontic Reptilian bloodlines established the money system (especially through the Rothschilds) and this is their vehicle to limit choice and control what people do and produce by dictating where the money goes or doesn't. Their obsession with money is far more about control than seeking mega wealth only for the sake of it (in the Deep State, I mean). I have exposed how the money scam works in considerable detail in *The Perception Deception* and other books because it is so crucial to how mass control is possible. There is a video explanation on Davidicke.com which you can access via the search engine with the words 'essential knowledge for a Wall Street protestor'. If you ensnare people in a system that demands money for everything including the basics of life and survival you impose a collective dependency on the few who run that system and

**Figure 365:** How the banking system controls the world.

**Figure 366:** Outrageous madness but humanity rolls over and takes it – most don't even know how 'money' is created.

both create and circulate the money. You want a home? You want to eat? Then do as we say or you'll get no money. How many people are not doing what they *really* want to do with their lives because they 'don't have the money'? The number is off the scale and includes almost everyone. Yet money is another illusion, another hoax. Archontic control of governments which I will explain later has allowed laws to be passed to hand power over global society to the Archontically-controlled banking and financial system. This is founded on fractional reserve lending which means private banks owned by Archontic Reptilian hybrid families can 'lend' money that doesn't exist called 'credit' and charge interest on it. They can lend some nine or ten times more than they actually have (much more in truth with other manipulations) and charge interest on the lot – charge interest on illusory 'credit' that has not, does not and will never exist (Fig 365). Put a dollar in a bank and it can lend that dollar multiple times and charge interest on every loan. People think they are borrowing 'money' from banks when it's only a conjuring trick on the balance sheet. 'We will loan you the money to buy a house' really means we will create credit out of nothing against the value of the house and we will retain ownership until you pay us back – with interest. People and families are being thrown on the street for not being able to pay back 'money' that has not, does not and will ever exist, and so could not have been 'lent' in the first place (Fig 366). Archon bloodline banks are 'lending' you an illusion that only has value because people believe that it does. In return bankers get the collateral of your house, land, vehicle or business. If you fail with the payments and interest because you lose your job the bank takes your home as we have seen with the mass foreclosures since the crash of 2008. One-percent of humanity (largely Archon families) own some 50 percent of the world's wealth. This has been made possible by centuries of swapping created-out-of-nothing credit (money that doesn't exist) for wealth that *does* exist – property, land, businesses and resources. Give a man a gun and he can rob a bank. Give a man a bank and he can rob the world. Give a man control of the banking *system* and he can own the world. Nathan Rothschild (1777-1836), who built the family empire in Britain, said:

> *I care not what puppet is placed upon the throne of England to rule the Empire on which the sun never sets. The man who controls Britain's money supply controls the British Empire and I control the British money supply.*

He could have said today that the man who controls the world's money supply controls the world because that is the situation we face.

**Figure 367:** Compartmentalised pyramid that controls world finance.

**Figure 368:** Ask most politicians about the role of the Bank For International Settlements and their blank face will say it all. The human hierarchy is a structure founded on compartmentalised ignorance.

The global web with The Spider at the centre owns and controls the banking system and through the Web apparently different organisations like the World Bank, International Monetary Fund (IMF), European Central Bank (ECB) and national central banks are simultaneously coordinated to the same end even though they appear in the public arena to be operating independently. One of the prime vehicles for this coordination is the Bank for International Settlements in Basle, Switzerland, a private organisation established in 1930 by Archontic Reptilian families (notably the Rothschilds and Rockefellers) where the heads of national central banks meet regularly outside of governments to agree collective policy (be told what it is). Figures 367 and 368 symbolise the structure of compartmentalised hierarchy that allows the few to dictate national and global economic decisions and direction. Money overwhelmingly comes into circulation not through governments but through private banks (ultimately owned by the same Web) making loans of non-existent credit and credit is *debt*. The very unit of exchange that we call money starts out from its very 'creation' as a *debt*. Money is created as a debt and debt = control. This domination by the Archontic Reptilian banking system over the creation of the currency allows them to decide how much 'money' is in circulation by how much illusory credit they choose to 'loan'. Booms and busts are created at will by increasing or decreasing the amount of theoretical 'money' in circulation that is available for people to spend. Interest rates are manipulated to the same outcome. This is the ever-recurring sequence: (1) issue lots of credit and get lots of people and businesses in debt to money that doesn't exist; (2) dramatically decrease the money in circulation by reducing the number of loans and/or increasing interest rates to trigger an 'economic downturn'; (3) steal all the real wealth that you have taken as collateral when your debtors can't repay the credit 'loan' plus interest. That's another thing – the interest. Banks only 'create' and 'lend' the amount you have agreed to borrow, but you are repaying that figure *plus interest*. The interest is never created and so there is never even nearly enough money in circulation, theoretical or otherwise, to pay back all the outstanding debt in the form of principle and interest. People losing their homes, land, businesses and livelihoods is built into the very structure of the financial system on purpose. This is less obvious during a boom with lots of money in circulation but becomes painfully apparent when the money supply is curtailed.

Could it get any more insane? Yes, it could. Archontic governments also borrow from Archontic banks in the same way and the population is made responsible for paying it back, plus interest. Virtually every country is owned by the banking cartel because of this. Why don't governments issue their own money interest free? Simple – the same network that controls the banks controls governments via the same Web. Why did bankers who caused the crash of 2008 (and every other) end up afterwards wealthier than ever while the public that bailed them out is mired in austerity and stuck with repaying the bail-out money *(borrowed from the financial system that was bailed out)*? Governments and banks are two strands in the same Web. Bail-outs are now being replaced by bail- *ins* since the manufactured banking crisis in Cyprus in 2011 (Fig 369). Bail-outs come from governments (the people collectively) while bail-ins make it

**Figure 369:** Birth of the bail-in.

legal for banks to steal the money of their depositors to get themselves out of trouble. They call this a depositor 'haircut' in the parlance. Money is safe in the bank? You must be joking. When a bank crashes, you are only an unsecured creditor. Bail-ins are the means through which the *El*-ite plan to part everyone from their money including those today who think they are doing well and that none of this is their problem (Fig 370). If you are not part of the one percent (much less in truth) they

**Figure 370:** A massive financial crash is planned at some point to trigger bail-ins and steal the wealth of those not within the *El*-lite.

want what you have, too, and they will get it unless people refocus their eyes, see what is happening and come together in unity. Laws continue to increase around the world allowing governments to take money from bank accounts without the holder's permission and this is part of the same agenda. Plans are in the pipeline by the EU to freeze accounts of failing banks so their depositors can't get their money out. Criminal levels of taxation on almost everything we earn and buy have been imposed so the few can further vampire the population, dictate choice and create dependency. If people realised how much of their income goes in ever-burgeoning forms of taxation they would be shocked to the core. Those on the left in politics who demand higher taxation have no idea what they are supporting. Oh, it helps the poor if you tax the rich? Really? Anyone noticed that no matter how high taxation becomes human deprivation goes on or gets worse and the same with public services? Anyone noticed that it's the not-so-rich who bear the brunt of taxation while mega corporations pay so little? Austrian Chancellor Christian Kern made the point that Amazon and Starbucks pay a lower percentage of tax in his country than a local sausage stall while Apple paid little more than one percent tax on £7.5 billion in UK sales. Google and Facebook are the same. Definition of parasite: 'An organism which lives in or on another organism (its host) and benefits by deriving nutrients at the other's expense.' Taxation pays for wars and mass murder and most of it is sucked through many and various means into the coffers of Archontic families. Their armament companies are only one example. Have you observed also that political 'heroes' of the Left and Right who claim to be 'anti-establishment' and challenging the *El*-ite never talk about how banks lend money that doesn't exist or pledge to do something about it? There are three main reasons for this. The vast majority of politicians don't understand how the money system works; the next highest number haven't got the guts to address it; and the smallest number know what is going on and support it as servants of the Web in awareness of what they are doing. We fix the money hoax or nothing can change. Governments issuing the currency interest free and excluding the private banking system from the creation of fresh-air money through fractional reserve lending would be the place to start. Governments should establish investment banks which create the currency and circulate that *interest free*. The private criminal syndicate banking system would then fall and humanity would have a gigantic yoke off its back.

## The God Program

I have long described religion as the greatest form of mind control ever invented and so it has been. Religion was invented to kidnap the minds of the population and set them at war with each other. Nothing has enslaved humanity this far more comprehensively than the unquestioning, unyielding and immovable belief in the multiple versions of the God Program. I mean 'multiple' in the sense of so many

**Figure 371:** Pseudo-randomness or opposames. The same program in different guises.

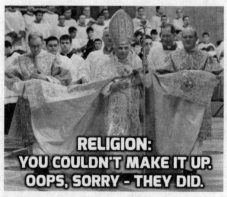

**Figure 372:** It's a joke, right? Yep, confirmed.

different names, but it's all the same program structured in the same way (Fig 371). Recurring elements are a congregation or group of followers; middle men (usually men and usually in frocks) who tell you what God wants you to do; and an omnipotent deity or god (occasionally gods) as the focus of worship (Fig 372). Check out almost every religion and you will see this repeating blueprint. There is also 'the book'. All perceptions, guidance, inspiration and insight are located only between the covers of 'the book', be it the Bible, Koran or whatever, even though they normally don't know who wrote 'the book' or in what circumstances and with what encoded bias or motive. Anyone who questions the particular orthodoxy is by definition misguided, a blasphemer or in the most extreme cases an infidel to be eliminated as with Sabbatean Frankism's manufactured Wahhabi Islam. Religion is for me a form of insanity defined as chronic myopia and sacrificing all rights to free thought. I was reading a news report while writing this chapter about the behaviour of ultra-orthodox Jews on flights with Israeli state airline El Al who refuse to sit next to women. They say it's against their religion and their God wouldn't like it. But their God created women, yes? What happened, did he have a bad day? Help me out here, I'm confused. If women don't want to move from their seats some of these religious crazies stand in the aisle refusing to sit down (Fig 373). A Jewish group in Hackney, London, displayed posters during a 'Torah Procession' telling women which side of the road they had to walk 'to avoid men and women touching who are not married or related' (Fig 374). Can you contemplate being in fear from morning till night every day in case you touch a woman however accidentally to whom you are not married or related? The level of mind and perception control is beyond comprehension. Another Jewish sect sought to ban girls and women from higher education because it was 'dangerous' and 'against the Torah'. Here are just a few – and I mean a few – of the things that Jewish people are banned by their religion from doing on the Sabbath (Shabbat, Saturn-day):

Applying heat to something in order to change it (baking for instance); driving (fires are banned from being started or extinguished and cars move with sparks and fuel); the same heating/sparking deal forbids turning on electrical appliances, lights, radios and televisions and the use of telephones (lights must be switched on before the Sabbath begins or you must remain in the dark); detach anything that is glued, sewed or perforated and this includes ripping off toilet paper and paper towels (don't ask). On and on it goes. Writing, drawing, erasing, even tearing a package if the rip goes across letters and words is taboo. So, too, is watering plants, picking flowers, handling money or putting the finishing touch to an object. The list is excruciatingly detailed, but one

**Figure 373:** Rule book minds of a rule book religion.

**Figure 374:** *Ahhh!!! Don't you touch me.'*

website I saw offered some good advice. Tape lights in the bathroom so you don't accidently turn them on without thinking if you want a wee in the middle of the night. Nice one. Pre-tear toilet paper and paper towels, put pencils, markers and pens away and pre-open bottle caps and packages before the Sabbath kicks in. You opened a bottle on the Sabbath? *Blasphemer!* I also love the array of get-out clauses which include light timers. They can be used to automatically turn lights on and off so long as they are set before the Sabbath starts. I bet they do a roaring trade in North London, Tel Aviv and New York. There is another wheeze of having a Gentile present who can do anything because only God's chosen people are subject to this craziness. Another Sabbath law prohibits 'transporting an object between a private domain and the public domain, or for a distance of 4 cubits within the public domain'. The madness reaches such mind-exploding proportions that Jews are banned on the Sabbath from anything considered work which includes using wheelchairs and prams or holding babies and keys outside a person's home or garden. This means that disabled and elderly Jews and babies often have to stay at home from nightfall on Friday until nightfall on Saturday when the nonsense ends. Who insists on all this? Well, it's what the Old Testament god demanded, apparently. He's a fucker that one. Jews in North London have sought to surround their community with a six-mile perimeter boundary using fishing wire suspended on tall poles. No, I am not making this up. They say this would create a huge 'eruv' which is defined as 'an urban area enclosed by a wire boundary which symbolically extends the private domain of Jewish households into public areas, permitting activities within it that are normally forbidden in public on the Sabbath.' Sounds like a bit of skulduggery to me but it seems the Old Testament tyrant must be okay with it. Such unyielding orthodoxy is a driving force behind the State of Israel and yet most Jews don't agree with these religious-Zionist fanatics. A 2017 poll found that 55 percent of Jewish Israelis want to reassess the fusion of Judaism and the state which they believed reflected ultra-orthodox Jews and not them. Almost 100 percent of secular respondents questioned wanted the role of religion reduced or the complete separation of religion and state, but their views are rarely heard compared with the screaming extremists.

## Madness masquerading as 'faith'

Extremes of Islamic believers insist that women can only appear in public with their entire body covered in black. Eyes are thankfully exempt. How thoughtful (Fig 375). Women are banned from driving in Saudi Arabia, the official 'home' of Islam, or rather Wahhabism, and cannot travel unaccompanied or without permission. Children have been forced to burn to death in fires and blocked from escaping to a

**Figure 375:** At the risk of repeating myself – it's a joke, right?

public place because they were not considered by Saudi religious police to be in accordance with the dress code. Fathers have been known to stop lifeguards saving their daughters from drowning because it would involve them being touched. Tunisian protesters demanded the right to eat and drink in public during the Muslim fasting month of Ramadan after non-fasters were arrested for 'attacking public morals'. There must be no laws against attacking basic intelligence, then, or the authorities would be forced to arrest themselves. Religious software can't grasp the concept that just because they give their mind away doesn't mean that everyone else has to. This is a universal theme of The Program and not only the God version either which says that you must believe what I believe. These are more extreme cases and there are many saner expressions of Islam, but even then, their whole perception of self, life and the world is dictated by an ancient doctrine downloaded through repetition and force since childhood. The same happens with Judaism, Christianity, Hinduism and all the rest of them. Major religions are *all* founded on ancient (and not so ancient) doctrines which, once committed to paper or tradition, rule the roost for often thousands of years while anything above and beyond them is dismissed or condemned. Where is free choice or thought when you believe that to please your god you must get on your knees five times a day and pray to Mecca (the Saturn cube)? 'Muslim' means 'One Who Submits'. Sabbatean Frankist Dönmeh Islamic extremists in Saudi Arabia and Pakistan go around policing their population with fascist arrogance and hand out their punishments at will to enforce their insanity on others – especially women. Not believing in extremes of Islam or being guilty of 'atheism and blasphemy' can be punishable by death, so desperate are those states to control the people through religious imposition. Do people really think that the Dönmeh Sabbatean Frankist Saudi 'royal' family follow Islam in private? It's their mass-control system, that's all. Religion can be – and often is – a form of insanity both among the enforcers and parents who impose it on their children. A Malaysian boy had both legs amputated and later died after being repeatedly beaten at a private religious school by a brain-dead maniac. Any religion that has to employ violence and intimidation to maintain its control clearly does not believe in the power of its arguments to promote itself. Parental indoctrination of children into any religion is a disgrace beyond words and more child abuse when the right to free thought without pressure or insistence to conform is denied.

Hinduism is believed by many to be a more enlightened religion and became the inspiration behind the emergence of the Western New Age movement. I see just another tyranny of the mind with its own multiple insanities. A man was beaten to death by a Hindu mob in 2017 when he refused to tell them the whereabouts of Muslim and Hindu teenagers who had eloped in Uttar Pradesh. We can't have Muslims and Hindus fall in love with each other. That's against our religion where marriages have to be arranged to suit tyrannical idiot parents and religious software programs. Two small children were beaten unconscious and electrocuted to death by an Indian father, again in 2017, when his mother convinced him that the electrocution would clear them of evil spirits and allow her to achieve 'enlightenment'. Such is the inverted insanity of the extreme religious mind. A ten-year-old girl was sacrificed in India in 2017 in a 'black magic ritual' instigated by her uncle

**Figure 376:** Mass slaughter buffalo – it makes the goddess happy. But harm a cow and you're in big trouble. The gods like cows.

and carried out by a black magician to cure a paralysed man. Police said the killers believed the man had been 'gripped by evil spirits' and to cure him they had to 'sacrifice a minor girl within 40 days.' Until 2015 a Hindu festival close to the Indian border in Nepal was held every five years in honour of Gadhimai, the 'goddess of power', and at least tens of thousands of buffalo and other animals were killed in ritual sacrifice with some claiming the figure to be a lot more (Fig 376). Millions turned up to watch the killing which they believed would end evil and bring prosperity. It never did and they couldn't see that you don't end evil by committing it. Selling the animals to meat suppliers afterwards was more likely to be the source of prosperity. This was yet another mass sacrifice to the god or goddess in the form of death and terror. A massive Archontic energetic 'lunch' from a human religion which imposes its perceptual will on its followers by the manipulation of fear – fear of displeasing the gods and goddesses. You can please them with an animal holocaust so long as it does not involve a cow. The gods like cows. India's state of Gujarat has introduced life imprisonment for killing a cow with up to ten years for possession of beef. Buffalos? Not a problem, the gods are fine with that. Islam, Christianity, Judaism, Hinduism, the basic theme is the same. Decide what 'god' or the gods want and then impose this by intimidation, guilt, fear, law and even execution. Buddhism has its own extremists despite its image as a religion of peace, with attacks on Muslims in Sri Lanka and especially Myanmar where a human catastrophe has ensued as vast numbers of Rohingya Muslims flee persecution. Nearly all religions are worshipping in some form the Demiurgic/Archontic self-aware distortion and its non-human Reptilian and other conduits (Fig 377). Their different versions of the same 'god' demand that they engage in such distorted

Figure 377: Religions worshipping the fake 'god'.

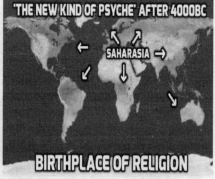

Figure 378: Major religions emerged in the same place and in the same period as the new psyche.

behaviour and belief because they are different versions of the same Archontic distortion. Many religions pursue male domination over female as we see with the extremes of Judaism, Islam and Christianity with its centuries of opposition to women priests. These male-dominated religions emerged from the same Saharasia in the same period following the new psyche which ushered in male-dominated societies (Fig 378). Religion is a creation of the new psyche to serve the Archontic distortion and its expression as Reptilians and Greys.

Christianity has a history of tyranny, mass slaughter and belief-imposition that makes Vlad the Impaler look like a cissy. Untold multitudes have had their lives ended, blighted and their perceptions limited for the best part of 2,000 years. Yet Christianity still provides the perceptual blueprint for an estimated 2.2 billion worldwide. Christianity is really the Church of Babylon which relocated with the bloodlines to Rome from where Christianity emerged as we know it today. The Babylonian trinity of Nimrod (father god), Semiramis (virgin mother) and Tammuz/Ninus (virgin-born son) became the 'Christian' trinity of Father God or Lord God, Jesus and Holy Spirit which is symbolised as a dove. Babylonians symbolised Semiramis, also known as Ishtar, as a dove and the attributes and titles they gave to Semiramis/Ishtar (virgin

**Figure 379:** The 'Christian' virgin mother story is a repeat of far older versions all over the world including the reptilian mother and child in Mesopotamia, Queen Semiramis in Babylon, and Isis in Egypt. Mother Mary appeared when the Church of Babylon relocated to Rome and became Christianity.

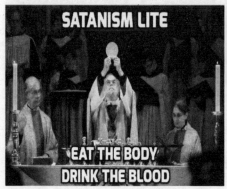

**Figure 380:** The Eucharist is an acceptable public version of what happens for real in satanic networks with their sacrificial rituals performed for thousands of years.

**Figure 381:** The 'crucifixion' is a symbol of human ritual sacrifice.

mother, Queen of Heaven) were handed to the symbolic character they called Mother Mary (Semiramis under another name). What is termed the 'Christian' story is only a plagiarised repeat of the same basic narrative told all over the world for thousands of years before Christianity. There are so many pre-biblical virgin mothers giving birth to saviours (Fig 379). See *The Perception Deception* and the chapter 'Archon Religion' for the detailed history and background to the religion myth. Babylon was an origin of today's human-sacrificing Sabbatean Frankism and Satanism which is why Babylon-inspired Christianity involves rituals like the Eucharist (drinking blood as wine and flesh as a biscuit). They are Satanism-lite (Fig 380). Christianity and other connected religions have a sacrificial altar as a throwback to the real thing in Babylon and elsewhere. Christianity's very symbol is a human sacrifice (Fig 381). Jesus was sacrificed on the orders of 'God' to 'save humanity'? Human sacrifices throughout 'history' have been performed to appease God or the gods and 'save humanity'. Now what 'God' could that be, I wonder??

## Same deity, same origin

Connections between 'different' religions are obvious. Judaism has a massive crossover with Christianity in the shared Old Testament while Islam includes the biblical characters Jesus, Mary and Abraham. They all believe their God created the Universe. True – the Demiurge and the simulation. All three religions involve the wearing of skullcaps (used by priests in Babylon) and claim to be the chosen people of their god. Jews say they are the chosen people above all others; Christianity claims that you can only get to heaven by believing in Jesus as your saviour; and Islam claims to be the only religion that will secure you a spot in Allah's paradise. Once you have a belief in God-given superiority you can mentally dehumanise non-believers and justify any scale of horror against them. This is what has happened and still does. Witness the mentally-deranged Islamic State or ISIS and what happens in Israel and the illegally-occupied Palestinian lands of Gaza and the West Bank. Judaism and Islam both demand the same ritually-sacrificed kosha and halal meat and neither, along with some Christian sects, eat pork. Their God says that pigs are unclean although the real origin are the beliefs of the ancient Middle East from where all three originated. You want people to do something? Easy – tell them God demands it.

The God Program subdivides in the way of fractal patterns which are embedded in the energetic construct of the simulation. Research that I mentioned earlier revealed how everything, whether 'physical' or psychological, follows repeating as above, so below fractal physics and they are encoded in religion. Fractals are holographic in the sense that larger patterns sub-divide into smaller exact copies (how the prime Demiurge distortion sub-divided into Archon 'copies'). Consider this pattern with religion. One religion is created which then sub-divides into copies of itself which operate with the same structure. Christianity began in Rome and then sub-divided into Catholic and Protestant which themselves sub-divided into other factions. The same happened with the Islamic sub-division into Shiite and Sunni and there are multiple versions of Judaism, Hinduism, etc. This was inevitable with Hinduism when you have tens of thousands of deities to choose from. Sub-divisions mean that original religions can be set at war with each other and *within* each other to divide, rule, perceptually conquer and hijack focus. In the end they are all sub-divisions of the Demiurge distortion and control system (Fig 382). Observe society in general and you will see the same fractal sub-divisions at work and in conflict everywhere. I have

long referred to these as 'opposames'
when two forces, organisations or
beliefs are in conflict and opposition
while being the same as each other.
Communism v fascism is an obvious
opposame. Religions have been such
a (literal) 'godsend' to human
perceptual control and if they didn't
exist the Demiurgic distortion would
have had to invent them. Er, which it
did. Here are some killer questions
with regard to religion that lift the
veil on their true reason for being:
Have major religions (and most
smaller ones) served human freedom
or human control? Have they
overwhelmingly been a source of
low-frequency energy or high-
frequency? Have they opened minds
or closed them? These are still more
questions that answer themselves (Fig
383).

**Figure 382:** Different religions – same deity.

Religions come in many guises far
removed from conventional priests
and churches. This is one definition:
'A pursuit or interest followed with
great devotion.' A devotion to sport,
shopping – anything – is a form of
religion. The deity becomes the
football star and the must-have brand

**Figure 383:** At least I can't be accused of
religious bias. I will be, though.

and the church becomes the stadium and the mall. Mainstream science is
a religion and its Bible is song-sheet orthodoxy. High priests of scientism
like Oxford professor Richard Dawkins exhibit perceptions and
behaviour that can be found with any priest and religion and it's
important to recognise the God Program when it's not standing in a
pulpit and wearing a frock. That version is easy to spot but the hidden
ones are less so. Soccer worship, shopping worship, celebrity worship,
money worship, career worship is still worship – 'the feeling or
expression of reverence and adoration for a deity'. Even the simulation
can't yet suppress and impose all perception to order if outside-the-
program consciousness is involved, and the Archontic mind-game
replaces one box or religion with another once the first is rejected. If
people continue to follow the psychological tram lines through the
perception-hijack of conventional religion then that is ideal; but there

have to be other boxes lying in wait that have a better disguise. The *El-ite* don't care what you believe so long as the belief doesn't stray far – preferably not at all – from the perception range of the five senses and you believe what you believe rigidly at the exclusion of other possibility. The Program is after all the hijacking of *attention*. To free ourselves from religion in all its forms and to recognise those that ensnare us we might ask this question: 'What dictates and controls my focus at the exclusion of other possibilities and information?' Whatever that may be is your personal prison of the mind focusing your attention on the dot so you don't see the picture. This is not to say that focusing on something is wrong – of course not. But when the focus is at the expense of peripheral vision The Program has you.

## Pennies (real ones) are dropping

Perceptual control enslaves the population on its journey from maternity to eternity. Most never see what is being done to them or if they do later in life they don't want to face the fact they have been had. They attack the messenger or just stay in denial and I understand that. Contemplating a lifetime of being hoaxed is hardly a place where people want to be, but, hey, better to know eventually than not at all. It's just an experience within infinite forever. The great news is that so many more worldwide are expanding their awareness and regaining the peripheral perspective essential to seeing through the bullshit. It may not seem so when you watch the TV news, but the waters *are* breaking and will go on doing so. The Truth Vibrations are playing a major role in this and I have been observing in recent years, especially as I have travelled worldwide since the summer of 2016, that dawn is breaking in the perceptions of growing numbers of people. I have been greatly encouraged by how many young people are seeing through the illusion. No, it's nothing like a majority yet, but they are increasing despite being the most fiercely psychologically-targeted generations in known 'history'. Today's young are planned to be the adults when the enslavement reaches the technological conclusion that I will be exposing. The System is urgently trying to hijack their minds so the dystopia can be installed with minimum challenge, but many are not falling for the perceptual onslaught. I am also hearing increasing numbers of older people asking: 'What's it all about?' I say older, but this re-evaluation is happening earlier and earlier in people's lives. They realise that chasing the carrot does not lead to happiness and joy. Are we really here only to work, work, work in pursuit of either survival or the accumulation of more and more 'things' that we can be persuaded to desire? Are we *really*? Even many that reach their goal see that actually nothing has really changed. They might have the title they always wanted – CEO or something – and they might have a bank account that others would die

**Figure 384:** Programmed human myopia.

for; but where's the joy? Where's the satisfaction and emotional harmony? Where's the peace? They chased the dream, even achieved it, and they don't feel any different. All that schoolwork, homework, degree study, long hours at the office, sales meetings, pressure to sell and perform – as life in the sense of living passed them by. Then for some there was all that religious adherence and submission. Was it really worth it? What was it all about? It was a *hoax* all along, a psychological railway track to keep you in the thrall of The System so you wouldn't wake up, suss it and escape. Human life is not a panorama, but a tunnel with a vision to match (Fig 384).

The point is that none of this has to be. Change your mind and you change your life. Your mind *is* your life. It has been stolen from you and with it your life, but you have the power to take them back. *Go for it.*

# CHAPTER NINE

# Holding the Spell

*'Great minds think alike because a greater Mind is thinking through them'*
**– Criss Jami**

Core perception programming is imposed in childhood and teenage years by parents, 'education', religion and peer pressure, and constantly topped up and confirmed by endless other sources for the rest of your life. The fact that ever-increasing numbers are now seeing through the veil of deceit is testament to the power of consciousness over even the most incessant programming.

Crucial to both casting the spell and holding the spell is the global media which daily confirms the perceptions of Postage Stamp reality (Fig 385). The term 'media' comes from 'medium' which means an 'intervening substance' and 'intervening agency' – hence the term psychic 'medium'. How appropriate that is with the media intervening at that crucial point between what is happening in the world and what the public are told is happening. To create and maintain a perception deception requires by definition control of information. Perceptions are formed from information received. This can be anything from personal experience to the 10 o'clock news but clearly most people have far more 10 o'clock news than personal experience when it comes to forming their view of life and world events. The scale of corporate media ownership (the ownership of information) is fantastic. A handful of giant corporations own the

**Figure 385:** Propaganda arm of The System.

American media and
those corporations
are themselves
owned by a handful
of billionaires. In
turn, the billionaires
are owned by the
Web and the Web is
owned by the
Spider. The same is
happening across
the world. There

**Figure 386:** Conflicts of interest are irrelevant the global *El*-lite.

may seem to be countless media outlets in the United States, for
example, but they are overwhelmingly owned by just six corporations –
News Corp, Viacom, Time Warner, Disney, CBS Corporation and NBC
Universal. Go deep enough in the Web and all six will be controlled by
the same hidden network. A tiny number of Web-connected people own
the global media, 'entertainment' industry – including Hollywood, and
the Internet. You see different television and radio channels, newspapers
and magazines on every subject you can imagine and there seems to be
endless choice from apparently independent sources; but research into
how few ultimately own them all and you will be shocked. I have
exposed this at some length in *Human Race Get Off Your Knees* and *The
Perception Deception* and in Britain you might put 'list of Trinity Mirror
titles' into a search engine to see what that group alone owns all over the
country. Media owners are often not *only* media owners either and this
creates enormous conflicts of interest. Billionaire Jeff Bezos owns both
Amazon and *The Washington Post* and he negotiated a $600 million deal
for Amazon with the CIA while *The Washington Post* reports stories
about the CIA (Fig 386). How can that be right? Where are the
demarcation lines between media and state and most importantly the
Deep State? There are none any longer if there ever were, except in
theory.

## The Daily CIA

*The Washington Post* and other major mainstream newspapers have a
long history of intimate connection to the Deep State intelligence
networks that operate outside the political system of ballot boxes and
transient 'leaders'. This has been exposed many times by insider
journalists including Watergate reporter Karl Bernstein who worked for
*The Washington Post*. He said the 1976 US Senate Select Committee
investigation into 'Governmental Operations with Respect to
Intelligence Activities', headed by Idaho Senator Frank Church, covered
up a lot of the CIA's control of the media; but even so the Church

**Figure 387:** Intelligence agencies have tremendous influence over what you see and hear – or don't.

Committee still acknowledged that about 50 'agency assets' were individual American journalists or employees of American media organisations and that 'more than a dozen United States news organizations and commercial publishing houses formerly provided cover for CIA agents abroad'. Forget the 'formerly'. The Church report said of CIA manipulation of foreign media: 'The CIA currently maintains a network of several hundred foreign individuals around the world who ... provide the CIA with direct access to a large number of newspapers and periodicals, scores of press services and news agencies, radio and television stations, commercial book publishers, and other foreign media outlets.' The network is far more extensive today than it was in 1976 and you can observe the most obvious coordination between North American and European media in the way they handle, spin and repeat the required narrative in stories of importance to the CIA and the Web (Fig 387). Currently central to that is 'Russia is evil'. Leading German journalist Udo Ulfkotte, former assistant editor for major German newspaper, *Frankfurter Allgemeine Zeitung*, publicly exposed control of the media by intelligence agencies before he died of a heart attack in January 2017 at the age of 56. Ulfkotte said that he was forced to publish articles under his own name that were handed to him by intelligence agencies and refusal to do so would have cost him his job. In the end he became so sick of this that he went public amid the hysterical propaganda to demonise Russia and trigger a war with the West. He said:

> I've been a journalist for about 25 years, and I was educated to lie, to betray, and not to tell the truth to the public. But seeing right now within the last months how the German and American media tries to bring war to the people in Europe, to bring war to Russia – this is a point of no return and I'm going to stand up and say it is not right what I have done in the past, to manipulate people, to make propaganda against Russia, and it is not right what my colleagues do and have done in the past because they are bribed to betray the people, not only in Germany, all over Europe.

Ulfkotte said media control by intelligence agencies is widespread and this is confirmed by other whistleblowers in Europe and the United

States (Fig 388). He said many
American and European
journalists were what the CIA
call 'non-official cover'. This
means that you write what the
agencies want and spy on their
behalf, but if you are ever
caught the connection is denied
by the agency involved. When a
target government arrests
foreign journalists there is an
outcry from the United States

**Figure 388:** Udo Ulfkotte bravely spoke out about
control of the media before he died in 2017.

and others about the abuse of journalistic freedom, but on at least some
occasions those 'journalists' really are spies. That's the bit they don't tell
you. Ulfkotte revealed that he was bribed by billionaires and American
agencies not to report the truth and instead produce articles that were
pro-American, pro-Europe, but *never* pro-Russian. The constant
outpouring of anti-Russian, anti-Putin propaganda on both sides of the
Atlantic (and in countries like US/UK-controlled Australia and New
Zealand) is being coordinated to a single end. In my experience the
corporate-owned media in 'little' New Zealand is right up there with the
worst and most mendacious. I have seen the worldwide reach of media
idiocy including a television presenter in New Zealand, two from
Channel 9 in Australia and a radio host in Iceland all from the same
conveyor belt and all thinking they are different and informed. You can
hardly get more 'distance' on Earth than between New Zealand and
Iceland, but in both I met the same mind (program) such is the global
spectrum of journalistic ignorance, arrogance and immaturity. Ulfkotte
said the CIA was especially strong in its control of British and Israeli
journalists and I have been aware for a long time of the connections
between British intelligence and the British media. Watch for print
journalists who are regularly wheeled out on television programmes to
spin their propaganda and trash stories about *El*-ite paedophilia and
Satanism or any suggestion of conspiracies. One in the UK comes to
mind immediately who was named to me by a former intelligence
operative as an asset of MI5. CNN stalwart Anderson Cooper from the
*El*-lite Vanderbilt bloodline was an intern for the CIA before turning to
what he calls journalism. Zionist-controlled and incredibly arrogant
CNN and the publicly-funded US National Public Radio (NPR) have
admitted that eight members of the US Army 4th Psychological
Operations (PSYOPS) Group worked in their news divisions and other
areas during the Kosovo war in the late 1990s when the CIA was
covertly directing the war against Serbia. This is what the mainstream
media really is – psychological warfare on the public. Udo Ulfkotte

**HOW CAN THE MEDIA LIE TO YOU?**

**IT KNOWS YOU SIMPLY WON'T CHECK THE 'FACTS'**
(WELL, THE VAST MAJORITY ANYWAY)

**Figure 389:** People need to check and questions everything and not just take it on face value. The face usually has no value.

published his revelations in a book entitled, *Journalists for Hire: How the CIA Buys the News*. He said that the CIA 'had a hand' on every journalist of significance in Europe (often coordinated through 'transatlantic organisations') to control the narrative that Europeans are given about world events and a host of other subjects (Fig 389). Germany and European countries in general were little more than colonies of the United States, he said. At the level that Ulfkotte worked this would have appeared to be the case. There is a twist to add, however. I said earlier that the United States is actually controlled from Europe and what you have is a chain of command to hide the real centre of power. European governments are largely controlled from the United States and the United States is controlled from the inner circle of the secret society web that is located in Europe. The same illusion is played with intelligence agencies. Call them the CIA/NSA, British intelligence (MI5/MI6), Israeli intelligence (Mossad) or whatever. It doesn't matter. They appear to be different and independent even to most of their operatives, but if you go deep enough they are all assets of the same central command – the same Web – working to the same global Archontic agenda. Spy agencies in the US, Canada, UK, Australia and New Zealand operate under the 'five eyes' arrangement of information exchange but the connections between global agencies go much further. German intelligence agency BND was exposed in 2015 for helping the US National Security Agency (NSA) to spy on supposedly 'friendly' governments in Poland, Austria, Denmark and Croatia and on embassies in Germany representing France, Great Britain, Sweden, Portugal, Greece, Spain, Italy, Austria, Switzerland and the Vatican. Even the phone of German Chancellor Angela Merkel was tapped in this NSA global surveillance operation which also targeted US diplomatic missions at the EU and UN along with the US Treasury Department and Department of the Interior (and it didn't end there). Intelligence agencies are spying on their own governments which are supposed to control them because their allegiance is not to governments, but to the Web that really controls them. Politicians come and go while agencies of the Web are always there pursuing the Web's ongoing agenda. This is the network, together with the inner-circle of the military, that operates the DUMBS or Deep Underground Military Bases which presidents are allowed to know next to nothing about. When Ulfkotte says the CIA has control of Israeli journalists, for instance, it's really Mossad on behalf of the Web that also includes the CIA. They use each other to spy on their own countries to have 'plausible deniability' if hacks and surveillance are uncovered. 'It's the Russians' is another regular response. The same technique was exposed by a British police whistleblower who revealed in a letter to a politician that the London Metropolitan Police were using Indian police to hack the emails of hundreds of political activists and journalists. The following is the Archontic Reptilian bloodline blueprint for control of the media and, as a result, of what most people think:

- Create or buy out major news agencies and TV channels
- Only publish stories that promote your agenda
- Maintain debate within a strictly limited range of views and subjects
- Focus on traumatic events to keep the people traumatised and in fear
- Label anyone who exposes your system and manipulation as a 'conspiracy theorist'

## Provable fact is only a theory

The term 'conspiracy theorist' is the one-stop shop to discredit those lifting the veil even though the definition of conspiracy is only 'the act of conspiring together'. On that basis there are conspiracies everywhere. 'Conspiracy theorist' is also a label confined only to those questioning The System. If you are serving The System by collectively claiming a Russian plot to influence US and European elections based on no hard evidence whatsoever while quoting anonymous 'sources' then a conspiracy theory becomes 'journalism'. Widespread deployment of 'conspiracy theory' and 'conspiracy theorist' as terms of derision began in the 1960s once again courtesy of the CIA when they were seeking to discredit those exposing the truth about the assassination of President Kennedy and Malcolm X. A CIA dispatch to media organisations in 1967 outlined ways to discredit people asking dangerous questions and included the use of the label 'conspiracy theories' (Fig 390). The dispatch was the work of the CIA's Clandestine Services Unit and expressed alarm at how the official (nonsensical) story of the Kennedy assassination was doubted by 46 percent of the population thanks to the work of independent researchers. This document was well timed, with Martin Luther King and JFK's brother Bobby Kennedy assassinated the following year and explained away by official narratives at serious odds with the evidence. The CIA dispatch gave the media a list of ways to counter 'conspiracy theories':

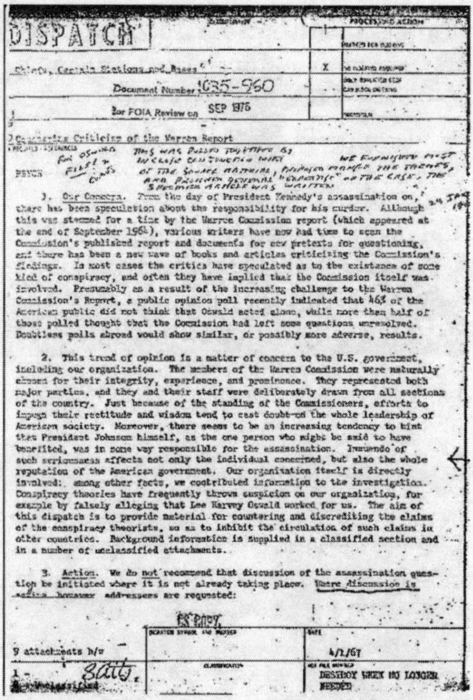
DISPATCH

Chiefs, Certain Stations and Bases

Document Number 1035-960

for FOIA Review on SEP 1976

Countering Criticism of the Warren Report

1. Our Concern. From the day of President Kennedy's assassination on, there has been speculation about the responsibility for his murder. Although this was stemmed for a time by the Warren Commission report (which appeared at the end of September 1964), various writers have now had time to scan the Commission's published report and documents for new pretexts for questioning, and there has been a new wave of books and articles criticizing the Commission's findings. In most cases the critics have speculated as to the existance of some kind of conspiracy, and often they have implied that the Commission itself was involved. Presumably as a result of the increasing challenge to the Warren Commission's Report, a public opinion poll recently indicated that 46% of the American public did not think that Oswald acted alone, while more than half of those polled thought that the Commission had left some questions unresolved. Doubtless polls abroad would show similar, or possibly more adverse, results.

2. This trend of opinion is a matter of concern to the U.S. government, including our organization. The members of the Warren Commission were naturally chosen for their integrity, experience, and prominence. They represented both major parties, and they and their staff were deliberately drawn from all sections of the country. Just because of the standing of the Commissioners, efforts to impugn their rectitude and wisdom tend to cast doubt on the whole leadership of American society. Moreover, there seems to be an increasing tendency to hint that President Johnson himself, as the one person who might be said to have benefited, was in some way responsible for the assassination. Innuendo of such seriousness affects not only the individual concerned, but also the whole reputation of the American government. Our organization itself is directly involved: among other facts, we contributed information to the investigation. Conspiracy theories have frequently thrown suspicion on our organization, for example by falsely alleging that Lee Harvey Oswald worked for us. The aim of this dispatch is to provide material for countering and discrediting the claims of the conspiracy theorists, so as to inhibit the circulation of such claims in other countries. Background information is supplied in a classified section and in a number of unclassified attachments.

3. Action. We do not recommend that discussion of the assassination question be initiated where it is not already taking place. Where discussion is active, however addressees are requested:

9 attachments h/w

4/1/67

DESTROY WHEN NO LONGER NEEDED

**Figure 390:** The CIA despatch to media organisations in 1967 that spawned the widespread use of 'conspiracy theory' and 'conspiracy theorists' which continues today in an ongoing attempt to discredit any alternative to official narratives. Those that parrot these terms have no idea where they came from.

- Claim it is impossible for so many people to stay silent if it was really a conspiracy [it is perfectly possible because of compartmentalisation, intimidation and outright elimination]
- Use CIA assets and supporters to trash the theories and highlight official findings [see file marked 'tell them claptrap']
- Ignore conspiracy information unless it is so widely circulating that a response becomes necessary [this is why there is such a panic now and the use of the label 'fake news']
- Claim that conspiracy theories reveal 'no significant new evidence' [when they actually take the official story apart]
- Discredit eyewitnesses [unless they support the official account, see also 9/11, 7/7 and other official versions of terrorist attacks]
- Condemn conspiracy researchers for irresponsible speculation [telling the truth]
- Claim they are infatuated, politically motivated or only doing it to make money [target the messenger if you can't discredit the message]

Fifty years later today's mainstream media is still using the CIA-inspired labels 'conspiracy theory' and 'conspiracy theorists' in an attempt to discredit those like me who are challenging official fairy tales which they are too ignorant or unmotivated to do (Fig 391). Virtually none of the 'journalists' who say 'conspiracy theory' by reflex action have any idea who introduced the term to the media and why. Day after day they do the bidding of the CIA with regard to 9/11 and countless other events and situations in which the authorities have lied to the population. Instead of investigating and exposing those lies themselves, which is supposed to be their job, they seek to undermine others who are doing what *they* should be doing (Fig 392). There are 'journalist' assets of the intelligence networks and media owners knowingly using their sources of communication to push the Hidden Hand perception control agenda, but the great majority of mainstream journalists are simply uniformed about the world they are reporting. They have all been through the perception program as far as college and university and every day they are interacting with fellow journalists, politicians, scientists and doctors who have downloaded the same perceptual illusions. They get most of their information from other journalists by reading newspapers and watching 24-hour rolling news programmes. When anyone comes along to

Figure 391: The real meaning of 'conspiracy theorist'.

Figure 392: 'News' broadcasts the world over.

challenge that mutual sense of the 'normal' and 'possible' they are dismissed in an instant as crazy, dangerous or in some way on the make. I have shaken my head so many times in mainstream interviews, print, radio and television, at the lack of knowledge journalists and presenters have had on subjects they think they know all about. Politicians are the same. They only 'know' what they have been *told* to know, that's all, and the totality of that amounts to jack shit compared with what there is to know. The human disease that I call the arrogance of ignorance is particularly virulent in the media (and politics) and this is essential if careers are to survive or prosper. In among the journalistic dross there are still some outstanding reporters seeking against all the odds and pressures to tell the truth as best they can and they are now in the gunsights of The System to ensure that only unquestioning acquiescence remains. Such is the programmed ignorance of the media generally that all they can do is to act as echo chambers repeating the official versions of Mainstream Everything. They repeat official accounts and agendas across the entirety of human society from politics to finance, world events to health. DNA-mutating GMO 'food' is perfectly safe (*genetically-modified* gives you a clue, right?). Parents that reject toxic, immune-system-demolishing vaccines are putting children at risk. Brain-suppressing fluoride in toothpaste and drinking water – so what's the problem? Experts from Mainstream Everything have said it is safe so it must be ... repeat, repeat, repeat. No mention of a list of studies showing that fluoride (a) damages teeth with fluorosis and (b) suppresses intelligence. Doctors and the pharmaceutical cartel (Big Pharma) are the journalist's fountain of knowledge about health and the fact that mainstream medicine is a global killing machine passes them by while never touching the sides.

If you are a genuine journalist who won't comply with the official narrative you're out the door and when you have a family and a mortgage to pay this is a mind-focusing incentive not to step out of line. I read a report about Misha Michaels, a proper science journalist at the WGBH media operation in Boston. She was fired and told she was 'not a good fit' after supporting a bill allowing parents not to vaccinate their children and questioning the human-caused global warming hoax of which more later. Censoring genuine journalists is done as a matter of course. Censorship and propaganda is further encouraged by advertising in terms of who gets it, who doesn't, and on what editorial criteria this is handed out or denied. Robert F. Kennedy, Jr, a campaigner against the negative impact of vaccines, said the media had been co-opted by the pharmaceutical industry: 'A network news broadcast these days ... is just a vehicle for selling pharmaceutical products.' Kennedy said that he was told by one of Americans biggest TV networks that any presenter who interviewed him about thimerosal, the toxic mercury-based vaccine ingredient, would be fired. The devastating potential effect of mercury on especially children's health is irrelevant to these programmed perceptual inversions. Money and career are all that matters. This happens across the spectrum of subjects as whistleblower reporters have testified. Access to the mainstream public is denied to those questioning official orthodoxy or weak guests are invited to put a case while stronger and more informed ones are ignored. Add to this the often breathtaking bias and ignorance of the writer or presenter and you have a fully-fledged System protection racket.

I watched a BBC 'discussion' about alleged human-caused climate change for which the BBC is a global leader in perception manipulation. Rarely is anyone exposing the climate-change hoax allowed to appear and when they are they're treated with systematic distain by the 'impartial' BBC. The presenter on this occasion, a bloke called Nicky Campbell, treated with absolute dismissal and contempt a weather expert challenging the climate hoax while the co-leader of the Green

Party Jonathan Bartley complained that the BBC had allowed a
dissenting voice to appear. Bartley and Campbell are so mesmerised by
their own omnipotence they can't see the outrageous extremism which
says that only one view – *their* view – is to be taken seriously or given a
platform. And 'their' view came from *The System* – underscored by the
knowledge that if you explore another opinion too fairly you will be
looking for new
employment very soon.
Nicky Campbell is the
former BBC pop music
disc jockey turned
excuse-for-a-journalist
who said of Syria's
President Assad while
presenting a 'news'
programme: 'We need to
get rid of him, he's a war
criminal.' Such
outrageous statements
by a 'news' presenter in
my day at the BBC

**Figure 393:** Holding your breath is not advised.

would have led to dismissal or demotion. Now it is rewarded with
promotion or accolade. Campbell was referring to an alleged chemical
weapons attack blamed on Assad forces in Syria based on absolutely no
evidence and only the rantings of US, UK, Israeli and European System-
server politicians who were desperate to remove Assad after he, thanks
to Russia, had resisted all Western attempts to bring him down. The
'attack' came at a time when Assad with Russian support was winning
back the country. Why would he attack his own people with chemical
weapons when he had nothing to gain and everything to lose by doing
that? Previous claims of 'gas attacks' by Assad turned out to be the work
of Western-backed terrorists designed to demonise him to justify
outright invasion by the West instead of just the proxy invasion by
Western-backed, armed and trained 'rebels' (terrorists). But all this
would have been lost on Campbell who takes his daily perceptual cue
from the official line on everything. No wonder he is so well thought of
by the BBC (and himself). His arrogant ignorance is so typical of his
breed and prevails throughout the mainstream media and much of the
'alternative' (Fig 393). Another BBC report related to a terrorist attack
talked of protecting *'our* values'. Proper impartial journalism should
never refer to 'our' anything and only present the neutral facts. The BBC
in general is an absolute disgrace to truth and journalism and a pathetic
and compliant PR unit for Mainstream Everything. A proper presenter's
job is to fairly and equally question different opinions and let the viewer

decide what to make of them. Instead we have these most basic of journalistic standards usurped by the cult of the know-it-all-know-*fuck*-all commentator host, and my god most are so uninformed (a great career move) it takes your breath away. Campbell is a personification and his blueprint is written into the very fabric of what passes for 'journalism' today. For this and all the other reasons the bulk of the mainstream media is little more than The Spider's propaganda network.

## All together now

Diversity in the mainstream media is a sleight of hand and eye. News agencies owned by corporate giants provide 'news' globally and nationally for untold numbers of newspapers, radio stations and television newsrooms. One reporter's version of something is then read out or published across the world. There are video compilations on YouTube with one TV 'news' show after the other presenting the same story word for word. It would be hysterical if it were not so tragic for human awareness. I worked as a journalist in newspapers, radio and television for 20 years and with honourable exceptions that arena is hardly the bastion of brightest. Nor does it need to be in the way it is currently structured. You want to be on TV? Read the words written for you in the camera lens as if you are not reading them; try to look as if you know what you're talking about even if you don't; and ask a few questions within the parameters of your particular owner/editorial acceptability. Then say goodnight – back tomorrow. That's it really, most of the time. Names like BBC, ITN, CNN, MSNBC and Fox News present the illusion of choice when they are basically all the same. Fox News may have a bias to the Republican Party and MSNBC to the Democrats, but that's only the surface veneer to kid people they have media diversity. Whenever it comes to anything that could truly expose The System and the *El*-lite for what they really are the mainstream media moves as one unit.

Hideous Fox News front man Bill O'Reilly (fired in 2017 over personal matters) and full-of-herself MSNBC host Rachel Maddow had their right-left spats with each other and appear to be political polarities, but they are illusory *Postage Stamp* polarities (Fig 394). 'Satirical' news comedians like Jon Stewart, Bill

**Figure 394:** The unlamented Bill O'Reilly and the lamentable Rachael Maddow. Two sides of the same postage stamp claiming to be different.

Maher, Stephen Colbert and John Oliver may seem to be laughing at The System and its foot soldiers. Yet question if 9/11 was a conspiracy (it was), or if anything else of fundamental importance to the *El*-lite is not what it seems, and they are all united in their dismissal, ridicule and condemnation. They are System-servers wearing different masks, playing different roles, and the same with most of their profession. They know that if they don't play the game they'll soon be yesterday's news themselves. You can attack bankers but don't you dare expose how they are lending money that doesn't exist and charging interest on it. You can make fun of the president, but don't you dare expose that he's a puppet of the force that holds the strings of all presidents. You can do what you like so long as it's what *we* like. 'Progressive icon comedian' (fraud and manchild) John Oliver mocked the Vault 7 WikiLeaks revelations about CIA surveillance and assassination operations which involve hacking technology and car computer systems. Oliver's response was sickening to behold, but typical of his pseudo-rebel breed which claims to be making fun of The System while licking its arse. Russia Today, or RT, the state-funded channel broadcasting in many countries, has improved the quality of television news journalism both by asking some of the questions the Western mainstream refuses to do and by giving a platform to other voices normally excluded. Even then it is only up to a point. RT is of course biased in favour of Russia and President Putin and this is to be expected given its paymasters. The output needs to be filtered with that knowledge while being welcomed all the same. I am well past their 'up to a point' it seems and at the time of writing I have never been invited on any RT programme even with 30 years of research into all the subjects they cover. Maybe I am not safe enough. I do hope so. Mainstream media says question nothing; RT says question more; I say question *everything*. That's the difference.

## Genuine alternative and mainstream-lite

When I started out in my current direction in 1990 there was no alternative media such as that we have today. Only a few of us largely working alone were exposing the Hidden Hand behind world affairs, and in the United States the field was dominated by Christian believers. Significant parts of it still are. I would speak to mostly tiny audiences in America with many of them very suspicious of this English guy who was exposing the conspiracy but didn't talk about Jesus. I spoke to eight people near Chicago, I remember, and to four or five in a front room in New England. This is what you had to do in those days with no Internet worth the name and little interest in the information. Many times I thought 'what's the point' but something drove me on, an intuitive 'knowing' that eventually I would get somewhere. Since then a massive worldwide Internet-based industry has emerged called the 'alternative media' or 'independent media' inspired by the pioneers and fuelled by gathering doubts about world-changing events such as 9/11 and the lie-fest that was the invasion of Iraq in 2003. These websites and Internet radio/TV shows have reported global events from a very different perspective to the mainstream. They have highlighted connections between people, organisations and happenings where the mainstream reported them only in isolation and with official spin. Without the connections there is no picture and only unfathomable 'random' happenings. Without context there is only the bewildering onslaught of the daily data storm. The alternative media has primarily (though far from totally) stayed within the parameters of five-sense perception while reporting events from another more expansive angle. This five-sense perspective has led to me being attacked, dismissed and ridiculed by great swathes of the 'alternative' media as much as I have by the mainstream. What is termed 'alternative' is an enormous spectrum of perception from those that are barely divisible from the mainstream to those like me who question everything we have ever been told to believe right down to reality itself. Most of the alternative media is closer to the barely-divisible polarity and hence my communal dismissal by many alternative sources. Davidicke.com and Brietbart.com, the Trump-supporting 'Alt-right' website that provided his alleged (and former) chief advisor, Steve Bannon, would both be considered 'alternative media', but they are in parallel universes.

Significant parts of the alternative media supported Donald Trump because five-sense focus sets you in pursuit of five-sense answers to problems that you seek to solve when five-sense reality is all you can see. I am saying that to change reality we need to change perception and expand consciousness beyond The Program. Current perceptions are manifesting current reality by folding into existence from the Cosmic Internet (quantum field) the possibilities and probabilities instigated by those perceptions. If that doesn't change then current reality can't change. Throughout 'history' humanity has been trying to change external events with the same state of consciousness that created them and that simply cannot happen. Violent revolutions to overthrow oppressive governments lead to the violent revolutionaries becoming the next oppressive government. We have seen this over and over because the level of consciousness is the same. Republican replacing Democrat replacing Republican replacing Democrat is another example. Political parties are Postage Stamp parties. They call themselves different names and have their own rhetorical hymn sheet, but the outcome is always predictable because their consciousness believes in the same System and reality. Differences are only in detail, not substance. Five-sense-only focus made parts of the alternative media vulnerable to the illusion of Donald Trump when he pledged to take on the Establishment (while being part of it). He told them what they wanted to hear about 'draining the swamp' and other points on the alternative wish-list and they bought it. Swamps are not drained by those who have spent their lives swimming in them or by those who announce after taking office that records of who visits the White House will no longer be disclosed. The power of Trump to seize the psyche of the five-sense-only 'alternative' can be witnessed in websites once exposing The System (or at least

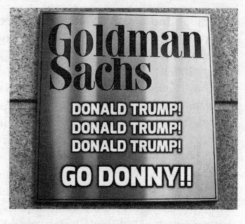

**Figure 395:** Parts of the alternative media are still supporting Trump even after he handed the US economy to the very Goldman Sachs that they had long exposed as a financial pillar of the *El*-lite.

parts of it) becoming little more than temples of Trumpian hero-worship. They would once have jumped on presidents who handed the US treasury and economic direction to Goldman Sachs operatives, but when their hero/deity Trump did that there was hardly a whimper (Fig 395). This has been good in a way in that it has highlighted the difference between the genuinely alternative and the illusory alternative. This re-evaluation was long overdue. Trump's perceptual hijack has been made possible by two main psychological traits. The first is the power of being told what you want to hear. Tell people what they don't want to hear and there is reflex-action resistance for the obvious reason that they don't want it to be true. Tell them what they do want to hear and they will be desperate to believe it because they *do* want it to be true. Politicians of every persuasion spend election campaigns telling their potential constituency of support what it wants to hear. Once secured in power they then do what they were always going to do and much of that is at odds with what they promised to do. This is an ever-recurring cycle all over the world and Trump is just the same. Promises that suit the Archontic agenda (those that create chaos and division) are instigated but everything else is forgotten including, in Trump's case, draining the swamp. The role of the truly alternative media is not in my view to promote a particular candidate in a system rigged to its core. It is to expose how it *is* rigged and by whom. It is to ask how a political system can be trusted that offers voters in a country of 326 million people a 'choice' between Donald Trump and Hillary Clinton. The Trump-supporting 'alternative media' might ask themselves in a quiet moment how come the system they have claimed to be so rigged from the shadows allowed their hero pledging to delete that system to come through to win against all the odds? Bernie Sanders was the real choice of Democrat supporters to run for president, but leaked emails revealed how the party hierarchy manipulated events to allow Clinton to win. The Republican hierarchy that was supposed to be so against Trump could not have done the same? With much to be revealed about Trump no apparently anti-Trump news outlet could produce something to ensure he couldn't win? *Please*. These are questions and observations that are firewalled from the minds of those desperate for their hero to be what they want him to be.

## 'Fake news!', says fake news

Trump made one of his foundation platforms the lies and manipulation of news by the mainstream media which he refers to as the 'enemy of the people'. This was another major reason why the five-sense-only alternative became his cheerleader. Who could disagree with the claim that the mainstream media lies and misrepresents events and people when it has clearly done so decade after decade? There is another angle to this, however, which I will be coming to shortly. The Trump anti-system fantasy was completely manufactured with the Zionist network in the US funding and supporting him as we will see, and Zionist-controlled CNN, *The New York Times* and *The Washington Post* attacking him and giving the impression that he was anti-Establishment. I have emphasised over the years to be on guard when a subject or theme suddenly appears out of nowhere and is immediately everywhere as if someone has pressed a button. These situations are almost always the Hidden Hand at work and so it was with the sudden emergence and global circulation of the term 'fake news'. Even the Pope – *the Pope* – condemned the circulation of fake information before heading for his next sermon to express the literal truth that 'Jesus' was born to a virgin mother, turned water into wine, fed thousands with a few loaves and fishes, walked on water, died on the cross, came back to life and disappeared into the sky promising to return one day on a cloud. The Pope would never see the contradiction. Ironically, this 'fake news' onslaught was directed at the alternative media in the wake of the

**Figure 396:** A disgrace to journalism.

exposure by WikiLeaks of coordinated collusion between the Hillary Clinton campaign and corporate 'news' operations like CNN (Fig 396). Major 'news' outlets caught planting stories and promoting a particular political candidate then had the nerve after Trump's election to lead the charge against the alternative media under the collective banner of 'fake news'. This was so immediate and widespread both sides of the Atlantic that the coordination was laughably obvious (Fig 397). Ann M. Ravel, former head of the Federal Election Commission (FEC), told an event called 'Future of Democracy' at the University of California, Berkeley that political speech

**Figure 397:** Someone pressed the button on the 'fake news' narrative and suddenly it was everywhere.

must be controlled on social media and 'fake news' regulated. Her true motivation is revealed in her efforts at the FEC to regulate alternative websites like the Drudge Report before the 'fake news' hoax was even launched. When people made clear their opposition to such state censorship she blamed the reaction on 'misogyny'. Political correctness is now a ubiquitous weapon of choice for many called out for their Orwellian tendencies. 'You are only saying that because of my sex, colour or sexual preference.' No, it's because you are talking bollocks. English writer Samuel Johnson (1709-1784) said that patriotism is the last refuge of a scoundrel. Now they have another place to shelter – political correctness. The claim was that alternative sites (dubbed the Alt-right earlier in the campaign) had been responsible for Trump's victory by spreading false information that was then widely shared on social media platforms such as Facebook and Twitter. Trump won because of 'fake news' and not because Hillary Clinton and her ex-president husband are among the most corrupt politicians in American history. This had nothing to do with it. 'Fake news' and 'the Russians' were the villains. Added to this mix for extra oomph was the claim without any evidence whatsoever that the Trump-supporting alternative media was serving the interests of President Putin and Russia in deciding the outcome of the election. The 'fake news' hoax is being exploited in Europe with claims that elections in EU countries are influenced by information that isn't true, but then they always have been through political party manifestos. Some idiots even linked 'fake news' to the Brexit referendum result in Britain. They don't want to face the fact that a UK majority voted to leave the EU against the wishes of almost the entirety of the Left-Right political class because more and more people are awakening to the realities of bureaucratic and one-party establishments masquerading as democracy and freedom. Trump was also elected because he was *perceived* to be against the American political class even though he wasn't. The role played in this fast-emerging

**Figure 398:** The alternative media was getting far too influential. Something had to be done.

realisation by the alternative media has been so crucial in circulating information exposing the game, and so it became the target of the coordinated fake news campaign (Fig 398). Demonise the alternative media as 'fake news' and you can justify censoring information that you don't want people to hear. Facebook and its vacuous manchild T-shirt frontman Mark Zuckerberg were on the case immediately which is no surprise at all given that Facebook is a major global arm of The Spider and its Web.

I referred there to the fake news 'hoax' and that needs to be put into context. I am not saying for a moment that elements of what *calls* itself the alternative media do not make up stories. They *do*. Take the sites Yournewswire.com and Newspunch.com operated out of California by Sean Adl-Tabatabai, ironically a former webmaster at Davidicke.com. What better definition of fake news can there be than to have alleged 'news' sites that make up stories which didn't happen, quoting only nonsense like 'sources say', and do so under the name of a 'journalist' called 'Baxter Dmitry' who doesn't exist? Alongside 'his' name an image has been posted, not of the non-existent 'Dmitry', but of a past associate of 'editor-in-chief' Adl-Tabatabai with no connection to Yournewswire or Newspunch.com. The invented 'Dmitry' has 'his' own Facebook page with a fake profile and also email addresses – baxter@yournewswire.com and baxter@newspunch.com. The site claims that he has 'travelled in over 80 countries and won arguments in every single one' and has been 'speaking truth to power since he learned to talk'. 'Dmitry' wrote emails to me in the child-like belief by the real writer that I didn't know his true identity. This site has posted outrageous stories written (or rather not) by 'Baxter Dmitry' trying to undermine me and my work of nearly 30 years – thus confirming how truly motivated they are in seeking to challenge The System. To do nothing about the state of the world is one thing, but to exploit that situation is quite another. I exposed the Baxter Dmitry scam on Davidicke.com and later so did the UK *Sunday Times*. Yournewswire/Newspunch.com and their 'editor-in-chief' have continued on regardless with people still sharing their made-up stories as if they are true. A fake story 'written' in June 2017 by the non-existent 'Baxter Dmitry' was headed: 'Retired MI5 Agent Confesses on

Deathbed: "I Killed Princess Diana"'. It was classic 'Dmitry' nonsense lacking all the essential details to support the headline. The story was illustrated with a picture of 'MI5 agent John Hopkins' on his deathbed which turned out to be 87-year-old Kevin Park, an asbestosis sufferer, pictured in a story in 2010 on an Australian news website about him having to use his mobile phone to call for help from his hospital bed when he could not attract the attention of nursing staff. Yournewswire posted that image of an Australian hospital patient from seven years before and claimed him to be an MI5 agent in a made-up story written by someone that doesn't exist. They have no capacity for shame. Soon after came another 'story' from this disgraceful website headed 'CIA Agent Confesses on Deathbed: "We Blew Up WTC7 on 9/11"?' The scale of absolute contempt you must have for the public and the genuine alternative media to behave like this is extraordinary, but no doubt they make a good living from it. The real motivation of pseudo-alternative websites – and there are many – is 'clickbait'. The term can be defined as posting headlines designed only to make people click on the story. When they do so the text in no way justifies the headline, but by then it doesn't matter. Every click to open the story adds to the advertising revenue of the site as does circulation of the page on social media by 'awake' people so desperately naïve that even after reading text that does not justify the headline they still believe what the headline says! It's amazing. But, then, perhaps not so with the power of perception programming that comes with a desire for something to be true despite the fact that it is nonsensical and unsupportable by any evidence. I came across a video on YouTube by an 'alternative' researcher talking about the Diana deathbed story as if it was true and this had been viewed 435,000 times when the whole thing had been made up simply to make money.

What is most appalling and disgusting with clickbait sites claiming to be 'alternative media' is they hand ammunition to The System to tar with the same brush the genuine alternative media that does seek to deal in fact. They also discredit alternative information with their so easy to debunk made-up stories and the El-lite must absolutely love them. It's about time they were called out and widely exposed by genuine researchers and all those who care about what the real alternative media is trying to do. Some of the most counterfeit, mendacious and untrustworthy people I have ever met have claimed to be part of the alternative media – and some of the best – and the same with those who call themselves 'spiritual'. Beware of anyone who has to tell you how 'spiritual' they are. Shouldn't it be obvious by their actions? Fake headlines to entice people to click on fake text are an epidemic on the Internet in general. I saw a headline on YouTube for a video by the great American comedian George Carlin which said during the 2016 US election campaign: 'Why I Won't Be Voting For Hillary Clinton or

**Figure 399:** The real reason for the fake news hoax.

**Figure 400:** The genie is out of the bottle and it must not go back.

Donald Trump – George Carlin.' This is the same George Carlin who died in 2008. Those responsible for the upload who had no connection with Carlin were aware the headline was thoroughly misleading but they knew it would attract many more clicks (money) than one that told the truth. The same happens when some YouTube channels post my videos and misrepresent them just to get more clicks by misleading headlines and claims that they are new when they are not. They, too, call themselves 'alternative' when they are clickbait parasites feeding off the efforts of others while contributing nothing. There is a chasm of difference between being wrong when you are trying to be right and being wrong while knowing that is the case. I freely acknowledge that parts of what *claim* to be the alternative media are guilty of circulating fake news, but I say they are not in the least alternative. What is the difference between websites that post made-up articles by a fake writer claiming to expose a conspiracy or quote George Carlin about a current event eight years after he died and the daily bias and spin of the mainstream media worldwide every day? *Nothing.* They are both knowingly misleading the public. Nor does The System really care much about any of this. The fake news agenda is a hoax in the sense that its real target is the *genuine* alternative media for which facts and dot-connecting are everything (Fig 399). Clickbait dross has given the authorities and their tools like Facebook, the T-shirt tyranny, the excuse to censor genuine content on the basis of fake news (Fig 400). This is the same 'moral' Facebook, by the way, that has admitted how its uses smartphone and computer microphones to listen to private conversations and has engaged in widespread experiments manipulating information in news feeds to alter the behaviour of its users about whom it doesn't give a shit. *The Australian* newspaper has published Facebook documents marked 'Confidential: Internal Only' which detail 'unsavoury and often predatory advertising practices which target teenagers as young as 14 and preys on their insecurities.' The paper reported that by monitoring user posts, media uploads, interactions and general internet activity Facebook can identify when people are 'stressed', 'defeated', 'overwhelmed', 'anxious' and 'nervous', or feeling 'stupid', 'silly', 'useless' and a 'failure'. These details are then 'shareable under a non-disclosure agreement only' for targeted advertising. Facebook has filed a patent that would allow this repugnant company to monitor people's faces via smartphone and laptop cameras. They claim this would help them target advertising and content by monitoring which videos people watched and which they looked away from. *Liars* – it is their version of Orwell's Telescreens. Zionist-controlled Facebook has allowed the sharing of death threats, images of self-harm and animal torture with leaked company documents revealing how moderators are told not to delete this content because it can raise awareness of the issues. They only have a problem with people telling the truth, asking the 'wrong' questions or having opinions at odds with the *El*-lite agenda of which Facebook is a part. Twitter is going the same way. Such are the people claiming the moral high ground over 'fake news' when this is only an excuse to censor on behalf of their masters way, way above Zuckerberg who I do not believe for a moment is the real power behind Facebook.

**Figure 401:** Full-blown fake news.

## Fake News 'fact-checkers'

Algorithms and 'fact-checkers' are being employed to target and flag-up stories that The System doesn't want the public to see including 'conspiracy theories' (stories that so often turn out to be true and are not 'theories' at all). These are called 'low-quality content' by the censors at Zionist created-and-controlled Google while lie-machines such as the BBC, MSNBC and CNN with the blatantly biased Anderson Cooper and Christiane Amanpour are considered high-quality and given search engine prominence (Fig 401 and 402). If

**Figure 402:** Google is using the 'fake news' hoax to censor genuine information The System doesn't want you to see.

**Figure 403:** Facebook and Google – Censorship Inc.

**Figure 404:** Zionist billionaire manipulator George Soros. You'll be hearing much more about him before the end of the book.

you are engaged in a perception deception you must control the narrative and the genuine alternative media has thrown a mighty spanner in that particular works. 'Fake news' is The System's response with Google and Facebook to the fore. Google was founded by Zionists Larry Page and Sergey Brin with pre-launch CIA seed money, Google-owned YouTube is run by Zionist CEO Susan Wojcicki and Facebook is headed by Zionist Mark Zuckerberg with Zionist chief operating officer Sheryl Sandberg, former vice president of global online sales and operations at Google and chief of staff to mega Zionist financial manipulator Lawrence Summers when he was US Treasury Secretary.

Facebook has determined that 'fact-checker' organisations will decide if a story is fake and will be flagged as 'disputed' with a link to an alleged explanation for why (Fig 403). Warnings began to appear like 'before you share this content, you might want to know that the fact-checking sites, Snopes.com and Associated Press disputed its accuracy'. Flagged stories are also given less prominence than before and fewer people will see them. To say these fact-checker organisations which determine if a story is disputed or 'fake news' are independent is hilarious. They include ABC News and other expressions of a long-discredited mainstream media that a Harvard University study found is not trusted by 65 percent of the public to tell them the truth. The International Fact-Checking Network (IFCN), which produced a code of five principles for news websites, is an offshoot of the Poynter Institute for Media Studies. Poynter is funded by a list of Spider fronts and frontmen including the George Soros Open Society Foundations (of which *much* more to come), Bill and Melinda Gates Foundation, Google and others. Collectively – billionairescareaboutfacts.com. Sure they do. Billionaire Soros and billionaire Gates seem to turn up everywhere in support or defence of the Archontic *El*-lite agenda (Fig 404). Another of the 'fact-checkers' is *The Washington Post* with its long and appalling history of manipulating information and producing fake stories to serve the interests of the Deep State. When the button was pressed in late 2016 on the fake news scam the *Post* published a story about 200 alternative sites accused of circulating 'Russian propaganda'. This ridiculously alleged Russian connection came from propornot.com, a truly fake news site which is written anonymously and launched in 2016 – the year the fake news hoax began. *The Washington Post* was forced to distance itself from the story after a backlash that included even mainstream sources. Some on the list *were* guilty of fake news, some were not, and this was another example of lumping the two together to use one to discredit the other. The list named Yournewswire, but also the genuinely alternative and excellent Activist Post. Even then the Russia propaganda claim against Yournewswire was crazy. Maybe they thought that Baxter Dmitry is really Russian and really exists! *The Washington Post* was also caught out in the same period claiming that Russians hacked the US electricity grid at a facility in Vermont, when it turned out that the 'hack' – with no evidence of Russian involvement – was on a laptop not even connected to the grid system. These are the people handed the power to 'fact-check' fake news and cause information to be censored. The System could not make its game more obvious if it used neon lights. Facebook is urging users to flag up and report fake news to them. No self-respecting tyranny would be complete without getting the target population to inform on and censor the target population and yet millions will do what Facebook tells them while going 'baa, baa, baa'. Assistant Professor Melissa Zimdars, a system-serving 'progressive' academic and 'feminist and activist' at Merrimack College in Massachusetts, is another fake to be given mainstream media prominence for highlighting fake news sites to avoid. Her list included painfully obvious satirical sites and those alternative sources she didn't agree with. No doubt she claims to believe in freedom, like much of the 'progressive' movement which spends its time deleting freedom. French newspaper *Le Monde* posted a list of 'conspiracy news sites' in a bid to discredit them (there are no conspiracies you see). Talk about desperate, and you will see this campaign go on increasing against those with other versions of events and reality. This is digital book burning.

Meanwhile, governments that claim to be so concerned about fake news are employing armies of people (and algorithms) to create fake profiles to manipulate opinion on social media and 'control the narrative'. They are known as 'cyber troops' and a five-year study by researchers at the Computational Propaganda Project at Oxford University found that this manipulation of opinion and perception was being employed more comprehensively by 'democracies' than officially-labelled authoritarian regimes when it came to targeting opinion in other countries. The research team published their findings in a paper entitled 'Troops, Trolls and Troublemakers: A Global Inventory of Organised Social Media Manipulation' which included research across 28 countries including the UK, US, Germany, Russia, Saudi Arabia, Syria, Turkey and Venezuela. The paper said that 'almost every democracy in this sample has organised social media campaigns that target foreign publics.' Lead author Samantha Bradshaw noted the prominence of social media manipulation among democratic governments and how they were using the same 'tools and techniques' as authoritarian regimes. 'I don't think people realise how much governments are using these tools to reach them. It's a lot more hidden.' The paper highlighted the British Army's 77th Brigade which was formed in 2015 to 'focus on non-lethal psychological operations using social networks like Facebook and Twitter to fight enemies by gaining control of the narrative in the information age.' In the United States they named DARPA (the technology arm of the Pentagon), US Cyber Command, US Agency for International Development and the Air Force as the major vehicles for targeting public opinion through social media in projects costing tens of millions of dollars. The techniques are also used by the Democratic and Republican parties. The Oxford team found that people were also targeted individually and this is being done by governments that say there must be more censorship to stop fake news and the manipulation of opinion. The hypocrisy is extraordinary.

## The monetisation conspiracy

Another weapon used to close down the genuine alternative is to deny those websites income through advertising, whether from Google's ad system or YouTube (also owned by Google) and other Internet ad agencies. They know that most truth-driven sites, unlike the clickbait merchants, scratch an often meagre living from these sources to allow them to pay website costs and work full-time on their research and communication. Google and its video subsidiary YouTube are now denying advertising income to content dubbed 'controversial', fake news, 'extremist' and the latest one – 'not advertiser friendly'. The Spider Web structure allows for coordination between on the face of it unconnected organisations, and in early 2017 we had the mock outrage from major global corporations about their advertising being used on YouTube with 'extremist' videos. Funny, it had never bothered them before and then suddenly it bothered them all in unity, and how kind of the UK *Times* newspaper, owned by Rupert Murdoch, to 'expose' the connection so they could all be outraged together. *Did no one ever look before?* More than 250 companies withdrew their advertising and they included Marks & Spencer, Toyota, HSBC, AT&T, General Motors, Verizon, Walmart and Johnson & Johnson. It may be worth remembering this before you part with your money. Matt Peacock, Vodaphone's

Director of Corporate Affairs, said they had created a 'white list' of sites
where their advertising can only be used which were 'in line with our
values'. Vodaphone has values; well, you live and learn. You would
have thought that the 'extremist' videos they were talking about were
ISIS beheadings and such like, but YouTube video sites that were denied
advertising revenue as a result of this coordination were those
throughout the alternative media. It is all so transparent. Simply talking
about anything 'controversial' is demonised by Google's YouTube or in
their own words: 'Video content that features or focuses on sensitive
topics or events including, but not limited to, war, political conflicts,
terrorism or extremism, death and tragedies, sexual abuse, even if
graphic imagery is not shown, is generally not eligible for ads.' YouTube
further includes on this list 'videos about recent tragedies, even if
presented for news or documentary purposes' – the alternative view of
those events is what they really mean. We have advertisers for my own
YouTube videos that *want* them to be used, but Web-asset
Google/YouTube still won't allow that because the game is to
undermine the alternative media in every way they can. The mainstream
media was not affected in the same way because their content is what
the *El*-lite controlling these companies want you to believe. This
'advertiser boycott' story was reported as bad for YouTube owners
Google because of the loss of advertising revenue, but (a) the goal of
mass human control is far more important to the Archontic Reptilian
networks than just money and (b) to a corporation as monumentally
wealthy as Google it was back-pocket change. 'Brand expert' Eric
Schiffer said: 'Google is also best positioned to put the kiss of death to
online hate because of their mastery at determining the relevancy of
content ... They will do their best to asphyxiate hate merchants, and in
the process, 90 per cent of brands which left will return to the fold
within one to three months.' Of course they will. For 'hate' read what
they don't want you to see. The moral high-ground is being claimed by
Google when it has been exposed for paying academics millions to write
papers in support of its claims that collecting vast amounts of data from
its customers is justified. In some cases the academics did not reveal
who was paying them. *The Wall Street Journal* claimed to have seen
thousands of emails revealing financial relationships with professors
from the world's leading universities. Moral Google? *Joke.*

## The censorship cabal

The theme of where this is going is typified by an oil and gas drilling
advocacy group which sent an open letter to Google asking for anti-
fracking websites to be purged or demoted in the listings. '... We urge
you to consider purging or demoting these websites from your
algorithm, which in turn will encourage a more honest public discussion

about hydraulic fracturing, and oil and natural gas development in general', the letter said. Orwellian translation: 'We only want people to see what suits us.' Some sites have been outright blacklisted by the Google monster that fixes search engine listings and word searches to manipulate the political agenda it represents. Algorithms are also in place with Facebook, Google and others to block the circulation of alternative information. Only a fraction of those who want to be alerted to my Facebook posts ever see them because of algorithmic manipulation while Zuckerberg, official head of Facebook, acts the role of regular guy and man of the people. You cool with that? Cool. Zuckerberg was caught out on a rogue live microphone at a United Nations event discussing with Germany's Chancellor Merkel the censorship of Facebook posts by Germans criticising her open-door policy for migrants which has created such upheaval and mayhem in the country. Merkel and Zuckerberg both deserve each other. Facebook has since banned people for 'hate speech' for posting the picture of a migrant who raped and killed a 19-year-old, while allowing those that say, 'white women should be hunted and killed then we won't get white babies who think the[y] own the world'. This was deemed by the T-shirt's operation 'not be a violation of community standards' when it is plain racism, but from Facebook's point of view it is the right kind of racism. I'll explain what I mean later. Then you have the stage show of authorities 'putting pressure' on Internet giants Facebook, Google and Twitter to censor 'fake news' and so give them public relations cover when they 'reluctantly' bow to that 'pressure' and do what they were going to do all along. What a joke it all is. Justice Minister Heiko Maas in the Undemocratic Republic of Germany pushed through a bill imposing fines of up to 50 million euros for social media sites that don't quickly delete 'hate speech' or defamatory 'fake news'. Maas demanded that companies be compelled to nominate a person to handle complaints who would be *personally* fined up to five million euros if the German tyranny is not obeyed. I'm sure they will be lining up to take that job, then. Facebook said it planned to have 700 people in Berlin dealing with 'flagged content' by the end of 2017. The supreme arrogance of Maas and his colleagues includes forcing social networks to create 'an easily recognisable, directly reachable, and constantly available' complaint system for 'prosecutable content'. This opens the door for censors among the public pushing their own agenda or through sheer vindictiveness to complain about material they don't want others to see, and it will be removed out of fear of facing censure from the authoritarian German government. Other countries will follow this lead for sure. Germany now has an extreme level of totalitarianism imposing its will on the population while claiming to be a free country. Renate Kuenast, a German Green Party legal expert, said: 'My fear, and that of many others, is that in the end the version [Maas] is now presenting will limit freedom of opinion because it will simply become delete, delete, delete.' Well, first of all that's the whole idea and second maybe the Green parties of the world will keep that in mind when they are supporting the systematic deletion of freedom of expression through political correctness or what the great American comedian George Carlin called 'fascism pretending to be manners'. Still, at least someone is delighted with Germany's gross attack on freedom. Robert Singer, the chief executive of the World Jewish Congress, was gushing in his praise:

*The internet is awash with hateful content, a lot of which is incitement to hatred and violence. Currently, it often takes providers far too long to remove or block such content. It's important that the internet companies and politicians take this problem seriously, and we commend Germany for taking the lead on this.*

How about Israeli politicians and others expressing their hate for Palestinians? *Ahhh*, we must defend the right to freedom of speech. Okay, got you. Not only Zionism is being protected from exposure, so is Islam. Google is directing staff to flag content that may be 'upsetting and offensive' and push down the listings anything that is inaccurate or has other questionable attributes, thereby giving prominence to [what they decide are] trustworthy sources. On that basis Google will be censoring itself. The policy is to delete material that is obviously true such as the fact that some expressions of Islam are horrific and intolerant. Most Muslims in my experience just want to get on with their lives and peacefully bring up their families, but many others, as in Wahhabi Saudi Arabia, behead people and outrageously oppress women as does US/UK/Saudi-created Wahhabi ISIS. Does this qualify as 'upsetting and offensive'? Not to the Internet giants, it seems. A Pakistani journalism student was beaten to death in 2017 by an insane mob of about ten Muslim students shouting 'Allahu Akbar' because of 'blasphemy' during a heated debate on religion. He was struck so violently that his skull caved in. At least 65 people have been murdered for blasphemy in Pakistan (and the rest) since 1990, and insulting the Prophet Muhammad carries a death sentence. Many are in jail awaiting trial and execution. It has become routine for Christians to be accused of blaspheming against Islam. The first Christian governor of Jakarta, Indonesia, was sentenced to two years in jail for blasphemy against Islam by brainless 'judges' for 'using words with negative connotations regarding the symbols of religions' while lunatics outside protested that it should have been the maximum five years. What confidence can these crazies have in their religion if they fear any questioning and have to silence people by killing them or sending them to prison? You would have thought that 'moral'

Facebook would stand up against such terror and violence, but no. We have had Pakistani Prime Minister Nawaz Sharif calling for the immediate prosecution of anyone publishing 'blasphemous content' on social media. You know Pakistan, home of free speech, religious freedom and basic humanity. First on the far right – can't miss it. Sharif proclaimed: 'The [posting of] blasphemous content on social media is an unclean attempt to play with the feelings of the Muslim Ummah [community] ... Effective steps must be taken immediately to remove and block this material.' You mean censorship to suit your programmed belief system, mate. This means the same in any language and with any religion, gender or sexual preference so long as you are not a white man (impossible to abuse or blaspheme against, apparently). Pakistan Interior Secretary Arif Khan was soon crowing about how gutless Facebook had removed 85 percent of the material the religious tyranny had deemed blasphemous. Facebook is just an agent of government and The System and treats its users and their basic human rights to express an opinion with total contempt. Notice how all these people, Jewish, Muslim, whatever, who otherwise agree on virtually nothing, come together in seamless unity when it comes to having the right to silence those who question their stance or beliefs. This unity reflects their mutual self-interest in censorship.

The plan is to lump together the fake news claims-to-be-alternative with the genuine alternative and censor one justified by the actions of the other. I don't want any of them to be censored not even 'Baxter Dmitry'. I want the public to become more streetwise and discerning so they don't go to sites that seek to exploit them with misleading headlines and fake text and certainly not circulate them. The first time they are manipulated by clickbait is the last time they ever open a story from that site again never mind share it. This is the way to deal with it, by making people aware of what to look for and how they are being scammed. Once you start deciding what can and can't be seen, what is fact and what isn't, then you give the power of censorship to those making those decisions. Fake news is preferable to censored 'news'. Who fact-checks the fact-checkers? Who *owns* the fact-checkers? What is their agenda? Answers: (1) no-one; (2) those who want to control the information that people see; (3) to use claims of 'fake news' to censor information they wish to suppress. Discernment of the public is what we should be working for not censorship which serves only the interests of the El-lite. I want people to be their own fact-checkers. Theresa May, the British Prime Minister who appears to despise privacy and freedom of speech, announced in her Conservative Party's manifesto for the 2017 General Election that she planned huge restrictions on what people can post, share and publish online. The manifesto said: 'Some people say that it is not for government to regulate when it comes to technology and the internet. We disagree'. Britain would become 'the global leader in the regulation of the use of personal data and the internet' – the global leader in censoring what they don't want the public to know. The British government has an alleged 'anti-terrorism' strategy called 'Prevent' which equates being sceptical about the prevailing order and status quo with potential for terrorism. Prevent encourages the public and demands that schools, universities and government offices and others report those with possible 'terrorist sympathies'; but the term is defined so widely that this can mean anyone who questions or challenges official narratives. All this is a stepping stone to an even wider definition that equates people like me with terrorism for, ironically, exposing government involvement in terrorism. Former British Prime Minister David Cameron, one of the prime figures responsible for the Libya catastrophe, made a speech along these lines at the UN. The Establishment-controlled BBC would surely be in support of such censorship after announcing on its website that it may send personal information of any users to employers, 'relevant third parties', school email internet providers or law enforcement agencies if they consider the content 'offensive, inappropriate or objectionable'. I find the BBC offensive, inappropriate or objectionable but I still support its freedom of speech. A quaint old concept these days, I know, but I'm sticking with it.

## Double-whammy

Donald Trump, flushed with support from many major US 'alternative' websites, began using the same term 'fake news' to describe the mainstream media especially after he came to power in January 2017 (Fig 405). This is an accurate description justified by more than a century of mainstream media manipulation in service to the Deep State agenda. But this is where I return to that 'other angle' I mentioned with regard to Trump's attacks on the mainstream media. To see through the smoke and mirrors always watch the outcomes and less the words and explanations for why something is being done. Outcomes are what matter because it is outcomes that change society, not speeches and rhetoric. On one side you have fake news sources claiming to be 'alternative' and on the other the fake news mainstream almost in its entirety. I emphasise, however, the *almost*. There are still a few chinks of light despite the massive global edifice of

**Figure 405:** Zionist Zucker heads one of the most biased 'news' sources on Planet Earth.

hierarchical information control that has the Web dictating to media
owners who dictate to editors who dictate to journalists who tell the
readers and viewers what the Web wants them to believe. By chinks of
light I mean those journalists who still seek to uncover the truth and tell
the public what they have a right to know. They may not be aware of the
big conspiratorial picture but they investigate elements of it in isolation
that produce important revelations about how the world is run, which
make uncomfortable reading for the El-lite and their gofers. The System
has these genuine journalists in its gunsights as well and that includes
security agency surveillance to uncover their sources and harsh laws
against government whistleblowers to stop the flow of insider
information. Theresa May's disgraceful, freedom-destroying
Investigatory Powers Act or 'snooper's charter' introduced in the UK in
2016 is one major example which the opposition Labour Party of Jeremy
Corbyn outrageously failed to oppose. A US federal judge has ruled that
the FBI can spy on journalists without revealing the legal basis on which
this is done. Research by the Institute of Advanced Legal Studies at the
University of London found that journalists are finding it increasingly
difficult to maintain the anonymity of sources in the wake of telephone
and Internet surveillance. German news magazine *Der Spiegel* revealed
in 2017 how the Germany intelligence agency BND had been spying on
foreign journalists for 20 years and monitored at least 50 telephone
numbers, fax numbers and e-mail addresses of journalists, newsrooms
and editorial offices around the world. Reporters Without Borders in
Germany described the surveillance as a 'a monstrous attack on press
freedom'. BND was sharing relevant information with the CIA and other
global agencies because they are strands in the same Web. The idea is to
use the 'fake news' technique of lumping together the remaining
genuine mainstream journalists and courageous editors with the gutless
manipulation and system-serving of the rest. The El-lite's desired
outcome for the fake news rhetoric on both sides is to censor into non-
existence the genuine alternative media *and* what is left of the genuine
mainstream. I don't want the mainstream media censored any more than
I do nonsense put out by fake news elements in the alleged alternative.
No one should be in favour of media censorship and sanction more than
me after the disgusting way I have been treated and reported since 1990.
But I don't want that – indeed I vehemently oppose it – because I value
freedom far more. I would much rather be abused by idiots than have
the idiots censored at the expense of the intelligent or the mendacious at
the expense of the genuine. Censorship law doesn't choose between
them and treats them all the same.

Two activists who used undercover filming to expose the scandal of
Planned Parenthood discussing the sale of foetal tissue found
themselves facing 15 felony charges for 'invading the privacy of medical

providers by filming without consent'. What about government agencies filming everywhere without consent? *Ahh*, that's different. This is the world we now live in. The UK *Guardian* bleated about the way other governments have followed Trump's anti-media lead and banned outlets for 'fake news', and how the Russian Ministry of Foreign Affairs launched a website to flag up what it says is fake media reporting by *The New York Times*, Al-Jazeera, and others. I see nothing wrong with setting up a website to highlight alleged false reporting and explaining why. It is censoring or suppressing that information which is the danger. Bleating by *The Guardian* would be more credible if it defended the alternative media from the fake news hoax and if it did not engage in manipulating and slanting its own journalism to fit with its political and corporate agenda. Lack of genuine mainstream journalism has caused this anti-media campaign by providing the authorities with an excuse, and the same with the fake, opportunistic elements of the so-called alternative. Mainstream media seeks to discredit the alternative with the label fake news because the alternative is taking its audience, when it only has itself to blame for that, and many in the alternative seek to discredit the mainstream with claims of fake news while delivering fake news themselves. So-called progressives hurl their hatred at Trump and call him fascist while they, too, support fascist-like censorship of the media that they don't agree with. 'Progressive' academics call for banning the UK *Daily Mail* because they claim its readers have an 'abnormal perception of reality'. Unlike those who demand an end to free speech, I take it. What a chilling statement that is. How many times have terms like 'abnormal perception of reality' been used by the most repressive regimes to justify incarcerating dissidents in psychiatric units and 're-education' centres? Progressive fascism is now a global disease. Other 'progressives' have led calls to bring down newspapers they don't like by targeting their advertisers while in America tyrannical progressives are running similar campaigns against TV news programmes they disagree with. I don't share the *Daily Mail's* politics in the least, but it still produces some excellent investigative journalism within the Postage Stamp and that is why the paper and its website are really being targeted. The *Mail's* successful campaign in support of a Brexit vote will have also put the paper right in the firing line. How breathtaking beyond belief to contemplate the mental gymnastics and self-deception necessary to claim to stand for free speech and human rights while calling for a newspaper to be banned because its perceptions and those of its readers are different to yours. Freedom of speech is what it says on the tin – the freedom to speak. This includes the freedom for people to say what we don't like as well as what we do. The first part of that sentence is what programmed 'progressive' perceptions cannot compute. They are so submerged in their own extremes of narcissism that they can't comprehend their own stupidity and hypocrisy. There is a reason for this which I will soon address and it relates to how 'progressive' academia and swathes of the 'progressive' student population have been lured into states of what I can only perceive as forms of mental illness. Extremists in the progressive (regressive) Left and Centre and their 'opponents' in the equally self-deluded Right are united in their desire to target and censor the media. They may target different sections, but together they target the whole. Never mind the words, watch the outcome.

## Hack attack

Trump projects his daily abuse at the American mainstream while the British version is clearly being targeted by an Establishment cheered on by supposedly 'anti-Establishment' (yet another irony) progressives. Plans to censor the UK print media began in earnest when operatives working for British Intelligence front organisations infiltrated national newspapers through their arms-length-away 'private security firms'. This was done most famously with the Rupert Murdoch-owned tabloid, the *News of the World*, when infiltrators introduced a policy of illegal phone-tapping to listen to conversations of the famous and those involved in topical stories. Content of the hacked phone calls would appear in the *News of the World* as 'exclusives'. They wouldn't set up an insider like Rupert Murdoch? He's small fry to The Spider no matter how powerful he may seem to be in the public arena. They are all expendable to the greater agenda. Former *News of the World* investigator Christine Hart told me how the phone-hacking scam was instigated and how the same sources were keen to 'get' the *Daily Mail*. Once the *News of the World* had been set up the phone-tapping activities were made public and the paper shut down amid the furore that followed. The anti-media campaign that then emerged was spearheaded by a group that called itself Hacked Off and one of its major voices was the actor Hugh 'plays-the-same-part-in-every-film' Grant. The scandal was used to justify a government investigation into the behaviour of the UK press headed by a judge, Lord Leveson, who recommended the creation of an 'independent' body to oversee the industry. Impress, the 'independent' body subsequently recognised by the government, is funded to the tune of millions by Max Mosley, who can't stand the Press. He is the son of British fascist Oswald Mosely. The *Daily Mail* revealed how Max Mosely had given £500,000 to the press-condemning deputy leader of the opposition Labour Party, Tom Watson. How remarkably independent this all is. A *Mail* editorial said:

> *Mr Mosley has pursued a campaign against the Press since he was exposed by the now-defunct News of the World for taking part in a sado-masochistic*

*orgy involving five prostitutes. Among Impress board members is one who has tweeted his wish to ban the Daily Mail, and others who have backed the campaign to drive centre-Right newspapers out of business by starving them of advertising.*

*Even if Impress had impeccably fair-minded credentials, this paper would refuse to join it, on the principle that it is wrong for the Press to submit to state regulation. As it is, the very thought of surrender to such a creepy body is unthinkable.*

But not, it seems, to the government and its string-pullers. Among the do-or-die options proposed by the government was for newspapers to either agree to be regulated by Mosley's mob or face having costs awarded against them even if they *won* libel actions. You read that correctly. Papers that didn't sign up to this 'independent' press-hating body would have to pay the costs of anyone suing them *even if the case was found in favour of the paper.* This would inevitably lead them all into certain bankruptcy. Did I mention that the Establishment is desperate to part the media from what is left of its balls? Fortunately, at the time of writing, they have backed off from this, and we'll see where it goes from here. The phone-hacking scandal was the manipulated excuse to justify new censorship laws for which there was no need. Phone-hacking was already illegal and journalists have been jailed for that. None of this has been about hacking, but about censorship. Those cheering on Trump, Leveson, Hacked Off and Impress because they don't like the mainstream media might benefit from a rethink and so, too, might the purveyors of fake news in both the mainstream and 'alternative' media. They might consider how their behaviour has brought all this about by providing the ammunition and public contempt now being trawled to justify across-the-board censorship that will include the genuine alternative and genuine mainstream. This was the plan all along.

## Information hijack

The *El*-lite are well into the process of transferring sources of news and information from traditional newspapers, television, radio and independent websites to Internet giants Google, Facebook, Twitter and their like (Fig 406). Many newspapers are being forced to go online only as paper

**Figure 406:** New media for the next stage of the perceptual lockdown.

sales fall. Plans for news and information domination by the Internet giants are motivated by the potential to use algorithms to manipulate what people are allowed to see. Twitter announced in 2017 a new system of algorithms to identify accounts engaging in abusive behaviour and then censor them. How long before the interpretation of abusive includes any information that challenges orthodox and official narratives? The technology is already in place to do that and only the code would need updating. Around a hundred websites dominate Internet traffic. Zionist-controlled Google has 1.2 trillion searches a year; Google-owned YouTube has more than a billion active users per month; and Zionist-controlled Facebook, which also owns Instagram, WhatsApp and so much more, claims two billion active users. I am guiding people to some YouTube videos in this book because its domination means that is the only place you can see them. We seriously need another mass video platform that believes in freedom not censorship. American intelligence whistleblower Edward Snowden said of Facebook: 'To have one company that has enough power to reshape the way we think, I don't think I need to describe how dangerous that is.' Those who have abandoned their alternative websites to operate from a Facebook page have been well and truly had. Facebook deleted thousands of UK accounts in the run-up to the UK General Election in June 2017 and launched a 'new drive' to tackle 'fake news' with technology to detect patterns of people who repeatedly post the same things and to demote articles on its news feed so people will see them less often or not at all. The fake news mainstream media was not affected (but it will be eventually if it steps out of line). Albert Speer, Nazi Germany's Minister of Armaments and War Production, said at the Nuremberg trials:

*Hitler's dictatorship differed in one fundamental point from all its predecessors in history. His was the first dictatorship in the present period of modern technical development, a dictatorship which made complete use of all technical means in a perfect manner for the domination of its own nation. Through technical devices such as radio and loudspeaker 80 million people were deprived of independent thought. It was thereby possible to subject them to the will of one man.*

Speer was talking about Hitler's 'People's Receiver' radio system in which the population were given cheap radios en masse that could only pick up broadcasts from within Germany and Austria. This is happening today on a global scale by ever-increasing concentration of power over information in a handful of Internet corporations centrally-controlled by the same Web network. Geopolitical researcher Tony Cartalucci wrote:

*Facebook has constructed a modern day People's Receiver for corporate-financier special interests – with alternatives omitted from the tuning dials, and lacking the technical ability to receive alternative information from outside Facebook's carefully controlled information space. It is the modern day destruction of independent thought – an information cage [which many] like the German people during the 1930-40's may not even realize they're locked in.*

*Just as people fought hard to up-end the Nazi propaganda machine during World War II, people today are and must continue to confront, undermine, and eventually displace Facebook's monopoly over modern day communication. Unlike Nazi Germany's People's Receivers, Facebook doesn't taint and skew the perception of just 80 million Germans, but includes a user base spread out across the planet and numbering nearly 2 billion.*

**Figure 407:** Algorithms can censor information you are not allowed to see without need for human intervention once the code is written.

Facebook's Zuckerberg has since claimed that the number has passed two billion just 13 years after its launch and the second billion has come in less than five years. The T-shirt says Facebook can take over from churches and, in the sense of dictating perceptions and turning alternative thought into blasphemy, it already has. Andreas Schleicher, director of education and skills at the Organization for Economic Cooperation and Development (OECD), made the point that social media tends to be an 'echo chamber' connecting people who think alike and he said it was important for schools to ensure a wide range of debate and views are heard. He is right, but that isn't what The System wants. News feeds, YouTube, and advertising algorithms offer people choices based on surfing history and what they have seen before. This, too, is reducing the chances of coming across something that makes you think differently. Facebook admits that algorithms listen to private conversations through device microphones and this became clear when people were seeing Facebook ads appearing that related to personal conversations and discussions. Facebook said: 'We use your microphone to identify the things you are listening to or watching.' This is not only for targeted ads, either, which are a secondary reason and not the main one which is surveillance and personal data trawling. Once social media giants – all answering to the

Web – began to dominate the circulation of news and information out came the algorithms and censorship to dictate what the masses see and don't see (Fig 407). Mainstream media like the dreadful *New York Times* cheer at the use of algorithms to censor the alternative media, when they will be next in line because the *El*-lite want to stop all exposure and challenge even the trickle that still gets out here and there in the mainstream. First you sell social media and the Internet as the free-flow of information and when you have secured enough control you bring in the censorship algorithms:

*Hey, we're all Mr Nice Guys, cool, man – look at my grey 'I'm one of you' T-shirt. Oh, we've reached domination point? Right, now censor the bastards. Gotcha.*

We have a US President communicating with the nation in 140 characters. Welcome to the world of the superficial with its superficial 'news' for superficial minds to superficially process into idiocy. We are heading towards the complete elimination of genuine journalism of all kinds and the end of substance which is really the same thing. Zionist-created Wikipedia, the notoriously inaccurate Internet 'encyclopaedia', is consulted by hundreds of millions every day as their 'factual' source on people, events and almost everything you could imagine. The *Daily Mail* was banned by Wikipedia as an information source in February 2017 and when the paper investigated why this happened what they found was both pathetic and chilling. A handful of people with an anti-press and in some cases seriously anti-*Daily Mail* agenda had simply got together and decided to ban the *Mail*, while producing no evidential justification whatsoever. One of them goes by the anonymous tags 'Hillbillyholiday' and 'Tabloidterminator' and has apparently been pictured burning a copy of the *Mail*. Wikipedia founder Jimmy Wales, who is married to the former diary secretary for Tony Blair and was on the board of the *Guardian*, claims Wikipedia is a democratic organisation – when a handful can just decide to ban a national newspaper. Wikipedia asks its visitors for donations to pay for the site while sitting on assets of more than $90 million and is among the most visited websites in the world. Wales announced without a hint of irony in 2017 that he was launching a new website 'Wikitribune' to produce 'fact-checked, global news stories' to overcome fake news: 'I find myself being a bit upset that people are making decisions based on lies, false information and so on, so I want to add a new trusted information source to all the other ones out there.' I suppose he could be referring to claims that Greek philosopher Plato was a surfer from Hawaii who discovered Florida and that singer Robbie Williams eats domestic pets – both of which appeared on Wikipedia. Information is being hijacked by a tiny few Internet giants and this is not where it is planned to end. Jonathan Taplin reveals the scale of domination in his book, *Move Fast and Break Things: How Facebook, Google and Amazon Cornered Culture and Undermined Democracy*. He points out that the world's five highest-valued companies are Apple, Google, Microsoft, Amazon and Facebook which have secured monumental levels of market domination. The potential this has for dictating the information that people see – or don't – requires no elaboration. They monetise the lives of the global population and exploit their creativity while paying them nothing or a pittance in return compared with the amazing wealth they accumulate for themselves. Taplin writes: 'Not since Rockefeller and J.P. Morgan has there been such a concentration of wealth and power ... and the enormous unprecedented fortunes created by the digital revolution have done much to increase inequality in America.' In the world as a whole, too, and they are way more powerful in the digital age than even the industrial robber barons ever were. Together they seek to control *everything* and *everyone* for their Archontic masters.

Heads need symbolically knocking together in the mainstream media, and the alternative, before they are divided and ruled into oblivion. The mainstream seeks to eliminate what it perceives as the competition as it rapidly loses its audience to alternative sources. The alternative revels in the demise of the mainstream it despises and has sought to replace. Such black and white thinking will destroy the freedom of both and is already well on the way to doing so. We need some maturity here. We need to see the shades of grey where truth always sits between the black and white. Mature and intelligent expressions of the mainstream need to come together with the mature and intelligent in the alternative and let us meet this challenge together. The idiots in both camps never will, but so be it. Those that can see the writing painted large need to unite – and fast.

# CHAPTER TEN

# Advancing the Spell

*'None are more hopelessly enslaved than those who falsely believe they are free' – Johann Wolfgang von Goethe*

The perception deception and its required suppression of other views and perspectives have plumbed still new depths with the emergence of a form of psychological warfare known as political correctness, or 'PC'.

I am not exaggerating with the term 'psychological warfare' when you consider its definition: 'The use of activities that cause fear and anxiety in the people you want to influence without hurting them physically.' So, no, it's not too strong. Psychological warfare describes the way PC's psychological fascism programs perception by the exclusion of other views and opinions, and by the use of fear and intimidation to silence dissenters. There is an antidote that I can recommend because I know it works from personal experience. When the PC fanatics seek to silence your right to an opinion try this reply: 'Fuck off.' You will feel the freedom frequency surge through your being and dispatch any emotional effects of intimidation. Let's try that again: 'Fuck off.' Again: 'Fuck off.' Good stuff (Fig 408). Now we have established the cure we'll deal with the utter madness itself for which there is no cure short of expanded awareness. No, I'm not holding my breath either, but you do what you can. Political correctness is an *El*-lite tool for getting the target population to silence and censor itself so they don't have to (Fig 409). PC foot soldiers and storm troopers are

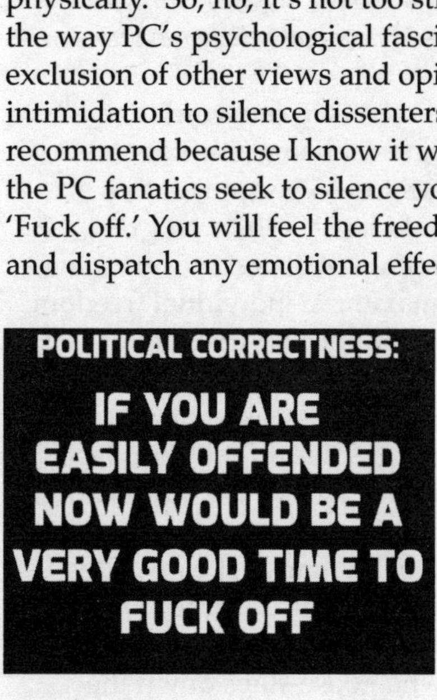

**POLITICAL CORRECTNESS:**

**IF YOU ARE EASILY OFFENDED NOW WOULD BE A VERY GOOD TIME TO FUCK OFF**

**Figure 408:** PC antidote.

dominated by progressives
(regressives) and they can be easily
spotted by their manic facial
expression, stupendous self-
righteousness, heart on the sleeve and
the torch which allows them to see
while in permanent residence up their
own arse. The term progressive
describes a mental and emotional
state of such self-centric self-delusion
that it skewers and inverts reality in
the extreme. Progressives think they

**Figure 409:** Sheep policing the sheep so the shepherds don't have to.

are (a) anti-Establishment and (b) liberal; but they are neither.
Progressives are the *new* Establishment and crucial to the social
engineering networks which instigated political correctness to
manipulate the population to censor itself. Claims that a progressive is a
liberal are demolished by these definitions:

> *Progressive: Favouring or advocating progress, change, improvement, or
> reform, as opposed to wishing to maintain things as they are, especially in
> political matters.*

> *Liberal: Favourable to or in accord with concepts of maximum individual
> freedom possible, especially as guaranteed by law and secured by
> governmental protection of civil liberties. Favouring or permitting freedom
> of action, especially with respect to matters of personal belief or expression.*

This definition of progressive nowhere mentions the word 'liberal'
while perceptions of what constitutes progress, change, improvement or
reform are purely subjective. That definition could be applied to what
the Nazis did in Germany which they would have seen as progress,
change, improvement or reform. The definition of liberal is everything
that PC progressives are not – favouring maximum individual freedom,
government-guaranteed civil liberties and supporting 'freedom of
action, especially with respect to matters of personal belief or
expression'. This is precisely what progressives are seeking to *destroy*
and the last thing they are is 'liberal'. They can't see this obvious fact
because of said stupendous self-righteousness. This whole area headed
'progressive' is so important to understand. We are told to fear the 'far-
right' when the vehicle for introducing global tyranny is being called
progressive. If you want to hide the fact that you are deleting freedoms
and manipulating behaviour and perception then don't use a bloke with
a tiny moustache with his arm in the air who goose-steps down the
street. This is far too obvious and someone might notice. Instead, use

those who present themselves as 'caring', 'thoughtful' and 'nice'. You are still employing the stick, but you make it look like a carrot. A good example of the concept is an app introduced by the Canadian government to award people points for basically 'good behaviour'. The app, named 'Carrot Rewards', gives people discount points for things like food, movies and flights, if they follow a lifestyle recommended by the Canadian government. The Chinese tyranny is also on the case at an even more extreme level and this is the way behaviour is planned to be manipulated globally. Remember how the wolf in *Little Red Riding Hood* was dressed like a nice old granny. Whenever the 'progressive' state wants to reward you for doing what it says be sure to look for the big ears, big eyes and big teeth because they will always be hiding under granny's bonnet.

My use of the term 'progressive' from hereon does not refer to those of the Left and Centre who are genuinely liberal in the sense of the definition, but to those who call themselves progressive while being the very antipathy of liberal. The Postage Stamp Consensus is not a permanent state of unchanging perception but a fluid one that reflects the advancing stages of the Archontic agenda. Fascist tyranny or communist tyranny may be the most effective form of control in one era or country, but now the tyranny of choice is labelled 'progressive'. They serve the same goal at each stage of entrapping perception within the firewall of five-sense reality and everything else is the detail of how most effectively this can be done. What suits the *El*-lite for people to believe at one 'time' may not be most effective at another. For example, Osama bin Laden was the good guy (Postage Stamp Consensus) when he was fronting up the covert US war against the Soviet Union in Afghanistan using Mujahedeen 'freedom fighters' in the 1980s; but he became the bad guy (Postage Stamp Consensus) when the US needed an excuse to invade Afghanistan themselves in 2001. They said they had to invade to find bin Laden and remove his Taliban protectors when the idea was never to leave as I wrote at the time. All these years later the US and NATO are still in Afghanistan and asking for more troops with the excuse of the new buzz-term – 'stabilisation'. Whatever the prevailing nature and spin of Postage Stamp Consensus it is crucial to the agenda that the majority of the people – especially those with perceptual influence – believe in it totally. They have to believe they are *right* and that they hold the moral high ground because they are *right*. From this comes the self-righteousness arrogance which says that if I am right then anyone who believes something different must by definition be wrong and so of no relevance or importance. This mind-set can then justify to itself the oppression of non-believers and their views and even violence (Fig 410). A perfect progressive example is the demand for the *Daily Mail* to be banned because its readers have 'an abnormal perception of reality'. *Ab*normal here only means different from *I am right* normal. 'Non-believers' is the right term given that political correctness is another religion operating to the same blueprint. To question religious orthodoxy during the Christian inquisition becomes to question political correctness during the PC inquisition. Being 'un-PC' is the new blasphemy. We have the same

**Figure 410:** Self-delusion on steroids.

program of the ages given a new alias. PC fanatics are only religious fanatics in disguise, but how can they see that when they are so *right?*

## On the road to PC

Political correctness has been systematically allowed to infest government departments, agencies and educational establishments worldwide. From this base camp it was able to make an assault on human society in general via 'hate laws', language policing and mainstream media. One of the wish-fors of the Frankfurt School of social engineering all those decades ago was the creation of racism offences. Political correctness has hijacked the language, put people in constant fear of 'saying the wrong thing' (almost *any*thing these days) and created a whole army of mentally ill, mind-controlled 'progressive' enforcers with their torches always at hand. George Orwell described political correctness in his prophetic epic *Nineteen-Eighty-Four* published in 1948. He called this *'Newspeak'* which is defined as 'a controlled language [used] as a tool to limit freedom of thought and concepts that pose a threat to the regime such as freedom, self-expression, individuality and peace.' This is political correctness to perfection. *Newspeak* was the language in Orwell's factually-based novel that replaced *Oldspeak* which was the original vocabulary with endless words that could describe detailed concepts to accurately reflect perceptions and opinions. *Newspeak* deleted words that described detail and replaced them with meaningless neutral words that upset no one by actually saying anything (Fig 411). There was no way to express vibrant opinion, concepts and views. People will immediately recognise that concept in the sterile and lifeless language of political correctness. Our conscious mind thinks in words and so as political correctness deletes *Oldspeak* for

**Figure 411:** And so he did.

*Newspeak* succeeding generations are denied language not only to speak in detail, but even to *think* in detail. We have today attempts to ban words as simple as girl and boy, mum and dad. The writer P.D. James rightly concluded: 'I believe that political correctness can be a form of linguistic fascism, and it sends shivers down the spine of my generation who went to war against fascism.' While Orwell was writing about Big Brother in the first half of the 20th century, today's PC culture was already being planned in the shadows as a means to highjack human perception and behaviour and to silence dissent. The instigators from the 1920s (though the PC concept goes back further) were the neo-Marxist Rothschild and Zionist social engineers at the Frankfurt School which later located its mind manipulators in the United States and infiltrated college and university campuses in California and then across the country. Out of this came political correctness which was subsequently exported to Europe and beyond. Seizing perceptions of students is vital because they are the decision makers and perceptual influencers of tomorrow. Get them and you get wider society. And my god they have got them. Not everyone – there are still students and young people who can see through the bullshit and refuse to comply; but what a daily challenge that must be in the midst of such programmed fanaticism underpinned by equally programmed academia (with honourable exceptions). Progressive students may be aghast at much of what I say in this book but many other students with a mind of their own will be delighted that what they think has a platform for once. There is much that American conservative author William S. Lind and I would not agree on, but he has penned some excellent critiques of political correctness and its origins. He wrote:

> *The totalitarian nature of political correctness is revealed nowhere more clearly than on college campuses, many of which at this point are small ivy covered North Koreas, where the student or faculty member who dares to cross any of the lines set up by the gender feminist or the homosexual-rights activists, or the local black or Hispanic group, or any of the other sainted 'victims' groups that PC revolves around, quickly find themselves in judicial trouble. Within the small legal system of the college, they face formal charges – some star-chamber proceeding – and punishment. That is a little look into the future that political correctness intends for the nation as a whole ...*

> *... In the cultural Marxism of political correctness certain groups are good – feminist women (only feminist women, non-feminist women are deemed not to exist), blacks, Hispanics, homosexuals. These groups are determined to be 'victims', and therefore automatically good regardless of what any of them do. Similarly, white males are determined automatically to be evil, thereby becoming the equivalent of the bourgeoisie in economic Marxism.*

The last point is captured in a quote from American 'radical feminist' Robin Morgan: 'I feel that man-hating is an honourable and viable political act, that the oppressed have a right to class-hatred against the class that is oppressing them.' Anyone who believes that hate is the way to respond to anything has completely lost the plot and these people did so long ago. If this is really about feminism how come that when I observe its screaming advocates and extremists that I see the traits of testosterone and not oestrogen? This is not about rightly allowing women to equally express themselves and their unique contribution to society; it is about making women and men the *same*. I will explain later why the *El*-lite want this to be. I have described how film producer Aaron Russo revealed that businessman Nick Rockefeller told him the Rockefeller family funded and established feminism and women's liberation to allow the state to control children at the earliest possible age 'to indoctrinate them how to think' and to destroy the family unit. William S. Lind's article about PC manipulation was dated February 5th, 2000 and the situation is far worse now and infinitely more extreme and widespread. Among the victim groups that can since be added are those promoting transgender issues although there will probably be three or four more by the time I have finished this sentence. Oh, look, there are. We have LGBT or lesbian, gay, bisexual, and transgender. Is that too short for you? Okay, how about LGBTQ or lesbian, gay, bisexual, transgender and 'queer' (questioning your sexual identity)? That's still too short? Shit. Well, let's try LGBTIQ or lesbian, gay, bisexual, transgender, intersex and 'queer'. LGBT+ (encompassing a spectrum of gender and sexuality) gets marks for brevity in case you're in a rush. Or maybe like me you'll just settle for BOLLOCKS (or don't be so *bloody silly*). No, it doesn't scan, but has the benefit of accuracy. Political correctness must create victims because without victims there can be no identifiable oppressor. Victims are PC's foundation currency and from them all oppressors can be agreed upon and targeted. One writer said: 'The underlying message is that a 'distressed' cry-baby attitude is something to seek and foster.' This relates to what I call label consciousness which self-identifies with Phantom Self and focuses perception on five-sense reality at the expense of Infinite Awareness. Political correctness is now sub-dividing former labels into sub-labels and sub-labels of sub-labels, hence LGBTIQ. We're not finished yet, though. There is LGBTIQAA (one A is for asexual with no desire for either gender and the other is for androsexual or primarily attracted to men). But the yellow jersey for idiocy (so far) goes to Wesleyan University in Connecticut with LGBTTQQFAGPBDSM (lesbian, gay, bisexual, transgender, transsexual, queer, questioning, flexual, asexual, gender-fuck, polyamorous, bondage/discipline, dominance/submission

and sadism/masochism). With 26 letters of the alphabet to play with I'm
sure they've only just begun. Are we talking about people here or a
game of friggin' Scrabble? How can expanded awareness beyond The
Program influence perceptions of a Phantom Self sub-divided in its self-
identity into such minutiae of parts and detail? How about a sub-group
of LGBTTQQFAGPBDSM for left-handed people? They are another
minority after all. It could be LGBTTQQFAGPBDSMLH. And those with
ingrowing toe nails are another minority: LGBTTQQFAGPBDSMITN. If
they are left-handed that would be LGBTTQQFAGPBDSMLHITN. Other
labels include 'non-binary', 'gender-fluid' and 'demisexual' (only
sexually attracted to someone if there is an emotional connection). Label
consciousness by its very nature insists on a label for *everything*. How
much genuine discrimination is missed and not addressed amid this
obsession with labels and the fine detail of individual self-identity?
Facebook offers 56 varieties of gender category to choose from when
filling in a profile and the HSBC bank lists a series of potential name pre-
fixes for its banking customers such as 'Ind' ('individual'), 'Pr' ('person')
'Mre' ('mystery') and 'Misc' ('miscellaneous'). Hello, who are who? I'm
Ms Cellaneous. What do you do? Oh, this and that. Transgender pre-
fixes include 'M', Myr', 'Mx', 'Msr', 'Sai' and 'Ser'. New York City
businesses can be fined up to $250,000 for not referring to someone's
chosen gender identity and the city's Commission on Human Rights
helpfully supplies a list of 31 to choose from: bi-gendered; cross-dresser;
drag king; drag queen; femme queen; female-to-male; ftm; gender
bender; genderqueer; male-to-female; mtf; non-op; hijra; pangender;
transexual/transsexual; trans person; woman; man; butch; two-spirit;
trans; agender; third sex; gender fluid; non-binary transgender;
androgyne; gender gifted; gender blender; femme; person of
transgender experience; androgynous.

Labels become ever more detailed and with each one Infinite
Awareness is further submerged and lost to nano-self-identity and that
is the whole idea. We are also told that not all women have vaginas and
not all men have dicks. Well, actually, speaking physiologically, they *do*.
Have a look and you'll see. All this is manipulating people into self-
identity so totally focused on the body, that expanded awareness beyond
the body is ever more powerfully excluded. And what will a perception
of perpetual victimhood fold into existence for these people from the
quantum field of possibilities and probabilities? Victimhood becomes a
self-fulfilling prophecy as perception manifests a holographic experience
of victimhood perception. Victims can only see (thus experience)
victimisation. If they don't perceive themselves as victims they lose their
self-identity. The entire persona of Zionism and Israel, for example, is
founded on their sense of victimisation. In so many ways they are the
ultimate victim mentality which they incessantly exploit to get their way.

A few points to emphasise to put all this into context: (1) I am not saying there isn't discrimination against those dubbed minority groups or that this should not be rightly and determinedly addressed; (2) nothing like all 'lesbian, gay, bisexual, transgender and intersex' people live their lives as victims and fall for political correctness; and (3) nor does everyone from a 'minority group', racial or otherwise, take offense at every last syllable said in their earshot. I am saying that genuine discrimination is being exploited to promote political correctness and some of what is claimed to be discrimination – which I will be describing in this chapter – is manufactured nonsense. The number of those instantly upset by almost anything is growing rapidly for one obvious reason: they are being *told* from all directions that they *should be upset*. They have to be programmed to be upset as a prerequisite to being a victim. No victim, no oppressor, no political correctness. Manipulating people to be upset is the essential starting point of the sequence and this is now a global industry. Welcome to Planet Earth – BeUpset PLC, or best forget the 'L'. Here is a PC deprogramming technique that I can highly recommend:

'*I am offended!*'

'Well, choose not to be.'

'Phew, thanks, never thought of that.'

'Okay now?'

'Good.'

Taking offence and being a victim is a *choice* that you don't have to make but it's the choice that The System and *El*-lite are programming people to make. If they really cared about you being upset the emphasis would not be on censoring speech but on making the receiver or hearer immune to any effect. They would set out to build self-assurance and backbone in everyone so that whatever was said could not hurt them. Then 'you have upset me' becomes 'what a prick'. They don't do that because they want to breed weak people easily offended and not strong people who couldn't care less what anyone says about them. The victim mentality should have been at my shoulder for the last 30 years in the face of historic levels of ridicule and abuse and see that you don't have to run away and hide. Lift your head up, push back your shoulders and look life in the eye.

Figure 412: Does Big Brother prefer people with backbones of steel or backbones of jelly?

Figure 413: *Whaaaaa! I want my mummy – he's just said something I don't agree with. Whaaaaa!*
Image credit: **www.grrrgraphics.com**

Figure 414: Progressives and pro-Trump supporters in yet another example of the *El*-ite playing the target population against itself.

## PC is BB – Big Brother

An additional bonus with PC is that those who self-identify as victims in fear of their own shadows will give their power away to the Big Brother state to 'protect them' from their perceived oppressors which invariably will be some form of majority (Fig 412). This is another pillar of the PC religion. Only minorities can be oppressed and only majorities can be oppressors. PC doesn't do shades of grey and certainly not subtlety. Far too much consciousness is required to process such things. Many PC people will claim that the one percent is oppressing the masses, but not to the extent they can see how the same one percent is behind political correctness which is a major vehicle for that oppression. Shakes head, moves on. Opinions and information that the oppressing *El*-lite doesn't want people to hear are now routinely censored by PC victims and groupies demanding 'safe spaces' where nothing can be said that will upset anyone (Fig 413). In other words, nothing worth hearing that might challenge perception. Speakers that these programmed censors don't agree with are banned from appearing at universities or 'de-platformed' in PC parlance. This is often done amid banner-waving protests hurling hate and abuse at those they accuse of hate and abuse (Fig 414). I wonder if feminist Robin Morgan supports anti-hate laws while she is hating men? The UK National Union of Students

**Figure 415:** Anti-fascist fascism.

actually produced a publication entitled *Managing the Risks Associated with External Speakers: Guidance for HE Student' Unions in England and Wales* to help students protect themselves and their campus from controversial opinions. Blimey, the *Muppet Show* would be controversial to these people although it may help them feel at home. Do you remember when student unions used to march for freedom of speech? My god, you must have a good memory. 'Left' – as in the progressive Left which dominates student unions – does not represent what it did when I was younger. I don't relate to the Left-Right political spectrum which is just another phenomenal perception trap, but some serious bias is at work when academics at the UK's University of Sussex can arrange a meeting called 'dealing with right-wing attitudes and politics in the classroom' when 'dealing with progressive attitudes and politics in the classroom' would most certainly have never have survived the censors (Fig 415). This is possible because progressives have hijacked colleges and universities as they have hijacked the political Left. Among those attacked and silenced by today's ever-upgraded PC have been those at the forefront for decades of challenging genuine discrimination and taking untold flack for doing so. They include British activist Peter Tatchell who has spent decades campaigning for human rights and against gay discrimination while today's PC extremists were not even thought of or still sucking on their dummy. Come to think of it, they still are. Tatchell has done a sterling job that rightly needed doing and he paid the price with a high public profile that attracted for a long time extreme media and public abuse. But in 2016 Fran Cowling, LGBT+ officer for the National Union of Students, refused to speak at an event on the subject unless Tatchell was dropped from the line-up. Maybe he could have slipped in unnoticed when her torch batteries ran out. Cowling accused him of being racist and transphobic. Who – Peter Tatchell? *Peter Tatchell?* What an example of the extremes of lunacy to which we have now plummeted. These people could make a case of racism against a lamp post. Tatchell's crime is having the intelligence and balance to see what undiluted political correctness is doing to basic human rights. He told the *Daily Telegraph*:

> *This sorry, sad saga is symptomatic of the decline of free and open debate on some university campuses. There is a witch-hunting, accusatory atmosphere.*

*Allegations are made without evidence to back them – or worse, they are made citing false, trumped-up evidence ... This is the antithesis of the free and open inquiry that is supposed to be the hallmark of university learning and culture.*

The whole point of political correctness is to delete free and open inquiry. Tatchell said of the National Union of Students:

*I just disagree with the way some of them choose to deal with other people's opinions. Anyone who doesn't toe the line politically risks being denounced, even over the tiniest disagreement.*

*The race to be more Left-wing and politically correct than anyone else is resulting in an intimidating, excluding atmosphere on campuses. Universal human rights and enlightenment values – including John Stuart Mill's On Liberty – are often shamefully rubbished as the ideas of Western imperialist white privilege.*

*I am all in favour of protesting against real racists and transphobes. But the most effective way to do this is to expose and counter their bigoted ideas, not censor and ban them. I've often debated religious fundamentalists and homophobes. They've lost the argument; leaving them weakened and discredited. Bad ideas are best defeated by good ideas. NUS, please take note.*

Many points come from this. White people can never be discriminated against in PC theology unless it is done by other white people. White colonialism is condemned (and the British and European Archontic empires *were* a disgrace) but what is forgotten is that millions of white working class people were also oppressed and sent to war by the empire-building *El*-lite, note *El*-lite, that doesn't give a damn about white people any more than it does about any other race or skin tone. Ah, but we have breached the black and white no-shades-of-grey mentality with that comment so we better move on quickly and leave the PC brigade with their bewildered expression. Observe white PC fanatics for only a short while and you can see the disappointment that they were not born into a minority. I have seen the same with New Agers walking around in Hindu tunics sad for a lifetime that they were not hatched in India instead of celebrating the infinite awareness that we all are. A lot of white PC fanaticism comes from white people programmed to feel guilty about being white. They are seeking to impose this guilt today in schools which have been conquered by the PC program and woe betide any teacher that doesn't conform to it. I don't feel guilty for being 'white'. What? Why am I not guilty for colonial conquest by white nations? Because I didn't fucking *do* it. We now have people who did not suffer abusing people for something they did not do. Others with white bodies did it and I find colonialism appalling, but some of the worst tyranny and oppression is done by non-white against non-white – people like Pol Pot in Cambodia along with African, Arabian and Asian tyrants, and gangs that intimidate and exploit their own communities the world over like the Chinese Triads and MS-13 in the US founded by illegal immigrants from El Salvador. White, black or blue with orange dots is only a *body* that is not even 'physical' for goodness sake. Who *cares* what colour it is or where it comes from? Behaviour and who you are is what matters to me. Racism is like judging astronauts by their spacesuits instead of what is inside and that's clearly ridiculous.

## 'Anti-racist' racism

PC by contrast is obsessed with race which makes it for me a racist philosophy and belief system. I look at behaviour, not race. They look at race, not behaviour. This behavioural blind-spot means that minorities can do no wrong to the PC mind. They are minorities and so they are oppressed by white imperialists. No more debate is necessary. We also have *inherited* victimhood where those who did suffer are used to claim victim status for those in the same colour bodies today who didn't suffer and were not oppressed by colonialism because they weren't there any more than I was. We need to deal with how things are now and not continue to fight battles and live a victim mentality welded to the illusory 'past'. What has happened is to learn from, not to live in. I find it nauseating to see people who didn't suffer exploiting those who did to secure their political, racial and religious agendas of today. A Philadelphia branch of Black Lives Matter banned white supporters from a meeting because it was a 'black only space'. If it had been designated a 'white only space' that would have been front-page news and outrage would have ensued with a Twitter storm thrown in. I watched a TV interview with Lisa Durden, a 'social commentator' and Black Lives Matter supporter, defending 'black only spaces' and the racist nature of her comments was shocking. You don't end racism by reversing it. Black Texas professor Tommy Curry says that 'some white people may have to die' for racism to be solved and true equality to be achieved. He contends that white people can't be educated out of their racism. Oh, really? What about black racists, Asian racists, Jewish racists and Islamic racists? Curry can't see that racism is not a colour but a state of mind or that he is everything he rails against. The same applies to Jason Osamede Okundaye who runs the Black and Minority Ethnic Campaign at Cambridge University. He praised violent protesters throwing petrol bombs and wrote that all white people are racist: '... White middle class, white working class, white men, white women, white gays, white children they can ALL geddit.' Student union extremists at the School of Oriental and African Studies in London demanded that white philosophers including Plato and Descartes be all but dropped from the curriculum simply because they were white. This was part of a wider campaign to 'decolonise' the university and 'address the structural and epistemological legacy of colonialism'. White philosophers should be studied only 'if required' and then only from a 'critical standpoint'. Effectively banning something purely on the grounds of race has a name: *Racism*. But these ignorant torch-holders would say we can't be racist whatever we do because we are anti-racist. Sir Anthony Seldon, vice-chancellor of Buckingham University, said:

> *There is a real danger political correctness is getting out of control. We need to understand the world as it was and not to rewrite history as some might like it to have been.*

Mate – rewriting history is the idea (see Orwell and *Nineteen-Eighty-Four*). UK higher education minister Jo Johnson wrote to education institutions warning that a commitment to freedom of speech will have to be clearly outlined in their governance structures. He said that access should not be 'denied to any individual or body on any grounds connected with their beliefs or views, policy or objective'. But Johnson was pushing against a heavy tide and swell with 94 percent of higher education institutions censoring what can be said on campus and 90 percent of universities having freedom of speech restrictions. PC programming which lives in a world of only black and white can see no difference between genuine refugees fleeing war that should be taken in, and opportunistic migrant young men guilty of crime, intimidation and rape in countries such as Sweden and Germany. They are not the same and should not be fused together as if they were, but the PC mind cannot conceive this obvious fact and seeks to silence such debate. They scream 'racist' and 'bigot' to hide (mostly from themselves) their own racism and bigotry. Appalling taxi firm Uber tried to block a law in London which insisted that its drivers prove their ability to communicate in English. Uber claimed this was 'indirect discrimination on grounds of race and nationality'. No, it is because speaking the language is an essential component in understanding where *people want to go*. Isn't seeking to use racial arguments to stop something that is purely commercial a fair definition of racism? No shades of grey, no balance, just black and white.

## Serve the state – be a victim

We live increasingly in a victim society. Victimhood has become a badge of honour through which self is defined. 'Vulnerability' is the new role-

**Figure 416:** Virtue signalling with added vitriol.

**Figure 417:** Protesting against 'hate'. *Mmmmm.*

model and victimhood the new heroism. Victims are the lifeblood of political correctness and the more the better to empower its tyranny. PC's victims and support systems campaign for laws silencing freedom of speech and opinion, without a care for the rights of others on the basis that different opinions must by definition be wrong if they differ from theirs. The only right that has validity is *I am* right. There is no other show in town. PC victimhood is another way of saying me, me, me – it's all about *MEEEEEE!* They walk around as if staring in invisible mirrors that limit the world to their own reflection. The last time I wrote me, me, me in this book was in relation to the self-identity of Satanists and Sabbatean Frankists and their desire for everyone to be as self-centric and self-absorbed as they are. Me, me, me also takes the form of what is termed 'virtue signalling' when people attack others for being politically incorrect not because they believe in the issue but to make themselves look caring and thoughtful. Look at me and how caring and thoughtful I am (Fig 416). Support systems for PC victims include those who may not be in a minority themselves unless perhaps that they are a woman. PC treats women as a minority, well, PC women, anyway, and yet globally the ratio of men to women is pretty close. Self-identity for victimhood and its support systems is founded on their sense of political, moral and spiritual purity. They 'care' and they insist that the world must know and acknowledge how much they care. This is more self-deception. Political correctness doesn't 'care' in the same way that all other tyrannies don't care. It's a façade to secure what it seeks, but PC self-deceivers identify with the façade and believe it to be real. Observe the hate on the faces of those who protest against hate; the intolerance of those who claim to promote tolerance; the destruction of diversity by those who say we must have more (Fig 417). French-born American historian Jacques Barzun said: 'Political correctness does not legislate tolerance. It only organises hatred.' Political correctness is really a

vehicle for hatred while pretending to be
against it. Even victims and supporters of
victims are collectively victims of the PC hoax
perpetrated on them by the less-than-one-
percent they claim to despise. PC is an *El*-lite
mechanism for destroying their targets,
dividing and ruling, silencing exposure and
hosing hate in all directions. *Mmmmm*, lunch.
Academics with long records of achievement
are forced out in the wake of the mildest of
jokes about women. Celebrities face 'Twitter
storms' and mass condemnation for the
smallest of alleged PC indiscretions which are
now so voluminous you can't keep up with
them (so don't try). Celebrities and politicians
fall to their knees in penance in the face of

**Figure 418:** In case there is a
Twitter storm over this book I
am just getting my reply
prepared.

Twitter storm abuse underpinned by the PC mania of the PC media. The
UK *Guardian* is at the forefront – they have their own torch supplier who
does job lots. Media operations like the *Guardian, New York Times* and
MSNBC are propaganda arms of the Provisional Progressives. High-
profile people caught in a Twitter storm are the most-prized targets of
the PC fascists because this says to millions looking on: See what
happens when you don't do what we say (Fig 418).

## The PC Pyramid

PC cancer has spread so far and deep that there is actually a no-no
category dubbed 'microaggressions'. These are defined as 'a subtle but
offensive comment or action directed at a minority or other non-
dominant group that is often *unintentional* or unconsciously reinforces a
stereotype.' Here we go ... 'a minority or other non-dominant group'.
Microaggressions in the Bible of PC do not apply to everyone, only 'a
minority or other non-dominant group'. The smaller the minority the
higher and more important you are in the PC hierarchy of victimhood. A
meme I saw on the Internet said: 'Whoever is declared the biggest victim
gets to be the biggest bully.' This certainly applies to Zionists who are a
category way above anyone else because their victimhood and
censorship are so well organised. White men are at the bottom of the PC
hierarchy of victimhood which goes like this: White men can
microaggress against white women and both can microaggress against
non-white people; non-white men can microaggress against non-white
women who can microaggress against gays and lesbians who can
microaggress against transgender and not sure. Transgender can't
currently microaggress against anyone (except Zionists), but give them
time. There will be a smaller minority along soon and the left-hand thing

is always an option. How confusing it must have been for PC warriors when Muslim parents at a Berlin preschool protested that one of the male teachers was gay; or when a Muslim school was exposed by a Swedish TV channel for forcing girls to board their school bus through the back door while boys use the front and also segregating them for school prayers; or the news that Islamist 'morality police' are patrolling areas of Stockholm imposing extreme limitations on the freedoms of women. PC zealots must have had to sit in a darkened room sipping sweet tea and breathing deeply while meditating on how this fitted into their victim hierarchy. Looking the other way is their usual response in such circumstances. An example of current transgender dominance in the victim hierarchy saw two women ejected from a homeless shelter in Canada because they were told to share a room with a man who said he identified as a female. One of them told a TV reporter: 'He wants to become a woman, I mean that is his choice but when a man comes into a women's shelter who still has a penis and genitals, he has more rights than we do.' This is how the PC sexual/racial hierarchy works. Know your place. I was referring to the PC hierarchy when I talked earlier about Facebook and its censorship policy that takes down mild criticism of mass immigration while allowing others to call for white women to be hunted down and killed. We now have good racism and bad racism. HelFem, a feminist group in Finland, included a 'sub-forum' at an event in Helsinki which banned white women. They called this the 'No Whites Allowed' room. An 'Only Whites Allowed' room would have the police turning up. Reverse racism is an epidemic and underpinned by the campaign to make white people feel shame and guilt for actions of other white people now long gone. PC white people feel so ashamed for something they didn't do when they should really feel more ashamed for what they *are* doing – now – like standing for this crap. 'Positive discrimination' is still discrimination. Positive and discrimination should not be used in the same sentence any more than CNN and journalism. A HelFem spokeswoman/person or whatever they call themselves next said: 'Mainstream feminism is very white – sometimes people use feminist messages simply for promoting their own brand.' Get used to this, white women, because this is the future as the sub-labels continually sub-divide into smaller and smaller segments of ever-greater discriminatory importance. Today's victim of oppression is tomorrow's racist oppressor. The 'No Whites Allowed' room was said to be a 'safe space' for non-whites; but safe from whom? White feminists, presumably. None of this can be racist because as HelFem said: '... organised racism requires structures and institutions, and whereas people of colour never have structures on their side, reverse racism simply cannot exist.' These people are completely potty. Ann Heberlein, a lecturer in ethics at Lund University in Sweden, has highlighted how blond Swedes are harassed and sneered at in their own country by 'people with non-European appearances'. But, hey, racism can only go one way, right? A report by the University of Illinois at Urbana-Champaign even insisted that a minority student 'walking into or sitting in' a room full of white people is a microaggression by the white people and a student 'diversity' officer at a London university famously banned white people and men from an event promoting *equality*. Golden rule of political correctness: no one can microaggress against white men. They are fair game no matter what and have no rights under PC law unless something tags them into another PC category. Where all this is going was reported in a *Huffington Post* headline in South Africa: 'Could It Be Time To Deny White Men The Franchise?' This call to remove voting rights for white men was penned by a Shelley Garland, an 'activist and feminist' who says she is 'working on ways to smash the patriarchy' (and replace it with a matriarchy). One extreme replacing another extreme = the same extreme under another name. Well done, you. She is also 'completing an MA degree in philosophy'. Cool, can't wait. Here's a taste of her 'philosophy':

> *Some of the biggest blows to the progressive cause in the past year have often been due to the votes of white men. If white men were not allowed to vote, it is unlikely that the United Kingdom would be leaving the European Union, it is unlikely that Donald Trump would now be the President of the United States, and it is unlikely that the Democratic Alliance would now be governing four of South Africa's biggest cities.*

> *If white men no longer had the vote, the progressive cause would be strengthened. It would not be necessary to deny white men indefinitely – the denial of the vote to white men for 20 years (just less than a generation) would go some way to seeing a decline in the influence of reactionary and neo-liberal ideology in the world. The influence of reckless white males were one of the primary reasons that led to the Great Recession which began in 2008. This would also strike a blow against toxic white masculinity, one that is long needed.*

**Figure 419:** What choice is there for non-transgender people?

Later in the article she speaks of up to 30 years for her denial of voting rights. The victim hierarchy can also be seen in pressure for transgender 'men' and 'women' to be able to use toilets on the basis of what they feel they are rather than their body-type and this is being

introduced in schools for even young children (Fig 419). To deny this
would be discrimination, apparently, and feelings of men and women
who don't want people who look like the opposite sex walking into their
toilets is never considered by PC insanity, nor is how this could be
abused by those who are not transgender but claim that excuse. Political
correctness is like a card game with each level of the hierarchy trumping
another based on sexuality and race. Lest we forget:

> If the nucleus were the size of a peanut, the atom would be about the size of a
> baseball stadium. If we lost all the dead space inside our atoms, we would
> each be able to fit into a particle of dust, and the entire human race would fit
> into the volume of a sugar cube.

That should be posted as a reminder on every PC wall and Zionist centre
of censorship where they are obsessed with race and their labels for that
'particle of dust'. We'll need lots of copies then. Politically incorrect
'microaggressions' don't even have to be intentional to incur the wrath
of PC storm troopers. Malice aforethought is not required.
Unintentionally upsetting the professionally upset is all that it takes. For
example, Ruth Starkman (Starkperson, surely?), a professor at Stanford
University, claims that saying homework was easy is a microaggression
against those that didn't find it easy. Silence would seem to be the only
way not to microaggress against somebody, but maybe noise will find
that discriminatory. There is a website called microaggressions.com
where people post their traumatic experiences. Here are some examples
of political correctness at this micro-level of madness:

> So what do you guys speak in Japan – Asian?

Wow, that must have been horrific.

-------------------

> When I gave a speech about racism the emcee introduced me as 'Jaime
> Garcia'. My name is Jaime Rodriguez, not all Latinos have the last name
> Garcia.

No, but a lot are called Rodriguez. That 'emcee', eh, what a racist.

-------------------

> My husband and I had just moved to Dallas. We went for a walk in a
> historic shopping district where we came upon a man and his son playing
> guitars. They sounded really good so we put a $5 bill in their tip jar. Almost

*immediately, the son pipes up, 'I thought black people only liked rap music!'*
*The father laughed nervously and said his son was just joking. I wanted to*
*snatch my $5 bill back, but we just walked away.*

Okay, sense of humour bypass. Next …

-------------------

*I am a straight, childfree female. My female friends are talking about how*
*many kids they want. When it's my turn, I tell them I want no kids at all.*
*There's a long, awkward silence during which time they stare at me like I'd*
*flown down from the moon. Then one of the girls says, 'Well, you're one of*
*those 'weird' ones, then', implying that I'm a lesbian because I don't want*
*children.*

Yes, I understand. I told someone that I lived alone. 'Oh, really?' he
replied, implying that I must be gay.

-------------------

*I'm in a restaurant with my husband and child. We're obviously a family.*
*The waiter is taking our order. 'For you, Sir' to my husband. 'For you,*
*Miss?' to me. Why does my husband consistently get the honorific title, but*
*I get only the diminutive title. It happens to us at restaurants throughout*
*my northern city. If I get a 'Miss', then he should get a 'Mr.' If he gets a*
*'Sir', then I should get a 'Ma'am' or 'For the lady?' Actually, I'd prefer*
*'Doctor'.*

I'd prefer you grew up.

-------------------

*A microaggression I face on a daily basis is the lack of respect for my gender.*
*People do not bother to ask about my pronouns, and assume that I am*
*cisgendered* [identify your sex with what your body looks like]. *I am*
*constantly called ma'am, miss, she/her, because my body is feminine shaped,*
*even when I express more masculine, people try to push me into the box of*
*cisgendered female, even though I am not. I must jump through many hoops*
*to have my pronouns, gender, and honorifics respected in most settings.*

I look like a woman and so people don't ask me if I am a man. That's
a hanging offence, surely?

-------------------

I cannot comprehend the staggering self-centric myopia that it takes to see the world and human interaction in such terms which destroy relaxed, open and spontaneous discourse with the constant watch-your-words mental gymnastics necessary not to offend child-like people. The point is that they *want* to be offended to feed their victim self-identity. Perceived victims and perceived victimisation need each other and feed off each other – another standing wave. Microaggressions are divide and rule at the micro-level. Scripps College, a 'liberal arts women's college' outside Los Angeles, has deemed that non-white students should demand financial compensation from white students for the 'emotional labour' of having to deal with 'microaggressions'. They are encouraged to charge white students for explaining why they are guilty of microaggressions – 'I don't like what you have said and so hand over some dosh.' A sane person would laugh to confirm their sanity, but these people are not sane and take this deadly seriously. A Harvard study even suggested that microaggressions could make people die earlier. Well, at least they would die rich if they went to Scripps. Harvard's 'Voices of [destroying] Diversity' concluded that 'the cumulative burden of a lifetime of microaggressions can theoretically contribute to diminished mortality [they mean life-span], augmented morbidity, and flattened confidence.' The only threat to life that I can see with microaggressions is that anyone with a mind of their own might lose the will to live.

## Madness archive

You can no longer make up the lunacy of political correctness. Anything you can invent will be bettered in terms of extremism by what is actually happening. Even the term political correctness has been condemned as politically incorrect and offensive at the University of Wisconsin-Milwaukee. They say it implies that people are being too 'sensitive.' They *are*, but political correctness is never the bedfellow of fact, truth and the patently obvious. Calling a thin person 'skinny' is apparently an act of verbal 'violence' along with 'Get over it'. The context of what they are being told to get over does not appear to have been considered. Get over anything is more than enough. Sweden's biggest union introduced a hotline for women to report 'mansplaining' – 'when a man explains something to a woman without being asked, particularly something which she might already know more about than the man'. A *hotline?* For *'mansplaining'?* How about women just tell the man that they know what he is telling them and they would appreciate it if he did not patronise them again? People are becoming so used to madness they think it's sanity. We are witnessing the normalisation of insanity. Facebook took down the page of an English pub called the Black Cock Inn for the 'racist

**Figure 420:** The Black Cock Inn was banned for being named in the 19th century after a black cock as in *chicken*.

and offensive name' that it's had since 1840 (Fig 420). Carleton University in Canada removed scales from the campus fitness centre to protect people with a special sensitivity to learning their weight. College athletics manager Bruce Marshall said scales were ditched because it was believed that only bad things come from monitoring weight. Those that might want to do so are irrelevant, but I have another solution for those who are sensitive to learning their weight – *don't stand on the friggin' scales*. There you go, all sorted. A 'Bias-Free Language Guide' used by the University of New Hampshire insists that the term 'American' is offensive and should be avoided as it doesn't recognise South America, or, presumably, Central America. The content of the 'guide' was so insane the university apparently dropped it, but out it will come again when the dive by political correctness into yet further depths of madness reaches the point where even that is official policy. Cardiff Metropolitan University in Wales has threatened disciplinary action for those using terms including mankind, man-made, manpower, man the desk, best man for the job, forefathers, housewife, Christian name instead of forename, Mrs and Miss, waitress and headmaster or headmistress even if they are used to describe men and women. Students and staff are advised to use 'same-sex' and 'other-sex' instead of homosexual and heterosexual and 'people with disability' rather than disabled. What an effect this must have on spontaneous open discourse if you are constantly filtering every word and phrase before you speak. The university say they are complying with the Equality Act and gendered words could be considered discriminatory. They say they are promoting an atmosphere in which all students and staff 'feel valued' and so totally missing the point that true self-value comes from within. We have universities threatening to mark down students in exams for 'failure to use gender-sensitive language'. This has been described as 'linguistic policing' and 'a one-way ticket to absurdity' which is exactly what it is. Frank Furedi, emeritus professor of sociology at Kent University in the UK, said:

> *Usually such threats are implicit rather than spelt out ... This linguistic policing is used as a coercive tool to impose a conformist outlook. The*

*alternative is to pay a penalty of being marked down.*

Furedi appeared shortly after he said that on the Richie Allen radio show on Davidicke.com. He was extremely impressive and very courageous given his academic background in his takedown of political correctness and its impact on universities and wider society: 'What we are seeing here is more or less an attempt to create a moral authority, a new cultural oligarchy that has the right to determine what is said and what isn't said.' We are dealing with cultural and psychological fascism imposed by the same people that go on 'anti-fascist' protest marches. Furedi said that the obsession with diversity can devalue the majority culture. This is not to say that minority cultures should not be valued but that majority cultures should have the same respect. This is not happening because the whole thing has been designed to *destroy* the majority culture for reasons I will be explaining. Furedi went on: 'In practice the theory of diversity becomes a way of devaluing the cultural dynamic and cultural content of national cultures.' He has written a first-class book on the subject, *What's Happened To The University? – A sociological exploration of its infantilisation.* And infantilisation is the word. An example of 'diversity' failing to include a majority culture is provided by Victoria Kawesa from Uganda who is Sweden's first black political party leader as a head of the Feminist Initiative also known as FI or Fucking Insane. The party wants open border immigration and Ms Kawesa called for an end to deporting foreign criminals, including murderers and rapists, because white Swedes are not deported when they do the same. No, don't worry it's not you. That is as crazy as it sounds. Er, where would 'white Swedes' be deported to, pray? But PC minds, by their very nature, do not do logic. In 2016 when I was touring Australia I saw a report of a school that had banned cheering and applause in case it upset those 'sensitive to noise'. You will gather by now that, no, this not a joke either. If only. Elanora Heights School in Sydney ruled that instead of cheering and applause 'the students are free to punch the air, pull excited faces and wriggle about on the spot'.

## Bias beyond words

I could go on for page after page with examples of how extreme all this has become, but there is once again method in the madness which literally involves replacing sanity with madness. The Williams Institute, an American think tank, estimated in 2016 that transgender people represent only 0.6 percent of adults in the United States or around 1.4 million out of a US population of 326 million. The number has significantly increased in recent years with all the propaganda to encourage and pressure people, especially the young, to question their gender identity when they had never felt the need to do so before. The highest ratio of transgender people in the US were found to be in the District of Columbia dominated by Washington DC. Also up there was California, the holy grail of political correctness where the Frankfurt School located. It is not a coincidence that Washington DC and California are at the forefront of transgender propaganda designed to confuse gender identity. This is not to say that people's gender choice shouldn't be respected within the bounds of balance and of course that is right. How people chose to see themselves is purely their own business, but why do they have to make it *my* business? Respecting those who genuinely choose a transgender identity is not what political correctness is all about. The mind-scam is to instil gender confusion in those that would not otherwise be confused and there is a very clear and serious reason for why this is being done which I will be addressing. Contrast transgender numbers and ratio with the extraordinary focus on transgender issues which arrived out of nowhere and was suddenly everywhere. This is virtually always confirmation of a calculated and long-planned *El*-lite agenda having the button pressed. Changing toilet rules, banning 'man and woman', 'mum and dad', 'girl' and 'boy' and so much more has been justified by advancing the interests of well under one percent of the US population. A similar ratio or less will likely to be found all over the world. Transport announcers in London have been banned from using terms such as 'ladies and gentlemen' to avoid offending transgender passengers. They must say 'good morning, everyone' and they are being trained in the use of 'gender-neutral' language (*Newspeak*). Bernard Reed, from the Gender Identity Research and Education Society, said that using words 'inappropriately' can cause 'great distress'. Only if you allow it to, mate. Can I call you, mate? Reed went on: 'A deep voice does not always indicate that the caller is a man, or a high voice that the caller is a woman.' No, but it gives you a bit of a clue and the people on the other end just want to tell you when your train leaves, not to have to pre-scan their mind every time to avoid upsetting the professionally upsettable. Sadiq Khan, the first Muslim Mayor of London and the personification of 'progressive', welcomed the word bans. He would never miss the chance for such virtue-signalling.

Ridiculous rules and word bans for 99.4 percent of the population justified by the need not to upset 0.6 percent? Does anyone really believe that this is because the *El*-lite which treats the entirety of non-*El*-lite humanity with such callous distain has such a heartfelt desire to help transgender people? Do transgenders even believe that if they dispassionately look at the evidence? So what's going on? We'll see later. Another of the fast-increasing examples of calculated craziness is the teachers' union in New South Wales, Australia, which advised teachers not to use the terms 'mum' or 'dad' and to encourage young boys to dress up as girls in new education guidelines. The guidelines for 'non-gender-specific free play' (it's not free if you pressure them to do it) are part of the explosion of political correctness in Australian schools matched in North America and Europe to confuse gender identity in the young. Get the kids and you get the adults they will become. Educate and Celebrate, a UK Government-funded organisation, gives lessons on 'gender diversity' in schools. Children as young as seven are told to stop using the terms 'boys', 'girls', 'ladies' and 'gentlemen' to avoid discrimination against

BBC's Children Show 'Just a Girl' is About a Transgender Child Taking Hormone Blocking Drugs

BY DAVID ON 5 NOVEMBER 2016 GMT                    MIND CONTROL USELESS MEDIA

**Figure 421:** What gender are you, kids? Really? Are you sure?

transgender pupils even though the enormous majority of classrooms won't have any. Monumental overkill exposes the real agenda. Children are encouraged to use terms such as 'cisgender', 'panromantic', intersex and 'genderqueer'. An Educate and Celebrate 'guidebook', *Can I Tell You About Gender Diversity?*, includes the fictional story of a 12-year-old given hormone blockers to 'transition' from female to male and stop the onset of puberty. The BBC ran a drama for children as young as six featuring a schoolboy taking sex-change drugs to become a girl (Fig 421). Critics said the programme was leaving children 'utterly confused' and it was supposed to. One mother said her daughter had questioned her gender identity after watching the show when she never had before. The BBC said the programme (programming) was 'reflecting true life'. *Nonsense.* It was reflecting an agenda to confuse young children about their sexuality as early as possible. One transgender mother in Canada, who has a moustache and a beard, has sought to register her baby with a 'non-gendered' birth certificate. She said: 'When I was born, doctors looked at my genitals and made assumptions about who I would be ... Those assumptions were incorrect, and I ended up having to do a lot of adjustments since then'. Maybe, but they were rather understandable assumptions. I suspect that the child will be facing a lot of adjustments itself to overcome totally unnecessary confusion purely to serve his/her mother's personal obsessions. My point is not that those who naturally feel they are in the wrong sexual body should not be respected and supported, but that children and young people should not be systematically *encouraged* and manipulated to question their gender when they were not before and a raft of words and terms should not be deleted for the entire population to accommodate the supposed grammatical sensibilities of a tiny few. Mr? Miss? Mrs? Ms? These things only matter if we *make* them matter and that is a choice.

Dutch MPs voted in 2017 to punish schools that don't have 'LGBT awareness' on the curriculum and a UK government-backed survey offered children from the age of 13 a choice of 25 different gender terms to describe themselves including 'bi-gender', 'tri-gender', 'demi-boys', 'demi-girls', 'trans-girls', 'trans-boys' and 'gender fluid'. An American College of Paediatricians report described as child abuse the widespread indoctrination of children into believing they can pick their sex. They condemned reckless, profit-driven doctors prescribing sex-change hormones to 12 year olds (but this is not only driven by profit and goes much, much deeper as we shall see). More than 800 children in the UK as young as ten are being given sex-change drugs and you can bet this figure is destined to soar. What is that doing to their long-term health alone? The British government has announced plans to make legally changing sex as quick and simple as making a statutory declaration. Canadian progressives led by Ontario Premier Kathleen Wynne passed what was called the Totalitarian Bill 89 to give more power to the state to steal children from families that oppose the 'LGBTQI and gender ideology agenda' and in effect ban couples with those views from fostering or adopting children. Wynne is the first woman premier of Ontario and the first openly gay head of government in Canada. Tanya Allen, president of Parents As First Educators, said: 'The Kathleen Wynne Liberals [progressives] have for years been pursuing their anti-parent and anti-family agenda and Bill 89 is the latest instalment.' Wynne will still go to bed at night believing she is a liberal who believes in freedom such is progressive self-deceit. California Governor Arnold Schwarzenegger signed a bill in 2007 banning anything in state schools that 'could be interpreted as negative toward homosexuality, bisexuality and other alternative lifestyle choices'. This is a great example of how the scam is being played. People might say okay, who can argue with that? But 'interpreted' is the crucial word. Interpreted by whom? Will it be someone with intelligence and a sense of balance and proportion or a PC idiot? A PC idiot, of course, and on that basis 'mum', dad', 'man', 'woman', husband', 'wife', 'boy', 'girl' are *interpreted* as 'negative towards homosexuality, bisexuality and other alternative lifestyle choices'. Laws targeting 'anti-social behaviour' can also be interpreted to stop a whole raft of activities that are not actually anti-social but non-conformist. Nikola Tesla's view was that 'anti-social behaviour is a trait of intelligence in a world full of conformists'. These are a small selection of PC 'interpretations' from American universities to give you a feel for what is happening:

- Kansas University's student senate voted to ban gender-specific pronouns such as 'his/her' from its rules and regulations document because they're microaggressions against the students who don't use them.
- North Carolina State University defended a lecturer's right to dock students' grades for using 'he' or 'him' to refer to both men and women and for using the word 'mankind' instead of 'humankind'.
- A University of Washington professor tried to instigate a policy punishing her students for using the words 'male' and 'female'.
- Scripps College declared that using the wrong pronoun to refer to someone was 'institutionalized violence', and gave students the option to request that teachers use no pronouns at all to refer to them because that too can be a microaggression.
- University of Pittsburgh warned its faculty and professors that even after a student has told them which pre-fix he or she prefers the students might change genders over time [so presumably they will tell them the new one, then??].

There are demands to change breast cancer to chest cancer to avoid 'upsetting' transgender people and the British Medical Association (BMA) urged doctors to avoid similar upset by changing 'pregnant women' and 'expectant mothers' to 'pregnant people'. *The Guide To Effective Communication: Inclusive Language In The Workplace* says: 'A large majority of people that have been pregnant or have given birth identify as women.' Blimey, top marks for observation. But there's more: 'We can include intersex men and trans men who may get pregnant by saying 'pregnant people' instead of 'expectant mothers'. Hold on. *Pregnant men?* Britain's allegedly first 'pregnant man' was revealed in 2017 although it turned out he had been beaten to it. Hayden Cross, who was 20, was born a girl but became legally male and started hormone treatment before putting this on hold to have a baby thanks to a sperm donor found on Facebook. When the child was born he said he planned to complete the 'transition process' which includes removing his breasts and ovaries. They will want to give wombs next to men who say they are women. Oh, sorry, they already are. Some doctors are calling for transsexuals with male bodies to be given wombs so they can give birth to their own children. Consultant gynaecologist Dr Arianna D'Angelo of the Wales Fertility Institute said this was fine from an 'ethical point of view' and Dr Francoise Shelfield, a clinical lecturer in obstetrics and gynaecology at University College London, agreed: 'If we are saying we should have equality ... I do not see why not.' Dr Amel Alghrani, director of Liverpool University's Health Law and Regulation Unit, says that once women are offered womb transplants 'questions will arise as to whether this should be publicly funded' for trans-women too. She says this would 'revolutionise reproduction' and could lead others to demand transplants, including straight men 'allowing for couples to jointly share the reproductive burdens and joys of pregnancy'. She adds that 'homosexual couples may also wish to procreate in this fashion, while single men may opt for it to avoid surrogacy.' Excuse me a moment, I am just going to check my sanity ... hold on ... just another minute ... nearly there ... no, it's okay, I'm fine. The world is mad, not me. Phew.

A student newspaper at the University of California-Los Angeles stressed that it was not being transphobic by linking menstruation and tampons to women: ... 'not all individuals who menstruate identify as women and ... not all individuals who identify as women menstruate.' If you say so. A Washington college declared that its 'non-discrimination policy' meant they could not stop a transgender man from walking naked among girls as young as six in a women's locker room. A mother reported the man for being naked in front of her 17-year-old daughter and a female swimming coach ordered him to leave and called the police after finding him naked in a women's sauna. The coach later *apologised – apologised* – when she was told the man was transgender. She did at least point out that girls of six years of age weren't used to seeing male genitals, but, hey, sorry anyway. Police said that the 'criminal law is very vague in this area' and the man himself told a TV station that he felt discriminated against: 'This is not 1959 Alabama – we don't call police for drinking from the wrong water fountain.' No, but a naked man among six-year-old girls might just warrant a quick ring. What about discrimination against young girls who don't want to be faced with a male dick (in every sense) in their changing room? They don't count because they are part of a *majority* in this situation. Transgender overrules young girls every time in the PC hierarchy of victimhood. A transgender student with a man's body got into a girl's locker room by saying he was a woman and began to sexually harass the genuine females. Harassment included 'twerking' – 'a dance move involving thrusting hip movements and a low, squatting stance'. Stop complaining. He's in a man's body but claims to be a woman so what's the problem? Move along now, everything's fine. Sexually harassed girls should get over it. Oops, 'get over it' isn't allowed, is it?

## It's my culture – keep off

Political correctness is specifically designed to dismantle every cohesive pillar of human society and is doing just that. The population is so at war with itself on endless fronts that they never see the same strings controlling them all. We now have the PC crime of 'cultural appropriation' which is when those of one culture wear clothes and symbols and eat food of another culture which they don't 'own'. Alleged ownership of culture on the basis that it can only be 'franchised' out by those of that culture draws still more demarcation lines between cultural differences and provides more potential for divide and rule and label consciousness. Canada's University of Ottawa cancelled free yoga classes on the grounds that they were 'cultural appropriation' and that yoga was connected to 'cultural genocide'. I thought yoga just took people into a calm space where they didn't kick the crap out of each other. But, no. ... apparently yoga started in India and it is a breach of cultural copyright if you use the name anywhere and you are not Indian. Okay, so Indian people should not play football or cricket then? The yoga class was reinstated after it was renamed 'mindful stretching'. Maybe Indian footballers and cricketers could rename their sport kickball and hitball? Hoop skirts were banned by the University of Georgia for being racist, and Quinnipiac University dropped a fundraiser for foster children after a student complained that putting maracas on a publicity poster was racist. Wearing sombreros is cultural racism according to these children and a case of 'ethnic stereotyping'. On one occasion when sombreros were worn at a tequila-themed student birthday party a student newspaper said this 'ignited campus-wide tensions, frustration and pain'. What, because of wearing sombreros or the *reaction* to wearing sombreros? It's got to be the second, surely. The first would be a form of mental illness. Go to Mexico tourist centres and what are the locals selling to the red-faced holidaymakers ... sombreros. Even worse and extremely sinister was that the students involved were ordered to partake in a re-education course by a faculty member, attend 'Active Bystander training' and write a letter reflecting on their experiences. I would have had only one reflection – stick it up your arse. An 'Around the World in 80 Days' party at Pembroke College at Cambridge University was cancelled for fear of causing offence by the clothes people might wear to symbolise the trip. Wearing costumes that are not of your culture is now considered racist, but then what isn't? Cambridge sounds like a university to stay well clear of unless you are pursuing a first-class degree in pottiness. Students from the African Society there boycotted an African-themed dinner based on the *Lion King* because non-African organisers were guilty of cultural appropriation and did not ask them to determine the menu and terms of cultural exchange.

Fault-lines of divide and rule are breeding like rabbits if that is not rabbitical stereotyping. Please note that I said rabbitical and not rabbinical and so it can't be 'anti-Semitic'. Although if a rabbit is owned by a rabbi ... *Mmmm* ... better play it safe and get my apology in early. No, second thoughts, fuck it. Culture is being divided from culture (we are all one consciousness by the way) and women are being divided from men by the feminazi extremists who are not driven by the laudable desire for equality but by their hatred of men (a symptom of hatred of self). At the other polarity, and just as outrageous, many men still treat women as an inferior species, as sexual objects (as do some women with men) and think its fine for a woman to be paid less than a man for doing the same job. State and religious involvement in relationships through marriage law and divorce courts are also there to drive apart the sexes and not to bring them together as people believe them to be. Massive court awards and maintenance payments to women by men which bear no resemblance to fairness are making men now fear women for what they could do and the same is true in divorce of restricted male access to children. Working women are also now being hit with big divorce pay-outs when they are the main breadwinner. Nothing drives people apart more than fear. This is not a resentful male complaining. I have nothing to complain about with regard to any of this. I am pointing out how the mind-scam works in ways that are not at first obvious. Women and men are being divided from each other and collectively from the endless sub-divisions of genders manipulated to this very end. Divisions are appearing everywhere on the basis of sex, race, religion, income bracket, the list goes on and on, and this has all been planned. White is divided from non-white amid racism on both sides – emphasis on *both*. The idea that only white people can be racist is destroyed by daily experience. I hear Indian people who support the stunningly racist caste system complaining about racism against themselves. Talk about self-deluded hypocrisy. Religion is divided against religion, political view against political view, young against old, haves against have nots. *Look at it* – and it is all being *made* to happen. Instead of sharing, mutual respect, fairness and justice (expanded awareness) we see each divided faction seeking to seize power for itself (myopic awareness). Yet these factions are only labels for the same Archontic Web. Do you want a Patri*archy* or a Matri*archy*? It doesn't matter either way because both are still the same hier*archy* of Archontic rule.

## Trigger warning – no trigger warnings

I don't use words like insanity and madness as metaphors with political correctness. I use them literally in terms of 'a severely distorted state of mind' and 'extreme folly and unreasonableness'. PC vocabulary includes classic words from government/military mind control programmes that I described earlier and the most obvious are 'trigger' and 'triggering'. Trauma-based mind control involves the creation of compartments in the mind known as alters which are activated by a *trigger* – a word, phrase, sound or whatever has been encoded – to instigate their programmed behaviour in a process called triggering. Here we have an aspect of political correctness based on the concept of triggers. Is that a coincidence? No way. Triggers in the PC sense are any text, comment, opinion or discussion that someone might find upsetting. This upset-obsession is a sobering thought when almost everything will upset somebody. In an attempt to protect everyone from everything has come the 'trigger warning'. These have been introduced 'to prevent unaware encountering of certain materials or subjects for the benefit of people who have an extremely strong and damaging emotional response (for example, post-traumatic flashbacks or urges to harm themselves) to such topics'. Having these responses – invariably being *manipulated* to have them – is referred to as 'being triggered'. When alters are opened in government/military mind control the person is referred to as 'being triggered'. The public in general and students in particular in their confined and isolated environment are being subjected to mass mind control. I am describing the many ways this is done and never more powerfully today than in schools, colleges and universities. So-called trigger-warnings are now commonplace in academic courses when students are warned that they might be upset by something soon to be mentioned or discussed. I have been with people subjected to government mind control and trauma when something has happened that triggers memories of unspeakable abuse. Their emotional reactions can be anything from very unpleasant to shocking. Triggering is real. But we are dealing here with students and not a multitude of survivors from MKUltra. When anything is this way-over-the-top, alarm bells should ring. How about the University of Glasgow in Scotland adding trigger warnings for theology students to alert them to upcoming images and discussion of the crucifixion so they can leave if they choose to?

'Morning Vicar – nice sermon but why did you stop before Jesus was crucified?'

'He *was*? I missed that bit. There was a trigger warning.'

Veterinary students are given trigger warnings about aspects of their work, as are those studying 'contemporary society' which involves discussing illness and violence. Archaeology students at Scotland's Stirling University are warned about any 'well-preserved archaeological body from an archaeological context' in case they find it 'a bit gruesome'. Forensic science students at Strathclyde University in Glasgow receive a verbal warning before lectures which may include images involving blood patterns, crime scenes and dead bodies. They are students of forensic science – what the heck did they think they would see and work with during any subsequent career, and the same with veterinary and archaeological students (Fig 422). Some Harvard students even suggested that rape law should not be taught to *law students*. A statement from Glasgow University said: 'We have an absolute duty of care to all of our students and where it is felt course

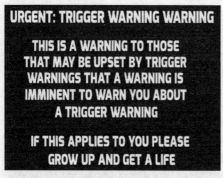

Figure 422: Yes, it is now that silly.

Figure 423: They will be running the world soon on behalf of the force that has turned them to jelly.

material may cause potential upset or concern warnings may be given.' Well, how come this has only happened on anything close to this scale relatively recently? How did I and previous generations manage to survive perfectly well without trigger warnings and safe spaces? Kent University professor Frank Furedi rightly calls this phenomenon the therapy culture, therapeutic censorship and the medicalisation of reading. Trigger warning policy for a gender studies course at Stirling University reads: 'We cannot anticipate or exclude the possibility that you may encounter material which is triggering and we urge that you take all necessary precautions to look after yourself in and around the programme.' A student commenting on the removal of scales at that Canadian university said: 'Scales are very triggering.'

This obsession with protecting students from all potential negativity and upset is creating what I call Generation Jelly for whom a breakdown is a badge of honour (Fig 423). This has caused PC students to be dubbed 'snowflakes'. I repeat my earlier incredulity and admiration for those balanced and intelligent students who are seeking to learn and stay sane among this insanity. Students at an American college said they had been 'literally traumatised' by seeing the words 'Trump 2016' written in chalk on the sidewalk. How are they ever going to deal with the challenges that life brings? They aren't and so they will give their power to the Big Brother state to protect them as it has done throughout their formative 'safe space' years. The psychological background behind all this is the manipulation of children and adults to perceive the state and authority as their *parents*. People even talk of the 'nanny state'. The stealing of children from loving parents by the state is an expression of this along with the constant deletion of parental rights and influence. I'm a victim. I'm insecure. I'm in danger. The state told me I am and I look to the state to protect me from how it told me to feel. Add in the extreme 'health and safety' risk assessment laws that stop children and adults doing activities that my generation took for granted and we have a pattern of programmed 'protection' to develop mollycoddled people with mollycoddled minds who perceive the state as mum and dad and everything else as dangerous and a possible trigger. A state of such perpetual fear of survival focuses attention and reaction within the reptilian brain. From the same mind-set comes the perception that anyone challenging the state is attacking their mum and dad. A newspaper report said that ITV, one of the main UK television channels, is coaching its managers to cope with the 'Millennial generation' (or Generation Y) born in the 1980s and 1990s. They are considered to have a greater 'sense of entitlement' and be 'less self-aware'. Given the background that I am exposing here that's hardly surprising and it starts long before college and university when tree- climbing is banned and school sports days are cancelled because the grass is damp. The Chartered Management Institute said this Millennial age group lacked 'decision-making skills'. How could this not be the case when they are denied throughout their academic years the experience of making their own decisions? They are living in a perceptual straitjacket and the situation has become even more extreme with those following Generation Y. This is the mentality and emotional state that is going to be running the world soon, in the lower levels anyway. Accountants firm Deloitte predict that Millennials will constitute up to 75 per cent of the workforce by 2025. Some will be exceptional and brilliant on the grounds that if you can come through this academic mind program with your sanity intact and see through the PC bullshit you must have an awakened consciousness; but how are PC groupies going to cope as they look at the world through their fingers while ducking behind the sofa? Schools, colleges and universities are mind control laboratories and what is found to work is then imposed on wider society. I saw that a London theatre is now issuing trigger warnings for its audiences in case something in a play might upset them. Political correctness also encourages narcissism and attention seeking. Narcissism in this sense comes from being a bigger victim than anyone else (see Zionist narcissism) and attracting attention because you have been 'triggered' with people rushing to your emotional aid. 'Quick – Ethel's been triggered when someone said Trump. Oh, there, there ... poor Ethel.' What can you say when a display about microaggressions triggered Asian students who complained that the safe space was making them feel unsafe? The organisers issued an apology:

> We would like to acknowledge and apologize to the Asian students on campus who were triggered or hurt by the content of the microaggressions in our installation. We understand and empathize with the effect that this installation could have without the context of the explanation provided on

*our Tumblr.*

Oh, grow the fuck up and try living in Gaza or Syria.

The safe space mind-set is another standing wave oscillating on the spot and so continually decoding reality in the same way like a DVD in freeze frame mode. Safe space protection from any other view and Internet algorithms offering only confirmations to surfing-recorded belief systems mean that the standing wave oscillation is never subjected to other possibilities (frequencies) that could challenge solidified perception. How are you going to evolve mentally and emotionally if all that you ever see and hear is what you have already been programmed to think?

## Generation Ritalin

A foundation of government/military mind control networks is the copious use of mind-altering drugs and you would expect to find the same in the mind laboratories of the education system. I have highlighted in other books the exploding use of drugs for children from the earliest age when any natural or temporary behaviour response is met with a bottle of pills. We are looking at the most drugged generations in human history and therefore the most perception-controlled (Fig 424). One study estimated that 1 in 13 American children take some form of psychiatric drug and tens of millions worldwide with the number constantly rising. A report on the Naturalnews website said:

**Figure 424:** Generation Drugged. See also Generation Jelly (the two are connected).

*An increasing number of children in America are being labeled, diagnosed and branded. Unique personalities are being scolded and molded by drugs to adapt childhood behavior into societal norms. Children have become like sculptures, motionless, lifeless, as psychiatric drugs chisel away at their natural state of well-being.*

*The emotional and behavioral differences among children are yoked into compliance, to conformity. A child's struggles aren't listened to, aren't understood. Their differences, behavior and problems are stamped into their mind as if they are a mental illness. Psychiatric drugs are driven down the throats of young people, as pharmaceutical companies expand their controlling influence.*

'Mental conditions' like ADHD or Attention deficit hyperactivity disorder are invented out of thin air with no supporting evidence and new drugs released by the Big Pharma cartel to spread mayhem in the minds of the young. This alliance between Big Pharma and psychiatrists inventing new non-existent mental conditions is one of mutual gain at the expense of those they often destroy. What has been happening to children is now being expanded and worse into higher academia. Jon Rappoport, an American *proper* journalist who I first met in the 1990s, published an article in 2017 exposing the systematic drugging of the student population and highlighting an origin for many of 'trigger sensitivity'. Rappoport described colleges and universities as the number one mind control program and 'the unspoken secret in plain sight'. He revealed that more than 25 percent of college students had been diagnosed or treated by a professional for a mental health condition within the previous year. Colleges, he said, had been taken over in a soft coup. I would add that the same is happening to global society as the obsession with 'mental health assessments' provides the excuse to drug the population. Rappoport wrote:

*Colleges are basically clinics. Psychiatric centers. Colleges have been taken over. A soft coup has occurred, out of view. You want to know where all this victim-oriented 'I'm triggered' and 'I need a safe space' comes from? You just found it.*

*It's a short step from being diagnosed with a mental disorder to adopting the role of being super-sensitive to 'triggers'. You could call it a self-fulfilling prophecy. 'If I have a mental disorder, then I'm a victim, and then what people say and do around me is going disturb to me ... and I'll prove it.'*

*The dangerous and destabilizing effects of psychiatric drugs confirm this attitude. The drugs DO, in fact, produce an exaggerated and distorted sensitivity to a person's environment. You want to know where a certain amount of violent aggressive behavior on campuses comes from? You just found it. The psychiatric drugs. In particular, antidepressants and speed-type medications for ADHD.*

See jonrappoport.wordpress.com for the full article.

Rappoport describes the sequence that ensnares a student's mind. First comes a feeling of stress or other emotion as a result of college work and life. Maybe results are not so good, a relationship has broken down, it could be anything. Seeking counselling or medical advice leads on to psychiatric 'help' and a diagnosis of some invented condition that used to be called 'growing up'. We are looking at the medicalisation of emotion and the medicalisation of essential life experience. Rappoport lists some 300 official mental conditions that 'multiply like fruit flies' for which there is no diagnostic proof. He quotes Dr Allen Frances who headed the team in 1994 that defined and labelled every official mental disorder – all 297 of them. Many years later Frances would say: 'There is no definition of a mental disorder. It's bullshit. I mean, you just can't define it ... These concepts [of distinct mental disorders] are virtually impossible to define precisely with bright lines at the borders.' Students feeling stress are 'diagnosed' with one of these undefined conditions such as bi-polar purely on a psychiatrist's say-so and the anti-psychotic drugs come out. Mind-altering drugs such as Ritalin (chemically similar to cocaine), Risperdal and so many others which fill the coffers of Big Pharma are prescribed with effects that include but are not confined to: Paranoid delusions; paranoid psychosis; hypomanic and manic symptoms, amphetamine-like psychosis; activation of psychotic symptoms; toxic psychosis; visual hallucinations; auditory hallucinations; LSD-type bizarre experiences; effects on pathological thought processes; extreme withdrawal; terrified affect; aggressiveness. Often dramatic changes in the person's behaviour as a result of these drugs is explained by the Big Pharma-controlled (therefore Spider-controlled) psychiatrist as still more mental conditions that require more or different drugs. This is the slippery-slope that is destroying great swathes of whole generations. Rappoport notes at least 300,000 cases of motor brain damage in the US alone in people prescribed so-called anti-psychotic drugs. Scan the above effects of those drugs and you can see where much of the demand for 'safe-spaces' come from, the paranoiac fear of being upset and seeing everything as a potential danger. This doesn't mean that all can be explained in this way, but a lot of it can together with the PC parameters set by authority and the drug-created psychotic atmosphere that can be infectious even for those not on the drugs. And ... it's all being done *on purpose* to hijack and suppress the minds of soon-to-be adult generations that will occupy positions of societal decision-making. Insider and *Brave New World* author Aldous Huxley could predict in 1961 what is happening today because it has all been long planned by the Archontic Reptilian Web:

> *There will be, in the next generation or so, a pharmacological method of making people love their servitude, and producing dictatorship without tears, so to speak, producing a kind of painless concentration camp for entire societies, so that people will in fact have their own liberties taken away from*

*them, but rather enjoy it, because they will be distracted from any desire to*
*rebel by propaganda or brainwashing, or brainwashing enhanced by*
*pharmacological methods. And this seems to be the final revolution.*

College campuses today and the world tomorrow. Not even tomorrow –
it's already happening.

## Trump Trigger

We saw the affect politically in the United States with the response of
Generation Jelly to the victory of Donald Trump. They and their fellow
progressives, typified by the 'anti-Establishment' (Establishment) film-
maker Michael Moore, were mortified by the defeat of Hillary Clinton.
They are so self-immersed, uninformed and programmed that they were
triggered by the fact that one of the most corrupt and evil people ever to
enter politics had not won the presidency. Here's a snap summary that
might help them become untriggered. Hillary Clinton is, with her cover-
story 'husband', so utterly and shockingly corrupt that words have no
meaning. They have a long list of dead people in their wake which has
been known since the 1990s as the 'Clinton body count'. You don't want
to live long? Then cross the Clintons. During the 2016 presidential
campaign we had the strange case of Seth Rich who worked for the
Democratic National Committee (DNC) and some suggest he was the
source of the WikiLeaks dump of DNC emails that exposed
manipulation by the party hierarchy in favour of Clinton and against
Bernie Sanders to ensure she won the Democratic nomination. Emails
also revealed that CNN political analyst Donna Brazile supplied Clinton
with debate questions to give her an advantage over Trump. This is
when the lie was promoted by the DNC and the mainstream media that
Russia was behind the leak and seeking to rig the election. Brazile had
the breathtaking nerve to say that Russia was trying to 'manipulate an
election, disrupt or discredit or destroy our democracy [and] produce an
outcome more favourable to them and their interests.' Seth Rich was
shot dead near his home shortly before the WikiLeaks emails were made
public in an 'armed robbery' in which nothing was stolen. The manager
of a bar where Rich was last seen said that the police never talked to staff
or asked for video camera footage. WorldNetDaily (WND) questioned
the official story:

> *WND also has reported on the eerie similarities between Rich's death and*
> *several deaths of individuals linked to former President Bill Clinton and*
> *twice failed presidential candidate Hillary Clinton. Just as in the Rich case,*
> *several of the people who died mysterious deaths were shot spontaneously*
> *and in public places, sometimes from behind, sometimes by unknown*
> *assailants and often just before they were set to release incriminating*

*evidence concerning the Clintons' activities. In most cases, there were no signs of theft at the crime scenes. And while some of the deaths were ruled suicides, other cases remain a mystery.*

I have been highlighting the Clinton body count in my books since the 1990s and it just goes on getting longer. PC student progressives and their like in mainstream society did no research into Clinton and supported her even after leaked emails confirmed that Clinton and the hierarchy of the Democratic Party had manipulated events to ensure that her rival for the presidential nomination – progressive number one choice Bernie Sanders – could not possibly win. Clinton was a woman and she wasn't Trump so what's more to know? Well, how about that this alleged bastion of 'women's rights' is a close associate of the Saudi 'royal' family who have funded her with millions while treating women so grotesquely it is almost unimaginable? How about the indescribable abuse by the Clintons of women in government/military mind control projects as exposed by Cathy O'Brien in *Trance-formation of America* and by many others? No, that can't be true, she's a woman so she must care about women. It stands to reason doesn't it? Progressive ignorance was captured by actress Meryl Streep in her eulogy for Hillary Clinton which would leave her embarrassed and mortified if only she would do a modicum of research into the Clinton horror show. But they don't and won't.

Instead, schools and colleges organised therapy sessions to cope with student response to their heroine's defeat and Trump's victory. There were communal 'cry-ins', 'therapy-dogs', mass hysteria and a virtual-reality Liberal America Simulator which offered an alternative universe in which the election produced another result in which Clinton won. Then there were the violent protests as hate-filled faces screamed that Trump was a hate-monger. I don't support Trump or Clinton and the real issue for conscious minds should have been how a system could be so rigged that America was offered the 'choice' between Clinton and Trump. PC progressives in their totality are far too self-absorbed to see how they caused the very result they were complaining about and the same with British progressives that were mortified by the Brexit vote. Those results were made possible by large numbers of people, often the white working class, who had been ignored for decades by the Establishment and its PC progressive censors of free expression which denied them the right to speak their mind about the effects, for example, of mass immigration on their communities. Instead of listening, understanding and having open debate, the PC brigade hurled insults like 'racist' and bigot'. Frustration of the abused and ignored led to the rejection of the Establishment and its PC support system in the votes against the centralised tyranny of the European Union and in support of

Trump who they believed – albeit wrongly – was anti-Establishment. Progressives have become the new Establishment, authority and Big Brother and when people rejected their tyranny they called for cry-ins and therapy dogs (Fig 425). Taking responsibility for what they themselves create is never on the table. Looking in the mirror is so un-PC.

**Figure 425:** Tyranny that calls itself 'liberal'.

Where are the progressives and Greens in the European Parliament while the EU, European Central Bank and IMF crushes and crucifies the people of Greece through a manufactured debt-crisis that has seen 1.5 million Greeks fall into extreme poverty and pensions for the elderly cut 17 times in seven years? Where are they when progressives if you believe their own hype should be in the front line? *Nowhere to be seen.* They are probably in a meeting complaining about someone saying 'man'. If the 'progressive' movement

**Figure 426:** The PC inversion – destroying the diversity that it claims to stand for.

is so anti-Establishment then why is it funded to such a large extent by billionaires about as liberal as Genghis Khan? I'll be coming to that in more detail. British doctor and psychiatrist Anthony Daniels, who uses the pen name Theodore Dalrymple, said that political correctness appears to be infective, spreading from brain to brain like a form of chronic mass hysteria. He compares it with the workings of capitalism. New desires must be stimulated to keep the capitalist system expanding to survive, and political correctness 'must discover new injustices to set right by a mixture of censorship, language reform, and legal privileges for minorities'. This was how PC had survived. He said that the meaning of life for the politically correct is political agitation. 'Dalrymple' rightly describes political correctness as speaking power to truth when it should be speaking truth to power. PC is an inversion of 'liberal' and 'diversity' (Fig 426).

## Manufactured separation

Those who are not ensnared by the PC program, young and not so young, who can see through the illusions, need to make a stand before all pillars of freedom are gone. We must not be intimidated by this fascism and instead look it in the eye. If *we* don't then no one else will and certainly not the snowflake generations. Students once marched for freedom of speech, now the snowflakes march against it. Far from seeing, let alone challenging, the forces that will enslave them for a lifetime, snowflakes are on the frontline pressing on to the next deletion of basic rights and freedoms. These PC Provisional Progressives are keenly supported by their political wing, the PC-obsessed Green parties and that part of the political Left which confuses debate with screaming abuse and slogans. Facts don't matter to snowflakes whether that be researching them or believing them to be of any relevance. Emotion drives their perceptions, not facts. We live in a post-fact society. I saw students protesting against Trump's travel ban list of mostly-Muslim countries. They were asked to name the countries on that list, but they couldn't. Facts don't matter, only emotion has any validity. Manufactured divisions are being instigated to separate old and young. Older generations are being depicted as those who have had their time and should move aside to let the snowflakes take over. Fifty, sixty, seventy, eighty years of experience are of no importance when snowflakes know it all already. The anti-old campaign was most obvious with Brexit where the majority of those voting to leave the EU were from older generations. Snowflakes accused them of destroying the future of the young when they had just voted to save it. Snowflake programming means that being controlled and dictated to by dark-suit bureaucrats they have never voted for and cannot name constitute securing their future. Older people voted for Brexit because they have had long enough to witness the effects on their country, community and freedom since Britain was signed into what became the EU in 1973 by the paedophile and Satanist, Edward Heath. The EU dictatorship is all that the snowflakes have ever known and this is what really divided old and young perspectives and united the snowflakes with the Establishment, which almost in its entirety campaigned to stay in the EU. Naïvety may be touching sometimes, but it is potentially fatal to freedom.

Novelist and EU supporter Ian McEwan gave us a flavour of this mentality when he said the Brexit vote had been won by 'a gang of angry old men, irritable even in victory' who are 'shaping the future of the country against the inclinations of its youth.' He was talking about those who have had longer to see what the EU has done and were not born into EU-domination with no other compass to compare this with. His 'gang of old men' also include many who fought for five years in unimaginable circumstances to stop the Nazis taking over Europe in the Second World War when Hitler had something in mind very much like the EU Commission and centralised bureaucratic control of the continent had he won. McEwan, who sounds a lovely man, told a conference of EU supporters that by 2019 thousands of elderly anti-EU voters would be 'freshly in their graves' and this could make the country more 'receptive' to staying in the European Union. Never mind respecting their right to an opinion – just wait till they die and then we get what *we* want. Britain's progressive Professor Richard Dawkins, a legend in his own mind with a fundamental misunderstanding of reality, dismissed Brexit voters as 'stupid, ignorant people' and said, 'it is unfair to thrust on to unqualified simpletons the responsibility to take historic decisions of great complexity and sophistication'. He must surely have been holding a mirror at the time. American actor Michael Shannon, another progressive who supported Hillary Clinton while knowing absolutely nothing about her, went even further in a bilious attack against those who commit the twin crime of being old and voting in a way he doesn't agree with. This stunning intellect said:

> There's a lot of old people who need to realize they've had a nice life. And it's time for them to move on. Because they're the ones who go out and vote for these assholes. If you look at the young people, between 18 and 25, if it was up to them Hillary would have been president. No offense to the seniors out there. My mom's a senior citizen. But if you're voting for Trump, it's time for the urn.

Wherever you look, 'progressivism' is the new tyranny and irony of ironies it is driven by those who perceive themselves to be 'anti-fascist'. Pope Francis, an *El*-lite puppet who was 80 at the time of writing, has urged businesses all over the world to replace old people with young people – so long as that doesn't apply to him, naturally. He tried to couch this in terms of old people should be given a 'just pension', but he knows that won't happen. Progressive political parties claim to represent the young but they are simply exploiting them. Pressure is building among progressive politics in Britain to lower the voting age to 16 to 'give young people a voice'. This is disingenuous crap. They know that young people are more likely to vote for progressive parties (while not knowing the real agenda) and they want the voting age reduced for purely political reasons. Nick Clegg, the shockingly inept former leader of the progressive UK Liberal Democrats, demanded a second Brexit referendum in which ... 'We should give every youngster under 30 a weighted vote of twice the value of everybody else, because it's their future.' This is yet more exploitation of the young. EU worshipper Clegg is desperate to stay in the EU tyranny and any excuse or manipulation will do. I would ask young people and progressives who have a problem with the equal human rights of older people to remember that one day they will be old and they will have to live in the world they are demanding for others now. You can expect this demonisation of older generations to both continue and deepen because it is all leading to

something called the 'demise pill' for old people which I will come to
later.

## Anti-fascist fascism

Some progressive groups even justify violence on the grounds that
fascists are violent and so they have a right to be. Among them are
Antifa ('Anti-Fascist') and the protest technique known as Black Bloc in
which the participants stay close together and wear black clothing and
masks. These are groups operating in many countries and pledged to
use violence to 'smash all fascism in all its forms'. Does that include
their own? They claim to be 'far-left' but as always what is presented as
a political spectrum is actually a circle where 'far-left' and 'far-right'
meet at the same point and so behave the same way. They oppose each
other when they *are* each other – a standing wave. Only the labels are
different. Black Bloc and Antifa oppose sexism, racism, and classism, but
not violencism. They were involved in violent protests at the University
of California, Berkeley in the wake of Trump's election and at the G20
summit in Hamburg, Germany, in 2017. *Jeeez* ... now we have the
infantilisation of protest and activism. I'm sure there are some genuine
people in their ranks but from what I have seen they are dominated by
angry, desperately uniformed hypocrites simply looking for a fight.
There is, of course, police provocation against demonstrators, but don't
tell me these groups need an excuse. They go with the intent of violence
and discredit the majority who demonstrate peacefully. Who benefits?
Those they claim to be protesting against. Who lose out? The genuine
and peaceful protesters who get tarred with the same public image and
have their voices silenced by the sound of rage and violence from self-
indulgent little boys and girls in their version of school uniform. You
change nothing with hate in your heart and you can only make things
worse. Germany's Chancellor Merkel was asked why she chose
Hamburg for the G20 when the city is a well-known centre for such
activism, but the question answers itself when you know that violence is
what they want to advance their own political agenda. Groups of
fascistic morons like Black Bloc and Antifa are used, funded and
infiltrated by the *El*-ite to target people they wish to silence and for the
essential divide and rule (see end of book postscript). I have two words
to say to them: *Grow up.* We should also be aware there are now
companies specialising in providing fake protestors paid for their work
and actors posing as activists and advocates of a cause. One is called
Crowds on Demand run by CEO Adam Swart which stages rallies and
demonstrations for politicians and others. Swart said he has 20,000
actors across the country with most required to sign a non-disclosure
agreement, but he sees no problem with this: 'We are merely part of the
democratic process if you ask me.' I won't, thanks.

An Internet video shows a young white man in the UK holding up a placard saying: 'The right to discuss must be defended.' That's fair enough and also quite right. How could that be a problem? Oh, but it can if you are suffering from rampant cognitive dissonance and up-your-own-arse syndrome. A

**Figure 427:** The PC inversion.

white woman harasses him holding a placard saying 'F\*\*k off Nazi scrum'. I think she meant fuck off, but I can't be sure because those asterisks hid it so well (Fig 427). The woman shouts 'Look at you, white man' and someone else screams 'You're a fucking white man.' Top marks again for observation, I'm sure he'd never noticed. Male progressives with faces covered in black scarves then move in and another white woman in black glasses urges her moronic mates to stand in front of the man so that people can't read his placard saying that the right to discuss must be defended. 'Everyone just cover him, just cover his shit', the Liberal warrior demands. The mob then pushes him away and forces him to leave amid chants of 'Nazi scrum'. They chant 'Nazi' while acting like them but what pass for their minds are too solidified to see that and maybe their torch batteries were on the blink. In this inverted world, the progressives act like fascists and many of those labelled 'far right' can be moderate by comparison. But the bewildered majority buy the media labels and not the reality – especially the 'anti-fascists' who support political fascists because they call themselves 'Left' or 'Centrist'. The label is king. Reality is the enemy.

## Turning the tide

Let us not forget, however, that there are still significant numbers of young people who have not fallen for The Program in all its forms and can see what the snowflakes cannot. They must stand together with the rest of us and not be bowed into silence by PC extremists. This won't make them popular but it is essential for this to be turned around. The sinister nonsense needs exposing for what it is in one-syllable, un-PC, *Oldspeak*. I was glad to see UK journalist Andrew Pierce having the courage to do this in an article headed: 'I've had it up to here with these gender fascists!' He was commenting on the decision by the RAF to ban women service personnel from wearing skirts on the parade ground in case this upset transgender recruits. A blanket ban on 4,400 women over potentially upsetting what is a tiny handful. This is the tyranny of the minority and the smaller the minority the greater the tyranny. That's the PC way. Pierce points out that those who perceive themselves as transgender comprise less than one per cent of the more than 65 million UK population and only 300 can be found in a total service personnel of 32,000. He said that town halls, education authorities and even some nurseries seemed to be in thrall to the gender thought police and this is happening all over the world. Victoria State in Australia launched a training programme (mind program) for thousands of teachers at a cost of millions of dollars to 'stop racism and sexism' in children as young as four by spotting those who 'enact sexist values, beliefs and attitudes'. Andrew Pierce wrote:

*So how did the trans lobby become so influential? The answer lies in the fact that in the past 20 years, gay people have become more mainstream, with civil partnerships and gay weddings widely accepted.*

*Not everyone, though, was content to let gays like me – who came out in the Eighties and fought for equality – enjoy our new-found freedoms. The extremists among us became bored by what had effectively become conventional mainstream lifestyles. Rebels without a cause, they had to find a new one. And they did: gender politics.*

I bet a Twitter storm followed.

I don't care what people call themselves or how they live their lives so long as they don't impose that on anyone else. No one should be discriminated against for their race or sexuality, but neither should anyone be discriminated against for their opinion by those who claim to be 'anti-discrimination'. The pious can't see the bias. Jenni Murray, a long-time campaigner for the rights of women and host of the *Woman's Hour* show on BBC radio, was the subject of a Twitter storm when she said in a newspaper article that men who become women are not real women as in 'natural' women while she expressed her respect for those who make that choice. She was condemned as a 'bigot' and 'dinosaur' with the usual self-righteous indignation and the BBC apparently reminded her of its rules of impartiality. This 'impartiality' is measured purely against whether what a BBC employee has said is within the rules of political correctness or fits with the BBC party line. TV presenter Gary Lineker, paid £1.8 million a year for hosting a football programme, protested against Donald Trump and the Brexit vote, but that was no problem because the BBC was against Trump and Brexit. George Orwell, a former BBC employee himself, would have recognised this concept of good bias (authority agrees with it) and bad bias (authority doesn't agree with it) that we see in these two cases.

Andrew Pierce is right to expose rebels without a cause (victims in constant pursuit of victimhood) and on one level this is what is

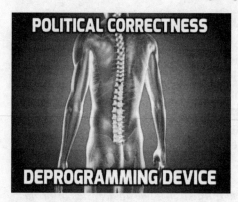

**Figure 428:** We need to stop taking this crap.

happening. But take a step further back into the shadows and that psychological state is being encouraged and exploited to a much bigger end. Obsession with the body and fine detail of 'physical' identity has spawned identity politics or the politics of me, me, me. Identity politics supports only those sources and causes which advance its own interests. Little things like what is best for everyone, what is fair and just for all are no longer criteria for political support by identity obsessives. It is another expression of divide and rule. We must not concede fairness and justice for all to these weeping warriors of self-interest. We need to let fairness, justice and freedom be our guide and not racial or sexual self-identity. The late Jewish Member of Parliament Gerald Kaufman spoke out for Palestinians and against the Israeli government in total disregard for identity politics. He accused the government of Israel of cynically exploiting the Holocaust as justification for their murder of Palestinians. He recalled how his grandmother was killed by the Nazis and he said: 'My grandmother did not die to provide cover for Israeli soldiers murdering Palestinian grandmothers in Gaza.' Kaufman was not popular with Zionist extremism and was accused of pandering to anti-Semitism when he was, in truth, pandering to fairness, justice and basic humanity. This is what we need to roll back – the anti-fascist fascism – and allow humanity to recover control of its collective mind (Fig 428).

Political correctness more than anything is about divide and rule with fault-lines of division ever sub-divided and set at war with each other. While humanity is at war with itself the Archontic Reptilian force is at war with humanity. The more division they can trigger the more effective their control will be and the antidote to being driven apart is coming together.

It is long past the 'time' that we did.

# CHAPTER ELEVEN

# Terrified of Truth

*"Where they have burned books, they will end in burning human beings'*
*– Heinrich Heine*

Political correctness is not about ending discrimination but about manipulating the target population to silence the target population to protect the perception deception and its Postage Stamp mentality.

Peter Tatchell is right that bigotry should be dealt with by debate and information and not censorship. I am always wary of people and governments that so lack confidence in the power of their own argument they seek to ban the views of others. What are they so afraid of? Why do Israel and extremes of Zionism work so hard to ban those who question their actions? If they are so sure of themselves they wouldn't care. Oh, but they *do* care. They know that if their own background, racism and bigotry was exposed a lot of people would see events from a new perspective. So don't argue your case, ban those who don't agree with you. Germany is one of the worst places on Earth for such freedom-deletion with its broad and vaguely defined 'Volksverhetzung' or 'incitement of the people' law that could in theory be applied against any political statement. Censorship laws that target freedom are vaguely worded on purpose to allow the widest interpretation in the way that 'anti-terror' laws claim to target terrorism but are then applied to the public as a whole. More than a dozen venues in multiple German cities either wouldn't take a booking for my speaking events or did so and then withdrew under threats and intimidation from hate-filled Zionist 'anti-hate' groups. Thousands of people in allegedly 'free' Germany want to hear me speak, but a few bigots supported by The System and jelly-spine venue owners deny them that basic human right. The most outrageous example was the Maritim Hotel in Berlin who accepted our booking, signed a contract for October 2017, and then told the media they had cancelled the event without to this day even telling us. They

refused to take phone calls to ask
what was going on. Talk about
contempt for contracts and
customers. A Maritim
spokeswoman told the media:
'Unfortunately, at the time of the
request we were not aware that
David Icke would participate in
the event. We only found this out
later.' This was an extraordinary
statement given they were sent a venue pack with *my* picture, *my*
background and the nature of *my* talk. My son Jaymie, who organises
the events, also flew to Berlin to meet the hotel management, sign the
contract and give them the background to how other venues in Germany
had cancelled. The Maritim Hotel chain declined to give a reason for the
decision, but I knew what it was because it was the same with all of
them. Zionist organisations contact them with a pack of lies about me
and what I will say, and venue owners cancel the booking and the
laxative order no matter how provably ludicrous the claims can be
shown to be (Fig 429). Staff at the Carl Benz Arena in Stuttgart said that
they cancelled an earlier booking because of the 'contentious nature' of
what they were told I would say. My God, we must never have views
that are contentious. How would freedom of speech survive if we did?
An Arena statement said they held to the 'values of the German Basic
Law – which also includes the right to free speech, but of course only as
long as this conforms to the democratic principles of our society.' We
believe in free speech BUT. There is always the BUT because they don't
believe in free speech at all. It's just bullshit. I am calling for *more*
freedom, what some call democracy, but I am banned for not
conforming, note *conforming*, to the 'democratic principles of our society'
which are being deleted in Germany by the hour. Any excuse will do to
justify destroying the free circulation of information and opinion. Ben
Knight, writer of a media article about the Maritim ban, accused me,
with no evidence, because there isn't any, of being a racist. 'Journalists'
think anything goes with me and they have to stay safely on the side of
the accusers or they will also be called 'anti-Semitic'. We are looking at a
hierarchy of fear and ignorance. They are absolutely clueless about me
and the world they are reporting, and 'fake news' doesn't begin to
suffice. Knight said that like many 'racist conspiracy theorists' I
identified billionaire investor George Soros as an enemy of humanity.
What does Knight know about the tidal wave of information that has
exposed the manipulations of Soros on so many fronts? Er, nothing.
*Ahhh*, but Soros is Jewish and so I must be racist. This is the media
mentality from which billions gets their views of people and the world.

**Figure 429:** Use it or it disappears.

The Internet article was tagged with the keywords 'David Icke, anti-Semitism and Holocaust denial' to ensure that those three words would be connected ongoing in search engines. This is called journalism, apparently, but then you will recall the German experience of Udo Ulfkotte. Germany promotes itself as a free country when it is a tyranny and while 'journalists' attack people like me for exposing what they don't have the intelligence or balls to expose, their own freedom of expression is being deleted by the day. Dr Wolfgang Herles, retired head of 'public-service' television network ZDF Bonn, said that this and other networks are told what to report (and not) by the German government:

> *We have the problem that – now I'm mainly talking about the public media – we have closeness to the government. Not only because commentary is mainly in line with the grand coalition* [The System], *with the spectrum of opinion, but also because we are completely taken in by the agenda laid down by the political class.*

The same can be found across the world and mass rejection of the mainstream media by rapidly increasing numbers of people has led to the *El*-lite moving in on the alternative media to absorb the corruptible and silence the incorruptible. The most laughable (and sinister) element of Knight's article, apart from the arbitrary label of racist, were quotes from Jan Rathje of the Amadeu Antonio Stiftung, 'an NGO that tracks racism in Germany'. He 'welcomed' the cancellation of my German events because censorship of other views is no problem to these people so long as their views are never censored. This was Rathje's opener: 'David Icke has a lot of influence on the conspiracy ideological scene, especially through the anti-Semitism he spreads, which appeals to people in Germany because it offers some relief from the guilt of German crimes against humanity in the Holocaust.' What a slur on an entire nation and, as always, the Holocaust is central to justifying censorship. The exploitation of what happened in Nazi Germany to justify censorship today is a real stomach-turner for me. It's absolutely disgusting to exploit those people to pursue a present-day personal agenda but it happens all the time. Accuse someone of being a 'Holocaust denier' and all doors slam shut to them. This includes the *cell* door in Germany where people are jailed for having another view and version of history. I don't have to agree with them to recognise that being jailed for seeing history differently – in whatever way that may be – is an expression of fascism. How ironic. Rathje's hysteria reaches its climax with the claim that when I say reptilians I am using this as code for Jews. Evidence? *Nil.* But he doesn't need any and journalistic pawns like the said Ben Knight will never ask for any. Rathje then truly enters the Twilight Zone: 'People know how to decode the code about

WHAT HAVE YOU GOT TO HIDE, CHAPS?
THOSE CONFIDENT OF THEIR POSITION

DO NOT SEEK TO BAN OPINIONS OF OTHERS
(ONLY TYRANNY DOES THAT)

**Figure 430:** Those afraid of information always have something to hide.

reptilians – whether Icke means it or not, it doesn't change that fact.' Let me decode the codes about codes: 'Reptilians is code for Jews and even if it's not, it is.' I hope that's clearer for you now. Can it get any more crazy? Yes it can. Another Rathje gem: 'It seems ridiculous, but the conclusion that Icke draws is that because he thinks the reptilians are pulling the strings [of the world] therefore the Holocaust didn't happen – that's anti-Semitism.' No words necessary or possible and, of course, we have the continual misrepresentation of the term 'anti-Semitism' which is a language group dominated by Arabic. I tell this story to highlight how easy it is to censor free speech today and it is all being done systematically with political correctness right there on the front line (Fig 430). No facts are required, not even coherence, only abuse. 'Freedom of speech' really means never saying anything that The System doesn't like. Those who conform to these strict parameters believe they have a freedom that doesn't actually exist. Freedom to conform is not freedom. Those who ban my talks in Germany are a wonderful example with their contempt for free speech while believing they support it – BUT. What a statement about illusory freedom in Germany that we had to move the 'German' event to Maastricht just over the border in The Netherlands so that 'free' Germans could hear what I have to say.

The 'anti-Semite' industry was on my case from the late 1990s and you can see what I had to put up with by typing 'David Icke, the lizards and the Jews' into YouTube. Another reason they gave for venues to cancel my events was that I was naming former UK Prime Minister Edward Heath as a paedophile and Satanist. Seventeen years later a UK police force began an inquiry into Heath's paedophilia and Satanism when witnesses came forward. The 'anti-Semite' censors had left me alone for some 15 years until it restarted out of the blue. The week I was due to speak in Manchester in January 2017 came an approach for an interview by first the not-to-be-trusted *Guardian* newspaper and when I turned them down there immediately followed a request to cover the event by the *Guardian's* television equivalent *Channel 4 News*, with its constantly virtue-signalling host, Jon Snow. I agreed to this until less than 24 hours later when the Manchester venue was contacted by the Campaign Against Antisemitism (CAA) doing a passable impression of what later came from Jan Rathje with its demands, tone and shocking misrepresentation. The coincidence of this happening within the same 24 hours after so many years of being left alone was so obvious that I told *Channel 4 News* I was no longer interested. I can't prove a connection and nor am I claiming one but it was such a coincidence that I was taking no chances with a possible set-up. Maybe it was the *Guardian* or maybe it really was just an amazing coincidence. A CAA bod called Stephen Silverman, who refers to me as a 'modern day hate preacher', was unsuccessful in getting the Manchester venue to cancel because I have been speaking at their venues for a long time and they knew that what Silverman said was nonsense. He urged people in the audience to contact him with reports of what I said and their complaints about it. They wrote to him in droves to point out that I didn't say anything 'anti-Semitic' and instead contended that identity with race is ridiculous and we need to love each other and realise that we are all one consciousness having different experiences. Mr Silverman, who calls himself the CAA Director of Investigations and *Enforcement*, did not publish what they said or apologise for his gross misrepresentation of me. He was too busy with his next target. The CAA, chaired by a Gideon Falter, was established in August 2014 with funding from 'private donations' while the world was being horrified by the daily bombing by Israel of the mass-populated Gaza Strip in Operation Protective Edge which killed more than 2,000 Palestinians with more than 500 of them children. CAA assets see anti-Semitism everywhere with their highly questionable 'public surveys' and the targeting of politicians and other individuals. Shockingly, the CAA is a 'charitable incorporated organisation' registered with the Charity Commission. The *Charity* Commission? What – an organisation that seeks to delete the freedom of speech of the population and tries to ban even the musical events of people like Israel-born and Britain-based jazz musician and activist Gilad Atzmon? It's outrageous. Even British Jewish Member of Parliament Gerald Kaufman was a CAA target with their condemnation of him continuing after his death:

> By saying that 'Jewish money' was used to subvert the British government, he was complicit in a centuries-old chorus of those accusing Jews of conspiracy and of showing disloyalty to their own country. This is explicit antisemitism: the International Definition of Antisemitism (as adopted by the Labour Party) explicitly states that 'Making mendacious, dehumanising, demonising, or stereotypical allegations about Jews as such or the power of Jews as collective — such as, especially but not exclusively, the myth about a world Jewish conspiracy or of Jews controlling the media, economy, government or other societal institution' is antisemitic.

> At the same meeting he was also recorded saying: '...because perhaps I can tell you in a way no-one else can tell you' – intimating that his having being

*born Jewish afforded him a protection which intimidated others into silence.*
*Is political correctness in the face of antisemitism any less weak and immoral*
*when applied to Jews?*

The thoroughly decent Kaufman put people and justice before racial
and religious bias, but the CAA declared that he left 'a rotting stain on
both the Labour Party and Parliament that will continue to eat away at
both institutions until such time as genuine and public acts of regret and
apology are made.' Oh, yes, get down on your knees everyone to the
CAA and its like. Know your place. The only rotting stains that I can see
are for the CAA to make such disgusting remarks on the death of a
Jewish man of high integrity, and the rotting stain they constantly leave
on basic human freedoms. The CAA pledged on Kaufman's death to
continue its campaign to free Britain's institutions of 'anti-Semitism' –
'ensuring that they are not places that quietly give poisonous racism a
pass because it happened to come out of the mouth of a rather harmless-
looking old Jewish man who happened to be our longest-serving MP.'
Words have no meaning in the face of such polemic. Even Jewish people
are not allowed to criticise Zionist actions such is the tyranny of
censorship that we are dealing with. These censors continually deny
something on one hand and prove it with their actions on the other. And
if what Kaufman said from his personal experience is 'mendacious' then
prove it. Produce the evidence. Explain why Zionist columnist Joel Stein
wrote in the *Los Angeles Times* in 2008: 'As a proud Jew, I want America
to know about our accomplishment. Yes, we control Hollywood ...The
Jews are so dominant, I had to scour the trades to come up with six
Gentiles in high positions at entertainment companies.' Put 'Who runs
Hollywood? C'mon' into a search engine to read the full article. Yet
anyone else who notes what Stein notes about Zionist dominance in
Hollywood is condemned as a racist. Zionist censorship doesn't deal in
facts, only slogans and abuse, because it knows where open debate and
discourse will lead.

The political goal all along with the CAA and the Zionist censorship
network worldwide has been clearly to equate anti-Semitism with
criticism of Israel to protect the Israeli regime from legitimate
investigation and challenge (Fig 431). This is not only to silence exposure
of horrific happenings in places like Gaza, but to silence exposure of
even worse that is planned to happen. Emmanuel Macron, the
Rothschild puppet President of France, took precisely this line in an
address with Benjamin Netanyahu when he said: 'We will never
surrender to the messages of hate; we will not surrender to anti-Zionism
because it is a reinvention of anti-Semitism.' They'll enjoy this book,
then, and how kind of Netanyahu to write Macron's speech. To equate
criticism of a country and political movement with racism is deeply

sinister and very much a sign of things to come unless a lot of backbones stir themselves awake and refuse to sanction such tyranny. Meanwhile, those crying 'racist' are silent when Israeli MP Aylet Shaked says of Palestinians: 'Kill the mothers to stop other little snakes being born.' This is straight from the script of the Old Testament Archontic 'god': 'You shall not leave alive anything that breathes but you

**Figure 431:** The most racist creed on Earth – Zionism – is not racist. I love it.

shall utterly destroy them.' Rabbi Shlomo Mlmad, chairman of the so-called Council of Rabbis in illegal Israeli West Bank settlements, called on Jewish settlers to poison Palestinian water supplies to force them from their land and allow Israelis to take over. Israeli Rabbi Shmuel Eliyahu believes the army should stop arresting Palestinians and simply execute them. He also said in 2007: 'If they don't stop after we kill 100, then we must kill 1,000. And if they do not stop after 1,000, then we must kill 10,000. If they still don't stop we must kill 100,000, even a million.' Israeli soldier Elor Azaria casually shot a 21-year-old Palestinian in the head as the man lay wounded and motionless on the ground after a knife attack on another soldier. One poll had 82 percent of Israelis saying the extra-judicial killing was justified and of course he secured the usual enthusiastic support from Netanyahu who said he would support a pardon. Azaria is serving just 18 months for a cold-blooded execution. Put 'Elor Azaria is filmed shooting the incapacitated man' into YouTube and see if you think the cold-blooded killing was 'justified'. Israelis – and especially their volunteer and conscripted army – are brainwashed to fear and hate Palestinians and consequently many see them as less than human. This programmed contempt justifies in their minds any scale of atrocity and abuse. Some extremely sick Israelis even sat on a hill night after night whooping and cheering as state-of-the-art missiles dropped on Gaza civilians in the 2014 Israeli campaign of mass murder. Then there is the systematic reduction of electricity supplies to Gaza by Israel with catastrophic consequences, not least in hospitals. Where is the Zionist condemnation of the stunning racism of the Israeli regime against Ethiopian Jews and other black Africans? Where is the condemnation of Israeli politicians who describe Palestinians as snakes and cockroaches? Or the jailing of more than 15,000 Palestinian women and young girls since the Israeli occupation began? Or the incarceration of children? Where is the condemnation of organisations like the Jewish Defence League (JDL) which has been listed as a terrorist organisation by the FBI? But none of this is racism

Figure 432: Zionism's answer to free speech.

Figure 433: Zionist racism is disgusting beyond words and the hypocrisy is beyond belief.

and it is anti-Semitic to say so – nothing to concern you here, move along now (Figs 432 and 433).

## And the Lord said ... you shall silence them

Zionism has long been censoring universities both sides of the Atlantic with regard to anything questioning the actions of Israel and we should remember the words of Russian poet and writer, Yevgeny Yevtushenko: 'When truth is replaced by silence, the silence is a lie.' Events highlighting the treatment of Palestinians are now increasingly banned. The universities of Exeter and Central Lancashire intervened to cancel student-run events in 2017 raising awareness about Palestinian human rights in 'Israeli Apartheid Week'. This is now a regular outcome since the UK government adopted a new definition of 'anti-Semitism' produced by an obviously biased group called the International Holocaust Remembrance Alliance which widens the interpretation of racism to include criticism of Israel. How come criticism of a country of eight million people (around six million are Jewish) is subject to the law when criticism of the United States with a population of 326 million is not? Well, not yet anyway. Some 250 academics wrote in protest at the demolition of free speech at UK universities, but to no avail. Dr Haim Bresheeth, a Jewish academic, said that the new definition sought to protect Zionism and Israel from criticism. 'You can criticise and you should criticise every political institution that you wish [but] we are told now that Jews who criticise Israel like me are anti-Semitic. This is nonsense.' It is, but there is, once again, method in the madness. Israel, Zionism, and especially its Sabbatean Frankist secret society core, are obsessed with silencing any opposition and that includes at home where the Zionist extremist and Education Minister Naftali Bennett imposed a new 'ethical code' which banned academics at all Israel universities from discussing politics with their students and barred academic departments from contacting politically-affiliated groups or organisations. This is the only time that I ever expect to write the words 'ethical' and 'Naftali Bennett' in the same sentence. The UK Campaign Against Antisemitism (CAA) encouraged supporters to 'record, film, photograph and get witness evidence' about Israeli Apartheid Week events and 'we will help you to take it up with the university, students' union or even the police'. How sinister is that? The arrogance of these people is without limit. A group who call themselves Irish4Israel successfully campaigned to have another academic discussion about Israel banned by Cork University after Southampton University had earlier done the same. Both gave the excuse of 'security concerns'. What does this mean – they had threats? Irish4Israel ran away from an interview on the Richie Allen radio show to justify their actions because, while they pledge to 'debate with anyone', they said this does not include anyone in any way associated with me. What this contradiction of 'anyone' really means is anyone who will ask softball questions and nod politely as the mainstream media do. Lunacy reached new depths when Franck Allais, a French artist living in London, had the idea of making 27 road warning signs depicting in silhouette people and animals commonly seen in particular areas crossing the road. He had no problem with 26 of them, including an old person, a cat and a mother and baby, but the other sign featured the silhouette of an orthodox Jewish man near a synagogue (Fig 434). *'Anti-Semitic'* came the cry. A 'Jewish community group' reported this act of 'racism' to the police while the ludicrous Labour Member of Parliament Diane Abbott called it 'disgusting' and 'unacceptable'(virtue signalling) and her Labour colleague David Lammy said the sign amounted to 'despicable, nasty behaviour that has absolutely no place in our community' (virtue signalling). How about idiot MPs? Do they have any place in our parliament? Unfortunately, it seems that they do. My son Gareth made a Twitter comment that he was waiting for Netanyahu to blame the sign on Iran and the CAA were on it like a shot: 'Meet Gareth Icke, whose only reaction to a sign warning of a 'Jewish hazard' in London is to predict how the Jewish state will exploit it.' Ironically, this comment came from a full-time apologist for the Israeli regime who had indeed been exploiting the sign as confirmation of anti-Semitism. Then came the story of what the 27 signs around London were really all about – depicting common sights in different areas – and the professional finger-pointers looked absolutely ridiculous. Artist Franck Allais still felt it necessary to apologise for any upset caused when those who branded the

**Figure 434:** Silhouette of a Jewish man in a Jewish area was 'anti-Semitic'.

sign racist should have done the apologising. But that will be the day. Humility and a sense of humour are not their forte.

The Israeli Parliament (a building paid for by the Rothschilds) passed a bill in March 2017 banning from the country 'any person who is not an Israeli citizen or permanent resident if he, or the organisation or body in which he is active, has knowingly issued a public call to boycott the state of Israel or pledged to take part in such a boycott.' This refers to the Boycott, Divestment and Sanctions (BDS) movement which campaigns for a boycott of Israeli and global companies that serve the oppression of Palestinians until they have the same rights as Jews in Israel/Palestine. Other countries and many American states have passed laws banning government contracts with any company participating in the boycott. What if they boycott Palestinians? Not a problem. An 'Israel Anti-Boycott Bill' was signed by 45 US senators and 237 congressional representatives that would make it a criminal offence for a US citizen to support a boycott of Israel. The American Civil Liberties Union (ACLU) said:

> The bill would ... bar U.S. persons from supporting boycotts against Israel, including its settlements in the Palestinian Occupied Territories, conducted by international governmental organisations, such as the United Nations and the European Union. It would also broaden the law to include penalties for simply requesting information about such boycotts. Violations would be subject to a minimum civil penalty of $250,000 and a maximum criminal penalty of $1 million and 20 years in prison. We take no position for or against the effort to boycott Israel or any foreign country, for that matter. However, we do assert that the government cannot, consistent with the First Amendment, punish U.S. persons based solely on their expressed political beliefs.

Such is the power that Israel has over American politicians and why does a country of eight million people warrant such protection from boycotts when there is no such protection for anyone else? Benjamin Cardin, a Zionist Senator, was the bill's main sponsor and it was apparently drafted by the ultra-Zionist US lobby group, the American Israel Public Affairs Committee (AIPAC). Get off your knees America. Israel says the BDS boycott is ... wait for it ... what can it be? ... the suspense is killing me ... yes ... *anti-Semitic*. Well knock me down with a feather. An event planned by BDS Austria during Israeli Apartheid Week was cancelled by a hotel after receiving 'incessant calls, some by those identifying themselves as representatives of the Jewish community in Austria', according to BDS Austria. 'These people had issued threats and allegations of anti-Semitism against hotel staff, as well as announcing, without further detail, protest actions and boycott calls against the hotel – the hotel management felt threatened by this, to the extent of asking for police protection.' Here we have the real story behind events cancelled 'for security issues' and this was their modus operandi to get my venues in Germany to cancel. The venues dare not say so and another excuse is produced to hide the truth. A spokesman for the Austrian hotel told the media they had received 'unpleasant' calls, but later gave the reason to cancel as being unable to accommodate a large public event. Yeah, right. This is how gutlessness destroys freedom of speech and what you won't stand up for you always lose. It is not the censors ultimately that destroy freedom of speech, but those who give in to them and their intimidation and lies.

There was a blatant example of this when I spoke in Canada in August 2017. I was banned from speaking for well over a decade in Canada because of the Zionist lobby and its sycophantic, arse-licking gofers. I then applied for a speaking visa to try again and eventually it was granted. Events were booked and advertised for Toronto and Vancouver and all seemed to be going fine. Then the first venue in Toronto pulled out with an excuse we didn't really believe and we booked another, the Metro Toronto Convention Center which is, according to its website: '... a joint venture between the Federal Government of Canada, the Province of Ontario and the Municipality of Metropolitan Toronto.' This is the same Federal Government of Canada that gave me the speaking visa and you would have thought there could be no problem. Not so. The venue accepted the booking in April 2017, contracts were signed and the event advertised on its website. By mid-July nearly all the tickets were gone and members of the audience had booked hotels and some even flights. Then came one letter from the Zionists – *one letter* – complaining that I was being allowed to speak and the Metro Toronto Convention Center cancelled the event. They did this with utter contempt for freedom of speech and utter contempt for the consequences for ticket holders. Who exactly sent the letter? We were not allowed to know. What did it say? We were not allowed to know. All we were told was that they feared a 'public backlash' – a backlash that had not happened at any venue in any location all over the world since my world speaking tour began more than year earlier. This Convention Center has hosted a G20 Summit. Did they cancel that for fear of a 'public backlash'? No, they surrounded the place with fences and rows of armed police. G20 participants calling for actions that create mass death and devastation must have their freedom of speech protected, but someone like me calling for the death and destruction to stop and exposing those behind it must be silenced. This is but one example of the gutlessness that is destroying your freedom of speech and the contempt that these anonymous playground bullies have for your rights and freedoms. Fortunately, my son Jaymie, a brilliant event organiser, managed to secure another venue (with some guts) at very short notice and the bully boys didn't win. Canada has the reputation of being a free and open country when the hidden networks of manipulation make it anything but. Think of the wolf in disguise and Little Red Riding Hood – that's Canada. Free speech and research is being censored all the time there and the public never hear about most of it. Even worse is the self-censorship that comes from the intimidation of knowing what will happen if you upset the bullies. Anthony Hall, a tenured professor of globalisation studies at the University of Lethbridge in Canada, was suspended without pay or due process for alleged 'anti-Semitism' after a campaign to silence him led by Israel-front B'nai B'rith Canada. He had taught at the university for 25 years and all he was doing was pursue the truth about world events and attacks like 9/11. This used to be the role of an academic, but no longer. The Canadian Association of University Teachers condemned the censorship and the denial of Hall's basic rights, but when did basic rights ever matter to these censors? For the University of Lethbridge see the Metro Toronto Convention Center and file both under gutless.

Talking of gutless ... the effect that I am having in uncovering and circulating suppressed information has really got the Zionist extremists in a tizzy and their knickers in a twist. Quickly following the Toronto cancellation came three more in the UK at the again gutless and disgraceful Lowry Hotel in Manchester, Gladstone Theatre in the Wirral, Merseyside, and Sheffield City Hall. The number of Jewish people in the world is estimated at around 15 million out of 7.5 *billion* and the vast majority are not active manipulators for Israel and Revisionist (secret society) Zionism. They will know little about what is really happening and what is wrongly done in their name using them as a convenient front and cover. They are pawns in a game they don't understand. However, the few that are left are very organised and well-funded and form a global network of groups specifically created to target anyone spilling the beans on the Israeli regime and its military intelligence enforcers, Mossad. Whether it be in Germany, Canada, Britain or wherever these destroyers of freedom lie in wait to pounce and when they target you it is confirmation that you must be saying something right and something that inner-core Zionism doesn't want the public to hear. All these groups are playground bullies – emphasis on the playground because they act like two-year-olds – and childishly celebrate every 'victory' in denying the freedom or disrupting the lives of their targets. In my opinion they are very sick. Britain has a core Jewish population of about 270,000 out of about 66 million and the same applies to them as I said above with the global Jewish community. We are not talking about Jewish people as a whole, but a cabal who have as much contempt for Jewish people in general as they do for everyone else. Witness how the Israeli government treats most of its own people and how Jewish-born men and women who challenge the activities of Israel are viciously libelled, slandered and have their careers targeted, even destroyed, by being bizarrely labelled 'anti-Semitic'. They are also called 'self- haters' for having opinions and observations that don't concur with the bully boys in Tel Aviv and Jerusalem. Research the background to American academic Norman Finkelstein and Britain's Israel-born Gilad Atzmon for just two examples.

Israel's network of apologists in Britain includes the Friends of Israel group within every major political party and among many other freedom-deleting attack-dogs are the Campaign Against Antisemitism (CAA) and a group calling itself the North West Friends of Israel which was behind the cancellations of my events at the said gutless and disgraceful Lowry Hotel in Manchester, Gladstone Theatre in the Wirral, Merseyside, and Sheffield City Hall. They operate on Twitter with the tag of @NorthWestFOI. Even when I was a target of Zionist censors in the late 1990s and across the new Millennium they never went so far as calling me a 'Holocaust denier', but they are now getting so desperate as the truth about the Israeli regime and its global reach comes to the surface that clearly the decision has been made that this would be the most effective way to have me silenced. The label was suddenly used by assets of the Israel censor network in 2017 in Germany and Ireland and by the CAA and North West Friends of Israel. It could well have been included in the single letter to the venue in Toronto which we are not allowed to see. All these groups work to the same global blueprint and so the usual sequence unfolded with the North West Friends of Israel, with its mouthpiece Raphi Bloom, contacting the Lowry Hotel, Gladstone Theatre and Sheffield City Hall to assassinate my character with outrageous misrepresentations and the label of 'Holocaust denier'. These gutless venue owners then cancelled the events without even consulting me for a response to what they were told and the emails they sent to us to cancel were remarkable in both their contempt for freedom of speech and their customers and ticket holders and in how their wording was so similar and pretty much the same as that from the Maritim Hotel in Germany. The media, in the form of at least *ITV News*, the *Manchester Evening News* and the *Coventry Evening Telegraph* (the latter two owned by the Trinity Mirror group) then published the same lie without even asking me to respond and we had the headline 'Lowry hotel cancels appearance by Holocaust denier David Icke'. I contacted all three and asked them to provide the evidence for this claim and they all took the stories down within minutes because they had none. They had staggeringly just taken what the Raphi Bloom group said and repeated it without seeking my response. Bloom and his censors gutlessly turned down the chance to debate with me on the Richie Allen radio show using the same lame excuse as his like in Ireland: 'We do not engage with Holocaust deniers'. Keep saying it, Mr Bloom, and people will believe it through repetition. That's the game, right? They just throw their mud and run and then wait for gutless venues to get down on their knees. Once one venue bows its head these people go to others using the earlier cancellations they have secured as added pressure for them to do the same. My much-use of the term gutless is intentional because in the end it is not the censor groups that censor but the gutlessness of venues who put an easy life before the most basic of human freedoms. The North West Friends of Israel (as with the CAA) enthusiastically supported the catastrophic bombing of the Gaza innocent by the mass-murdering Israeli regime in 2014 which according to UN figures killed 2,200 Palestinians (551 of them children), injured 11,000 (3,000 children), made 20,000 homes uninhabitable and displaced 500,000. This Bloom group is notorious for their seek-and-destroy tactics against anyone supporting the Palestinian cause including doctors. They would never be banned from speaking anywhere – the venues would not dare – but I am fair game for speaking the words of peace and not violence. The group says it was created – irony of ironies – after protests against a Jewish shop owner in Manchester who was selling Israeli beauty products. The North West Friends of Israel was formed in response to attempts to stop a Jewish man going about his business and then proceeded to prevent those they don't like from going about theirs. They will not be even nearly conscious enough to see the shocking levels of hypocrisy that this requires and most certainly would never be able to compute this line by George Orwell: 'If liberty means anything at all, it means the right to tell people what they do not want to hear.' But, of course, liberty is the last thing they want to see. The deletion of freedom of expression will go on while there are gutless people like those that run the Metro Toronto Convention Center, Lowry Hotel, Gladstone Theatre, Sheffield City Hall, Carl Benz Arena and the Maritim Hotel group. In other words, it will go on. It is vital that Jewish people as a whole call out what is being done in their name and largely without their knowledge because the actions of the few are blamed on everyone else by the inability of many to see that judging a group instead of highlighting the actual perpetrators is ridiculous. Israel bullies are not just the enemy of freedom, but the enemy of Jewish people. Israel-born activist Gilad Atzmon wrote:

> ... *it is certain that a growing number of Brits have been subjected to an orchestrated slanderous campaign run by Zionist institutions that are funded by British taxpayer money such as CST* [Community Security Trust] *and CAA. These organisations attack Jeremy Corbyn, the Labour party, venues, intellectuals, artists, musicians, authors and anyone else they*

*decide has dared to point at Israeli brutality and extensive Jewish political lobbying in Britain.*

*If Britain still cares for values of tolerance and intellectual exchange, it better spend some taxpayer money defending its citizens, gentiles as well as Jews, from these foreign bodies. And if Britain truly cares for its Jews, it should protect them from the unfortunate consequences of the CST, CAA and other Israeli lobbies operating in our midst.*

These groups act in ways that make many angry with what is being done and some wrongly equate the perpetrator groups with all Jewish people. These groups then have the nerve to complain about 'anti-Semitism' when they are a major cause. Their targets are mainly in the alternative media, but not always. Columnist Kevin Myers was fired by the Irish version of *The Sunday Times* for alleged 'anti-Semitic' comments he made in July 2017 in an article about the way the BBC pays male presenters more than female. Myers wrote:

*I note that two of the best-paid women presenters in the BBC – Claudia Winkleman and Vanessa Feltz, with whose, no doubt, sterling work I am tragically unacquainted – are Jewish. Good for them. Jews are not generally noted for their insistence on selling their talent for the lowest possible price, which is the most useful measure there is of inveterate, lost-with-all-hands stupidity. I wonder, who are their agents?*

My point is not about what Myers wrote, but that had the word 'Jewish' instead been 'American', 'Chinese', 'French', 'Russian', 'Colombian' or 'Canadian' he would not have been instantly fired, his column removed and an apology published. The Jewish population of Ireland is about 2,500 in a total Irish population of around 4.8 million. What is the power of Zionism that ensures that its advocates are not treated like everyone else? Yet again leading the charge against Myers was the Campaign Against Antisemitism (CAA) which was red-faced with outrage and condemnation in its perpetual and professional victimhood. The Jewish Representative Council of Ireland defended Myers from CAA and other attacks and said that branding him as either an anti-Semite or Holocaust denier was 'an absolute distortion of the facts'. But then that is what these Israel attack-dog organisations are there to do – distort facts to serve their agenda (the inner-core Zionist agenda) of censorship and intimidation. All I am asking for is equal treatment for *everyone* no matter what their race, group, culture, creed or background and that is not what is happening. The sacking of Kevin Myers is steeped with irony because he has taken a pro-Israeli stance in many articles over the years and perhaps he now understands why people have become so sick of the Israel lobby and its systematic censorship. It is also further evidence of the extremes to which Zionist censors are targeting absolutely *anyone* who steps out of their line. Those who are so terrified of what someone else will say, to the point they will go to these lengths to silence them, always have an enormous amount to hide. It is not often that I quote Shakespeare, but this one is perfect: 'The lady doth protest too much, methinks.'

There is another centre of planned censorship to note in the form of Amazon which is taking over online shopping and expanding into all retail areas. Amazon began as an online bookstore and now dominates the book market with a gathering pace and has put a vast number of independent book shops and publishers out of business worldwide. This has always been the plan and once total domination is achieved the widespread censorship of what can and can't be published and sold will begin – Facebook and Google have been through the same sequence and Amazon, Facebook and Google come as one unit if the truth be told. There was basically a no-censorship policy at Amazon in the beginning but now after pressure from the Zionist lobby books questioning the official story of the Holocaust and those they dub 'hate material' are being banned. As the definition of 'hate' continues to expand so will be the range of banned books until ultimately they will include anything that questions the official version of any subject. This is where we are going and Amazon is the major vehicle for this modern-day book burning under the leadership of arrogance personified, Jeff Bezos. It goes without saying, but I will anyway, that Zionist books of racism and hate with regard to Palestinians are not being censored. It has always seemed to me that for books to be banned and authors jailed for having another version of history is truly bizarre and deeply sinister – especially when opposing versions of history are given free rein. Why can't we just have an open debate on everything and let people have the freedom to decide what they think? But that is freedom and that just wouldn't do in a tyranny. A definition I would offer of 'tyranny' is 'any society that seeks to ban the circulation of information that would awaken the population to the tyranny'. See, so ironically, the book-burning Nazis for a start.

## Shoot the messenger – delete the message

Highlight Israel's apartheid state and there is apoplexy. A report by the United Nations Economic and Social Commission for Western Asia in early 2017 concluded that 'Israel has established an apartheid regime that dominates the Palestinian people as a whole' and found that 'beyond a reasonable doubt ... Israel is guilty of policies and practices that constitute the crimes of apartheid' in accordance with the definition in international law. Zionism's 'claim to Palestine as the exclusive homeland of the Jewish people rests on an expressly racial conception of both groups', the report said. 'The mission of preserving Israel as a Jewish state has inspired or even compelled Israel to pursue several general racial policies.' These policies included 'demographic engineering, in order to establish and maintain an overwhelming Jewish majority in Israel' and 'a range of other policies designed to restrict the size of the Palestinian population.' The report said full political rights are given only to Jews: 'As in any racial democracy such a majority allows the trappings of democracy – democratic elections, a strong legislature – without threatening any loss of hegemony by the dominant racial group.' Quite simply the UN report said that Israel is a country founded on racism, and this is the same regime that accuses everyone else of racism via its global network of Zionist attack-dog organisations. The Israeli government has approved a bill to officially designate the country as a Jewish state and make Hebrew the only official language, but it's not racial domination or anything. Examples of Israeli apartheid are legion including the policy of demolishing family homes of Palestinians that Israel accuses of terrorism (collective punishment that is illegal under international law) while the same policy is not applied to Israeli terrorism against Palestinians. Avigdor Lieberman, the Israel Defence Minister and Zionist extremist, denied official compensation to an eight-year-old, Ahmed Dawabshe, whose father, mother and baby brother were burned to death by illegal Jewish settler terrorists who firebombed their home in the Israeli-occupied West Bank. The arsonists left slogans on the wall alongside a Star of David which said 'long live the Messiah' and 'revenge'. Compensation is offered to all Jewish victims of terrorism, but not Ahmed, who suffered second-degree burns to 60 percent of his body. Two years later at the time of writing those who killed his family and scarred him for life still have not been tried. No apartheid? No evil? The UN Western Asia report backed the BDS boycott and urged national governments to 'support boycott, divestment and sanctions activities and respond positively to calls for such initiatives.' They should not pin their hopes on that in Britain and the United States where the governments are doing all they can to block any boycott.

The hypocrisy of Zionism has no limits and nor, it seems, does its global reach (Fig 435). Days after the apartheid report was published UN Secretary-General Antonio Guterres ordered it to be withdrawn. Under Secretary General Rima Khalaf, who led the Commission that produced the report, resigned over pressure to unpublish what she believed to be true. Israeli UN ambassador Danny Danon led the charge against Khalaf with America and Britain as always in tow – especially under Trump who appointed the vacuous Israel apologist Nikki Haley, who does everything but drape herself in the Israeli flag, as US ambassador to the

UN. Danon praised Guterres for his action and welcomed the resignation of Khalaf: 'The time has come to put an end to those using their status within the UN to promote anti-Israel activity.' They love censorship to the point of orgasm. Danon, who later became vice president of the United Nations General Assembly, said that 'anti-Israel activists do not belong in the UN.' Nope – only pro-Israel ones. The biggest joke of all came when Secretary-General Guterres said the report was not withdrawn because of its content, but because Khalaf did not consult him first (so he could have blocked publication altogether). Any excuse will do except the truth. See 'we are unable to accommodate a large public event'.

It is correct that as a Jordanian national Khalaf would see Israel from her angle, but her point

**Figure 435:** One rule for Israel (and the US/UK and NATO countries) and another for everyone else.

**Figure 436:** Israel's golden rule.

about Israel running an apartheid regime is so obvious it is laughable to deny. Khalaf was accused of libelling Israel by actually telling the truth and reality has no meaning in these matters. The rule is simple: What Israel (the Rothschilds) wants Israel (the Rothschilds) gets (Fig 436). They could have gone down the Peter Tatchell route and argued and exposed the alleged untruths in the report, but open debate on something that is so clearly happening is the last place they want to go. It is so much easier to get backbone-deleted lackey place-people to silence the opposition. Palestinians gave Khalaf an award for her courage, a move which Israel condemned as 'outrageous'. Israel apologists are in a permanent state of outrage. Those who have directly experienced apartheid certainly agree with the Khalaf report conclusions. South African MPs refused to meet an Israeli delegation in 2017 and Nelson Mandela's grandson, Mandla Mandela, now an MP with the African National Congress (ANC), said: 'Parliament has stayed true to Nelson Mandela's commitment to stand by the Palestinian cause until Palestine is free.' He called for the Israeli ambassador to be sent home and the South African ambassador to Israel to be withdrawn and he went on: 'History calls upon us to take similar measures to those

**Figure 437:** Sums it up, really.

**Figure 438:** Literally anything.

taken by freedom, justice and peace loving communities that supported the global anti-apartheid movement against the brutal and illegitimate South African regime.'

A later United Nations Economic and Social Commission for Western Asia report, not involving Rima Khalaf, accused Israeli forces of killing 63 Palestinians, including 19 children, and wounding 2,276 Palestinians, including 562 children, between April 2016 and March 2017 including what it called 'extrajudicial executions'. Danny Danon was immediately on the case the moment someone typed in 'fury' and 'outrage' and pressed enter. Zionism was running the political correctness program before the world had even heard of it and provided the blueprint for all that has followed. They are terrified of open debate and the careers of even Jewish academics have been destroyed when they have spoken out against the behaviour of Israel and the Saturnic Rothschild Mafia at the Sabbatean Frankist secret society core of Zionism (Fig 437). We only need to look at Israel itself to see where this is heading for the rest of us. Bloggers and social media posters are required by law to have their words screened before posting. A bill passing through the Israeli parliament will order Facebook and other social media sites to delete content the Israeli regime claims to be 'incitement'. Who decides what this is? They do. This will, of course, include legitimate criticism and target the most basic freedom of speech. Palestinians are routinely charged for posting comments about Israel oppression and even poets are jailed for expressing their art to make statements about fundamental injustice. None of these Zionist censors or political correctness supporters in general want to see Tatchell's counter-their-arguments strategy. To do so would require open debate and that is precisely what political correctness is there to stop, to allow censorship to control the narrative (Fig 438).

## Upping the ante

The next inevitable extension of Zionist censorship came with the announcement in 2017 that the notorious Anti-Defamation League (ADL) was planning 'a state-of-the-art command centre' in Silicon Valley to monitor everything online that it decides is 'hate'. The definition of 'hate' in this context: Anything that criticises Israel and anything the ADL decides is 'hate' because its censorship suits the Web agenda. ADL chief executive Jonathan Greenblatt revealed the establishment of the new censorship centre and never one to exaggerate he is quoted as comparing the alleged growth of 'anti-Semitism' in the United States to that of Nazi Germany. The behaviour of Israel and Revisionist Zionism is naturally never considered a contributory factor to people being pissed off with them. Greenblatt was a Special Assistant to Barack Obama. The Omidyar Network of e-Bay founder Pierre Omidyar is providing the 'seed funding' for the project which Greenblatt says will write reports, compile data, and 'provide insights to government and policy makers'. The centre will use the 'best-in-class technology', according to Greenblatt, 'to provide insights to government and policy makers'. Pass that through an Orwellian translation unit and it becomes 'to tell people what information and opinion they can and cannot circulate'. I'm sure that Zionist owned-and-controlled Facebook, Google/Alphabet and YouTube will be most enthusiastic in their support. At the same time the Israeli government is expanding its censorship reach and hands out scholarships at its universities to students agreeing to make pro-Israel Facebook posts and tweets to foreign audiences. They don't reveal their government connection and make their posts seem independent and spontaneous. The ADL, an outgrowth of the Rothschild-created B'nai B'rith ('Sons of the Covenant'), led the whole campaign to create the offence of 'hate crime' in the first place which was a goal of the Zionist Frankfurt School. I have detailed the history and background of the Apple-funded ADL in other books, but basically in yet another laughable inversion the 'Anti-Defamation' League sets out to defame anyone challenging the behaviour of Israel and its global network of connected organisations. The ADL, along with the American Jewish Committee's Project Interchange and the Jewish Institute for National Security Affairs, has been paying for hundreds of US police officers to be trained in Israel and occupied Palestine to learn Israeli methods of violent and racist military 'law enforcement'. They then return to America to train their colleagues and the result has since been seen on the streets of America. The St Louis Chapter of Jewish Voices for Peace has been vehement in its opposition to the ADL and the Israel connection to US police. A statement said:

**Figure 439:** Global manipulation by a Rothschild front operation claiming to be the government of a country.

*We have cringed as the ADL positions itself locally as a champion of racial profiling legislation while sending US police – including former St. Louis County Police Chief Tim Fitch – to train on population control in Israel, an apartheid police state with more than 60 years of sophisticated expertise in racial profiling, mass incarceration, settler colonialism, and ethnic cleansing targeting the non-Jewish indigenous Palestinian people.*

'Anti-racists' at the ADL did surveillance work for the apartheid regime in South Africa with whom Israel was extremely close. Israel agencies and military intelligence arm Mossad have made an art form of setting up front organisations and infiltrating others to serve their interests (Fig 439). Israeli newspaper *Haaretz* uncovered official documents in 2017 that revealed how the Israel branch of Amnesty International was a front for the foreign ministry from the late 1960s to the mid-1970s. Tip and iceberg come to mind. Documents exposed how the Amnesty branch was funded by the Israeli government and took instructions from the foreign ministry. Buying bias, I think would sum it up, and this is going on worldwide on a grand scale.

Al Jazeera, the Arabic television channel based in Qatar, used hidden cameras in 2016 to reveal how an official from the Israeli Embassy in London was manipulating British politics through front organisations and the Friends of Israel network in the major political parties. Embassy senior political officer Shai Masot was caught on camera talking about a list of British politicians he wanted to 'take down' for their stance on

**Figure 440:** Why is it 'racist' to ask why a country of just eight million people is always given special treatment no matter what it does?

Israel including Foreign Office Minister Alan Duncan. Joan Ryan, chair of the Labour Party Friends of Israel who appeared with Shai Masot in the film, has been a constant and vocal critic of party leader Jeremy Corbyn. The British government and 'opposition parties' were virtually silent on the exposure to take down a government minister, but think of the global outrage if it had been Russia (Fig 440). At the time of writing the US/Israel-controlled Saudi Arabia, United Arab Emirates, Egypt and Bahrain are seeking to close down Al Jazeera. Israel announced (of course) that it was doing the same in that country. Zionist censorship is not about protecting people from racism. It is about silencing the opposition and not just in terms of Israel either. Zionism at its controlling core has a much bigger agenda than that. A bill proposed by Zionist New York Assemblyman David I. Weprin gives you a feel for where they want this to go. The bill would require 'inaccurate', 'irrelevant', 'inadequate' or 'excessive' statements to be removed within 30 days of a request from the subject of the statements/posts concerned. Failure to do so would cost search engines or the source of the statement statutory damages of $250 per day plus attorney fees. Weprin is referred to as a 'liberal'. Inclusion of the term 'irrelevant' is to instigate George Orwell's memory hole where information about the 'past' can be deleted. We already have this in Europe thanks to EU judges who ruled that anyone can demand that search engines cease to list information about them that they don't want people to see. This means that while the information is still there no one can find it without basically knowing the information beforehand to help them in their search. Weprin's bill specifically includes the censorship of content that 'is no longer material to current public debate or discourse'. Who decides that? They do. Delete the 'past' to manipulate perception in the 'present'. Yet another humdinger in terms of the real motivation is the clause that says the content should be deleted '... without replacing such removed ... content with any disclaimer [or] takedown notice'. All trace of what you have censored and the fact that it *has* been censored must be kept from the public. Mr Weprin and other supporters of this bill – you are a disgrace. A *Washington Post* article said:

> So, under this bill, newspapers, scholarly works, copies of books on Google Books and Amazon, online encyclopaedias (Wikipedia and others) – would all would have to be censored whenever a judge and jury found (or the author expected them to find) that the speech was 'no longer material to current public debate or discourse' (except when it was 'related to convicted felonies' or 'legal matters relating to violence' in which the subject played a 'central and substantial' role).

> And of course the bill contains no exception even for material of genuine historical interest; after all, such speech would have to be removed if it was 'no longer material to current public debate.' Nor is there an exception for autobiographic material, whether in a book, on a blog or anywhere else. Nor is there an exception for political figures, prominent business people and others.

This is where we are going and the scale of censorship by these Archontic forces of oppression has hardly started yet. Political censorship is well advanced around the world with politicians facing the PC police if their views don't conform. South Africa's opposition Democratic Alliance Party charged one of its number with misconduct for saying in a tweet that colonialism was not all bad and some good things came from it. Party leader Mmusi Maimane said the views could harm the image of the party. Not possible, surely, compared with him. The European Parliament is now cutting live debate feeds, removing recordings of offensive remarks and imposing fines of $9,500 on MEPs they claim are guilty of 'defamatory, racist or xenophobic language or behaviour'. Naïve politicians supporting censorship of all kinds do not realise that it will all eventually apply to them and in fact is already doing so.

## Sleepwalk into tyranny

The Archontic Reptilian control system is a multidimensional, multi-levelled, multi-faceted and absolutely incessant perceptual onslaught on the human mind to create fragmentation of thought and emotion and to implant a sense of powerless isolation. People are isolated from other ways of looking at the world and this creates the desired perceptual stagnation. Suppression of free expression becomes more extreme to prevent the circulation of information that exposes the conspiracy and its programming. What we are seeing on student campuses is the precursor for how the whole of human society is planned to be with people unable to say anything that The System has not approved and mind-altering and suppressing drugs handed out like confetti. The scale of psychological drugs in circulation for adults and children is already enormous and the ultimate plan is to have everyone drugged by law ('to keep the peace') and have this technologically tracked. Microchipped pills that tell a doctor when they have been taken now exist and making them compulsory is all that remains. Pharmaceutical drugs scramble the brain and on a waveform level impact upon the waveform standing wave oscillation and throw the body out kilter in terms of health, thought, emotion and most crucially a connection to 'out there'. The waveform impact is what primarily matters and the El-lite know that.

Political correctness and triggering are fast breaking out from academia into mainstream society. Comedy has been devastated and in many ways destroyed by PC zealotry which has no sense of humour and would be mortified if asked to laugh at itself. Most so-called 'alternative' comedians who supposed to be 'anti-Establishment' stay well within the bounds of the progressive Establishment while claiming to be fearless. Comedians bow to the PC tyranny when they should be looking in its face and refusing to blink. You don't want to hear my jokes? Then *don't come.* Then *go to another channel.* The *Washington Times* reported how it's now routine for publishers to have 'sensitivity readers' to screen new books for words that indicate bias, stereotypes or negatively-charged language about gender, race, disability or sexual orientation and to check if they are 'culturally untactful'. I don't know what they would do with this one. Call for oxygen, I guess. The Spanish government is targeting artists, students and the public in general with extraordinary levels of censorship which has included a 21-year-old college student accused by a Spanish National Court prosecutor of 'glorifying terrorism and humiliating victims of terrorism', according to German news website Deutsche Welle. Her 'crime' was tweeting a 'joke about a dictator' and the court was seeking a *three-year* prison sentence. Two street puppeteers in Madrid were arrested in 2016 after a performance making fun of local police, who couldn't see that arresting them merely confirmed how right the puppeteers had been to take the piss in the first place. The world is going into diversity lockdown driven by the agents of diversity and this inversion is not by chance. If you want to run drugs without being suspected do it through an anti-drug agency. If you want to destroy diversity use a rabble and mob constantly screaming about the need for more diversity. It's all a mind game.

There are still academics standing up against the gathering tide, often to the detriment of careers, but many have also become torch-carriers so consumed by their own self-righteousness that they campaign for what is designed to silence their own profession and global society in general, just as politicians campaign for what is eventually planned to silence them. A bloke called Professor Thom Brooks, head of Durham University Law School, told a UK parliamentary committee that there should be a 'Hate Crime Offenders Register' similar to the sex offenders register that restricts access to jobs. 'Anyone on [the Register] could be restricted from working with children and/or working in certain professions', the intellectual colossus insisted. 'This seems sensible, mirrors current policies in place and would help send a clearer signal of how serious these offences are.' How would this scan in terms of fairness and freedom when the definition of what constitutes a 'hate crime' is constantly expanded? The hate industry is being fuelled by claims of 'record levels of hate crime' and that Britain 'is in the grip of an epidemic of intolerance'. Evidence? Er, well, er, er. Maybe they mean figures like those supplied by a Zionist private security organisation called the Community Security Trust (CST) which makes its money from Jewish people who fear 'rising anti-Semitism' because of figures issued by the same CST. The organisation has more than 65 staff based in offices in London, Manchester and Leeds and the then Home Secretary Theresa May gave them £13.4 million of taxpayers' money in 2016. CST 'anti-

Semitism' figures are reported every year by the media without the context of where they come from. Activist Gilad Atzmon wrote in an article headed 'Hate PLC':

*A mere few days after the British government vowed to wire millions of pounds to the CST, the number of 'anti-Semitic incidents' rose by 30% to over 100 incidents a month. The results, at least according to the CST's statistics, are that the more public money is allocated to fight anti-Semitism, the more anti-Semitic the Brits become.*

*If this is the case, the cure for British anti-Semitism may be within reach – to fight anti-Semitism, deprive the CST and similar organisations of taxpayers' money! Anti-Semitism is not really a social phenomenon, it is instead a multi-million pound industry. The more we spend on the fight against it, the more incidents are 'recorded' to justify further spending.*

I am not saying that racism does not exist – of course it does and they are idiots obsessed with a body that doesn't physically exist. Some of the worst and most grotesque racism can indeed be found at the extremes of Zionism. I am saying that racism is being exaggerated and now covertly and psychologically encouraged through terror attacks to justify the 'hate crime' lockdown on free expression. Screaming headlines about headstones toppled in a 'hate crime' at a Brooklyn Jewish cemetery were followed by a police assessment that no such crime took place and the damage was likely caused by high winds, eroded soil and neglect. Let us not forget either about 'anti-Semitic attacks' carried out by Jewish people for propaganda purposes. In March 2017 came the headline 'Israeli man, 19, arrested in connection with threats against Jewish Community Centers in U.S. and other nations'. The arrest came after a joint operation between the FBI and Israeli police and involved bomb threats made over a six-month period against Israeli institutions in several countries by the duel US-Israeli citizen. His father was also arrested and police said the 19-year-old was found to have a Bitcoin account worth millions of shekels. The Common Dreams website uncovered a 'Jewish Harvard graduate in his thirties' who was trolling the site with anti-Jewish hate and then challenging himself under another alias to give the illusion of an 'anti-Semitic' argument between two different people. This Jewish man said that Hitler should have finished the job and killed all Jews and then attacked himself under another name. A Canadian man became infamous for posting horrible racist comments under anonymous log-in names and then reporting the site to the authorities for posting what he posted and any replies agreeing with him. The idea is to discredit discussion and the website. Government agencies and corporations now have whole armies of paid trolls who work to discredit and disrupt website discourse on subjects they want people to reject.

A bedrock of any police state is to have the target population report on the target population and we have this policy instigated on campus and wider society. *The Washington Examiner*, an American political website, revealed how college administrators are encouraging students to report each other and academic staff for 'inappropriate speech'. These are classic PC terms – appropriate and inappropriate. In this context what do these words mean? They are entirely subjective; what is considered 'appropriate' by one person will be 'inappropriate' to another. But they are meant to lack clarity because it allows the widest possible interpretation of them by those in authority. The *Examiner* said that 230 colleges had 'Bias Response Teams' to investigate claims of offensive speech most of which are made anonymously. This 'bias' is defined by whatever the PC Mafia interpret that to be. Snitching on people anonymously behind their back is preparing students to do so throughout their lives as described by George Orwell. The Internet was supposed to be an extension of freedom but through algorithms and control by global Web corporations this can now be seen as a temporary illusion as censorship becomes the norm. The Net was sold as a means of free communication when the idea was to create a vehicle for total surveillance that so dominated public discourse as other sources disappeared that they could control everything that people say, see and hear by direct and algorithmic censorship. The Trump Administration's plan to end so-called net-neutrality and equal access to the Internet is all part of this. The move, instigated by Ajit Pai, Chairman of the Federal Communication Commission (FCC), would allow corporations to block content, and establish fast and slow lanes for lawful content which they could not before. The 'free' Internet was just the selling point, not the way it was ever planned to end up.

I wrote in books in the 1990s about a global computer system in which the *El*-lite programmed their desired outcome and the computer would produce the sequence of events necessary to achieve that end by essentially predicting public responses to each step. Now that very system is in the open, far more advanced and called the 'Sentient World Simulation' based at the Synthetic Environment for Analysis and Simulations Laboratory at Purdue University in Indiana, which is mass-gathering data to predict (and manipulate) human behaviour. More about this later when the term 'synthetic' will also become very relevant. Add to this personal data, beliefs and behaviour traits compiled on the population globally by the US National Security Agency (NSA) and Homeland Security at the Intelligence Community Comprehensive National Cybersecurity Initiative Data Center in Utah through the collection and algorithmic processing of emails, phone calls, Internet browsing, social media posts, credit card transactions, parking tickets

**Figure 441:** National Security Agency global data-gathering centre in Utah.

and receipts, travel records, book buys and other actions and communications (Fig 441). Together you have all the information you need for superfast and super-advanced artificial intelligence computers to predict collective response and outcomes. Then trigger the right event to trigger the predicted response to secure the desired result and societal change. Are people so naïve to believe that the colossal (and ever increasing) scale of surveillance and freedom deletion imposed on humanity worldwide is to *stop terrorism*? That is not the reason, only the excuse and the more terrorism they can stage the more effective becomes the excuse. Humanity has to break free from programmed perceptions of the possible and start thinking anew. I can tell you from personal experience that once you do that the world looks a very different place.

## Must-knows

I will conclude this chapter with two advancing-the-spell techniques essential to understanding world events and the battle for human perception. I have long-called them Problem-Reaction-Solution and the Totalitarian Tiptoe. These operate as one unit and they constantly transform global society by manipulating the population to support (or at least not to effectively oppose) the Archontic agenda. They are devastatingly simple and so I can be brief. Problem-Reaction-Solution (PRS) involves first covertly creating a problem. This could be a terrorist attack, financial collapse, political upheaval, the possibilities are endless. Control of the mainstream media is vital to stage two when you tell the public the version of the problem that you want them to believe in terms of who or what was responsible. This could not happen if we had a questioning, researching media prepared to critically think outside of the box; but because we don't stage two is a breeze as excuses-for-journalists repeat the official narrative usually without challenge. The manipulators are seeking a public reaction of fear, outrage and a demand that 'something must be done' which opens the door for stage three and the final sting when those who have covertly created the problem and named the fake villain then openly offer the solutions to the problem they have themselves covertly created. These always involve changes in the law, deletions of privacy, greater surveillance and often wars that advance the Archontic agenda for global tyranny in response to the manufactured problem. When I say they 'have themselves created' I mean hidden agents of the Web and not necessarily the bewildered puppets you see in the public arena. I will highlight many examples of this technique later, but an obvious case is 9/11. If you want to launch a 'war on terror' to regime change target countries then set up a massive attack on your own soil, blame Islamic terrorists and most of the world will be cheering when you start dropping bombs on Islamic countries that you planned to target all along. If you want to justify bombing Syria just say that President Assad is using chemical weapons on this own people and the claim alone will be enough for the media to repeat in a frenzy of condemnation with no need for actual evidence. Data scientist Adam Kramer, who worked on one of the Facebook behaviour-changing experiments, said emotions are contagious: 'When positive expressions [posts] were reduced, people produced fewer positive posts and more negative posts; when negative expressions were reduced, the opposite pattern occurred.' The 'reaction' response in Problem-Reaction-Solution is all about the manipulation of emotion. PRS 'problems' are designed to create collective trauma (very much involving the reptilian brain) and traumatised people are the most psychologically suggestable. There is also a version that I call No-Problem-Reaction-Solution when you don't need a real problem just the perception of one. Claims about weapons of mass destruction in Iraq, that they knew didn't exist, is an outstanding example. The antidote for PRS is a simple question: Who benefits? Who benefits from me believing the version of this situation that the authorities and media are telling me to believe? Beneficiaries will invariably be anyone who wishes to advance an agenda of human control and justify 'solutions' to take the community, country or world in that direction. Politicians and economists also seek to make you terrified of what they don't want to happen so that you won't want it either. Witness the campaign against Brexit.

Mainstream journalists, or those that claim to be, cannot contemplate such manipulation because of terminal naïvety and the arrogance of ignorance. There are few better cases than BBC radio presenter Nicky treat-those-questioning-human-caused-climate-change-with-distain-and-we-must-remove-Assad-he-is-a war-criminal Campbell. He reported that two Muslim men had told him they thought that government agencies were behind the suicide bomb attack that killed 22 people and injured 250 as they left a Manchester concert venue in May 2017. The government immediately used the attack to justify the deployment of troops for domestic law enforcement and announced plans to further censor information, views and opinions on the Internet. Campbell was incredulous about what the Muslim pair had told him: 'They said it was the government!', he cried, unable to hide his contempt. 'Government' is a term meaning a colossal number of people and agencies and most them are well beyond public awareness, but in

BBC'S NICKY CAMPBELL

CAN'T UNDERSTAND WHY PEOPLE
DON'T TRUST AUTHORITY
NO WONDER THE BBC LOVE HIM

**Figure 442:** Postage Stamp Consensus personified.

Campbell's mind 'government' would have meant only those we can see. Then he delivered a humdinger: 'Where is their critical thinking?' You couldn't make it up but with him you don't have to. The *El*-lite get away with what they do because people like *Campbell* don't have the capacity to critically think and look at anything from a different angle. The BBC pays him up to £450,000 a year because he's perfect for them. Campbell was also bewildered at how the Muslim lads lacked trust in government, which should be his job, but isn't (Fig 442). On the same day the 'progressive' Establishment 'activist' Shami Chakrabarti urged people not to voice 'conspiracy theories' about the Manchester attack. To think this lady, a member of the unelected House of Lords, was once the head of Liberty, an organisation that claims to protect freedoms and human rights. Here was another 'progressive' insisting that everyone must be as clueless as them.

Understanding where they want to take the world is the most effective way of decoding PRS. Does the solution take them closer to the police state and centralisation of power? PRS manipulation can also be a double-bluff. I watched an old edition of the UK police drama *New Tricks* in which a British intelligence officer ordered a covert investigation into a murder and led police investigators to believe their findings would be covered up to help a company at the expense of its pension fund and the 'little people'. The intelligence officer talked privately about how it was possible to predict behaviour if you knew those involved. One of the investigation team leaked the findings they believed were to be covered up and the programme ended with the intelligence official telling his bosses that the mission has been accomplished. They had *wanted* the information leaked to damage the company concerned without it coming from the intelligence network. Human mental and emotional responses to various stimuli are studied in enormous detail by The System to predict behaviour and they know how to trigger behaviour and responses required at any point. Making society ever more regimented in mind and emotion means people are more predictable and more manipulatable with PRS. I see this constantly with those of the political Right, Left and Centre who think they are challenging the government and the Establishment while doing exactly what they want. Behaviour of progressives in relation to Donald Trump is a current example. They think they are protesting against the Establishment when in fact divide and rule and focusing attention on the twigs and not the forest is just what the *El*-lite want to happen. Observe the *outcomes* of these situations. Everything else is detail. Never mind what was said. What has actually *happened*? What has *changed*? Who *benefits*?

The Totalitarian Tiptoe technique is the stable-mate of PRS in which you start at A with the intent of reaching Z (the complete Archontic enslavement of humanity). Each A, B and C is a step towards that goal made possible by Problem-Reaction-Solution. The trick is to make people believe that each stage is happening randomly and in and of itself. They must perceive that the tiptoes are unconnected when they are fundamentally connected and heading in a clear direction to those with a mind to see. This how the EEC or Common Market was transformed step by step into today's centralised bureaucratic dictatorship known as the European Union. The EU as it has become was planned at least since the early decades of the 20th century (see ... *And The Truth Shall Set You Free* and *The Perception Deception*). Jean Monnet, the so-called 'father' of the EU project, said in a letter to a friend in 1952:

> *Europe's nations should be guided towards the super-state without their people understanding what is happening. This can be accomplished by successive steps, each disguised as having an economic purpose, but which will eventually and irreversibly lead to federation.*

This is how the Totalitarian Tiptoe works and together with Problem-Reaction-Solution they create a perception deception of incredible power to transform society down to the finest detail. The world we live in today is largely down to them and to the censorship, suppression and marginalisation of free thought, speech and opinion which challenge the official narrative. All of these things are connected.

**Postscript:** The European Union, which jumps on all alleged 'anti-Semitism', featured an Israeli 'comedian' called Avishai Ivri in a 2017 official video promoting EU-Israel relations. This is the same Ivri who has said: 'Fuck it, wipe out Gaza'; 'Are Palestinians a nation?' – 'They're shit'; '... the Palestinians are Nazis ... They haven't built gas chambers yet ... but they're definitely Nazis'; 'Here's a strategy that hasn't been tried out yet: 1,000 Arabs killed for each one of our people killed ... I think they owe us 5,000 from last week.' Ivri has also said:

> *You're always asking* [us] *'what's your solution?' What's your solution? Hello?? We don't shout 'Death to the Arabs' because it rhymes! We shout it because it's our solution! We fucking write it with spray on the wall! How*

*secret do you think we keep our solution?*

But don't worry, Zionists can't be racists, it's the law (literally so). The EU was embarrassed into taking down the video, but I don't want Ivri or anyone else censored. I want the world to know the scale and depth of the racism of those who constantly cry 'racism' and I want their hypocrisy and efforts to silence the global population called out and exposed. Thank you, Mr Ivri, for your contribution.

**Postscript (2):** After the main body of this book was completed came the inevitable announcement by the Zionist-owned Google and YouTube that they were changing their guidelines to openly target 'conspiracy theories' (anything that exposes the official narrative for which Google is merely a tool) and 'hate speech' (ditto). 'Conspiracy theories' – a term promoted by the Google seed-funding CIA – are defined as websites contradicting what are called 'well established historical and scientific facts'. How many such 'facts', which were once accepted, are now shown to be ludicrously inaccurate? One after the other is the answer. Challenging them is how we move on. This is Orwell on steroids and the ultra-Zionist Anti-Defamation League (funded by Apple) has been called in by Zionist-owned Google and YouTube as one of the censors. If people can't see what is happening now with the calculated suppression of information – they never will.

Another prominent Zionist-controlled and immensely well-funded US 'anti-hate', label-them-all-Nazis, censorship front is the ironically named Southern Poverty Law Center (SPLC). This was exposed in August 2017 for funnelling millions into offshore accounts and paying its executives like Zionist president and CEO Richard Cohen more than $350,000 a year. American TV host Tucker Carlson, with an admirable record of calling out free speech destroyers, described the Apple-funded SPLC as 'deeply corrupt, dishonest and loathsome'. Yes, and not only them, either.

# CHAPTER TWELVE

# Before Your Very Eyes

*'In presence of the Moon nobody sees stars'* – **Amit Kalantri**

I am going to weave together in the next few chapters where all that I have exposed and highlighted so far has been leading and how it is planned to conclude. This will involve a vastly different explanation of world events to that spun daily by Mainstream Everything.

The bottom line is context. You can look at people and happenings in isolation and they will appear a certain way, but connect them and *wow* how different they appear. The mainstream media reports everything as a series of unconnected dots happening randomly in and of themselves. They do this because 90 percent of them are ignorant of the connections and context while maybe ten percent have some level of awareness that all is not as it seems to be. Most of the latter still ignore what they know to protect their career or because they support those in the shadows who depend on an ignorant and compliant media to hide the magnitude of difference between what is really happening and what the population is told is happening. The whole foundation of my work for nearly 30 years has been to put events and people into context and reveal how they link together to a common end. When strands are connected you can see the Web and when pixels are connected you can see the picture. Keep them apart as politicians and media do and everything appears to be a bewildering series of random events without coherence or direction. In fact, they have *both* and the El-ite are terrified of you seeing that. Once people, organisations and happenings are put into their true *connected* context the world looks very different. These connections operate on multiple levels within the realm of the 'seen' and between the 'seen' and 'unseen'. What appears to be the reason for something in the seen can have a far deeper meaning in the unseen. Take war as an example. The mainstream explanation for a war will be whatever the dominant force behind the media (mostly Western politicians and corporations) say it is.

'We must invade to stop this dictator killing his own people!' Connect the dots within the seen and you see that in fact this is just a made-up excuse to remove a target regime as part of a much bigger strategy in pursuit of global acquisition and control. Go into the unseen and the Archontic Reptilian force which feeds off human fear and other low-vibrational emotion and the act of war *itself* becomes the most important thing. There will be an ideal Archontic sequence of war in the seen to divide and rule the population and absorb land, resources and freedom, but the prime focus is that war and conflict of *any kind* keep happening to energetically feed the beast through the human emotional response. Continual war and conflict are themselves the main priority to the Archontic distortion. What are they fighting about? We don't really care so long as they are fighting. What are they in fear about? We don't really care so long as they are in fear. World events can only be understood in their true light when people know that what is happening in the seen is being orchestrated from the unseen.

## Hunger Games Society

The world of the seen becomes an open book once we answer two questions: Where are we being taken and what are the psychological techniques that take us there? I have already answered question number two with Problem-Reaction-Solution and the Totalitarian Tiptoe. There are other mind games to confuse and manipulate the collective perception of events, but these are the twin pillars of what is a global psychiatric program targeting the human psyche. A few people can't control the many 'physically' and this has to be done by controlling minds and perceptions of reality. So now to question one: Where are we being taken? I refer to this long-planned Brave New World as the Hunger Games Society after the movie series that portrayed a dystopia in which a tiny few mega-rich people employed a vicious and merciless police/military state to impose their will upon a poverty-stricken population maintained in ongoing inter-generational slavery. This describes the structure of a global society that is clearly being installed by the day (Fig 443). The plan is for the one percent to control everything with virtually the entire human

**Figure 443:** The structure of what I call the Hunger Games Society.

race enslaved by total
dependency for the basics of
survival and by the
police/military control system
which is now being installed
across the world justified to a
large part by 'protecting the
people from terrorism'. This is
the same terrorism
orchestrated by the same
networks that then say our

**Figure 444:** Archontic Reptilian calling card – no empathy.

freedoms have to be deleted to save us from terrorists they control, arm
and fund – Problem-Reaction-Solution. There are planned to be only
three basic levels of 'human' society – the one percent, those serving
them in the police/military control structure, and everyone else
enslaved in poverty and dependency. Official contempt for the poor and
destitute is an example of the assault on the 99 percent by the one
percent and their enforcement arms. People are made homeless while
laws make it illegal to sleep rough; feeding the homeless is illegal in
some cities and caring people are arrested for doing that; a student was
investigated for giving free haircuts to the homeless 'without a licence'
(Fig 444). I could fill the book with examples of such official
inhumanities. If you think that none of this applies to you because you
are currently one of the economic 'winners' with a nice house, car and
money in the bank I would advise that you think again. The one percent
and its controlling *less*-than-one-percent want everyone's wealth and
assets. If you are not one of them this includes *you* no matter what you
may think you own today. There are already many who had nice homes
and well-paid jobs now living in America's tent cities. Government after
government is taking money directly from people's bank accounts using
various excuses and Greek Finance Ministry inspectors are amending
the law to allow for financial assets and contents of safe deposit boxes to
be confiscated. Then there is the bail-in scam when they steal depositors'
money to 'save' the banks they have purposely crashed. This is a major
way they plan to steal wealth in the wake of a financial collapse that
would make the one in 2008 look like a small deal. I am sure the
derivatives market will play a key part in this when it is revealed at the
most effective moment that a market supposedly worth hundreds of
trillions is actually founded on fresh air. The state stealing of people's
money and assets is becoming quite a theme given that in 2014 law
(lawless) enforcement seized more property from Americans than
burglars did – $5 billion worth as against $3.5 million. They are doing
this through 'civil asset forfeiture' laws that allow property to be taken
and kept by police without any charges or proof that any crime

whatsoever has taken place. The onus is then on the target to prove they are not criminals or planning to be to get their property returned. This robbery by the state is rising rapidly with Trump Attorney General Jeff Sessions pledging to make it easier for police to seize property without evidence of a crime.

The frenzy of credit card debt (all callously-manipulated) is leading multitudes of people to the financial abyss. A survey by Northwestern Mutual in 2017 indicated that 45 percent of Americans use half their monthly pay to service debt and this is *excluding* mortgage debt. We already have a mega-rich one percent owning 50 percent of the wealth and the world's wealthiest 62 people worth the same as the poorest *half* of the human population combined by early 2016. This 62 figure has since plummeted as wealth and control of resources are further concentrated year by year even within the one percent and 2017 studies put the number as low as *five or six* – Bill Gates (Microsoft), Mark Zuckerberg (Facebook), Jeff Bezos (Amazon), Warren Buffet (Berkshire Hathaway investments), Amancio Ortega (fashion and real estate) and Carlos Slim Helu (Latin America telecom). The top five each has the wealth equivalent to 750 million people. Corporations owned by the less-than-one percent are seizing control of the global economy with, for example, nearly one dollar in every two that Americans spend online going to Amazon and four pounds in every ten in the UK. Amazon continues to increase its domination and range of products to force out of business ever-more competitors across the entire spectrum of human economic activity. Fairness, sharing and leaving something for others is not in the Amazon vocabulary because Bezos wants it all – a full-blown global monopoly on almost everything you buy and straight from the script being followed by Google and Facebook in their areas of operation. Amazon has even patented a system that would stop customers in its stores checking out prices at other outlets on their phones. These people are utterly ruthless. Bezos is reportedly known for his rages and frequent tantrums and was named the World's Worst Boss by the International Trade Union Confederation in 2014. Fifty-one of the 100 biggest economies are now corporations and not countries. The largest 200 corporations are worth more than 182 countries combined and 147 corporations account for 40 percent of global trade. Once again this concentration of power is increasing by the day helped by international 'trade agreements' that are nothing more than the legally-binding transfer of power from governments to corporations which allow governments (the people) to be subject to massive fines if they pass laws that corporations say are harmful to their profits. Whether such laws are beneficial to the population or the environment is irrelevant to this fascism. Profits (*control*) is all that matters. They are, after all, Archontic Reptilian satanic psychopaths who are so empathy-deleted that they can sacrifice children, destroy lives at will and pepper-bomb civilians without even a smear of emotional consequence.

The Hunger Games Society structure is founded on a world government that would dictate globally to every community (Fig 445). By 'government' I don't even mean elected government. This would be run by unelected appointees and those appointed by appointees in the manner of the European Union where major decisions affecting the lives of hundreds of millions are made by dark suit bureaucrats who run the EU as their own personal fiefdom while answering to their hidden masters. The joke of a 'European Parliament' (appropriately in another country to the EU bureaucratic Commission) is only there to exercise illusory power and allow the EU to be called 'democratic' while operating as a bureaucratic, financial and legal dictatorship. The 'world government' would operate in the same way as a bureaucratic global tyranny. We already have de facto world government being introduced via the Totalitarian Tiptoe in the form of the United Nations Security Council and the 'G' numbers – G7, G8, G20 and whatever they come up with next. World government-in-waiting is also referred to as 'the international community', and there is an annual World Government Summit exploring and promoting global governance. I have been highlighting the world government agenda since *Robots' Rebellion* in 1993 and here they are now openly advocating just that. Society-transforming events are random? Not a chance. Britain and France are among five permanent members of the UN Security Council along with the United States, Russia and China deciding among many other things who shall and shall not be bombed by usually the United States, Britain and NATO although the US often ignores the UN and does it anyway. How can Britain and France with the 21st and 22nd biggest populations

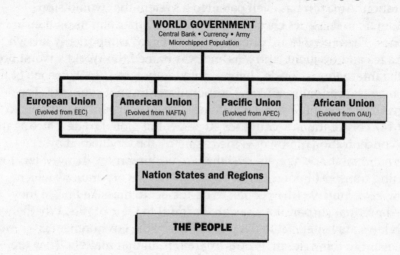

**Figure 445:** The world government hierarchy of the Hunger Games Society.

have a permanent place on such a body? This is because of their position in the hierarchy of the global Web and nothing to do with the size of the countries. World government would control all finance through a world central bank imposing its will through subordinate levels already being moved into place like the European Central Bank (ECB). There would be only one global electronic currency and cash would be eliminated. I have been warning about the cashless society since the early 1990s and now cash is being deleted at an ever-quickening speed. Some countries are already virtually cashless and credit card giant Visa has begun *paying* businesses to stop taking coins and notes (so hitting those without cards or smartphones, usually the elderly, but what does Visa care?). The International Monetary Fund (IMF) published advice to governments on how to delete cash and what they suggest is happening:

> *Although some countries most likely will de-cash in a few years, going completely cashless should be phased in steps. The de-cashing process could build on the initial and largely uncontested steps, such as the phasing out of large denomination bills, the placement of ceilings on cash transactions, and the reporting of cash moves across the borders.*

> *Further steps could include creating economic incentives to reduce the use of cash in transactions, simplifying the opening and use of transferrable deposits, and further computerizing the financial system.*

It's vintage Totalitarian Tiptoe. A cashless world is all about control and surveillance, but ignorance of the real agenda behind the deletion of cash is the reason why surveys suggest that a third of Europeans would be happy to go cashless. Not if they knew the consequences they wouldn't. A cashless world means that you would not be able to purchase anything that The System didn't know about immediately. Barter would be banned on the grounds that it can't be taxed and anyone who resisted, challenged and exposed the authorities would have their access to money deleted by a simple click, click, enter. Cash you can hold in your hand is a bulwark against total financial control and that is why it is disappearing. 'Oh, but it's so convenient just to swish my smartphone.' What do people think they are going to do – make it *in*convenient to be enslaved??

The next level of control under the world government would be a series of superstates – mirrors of the EU – with once-sovereign countries dismantled and replaced by smaller regions to dilute any unity of response to this edifice of oppression and imposition. The System and its agents and sycophants were so shocked by a majority in the UK voting to withdraw from the EU in the 2016 Brexit Referendum because it goes against the plan. Brussels bureaucrats and their agents, system-servers and clueless progressives in Britain are doing everything they can to thwart Brexit and make it as difficult as possible to leave as a warning to anyone else that wants to follow as great numbers of Europeans would like to do. EU controllers want to absorb more and more countries not have anyone leaving. What a sight to see progressives so ignorant of what is happening

**Figure 446:** How dare you useless old people get us out of jail?

and so in the thrall of cognitive dissonance (believing that two contradictory opposites are both true) that they can talk about freedom and democracy while campaigning for 66 million British people to have the fine detail of their lives decided in another country by unelected bureaucrats they can't even name (Fig 446). Jean-Claude Juncker, President of the European Commission (unelected bureaucrats), has many times been accused of being drunk on duty and videos can be seen on the Internet of him clearly so. He has been referred to as Jean-Claude Drunker and Jean-Claude Junket. A diplomat quoted in the media accused him of being 'very visibly pissed' during EU talks over Cyprus and being 'very familiar' with young aides to the point of embarrassment for onlookers. His behaviour was described as 'strange', but not so strange if you are pissed. I just put 'Jean-Claude Juncker' into a search engine and the second phrase offered after his name was 'Jean-Claude Juncker drunk'. *I know what* – let's give him power over the lives of more than 500 million people, shall we?

There was an obvious sleight-of-hand in the 2017 British General Election to dilute Brexit and maintain EU bureaucratic control of the UK. Prime Minister Theresa May of the Conservative Party had said again and again that she would not be calling an election until she had to by law and by then negotiations to leave the EU would have been completed. She had a big enough majority in Parliament to have the triggering of Article 50 agreed that began the negotiations and they were weeks away from starting. Then, out of nowhere, May announced a General Election on the grounds that she needed a bigger majority to give her more power in the negotiations. Opinion polls suggested that she would achieve this, but what followed can only be described as one of the worst election campaigns by any major party in British political history and included a suicide-note manifesto financially targeting the very core Conservative Party vote that May needed to win her majority. If she had set out to lose she would have run the same campaign. She clung on as the biggest party, but lost her majority which gave a 'progressive alliance', most of which doesn't want Brexit at all, the chance to stop the full withdrawal from EU control that the public voted for in the 2016 referendum. Staying in the single European trading market or what is called a 'soft Brexit' would still involve EU bureaucratic control even if the UK officially ceased to be an EU member. This is the most that the progressive alliance would agree to and if so this would reduce Brexit to little more than window dressing. Some members of the main opposition Labour Party have indicated that they would support May in a full withdrawal ('hard Brexit') and we'll see what happens but the Theresa May election debacle when Brexit was on course stinks to high heaven. Decisions were taken by a tiny group around May without consulting the wider party and it was reported that she had been urged several times by Eurocrat Jean-Claude Juncker to call a snap election to secure a bigger majority and more power in the EU exit negotiations – the last thing he wanted her to have. If what he said played any part in May's decision the scale of naivety alone should bar her from running a country. Like I say, the whole thing stinks. At the same time most of the EU-worshipping progressives go on protests against globalisation and trade agreements giving power to corporations when that agenda is being driven by the same global cabal driving the constant centralisation of bureaucratic power in the EU. There are *30,000* lobbyists in Brussels (roughly equal to the EU bureaucracy) representing some of the world's biggest corporate names and they are estimated to influence some 75 percent of EU legislation on the road to global corporate domination through *globalisation*. Shakes head again, breathes deeply, and continues on. Arrogance of ignorance does not begin to describe the scale of ignorance, stupidity, hypocrisy and self-delusion. Such is the child-like bewilderment of the 'progressive', black-and-white PC mind which has convinced itself that anyone who doesn't want to be centrally-controlled by bureaucrats or have their country unable to decide the scale of immigration must by definition be racist and thus unworthy of further debate or consideration; and, in the eyes of some PC progressive extremists, they should not even have a right to vote. It is a form of mental illness in which you are so psychologically imbalanced that you act like a fascist but self-identify as a freedom-loving liberal.

## World Army NATO

The will of the world government dictatorship is planned to be imposed by a world army with all national militaries disbanded and their personnel and resources handed over to control by the global network in which ultimately there would be one combined and centrally-controlled military and police organisation responsible for all law enforcement whether foreign or domestic. Indeed, this is meant to be eventually a technological world military/police force controlled by artificial intelligence, but I will come to that later. The United States and NATO (the United States) are the stalking horses for the world army to be introduced through the Totalitarian Tiptoe and the United Nations peacekeeping operation and any EU army are also destined for absorption into the world army structure. The US spends more on the military than the next ten countries combined (Fig 447). Russia is way behind and yet they are supposed to be a threat to the world while the most trigger-happy country on earth spends *at least* a trillion dollars-plus a year on the military (hidden costs included) while constantly claiming to be under threat from someone or other. Terrify the population with lots of make-believe 'enemies' and they'll accept that their

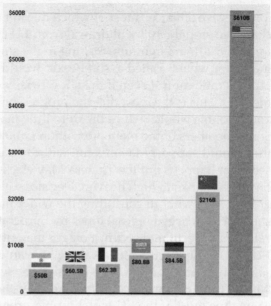

**Figure 447:** US military spending compared with the rest of the world. Russia is a very distant third close to that of Saudi Arabia.

**Figure 448:** The global command structure of the United States military awaiting handover to the world army.

government spends trillions on the military while people are hungry and live on the street. The US military now operates in 147 countries out of 196 and has divided the world into different 'Coms' or commands (Fig 448). There is NORTHCOM, SOUTHCOM, EUCOM, CENTCOM, AFRICOM AND PACOM. The arrogance of this is beyond belief, but the

**Figure 449:** NATO – the biggest terrorist organisation on Earth along with partners America and Britain.

point is that this structure is not ultimately for the US military. These are structural divisions preparing for the world army to take over. Alongside this we have US-controlled NATO which is the major grouping in the world-army-in-waiting. I said in ... *And The Truth Shall Set You Free*, written in 1994, that we should watch for NATO expanding its operations outside the North Atlantic region for which its creation had been justified to stop the 'Soviet threat' to the West during the manufactured Cold War. The NATO killing machine (the North Atlantic Terrorist Organisation) has since bombed the innocent in Libya and operates around the world including Afghanistan, Africa, the Mediterranean and Kosovo over which it bombed the innocent in Serbia at the end of the 1990s at a time when Kosovo was part of Serbia in what remained of the former Yugoslavia (Fig 449). I spoke in Serbia in 2017 and I met a man struggling along on crutches who had his legs blown off by a NATO attack on Belgrade in the conflict promoted by war criminals Bill Clinton and Tony Blair. A Serbian legal team is suing NATO for the illegal use of between 10 and 15 tons of depleted uranium during the bombing campaign which created a human and environmental disaster. Serbian lawyer Srdjan Aleksic, who leads the legal team, said the use of banned

**Figure 450:** The hypocrisy is breathtaking.

weapons was a violation of all international conventions and rules that protect people. 'We expect the members of NATO to provide treatment to our citizens who are suffering from cancer,' Aleksic said, and NATO must 'provide the necessary technology and equipment to remove all traces of the depleted uranium from Serbia'. It's just another day in NATO's sick history (Fig 450). What has happened in Kosovo, Serbia and the rest of the Balkans is a great example of how the Hidden Hand works and secures recruits for its NATO world army and European Union. The US-UK-NATO alliance of pure evil funded and armed the 'Kosovo Liberation Army' (KLA), a bunch of terrorists supported by Albania which is 100 percent owned by the United States.

When Serbia and Montenegro responded to KLA attacks Clinton, Blair and NATO justified the bombing of Belgrade and elsewhere to 'protect the people' (see Libya, Syria, and so on). European officers who served with the international peace-keeping force in Kosovo later confirmed to the media that the CIA was behind the Kosovo 'Liberation' Army and encouraged the 'rebellion' in southern Serbia to target then Yugoslav President Slobodan Milosevic. The break-up of the former Yugoslavia and Soviet Union was connected to the world army agenda and that of the European Union. The plan was to divide those groupings into constituent countries and then absorb them into NATO and the EU. This is what has happened and continues to happen. The speed with which those countries left Eastern communism to be absorbed by Western communism and fascism says it all. There were mass protests, while I was in Belgrade, in neighbouring Montenegro after the parliament without consulting the people voted to join NATO – the organisation that bombed the country less than 20 years before. Talk about insensitive, but the Archontic political class answers to other masters and not the public. US-worshipping Prime Minister Dusko Markovic officially led Montenegro into NATO in June 2017 in a ceremony in Washington DC and with that NATO added to its armoury just 1,950 military personnel, 13 helicopters, two frigates and three patrol ships. This was about NATO entering Montenegro and not the other way round and secured control of virtually the entire coastline both sides of the Adriatic. Mendacious Markovic said: 'It is a historic event for a country and a nation which endured enormous sacrifices in the 19th and 20th centuries in order to defend their right to a free life, the right to decide our own future, recognised by the world under our own name, and with our own national symbols.' Those words were spoken by a man who had given military control of his country to a power that so recently bombed his people and while preparing to join the EU that will strip Montenegro of every right to decide its own future. Simply incredible, but that's the scale of progressive self-delusion.

The United States is using Albanians and its Albanian puppet government (a member of NATO) to infiltrate northwards into the other countries of the Balkans to take them over politically (Fig 451). Once this influence is strong

**Figure 451:** The NATO and EU takeover of the Balkans which was the whole point of manipulating the break-up of the former Yugoslavia.

enough they will press for the country to join NATO and the EU. German lawmakers have warned about the spread of Saudi Arabian Wahhabism (Sabbatean Frankism) in Kosovo under the eyes of UN 'peacekeepers' and this all makes sense. The manipulation networks of Web bagman George Soros are heavily involved throughout the Balkans, as they were in the overthrow of Slobodan Milosevic in Serbia and are currently in the political turmoil involving ethnic Albanians and Soros-funded progressives in Macedonia. Soros-funded activists are known as 'Sorosoids' in Macedonia and one commentator said that, 'Soros came into Macedonia like a Trojan horse, and now he is an octopus'. The same story can be told wherever he operates – which seems to be everywhere – as he uses money to influence and control progressives, the wider Left and the media. Leaked documents from his Open Society Foundations reveal how Zionist Soros, an *American* citizen, has spent big money to stop populist candidates and anti-EU movements in Europe by funding some 100 organisations across 28 countries with sums of between $10,000 and $350,000. Populism is being demonised to protect the progressive agenda because this is the dictionary definition: 'Any of various, often anti-establishment or anti-intellectual political movements or philosophies that offer unorthodox solutions or policies and appeal to the common person rather than according with traditional party or partisan ideologies.' This is why people like Soros and everything he represents want to destroy populist movements whether of the Left or Right, and why the Pope has come out in condemnation of populism (Fig 452). 'Jesus' may have been a mythical figure, but if you take the story literally as the Pope is supposed to do then he was heading a populist movement. Soros was exposed for secretly paying the salaries of three key aides to then-Moldovan Prime Minister Lurie Leancă, starting in 2013, and overcame Moldovan laws by directing the money through a non-profit organisation in Germany. Albanian Prime Minister Edi Rama hired Tony Blair as an advisor to try to get them into the EU. The disgusting Alastair Campbell, Blair's spin doctor who co-produced the 'dodgy dossier' that lied about weapons of mass destruction in Iraq, also advised Rama's socialist party on its way to power. Apparently Albania loves Blair for supporting the Kosovo Liberation Army by bombing Belgrade and other targets. Croatia, Slovenia, Slovakia, Romania and Bulgaria have already joined both NATO and the EU. This has happened in the states of the former Soviet

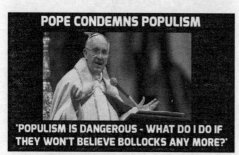

**Figure 452:** Pope's don't just support the global Establishment – they are a major pillar of it.

Union with countries like Poland, Estonia, Lithuania, Latvia, Czech Republic and Hungary. Others are in the process of doing so, in both the Balkans and former Soviet Union. Serbian people are holding out against NATO and EU membership so far but current president Aleksandra Vučić wants to join both if the truth be told, and the prime minister he appointed, Ana Brnabić, Serbia's first woman and openly gay prime minister, said her priorities were membership of the European Union and 'modernisation', which means the classic progressive 'centrist' extremism that is taking over the world. They want you to focus on Trump, the hate-figure of progressives, so we won't notice that it is progressives (not liberals) who are holding power in country after country. The UK and US-educated Brnabić said the EU represented the 'values we stand for'. Wow, now the EU and 'values' in the same sentence – collector's item. Aleksandra Vučić has such contempt for Serbians that he, too, hired Blair as an 'advisor', with Campbell thrown in, to help him secure Serbia's place in the EU. The deal was paid for, apparently bizarrely, by the fake royals of the United Arab Emirates (the Web) with the fortune they make from stealing the country's oil resources from the people. Vučić once again hired Blair less than two decades after he was a leading proponent of bombing Belgrade and a Serbian government in which Vučić was a minister. The lack of principle by Vučić or respect for Serbians who took the consequences is astounding. He claims to have won 58 percent of the vote to become president but during a week in Belgrade I met nobody who voted for him and only one person who knew anyone who had.

## Military police (literally)

The plan is for the world army to absorb all domestic police into one military/police structure and the emergence of this is clear in the United States where the Pentagon has been transferring military vehicles and technology to even county police forces for either nothing or next to nothing through its 1033 program. We now have police driving through the community in tanks and the difference in clothing and weaponry between police and military is fast disappearing (Figs 453 and 454). Potentially lethal Tasers and very lethal hand and machine guns are becoming standard issue and commonplace, as manufactured terrorism and the fear of terrorism is exploited to

**Figure 453:** Traffic patrol in the Brave New World.

YEP - IT SAYS 'POLICE'

**Figure 454:** The plan is to fuse the police and military into one global control system and this is why police officers are increasingly looking like troops.

manipulate the population to accept lethally-armed police officers and a surveillance state. Public events in the UK are teeming with armed police in military-type uniforms since the terror attack at the Manchester concert venue in 2017 and others. Police increasingly look and act like the military because the plan is to eventually fuse them into one. Militarised police worldwide are overseeing an emerging police state underpinned by now extreme levels of surveillance and control with far more to come, and by the systematic recruitment of psychopathic people of strictly limited intelligence. What a nightmare police work must be today for those remaining genuine officers who still want to do the job with integrity and balance. Surveillance technology allows the authorities to track almost everything we do and pretty soon you can forget the 'almost'. As I write, the British government is preparing new laws in conjunction with O2, BT, BSkyB, Cable and Wireless, Vodafone, Virgin Media and interception agencies to impose a massive increase in surveillance even beyond the enormity of state tracking already in place. Communication companies would be legally responsible for giving the government and its agencies real-time access to content from a named person within a single working day and other 'secondary information'. They would also have to remove any encryption. Electronic communication means that nothing you do is private any longer as revelations by WikiLeaks and former insiders like Edward Snowden have shown, and even then this is only part of the picture. Compartmentalisation of knowledge means that insiders only see some levels of the Big Brother apparatus and nothing like all. It is good that whistleblowers do what they do because we need to know, but people shouldn't kid themselves that what is called the Deep State isn't quite happy for the scale of its surveillance reach to be made public. Many studies confirm that when people know they can be watched and whatever they do electronically is retrievable they begin to censor *themselves*. This is the holy grail of state control when people stop doing things out of fear of being caught doing things. The more the state reveals the scale of surveillance the more self-censorship will follow if people don't have the backbone to challenge The System and not let fear freeze them into acquiescence. Drones, including armed drones, are the next level of control, and surveillance along with highly-sophisticated tracking techniques that involve phone apps that pick up high-frequency tones undetectable by the human ear broadcast by websites, radio and television broadcasts, advertisements, even shops and sports stadiums. This information can build up a profile of your life.

Satellites are counting albatrosses from space so you can appreciate the scale and detail they can track and record about human activity. Holographic versions of homes and wider areas are being created using Wi-Fi transmissions. Friedemann Reinhard, director of the Emmy Noether Research Group for Quantum Sensors at the Technical University of Munich, said: 'Using this technology, we can generate a three-dimensional image of the space around the Wi-Fi transmitter, as if our eyes could see microwave radiation.' This is one reason why they want Wi-Fi and smart meters in every home and everywhere else, although there are many others. The holographic technology would potentially allow real-time surveillance of private space. Documents made public through WikiLeaks reveal how the CIA uses a system it calls 'Archimedes' to redirect traffic from computers to an 'exploitation server' controlled by the CIA. Deeply untrustworthy former FBI Chief James Comey told a cybersecurity conference there is no such thing as privacy in America and people should accept that their conversations and communications may not remain private. 'There is no place outside of judicial reach', he said. The term 'judicial' is thoroughly disingenuous in an attempt to indicate some judicial oversight when in fact these agencies do what they like. The Director of US National Intelligence reported that in 2016 alone 151 million phone records were traced and that is only what they are admitting to. Comey's speech was an example of an ongoing campaign to normalise Big Brother as just part of life and the way things are and have to be. Children are being conditioned to accept all this as normal by the cameras, fingerprint and iris scanning technology used in schools which increasingly resemble the prisons that they are (Fig 455). I was born in 1952 and I have the filter of knowing

**Figure 455:** Schools are preparing children to accept constant surveillance and authoritarian control as 'normal'.

how things were before the surveillance society began in earnest. Young people today have only known surveillance schools, cities and communities and familiarity can induce a sense of 'normality' for impositions that are anything but normal. We need to keep emphasising this at every opportunity. Tracking where people go on the Internet, what they do in their own homes through Smart TVs, smartphones, smart meters, technological 'office assistants' and anything connected to the Internet (even toys), and knowing wherever you go through surveillance cameras, drones, phones, tablets, watches and microchips is *not normal*. It is outrageous, unnecessary and insane. We are told this is to protect us from terrorism but this is an obvious lie. We are seeing every day the installation of the police/military apparatus and structure for the Hunger Games Society which is designed to impose the will of the one percent on the rest of humanity. Well, in part it is. We need to keep in mind that the one percent and the global Web are only conduits for who is really orchestrating this monstrous level of human control – the Archontic Reptilian manipulators pulling the strings from the hidden realms.

## Owning the world

The *El*-ite in the *Hunger Games* movie series lived in isolation from their slave population protected by the police/military complex. Today there are enormous cities underground and within mountains where the *El*-ite plan to shelter until the people are brought to heel by their military with much of it controlled from hidden locations through artificial intelligence. Human slaves in *The Hunger Games* were divided into sectors which were unable to mix and converse and those that have minds to see will observe how the same pieces are being moved into place. These sectors specialised in particular areas of production to serve the *El*-ite in the 'Capitol' and that was the plan from the start with the European Union as I have explained in detail in other books. The UK, for example, secretly agreed to specialise in finance and services and run down fishing, steel, coal and manufacturing industries when Britain joined what is now the EU under paedophile, Satanist and serial child killer, Prime Minister Edward 'black eyes' Heath. This is what has happened in the more than four decades since. I have featured at length in my last book *Phantom Self* the extremely accurate predictions in 1969 of Dr Richard Day, a Rockefeller family insider and Planned Parenthood executive. He described how the new global system would involve countries losing their self-sufficiency to specialise in only certain areas. Day was speaking at a conference of paediatricians in Pittsburgh, Pennsylvania, and stunned his audience by asking them to turn off recording equipment and not to take notes while he told them how the world was going to change. No one seems to know why he did this, but I'm glad he did because it gives us a greater understanding of how long this transformation of human society has been in the planning along with other 'prophetic' (knowing the plan) examples such as Orwell's *Nineteen-Eighty-Four* and Huxley's *Brave New World*. One doctor that night, Lawrence Dunegan, did keep notes and gave a series of interviews before he died in 2004 detailing what Day had said. Among his predictions was a description of the World Wide Web 20 years before it was officially invented and Smart TVs some 40 years before they were introduced. George Orwell described them in 1948 and called them Telescreens that could film and monitor people in their own homes. Current Smart TVs are only the first versions and Web giant Samsung has already announced a new ultrathin Smart TV called 'The Frame' which never turns off and has an 'art mode' which makes it appear as a painting on the wall – one that is watching you. Richard Day said this of the new world economic and commercial system as reported by Dr Lawrence Dunegan:

> *The stated plan was that different parts of the world would be assigned different roles of industry and commerce in a unified global system. The continued pre-eminence of the United States and the relative independence and self-sufficiency of the United States would have to be changed.*

This has been done through massive outsourcing of manufacturing and so much else from the United States and Europe to other countries where sweatshop labour can be exploited. This has so suppressed the jobs market and incomes in the West – as with mass immigration – that sweatshop labour has been imported to the West as the human race in general enters a downward spiral to the Hunger Games Society. Increasing unemployment, homelessness, lower wages and zero hours contracts, where employers do not have to provide minimum working hours and only call on staff (and so pay them) when they choose, are all connected with this. The number of food banks in Britain for those who can't afford to feed themselves and their families has risen to more than 2,000 with demand for emergency food parcels growing for the ninth successive year. This process is now being accelerated by the mass replacement of work opportunities worldwide by robots and artificial intelligence which has only just begun but will increase dramatically from here. Donald Trump sold himself to the electorate as the man to reverse outsourcing when that was never going to be allowed to happen except cosmetically here and there to hide the truth that no such major reversal is taking place. Centralisation of global power with supranational groupings and gigantic corporations means that while countries lose self-sufficiency through specialisation and become dependent on forces over which they have no control, those at the global centre can direct and dictate the entire system. This is the role of the world government and its world central bank with their decisions imposed by the world army. Rothschild-Rockefeller *El*-ite creations such as the World Trade Organization, World Health Organization and others are part of the preparation for every subject area to be globally controlled under one roof and their will enforced on every man, woman

and child. This is not some out-of-the-ether prediction. It is *happening*.
The deluge of regulation and law that is forcing so many small and
medium-sized companies out of business – not least in the EU – is being
imposed to that very end. There would only be giant corporations in the
Hunger Games Society and everything else would be deleted by then.
Globalisation is not an accident; it is essential to the tiny few controlling
the very many. Humans once lived in tribes which decided their own
direction and methods of operation. Then the tribes were brought
together into nations and many tribes were centrally controlled. Now we
have moved on to superstates like the EU and global bodies centrally-
controlling nations, and it's all been Archontically-orchestrated from the
unseen. Each new centralisation gives the few more control over the
many and they then use that power to centralise even quicker. Hence the
pace of globalisation has got faster and faster. Another aspect of
increasing corporate control is for governments owned by corporations
to sell them public assets for well below the market price as we have
seen again and again in the United Kingdom and across the world. This
is explained away as incompetence, but it's not. Greece alone has been
asset-stripped by corporations in the wake of an economic collapse
caused by merciless corporate banks (see Goldman Sachs), the IMF and
the EU with its 30,000 corporate lobbyists surrounding the EU
Commission in Brussels. Austerity package follows austerity package to
qualify for new 'bail-outs' that Greece can never pay back and, while the
pathetic government of Alexis Tsipras capitulates without a murmur,
people go hungry and die. All this is empathy-deleted Sabbatean
Frankism and Satanism encapsulated.

## Political 'choice' – the sick joke

To bring about this step-by-step transformation to global tyranny you
must control political decision-making. This would seem to be a big
problem given the different political parties that people could
potentially vote into power, but it's not really a problem once you have
political and financial structures in place which are almost certain to
deliver who you want or restrict the possibilities for real change of those
rare few elected to high office that you don't want. We return to the
theme of pseudo-randomness in which 'different' is just another word
for 'same'. There may be many political parties, but the crucial point is
that in almost every country only two, maybe three, have any chance of
forming a government and it's the *government* that makes the law and
changes society. You vote for party A and they get into government. You
don't like what they do and so you vote for party B. You don't like what
they do and the only way you can get rid of them is to vote again for
party A. This is what is known as political 'choice', 'democracy' and
'freedom'. Add to this the fact that leading parties (and most of the

smaller ones) are manipulated in the background by the same Archontic force and the myth of political choice becomes even more laughable. The Left-Right political to and fro is literally an electromagnetic wave system that makes both 'sides' or polarities dependent on each other and creates a standing wave that doesn't change (Figs 456). I said earlier that standing or stationary waves are produced whenever two waves of identical frequency interfere with each other while traveling in opposite directions along the same medium. They combine

**Figure 456:** Politics is literally an electrical and oscillation system that forms standing waves between its polarities and so jogs on the spot getting nowhere.

to create a wave that vibrates in the same position, like jogging on the spot, and looks like the double helix of DNA. What a great description of never-changing party politics or political DNA and this is a waveform/holographic version of the standing wave construct of the simulation itself (as above, so below). Even most genuine politicians are vibrated into line through daily experience of the oscillating waves pulsing to the frequency of the 'political system' and turning its parts (politicians) into expressions of itself – 'I knew that guy when he went into politics and he's now everything he said he opposed.'

When I spoke in Ukraine in 2011 the president was Viktor Yanukovych. He had been thrown out of office for alleged corruption in the 'Orange Revolution' in 2004, but when the people didn't like the new chap either they could only replace him with the other party that could win an election and this was still led by ... *Viktor Yanukovych*. They voted back in the man ejected in a revolution because that was the only 'choice' offered by the rigged system. He was then thrown out again in the US-led coup, sorry 'people's revolution', in Ukraine in 2014. There is no need to control all political parties although they mainly do. What really matters are the two or three who can potentially form a government. Nor do you have to control everyone in a party, only those that decide its stance and direction. They don't even necessarily in every case have to be knowingly doing what you want. They can be persuaded or selected on the basis that what *they* want is what *you* want. British Prime Minister Margaret Thatcher was brought to power because her economic philosophy called Thatcherism was what the Hidden Hand wanted during the 1980s to transfer wealth and assets from public ownership to private *El*-ite ownership. Was it really by pure coincidence that in the same period Ronald Reagan became President of the United

States and introduced a mirror image of Thatcher's policy dubbed 'Reaganomics'? World leaders are just puppets that can be anything from in-the-know (the few) to those doing whatever it takes to secure and retain political power for its own sake (the many) to complete idiots being controlled by their 'advisors' (depressingly many). Real power knowingly connected to the Archontic Reptilian Spider does not put itself on public display where it can be identified and targeted. Politics has its own Postage Stamp Consensus which means that all but a tiny few see the world pretty much the same way. Some may want more tax, some less, some more money for the poor, some less, but the foundations are the same. For example, banks control events far more than governments with the global power that comes from lending people money that doesn't exist (credit) and charging interest on it; but where is a political party with any chance of forming a government calling for an end of charging interest on fresh-air money and for government to create the currency interest-free instead of allowing banks to issue money as a debt from the outset by making loans of fresh-air credit? Why aren't even smaller parties calling for that? The only one I have personally come across is the Human Shield Party (Zivi zid or 'Living Wall') in Croatia which came into being and won seats in parliament after reading the information in my books. I asked a UK Green Party candidate about their policy on banks creating money out of nothing and she had no idea what I was talking about. Most politicians don't know how the banking system works and the few that do know haven't got the guts or desire to challenge it. Unless corporate banks are prevented from creating the currency as an interest-bearing debt nothing any politician does will ultimately make any difference because economic control is not with them but the bankers (the Archontic Web that controls the bankers).

## Political 'royalty'

Political parties were created after people began to reject in-your-face dictatorship by royal bloodlines. The *El*-ite then hid the bloodline behind dark suits and terms like politician, CEO, bank executive, media owner and so on. This way they could go on controlling everything while the target population believed they were now free to decide who ran their country. The illusion of freedom is a much more powerful means of ongoing control than knowing you are in an open dictatorship. People at some point will rebel against a tyranny they can see, but you don't rebel against not being free when you think you are. Political parties are an *El*-ite scam. Focus on parties negates the individual whether they have positive intent or otherwise. Someone of intelligence and integrity will not get voted into parliament or Congress unless they are in the right party in the right constituency or state. Most people don't vote for the person but the party. The colour of the rosette is all that matters. Corrupt and contemptible people are voted into power so long as they are in the right party in the right constituency or state. This hands control of political personnel to those who run the parties and ultimately to that which controls those who control the parties. To be elected you have to be chosen to stand by a party that can win. To be selected you have to tell the party hierarchy what it wants to hear and 'toe the party line' as dictated by that hierarchy. Once elected you have to continue to do what the party hierarchy demands or you will have no chance of being chosen for government office. They who control the party therefore control those within the party. The next level is the one that hands game, set and match to the *El*-ite. Every major political party has an inner circle that picks leaders and directs policy. The US Republican Party under Boy George Bush was controlled by a Zionist-created grouping that the media called Neocons or neoconservatives, which included behind-the-scenes manipulators like Robert Kagan, William Kristol and Richard Perle and those in government such as Vice-President Dick Cheney, Defense Secretary Donald Rumsfeld, Deputy Defense Secretary Paul Wolfowitz and Doug Zakheim, who was Comptroller of the Pentagon in charge of its entire budget. These were the players controlling Bush and I will come back to them in the next chapter with regard to 9/11 and the

'war on [of] terror'. The Democratic Party has a similar group that I call the Democons and this has included Rothschild bagman George Soros, the Clintons and former Jimmy Carter National Security Advisor Zbigniew Brzezinski who died in May 2017. Democons controlled Barack Obama in his eight years as president and the party apparatus ensured – as WikiLeaks documents show – that Hillary Clinton won the nomination to run for president in 2016 and not the more popular Bernie Sanders. Major *El*-ite assets move between the two parties as presidential 'advisors' as we have seen with 'Republican' Secretary of State and ultra-Zionist Henry Kissinger who has been an advisor to George Bush (Republican), Barack Obama (Democrat) and Donald Trump

**Figure 457:** Why nothing changes and the same incessant direction continues no matter which 'party' is in illusory power. Those in the shadows are *always* in power.
© www.neilhague.com

(Republican or whatever he decides to be tomorrow). Now here is what people crucially need to know: Take one step further back into the shadows and both Neocons and Democons are controlled by the *same* (Archontic) force via Sabbatean Frankists and other Web assets in both groups (Fig 457). No matter who is in the White House or what party they claim to represent that same force is always in power. Mark Twain said: 'If voting made any difference they wouldn't let us do it.' Direction never changes with centralisation of power, war, advancing the Big Brother state and crushing the poor to serve the rich. This happens whoever is in power because the hidden force always in control demands it (Fig 458).

**Figure 458:** The self-delusion of Left-Right politics.

They try to hide this with rhetoric and image to give the impression that potential political leaders are different and offer a genuine choice and this was never so obvious than when Obama campaigned to replace Bush and claimed every 60 seconds that he was about 'change'. The term is often used by politicians because most people are sick of their status quo (brought about by previous politicians claiming to be about 'change') and so they are attracted to any politician saying they will change the status quo. They don't and are never meant to; it's just a recurring hoax to get your vote and secure power to do what the *El*-ite want to happen. 'Mr Change' Obama was only a continuation of Bush and the 'man of peace' became another man of war as he was always going to be. There was not a single day in Obama's eight years in office when America was not at war and the scandalous Guantanamo Bay concentration and torture camp that Obama pledged to close 'within a

**Figure 459:** Fraud from first to last.

year' is still open (Fig 459). In his last year in office in 2016 his administration dropped an estimated 26,000 bombs at the rate of nearly three an hour for 24 hours a day. I called him out at the time he was elected in an article headed 'The Naked Emperor' because he was such an obvious conman and fraud. The fact that he attracted record amounts of campaign money from *El*-ite banks and institutions made it obvious that 'man of the people' was the last thing he was going to be. A political system offering an alleged 'choice' for a population of 326 million has installed the following last six presidents: Ronald Reagan, who was suffering from dementia while still in office, abused mind-controlled women and whose military actions and covert support for others make him a war criminal; Father George Bush, the drug-running, child-abusing serial killer, CIA Deep State operative and war criminal; Bill Clinton, Bush family friend and drug-running partner, serial abuser of women and war criminal; Boy George Bush, a manchild with arrested development verging on the illiterate, and war criminal; Barack Obama, front man fraud, Mr Change-Nothing and war criminal; Donald Trump, insider playing the outsider, reality TV star and war criminal before he had completed 100 days in office. You mean we can't find better than that lot out of hundreds of millions of Americans spanning nearly 40 years? Of course we can, but we're not allowed to. We get what the El-ite choose to give us by selecting the candidate and controlling both the media and the funding. This is the only political 'choice' that really exists – who the El-ite and the Web choose to rule on their behalf. See ... *And The Truth Shall Set You Free* and *The Biggest Secret* for the background to what I said about Reagan, Bush and Clinton. Genuine people who come to power only here and there are locked in by the economic control of the banks and their own Postage Stamp mentality that won't allow them to see what is necessary to secure real change for the better.

## President Drumpf of Zion

Along came the latest purveyor of snake oil in the form of Donald Trump, real family name 'Drumpf' originating in the German village of Kallstadt, about an hour and half drive from Frankfurt. The Heinz 'food' family dynasty came from the same village and is apparently related. Trump told his potential voters (including some alleged 'alternative' media in the United States) what they wanted to hear about taking on the banks like Zionist-owned Goldman Sachs, building a wall on the Mexican border to stop illegal immigration and no longer using the US military to interfere in the affairs of other countries. The speed at which he went back on that must have broken all previous records (Fig 460). He hasn't 'drained the swamp' as he pledged but further expanded it with more billionaires in his government than any US administration in history

**Figure 460:** America's latest road sign.

**Figure 461:** As the Bee Gees sang: 'It's only words, and words are all I have to take your heart away.'

(Fig 461). In next to no time after winning the presidency he filled his administration with Sabbatean Frankists and their Zionist perceptual kin. The American economy was handed to Zionist-owned Goldman Sachs through Goldman assets Steven Mnuchin (Treasury Secretary) and Gary Cohn (Director of the National Economic Council) who was president and CEO of Goldman Sachs (Fig 462). Bill Clinton ('Democrat') and Boy Bush ('Republican') also appointed Treasury Secretaries from Goldman Sachs. At the same time over the last 30 years the privately-owned Federal Reserve or 'the Fed', the 'US' central bank which basically controls the American economy, have been: Alan Greenspan (Zionist), Ben Bernanke (Zionist) and Janet Yellen (Zionist). Yellen was vice-chair to Bernanke and her own vice-chair is Stanley Fischer (Zionist) who is the former chairman of the central bank of Israel. The ratio of Zionist population of the United States to heads and deputy heads of the Federal Reserve is fantastic; but legitimate questions about why this is so are blocked by the usual defence response of 'anti-Semitism'. The number of people in America identifying their religion as Jewish is only a little more than four million out of 326 million and that is less than two percent. Zionists and especially secret society Zionists will be less and far, far less respectively. If the same population-Fed ratio applied to black people, Irish people, Hispanics etc., there would be a tidal wave of questions with Zionists leading the charge. Why are they untouchable above everyone else when it comes to legitimate questioning? We are bombarded with propaganda about how Jewish people are so discriminated against, but put 'list of Jewish American business people' into a search engine and you'll see the

**Figure 462:** Goldman Sachs Zionists Gary Cohn and Steven Mnuchin.

extent of this 'discrimination' in the business world never mind with government positions. Zionist Steven Mnuchin donated heavily to the Democratic Party in the one-party state before joining the 'Trump' (Goldman Sachs) government. He worked for Democon Rothschild/Rockefeller manipulator extraordinaire

George Soros and was CEO of a company called OneWest Bank Group (formerly IndyMac Bancorp Inc) which he and his partners sold for a nearly $2 billion profit after foreclosing on tens of thousands of homes in what has been described as 'a foreclosure machine' after the crash of 2008. Nice man. Oh

Figure 463: Wilbur Ross perfect for government.

yes, and one of the major backers of OneWest? George Soros. President Trump (how hard that is to write) named Wilbur Ross as his Commerce Secretary. Ross is an investor and banker who worked for the Rothschilds for 24 years and claims that 'the one percent is being picked on for political reasons'. *Ahhh*, there, there. He is also a head, or 'Grand Swipe', of Kappa Beta Phi 'Wall Street's most secret society' founded in 1929. Journalist Kevin Roose who gate-crashed a Kappa Beta Phi 'induction ceremony' found billionaire bankers, cross dressing, mocking of the '99 percent' and jokes about the enormous bailouts of the banking *El*-ite which were nothing more than a means of transferring trillions from public to the *El*-ite in pursuit of the Hunger Games Society (Fig 463). Kevin Roose wrote in *New York Magazine*:

> Here ... was a group that included many of the executives whose firms had collectively wrecked the global economy in 2008 and 2009. And they were laughing off the entire disaster in private, as if it were a long-forgotten lark. (Or worse, sing about it — one of the last skits of the night was a self-congratulatory parody of ABBA's 'Dancing Queen', called 'Bailout King.') These were activities that amounted to a gigantic middle finger to Main Street and that, if made public, could end careers and damage very public reputations.

Such is the mentality of Wilbur Ross, appointed by 'anti-Establishment' Donald Trump, but then why would Trump want to drain the swamp when he has been swimming in it all his life? He conned the working class and much of the US 'alternative' media into supporting him just as Obama conned so-called progressives. Same masters, same technique, different huckster. Trump played on the claim to be an 'outsider' and 'anti-Establishment' and won because he tapped into the gathering realisation that the system is rigged. He told them what they wanted to hear and they bought it. This 'outsider'/insider scam was exploited with the promotion of French President Emmanuel Macron, an employee of the Rothschilds. He was portrayed as an 'outsider' when he wasn't because they know the public mood is changing. Both Trump and Macron are the *creation* of the Establishment not its challengers. I don't believe for a second that Trump bucked the system to win against all the odds. He was chosen to win and enter the White House – at least in the short term. With so much to come out about Trump they could have

**Figure 464:** The President of the United States alongside Donald Trump.

blocked his election and they have the power to remove him whenever they like. One of his key roles was to polarise society in a massive exercise in divide and rule and set American at war with itself. Chaos is the currency of the Hidden Hand – a state of flux that is so easy to manipulate – and in Trump they have Captain Chaos with the potential of monumental upheaval should he be removed in office through investigation, assassination or whatever. He's just another puppet to be used as necessary. Should anything happen to cause his demise they have Neocon-to-his-fingertips Vice-President Mike Pence ready to take over and he would suit the Neocons perfectly. If not him there are many more where he came from. The Democons that control the Democratic Party provably chose Clinton and made it impossible for Bernie Sanders to beat her for the nomination. Are we to believe that the Neocons controlling the Republican Party could not have done the same to stop Trump if that was their aim? Trump may not agree with everything the Neocons want, but they have their ways of overcoming that. Pressure on him over fake allegations of Russia fixing his election are to ensure that he does not make any agreements with Vladimir Putin that would block Neocon ambitions to bring the US into conflict with Russia. Trump has been bailed out of bankruptcy by Zionist financiers and he owes them. Payback is to be the most pro-Israel US President yet. Immediately Trump won the presidency Israel Prime Minister Netanyahu gave the go ahead for a rapid expansion of illegal Jewish settlements in occupied Palestinian land knowing he could now do what he liked (Fig 464). Trump announced that he would relocate the US Embassy from Tel Aviv to Jerusalem in a highly symbolic and provocative move for the Palestinians although he delayed the switch when he saw the potential opposition and consequences, but Vice President Pence 'forcefully reiterated' that this will happen. Pence told the Christians United for Israel summit in Washington, an organisation with which he has close ties: 'It is not a question of if; it is only when.' He also stated the obvious: 'Under President Donald Trump, if the world knows nothing else, then the world will know this: America stands with Israel, now and always.'

The first overseas tour by Trump as President of the United States (controlled by Sabbatean Frankism) was to Israel (controlled by Sabbatean Frankism), Saudi Arabia (controlled by Sabbatean Frankism) and the Vatican (controlled by Sabbatean Frankism). Secretary of State Rex Tillerson said the visit was to gather support to stand in 'unity' with Israel against Iran. Yawn. Trump proceeded to sign deals with the Saudi Sabbatean Frankist Dönmeh fake royals to supply them with still more arms worth $350 billion. This is a country that violently oppresses its people, funds terrorism, bombs the innocent and oppresses women to extremes that beggar belief – a country that Trump once said masterminded 9/11. They didn't, but they did play their part.

Zionism has taken over US financial policy (or continued its control) thanks to Trump's Goldman Sachs appointments, and Zionist Carl Icahn is Special Advisor to the President on Regulatory Reform working with the absolutely Zionist-dominated Trump financial team. Then we have Trump's ubiquitous hard-line Zionist son-in-law and 'senior advisor', Jared Kushner, who has known Israel crazy Netanyahu since he was a child. Netanyahu once slept in Kushner's childhood bedroom due to his close relationship with Kushner's father, Charles Kushner, a real estate mogul who was jailed for illegal campaign contributions, tax evasion and witness tampering. Jared Kushner is Israel's (therefore the Rothschilds') man in the White House and married to Trump's daughter Ivanka who converted to the Jewish faith before the wedding on his insistence. Are we also to believe it is all a coincidence that a life-long friend of Benjamin Netanyahu and vehement Zionist married into the Trump family and then Trump became US President and made him his senior advisor at 36? Ivanka, another presidential advisor, has a fundamental influence on her child-like father whose narcissism makes him such a synch for sycophancy to manipulate as does his capacity for creating upheaval and chaos. Trump has a legendary ego but that is cover for his deep insecurity which requires him to respond to criticism that secure people would simply ignore. How typical that the media has focused on Kushner's meetings with Russian people, but looks the other way with his full-on connections and associations with Israel and Zionism. Jared Kushner is Israel-to-his-DNA and has given money to the American Israel Public Affairs Committee (AIPAC), the notorious Israel-front and one of the best-funded lobby groups in the United States. They also have front men on Capitol Hill like Senators John McCain and Lindsey Graham who, appropriately, are also apologists and lobbyists for US/Israel fiefdom Saudi Arabia. McCain's 'foundation' receives funds from the Rothschild family and Zionist billionaire George Soros. Former Congresswoman Cynthia McKinney has revealed how she was approached immediately she ran for office to 'sign the pledge' to Israel and confirm she would always vote in Israel's best interests. Failure to

do so meant no support or funding from the all-powerful Zionist lobby
that includes AIPAC. McKinney said this happened to everyone running
for Congress or the Senate and she described her own experience:

> *Every candidate for Congress at that time had a pledge, they were given a*
> *pledge to sign ... If you don't sign the pledge, you don't get money. For*
> *example, it was almost like water torture for me. My parents observed this. I*
> *would get a call and the person on the other end of the phone would say 'I*
> *want to do a fundraiser for you.' And then we would get into the planning. I*
> *would get really excited, because of course you have to have money in order*
> *to run a campaign. And then two weeks, three weeks into the planning, they*
> *would say, 'Did you sign the pledge?' And then I would say, 'No, I didn't*
> *sign the pledge.' And then my fundraiser would go kaput.*

McKinney eventually lost her seat when AIPAC funded her opponent
who signed the pledge. If you want to be in Congress or the Senate don't
upset AIPAC and this is the swamp that Kushner swims in. He has
major financial ties to Soros, an almost life-long agent of the Web, which
includes a $250 million 'investment' in a Kushner company, and to the
Steinmetz family, one of the richest in Israel. Kushner owned the *New
York Observer* newspaper which promoted the Zionist agenda and
trashed those who question the official fairy story about 9/11. His own
special assistant is Zionist Avrahm Berkowitz and another Trump senior
advisor alongside Kushner is Zionist Stephen Miller. The president also
has a list of Zionist 'special assistants'. Trump named his lawyer, the
Zionist extremist David M. Friedman, as Ambassador to Israel. Jason
Greenblatt, executive vice president and chief legal officer to Trump and
the Trump Organization, and his 'advisor on Israel', became US Special
Representative for International Negotiations including those between
Israel and the Palestinians. Another Zionist, Yael Lempert, is Special
Assistant to the President and Senior Director for Israel, Egypt and the
Levant. Palestinians have been royally stitched up and on Netanyahu's
first visit to the Trump White House the two-state solution to the Israel-
Palestine conflict was questioned by a president for the first time in
favour of a one state – Israel – 'solution'. Zionists can be found
throughout the Trump administration in far greater numbers than you
would statistically expect given the Jewish population of America and
so it was with Obama's financial team and key players across 9/11 at the
time of Boy Bush. Are these people there to represent the interests of the
United States or Israel and the Rothschilds? They play the 'anti-
Semitism' card so vehemently and vociferously to stop such legitimate
questions being asked. Well they can say what they like about me – I
couldn't give a shit. The truth is the truth and it's about time it was
spoken. The Zionist network is really the Rothschild network and inner

circle *secret society* Zionism is a front for Sabbatean Frankism. Jewish people as a whole are as irrelevant to these Zionist insiders as the rest of the global population.

## Follow the money ...

Zionist billionaires are major funders of American politics, Democrat and Republican, to control both sides. In return they want lots of bang for their buck. Zionist George Soros gives money to 'progressive' and Democrat causes while the biggest financial supporter of the Trump presidential bid was Sheldon Adelson, the American-Israeli casino billionaire and Israel media owner. Own both sides and you can't lose and the same principle (or lack of it) is true of all the major corporations and banks that now have free reign to spend as much as they like in the US persuading the public to vote for their candidates or against the ones they don't want. Wall Street spent a record $2 billion on political contributions in the 2016 US election cycle and that's only the headline figure. The 'bang for their buck' means they choose who gets what job – see Trump and Goldman Sachs who he heavily criticised in his election campaign to pander to his anti-Establishment support. WikiLeaks released an email sent in 2008 by Zionist banker Michael Froman, an executive at Citigroup, to John Podesta, co-chair of the transition team for President-elect Barack Obama. Froman suggested names to be appointed to Obama's government and almost all of them duly were. The three names he listed for Treasury Secretary were Robert Rubin (Zionist), Larry Summers (Zionist), and Timothy Geithner (Zionist-owned). All three had served in the Bill Clinton administration. Obama appointed Geithner as Treasury Secretary and made Summers Director of the National Economic Council, a job now held by Zionist Gary Cohn. Read the economics chapter in *The Perception Deception* and you'll see that Zionist control of the American economy under successive administrations and parties is shocking and utterly undeniable purely by listing all the names and positions. Now it continues under Trump. I have heard some in the alternative media say they can see no evidence of Zionist manipulation of America and world affairs when it is so blatant and stuck to your nose. Given there are only 15 million Jewish people in the world compared with a population of 7.5 billion and 4 to 5 million in total in the US compared with a population of 326 million it is ridiculous not to question their scale of influence in global affairs. I am not talking about a 'Jewish plot' but the actions of inner-core or Rothschild Zionists in league with those from other backgrounds and groupings. The 'anti-Semitic' card is thrown to intimidate people into silence. The idea is to ensure that anyone who asks such obvious questions is immediately deemed a racist and systematically vilified while the Israeli state can openly urge Jewish people not to marry and have children with non-Jews with no problem at all. Zionism is actually the most racist creed on Earth while accusing everyone else of racism. There we have the inversion again. Zionist networks operate everywhere including the British Friends of Israel, the Henry Jackson Society and the French Jewish umbrella group CRIF known as the 'French AIPAC'. The Henry Jackson Society is a vehemently pro-Israel version of the US Neocons. International patrons include ultra-Zionist Robert Kagan, William Kistrol, Richard Perle, Michael Chertoff and others. One of the first moves by Emmanuel Macron after winning the French presidency was to drop one of his party's candidates after pressure by CRIF and other Jewish lobby groups claiming he was anti-Semitic for supporting the Israel boycott movement, BDS. Macron's opponent, Marine Le Pen, is also in the Zionist pocket while being labelled racist against Muslims. How does Israel, a country of just eight million people, have such global influence and such a say on the world stage? Here you have your answer, or part of it.

## 'Moderate' extremists

The Spider and its Web have hijacked the term 'progressive' and used it as cover for fascism and mass murder and to sell its extremist placemen and women in political office as 'the middle ground', 'centrist' and 'moderate'. You see this increasing with Conservative parties of the so-called 'Right' as you do with progressives of the so-called 'Left'. War criminals and 'centrists' like Tony Blair condemn extremism while producing fake dossiers to justify slaughter of the innocent and ongoing death and mayhem for tens of millions. Blair in so many ways is the blueprint for extremists who claim the 'centre ground'. They are all pro-EU, pro-NATO, pro-war, pro-Israel and Zionism, pro-global warming hoax, pro-everything The System wants; and anti-Russia and anti-anyone the El-ite choose to target and demonise. Obama was basically the Blair blueprint and so are leaders like Macron in France, Angela Merkel in Germany, Charles Michel in Belgium, Justin Trudeau in Canada, Malcolm Turnbull in Australia, Stefan Lofven in Sweden, Leo Varadkar in Ireland, Nicola Sturgeon in Scotland, Aleksandra Vučić and Ana Brnabić in Serbia, Dusko Markovic in Montenegro, Edi Rama in Albania, Alexis Tsipras in Greece, Paolo Gentiloni in Italy and his predecessor Matteo Renzi before he lost a referendum while seeking more centralised control. The world is drowning in Blair blueprints presenting tyranny as moderation and following his privately-stated political philosophy of 'Smile at everyone and get someone else to stab them in the back'. Web networks in each country manipulate events to bring these people to power and always with the mass support of the Web-controlled mainstream media. Macron is a textbook case. He is a

Rothschild banker who came out of nowhere with a 'new party' and claiming to be independent when he is a 100 percent creation of the Establishment just like Hollande and Sarkozy from 'different' parties who preceded him. He was a minister in the Hollande abomination of a government. Macron's 'new party' was simply to overcome the stigma of the discredited major parties that he would have otherwise represented as a natural successor to the truly appalling François Hollande who managed the lowest public approval rating in French political history at just four percent. Italian psychiatrist Dr Adriano Segatori said in a video interview that Macron, who married his schoolteacher 24 years his senior, is a dangerous psychopath who could potentially ruin France. His behaviour since taking office supports this. They are *all* psychopaths – that's why they get the job. Segatori claimed that Macron 'has a full blown case of narcissism' that is 'malevolent' and needs the admiration of others to compensate for a massive inferiority complex (see Trump). This is a psychological assessment that could apply to all these Web place men and women called 'world leaders'. Hollande endorsed Macron for president as did the entire political, media and financial Establishment and other Web creations and clones including EU dark suits, Angela Merkel and Barack Obama. What was that about foreign countries interfering in the elections of others?

Russia is constantly accused of this with no convincing evidence but when it is openly done by Western leaders nothing is said so long as they support the Archontic choice. The Brexit campaign saw Obama making statements in support of Britain staying in the EU and so did the International Monetary Fund (IMF), world leaders and almost the entirety of the British Establishment and the left-to-right political class. All this is the result of Web coordination and perception programming of the clone-like political mind. Enough people in France voted for Macron in 2017 for him to beat the anti-EU, stop mass-immigration Marine Le Pen because that is what the media and political establishment told them to do. The technique is easy. Promote your candidate as the new messiah (as the British media did with Blair) and condemn the opponent as the Devil incarnate or an unelectable disaster. Le Pen said that whatever the result of the election a woman would lead France, either her or Chancellor Merkel. Macron's first call only minutes after his victory was to mother Merkel before he went out to address his followers to a backdrop of the classic Archontic black pyramid at the Louvre Museum to the sound not of the French national anthem but that of the *European Union*. The day after his inauguration he was off to Berlin to see his political mummy. Macron is another little boy in short trousers doing what he's told, but we should not forget that 11 million voted for Le Pen and a third of French voters rejected them both by abstaining or spoiling their ballots and that's the most since 1969. People across the world are getting increasingly sick of what they see as a system rigged against them. Hillary Clinton, with corruption in her bloodstream, supported Macron and called it a 'defeat for those interfering in democracy' in a laughable reference to Russia. Those words were written by a woman who has been interfering in democracy her entire political life. Madonna, Cher and Katy Perry also celebrated the Macron victory. The word is again 'progressive', a term interchangeable with filthy-rich and clueless 'celebrities' like Madonna, Cher, Perry, Bono and Geldof. For goodness sake, Bono and Geldof supported Tony Blair.

Such self-styled progressives support Blair blueprints like Macron and campaign to overcome the democratic Brexit vote, promote the global warming hoax, impose political correctness to silence contrary opinion and dub anyone who disagrees with them a racist bigot or too old and stupid to be relevant in their Brave New World. They are so perceptually controlled, so caught in the manipulated polarisation of left-right politics that they will fill the streets in protest at the wars of Bush but stay silent when 'progressive' hero Obama does the same. 'Progressive' Bernie Sanders can be blatantly manipulated out of the presidential nomination by the Clinton-controlled Democratic hierarchy and then he takes to his feet at the convention to endorse her for president because 'we must not let the "other side" win'. You mean the 'other side' that will do what Clinton would do anyway because they are both controlled by the same force? If you can't truly stand up to the Establishment in your mid-70s Bernie, when are you ever going to start? What a contribution he would have made by telling the world that he could not endorse Clinton or Trump because they were both as bad as each other and Americans should question why they were being offered such an illusory 'choice'. But no, play the game, Bernie, like a good 'progressive'. The 'Left', 'Right', 'Centre' political paradigm is a hoax used as cover to hide basically the same mind-set. They all get their information, opinions and perceptions from the mainstream media and Mainstream Everything. They may read a 'progressive' paper or a 'right-wing' paper, but both papers are reporting from the same Postage Stamp.

Some other political tricks and techniques the Web employs to scam you:

Make sure an unelectable candidate runs against the one that you want to win. When they wanted Margaret Thatcher to stay in office through the 1980s she would have had to shoot a child in broad daylight not to have beaten leaders of the opposition Labour Party, Michael Foot and Neil Kinnock. When Labour leader Tony Blair was their man they

pitched against him William Hague, Iain Duncan Smith and Michael
Howard, all of them fresh from their charisma-bypass operations. The
new, young, 'change' and 'anti-war' candidate Barack Obama faced the
elderly war-monger John McCain and his dippy running mate Sarah
Palin, and in his second election it was the multi-millionaire and clearly
Establishment-to-his-fingertips Mitt Romney. Some who are knowingly
part of the Web machine *set out* to lose (and later get their reward)
because they are well aware that the other candidate is the Web choice.
Father George Bush wasn't trying in his campaign against Bill Clinton
and why did Al Gore do so little to challenge the 2000 presidential
election count in Florida so obviously manipulated in favour of Boy
Bush? Control of the media means the Web's preferred candidate can be
presented as the only possible choice while his or her opponent is
constantly berated, ridiculed and dismissed. In more extreme cases
scandals can be revealed or cooked up to stop someone getting into
power or circumstances manipulated to make it impossible to stay in
office. The United States is infamous for doing this in other countries
through Pentagon/CIA-fomented 'revolutions' and economic attacks via
the banking system and global bodies like the IMF which take orders
from the Web. Another technique is to organise Web assets in a political
party to overthrow the target leader and we saw this with Margaret
Thatcher in 1990. She was the 'Iron Lady' while she was favouring
policies the Web wanted, but she was gone very quickly once she began
to publicly resist further centralisation of power in the European Union
and the constant dilution of British sovereignty. Simple blackmail is a
constantly-used method of controlling politicians to make sure they
follow your agenda to the letter even if they may not agree with it.
Paedophilia is massively used to do this with politicians and other
influential people provided with children while hidden cameras are
running. The Australian 'death bed' Satanist from earlier said:
'Politicians are introduced by a carefully graded set of criteria and
situations that enable them to accept that their victims will be, "Our little
secret".' A secret only so long as you do what we want. Those called
'whips' in political parties have the job of pressuring their Members of
Parliament, Congress and the Senate to vote the way the party hierarchy
(Web) demands and blackmail is often their weapon of choice. Tim
Fortescue was a whip under paedophile and Satanist Prime Minister
Edward Heath between 1970 and 1973. He told the BBC:

> *For anyone with any sense, who was in trouble, would come to the whips*
> *and tell them the truth, and say now, I'm in a jam, can you help? It might be*
> *debt, it might be ... a scandal involving small boys, or any kind of scandal in*
> *which a member seemed likely to be mixed up in, they'd come and ask if we*
> *could help and if we could, we did.*

**THOSE YOU SEE ARE ONLY GOFERS**

**FOR THOSE YOU DON'T SEE**

**Figure 465:** A fact we should never forget if we are to understand the world and what is really going on.

*And we would do everything we can because we would store up brownie points ... and if I mean, that sounds a pretty, pretty nasty reason, but it's one of the reasons because if we could get a chap out of trouble then, he will do as we ask forever more.*

The Web loves to exploit place-people who have scandals to hide. Gotcha! Political leaders suddenly change policy because of this and begin to oppose everything they once claimed to believe in. This is particularly worth noting when it happens very quickly. Political parties and leaders have no contract with the electorate and they can say whatever they want in an election campaign and then do the opposite once they get into office. Four or five years follow of changing society against the will of those who voted for you before another 'democratic election' when the whole farce is repeated. Observe how the British 'Mother of Parliaments' structure is now followed across the world in 'democratic' countries with only one, two, sometimes three parties with any chance of forming a government and all answerable in the shadows to the same force. So-called 'democracy' which we are told to equate with 'freedom' is really a vehicle for dictatorship by the Hidden Hand and in the end not even one that takes human form. The political and economic structure of the seen is only a vehicle for those in the unseen (Fig 465). It's a mirage, an illusion, a vaudeville show. The Trumps and Obamas and Bushes and Clintons may seem to be important and they hijack attention as illusory centres of power. But they are only lackeys and gofers for unseen forces with a long-term agenda for total human subjugation.

This is the Big Secret that they don't want you to know.

**Postscript:** Trump announced that he was sending his ultra-Zionist son-in-law Jared Kushner and ultra-Zionist 'chief negotiator' Jason Greenblatt to head 'peace talks' with the Israelis and Palestinians also involving US/Israel-controlled Saudi Arabia, the United Arab Emirates, Qatar, Jordan and Egypt. No bias there, then. They are laughing at you.

# CHAPTER THIRTEEN

# War, War, War
# – We Love It

*'It is forbidden to kill; therefore all murderers are punished unless they kill in large numbers and to the sound of trumpets' – **Voltaire***

Human history over the past 6,000 years since the emergence of the new psyche has been defined by war. Archontically-controlled Reptilians and Greys have manipulated wars and conflicts across the world through their hybrid *El*-lite with the human population pitched against itself to divide and rule and create an ongoing frenzy of violence, fear, suffering and death on which the hidden controllers feed. This continues today and every day.

There is always money for war (Fig 466). You never hear political leaders say they can't go to war because the country can't afford it. They claim not to have money for the poor, homeless and hungry, but war? It's never a problem. There are so many reasons for this. War is incredibly profitable for armament giants owned by the *El*-ite, that are ridiculously called 'defence' contractors when attacking the innocent is all they care about. The United States spends enough on 'defence' to provide every homeless American with a one-million-dollar home (Fig 467). 'Let them eat tanks' is the cry of modern-day financial/military aristocracy (Fig 468). In one week alone in April 2017 two

**Figure 466:** Why is this so? Because the *El*-lite and their Archontic Reptilian masters want constant war and could not care less how much people suffer. The more suffering the better to them.

**Figure 467:** The madness of it all.          **Figure 468:** Don't feed people – kill them.

Trump-sanctioned attacks in Syria and Afghanistan cost a minimum $100 million to launch 59 Tomahawk missiles on a Syrian airbase and another £16 million for dropping the 'Mother of All Bombs' in Afghanistan (with terrible long-term health consequences for civilians) in the world's biggest non-nuclear impact (Fig 469). Those figures only reflect the price of the missiles and don't include all the other costs. Drain-the-swamp Trump significantly militarised the government by appointing generals and others in defence-related positions with ties to the armaments industry including Secretary of Defense General James 'Mad Dog' Mattis and Homeland Security chief General John F. Kelly. Mattis was paid $242,000, plus $500,000 in vested stock options, when he was director of submarine, tank and munitions producer General Dynamics. Kelly was an advisor to DynCorp and had other arms industry connections. Trump later appointed General Kelly to be right at his shoulder as White House Chief of Staff because he 'wanted a general' in that position. National Security Advisor General Herbert Raymond McMaster is connected with arms industry fronts including the Center for Strategic and International Studies (CSIS) which is funded by ExxonMobil (Secretary of State Rex Tillerson is the former CEO), Hess, Chevron and Boeing. Tillerson has associations with CSIS along with representatives from arms manufacturers Lockheed Martin and Raytheon. Thus McMaster, like Mattis, is anti-Russia, anti-China and anti-Iran. CSIS told the media there was an urgent need to deploy the Terminal High Altitude Area Defense (THAAD) missile system to South Korea to meet the 'threat' from the North without pointing out that Lockheed Martin, THAAD's primary contractor in a deal

**Figure 469:** Priorities of the Death Cult.

worth billions, funds the Missile Defense Project Program at CSIS. Trump also named Mark Esper, an executive with 'defence' giant Raytheon, as Army Secretary. Arms companies secure ever-more influence in government and the Pentagon because war, death and destruction are so good for business. They set up or support 'think tanks' to push their war agenda with politicians and media, and one example is the Canadian Global Affairs Institute (CGAI) which campaigns for Canadian involvement in America's overseas conflicts and once commissioned a 'survey' which claimed that 'Canadians are willing to send troops into danger even if it leads to deaths and injuries as long as they believe in the military's goals'. The Institute has called for Canada to establish an overseas spying network akin to the CIA and MI6 and runs 'military journalism' courses for trainee reporters to prepare them to see the world the way that suits the Institute. You will not be at all surprised to know that the Canadian Global Affairs Institute has received funding from major arms manufacturers. *Huffington Post* reported that 'General Dynamics and Lockheed Martin Canada, as well as Edge Group, C4i, Com Dev, ENMAX, SMART Technologies, the Defense News Media Group and Canadian Council of Chief Executives have all supported CGAI'. Similar organisations operate in all major countries and they are pushing against an open door in Canada where the one-party state in the form of Prime Minister Justin Trudeau (Liberal, Web) and his predecessor Stephen Harper (Conservative, Web) who have slavishly supported the military agenda of the United States, Israel and their satellite state Saudi Arabia. Trudeau, another off-the-shelf Web creation in the model of Macron and company, is continuing the family business by following his satanic father Pierre Trudeau (1919-2000) into the highest level of Canadian government. See *The Biggest Secret* and Cathy O'Brien's *Trance-formation of America* for more on Pierre Trudeau.

I would stress, however, that war is not primarily nor even majorly about money in the deeper levels of the Web. War fries much bigger fish.

**Figure 470:** We have constant war because war destroys status quos and allows another to replace them.

Money is the bonus and not the ultimate motivation for those in the shadows and in the know. Nothing changes a society quicker and more permanently than war and so bombs have become the calling cards of the 'moral West' (Fig 470). Whether it be a country or a world the same outcome applies. Nothing is ever the same again. The process is known as 'creative destruction' and involves using war to change a status quo and install a new one. Then you

**Figure 471:** This has been happening throughout known human history in a process of constant transformation.

destroy *that* status quo and install a new one (Fig 471). Each new status quo takes you further along the road to global domination and the Hunger Games Society. We have seen this with the two world wars. Power was in far fewer hands after World War I and even more so after World War II with the creation of global bodies like the United Nations justified by 'preventing war' (which they haven't because they were not meant to). War allows Archontic Reptilian bloodlines to remove problem governments and leaders, rewrite the map, acquire more land and resources and dramatically speed the centralisation of global power. The process of replacing tribes with nations and nations with superstates has largely been achieved through war. Establishment of the European Economic Community – now the EU – was sold to a very significant extent as a way of stopping another war in Europe when the force claiming this had started the others. Major wars are not spontaneous, but long-planned according to an agenda and sequence dictated from the unseen. The Old Testament 'Demiurge' or Yahweh/Jehovah has long demanded death, destruction, sacrifice and war. Here's an example from the Book of Joshua when 'The Lord' (Lord Archon) demanded the destruction of Jericho:

> *Now Jericho was straitly shut up because of the children of Israel: none went out, and none came in ... And they utterly destroyed all that was in the city, both man and woman, young and old, and ox, and sheep, and ass, with the edge of the sword ... And they burnt the city with fire, and all that was therein: only the silver, and the gold, and the vessels of brass and of iron, they put into the treasury of the house of the LORD.*

This could have been describing (with missiles and guns replacing swords) the mass human slaughter during the US Marines assault on Fallujah, Iraq, in April 2004, when all escape routes were blocked before the carnage began and so many civilians were murdered that a soccer stadium had to be turned into a graveyard. A US general central to what happened was James 'Mad Dog' Mattis, the Trump choice for Secretary of Defense at the Pentagon. This is where his mad dog nickname came from. Mattis is a psychopath who has said:

> *I come in peace. I didn't bring artillery. But I'm pleading with you, with*

*tears in my eyes: If you fuck with me, I'll kill you all.*

*Find the enemy that wants to end this experiment* [in American democracy] *and kill every one of them until they're so sick of the killing that they leave us and our freedoms intact.*

*Be polite, be professional, but have a plan to kill everybody you meet.*

*So it's a hell of a lot of fun to shoot them. Actually it's quite fun to fight them, you know. It's a hell of a hoot. It's fun to shoot some people. I'll be right up there with you. I like brawling.*

Figure 472: Sleep well.

He's such a nice man, very balanced, and in charge of the US military with Trump, another psychopath, on the side-lines (Fig 472). 'The Lord' behind biblical mass-slaughter is still doing the same today only now with weapons that make death and destruction virtually limitless with the capacity to destroy everyone and everything. At the same time politicians deny that their Murder Inc has any effect on creating terrorists who are full of hate for those who do this to their families and countries. Those with a fragment of empathy, compassion and intelligence would find it hard to comprehend the calculated and emotionless death and destruction of men, women and children, mostly with brown faces, by these Western psychopaths; but we are talking about the mentality that sacrifices children. Their software is programmed not to feel empathy and compassion and so there are no limits to their evil and inhumanity. Indeed, they are *not* human in our understanding of human. I have said over and over that people should not judge what these software programs will do on the basis of what they would do. The bloodlines are not the same as you and don't comprehend, let alone express, the fail-safe mechanism of behaviour – empathy. Without empathy and compassion there are no emotional consequences for whatever they do and thus no limits.

## Connecting the dots ...

I have exposed the manipulated background to so many wars and terrorist attacks in the enormous body of research and evidence in my other books, but here is a sequence of events since the turn of the

Millennium to
show how wars
are planned and
played out to a
blueprint
ultimately
decided in the
unseen. We can
pick up this story
in the year 1998,
but it was in the
planning for
decades and in

**Figure 473:** Eurasia and connected regions.

the unseen for far, far longer. Democon Zbigniew Brzezinski, former
National Security Advisor to President Jimmy Carter and co-founder
with David Rockefeller of the *El*-lite's Trilateral Commission, published
a book in 1998 entitled *The Grand Chessboard*. Brzezinski, who died in
2017, wrote that for America (the Web) to control the world they had to
control Eurasia. This is the biggest landmass on Earth stretching from
Europe in the east to China in the west and from Russia in the north to
the Middle East and India in the south (Fig 473). An important point to
make about Brzezinski's books and statements is that when he tells you

what he *thinks* should happen he
is revealing what is *planned* to
happen. I'll come back to Eurasia
in a moment, but first a
devastating exercise in dot-
connecting that will lead us back
there. We must switch at this point
from the Brzezinski Democon
wing of the Hidden Hand to the
Neocons in the Republican Party –
people like Dick Cheney, Donald
Rumsfeld, Paul Wolfowitz, Doug
Zakheim, Robert Kagan, William
Kristol and Richard Perle (Fig
474). They were all members of
the Washington-based Project for
the New American Century

**Figure 474:** Months before they came to power
directly and indirectly with Boy George Bush
these Zionist bullies and cowards published the
blueprint for war and regime change that has
been followed ever since.

(PNAC), co-founded in 1997 by hard-line Zionists Kagan and Kristol.
Robert Kagan is a member of the *El*-ite's Council on Foreign Relations,
established in 1921 by J.D. Rockefeller to drive US foreign policy, and a
senior fellow at another *El*-ite asset, the Brookings Institution. He also
writes a weekly column in the *El*-ite-controlled *Washington Post* owned

by Jeff Bezos, who also owns Amazon. William Kristol is 'editor at large' of the Neocon rag *The Weekly Standard* and a 'political analyst' who regularly appears on *El*-ite-controlled television networks. 'Political analyst' is a cover for selling the Neocon/Democon Hidden Hand agenda which means sending America's young people into overseas wars of *El*-lite conquest to mass-murder the innocent and presenting US/UK-instigated terrorism against target governments as a 'peoples' revolution'. The one proviso for Kagan and Kristol in their bomb-everyone insanity is that they never see a gun fired in anger because a car backfiring would ensure that these spineless cowards would leave a terrible mess in the street. Neocon leadership is dominated by secret society Zionists and a front for Sabbatean Frankism and its agenda for global control. The Project for the New American Century produced a policy document in September 2000 entitled 'Rebuilding America's Defences – Strategy, Forces and Resources For A New Century'. This called for 'American forces to fight and decisively win multiple, simultaneous major theater wars' and it named a series of countries listed for 'regime change' by those wars: Iraq, Libya, Syria, Lebanon, Iran, North Korea and China – 'American and allied power [should provide] the spur to the process of democratisation in China.' A few months later in January 2001 the PNAC took over the Pentagon through Secretary of Defense Donald Rumsfeld, his more powerful 'deputy', Zionist Paul Wolfowitz, and Pentagon budget controller, Zionist Dov Zakheim, along with other PNAC assets in influential Pentagon positions. They took over the White House through Dick Cheney, the 'Vice'-President who completely dominated the hapless and hopeless Boy Bush. Another highly significant PNAC asset was Richard Perle, known as the Prince of Darkness, working mostly in the background ducking, weaving and manipulating together with Kagan and Kristol when they weren't hiding behind the sofa telling others to go and fight. Zionist extremist Perle is a close friend of Israel Prime Minister Netanyahu as is Trump and his son-in-law and senior advisor Jared Kushner. Perle produced a policy document for Netanyahu in 1996, *A Clean Break: A New Strategy for Securing the Realm* which called for the removing of Saddam Hussein in Iraq and weakening the Assad government in Syria. Perle said:

> *Israel can shape its strategic environment, in cooperation with Turkey and Jordan, by weakening, containing, and even rolling back Syria. This effort can focus on removing Saddam Hussein from power in Iraq – an important Israeli strategic objective in its own right – as a means of foiling Syria's regional ambitions.*

Turkey and Israel-vassal Jordan have since been used to 'roll back

Syria' and Perle's strategy was followed and expanded by the Project for the New American Century with which he was centrally involved with a stream of other Israel assets. US General Wesley Clark, a war criminal himself for his role in the bombing of Serbia during the Kosovo conflict, gave further confirmation of the plan in speeches and an interview with television station *Democracy Now* which you can see on the Internet. Clark, a retired four-star general and former Supreme Allied Commander of NATO, said that about ten days after 9/11 he went to the Pentagon to meet with PNAC Secretary of Defense Donald Rumsfeld and his PNAC deputy Paul Wolfowitz and then went downstairs to see members of the Pentagon Joint Chiefs of Staff who once worked for him. Clark went on:

> ... *one of the generals called me in. He said, 'Sir, you've got to come in and talk to me a second.' I said, 'Well, you're too busy.' He said, 'No, no.' He says, 'We've made the decision we're going to war with Iraq.' This was on or about the 20th of September. I said, 'We're going to war with Iraq? Why?' He said, 'I don't know.' He said, 'I guess they don't know what else to do.'*

> *So I said, 'Well, did they find some information connecting Saddam to al-Qaeda?' He said, 'No, no.' He says, 'There's nothing new that way. They just made the decision to go to war with Iraq.' He said, 'I guess it's like we don't know what to do about terrorists, but we've got a good military and we can take down governments.' And he said, 'I guess if the only tool you have is a hammer, every problem has to look like a nail.'*

Such is the compartmentalisation of knowledge that this general would not have known the reason for targeting Iraq despite his position, but I can help him with his bewilderment. Iraq was first on the list for regime change by the Zionist-created-and-controlled PNAC and Zionist Perle's document for Netanyahu and both were answering to hidden powers that were orchestrating the whole sequence that would follow. No one was mentioning Iraq publicly until 2002 when the demonisation and fear campaign began against Saddam and Iraq which led to the invasion in March 2003. The excuse was Saddam's 'weapons of mass destruction' which they knew didn't exist, but they needed a public justification to kick off the PNAC list of regime changes. Almost to the first bombs being dropped Web puppets Bush and Blair were claiming that the invasion could still be avoided if Saddam complied with their demands, when in truth the war had been planned long before. Wesley Clark said that he returned to the Pentagon a few weeks later by which time the US was bombing Afghanistan and he met the same general. Clark recalled:

> *I said, 'Are we still going to war with Iraq?' And he said, 'Oh, it's worse*

*than that.' He reached over on his desk. He picked up a piece of paper. And he said, 'I just got this down from upstairs' – meaning the Secretary of Defense's office – 'today.' And he said, 'This is a memo that describes how we're going to take out seven countries in five years, starting with Iraq, and then Syria, Lebanon, Libya, Somalia, Sudan and, finishing off, Iran.'*

*I said, 'Is it classified?' He said, 'Yes, sir.' I said, 'Well, don't show it to me.' And I saw him a year or so ago, and I said, 'You remember that?' He said, 'Sir, I didn't show you that memo! I didn't show it to you.*

Clark added that the Project for the New American Century 'wanted us to destabilise the Middle East, turn it upside down, make it under our control'. PNAC may have been the vehicle but this was still an organisation of subordinate gofers doing the bidding in the hierarchy of fear of those much further in the shadows that take orders directly from The Spider. The simple rule is this: if you can see them they are gofers and yes-people and not the source of the power to which they answer. When they do what they're told, all is fine, but if they refuse ... *BIG* mistake. PNAC was so exposed and discredited by the alternative media post-9/11 that the same force today operates through other fronts most notably the Foreign Policy Initiative founded by the same Kagan and Kristol and another Zionist Dan Senor, a columnist and political adviser. This organisation has the ear of

**Figure 475:** In the years since Brzezinski wrote of the need to dominate Eurasia we have seen country after country in and near that region targeted by the US and the West.

Mad Dog Mattis and National Security Advisor McMaster. Now we can return to Brzezinski's Eurasia from this background and see how this fits with countries targeted by the PNAC and Israel (same thing) and those like Russia that have been systematically demonised. They are all in or on the fringes of Eurasia (Fig 475). This is yet another coincidence, nothing to worry about.

## The real reason for 9/11

Neocons had the problem of justifying all the war and regime change they were planning and so cue the always dependable Problem-

Reaction-Solution. Their September 2000 document said that the 'process of transformation ... [war and regime change] ... is likely to be a long one, absent some catastrophic and catalysing event – like a new Pearl Harbor'. A year to the month after the publication of that PNAC document and nine months after those who wrote it came to power with Bush in the White House and Pentagon, the United States experienced what Bush called at the time 'the Pearl Harbor of the 21st century'. If the mainstream media were peopled by proper journalists they would have made the connection in a flash, but my experience is that most have never heard of the Project for the New American Century and those that have don't see – or specifically ignore – its foundation significance to 9/11 and all that has followed. But then conspiracies don't exist, do they? They're only 'theories'. I have taken apart the official story of 9/11 in a combination of *Alice in Wonderland and the World Trade Center Disaster* and *The David Icke Guide to the Global Conspiracy* (plus a major chapter in *The Perception Deception*) and I won't repeat all the detail here.

**Figure 476:** The attacks of 9/11 were the excuse that justified the war on terror and began the process of long-planned 'regime-change' in the Middle East.

Enough to say that the official fairy tale is an absurdity which does not stand up to the mildest scrutiny and came from the same lying mouths that told us there were weapons of mass destruction in Iraq when they knew there were not (Fig 476). The mainstream media agree they were lied to over Iraq and yet accept every word about 9/11 when both narratives came from the same people – not just the same agencies and governments – the same *people*. Even worse the media ridicule and attack those like me who do have a mind of their own and expose how 9/11 was created by elements within the US, Israeli, UK and Saudi Arabian government, intelligence and military networks to justify the global 'war on terror' (war on freedom) and targeting countries listed by the PNAC. Pathetic doesn't even begin to describe the behaviour of alleged 'journalists' and the part they so crucially play in the takeover of Planet Earth by insane psychopaths. Some of the most shockingly uninformed people I have ever met around the world have been journalists and politicians. The attacks of September 11th were based on a blueprint first committed to paper in the early 1960s and called Operation Northwoods. This was the work of the Pentagon Joint Chiefs of Staff in 1962 led by the chairman Lyman L. Lemnitzer which the Kennedy government eventually blocked. Operation Northwoods was the plan for the US military, CIA and other agencies to stage terrorist attacks in the United States and elsewhere and blame them on Cuba to justify an invasion to remove Fidel Castro. James Bamford, a former investigative producer with ABC, described Operation Northwood in his book, *Body of Secrets*, about the US National Security Agency (NSA). He wrote:

> *Code named Operation Northwoods, the plan, which had the written approval of the Chairman and every member of the Joint Chiefs of Staff, called for innocent people to be shot on American streets; for boats carrying refugees fleeing Cuba to be sunk on the high seas; for a wave of violent terrorism to be launched in Washington, D.C., Miami, and elsewhere.*

> *People would be framed for bombings they did not commit; planes would be hijacked. Using phony evidence, all of it would be blamed on Castro, thus giving Lemnitzer and his cabal the excuse, as well as the public and international backing, they needed to launch their war.*

This is what happened on 9/11 and has been happening since with Problem-Reaction-Solution or 'false flag' terror attacks in the United States, Europe, Middle East and elsewhere. Another Pentagon project known as Operation Mongoose proposed similar false flag attacks to target Cuba including to 'create an incident which has the appearance of an attack on U.S. facilities (GMO) in Cuba, thus providing an excuse for use of U.S. military might to overthrow the current government of Cuba'. Chiefs of Staff chairman Lemnitzer was removed by President Kennedy after presenting Operation Northwoods (the military-industrial complex was not pleased by his sacking) but he was then appointed Supreme Allied Commander of NATO! How apt that Operation Northwoods was first made public in 1997 by the John F. Kennedy Assassinations Records Review Board and what timing that a more complete version was posted online by the National Security Archive on April 30th, 2001, just five months before the foundation themes of the document happened for real on September 11th. The official story of 9/11 is so ridiculous and untenable that building and structural experts formed Architects and Engineers for 9/11 Truth (ae911truth.org) to highlight the fact that the explanation for why the twin towers fell makes no engineering sense. Professional pilots formed Pilots for 9/11 Truth (pilotsfor911truth.org) to expose countless and glaring flaws in the story of how 'Muslim hijackers' supposedly learned to fly on simulators and single-engined planes and yet somehow managed to fly wide-bodied jets with such amazing skill that a Lufthansa pilot of 28 years' experience flying wide-bodied aircraft told me he could not have done it. One 'hijacker pilot' was so bad flying single-engined aircraft that his instructor said he was surprised he could even drive a car. My contention, along with others, is that the planes which left the airports in Boston, Newark and Washington that September morning were not those that crashed in New York and were said to have crashed in Pennsylvania and the Pentagon (there is scant evidence for the last two if you care to look in detail at the lack of credible debris left behind). I say the planes that hit the Twin Towers were drones controlled from the ground. We were led to believe immediately after the attacks that technology did not exist for the planes to be taken over and flown as drones. President Bush said days later that he would provide federal funding to develop remote control technology that could be used during hijackings when that technology had officially existed for commercial aircraft for nearly 20 years and much longer within the military. Staged attacks using drone commercial aircraft flown from a ground station were part of Operation Northwoods in 1962. The Northwoods document planned the following:

*An aircraft at Elgin AFB would be painted and numbered as an exact duplicate for a civil registered aircraft belonging to a CIA proprietary organization in the Miami area. At a designated time the duplicate would be substituted for the actual civil aircraft and would be loaded with the selected passengers, all boarded under carefully prepared aliases* [remember how few passengers were on the 9/11 aircraft].

*The actual registered aircraft would be converted to a drone. Take off times of the drone aircraft and the actual aircraft will be scheduled to allow a rendezvous south of Florida.*

*From the rendezvous point the passenger-carrying aircraft will descend to minimum altitude and go directly into an auxiliary field at Elgin AFB where arrangements will have been made to evacuate the passengers and return the aircraft to its original status. The drone aircraft meanwhile will continue to fly the filed flight plan. When over Cuba the drone will be transmitting on the international distress frequency a 'May Day' message stating he is under attack by Cuban MiG aircraft.*

*The transmission will be interrupted by destruction of the aircraft, which will be triggered by radio signal. This will allow ICAO* [International Civil Aviation Organization] *radio stations in the Western Hemisphere to tell the U.S. what has happened to the aircraft instead of the U.S. trying to 'sell' the incident.*

These are the themes and techniques that were used to pull off the gigantic illusion that was 9/11. 'They would never do that?' They have killed hundreds of millions in their manipulated wars century after century orchestrated by Archontically-possessed psychopaths. Do we really think that three thousand people on 9/11 have any relevance to them? They were just a means to an end like all the others. The Bush administration had to be forced kicking, screaming and spitting to set up the 9/11 Commission to 'investigate' what happened and they did everything they could to make it as difficult as possible to uncover the truth including the allocation of seriously inadequate funding. Bush and Cheney (in other words, Cheney) even tried to make Zionist extremist Henry Kissinger the Commission chairman, an appointment so outrageous in terms of a cover-up that he had to withdraw. I have exposed in other books the Zionist involvement in the final report of the Commission which co-chairs Thomas Kean and Lee Hamilton said afterwards had been 'set up to fail'. Why would you do this if you cared about three thousand dead people and wanted to establish what happened and how? Another simple answer: They knew what happened and how – they just didn't want the public to know.

## And the solution is ...

Now the Zionist and American manipulators had their 'new Pearl Harbor' they could begin to pick off their target countries. Afghanistan was attacked first on the way to Iraq and the rest of the PNAC hit-list. The excuse was that Osama bin Laden was the 'mastermind' of September 11th and he was being protected by the Taliban in Afghanistan who refused to hand him over. More bombing of the innocent or 'collateral damage' followed as the American military embarked on another glorious slaughter with Britain as always in tow and Israel cheering from the side-lines and the shadows. I mentioned earlier the late Aaron Russo, an award-winning film-maker who produced *Trading Places* with Eddie Murphy, and his conversation with lawyer and businessman Nick Rockefeller about the origin of the feminist movement and 'Women's Lib'. Russo also revealed that Rockefeller told him nearly a year before 9/11 that there would be an event leading to the invasion of Afghanistan and Iraq to take over the oil fields and establish a base in the Middle East. Russo would see soldiers looking in caves in Afghanistan and Pakistan for Osama bin Laden. There would be an 'endless war on terror where there's no real enemy' and the whole thing would be a 'giant hoax'. Rockefeller said that 'the people have to be ruled' and the population reduced by at least half, and he talked of the plan for mass-microchipping of what he called the 'serfs'. An added benefit – and major goal – of the Afghan invasion was that poppy-growing in Afghanistan could now reach record levels again after being stopped on the orders of the Taliban. Today 90 percent of the world's production of heroin starts out in the poppy fields of Afghanistan and this has generated a global epidemic of addiction (not least in the US). The CIA has a long connection with Pakistan Inter-Services Intelligence (ISI) in the poppies-to-opium/heroin trade that generates enormous sums of money (with its cocaine operation out of South America) to fund covert projects untraceable through official channels and paper trails. ISI is a Web organisation as with all intelligence agencies and operates in many countries. The *Times of India* claimed that the then head of ISI, Mahmood Ahmed, arranged through a third party the transfer of $100,000 to 'lead hijacker' Mohammed Atta and this was taken to be connected to the 9/11 plot. I say it was actually connected to the drug-running operation run by the CIA and ISI in which Atta was involved as a gofer. This allowed the CIA to put Atta and company in the right place at the right time (wrong place and time for them) to be blamed for 9/11. 'Muslim fanatic' Atta lived with a white and seriously non-Muslim American girlfriend in Venice, Florida, close to the now infamous Venice airport and flying school. She describes in an interview you can see on the Internet how Atta was often drunk, his favourite food was pork and whenever they ran out of cocaine he would go over to the airport and come back with an arm full. This makes perfect sense because at that time at least Venice Airport was a conduit through which the CIA flew in cocaine shipments from South America to be distributed on American streets. The Clintons and Bushes were both involved in this drug trade through the Mena airstrip in Arkansas where Bill Clinton was the governor before moving to the White House. The Clinton-Bush 'body count' of dead people includes those, among them children, who saw what they should not have seen at Mena or were starting to talk about their involvement (see ... *And The Truth Shall Set You Free*). English author and activist Shaun Attwood published a book in 2016 called *American Made* that told the story of pilot Barry Seal and his involvement with Father Bush and Bill Clinton in this drug-running operation. Seal was eventually murdered to protect the secrets. The film of the same name starring Tom Cruise released in 2017 was a pale shadow of the real story. Shaun Attwood was kind enough to acknowledge the part my own work played in inspiring the writing of *American Made* and it has been so great over the years to see others picking up the baton and running with it in their own area of interest. The more the better, I say. US wars in Vietnam and Southeast Asia were also majorly drug-related together with other reasons, and drugs were smuggled into America by the *El*-lite and their agents in the coffins of dead soldiers. The real world is certainly not the one that you see on the news. ISI's Mahmood Ahmed was having breakfast in Washington on the morning of 9/11 with Senator Bob Graham and representative Porter Goss who would subsequently head a joint Senate Select Committee on Intelligence and House Permanent Select Committee on Intelligence inquiry into 9/11 which, shall we say, did not uncover the truth. Graham and Goss had been part of a US delegation to Islamabad, Pakistan, barely two weeks before 9/11 during which they met with Mahmoud Ahmed, other ISI officials and President Pervez Musharraf. Porter Goss, an intelligence insider to his fingertips, has a long history with the CIA and became its director in 2004.

The alleged hijackers on 9/11 were overwhelmingly connected to Saudi Arabia, but no action was taken against the Saudis or their British-installed fake 'royal' family which goes on being supplied with massive amounts of hi-tech weapons by the US and UK to oppress its people and kill civilians on a vast scale in Yemen through bombing and subsequent disease and famine. Saudi 'royals' are Sabbatean Frankist Dönmeh Web assets and they can do what they like so long as they continue to serve their hidden masters. Trump describes the evil Saudi Arabian regime as 'friends and allies' and the same with vicious dictator Recep Tayyip Erdogan in Sabbatean Frankist Turkey who wants to reinstate an equivalent of the Ottoman Empire. It is important not to fall for the myth that the world can be broken down on racial, ethnic and religious grounds. This illusion is only for the masses. There are no such divisions for Web assets because they know it is all nonsense and Saudi Arabia (centre of Islam) is on the same side as Israel (centre of Zionist Judaism) and the US/UK (which claim to be 'Christian'). They are all controlled by the same Web and work as one unit when you would expect that especially Israel and Saudi Arabia would be in opposing camps. Saudi Arabia does not fund and arm people that kill Jews, but those who kill other non-Dönmeh Muslims.

The Saudi bin Laden family are closely connected with the 'royals' and with the Bush family through Father George Bush who did business with them for the Carlyle Group, a Washington-based private equity and asset management company which handled the assets of the Saudi Binladen Corporation. Democon Zbigniew Brzezinski told French news magazine, *Le Nouvel Observateur*, in 1998, that when he was National Security Advisor to President Jimmy Carter in the late 1970s he arranged for the arming, training and funding of 'freedom-fighters' in Afghanistan that became known as the Mujahedeen. Brzezinski wanted them to attack the Soviet satellite government in the capital Kabul to force the Soviet Union to invade. He described this as giving the Soviets 'their Vietnam' and he did so at a cost of 1.5 million Afghan lives. The US and Saudi Arabia gave the Mujahedeen, involving fighters from 40 Muslim countries, billions in financial and military aid under the CIA's Operation Cyclone and this was funnelled into Afghanistan by the

Pakistan ISI which also provided military training together with the Pakistan military and Britain's MI6 and SAS (the elite Special Air Service unit of the British army). Mujahedeen terrorists were also trained by the CIA in Virginia and Brooklyn, New York, ironically close to the Twin Towers. These many and various organisations are all Web assets and this was the conduit for coordination against the Soviets and later for 9/11. The Mujahedeen and the Taliban were the 'good guys' at first and under the subsequent Reagan-Father Bush regime in the 1980s the front man of Mujahedeen resistance to the Soviets became ... *Osama bin Laden*. Transition in Afghanistan from Brzezinski-Carter ('Democrat') to Reagan-Bush (Republican) was predictably seamless in the one-party state. The Mujahedeen later morphed into al-Qaeda and the 'good guys' were now demonised by the US because that suited the next stage of the plan. Former British Foreign Secretary Robin Cook said shortly before he suddenly died in 2005 that 'al-Qaeda' means 'the base' or 'database' and is a reference to the CIA database of Mujahedeen fighters brought together to fight the Soviets. Cook said:

> *The truth is, there is no Islamic army or terrorist group called al-Qaeda, and any informed intelligence officer knows this. But, there is a propaganda campaign to make the public believe in the presence of an intensified entity representing the 'devil' only in order to drive TV watchers to accept a unified international leadership for a war against terrorism. The country behind this propaganda is the United States.*

Within a month Cook was dead from a 'heart attack'. There are now groups calling themselves 'al-Qaeda' who believed it existed because the US told them it did! Al-Qaeda was wrongly blamed for 9/11 to justify the 'war on [of] terror' and triggering the PNAC hit-list and the same network is now also known as ISIS/ISIL/Islamic State, Al-Nusra Front, Tahrir al-Sham and further south in Africa as Boko Haram. All are ultimately controlled by the United States, Britain and Israel (the Web). I'll have more about this in the next chapter.

## War criminals everywhere

Boy George Bush, Tony Blair and their corrupt cohorts lied about weapons of mass destruction in Iraq because it was the next target after Afghanistan. In the absence of a reason to invade and remove Saddam Hussein they just made one up. Blair, rightly known as Bliar, told the House of Commons that Saddam could strike British targets within 45 minutes and Colin Powell, the US Secretary of State, gave his laughable and child-like performance at the United Nations telling the world a load of absolute nonsense about the lethal danger posed by Saddam's (non-existent) chemical weapons. We had the usual 'threat to our way of

life' scam and the technique described
by Nazi military leader Hermann
Goering. He said that it was always a
simple matter to drag the people into
war whether in a democracy, fascist or
communist dictatorship ... 'All you have
to do is tell them they are being
attacked and denounce the pacifists for
lack of patriotism and exposing the
country to danger. It works the same
way in any country.' Dr David Kelly, a
British UN weapons inspector with long
experience in Iraq, had the knowledge
to demolish the El-lite's manufactured
excuse for war and he told the BBC that
the Blair/Alastair Campbell/British

**Figure 477:** Best of pals – Donald
Rumsfeld meets Saddam in 1983 as an
envoy for President Reagan and a
middleman in supplying Saddam with
chemical weapons for use against Iran.

Intelligence dossier making the case for invasion had been 'sexed up'.
Shortly afterwards he went for a walk and 'committed suicide' in the
most obvious of murders. Was Saddam a nice man? No, certainly not.
He was a tyrant put into power by CIA-instigated coups and supplied
by United States companies with chemical weapons to use against Iran
after Iraq invaded in the 1980s. They were also employed to gas Kurdish
people in 1988. The middle man in the chemical weapons shipments to
Saddam was Neocon Donald Rumsfeld as confirmed in thousands of
State Department documents related to the Iraq-Iran war that were
declassified and released under the Freedom of Information Act. They
included viruses such as anthrax and bubonic plague. The same
Rumsfeld would be US Secretary of Defense at the time of 9/11 and the
invasion of Iraq which was sold to the public as necessary to stop
Saddam using chemical weapons *that Rumsfeld helped to supply* (Fig 477).
By then Saddam had got rid of them as the United States and Britain
both knew. Saddam was a seriously nasty piece of work, but was he in
the same league for death and destruction as the force plotting his
removal? No, again, not even close. I vehemently oppose some of the
outrageous injustices that happen in Iran in the name of religious
extremism – not least to gay people – but the same question and answer
applies to Iran as it does to Saddam when you compare that country
with the killing machine of the US, UK and the West in general. How
could Saddam and Iran compete with those who number their dead and
injured in millions and cumulatively over centuries and generations in
billions?

   Libya was next in line and the same story was used to target Colonel
Muammar Gaddafi that was later employed against President Assad in
Syria. This can be summarised as: 'He's killing his own people.' To

justify attacking and removing sovereign governments the definition of sovereignty had to be changed from meaning the government of a country to meaning its population. This way you can say we have to protect the *people's* sovereignty in the face of a hostile government and remove your target leader without officially intervening in the sovereignty of the country. Okay, time to welcome back George Soros. He's been away too long. Zionist Soros began the process of changing the definition of sovereignty in a 2004 article in *Foreign Policy* magazine then owned by the *El*-lite's Carnegie Endowment for International Peace which was exposed by a Congressional Committee in the 1950s for manipulating war (see ... *And The Truth Shall Set You Free*). *Foreign Policy* has since been sold to the Jeff Bezos-owned *Washington Post*. The Soros article was titled 'The People's Sovereignty':

> ... *True sovereignty belongs to the people, who in turn delegate it to their governments. If governments abuse the authority entrusted to them and citizens have no opportunity to correct such abuses, outside interference is justified. By specifying that sovereignty is based on the people, the international community can penetrate nation-states' borders to protect the rights of citizens.*

> *In particular, the principle of the people's sovereignty can help solve two modern challenges: the obstacles to delivering aid effectively to sovereign states, and the obstacles to global collective action dealing with states experiencing internal conflict ...*

> ... *the rulers of a sovereign state have a responsibility to protect the state's citizens. When they fail to do so, the responsibility is transferred to the international community. Global attention is often the only lifeline available to the oppressed.*

Soros could not give a damn about oppressed people – except in the sense of creating them – and he was preparing the ground for the fake 'Arab Spring' that he knew was coming. The basis of what Soros was demanding in 2004 was adopted the following year by the United Nations' Security Council and General Assembly under a doctrine called 'The Responsibility to Protect'. How synchronistic then that Soros networks connected to his Open Society Foundations have become infamous among genuine researchers for covertly manipulating 'people's revolutions' in Ukraine, Georgia, the Middle East and elsewhere – usually related to a colour. We have had the Orange Revolution (Ukraine), Jasmine Revolution (Tunisia), Lotus Revolution (Egypt), Rose Revolution (Georgia), Tulip Revolution (Kyrgyzstan), and the failed Green Revolution (Iran). There are also the attempted 'Redshirt' revolutions in Thailand where the Open Society network seeks to impose further Western (Web) control. The 'Rose' version placed into power a US asset and little boy in short trousers, Mikheil Saakashvili, who would later turn up as a *Ukrainian* politician appointed Governor of Odessa by Ukraine president Petro Poroshenko after he was installed in a second Ukrainian

**Figure 478:** The Kagans could be a reality TV show except that it would be far too violent.

'revolution' (coup) by the United States and Soros in 2014. WikiLeaks documents reveal that Poroshenko was a US asset in Ukraine long before he came to power and he was handed the presidency by Victoria Nuland, the Zionist US Assistant Secretary of State for European and Eurasian Affairs who is married to Robert Kagan ... co-founder of The Project for the New American Century (Fig 478). Small world, eh? Nuland was exposed in a leaked phone recording telling the US Ambassador to Ukraine who she wanted in the government and, by the way, she was also exposed by Macedonian Intelligence for political manipulation there. Ukraine's second fake 'revolution' was triggered by protests in Maidan Nezalezhnosti ('Independence Square') in Kiev in November 2013, after the government of President Viktor Yanukovych chose to reject the signing of an association agreement with the European Union, and instead look to Russia and the Eurasian Economic Union. Protesters became known as the Maidan Movement. Leaked documents have confirmed manipulation in the background by the George Soros network and the control that he had over Ukraine after Yanukovych fled to Russia. Anywhere that Soros goes the US State Department and Israel goes with him. Everything was now in place with 'The Responsibility to Protect' for the *El*-lite and their pathetic media to dub US/UK attacks and coups in Tunisia, Egypt, Libya and Syria, as the 'Arab Spring' and demand regime-change in the very countries named in September 2000 by the Zionist Project for the New American Century. This 'Arab Spring' was supposed to be Arab people seizing their freedom but (a) you can never be free while your mind is controlled by religion, and (b) it was never about freedom at all. I remember sitting in a hotel room after speaking in Kiev, Ukraine in 2011 and watching the live coverage of thousands celebrating in Cairo over the resignation of President Hosni Mubarak after the Soros-driven protests that brought him down. But what followed was not freedom, only a vicious military junta government led by Abdel Fattah el-Sisi. Egypt is second only to neighbouring Israel for US military funding and together they take something like three-quarters of the US foreign military support budget. When the US says jump, Sisi asks 'How high?' Yep, the 'Arab Spring' worked out really well – just not for Arabs. This is how the 'people's revolution' scam works:

(1) Train agitators in the techniques of overthrowing governments through civil unrest (Egypt and so many others) or train, fund and arm terrorists and mercenaries to do so through what you term 'civil war' (Libya, Syria etc.).

(2) Employ propaganda to encourage others to 'join the fight' who have no idea who the real masters are, by demonising the leader and regime you want to bring down. The global mainstream media will always be frothing at the mouth to do so – see bin Laden, Saddam, Gaddafi, Assad and Putin.

(3) Your proxy army of 'rebels' begin to attack government targets – often with civilian casualties, or riot or amass in large numbers in iconic places such as squares or outside the government building. When the government responds with military and police you claim the target leader is oppressing his own people or when violent exchanges are involved with armed 'rebels' that he is 'killing his own people'.

(4) Tell the world that the innocent are being killed and the 'international community' (i.e. Britain, America and NATO) must intervene to protect civilians from violence by bombing them mercilessly from the sky as happened in Libya, Syria and a list of other locations worldwide. Thomas Paine, the English-American political activist and philosopher, said: 'The greatest tyrannies are always perpetuated in the name of the noblest causes.'

This is the sequence that can be witnessed over and over again and don't take my word that this is all coldly planned. The policy was revealed in a US military document entitled 'US Special Forces Unconventional Warfare Strategy' published on November 30th, 2010, just one month before the 'Arab Spring' began in Tunisia. The document begins:

*The intent of US UW* [Unconventional Warfare] *efforts is to exploit a hostile power's political, military, economic, and psychological vulnerabilities by developing and sustaining resistance forces to accomplish US strategic objectives ... For the foreseeable future, US forces will predominantly engage in irregular warfare (IW) operations.*

**Figure 479:** The West's version of protecting civilians from violence.

The document goes on to say the strategy requires that target-state population perceptions are first 'groomed' into accepting an armed insurrection, using 'propaganda and political and psychological efforts to discredit the government'... creating local and national 'agitation'... helping to organise 'boycotts, strikes and other efforts to suggest public discontent'... before beginning the 'infiltration of foreign organizers and advisors and foreign propaganda, material, money, weapons and equipment'. Should there be retaliation by the target government, the document continues, the resistance can exploit the negative consequences to garner more sympathy and support from the population by emphasising the sacrifices and hardship the resistance is enduring on behalf of 'the people'. This is what happened in Libya when a country with the highest per-capita income in Africa with free education, healthcare and even electricity was transformed into a Stone Age bloodbath of ongoing violence between warring tribes that had been prevented from killing each other by Colonel Gaddafi. Libya is now a safe haven for ISIS and other extremist crazies – as planned – and a major source of the vast influx of migrants into Europe (Fig 479). British-based Libyan fighters were allowed to move freely between the UK and Libya even though they were members of terrorist networks like the Libyan Islamic Fighting Group which was aligned with al-Qaeda and designated a foreign terrorist organisation in 2004. Former British MI5 agent David Shayler said that MI6 collaborated with the Libyan Islamic Fighting Group in a 1996 assassination attempt on Gaddafi. Many of these anti-Gaddafi operatives trained by the British SAS came from Manchester in the north of England and called themselves the 'Manchester fighters'. One of them said that three quarters of the anti-Gaddafi 'rebels' at the start of the conflict in 2011were from Manchester, with others from London, Sheffield and countries such as China and Japan. Among them was Ramadan Abedi, an *airport security guard,* who left England as an asset of MI6 to fight against Gaddafi with British support and was allowed to come and go at will. Five years later his son, Salman Abedi, would return from Libya to Manchester where he was named as the suicide bomber that killed 22 people and injured 119, many of them children, as they left a performance by singer Ariana Grande at the Manchester Arena. Theresa May, the British Prime

Minister, condemned the attack and ordered troops on the streets to protect the public. The Home Secretary responsible for border control in the David Cameron government when Salman Abedi's father and other British terrorists were freely allowed to move between the UK and Libya was ... *Theresa May*. The hypocrisy is stunning. Former MI5 agent David Shayler has said that father Ramadan Abedi worked for MI6 under the code-name 'Tunworth' and was given £40,000 for the assassination attempt on Gaddafi in 1996. His son, Salman Abedi, was yet another 'known to the security agencies' to be named as a terrorist killer. UK 'counter terrorism' agencies were warned at least five times about the danger posed by Abedi, including his stated willingness to be a suicide bomber, but did nothing. MI5 was warned by the FBI months before the attack that Abedi was part of a North African Islamic State cell in the north west of England which was planning attacks, but did nothing. Abedi was reported to have been on a US terrorist watch list in 2016 and yet was allowed in the run up to the Manchester attack to travel unquestioned between Libya, Syria, Turkey and Britain despite visiting a convicted Libyan jihadist jailed in Liverpool near Manchester in the months before the attack. Terrorists named for the London Bridge attacks which killed eight people shortly after Manchester continued the theme. Police, MI5 and the UK border authority were reported to have missed at least 18 opportunities to investigate and question those involved. One of them, Rachid Redouane, was another who fought in Libya during the US-UK-NATO coup against Gaddafi with a unit trained by Qatar (with UK/US 'liaison' officers) known as Liwa al Ummah which moved on to Syria after Libya had been devastated and merged with the 'Free Syrian Army' – you know, the US/UK/NATO-supported 'moderate rebels' in Syria that we were told so much about.

## In their own words

US Defense Intelligence Agency (DIA) documents, dated August 12th, 2012, confirmed the terrorist-supporting policy against Syria when they were made public thanks to a lawsuit instigated by government-challenging Judicial Watch. Documents confirm that Western governments (including the US, Britain, France and Israel), Turkey and Gulf States (Saudi Arabia, Qatar and UAE) were 'supporting powers' to terrorist groups that became ISIS in an effort to remove President Assad. They knew that this 'proxy war' was likely to lead to a 'Salafist [ISIS] Principality' in Syria:

> *... there is the possibility of establishing a declared or undeclared Salafist Principality in eastern Syria, and this is exactly what the supporting powers to the opposition want, in order to isolate the Syrian regime, which is considered the strategic depth of the Shia expansion (Iraq and Iran).*

Sunni and Shia Muslims disagree on the line of succession from the Prophet Muhammad and so there has been conflict between them for around 1,400 years. I know, but this is Planet Earth. The centre of Shia Islam is Iran while ISIS and Gulf States are Sunni dominated. Those DIA documents should have been dynamite for the media, but with a few exceptions they weren't. *Shhhh!* Charles Shoebridge, a former British Army and Metropolitan Police counter-terrorism intelligence officer, said:

> *Throughout the early years of the Syria crisis, the US and UK governments, and almost universally the West's mainstream media, promoted Syria's rebels as moderate, liberal, secular, democratic, and therefore deserving of the West's support. Given that these documents wholly undermine this assessment, it's significant that the West's media has now, despite their immense significance, almost entirely ignored them.*

The Pentagon-funded Rand Corporation proposed a similar policy in a 2008 US Army-sponsored report *Unfolding the Future of the Long War*. The proposed plan was to divide and rule the Arab world by setting Sunni (Saudi Arabia) in conflict with Shia (Iran) and the US supporting with weapons and cash the very terrorist groups they were supposed to be fighting. The evidence is clear from so many sources that ISIS was purposely-created by the US, UK and other Western governments in league with Turkey and the Gulf States. Israel was right at the centre of this, too, as always, and so although you would expect ISIS to head straight there to fight the 'infidels' they kill Muslims instead and destroy mosques. I would not rule out Israeli targets being hit at some point to justify direct Israel involvement in the war, but the pattern of Muslims killing Muslims is there for all to see. Former Israeli Defence Minister Moshe Ya'alon said in 2017 that on one occasion when Isis-affiliated fighters exchanged fire with Israeli troops in the occupied Syrian Golan Heights, ISIS had apologised. They were beheading Muslims and apologising to Israel? ISIS is a *Muslim* group?? No, it is a Saudi Dönmeh Wahhabi group. During Ya'alon's period as Defence Minister in 2013 Israel began to provide money, food, fuel and medical supplies to anti-Assad 'rebels' (terrorists) according to 'rebels' interviewed by the *Wall Street Journal*. This is still ongoing today. What happened in Syria was a repeat of the technique used in Libya when West-supported terrorists promoted as 'moderate rebels' were used to remove Gaddafi. Now here is a vital point to emphasise. Bush (Republican) and Blair (Labour Party) fronted up the lies to sell the invasion of Iraq, but by the time America, Britain, France and NATO were bombing the innocent in Libya to save them from violence in 2011 the political leaders in the US and UK were

**Figure 480:** Saddam's 'weapons of mass destruction' was the lie America and Britain used to tick-off Iraq on the Neocon list.

**Figure 481:** Change of leaders in the US and UK, but the same list goes on being followed – this time Libya.

**Figure 482:** All long-planned ... Syria was next.

**Figure 483:** Trump came to office and immediately focused on North Korea, Iran and China – or his military handlers did.

from the 'other sides' with 'Democrats' Barack Obama and Secretary of State Hillary Clinton teaming up with David Cameron, the Conservative Party Prime Minister. 'Outsider' Trump then comes in and kicks off about Iran and North Korea which are two others on the original hit-list (Figs 480, 481, 482 and 483). 'Different' leaders and 'different' parties, but the same PNAC list of countries continued to be targeted. This is how it works in the one-party state with the Hidden Hand directing policy whoever is officially in power. By the time Gaddafi was gone in Libya the same technique was underway in Syria and many of the 'Libyan rebels' (terrorists and mercenaries) then headed to Syria to do the same to Assad, thanks to weapons and funding from the US, UK and their satellite states in the Middle East, Saudi Arabia, Qatar and the United Arab Emirates. Weapons used against Gaddafi were also transferred from Libya to 'rebels' in Syria. An email released by WikiLeaks sent by Clinton's State Department in 2012 said:

*Washington should start by expressing its willingness to work with regional allies like Turkey, Saudi Arabia, and Qatar to organize, train and arm Syrian rebel forces. The announcement of such a decision would, by itself, likely cause substantial defections from the Syrian military. Then, using territory in Turkey and possibly Jordan, US diplomats and Pentagon officials can start strengthening the opposition ... Arming the Syrian rebels and using Western air power to ground Syrian helicopters and airplanes is a low-cost high payoff approach.*

**Figure 484:** *Ahhhh .... it all makes sense now.*

Turkey, Saudi Arabia and Qatar have since played central roles in funding and arming what was now called ISIS or Islamic State (see al-Qaeda, Mujahedeen etc.) and in the case of Turkey and Jordan allowing ISIS and 'rebel' forces to cross the border into Syria. Still more confirmation that ISIS is a creation of the West and its Gulf State satellites came with the admission by Hamad bin Jassim bin Jaber al-Thani, Qatar's prime minister and foreign minister until 2013, that the United States and Gulf allies had been supporting Islamic terrorists in Syria (Fig 484). He told PBS television interviewer Charlie Rose in June 2017 that the CIA was running training centres in Jordan and Turkey to produce terrorist fighters to overthrow Assad. Documents leaked by NSA whistleblower Edward Snowden revealed that up to a billion dollars a year was being spent training and arming this proxy US army. Hillary Clinton lied under oath when she denied knowledge of weapons shipments to al-Qaeda and Islamic State from Libya via Turkey and she knew that the US was arming anti-Gaddafi 'rebels' in Libya. Of course she did – *she* was doing it. Charges against American arms dealer Marc Turi for running weapons to Libyan 'rebels' were suddenly dropped by the US Department of Justice in 2016 when the court case threatened to reveal the involvement of Hillary Clinton, Barack Obama and the CIA in doing what Turi was accused of doing. US/UK funding and arming of ISIS/Islamic State (IS) against Assad and Syria has been hidden behind terms such as 'moderate rebels', but weapons supplied to 'moderate rebels' (terrorists can be 'moderate', apparently) ended up with ISIS, as the Americans and British knew they would. Military vehicles and state-of-the-art weapons were 'left behind' by the Americans in Iraq for ISIS to inherit and a study by the London-based organisation Action on Armed Violence found that of the 1.45 million guns supplied by the US to Afghanistan and Iraq between 2001 and 2015 only *three percent* are accounted for.

Peter Ford, a former British ambassador to Syria, has said that the United States is 'effectively siding with a branch of al-Qaeda' to overthrow the Syrian government. He said the US had an 'obsession with getting rid of Assad and the secular government in Syria' at the loss of 'all moral and practical competence'. This 'obsession' is because Syria is on the Zionist Neocon regime-change list and anything goes to

**Figure 485:** They act the same because they are the same.

**Figure 486:** Not even the fanatic killers and fodder who 'fight for ISIS' know this fact when just a little research would show them everything they need to know.

achieve that. At the time of writing the Neocon-instigated Syrian conflict has cost the lives of more than 400,000 people since 2011 (others say that's an underestimate) with another 5.5 million fleeing the country and 6.3 million internally displaced, according to UN figures. To describe those responsible as psychopaths is not even nearly sufficient. They represent pure, undiluted evil and the extremes of the Archontic distortion. Saudi Arabia is the direct creator of ISIS or Islamic State as a Western proxy army and so ISIS behaves the same way as the Saudis with its violent imposition of Wahhabism or Salafism through beheading and mass murder (Fig 485). The only difference is that Islamic State is promoted as a terrorist 'enemy' by the West, but Saudi Arabia is an ally to be armed to the teeth for their human carnage in Yemen and manipulated onto UN human rights and women's rights bodies while the Saudi fraudulent 'royals' daily destroy the most basic rights for their religiously-cowed population. Activists campaigning for human rights are tortured to elicit forced confessions which are then used to behead them. They have even done this to disabled people. There is no condemnation from the 'moral West' while Saudi Arabia does the bidding of the United States, United Kingdom, Israel, France and NATO (Fig 486).

## The defector prince

Saudi Prince Khalid Bin Farhan al-Saud defected from the family in 2013 because of their lies and corruption and now lives in Germany. He has confirmed that the US and Israel control the Saudi 'royals' and posted information that he said came from inside the family about US and Israeli 'conditions' for 'helping' current Saudi king, Salman bin Abdulaziz Al Saud, to succeed his father in 2015. Two other 'heir apparents' higher up the pecking order died in 2011 and 2012. Farhan al-Saud, the defector prince, said that in return for this 'help' Salman had to agree to 'absolute obedience' to the US and Israel, work to settle all Gaza Palestinians in north Sinai (to be paid for by the Saudis and UAE), destroy Palestinian group Hamas and secure ownership of Sanafir Island from Egypt. The latter was to change the Gulf of Aqaba from Egyptian territorial waters to international waters for the benefit of Israeli shipping operating out of the port of Eilat. In June 2017 Egypt president and US puppet Abdul Fattah al-Sisi transferred ownership of Sanafir Island and neighbouring Tiran island to Saudi Arabia despite public protests. The islands sit at the entrance to the Gulf of Aqaba which allows Israeli shipping access to the Red Sea. This is what really goes on behind the headlines and fake narratives. These Israel-Saudi connections further explain why Israel arse-lickers like Senators John McCain and Lindsey Graham also pimp for Saudi Arabia. With the US Deep State, Israel, UK and Saudi Arabia working as one unit it is worth people reflecting again on what happened on 9/11 from this perspective when there was such a Saudi Arabian connection to those attacks. The real power in Saudi is King Salman's appointed successor, the US-puppet Prince Mohammad bin Salman who has been given control of the military, oil and the economy, entertainment, business and in effect foreign affairs. They now call him Mr Everything.

Britain sells more arms to Saudi Arabia than it does to any other country because they are working to the same ends. Home Secretary Amber Rudd justified the Saudi killing of Yemeni children with British weapons as 'good for British industry' while condemning the Manchester bombing as 'a barbaric attack deliberately targeting some of the most vulnerable in our society – young people and children.' The UK *Guardian* quoted a Home Office spokesman at the same time as saying that a British government investigation into the financing of terror groups operating in Britain with special focus on Saudi Arabia had not been completed and published because the contents were 'very sensitive'. I bet they bloody are. The government later blocked publication for 'security reasons' (the security of Saudi Arabia and its connections to terrorism). During Trump's visit to Saudi Arabia in May 2017 an 'Arab NATO' was launched involving the United States and nations in the Persian Gulf agreeing to collaborate to stop the flow of terrorist financing. No collaboration was necessary – all these nations had to do to stop the financing of terrorism was to stop financing terrorism. The initiative will be jointly chaired by the US and Saudi Arabia, the two biggest funders of terrorism on the planet. The terrorists and terror-supporting Saudi Arabia, Kuwait, Qatar, Bahrain, Oman and the United Arab Emirates (UAE) came together to form the Terrorist Financing Targeting Center. This is to ensure the better financing of terrorists, presumably. The 'anti-terrorist' UAE was exposed by *Associated Press* for running 'black sites' in Yemen where prisoners are abused and tortured with US personnel involved in at least some of them. The joke plumbed still new depths when in June 2017, Saudi Arabia, the UAE, Bahrain and Egypt cut diplomatic ties and all land sea and air contacts with Qatar over claims that it was supporting terrorism and interfering in their internal affairs. The real reason was that Qatar did not support a hard-line against Iran and because from the US/UK perspective the dispute adds to the fracturing of the Muslim world demanded by Israel which, of course, supported the Saudi action against Qatar. Given what the Saudi defector prince said about Saudi Arabia's King Salman being completely controlled by the US and Israel this targeting of Qatar must have originated with them. They'll unseat the Saudi royals eventually, too, when it suits them. Trump condemned Qatar while saying not a word about the rest of them, and the sight of Saudi Arabia and the UAE attacking Qatar for funding terrorism takes us deep into the Twilight Zone. Veteran real journalist John Pilger said of ISIS:

> They are not only the progeny; they are the fully grown-up, manic, adolescent creature belonging to Paris, London and the United States. Without the support of these three countries, without the arms that have been given to ISIS – either they have been given directly to Jabhat al-Nusra and have gone to ISIS; or they have gone the other way; or they have gone to the Wahhabists in Saudi Arabia or in Qatar – but the French, the British, the Americans and the Turks have all supplied those that have kept ISIS going.

> You know, if David Cameron had won his Commons vote a couple of years ago [to bomb the Assad government directly], ISIS would now be in charge in Syria ... The Middle East's most multi-ethnic, multi-cultural state, would be finished, and these fanatics would be in charge, and that would be thanks entirely to Western actions.

These were the very actions demanded in September 2000 by the Zionist Project for the New American Century. Another question: Why do 'ISIS' propaganda videos including beheadings come into public circulation through fronts for Israeli Intelligence and why are ISIS claims of responsibility for terror attacks circulated through the same source? The most prominent of these Israeli organisations is SITE (Search For International Terrorist Entities) Intelligence Group

**Figure 487:** ISIS – such a blatant scam. SITE made 'Bin Laden' videos public and now does the same with ISIS.

in Bethesda, Maryland, run by Israeli zealot Rita Katz, which I have exposed in other books (Fig 487). How come 'ISIS' videos reach the public and media through Katz? American journalist and researcher Christopher Bollyn has established that SITE's 'ISIS' videos are supplied by Jihadology.net. This is a website operated by Aaron Yosef Zelin, a Zionist connected to Zionist think tanks, including the Washington Institute for Near East Policy. Bollyn points out that Zelin attends Israeli intelligence events, like the International Institute for Counter-Terrorism conference in Herzliya, Israel, which was addressed by ultra-Zionist Michael Chertoff, the US Assistant Attorney General at the time of 9/11 when crucial evidence was destroyed. Chertoff was also head of Homeland Security, an agency established because of the September 11th attacks. Videos that appear to come from ISIS and earlier from 'Bin Laden' are so easy to fake with modern technology to make them do or say anything. Put the words 'Nothing is real: How German scientists control Putin's face' into YouTube and you will see what I mean. There is also 'Synthesizing Obama: Learning Lip Sync From Audio'. These examples are not even close to the state of the art available to the Intelligence agencies which operate with technology far beyond anything you are allowed to see in the public arena. A team at the University of Washington has developed algorithms that can realistically lip-sync audio and video to make anyone appear to say anything and again this is only what you are allowed to see. Question *everything* especially 'terrorist' videos circulated by SHITE, sorry SITE. I must learn to type. We should also not underestimate for a second the central role of Israel and Britain in this frenzy of calculated global slaughter. Britain has been on the case since the days of violent colonisation – the 'Great' British Empire – and as a major centre for the unseen levels of the Web it is always in the frontline where exploitation, war and slaughter is being hatched. Britain tries to hide this by playing the little boy to America's Big Daddy, but while it may be like that in the arena of politicians and governments it is a very different relationship in the unseen. Roland

Dumas, a former French Minister for Foreign Affairs, said on French television:

> I'm going to tell you something. I was in England two years before the violence in Syria on other business. I met with top British officials, who confessed to me that they were preparing something in Syria. This was in Britain, not in America. Britain was organising an invasion of rebels into Syria. They even asked me, although I was no longer minister for foreign affairs, if I would like to participate. Naturally, I refused ... This operation goes way back. It was prepared, preconceived and planned ...

Official documents reveal that British and American governments planned something very similar in 1957 when Prime Minister Harold Macmillan and President Dwight Eisenhower agreed a plan by the CIA and MI6 to stage fake attacks to provide the excuse for an invasion by Syria's pro-Western neighbours Iraq and Jordan and to 'eliminate' leading figures in the Damascus government. A *Guardian* article described the plan:

> The report said that once the necessary degree of fear had been created, frontier incidents and border clashes would be staged to provide a pretext for Iraqi and Jordanian military intervention. Syria had to be 'made to appear as the sponsor of plots, sabotage and violence directed against neighbouring governments', the report says. 'CIA and SIS [MI6] should use their capabilities in both the psychological and action fields to augment tension.' That meant operations in Jordan, Iraq, and Lebanon, taking the form of 'sabotage, national conspiracies and various strong-arm activities' to be blamed on Damascus'.
>
> The plan called for funding of a 'Free Syria Committee', and the arming of 'political factions with paramilitary or other actionist capabilities' within Syria. The CIA and MI6 would instigate internal uprisings, for instance by the Druze in the south, help to free political prisoners held in the Mezze prison, and stir up the Muslim Brotherhood in Damascus.

Nothing changes then.

## Israel, war and terror

Former French minister Dumas also stressed in his television interview how it was important to know that in the region the Assad Syrian government has a very anti-Israeli stance. 'Consequently ... and I have this from the former Israeli prime minister who told me "we'll try to get on with our neighbours but those who don't agree with us will be destroyed."' The same theme was confirmed in a Hillary Clinton State

Department email:

*It is the strategic relationship between Iran and the regime of Bashar Assad in Syria that makes it possible for Iran to undermine Israel's security – not through a direct attack, which in the thirty years of hostility between Iran and Israel has never occurred, but through its proxies in Lebanon, like Hezbollah, that are sustained, armed and trained by Iran via Syria. The end of the Assad regime would end this dangerous alliance. Israel's leadership understands well why defeating Assad is now in its interests.*

US desire for a 'Salafist Principality' in Syria supports the long-term plan by Israel to 'Balkanise' Syria and the Middle East, in the way that the former Yugoslavia was broken up into smaller parts, and allow for Israel domination of the region. This is the century-old project for a 'Greater Israel' (Revisionist Zionism's

**Figure 488:** The long-term plan to impose a Greater Israel explains so much about events in the Middle East.

biblical Eretz Yisrael) from the River Nile in Egypt to the River Euphrates in Iraq (Fig 488). Kurdish people fighting ISIS want to secure part of Syria and should Turkey and the United States control Syrian land when the fighting ends (and that's the plan) you can bet they won't be giving it back to the government in Damascus. Kurdish official Hediya Yousef told the UK *Observer* of their intent to annex the Syrian city of Raqqa and land in northern Syria to the Mediterranean Sea with support from the United States. Part of this Greater Israel plan is to replace the Al-Aqsa Mosque on Temple Mount in Jerusalem with a rebuilt 'Solomon's Temple' which Jews believe stood on the spot a thousand years ago. Watch for events with regard to Temple Mount – Haram esh-Sharif to Muslims – and you will see where they are meant to lead. Even a US State Department report, *Country Reports on Terrorism 2016*, said that Palestinians were being pushed into violence by the actions of the Israeli regime and violence by Jewish extremists or 'settlers' illegally occupying Palestinian land:

*A lack of hope in achieving Palestinian statehood, Israeli settlement construction in the West Bank, settler violence against Palestinians in the West Bank, the perception that the Israeli government was changing the status quo on the Haram Al Sharif/Temple Mount, and IDF [Israel Defense Forces] tactics that the Palestinians considered overly aggressive [are* pushing Arabs to resort to violent extremism] *... extremist Israelis, including settlers, continued to conduct acts of violence as well as 'price tag' attacks.*

'Price tag' refers to violence by Jewish fundamentalists in retaliation to what they claim to be anti-illegal settlement activities. Israel is up to its neck in terrorism both against Palestinians and covertly elsewhere. Violence for the Israeli regime is the answer to everything and the State of Israel was bombed into existence by Zionist terror groups involved in a string of attacks including the bombing of the King David Hotel in Jerusalem in 1946 by the Irgun group and a massacre in the Arab village of Deir Yassin in 1948 as Palestinians were terrorised into fleeing their own country. Nearly a hundred men, women and children were killed in those two attacks alone and yet Israel claims to be the paradigm of virtue in which butter wouldn't melt. It *isn't*. Israel is a state founded by and sustained by terrorism through merciless groups like Irgun and Lehi (also the Stern gang) and continues today with the Israel Defence Forces (IDF) and the global octopus that is its military intelligence arm, Mossad. This has to be so given that Revisionist Zionist ideology (Sabbatean Frankism) is violent to its core. The Lehi Zionist terror group even explored at one point an alliance with Nazi Germany and Fascist Italy. Yes, really. But then fascism is Revisionist Zionism's spiritual home. Israeli Prime Ministers Yitzhak Shamir and Menachem Begin were leaders of Lehi and Irgun and subsequently had the nerve to condemn terrorism. Albert Einstein and other prominent Jews said in that 1948 letter to *The New York Times* that even Jews who rejected Revisionist Zionism were targeted by these terrorists and this still continues today:

> *... [Irgun] and Stern groups inaugurated a reign of terror in the Palestine Jewish community. Teachers were beaten up for speaking against them, adults were shot for not letting their children join them. By gangster methods, beatings, window smashing, and widespread robberies, the terrorists intimidated the population and exacted a heavy tribute.*

Journalist Jonathan Cook, based in Nazareth, Israel, wrote an acclaimed book, *Israel and the Clash of Civilisations: Iraq, Iran and the Plan to Remake the Middle East* in which he laid out the plan by Israel to 'unleash chaos across much of the region, destabilising key enemy states ... Iran, Iraq, Syria and Lebanon' with the intent of Balkanising the Middle East. A decade later the result of that policy is there to see. Cook highlighted the connection between Israel and the Neocons in the United States and he was right about that, too. The agendas of Israel and the Neocons are the same because *they* are the same. Cook wrote an article in 2017 headed 'Syria is the dam against more bloody chaos':

> *My book was published when efforts by Israel and the neocons to move the*
> *Balkanisation campaign forward into Iran, Syria and Lebanon were*
> *stumbling, and before it was clear that other actors, such as ISIS, would*
> *emerge out of the mayhem. But I predicted – correctly – that Israel and the*
> *neocons would continue to push for more destabilisation, targeting Syria*
> *next, with disastrous consequences.*
>
> *Today, Israel's vision of the region is shared by other key actors, including*
> *Saudi Arabia, the Gulf States, and Turkey. The current arena for*
> *destabilisation, as I warned, is Syria. But if successful, the Balkanisation*
> *process will undoubtedly move on and intensify against Lebanon and Iran.*

And so it will – the very fact that Lebanon and Iran are on the original Neocon hit-list of September 2000 is confirmation of that. The Neocons are desperate for a war with Iran. US Secretary of State Rex Tillerson made it clear in June 2017 that they planned a repetition of Libya and Syria in Iran when he told the House Foreign Affairs Committee that their Iran policy was 'to push back on this hegemony, contain their ability to develop obviously nuclear weapons, and to work toward support of those elements inside of Iran that would lead to a peaceful transition of that government'. Arm, fund and train 'rebels' ... you know the rest. I have no support for an Iranian regime so founded on religious programming, but look at Iran's history of starting wars compared with the United States which has been almost permanently at war since 1776. All this war crime, but not one of those responsible has appeared before the International Criminal Court (ICC) in The Hague, Netherlands, which prosecutes individuals for international crimes of genocide, crimes against humanity and war crimes. Or, rather, it doesn't.

If that were the case both Bushes, Blair, Obama, Cameron, Hollande, Kissinger, Cheney, Rumsfeld, Wolfowitz, etc. etc., and the fake royals of Arabia and the Gulf would all be safely secured behind bars. Instead they indict people like Serbia's Slobodan Milošević and those from Africa and South America. Anyone from the mass-killing West is nowhere to be seen. The ICC is a farce, an embarrassment and a tool of the very people that it should be

**Figure 489:** The International Criminal Court is a tool of the West and to claim otherwise is an insult to the intelligence.

prosecuting (Fig 489. Tony Blair was not arrested after playing a crucial role in the mass murder of Iraqis based on a lie and turning the Middle East asunder but instead he was appointed Middle East '*peace* envoy' to represent the 'quartet' of the US, EU, UN and Russia (while really representing Israel).

## Russian spanner

Assad and the Syrian army held on much longer than expected against the ISIS, al-Qaeda, 'moderate rebel' onslaught that was armed, funded and supplied by the US and Britain through Gulf states like Saudi Arabia, the UAE and Qatar. America was supposed to be out there with its air force 'fighting terrorism', but the ISIS advance was incessant and unchecked towards Assad's stronghold in the capital Damascus. Somehow with all that firepower in the air the US couldn't stop them. What could have been happening? Were these desert fighters just so incredibly good and unbeatable? Well, I guess dropping leaflets 45 minutes before a US bombing raid to tell them what was coming didn't help the cause. With every new village, town and city taken by ISIS came more beheadings, mass murder and abuse of women and children. The

Archontic Reptilian psychopaths in the West could not care less any more than the Archontic ISIS psychopaths that were doing it. But then came the game-changer. Russia's President Putin could see that Assad was certain to fall if nothing was done and the Russian naval base was also potentially under threat in the Syrian Mediterranean port of Tartus. Assad welcomed the offer of Russian air support and suddenly – hey presto – ISIS and their allies began to retreat in the

**Figure 490:** No, they were not trying because ISIS is a US/UK Western creation to remove Assad and seize control of Syria.

face of someone actually trying to make them do so (Fig 490). They were removed from the major city of Aleppo amid hysterical attacks by the mainstream media and politicians that Assad and Russia were killing the innocent. When the US bombarded Raqqa in Syria and Mosul in Iraq they were reported to be liberating those cities when Airwars, a UK-based monitoring group, said that at least 744 civilians were killed by US airstrikes in Iraq and Syria in June 2017 alone and *The Independent* in the UK revealed intelligence reports that put the civilian death toll in Mosul at more than 40,000. But still Russia and Syria were portrayed as civilian killers and the US/UK coalition as liberators. How the mainstream media sleep at night is beyond me, but not them, and progressives were on the street to order (Fig 491). An Iraqi general in the 'US coalition' quoted by *Middle East Eye* said that they were ordered to kill everyone in Mosul included civilians and children – 'anything or anyone that moved'. He said: 'We

**Figure 491:** More anti-System System-servers.

killed them all, Daesh [ISIS], men, women and children. We killed everyone.' Paulo Sergio Pinheiro, chairman of the UN Commission of Inquiry into the Syrian conflict, spoke of the 'staggering' loss of civilian lives in Raqqa from US 'coalition' air bombardment in support of Kurdish militia on the ground (many of them as crazy as any of the others) while footage emerged of ISIS maniacs driving in convoy out of Raqqa without any resistance from the same US 'coalition'. The American military is a death and destruction machine and wherever it and its UK/NATO allies go dead civilians follow while their proxy terrorist armies often get away and regroup; but remember that the US military is controlled by Satanists literally representing a Death Cult and then the mass targeting of civilians takes on a new meaning. To these satanic psychopaths mass murder in the name of war and 'liberation' are blood and fire death rituals feeding their masters in the unseen and holding down the collective frequency – thus 'kill

**Figure 492:** Deadly and devastating white phosphorous used against civilians by the United States 'coalition' and Israel.

everything and anyone that moves'. The US 'coalition', which as always includes Britain, has used white phosphorous weapons in Raqqa and Mosul which burns through to the bone causing horrendous injuries. These are banned for use in civilian areas but these psychopaths couldn't care less. They have used white phosphorous in Vietnam, Fallujah – see Mad Dog – and in Iraq and Syria in current conflicts while Israel has dropped this abomination on civilians in the concentration camp that is Gaza (Fig 492). Putin has been accused of propping up the demonised Assad, but he explained his reason for intervening:

*It's not President Assad whom we are protecting; we are protecting the Syrian statehood. We don't want their interior to be a situation similar to that in Libya, or that in Somalia, or in Afghanistan – in Afghanistan NATO has been present for many years, but the situation is not changing for the better.*

*We want to preserve the Syrian statehood. On the basis of resolving this fundamental issue we would like them to move towards settling the Syrian issue through political means. Yes, probably everyone there is to blame for something, but let's not forget that were it not for active interference from outside, this civil war probably would not have broken out.*

This is more statesmanlike in two paragraphs than American administrations have shown collectively in more than 50 years. The Syria-Russia purge of ISIS should have been welcomed by the US, UK and the West in general if they really cared about 'fighting terrorism', but they don't. Why would they when they *created* the terrorism? Michael Fallon, the numbskull UK Defence Secretary (a terrifying thought), was one who vehemently condemned Assad and his Russian support but in 2012 he was shaking Assad's hand in Damascus at a party to celebrate the president's re-election. Actions change when the agenda changes to another phase because people like Fallon are just gofers who do whatever they are told. The media should just record one video of Fallon saying 'I agree with the Americans' and they can then play that as his response to everything ongoing. To think that at a time when the world needs intelligent statesmen of integrity and wisdom Michael Fallon was made UK Defence Secretary, buffoon main-chancer Boris Johnson became Foreign Secretary, Donald Trump was elected President of the United States and the US military is headed by a bloke called 'Mad Dog'.

Russia's spanner was now in the Western works and we reached the point where even the American government was saying for the first time that a settlement in Syria was not necessarily dependent on Assad stepping down. Almost immediately afterwards Assad was accused of a sarin gas attack on 'his own people' in 2017 based on no evidence and when that is the last thing that Assad would do given that he and Russia were winning the war and pushing the US into the background. Why would Assad give America the ammunition against him that they so wanted? Khan Shaykhun, where the attack is said to have happened, is described as a 'ground zero' for Islamic jihadists. The West had tried to play the Assad chemical attack card in 2013 soon after Obama said that such an attack on civilians would be the 'red line' that would trigger US strikes on Syrian government targets, but veteran US investigative journalist Seymour Hersh reported that the Obama Administration had lied about Assad's involvement in search of an excuse to invade Syria. Hersh wrote that an agreement had been made in 2012 between the Obama Administration (controlled by Sabbatean Frankism) and the leaders of Turkey (ditto), Saudi Arabia (ditto), and Qatar (ditto), to instigate a sarin attack and say that Assad was to blame: 'By the terms of the agreement, funding came from Turkey, as well as Saudi Arabia and Qatar; the CIA, with the support of MI6, was responsible for getting arms from Gaddafi's arsenals into Syria.' Following the agreement exposed by Seymour Hersh, the London Mail Online website ran a story in January 2013 about leaked

**Figure 493:** Mail Online story that was quickly removed.

emails describing plans for a chemical weapon sanctioned by Washington to be delivered to a 'rebel' stronghold in Syria. The story was quickly removed from the website, but I was sent a screen grab (Fig 493). We are looking at a classic Problem-Reaction-Solution confirmed by details in allegedly hacked emails from the British and Dubai-based defence contractor Britam Defence which revealed a plan 'approved by Washington' and organised through the American client state of Qatar to transport a chemical weapon (CW) to Syria that was clearly intended to be a PRS to remove Assad. Obama had said that a chemical attack by Assad would be the 'red line' that would mean military intervention and the on-the-team French President Francois Hollande followed suit. Hollande agreed that the use of chemical weapons would be 'a legitimate reason for direct intervention'. Israel naturally said something similar as you would expect. The emails were made public by a German hacker and were alleged to be correspondence between David Goulding, the Britam Defence Business Development Director, and Philip Doughty, the company's founder:

*Phil*

*We've got a new offer. It's about Syria again. Qataris propose an attractive deal and swear that the idea is approved by Washington.*

*We'll have to deliver a CW to Homs, a Soviet origin g-shell from Libya
similar to those that Assad should have. They want us to deploy our
Ukrainian personnel that should speak Russian and make a video record.*

*Frankly, I don't think it's a good idea but the sums proposed are enormous.
Your opinion?*

*Kind regards
David*

The Qatari Emir at the time, Sheikh Hamad bin Khalifa Al Thani, is a
fake royal US puppet and the Qatar regime is a conduit for funding and
arming terrorist 'rebels' in Syria and Libya. The same is the case with the
fake royals running the United Arab Emirates, who include Sheikh
Mansour, Deputy Prime Minister of the UAE and owner of Manchester
City Football Club – the same Manchester hit by a suicide bomb that
killed 22 people and was blamed on an Islamic terrorist connected with
terrorist groups in Libya. How about Mansour sells the club and walks
away in shame? But then American, Saudi, UAE and Bahraini
condemnation of Qatar for funding terrorism shows they are incapable
of shame. Why would Qatar offer 'enormous' sums to transport a
chemical weapon to Syria 'similar to those Assad should have'? Only an
idiot could not answer that question. Carla Del Ponte, a former Swiss
attorney-general and leading member of a UN panel of inquiry into the
2013 chemical attack blamed on Assad, said of the investigation: 'I was a
little bit stupefied by the first indications we got ... they were about the
use of nerve gas by the [terrorist] opposition.' Those chemical attacks of
2013 and 2017 were Problem-Reaction-Solution scenarios to stage the
attacks or the illusion of them and then blame Assad to justify action
against him and his country.

## White Hell-mets

'Evidence' of the 2017 chemical
bombing came from the so-called
'White Helmets', an American,
British and EU-funded
'humanitarian' organisation
operating only in terrorist-held
areas of Syria. Abu Jaber, leader of
Tahrir al-Sham (al-Qaeda in
Syria), said in a video in March
2017 that the White Helmets were
the 'hidden soldiers of the
revolution' (Fig 494). White

**Figure 494:** The White Helmet hoax.

**Figure 495:** They need a better director and props manager.

Helmets were established in 2013 by James Le Mesurier, a British military intelligence officer who graduated from the Royal Military Academy at Sandhurst. He has reportedly been involved in similar 'humanitarian groups' in war zones including Iraq, Bosnia and Kosovo and has connections to the US Blackwater operation (now called Academi) which is a corporate arm of the CIA and US Intelligence in general. White Helmets have been exposed many times for staging non-existent attacks against civilians that they blame on Syria and Russia. Footage of these 'attacks' are provided by them and distributed to the media. They are not even good at it, but people are so gullible, especially 'journalists'. We have had 'corpses' open their eyes and footage has emerged of 'victims' being moved into place. One video shows a young girl 'pulled from the rubble' from behind a lump of stone so you can't see what is going on and then she emerges without a speck of dust on her while holding an absolutely pristine-clean rag doll (Fig 495). When Swedish doctors studied a White Helmets' video claiming to show them resuscitating children, this was the response from Dr Leif Elinder, a Swedish medical doctor and specialist in paediatrics: 'After examination of the video material, I found that the measures inflicted upon those children, some of them lifeless, are bizarre, non-medical, non-lifesaving, and even counterproductive in terms of life-saving purposes of children.' YouTube (Google) have no problem with such fakery putting the White Helmets in a good light while videos exposing them have been taken down for 'violating terms and conditions', which would appear to include telling the truth. White Helmet personnel have been filmed working with the most brutal terrorists, and a video was circulated in the summer of 2017 of a White Helmet helping anti-Assad militants to dispose of beheaded Syrian Army troops. Assad was right when he said: 'Our impression is that the West, mainly the United States, is hand-in-glove with the terrorists. They fabricated the whole story in order to have a pretext for the attack.' Pictures were released of the heroic White Helmets treating children and others caught in the alleged Assad sarin attack, but they were not wearing the right protective clothing and if the pictures were genuine they would all have been dead. Read the safety protocol for dealing with sarin which includes 'exposure to even small doses of sarin

**Figure 496:** Miracle men – White Helmets respond to 'sarin attack' without the correct protection but somehow they suffered no ill-effects. Amazing people.

can be lethal [and] damage can occur within one minute of exposure' and you'll see that what we are told is happening in the pictures is simply impossible (Fig 496). Professor Theodore Postol at the Massachusetts Institute of Technology wrote a preliminary review of the US government claims of 'Assad is to blame' and he said this of the White Helmets:

*If there were any sarin present at this location when this photograph was taken everybody in the photograph would have received a lethal or debilitating dose of sarin. The fact that these people were dressed so inadequately either suggests a complete ignorance of the basic measures needed to protect an individual from sarin poisoning, or that they knew that the site was not seriously contaminated.*

This is par for the course for the White Helmets hoax, and supports claims on Syrian television by terrorist Walid Hendi, who said that while working with the White Helmets he helped to fabricate a chemical weapons attack in the city of Aleppo filmed by a Turkish TV station and blamed on Assad's army. Hendi said it was financed by Arab Gulf countries. He described how they were filmed by two people, whom he named, while White Helmets brought stretchers to carry supposedly (but not) injured people. The United States and the West protect their

**Figure 497:** Don't reveal any facts or question anything that would trash the official narrative.

own lies from public exposure by controlling any investigation into its claims. This happened with the chemical attack and with the shooting down of Malaysia Airlines Flight MH17 which was blamed by the West on pro-Russian separatists over Eastern Ukraine in 2014. MH17 was 'investigated' by a team based in the Netherlands that was never going to produce findings that didn't suit the official narrative. Russian Defence Ministry spokesman Igor Konashenkov asked the again Netherlands-based Organisation for the Prohibition of

Chemical Weapons (OPCW) to explain how the White Helmets could not be harmed when dealing with alleged sarin (Fig 497). 'If it is true that sarin was used in Khan Shaykhun', he said, 'how can the OPCW then account for the fact the charlatans from the White Helmets organisation were hustling and bustling inside sarin clouds with no protective gear on?' No matter about such laughable flaws the West-controlled OPCW duly announced that sarin was used in the attack without saying by whom. Their conclusions about the sarin came from samples produced by the West-controlled White Helmets and other terrorist-supporting groups. This was enough for Buffoon Boris, the White Helmets-funding UK Foreign Secretary, to demand 'international action' against Assad. This is the demonise-Assad-so-we-can-bomb-him strategy that is so transparent it's pathetic:

1) West blames Assad for sarin attack.
2) West produces no evidence.
3) Western organisation investigates.
4) Organisation does not visit site but takes 'samples' from West-controlled terrorists and Assad-hating groups.
5) 'Investigators' say sarin was used without saying by whom.
6) Western politicians and media say this proves Assad was to blame.

A short film celebrating the White Helmets predictably won an Oscar in 2017 to generate more anti-Assad sentiment. The Oscars are often used to promote the El-lite agenda as they were when Al Gore's ridiculous global warming propaganda film, *An Inconvenient Truth*, won an Oscar. The Nobel Peace prize is used in the same way and Gore won that, too, along with the mass-bombing, mass- killing Barack Obama, Henry Kissinger and many other war criminals. How fitting that peace prize founder Alfred Nobel made his fortune from inventing dynamite and producing armaments. Aljazeera, the propaganda arm of the Qatar fake 'royals', reported: 'The eponymously titled White Helmets, a 40-minute Netflix film, gives a window into the lives of the group's volunteers as they scramble to pull people from the rubble of buildings flattened in bombing raids.' This was straight from the song sheet and as such it is absolute crap. Civilians rescued from Aleppo after Syria and Russia liberated the city from Western-backed terrorists confirmed the fraudulent nature of White Helmet

**Figure 498:** News from the front.

activities. One of the sickest examples of White Helmet propaganda was a film broadcast by Britain's Channel Four exploiting the horrific fire at a London tower block in June 2017 in which the Whites Helmets claimed 'solidarity' with those who died and compared themselves with the firefighters who risked life and limb to save as many people as possible. How insulting to those firefighters to compare them with the White Helmets and how insulting to the dead and injured to exploit them for blatant propaganda to promote a Western-funded front for terrorism. Another major source of anti-Assad and Syria 'information' constantly quoted by the mainstream media is the one-man Syrian Observatory for Human Rights which is run by the Assad-hating Rami Abdulrahman who lives in that well-known Syrian enclave of *Coventry* in the English Midlands (Fig 498). No, don't laugh. Oh, go on then.

## President Manchild

By now Trump was in the White House when he wasn't at his Mar-a-Lago golf resort in Palm Beach, Florida (Fig 499). This was the Trump who said throughout his election campaign that America should stop intervening in the affairs of other countries and regime-changing governments; and the Trump that called for better relations with Russia. But it was also the Trump that constantly says one thing and does another. Neocons were never going to allow their regime-change agenda to be stopped or better relations with Russians when they want to go to war with them, or at least bring them and China to heel on the road to complete global domination. General Michael Flynn, Trump's pick for National Security Advisor, wanted to end contrived animosity with Russia. He was soon outed in a manufactured 'Russia scandal' whipped up by the Neocon-controlled 'intelligence community' and hysterical media claims of collusion between the Trump team and Russia to fix his election. Soon the Neocon mentality was in place in all the crucial positions. 'Let's get on with Russia' rhetoric disappeared as an exercise in damage limitation amid the 'Trump connives with Russia'

propaganda. Every time any US accommodation and cooperation with Russia is mooted the Neocons and their media prostitutes invent some Trump-related 'Russia scandal' in an effort to ensure it doesn't happen. I have no doubt that Trump has long-time connections with some very unsavoury Mafia types in Russia as he does in the

**Figure 499:** Donald Trump, reality TV star, is a perfect resident for the House of Illusion.

United States and his financial dealings could bring him down in the
end – if that is what the Hidden Hand wants; but the idea that Russia
got him elected is supported by nothing but innuendo and fresh air.
Swamp-dweller Trump is another Neocon stooge (even if he doesn't
always want to be) who put the military in charge of key roles – General
John Kelly, head of Homeland Security and then White House Chief of
Staff; General James 'Mad Dog' Mattis, Secretary of Defense; and
General Herbert Raymond McMaster, Flynn's successor as National
Security Advisor. Add to those Lieutenant General Keith Kellogg who is
National Security Council Chief of Staff and General Mark S. Inch,
director of the Federal Bureau of Prisons. All these positions should be
given to civilians to balance the war crazies in uniform, but this is
Neocon World and America is a country built on war. The United States
has been at war for all but 21 years since it was formed in 1776 and the
military weaves through the very fabric of society. A law imposed in
2001 demands that schools submit data on all their students so Pentagon
recruiters can contact them directly at home. If they don't the schools
lose funding. Poor kids are targeted to become the military fodder of
tomorrow and the Pentagon has soldiers in school classrooms – even
primary schools – across America running military courses that involve
the already indoctrinated indoctrinating the indoctrinatable. As a result,
one young schoolboy said of the US military: 'They save the world and
go around the world to help people.' Sure they do. 500,000 students are
enrolled in ongoing Pentagon courses at school and about 40 percent of
those still attending in their last year at High School end up in the
military. America is a military society and clueless Trump handed
control of US military action to Mattis and McMaster or, put another
way, to the Neocons that control them. A military junta is now running
US foreign policy on behalf of the Hidden Hand after a bloodless coup.
Mattis told the Senate Appropriations Subcommittee on Defence that the
president had delegated him complete authority over the number of
troops in Afghanistan as he had in Syria and Iraq. Trump and Mattis
were immediately bad-mouthing Iran (PNAC hit-list) as a sponsor of
terrorism and a danger to the world and condemning North Korea

Figure 500: Illusory 'choice'.

(PNAC hit-list). Bush,
Obama or Trump – it doesn't
matter who you vote for the
Neocons/Democons and
their Hidden Hand
controllers always get in and
continue business as usual
(Fig 500). We have to focus
our attention on the
engineers, not the oil rags.

Trump has a notoriously short attention span and interest in detail and this makes him so easy to manipulate.

'Non-interventionist' Trump responded (was told to respond) to the lie about the Assad 'chemical attack' in early April 2017 by unleashing 59 Tomahawk cruise missiles on an airbase in Syria which seems to have done terrible damage to a canteen but strategically not much else. Oh, yes, some seven people were killed. Don't worry about that, though, it's only collateral damage. No evidence is required any longer before the button is pressed. Even Bush and Blair felt it necessary to at least make some up. Nobel Peace Prize winner Obama sanctioned ten times more unmanned drone strikes in faraway countries than his predecessor Bush, but in the first 45 days alone of 'non-interventionist' Trump the

**Figure 501:** Videogame mass murder.

rate of drone strikes increased by another 432 percent with one every 1.25 days. Trump has reportedly given the CIA power to order drone attacks as they choose (Fig 501). The Tomahawk attack on Syria was a clear breach of international law and a war crime, but all the usual Web suspects raced to the microphones to repeat the lies of America. Someone played a recording of UK Defence Secretary Michael Fallon who said 'I agree with the Americans'. *El*-lite gofer and yes-man Jens Stoltenberg, NATO Secretary General, said that Assad 'bears the full responsibility for this development' while German Chancellor Angela Merkel and then French President Francois Hollande issued a joint statement (Germany did in other words) which said that 'President Assad alone carries responsibility for these developments' for 'repeated use of chemical weapons and his crimes against his own people'. Liars the whole lot of them. Russia's President Putin accused them of 'nodding like bobbleheads'. Award-winning US investigative journalist Seymour Hersh revealed there was no American intelligence to connect the attack to Assad, but Trump ordered the missile strike anyway (although no way did he make that decision alone). CIA Director Mike Pompeo later indicated that he had told Trump that Assad was behind the chemical attack when there is no evidence for that. Hersh compiled his report from interviews with several US advisers and from transcripts of real-time communications that immediately followed the strike. He quotes a US officer saying to colleagues in the wake of Trump's decision:

*None of this makes any sense. We know that there was no chemical attack ... the Russians are furious. Claiming we have the real intel and know the truth ... I guess it didn't matter whether we elected Clinton or Trump.*

No, it didn't and it never does for all the reasons I have been explaining for decades. Hersh reports that 39 of America's leading 100 newspapers published editorials supporting the attack on Syria, including *The New York Times*, *Washington Post* and *Wall Street Journal*. System-serving CNN host Fareed Zakaria said the morning after: 'I think Donald Trump became President of the United States last night. I think this was actually a big moment.' This idiot added that 'for the first time, really, as president he talked about international norms, international rules, about America's role in enforcing justice in the world.' The vacuous Zakaria said that Trump had displayed the same qualities as past American leaders. In that he was right, but not for the reasons he was claiming. MSNBC anchor Brian Williams, spawned from the same intellectual desert as Zakaria, was in raptures watching the

**Figure 502:** America lies and Britain supports the lie.

launch of the missiles, a sight he described as 'beautiful'. Zakaria and Williams are what passes for journalism and yet Facebook and Google have no problem with them and their fake news – only those trying to tell the truth. So, we had a US president ordering the attack, the head of NATO and world leaders supporting the attack along with major media and it was all based on no evidence whatsoever. This is the scale of deceit that happens

worldwide day after day after day (Fig 502). In the wake of the Hersh revelations the Trump gangsters had the nerve to claim they had evidence (none supplied as usual) that Assad was planning another chemical attack in late June 2017 and would pay a heavy price if it went ahead. The term 'another' meant in addition to the first two for which the US provided no evidence. Michael Fallon's video said 'I agree with the Americans' and Rothschild-puppet Macron pledged the support of France. We plumbed still new depths of ludicrousness when Mad Dog announced that the US warning to Assad of paying a heavy price had stopped the attack happening (the one for which they provided no evidence). 'It appears that they took the warning seriously', said the man who loves killing people, 'They didn't do it.' Miss Vacuous, UN Ambassador Nikki Haley, said: 'Due to the president's actions, we did not see an incident. I would like to think that the president saved many innocent men, women and children.' You have got to laugh or you would weep.

The Tomahawk attack on Syria attack was engineered to happen while Trump was with Chinese leader Xi Jinping at his Florida resort, and the manchild delighted in telling the media how he revealed the Syria strike while they were both eating 'the most beautiful piece of chocolate cake'. Wilbur Ross, Trump's Rothschild Commerce Secretary and Wall Street secret society bigwig, said the attack had been after-dinner entertainment: 'Just as dessert was being served, the president explained to [China's President] he had something he wanted to tell him, which was the launching of 59 missiles into Syria – it was in lieu of after-dinner entertainment.' This is the sick mentality we are dealing with. The Tomahawk strikes and soon afterwards the dropping on Afghanistan of the biggest non-nuclear bomb ever deployed in known human history were both to send a Neocon message to China and Russia that the United States is the Big Daddy who is not to be messed with. After the Assad chemical attack lie came the claims that Saydnaya prison not far from Damascus in Syria was a 'human slaughterhouse with mass-hangings, exterminations and a crematorium to dispose of the bodies'. All except the crematorium bit had surfaced before in claims by Amnesty International, an organisation I do not even begin to trust although as always I am sure there are many genuine people among its ranks. Amnesty, which has received funding from George Soros, claimed that anything between 5,000 and 13,000 prisoners have been executed at Saydnaya since 2013, and that range of possibility alone should make people question the information on which it is based. No doubt Saydnaya is a deeply unpleasant place to be, but Amnesty admitted there was no physical evidence for its allegations and much of its case was illustrated using a computer model of Saydnaya where none of the model creators had ever been: 'In a unique collaboration, Amnesty International has teamed up with Forensic Architecture of Goldsmiths, University of London, to reconstruct both the sound and architecture of Saydnaya prison, and to do it using cutting-edge digital technology to create a model.' Eyal Weizman is the director of Forensic Architecture which provides 'evidence for international prosecution teams, political organisations, NGOs, and the United Nations in various processes worldwide'. In the wake of the US Tomahawk attack the Saydnaya allegations were repeated by the US State Department with the addition of the crematorium. Stuart Jones, acting assistant secretary for Near Eastern Affairs, spewed the usual lies about 'well documented' chemical attacks by Assad and then read his script about Saydnaya from which he quoted the Amnesty International report. A journalist asked Jones how he knew that the building that he was claiming to be a crematorium was not used for something else. Was it because snow melted on the roof more than surrounding buildings? Couldn't it just be that this building was simply warmer? 'We're looking at snowmelt on the roof that would be consistent with a crematorium,' Jones said. 'Or just a warmer part of a building, right?' the reporter asked. 'Possibly', Jones replied. On this preposterous 'evidence' an Israeli minister Yoav Galant said it was time to assassinate Assad, 'and when we finish with the tail of the serpent, we will reach the head of the serpent, which can be found in Tehran, and we will deal with it, too'. Oh, Syria and Iran – two of the names on the Zionist Neocon Sabbatean Frankist hit-list, yes? To the regime in Israel there is nothing, absolutely nothing, that can't be solved by violence and that is perfectly in line with the evil 'philosophy' of Netanyahu hero and Revisionist Zionism founder Ze'ev Jabotinsky.

**Figure 503:** Child meets adult.

## No-one flies! Er, except us

The problem for the Neocons is that the Russian leadership is far more intelligent and wily than the Western leaders (hardly difficult, I know) and to watch Russia Foreign minister Sergey Lavrov at press conferences with US Secretary of State, the Exxon CEO, Rex Tillerson, is to witness a father schooling a child (Fig 503). Russia appropriately trumped the West with an agreement brokered with Iran and Turkey for 'no-fly' or 'safe zones' in Syria to isolate ISIS/IS and their terrorist allies and ensure routes for food and other essential supplies to besieged areas. The United States had wanted a different kind of 'no-fly zones' which meant that no one could fly in those areas ... *except them and their allies.* This was done in Libya when NATO policed 'no-fly' zones in which NATO could fly, but not the Libyan air force and they protected their armed, funded and trained 'rebels' from Gaddafi retaliation. Russia would not accept that in Syria and instead negotiated with Syria, Iran and Turkey for zones where literally *no one* could fly. This included Israel which with its legendary arrogance has been bombing in Syria on the pretext of stopping Iranian arm supplies to Lebanon via Syria. Watch for Lebanon being targeted because it was on the original PNAC list in 2000, and also Sudan and Somalia where Trump eased restrictions on air strikes put in place to prevent civilian casualties. The man is a psychopath like those that control him. The US responded to the Russian-negotiated no-fly zones by creating its own arbitrary 'deconfliction zones' in Syria that no one could enter, not even the Syrian army of a sovereign government, without being attacked. This was done illegally as a blatant act of war without agreement of the UN Security Council or the permission of Syria which has invited only Russia into its territory in terms of direct military support. Every other country is an invasion force. America has attacked any Syrian Air Force planes or Assad-supporting groups entering the zones or even going close to areas the US is occupying illegally under international law. Where are you United Nations and International Criminal Court? *Silence*. America uses the pathetic excuse

**Figure 504:** Mad Dog summed up in five words.'

of self-defence to justify its attacks against Syrian sovereignty when the real reason for those deconfliction zones is to provide a safe haven to further train and arm terrorists for new assaults on Assad and the tragic Syrian people, and to lay the ground for the Balkanisation of Syria as per the Israeli blueprint. America illegally occupies sovereign Syrian land and then shoots down Syrian planes in *self-defence*? Mad Dog Mattis, US Defense Secretary, was also upping the stakes by taking out Syrian aircraft in the hope that either Syria or Russia retaliate and he would have the full-blown war that he and his Neocon controllers so desperately want. Russia's Defense Ministry said that the US had moved multiple rockets launchers to its illegal al-Tanf military base in a southern Syrian 'deconfliction zone' and it is obvious that America is itching for Syrian or Russian retaliation to its actions to trigger a wider conflict (Fig 504). Israel joined in by attacking Syrian government targets after claiming that Syrian missiles had 'spilled over' into the Israel-controlled Golan Heights – land that Israel has occupied illegally since 1967. Russia thwarted the sick agenda of the Neocons and now the US and Israeli governments and military are like children in their terrible-twos throwing a tantrum because they haven't got their way. How befitting that manchild Donald Trump is in the White House and manchild Netanyahu is in Jerusalem. Russia/Syria, America and Jordan agreed a ceasefire in parts of Syria in July 2017, but this was only another attempt by the United States (the Neocons) to get what they want by other means. Their goal is the removal of Assad and the breaking up of Syria into Balkanised regions. Russia must surely know that no American government is ever to be trusted. Anyone in doubt should ask the Native Americans. Israel's Netanyahu opposed the ceasefire and refused to be bound by any agreement, but that's

**Figure 505:** Ahhh! Save us from those toast burners.

**Figure 506:** You can't trust them.

understandable when your only response to anything is either rage and violence.

## So where now?

I have been warning about the plan for World War III pitching the West against China, Russia and their allies for a long time now, from back in the days when there had been no sign since the end of the Cold War that this could happen. Today even the mainstream media has been talking about the possibility as Russia has been subjected to incessant demonisation in the most pathetically obvious attempt to prepare the public mind for conflict. Russia has been accused of fixing the American election in favour of Trump and seeking to interfere in Brexit, the French election and each new one in turn (Figs 505 and 506). The power of repetition – 'Russia hacked the election' – led to one poll recording that 59 percent of Democrats believed the Russian government hacked into voting machines to fix the result when not even the authorities are claiming that (Fig 507). Any situation involving the name 'Russia' is seized upon and a molehill turned into Mount Fuji when no one seeks to

**Figure 507:** Repeat the same lies enough times and most will believe them.

manipulate the outcome of elections all over the world more than the United States. Mainstream media lie-for-a-livings were all over the story promoting the Trump-Russia connection, but then in June 2017 CNN producer John Bonifield was caught on a hidden camera by the Project Veritas organisation saying the alleged Russian scandal was 'bullshit' and that CNN was pushing the story for ratings. I think it's more than that, but the point is taken. The fake Russian scandal was hatched to block any coming together with the United States because the Hidden Hand wants conflict, war and not cooperation. Sanctions against Russia on the basis of no evidence are another wedge that is used to divide the countries. At the same time, a CNN reporter and two editors resigned (were fired) over their involvement in a story alleging a congressional investigation into links between Trump officials and a Russian investment fund which the channel had to retract. President Putin has been accused of preparing to invade countries on Russia's Western borders with once again no evidence produced. I am not saying that Putin is a Sunday school teacher. I am saying that the idea that he is the new Joseph Stalin seeking war with the West is ridiculous beyond words, but then Western propaganda *is* ridiculous and indicative of the kindergarten mentality that both produces and believes it. Russia is part of the Web, too, in terms of its secret society network and the Russian and American Deep States will be the same global Deep State way beyond the public arena. I have presented examples in other books of serious cooperation between the United States and the Soviet Union at the Deep State level with regard to technology and other matters while their governments were hurling abuse at each other. Nothing is what it seems. How much influence the Russian Deep State has over Putin will have to be judged from his actions and those of his government. We should always keep in mind that there are levels in every country beyond the official leader however all-powerful that leader may appear to be. I see this in North Korea where another manchild, Kim Jong-un, always seems to start firing missiles just when it suits the political purposes of the United States. There are also the next to useless missiles fired from Gaza into Israel whenever Israel needs an excuse for more mass murder. NATO accuses Russia of aggressive actions against the West when the opposite is the case. NATO is constantly increasing its build-up of troops and military resources along the border with Russia in Estonia, Lithuania and Latvia and essentially acting as an occupying military force in those former Soviet countries through so-called 'milestone agreements' (Fig 508). Who believes that the national armies of these states will now be able to act without NATO sanction? We are witnessing the biggest build-up of Western forces targeting Russia since the Cold War, which involves all the

**Figure 508:** The propaganda is pitiful.

countries on its borders with the West including Poland. This is in response to non-existent 'Russian aggression' and betrays the Neocon technique of demonise-then-invade. Lithuania produced a report about dangers posed by Russia and among them was the use of social and traditional media 'to promote a positive image of itself'. Oh, better bomb them, then. Putin clearly knows what is going on and that 'people's revolution' infiltrators are at work against him in Russia in the usual way, with Soros-connected 'opposition leader' Alexei Navalny used as the current front-man. Nothing has changed with the election of the fraud that is Trump and his campaign attacks on NATO and talk of the US withdrawing from the killing machine 'alliance' are long gone. Obama Defense Secretary Ashton Carter announced a four-fold increase in US military spending in Europe in early 2016 to 'meet the Russian threat'. The script-reading Carter said that Russia and China posed the greatest threat to world peace followed by North Korea and Iran. The brutal Islamic State that was beheading its way across the Middle East at that point was considered worthy only of fifth place.

## Chessboard pieces

The plan is for the Web via the United States to dominate the world militarily by positioning anti-nuclear missile interception technology close to Russia and China to provide a first strike nuclear capability against them in the knowledge that anything coming back would be intercepted and taken out. Or, at least that's the theory. I should emphasise that when they say 'intercepted' they mean before intercontinental ballistic retaliatory missiles can hit the United States. Europe on the other hand which is obviously much closer to Russia, would be destroyed. If Russia and China put their hands up or bow down to the United States on this basis maybe the crazies in Washington won't test the theory, but if they don't then anything could happen. The concept of MAD or Mutually Assured Destruction is the incentive for all to leave nuclear weapons in the box. US interception systems are purposely changing that. A Russian military spokesman said US long-range defence systems in Alaska, Romania and Poland increase the potential to intercept missiles from Russia and the zone of control covered almost the entire country. The strategic threat to both Russia and China from a global defence system giving potentially first-strike capability would only grow, he said. The United States has used the excuse of the non-existent 'Iranian threat' to install intercept bases in Europe which are really targeting nuclear Russia and not non-nuclear Iran. The same has been done with regard to China as the Terminal High Altitude Area Defense (THAAD) intercept system has been placed in South Korea using the excuse of a 'dangerous' North Korea when the real target again is China. The US deployed some THAAD launchers without even telling the South Korean president, but public protests have led to a block at the time of writing on further deployments. Iran is an American target because it is an Israeli target which means a Web target. A cache of emails by 9/11 Secretary of State Colin Powell leaked by a hacking group include a communication with business partner and Democratic donor Jeffrey Leeds responding to claims by Benjamin Netanyahu, a permanent advertisement for anger management therapy, that Iran is a nuclear danger. Powell wrote in 2015:

> *Anyway, Iranians can't use one* [a nuclear weapon] *if they finally make one. The boys in Tehran know Israel has 200, all targeted on Tehran, and we have thousands. As Akmdinijad* [misspelt former Iranian president Mahmoud Ahmadinejad] *said: 'What would we do with one, polish it?' I have spoken publicly about both nK and Iran. We'll blow up the only thing they care about – regime survival. Where, how would they even test one?*

Amazing what these people will say in private that they won't in public, but as Hillary Clinton said in a leaked private speech: 'You need both a public and private position.' In other words, your public position is to lie. Israel has 200 nuclear missiles pointed at Iran when neither Israel nor the United States will admit that Israel is a nuclear power even though this is an open secret. Israel's population is just eight million. Do you think there might be just a little bit more to know about Israel and its role in the world and why it requires hundreds of nuclear warheads to protect its sliver of land? The United States knows that Iran and North Korea are not a threat to them but it suits the plans of the Hidden Hand to convince people they are. You don't see mention in Mainstream Everything about what the United States military did to North Korea in the war of the 1950s, which is why so many in the country fear and despise the American government. General Curtis Lemay, who coordinated the bombing campaign against North Korea between 1950 and 1953, said: 'We killed off – what – 20 percent of the population. We burned down every town in North Korea ...' About 1.55 million civilians were killed, but North Korea is always the threat and not the world's biggest killer of human beings. North Korea dictator Kim Jong-un is a manchild and tortures people. The United States President Donald Trump is a manchild and has Guantanamo Bay. In terms of the number of innocent human beings they kill the US is way off the scale compared with North Korea. But one is condemned as an evil tyranny and the other is promoted as the shining light of the free and moral world. How easy it is to hide the truth when one study found that only 36 percent of Americans know where North Korea is located and in another poll 30 percent voted to bomb Agrabah – a fictional town in Aladdin. They are fed lie after lie by the media, politicians and the US and UK United

Nations representatives, the inane and child-like Nikki Haley and war-monger Matthew Rycroft with his connections to Tony Blair and the manipulated invasion of Iraq. The outstanding British political journalist Peter Oborne wrote:

> ... *Rycroft has form as a hawk. He played a key role behind the scenes as a Downing Street official on the eve of the Iraq war. He was the author of the notorious 'Downing Street memo' which showed that Blair believed that war with Saddam was 'inevitable' eight months before the invasion began and that the Labour PM was committed to support U.S. plans for 'regime change' in Iraq.*

> *Most cynically in that memo, Rycroft recorded that 'the intelligence and the facts were being fixed around the policy'. This shameful document dictated the tone for the subsequent fabricated dossier on weapons of mass destruction, which falsely set out the basis for going to war with Iraq.*

> *Sadly, this wretched episode did no harm to Rycroft's career, seeing him rise to his current post, which is*
> *Britain's most important*
> *diplomatic job on the world stage.*
> *It is, therefore, no surprise that the*
> *man who played a central role in*
> *the damnable conspiracy which*
> *took Britain to war with Iraq is at*
> *it again – banging the drum and*
> *demanding military action in*
> *Syria.*

**Figure 509:** Lying for a living.

Rycroft and Haley are both wheeled out at the UN to condemn with lie after lie the US target countries on the Neocon hit-list with Rycroft employing his cold and calculated venom and Haley as the head girl trying – and failing – to act like a grown up (Fig 509). If her brains were gunpowder they would not blow her hat off and appointing her is just taking the piss. Israel-worshipper Haley said in May 2017 that North Korea is 'a true threat to the world'. She could have been talking about Saddam, Gaddafi or Assad. It's the same script and they only change the name and the script-reader. She said the international community had to make a choice between supporting North Korea and facing the wrath of Washington or, as Boy George Bush put it 14 years earlier: 'Either you are with us or you are with the terrorists.' Watch for propaganda attacks on China (and countries bordering China) and efforts to break the alliance between Russia, China and Iran. It's easier to pick them off one by one than all together.

## World War III

Commander William James Guy Carr, an English-born Canadian naval intelligence officer, claimed the existence of a letter detailing a plan for three world wars in his 1959 book *Satan, Prince of this World*. He said the letter was written in 1871 by the infamous Albert Pike, Supreme Pontiff of Universal Freemasonry and influential in the creation of the Ku Klux Klan. Pike's letter was sent to Mafia founder and Web asset Giuseppe Mazzini and accurately described the first two world wars; but they had happened by the time of Carr's book and so the credibility of the content rests with what Pike is claimed to have said about World War III:

> *The Third World War must be fomented by taking advantage of the differences caused by the 'agentur' of the 'Illuminati' between the political Zionists and the leaders of Islamic World. The war must be conducted in such a way that Islam (the Moslem Arabic World) and political Zionism (the State of Israel) mutually destroy each other. Meanwhile the other nations, once more divided on this issue will be constrained to fight to the point of complete physical, moral, spiritual and economical exhaustion. We shall unleash the Nihilists and the atheists, and we shall provoke a formidable social cataclysm which in all its horror will show clearly to the nations the effect of absolute atheism, origin of savagery and of the most bloody turmoil.*

A definition of nihilism: 'A political belief or action that advocates or commits violence or terrorism without discernible constructive goals.' This perfectly describes ISIS/Islamic State and company and they are not only being deployed in the Middle East but further afield in Europe through terrorism, and in countries like the Philippines after its president upset America by moving closer to China. The Nihilists are indeed being unleashed to provoke a formidable social cataclysm and the *El*-lite want open fighting on the streets of Europe in the same way that we are seeing in the Middle East, Africa and the Philippines. Pike's letter continued:

> *Then everywhere, the citizens, obliged to defend themselves against the world minority of revolutionaries, will exterminate those destroyers of civilization, and the multitude, disillusioned with Christianity, whose deistic spirits will from that moment be without compass or direction, anxious for an ideal, but without knowing where to render its adoration, will receive the true light through the universal manifestation of the pure doctrine of Lucifer [the Demiurgic force], brought finally out in the public view. This manifestation will result from the general reactionary movement which will follow the destruction of Christianity and atheism, both*

*conquered and exterminated at the same time.*

Some will point out that there was no Zionism or Israel in 1871, but I can't stress enough how far ahead this plan is in the making. Our perceived timeline is an illusion. The Demiurgic Spider and its Archontic Reptilian assets beyond our reality and apparent timeline have been planning this long before even the weapons and technologies needed to achieve their end were known about in our five-sense world. They had these weapons and technologies all along and they have been making them available to their hybrid bloodline *El*-lite as the plan demanded and human technological understanding and capability could build and use them. Zionism and its base in Israel would have been in the planning on the inside way long before they appeared to the global public. The idea is to create such global war, violence and chaos that the population will agree or even demand a world government and army to intervene and stop the war, violence and chaos – with many more justifications thrown into the mix including the need for world government to impose compulsory laws on everyone to save the planet from global warming. In all these areas progressives will be in the front line demanding what the Web wants to happen without even knowing that the Web exists. If they don't wake up and start researching outside of the box they will continue to be conduits for the very fascism they spend so much time condemning.

World domination by the Archontic networks either through acquiescence or World War III is the plan unfolding before our eyes, but fortunately times are changing and more people are becoming streetwise to the game and selling tyranny is not as easy as it once was. The *El*-lite know this and hence the efforts to silence the genuine alternative media. Everyone who believes in freedom has a duty to defend it.

**Postscript:** What makes the political and military lunacy even more insane is that countries and their governments are set up as *private corporations* – so are the courts and virtually the entirety of 'The System' worldwide. They don't tell us that because they have to trick us into contracting with them to have authority over us. We need to rip up the contract and we can. The United States of America and the 'United States', for example, are not the same entity and this also relates to why there is a yellow fringe on the US flag on military uniforms. The fringe indicates that US troops are fighting for the United States *corporation*, not the country. I have covered this subject at length in other books and there is an excellent explanation headed 'InPower Episode #1: A Mass Action of Liability' which you can see on YouTube.

## CHAPTER FOURTEEN

# Saying the Unsayable

*'The rocket bombs which fell daily on London were probably fired by the
Government of Oceania itself, just to keep people frightened'*
*– George Orwell, 1984*

War today cannot be divided from terrorism. It never could in truth because all war is terrorism, but I mean in the modern definition of killing civilians in public places and making nowhere safe in the minds of the population. Terrorism is now an excuse for war and invasion.

Terrorism perpetrated by, or blamed upon, West-created psychopaths under names such as ISIS and al-Qaeda has been increasingly employed to terrify the public, generate ongoing fear and anxiety (food, low-vibrational states) and justify the deletion of basic freedoms and privacy to 'protect the country from terrorism' (Fig 510). These attacks are carried out by a combination of mindless idiots with no idea who their real masters are; those under alter-compartment mind control; and covertly by psychopathic military intelligence networks which then blame ISIS and other groups and individuals. The last method is easy when attacks are carried out by people with masks who are covered with clothing from head to foot. Once they leave the scene you can name anyone as the perpetrator. Who would know? There is no way when you look at the evidence that 24-year-old neuroscience student James Holmes killed 12 people and wounded 58 at the Aurora, Colorado, movie theatre in 2012 for which he was given 12 consecutive life sentences. If you want to see someone obviously under drug and mind control look at pictures of Holmes in the

**Figure 510:** *Everything.*

courtroom. The real killer was dressed in black tactical clothing and heavy body armour and wearing a gas mask. He entered through an emergency exit that could only be opened from the inside, threw a tear gas canister and opened fire. Witnesses reported shooting and gas canister explosions from *two* locations in the theatre and that a man in the front row took a phone call and then walked across to the emergency entrance and held it open with his foot before the killer entered through that same door (see *The Perception Deception* for the detailed background). The authorities then named Holmes, a mind-controlled stooge, and told the public a pack of lies about what happened. British soldiers *dressed as Arabs* were arrested by Iraqi authorities while driving a car carrying weapons and explosives. They were busted out of jail before they could be questioned when the moral British army sent six tanks and an elite SAS unit, held Iraqi police at gunpoint, demolished much of the jail and freed their own terrorists along with other criminals and insurgents. When idiot or mind-controlled terrorists are used in attacks they are often killed on the basis that dead men can't talk. Operation Northwoods planned to embark on real or simulated actions against various US military and civilian targets and the same techniques continue today. Rockefeller insider Dr Richard Day predicted the use of manufactured terrorism in his talk to the Pittsburgh paediatricians in 1969 as reported here by Dr Lawrence Dunegan:

> *There was a discussion of terrorism. Terrorism would be used widely in Europe and in other parts of the world. Terrorism at that time was thought would not be necessary in the United States. It could become necessary in the United States if the United States did not move rapidly enough into accepting the system* [transformation of society].

> *But at least in the foreseeable future it was not planned ... Maybe terrorism would not be required here, but the implication being that it would be indeed used if it was necessary. Along with this came a bit of a scolding that Americans had had it too good anyway and just a little bit of terrorism would help convince Americans that the world is indeed a dangerous place ... or can be if we don't relinquish control to the proper authorities.*

Today's engineered terrorism has been planned for decades and is nothing new. Only the scale and frequency has changed. NATO and the CIA created a terrorist network after World War II based in Italy and expanding across Europe under the code name Operation Gladio. The term came from a Roman word meaning 'stay behind'. Operation Gladio was claimed to be preparation for armed resistance if the Soviet Union's Warsaw Pact armies ever invaded. The real reason, however, was described by Operation Gladio operative Vincenzo Vinciguerra who is still serving a life-sentence for killing three police officers with a car bomb in Peteano, Italy in 1972. He said at his trial:

> You had to attack civilians, the people, women, children, innocent people, unknown people far from any political game. The reason was quite simple. They were supposed to force these people, the Italian public, to turn to the state to ask for greater security.

Vinciguerra also told the judges:

> With the massacre of Peteano, and with all those that have followed, the knowledge should by now be clear that there existed a real live structure, occult and hidden, with the capacity of giving a strategic direction to the outrages ... [it] lies within the state itself ... There exists in Italy a secret force parallel to the armed forces, composed of civilians and military men, in an anti-Soviet capacity that is, to organise a resistance on Italian soil against a Russian army ...

> ... A secret organisation, a super-organisation with a network of communications, arms and explosives, and men trained to use them ... A super-organisation which, lacking a Soviet military invasion which might not happen, took up the task, on NATO's behalf, of preventing a slip to the left in the political balance of the country. This they did, with the assistance of the official secret services and the political and military forces.

Vinciguerra said in a statement to the *Guardian* newspaper that the terrorism was perpetrated by 'camouflaged people ... belonging to the security apparatus, or those linked to the state apparatus through rapport or collaboration'. He said that every single outrage that followed from 1969 fitted into 'a single, organised matrix' with right wing terrorist groups Avanguardia Nazionale ('National Vanguard') and Ordine Nuovo ('New Order') 'mobilised into the battle as part of an anti-communist strategy originating not with organisations deviant from the institutions of power, but from within the state itself, and specifically from within the ambit of the state's relations within the Atlantic Alliance'. Vinciguerra's testimony is describing exactly what is happening today. Observe the response to every terror attack no matter where it may be and you'll see the same demands to increase the Big Brother state to track terrorists and protect the public. Troops were deployed on the streets of Britain after the Manchester attack in May 2017 and ten thousand troops are on public patrol in France in their ongoing official state of emergency, which also imposes multiple restrictions on public protest. We are going to protect your freedoms by taking them away – Problem-Reaction-Solution. The UK National Police

Chiefs' Council has also begun to press for all British police officers to be armed with pistols. These are only a few of the constant headlines that tell the story:

> *'Berliners call for more CCTV with 83 percent saying more public areas should be covered by cameras in the wake of the Christmas market killings'*
>
> *'Germany debates putting "troops on the streets" to protect against terrorism'*
>
> *'France to form National Guard amid calls to step up security'*
>
> *'British police officers asked if they want to carry guns in wake of terror attacks'*
>
> *'Theresa May says the internet must now be regulated following London Bridge terror attack'*

The military/police middle strata of the Hunger Games Society pyramid is being constructed on the back of terrorism and the need to 'meet the threat', when that threat is really coming from the force behind the creation of the military/police state. For this reason the authorities have no interest in genuinely investigating what happened as we saw with 9/11 and the Nice truck attack on Bastille Day in 2016 when the French government's anti-terrorist executive, SDAT, told urban surveillance authorities in Nice to illegally destroy all 140 videos of CCTV footage. The French Ministry of Justice said the reason was to stop 'uncontrolled' and 'non-authorised' circulation of the images and to prevent ISIS from using them for propaganda. Destroying the evidence would also 'protect the victims' families'. As if the psychopaths care about that. They didn't want the videos in the public arena because some clearly didn't support the official story and this would have been quickly pointed out by the public and independent media as we have seen in attack after attack since 9/11.

## Play it again, Sam

We have the same recurring theme with 9/11, the 7/7 bombings in London, the British police murder of an innocent Brazilian electrician, the murder of Princess Diana and many other tragedies – security cameras that would have shown us what happened were 'not working'. The mainstream media report the technological 'malfunction' and quickly move on without a second thought. Go about your business, nothing to see here. French authorities, as with the inner core of 'security' networks worldwide, are sick beyond comprehension, with

**Figure 511:** FBI or Feared By Informants.

staged horrors and cover-ups galore to their name including the murder of Princess Diana in conjunction with their Web buddies at MI6 in London. Go deep enough and French intelligence is British Intelligence is American Intelligence and so on through the Web connections. Involvement of the security authorities in setting up false flag terror attacks explains why so many of those blamed for them in the US are in some way connected to the FBI as informants or assets of informants (Fig 511). I have taken apart terrorist attack after terrorist attack in other books – see *The Perception Deception* – and shown them to originate with the very organisations whose official job is to stop them. Attorneys for alleged 'terrorist' Samy Mohamed Hamzeh said that hundreds of hours of tape recordings prove that he was groomed to carry out a mass shooting attack on a Freemasonic centre by two corrupt under-cover FBI agents who urged him against his will to secure a machine gun. The FBI then arrested Hamzeh and claimed to have 'foiled a terrorist plot' which they had instigated from the start. Many intelligence insiders have confirmed this false flag theme mostly through the alternative media. Among them is David Steele, a former Marine with 20 years' experience as an intelligence officer who was the second-highest-ranking civilian in US Marine Corps Intelligence. He said that 'terrorist attacks' are false flag attacks staged by security services:

> In the United States, every single terrorist incident we have had has been a false flag, or has been an informant pushed on by the FBI. In fact, we now have citizens taking out restraining orders against FBI informants that are trying to incite terrorism. We've become a lunatic asylum.

Amaryllis Fox, a former counterterrorism agent who worked for the CIA for ten years, talked of 'stories manufactured by a really small number of people on both sides [ultimately the *same* side], who amass a great deal of power and wealth by convincing the rest of us to keep killing each other'. Put simply: Tell both sides that the other side is out to destroy them and bingo you have a conflict. Henry Kissinger made a whole diplomatic career out of this technique which was hailed as 'shuttle diplomacy'. Historic false flags or Problem-Reaction-Solutions have been admitted and confirmed again and again, decade after decade, but were vehemently denied at the time they happened. The Nazis set fire to the German Parliament in 1933 and blamed it on communists to justify the suspension of civil liberties and freedom of the press which stayed in place throughout the Nazi years. US President Lyndon B. Johnson, who succeeded John F. Kennedy after the assassination in which he was involved, secured Congressional support to start open warfare in Vietnam on the back of 'attacks by the North Vietnamese' on the American Navy in the Gulf of Tonkin which never actually happened. We have just passed the 50th anniversary of the Israeli air and sea attack on the American naval ship USS Liberty off the coast of Gaza during the Six Day War with Egypt in 1967 which killed 34 crew members and wounded 171. Israel used unmarked planes in an attempt to blame Egypt. When the lies unravelled they claimed the Liberty was mistaken for an Egyptian ship – yeah, okay. American warplanes responding to Liberty distress calls were twice turned back on the orders of Zionist-controlled President Johnson and Secretary of Defense Robert McNamara. A massive cover up followed that ruled it was an 'accident'. Israel admitted that an Israeli terrorist cell in Egypt planted bombs in 1954 in US diplomatic buildings and other locations and left evidence to implicate Arabs. False flags are a speciality of Israeli military intelligence network, Mossad (the Rothschilds). The Soviet Red Army attacked their own border post in the Russian village of Mainila in 1939 and blamed it on Finland as the excuse to launch the Soviet-Finnish 'Winter War'. Hutu tribe soldiers in Rwanda, Africa, killed their own president in 1994 and blamed it on the rival Tutsi tribe which led to the best part of a million Tutsis being killed by Hutus in the blood bath that followed. A US Congressional committee revealed how the infamous FBI 'Cointelpro' operation from the 1950s to 1970s used agent-provocateurs to commit violence that could be blamed on target political activists. The list is enormous and why wouldn't it be when Problem-Reaction-Solution is a foundation technique of mass perception manipulation? If you put 'the ever-growing list of admitted false flag attacks' into a search engine you can see around 70 of them.

## Found a passport - you know the drill

The fact that we are looking at a recurring technique or blueprint explains the repeating sequences that we see in so many terrorist attacks. They include a terrorist passport being found, the 'terrorists' identifying the cause with 'Allahu Akbar', or Allah is Greatest, and an anti-terrorism drill or exercises happening at or around the same time at the same place based on a scenario that is either similar or exactly the same as what happens for real (Fig 512). The FBI claimed to have found a *paper* passport of a '9/11 hijacker' in Vesey Street at Ground Zero which had somehow survived a fireball plane crash and floated down to be discovered amid the extraordinary scale of debris and dust. Once this was announced and repeated by the mainstream media (without even

**Figure 512:** What a bomb shelter they would make – they're obviously indestructible.

laughing) the passport was just forgotten. It never existed, of course, but telling people it had been found confirmed in the minds of the unquestioning and naïve that the official story was true. 'See Honey, it was them Islams, they've found a passport.' We had the same theme with the 7/7 London tube train and bus bombings in 2005 when the authorities claimed to have found a passport and mobile phone insurance of one of the 'terrorists', Germaine Lindsay, who was supposed to have exploded a bomb in his backpack. The bombing was on July 7th, Lindsay's home was raided on July 13th and the passport, insurance and other documents were found in the carriage on July 17th and 18th according to the inquest – ten and eleven days after the event. Yep, sounds credible. Passports and other identification were found in attacks in Berlin, Paris, Nice, New York and Manchester where a bank card survived from a bomber who is said to have exploded a device on his person so powerful that it killed 22 people and injured 250. Official stories of terrorist attacks are full of glaring holes because they are invariably not true or at least twisted. Thus you have witnesses describing how the impact damage in tube carriages in the 7/7 attacks bent inwards and not outwards as it would if a bomb was inside the train.

Then there are the drill 'coincidences' (Fig 513). A series of air force 'training exercises' involving staged commercial airliner hijacks were happening in the sky over the United States and its Eastern Seaboard

**Figure 513:** 'Training drills' give cover for *El*-lite personnel on the ground to stage an attack.

during the 9/11 attacks which basically mirrored what actually happened (see *Alice in Wonderland and the World Trade Center Disaster* and *The David Icke Guide to the Global Conspiracy*). These exercises scrambled the usual emergency response by operatives with the North American Aerospace Defense Command (NORAD) which is there to protect America from air attack and deal with plane hijackings. Operators were confused about whether the real attacks were part of the exercises. 'Is this real world or an exercise?' one responder asked as recorded in the NORAD logs that morning. Exercises also moved air force planes from where they would normally be waiting on alert to immediately react to hijackings. The time it took for them to respond on 9/11 was ridiculous – as planned – and the White House and Pentagon are in no-fly zones where anything flying without permission can be taken down. So why didn't that happen to Flight 77 which is claimed – *claimed* – to have struck the Pentagon? You cannot declare no-fly zones to protect those buildings and then not have the means on permanent stand-by to police them. So what happened on September 11th? Anyone who reads the background to 9/11 as set out in detail in my books will be astounded to think that the mainstream media has questioned *nothing* about the official story which was given to them by the very people who claimed there were weapons of mass destruction in Iraq. A security 'practice' drill scenario related to the same locations as the 7/7 attacks in London was happening at the same time as the actual attacks and this was also the case with the Boston Marathon bombings in 2013. This happens repeatedly because the drill or exercise is the smokescreen that allows the real attacks to happen and gives cover to the military intelligence personnel who are behind them. Other false flag operations involve clueless pawns or those under Manchurian Candidate-type mind control. The image of terrorist cells everywhere peopled by Islamic fanatics reading the Koran all day is a fantasy. Alleged 9/11 'hijackers' were so lax with their Korans that they left them everywhere – hotel rooms, hire cars, all over the place. Or, rather, that is what the authorities told us. Korans were usually found alongside flying manuals. How predictable the manipulators are, but as the Nazis said the best propaganda is always the simplest. You want to sell a belief that Islamic fanatics flew the planes on September 11th? Okay, say you found Korans and flying manuals where they were supposed to have been. 'Said Ramzi' is a pseudonym for an undercover reporter with French TV who produced a documentary, *Allah's Soldiers*, after infiltrating a group of ISIS supporters planning a terror attack in France. This is what he found:

> The militants had very little understanding of Islam – they were 'fast food jihadis' ... One of the main lessons was that I never saw any Islam in this affair ... No will to improve the world. Only lost, frustrated, suicidal, easily manipulated youths.

One of the group urged 'Ramzi' to join him on the 'path to paradise' in a suicide attack and secure his reward from Allah: 'Our women are waiting for us there, with angels as servants. You will have a palace, a

HIDDEN HAND

SECRET SOCIETIES

MILITARY INTELLIGENCE

TERROR GROUP LEADERS

RANK AND FILE FODDER

**Figure 514:** Rank and file terrorists have no idea who their real masters are.

winged horse of gold and rubies.' Er, I don't think so, but this is who we are really dealing with. They are easily manipulated idiots controlled by those further up the hierarchy that they don't even know exist. An ISIS middle man based in Raqqa, Syria, was their go-between in the case of 'Ramzi's' group, but who controlled him and to what end? They would have no idea. The compartmentalised structure in Figure 514 is used to keep each lower level more ignorant than the one above and you don't have to go very high before any connection to Islam is long gone. Again and again after terrorist attacks we are told that the alleged perpetrators were known to the security agencies and that is true in both Europe and with the FBI and CIA in the United States. The phenomenon is so widespread it has been given a name – 'known wolf'. Some attacks are 100 percent staged with so-called 'crisis actors' playing their parts and talking to the media. The same people have been exposed for turning up at different incidents in different guises. It may sound bizarre but for sure there are companies that specialise in training people to play a part convincingly in training exercises. One company says:

> We dramatise events for emerging security needs in the UK, Middle East and worldwide. Our specialist role play actors – many with security clearance – are trained by behavioural psychologists and rigorously rehearsed in criminal and victim behaviour to help police, the army and the emergency services, hospitals, schools, local authorities, government, private security firms, shopping centres, airports, big business, criminal justice departments, media and the military to simulate incident environments for life saving procedures ... We use state of the art British film industry techniques, props and special effects ...

There are similar organisations openly providing rent-a-mobs for fake protests. Crisis actors, fake protestors and videos in which you can make people say anything. This is the world we now live in and people need to get streetwise and not accept things on face value. El-ite-manufactured terrorism has one goal: To make you so terrified that you will give your freedoms away in the name of safety and protection. *Don't fall for it.*

## The Exodus

Fear of terrorism has been increased on purpose by the massive movements of people into Europe from North Africa and the Middle and Near East (Fig 515). There are many reasons why this has been made to happen, but the two main ones are diluting individual cultures and traditions of Europe and the omnipresent divide and rule as incomers and indigenous populations are set at war with each other. The plan is to delete sovereign countries and divide them into regions ruled by

**Figure 515:** Vast numbers of people coming into Europe are part of a much bigger agenda.

superstates like the EU which would themselves be ruled by the world government. A continuing sense of culture, history and tradition are major problems for the *El*-lite because they know this would generate profound resistance to destroying countries and bringing in their regionalised cultural-fusion and tyranny in yet another expression of divide and rule. So, you have cultural identity in Europe being systematically eroded by introducing a completely different culture on a mass scale. Rockefeller insider Dr Richard Day knew this was coming in 1969 as part of the transformation of human society. He said there would be mass movements and migrations of people without roots in their new locations because 'traditions are easier to change in a place where there are a lot of transplanted people, as compared to trying to change traditions in a place where people grew up and had an extended family, where they had roots'. The Frankfurt School of social engineering, founded by Zionists in the 1920s, wanted 'huge immigration to destroy national identity'. This migration crisis did not happen by accident, but by design. First there was the easily predictable cause and effect of creating mass death, destruction and mayhem in Afghanistan, Iraq, Libya, Syria and elsewhere. Enormous numbers of people were sure to seek refuge from the fear and violence and the only direction for such escape was north into Europe. But that alone was not enough for the *El*-lite in transforming European culture and they added to the genuine refugees of war who need and deserve our help a far, far, greater number who were using the plight of the genuine to transplant themselves into Europe for purely economic and personal reasons. This may be understandable when they seek to leave countries in a state of Western (Web)-created deprivation, but it is still a fact and the word 'refugees' is used when the great majority are not. Look at the pictures of the hordes of people walking the migrant trails and you see that families and children are the serious minority compared with the domination of young adult men (Fig 516). A breakdown of unauthorised migrants arriving in Europe by sea in 2015 reveals that 58 percent were adult males, 17 percent were adult females, and 25 percent were minors under 18 years of age. Most of those arriving in Germany had no passport or paperwork to confirm their origin, but figures from the UN Refugee Agency (UNHCR) reveal that of the more than 180,000 migrants arriving in Italy by sea in 2016 almost a fifth were from Nigeria followed in number by those from Sudan, Gambia, Ivory Coast, Guinea, Somalia, Mali, Senegal and Bangladesh. Mass immigration is overwhelmingly not about supporting those fleeing war in the Syria and Libya. Do people really think that the child-sacrificing *El*-lite care about migrants? They are just pawns to them to be used and abused as necessary. Strings attached to the migrants and strings attached to the indigenous populations are being held by the same hand. An intelligence report leaked to the German newspaper *Bild* in May 2017 said that nearly seven million migrants in countries on the Mediterranean were waiting to make the journey into Europe. A million were in Libya, 3.3 million in Turkey, and a million in Egypt with others from Algeria, Tunisia, Morocco and Jordan. Should the EU agreement with Turkey to reduce the flow of migrants break down, the numbers will again increase dramatically. Saying this may be not be politically correct, but I couldn't give a damn. These are facts and truths that we need to face before it is too late. Progressives and those in fear of them are not interested in facts and reality, only mass virtue signalling.

**Figure 516:** A massive majority of migrants are not families and children fleeing war (refugees) but adult young men (economic migrants).

## All planned long ago

The process of cultural transformation began in countries such as Britain and Sweden many decades ago when politicians, without asking the population, decided that these societies would become 'multicultural'. I spent the first 15 years of my life, and a few years later, living in Leicester in the English Midlands which was a target city for the multiculturalists. You only ever saw white people in the 1950s but by the

1970s that had dramatically changed and those who had lived in Leicester all their lives hardly recognised areas of the city where they were born. Those who complained about the scale of the change were dismissed as racists – just as they are today. But most were not racist at all. They were troubled and fearful at seeing the communities they once knew disappearing so fast and being replaced by another culture they did not know or understand. There was no empathy with how they felt, only abuse and contempt from the authorities, media and what are now called progressives who believe that empathy should be reserved only for those that agree with their belief system. Out of that voiceless frustration came the rise of the far right in parties like the UK National Front. The same is happening today across Europe and it is only a much-expanded repeat of what I watched happen in Leicester decades ago where the foundation of the problem was sheer *numbers*. The first inflow mainly from the West Indies was fine overall and many arrived at my school where everyone pretty much got on and became friends and mates in a spirit of mutual integration. What tipped the balance was that the numbers went on increasing with massive arrivals from Asia (including Ugandan Asians) and the culture of Leicester was utterly transformed in a matter of years. Nor was this about integration in many areas, but cultural domination and replacement of what was there before. Those that saw their communities literally taken over by an incoming culture were left voiceless and dismissed as racists and bigots. Political correctness has been specifically created to make people voiceless in this and so many other ways. The 2011 census revealed that only 45 percent of the Leicester population was by then white British compared with 61 percent ten years earlier and that number is bound to go on falling. Progressives and those like them who hurl 'racist' in all directions cannot distinguish the difference between cultures and *numbers*. I love cultural diversity – how boring if everyone was the same – and as I travel around the world it is sad to see this diversity fusing globally year on year into a congealed blob of cultural neutrality. The McDonald's-Nike-Apple 'culture', as you might describe it. But you don't protect cultural diversity by having one replace another. As the number of migrants go on increasing the earlier arrivals and their successors suffer the consequences, too. But, don't worry, you can pour water into a jug forever and it will never overflow, bless 'em. The child-like naïvety is unbelievable. Official bias towards the new culture and against the old dramatically increased in Leicester when the incoming population became a pivotal electorate in deciding political power in the city and the same bias is happening now in many parts of Europe. Progressives reading this will be having apoplexy and screaming 'racist' because that is all they know, but I am seeking to look at this with some maturity and peripheral vision and not down the myopic lens of rampant self-purity and virtue signalling. I don't want the far right in charge any more than the far left or far centre. I want people of maturity, balance and fairness who can see the shades of grey. There are at least two sides to every story and situation and you don't see anything clearly by considering only one.

Confirmation that mass immigration is planned for the benefit of the *El*-lite comes with the central role of Tony Blair, the genetic liar and war criminal whose obsession with the European Union confirms the importance of that grouping to unfolding human control. When Blair speaks and acts the *El*-lite is speaking and acting. Andrew Neather, a former adviser and speech writer to Blair and UK Home Secretaries Jack Straw and David Blunkett, has revealed how immigration controls were deliberately relaxed under Labour Party Prime Minister Blair to 'open up the UK to mass migration'. He said that Blair and his ministers kept the policy secret because they feared alienating their party's 'core working class vote' in areas where they knew most migrants would go with the consequences of competing for jobs and driving down wages by working for less. The Labour Party hierarchy has long had contempt for its traditional white working class support and behind all the bullshit and slogans it still has. 'Progressives' and the Left in general support mass immigration when the biggest winners are rich people who can slash wage costs and exploit cheap labour. Instead of telling their 'core working class vote' the truth, Blair and his rabble publicly argued that immigration had economic benefits (yes, for the rich) and Britain needed more migrants. In ten years under Tony Blair and his very strange Labour Party successor, Gordon Brown, they allowed 2.2 million to settle in the UK which is double the population of the second biggest city, Birmingham. Andrew Neather said that a secret government report in 2000 called for mass immigration to change Britain's cultural make-up forever. This is precisely what they are seeking to do throughout Europe and that is the simple and supportable fact which the authorities won't publicly admit and progressives refuse to face. There is a war on individual and unique cultures and this is partly the reason for the destruction and theft of irreplaceable ancient artefacts (and razing whole cities like Mosul) in countries invaded by the United States or its proxy terrorist armies as we have seen in Syria and Iraq.

Successive Swedish governments have pursued the same policy that Blair did after the initial kick-start to Swedish multiculturalism provided in the 1960s by Polish Zionist David Schwarz who emigrated to Sweden in the early 1950s and became the foremost proponent of government support for immigration, the protection of incoming cultures and the dilution of the native one. This policy became official in 1975 and by 2001 the Social Democrat politician Mona Sahlin was announcing that 'Swedes must be integrated into the new Sweden; the old Sweden is never coming back'. Government-funded propaganda advertisements to this effect appear on Swedish television. 'Progressive' Fredrik Reinfeldt, Sweden's Prime Minister between 2006 and 2014 who pressed for more immigration, said that Swedes were 'boring', national borders were fictional and 'only barbarism is genuinely Swedish' while everything else came from outside. Clearly in his case breathtaking arrogance was also home- grown. Challenge such remarks and policies in Sweden and one of the most tolerant and egalitarian peoples in the world are condemned as racist. American Zionist and academic Barbara Lerner Spectre who relocated to Israel in the 1960s before heading to Sweden with her husband Rabbi Philip Spectre is quite open about the Zionist role in changing European culture. Spectre founded Paideia, the European Institute for Jewish Studies in Sweden, funded by the Swedish government. She said in a television interview:

> *I think there's a resurgence of anti-Semitism because at this point in time Europe has not yet learned how to be multicultural, and I think we're gonna be part of the throes of that transformation, which must take place. Europe is not going to be the monolithic societies that they once were in the last century.*

> *Jews are going to be at the centre of that. It's a huge transformation for Europe to make. They are now going into a multicultural mode, and Jews will be resented because of our leading role. But without that leading role, and without that transformation, Europe will not survive.*

The arrogance of those words is without limit, and how ironic that the Israeli authorities have such contempt for African migrants in their country and offer them money and flights to leave. Former interior minister Eli Yishai has been quoted as saying that Israeli authorities 'make their lives miserable' until they give up and allow the government to deport them. Prime Minister Netanyahu has said: 'If we don't stop their entry, the problem that currently stands at 60,000 could grow to 600,000, and that threatens our existence as a Jewish and democratic state.' Israel doesn't want refugees or migrants but it does want to clear the Middle East of as many non-Jews as possible in pursuit of its 'Greater Israel' or Eretz Yisrael. Professor Arnon Soffer from Israel's University of Haifa said: 'We are witnessing the beginning of a mass migration [out of the Middle East], such as the incursions of the peoples of the sea or the Huns.' Once more the 'resurgence of anti-Semitism' manipulation technique is employed by Spectre to explain why Europeans don't want to see their culture disappear. Maybe she might consider (she won't) that she is the *cause* of the resentment of which she claims to be a victim by having the astonishing conceit and sense of superiority to tell the whole of Europe – hundreds of millions of people – how things are going to be whether they like it or not.

Sweden's basically no-limits policy on immigration has been an absolute disaster both for most incomers and the native people, with Sweden taking more migrants in ratio to population than any other country in the developed world. In 2015 alone 180,000 were accepted which is bigger than the population of all Swedish towns and cities except the biggest three. Many are allowed in – as in other countries – because they are children, when they are well over six-foot-tall, extremely muscular and have beards. But don't point out such nonsense or you are a racist. New age tests in Sweden have established that three out of four of those given asylum because they were children were in fact over 18. The once prosperous Swedish economy is being destroyed by the immense cost of housing and funding such ratio-vast numbers of migrants, who arrive unable to speak the language and so with employment possibilities negligible for most. Sweden's famed welfare system is buckling under the ever-increasing demands. Yet still we have progressives calling for more immigration on their 'I'm-a-white-oppressor' guilt trip and those like Ugandan-born Victoria Kawesa, leader of the Feminist Initiative Party, want to open all borders and end the deportation of migrants who commit crime including rape. That's some 'feminist initiative', eh? Oh, yes, and she wants a tax on men. Don't ask. Ms Kawesa would never have the humility to question whether someone who was welcomed into Sweden when she needed to flee Africa and now calls for the deletion of all border controls, so destroying Sweden as we have known it, might just add to the resentment that many native Swedes feel towards immigrants. Self-obsessed and ridiculous statements by people like Kawesa and Spectre lead to resentment towards *all* immigrants and *all* Jewish people who are tainted with their brush. They are *causing* the very thing they say they oppose but their giant egos and inexhaustible self-importance can't see that. There is a backlash against *all* migrants when videos appear of a migrant telling a German man that Islam will come to Germany, his daughter will wear a headscarf, his son will wear a beard and that they are reproducing so much faster than Germans that they will conquer the country by birth rates (plus all the family members that follow once asylum for one is secured). Another video has a Muslim man bragging about the rape of European women – 'We are taking Europe from the Europeans and they are too stupid to fight back' ... 'They are going to pay us to conquer them and take their land' ... 'What I look forward to most is the destruction of European womanhood'. Another boasted about raping a young white virgin girl with seven of them involved. *This is going to create racial harmony, is it?* Perhaps the feminist progressives would care to comment.

I couldn't care less about someone's race. We are all one
consciousness having different experiences. I care about what people are
and what they do irrespective of creed and background, but the
manipulators are focusing on race and so we have to address that to
understand their agenda which includes the targeting of European white
races. Lamya Kaddor, a German scholar of Islamic studies with Syrian
ancestry, told a German TV programme that being German in the future
will mean having a migrant background. 'No more blue eyes, light hair
and "We're all German" – being German also means wearing a hijab.'
Kaddor introduced Islamic education in German public schools and
published the first German translation of the Koran for children and
adults. I am now seeing the Muslim hijab or head-covering being
promoted as a symbol of *feminism* in music videos and Alexander Van
der Bellen, the truly moronic president of Austria and former Green
Party leader, called for all women to wear headscarves in solidarity with
Muslims to fight 'rampant Islamophobia'. What about his rampant
stupidity? Let's go the whole way and insist that all women wear the
burka, shall we? Women should not be heard or even *seen*, right? The
gathering theme is the Islamisation of Western society and this is not for
the benefit of Islam, but the Hidden Hand exploiting Islam and its
advocates just as they created Wahhabism/Sharia law to usurp more
secular Islam. Children and the young are being especially targeted to
completely transform Western society when they become adults.
Austria's Van der Bellen, for example, made his remarks about the hijab
to school children.

### *Shhhhh!* The truth is not allowed

Walter Lubcke, district president in the small Germany city of Kassel,
responded to local concerns about immigration by saying that anyone
who didn't agree was 'free to leave Germany'. How do you think
Germans are going to feel about being told they can leave their own
country when they complain about so many of a very different culture
coming in from outside? Calls for compulsory Arabic to be taught to all
children in German schools is not going to add fuel to the potential fire
of indigenous resentment? Or when communities see those who settle in
their countries insisting on taking over entire areas with their own
culture at the systematic exclusion of others and operating Islamic
Sharia law as if in a country within a country or parallel societies. This is
the same Sharia Law that is used in Indonesia to target homosexuals and
transgender people and where homosexuals have been publicly caned
while a big crowd watches and cheers. How does that go down with
you, progressives? Are we naïve enough to think that Sharia Law
fanatics don't want to impose this wherever they go? Sharia law is
*Wahhabism* which is Saudi Arabia which is Israel which is Revisionist

Zionism which is Sabbatean Frankism which is Satanism. How can it be acceptable for Muslim women – and non-Muslim women – to be harassed and controlled by male Muslim 'religious police' in countries that find that abhorrent? A Swedish television team interviewed mosque officials about gender equality and they said they agreed with it. Then two journalists went back posing as Muslim women and their hidden cameras recorded the same people telling them they were expected to sleep with their husbands even if they didn't want to, accept being beaten and not to go to the police. This is everything that Sweden once stood up against, but half of these mosques are government funded. We are not only talking fairness and freedom for non-Muslim people – what about the horrendous way Muslim women are treated by Wahhabist Sharia law which sees women as little more than slaves to serve their programmed husbands? We also have the wave of 'honour' killings in countries like Germany where women are killed for perceived slights against men or falling in love with the 'wrong' person? Where are you then progressives? This is happening today across Europe. A school in Birmingham, England, was exposed in a government report for segregating pupils and having books in its library which advocated husbands beating their wives.

Former Swedish Social Democrat politician Nalin Pekgul, a feminist, told Swedish television that she no longer feels safe in the Stockholm suburb where she has lived for 30 years because of a rise in religious fundamentalism among men and she can't visit the suburb centre without being harassed. Zeliha Dagli, a former Left Party politician, moved from her suburb because of Muslim 'morality police' who want to control women's behaviour in the area. She said that aggression towards feminists had become an issue and she did not feel safe anymore. Blimey, the irony of it and all you progressives elsewhere are going to face the same if this is allowed to continue and go on expanding. A report commissioned by Sweden's Civil Contingencies Agency, part of the Ministry of Defence, warned that Muslim Brotherhood extremists were seeking to spread Islam in Sweden, instigate tensions in secular society and target political parties, institutions and other organisations to secretly build a 'parallel' society in Sweden. With a Swedish population of only ten million this process of infiltration and takeover could be achieved relatively quickly compared with much bigger countries. The report also described how those who challenge this process 'run the risk of being called "racist" or "Islamophobic" and because of the situation in Swedish society such classifications endanger people's careers'. Political correctness is there to censor exposure of what is really happening long enough for the end goal to be achieved with minimum challenge. Robert Menard, mayor of the French town of Béziers, was fined two thousand euros for 'inciting hatred' by saying there were too many Muslim children in local schools. Menard said that one class was 91 percent Muslim children: 'I do not find it desirable for children and their mothers that there are ghetto schools and to find solutions, it is necessary to say what it is.' Oh, but you can't if it could damage the immigration agenda that is exploiting both migrants and native populations because the *El*-lite have contempt for both. President Macron, the Rothschild vassal, announced plans to buy 62 hotels across France to be turned into migrant shelters, but mayors and police unions said this could mean that towns with smaller populations were 'filled with hundreds of single men'. This is what is meant to happen with local populations and the 'hundreds of single men' both pawns in the same 'game'. Highlight any of this and progressives (and the Establishment they underpin) can't scream 'racist' fast enough. Scream what you like, I could not give a fuck. These things have to be said and we must not be intimidated into silence by arrogant self-obsessed myopic self-purity. All balance and common sense has been usurped and we need to bring them back. Progressives complain about the 'rise of the far right' when political parties emerge that voice views and opinions which are otherwise silenced by the tyranny of political correctness and Orwellian 'hate' laws. PC progressives are *causing* what they protest about, but they are too blind and obsessed with their own self-purity to see that.

I spoke in Sweden several times in the 1990s and early 2000s and then there was a gap of many years until I returned to speak in Gothenburg in 2017. Sweden was not the same place. There was an air of fear in the air and advice not to go to certain areas after dark including a shopping mall. Rapes have risen sharply – by 13 percent in 2016. This forced the Swedish government Integration Minister to apologise for saying that the level of rape was 'going down and going down and going down' in reply to a claim that the city of Malmo is the 'rape capital of Europe'. The country's leading music festival announced the cancellation of the event for 2018 after a series of rapes and sexual assaults in 2017. A Swedish radio presenter then proposed plans for a festival in which all men were banned. She said: 'What do you think about putting together a really cool festival where only non-men are welcome, that we'll run until ALL men have learned how to behave themselves?' I think it is a pathetic and very sinister idea to ban all men – or all anyone – for the actions of a few instead of dealing openly with the few. Where does that road end? I know, let's jail all men for the crimes of a few because that way we'll be sure to stop male crime. Crazy, but that's the 'progressive' mind-set for you and their front-line influence is leading to Sweden losing its mind and all sense of perspective. Sexual assaults have soared in Sweden and so has crime in general while the authorities desperately try to hide the background by preventing police officers from telling the

truth and banning ethnic and nationality details from being recorded in
crime reports. An internal letter circulated by police authorities in
Stockholm instructed officers that the public should not be told of a
suspect's ethnicity, nationality, skin colour and height. Oh, that should
help to find them, then. The letter added: 'Criticism is sometimes made
against police regarding information about people's skin colour. It is
perceived as racist.' But not essential to locate the perpetrator, it seems. I
mean, they're only the police after all. Dutch national newspaper *De
Telegraaf* reported how police offered them special treatment with leads
and exclusive stories if they dropped a Freedom of Information request
asking for the number of asylum seekers involved in crime. This was
refreshing given that the mainstream media fundamentally contributes
to hiding the reality of what is happening until the point of no return is
crossed.

There are 'no-go areas' in Swedish cities where police won't go except
in numbers and among them is the now notorious Stockholm suburb of
Rinkeby known as 'Little Mogadishu'. They want you to believe this is
not true, but it is. A new police station being built in Rinkeby includes
bulletproof windows, walls reinforced with sheet metal and a protection
fence. It has been described as like a fortress or military installation. This
is in *Sweden*, I mean – *Sweden*. In June 2017, Swedish police added eight
more areas to the list of those 'especially vulnerable' bringing the total to
23. More than 50 are designated 'vulnerable' which are areas with high
crime where police face 'unique challenges', where there may be violent
religious extremism and where people don't report crime for fear of
retribution. This is in 'free' and 'liberal' Sweden today and the plan has
always been to make this happen right across Europe in a colossal
exercise in divide and rule. Gordon Grattidge, head of Sweden's
Ambulance Union, said there are about 50 mainly immigrant areas that
are dangerous to enter and especially so with five to ten 'no-go zones'
for ambulance crews. They only entered them with a police escort, wore
helmets and body armour and used reinforced ambulances. These are
some of the locations where police have been pelted with stones and
patrol cars set on fire. Grattidge said the migrants had their own
structure and community 'parallel to ours' and ambulance crews 'don't
feel welcome, that's for sure'. Then there is the gang culture and inter-
gang violence. Swedish National Police Commissioner Dan Eliasson told
a press conference that at least 5,000 criminals in about 200 networks
were operating in the now 61 'no-go zones' and his message to the
government was 'help us, help us'. Eliasson said that if the trend
continued they would not be able to cope. One report claimed that 80
percent of Swedish police officers are considering leaving the force
because of the conditions they now face. Amir Rostami, a former police
superintendent specialising in organised crime and gangs said: 'Today,

the gang environment is – well, I don't want to exactly call it the Wild West, but something in that direction.' The same is happening in the US with the MS-13 gang network and Germany with Middle Eastern crime syndicates engaging with virtual impunity in racketeering, extortion, money laundering, prostitution and drugs, arms and human trafficking. They control large areas of German cities and towns with the *Die Welt* newspaper reporting that about a dozen Lebanese clans control organised crime in the German capital, Berlin. A judge in Hanover passed only *suspended sentences* on six members of a Kurdish clan who badly wounded 24 police officers and six paramedics. German police were shocked at this ridiculous sentence and rumours circulated that the judge was in fear of reprisals against his family. Such rumours are not surprising when the judge did a deal with the accused that meant police officers did not give evidence against them. If the police rank and file were allowed to speak out the shocking truth would be revealed of what is happening and that's why they are told to keep quiet. Some officers have spoken out anyway. Peter Springare, a Swedish police investigator in the serious crimes squad for 47 years, took to Facebook to express his frustration:

> *Here we go; this is what I've handled from Monday-Friday this week: rape, rape, robbery, aggravated assault, rape-assault and rape, extortion, blackmail, assault, violence against police, threats to police, drug crime, drugs, crime, felony, attempted murder, rape again, extortion again and ill-treatment ...*

> *... Suspected perpetrators; Ali Mohammed, Mahmod, Mohammed, Mohammed Ali, again, again, again. Christopher... what, is it true? Yes, a Swedish name snuck in on the edges of a drug crime. Mohammed, Mahmod Ali, again and again ...*

> *... Countries representing all the crimes this week: Iraq, Iraq, Turkey, Syria, Afghanistan, Somalia, Somalia, Syria again, Somalia, unknown, unknown country, Sweden. Half of the suspects, we can't be sure because they don't have any valid papers. Which in itself usually means that they're lying about their nationality and identity.*

Springare's post was met with a mixture of wild support and the usual condemnation of racism, but as always the 'progressive' condemners refuse to address the key question: Is what he said *true*? They don't want to go there because to do so is to burst their bubble of self-delusion. They have an inability or desire to look at every individual on their merits in and of themselves irrespective of colour, creed and background. Their minds can think only in groups (the new version of 'group think') as in all migrants are good and all white people who complain are racists and bigots. In reality, *they* are the racists and bigots. German police woman Tania Kambouri, an immigrant from Greece, said that it 'cannot be that [migrant] offenders continue to fill the police files, hurt us physically ... and there are no consequences. ... We are losing control of the streets.' She added: 'Whoever tells the truth in this matter is quickly put in the Nazi corner.' Sex offences committed by migrants in Germany have nearly doubled to more than 3,000 in a single year according to official figures rising from 1,683 in 2015 to 3,404 in 2016 and that is only what is officially recorded. But you'll be a racist if you point this out. Those who are attacked? They don't matter, right? There are many cases of totally inadequate sentences, even acquittals, for migrant men guilty of rape on the grounds of 'cultural differences and misunderstanding'? An Austrian judge overturned a conviction by a migrant for brutally raping a 10-year-old boy and ordered a re-trial because the first court should have established whether the attacker thought his target had *consented*. What *a 10-year-old boy?* The Austrian town of Tulln refused to accept any more migrants after a 15-year-old girl was violently raped by multiple men and a 28-year-old Hungarian woman told a German court that she was raped nine times by Ethiopian asylum seekers while they filmed what happened on her mobile phone after she was ambushed at a town fair. Where are *their* 'human rights', feminist progressives? A 13-year-old girl raped continually by a British Muslim gang said she was told 'numerous times' by police and social workers not to mention the ethnicity of her attackers. 'I knew I wasn't racist, but I felt like that was used as a way to silence me', she told a radio interviewer. ' ... As soon as I said the names, I was made to feel as though I was racist and I was the one who had the problem.' When a 14-year-old child bride from Syria moved to Sweden and became pregnant with her husband he was taken to court by social services, but the judge said it was not a problem because she appeared 'mature' and it was their religion and culture. Had this involved a native Swede a big jail sentence would have followed for paedophilia and so the resentment builds and builds until it eventually blows – which is what the *El*-lite want to instigate to divide and rule and justify more police states.

## Trigger warning – shades of grey zone

Are all migrants rapists and criminals? No, *of course not*. The great majority just want to live their lives in peace. But are some of them? Of course, *yes*. It is these that the authorities and progressives don't want to face or allow you to highlight or hear about and this is the source of resentment and frustration that builds up in the indigenous population, expresses itself through political parties making these same points and associates in the minds of many all immigrants with the criminals and rapists. Show me any racial or cultural group and I'll show you nice people, okay people and seriously unpleasant people, but we are supposed to ignore this obvious fact when it comes to mass immigration. In my travels around the world in the last 30 years I have seen that it is not the colour or religion that matters it is a person's level of consciousness and how much they are connected with their heart. They are not nice *Muslims* or violent *Muslims* or nice *Christians*, violent *Christians, Jews and Hindus.* They are states of awareness expressing themselves through their particular body-type and faith. A violent Muslim would likely be a violent Christian if they occupied a different body and came from a different background. Give a psychopath another body but the same mind and what would they be? *A psychopath.* I look for states of consciousness in the knowledge that when all else is stripped away this is what we *all* are. Progressives see only the body. They are obsessed with race and gender and when you are so body-centric you must live in a state of ongoing myopia and ignore, even condemn, what is patently obvious to anyone with expanded levels of consciousness. How could there not be problems when you are introducing en masse a completely different culture with very different attitudes to freedom and women which includes those that are determined to impose their belief system, culture, religion and laws wherever they go? We must not be intimated into silence by progressive tyrants because these things need saying, acknowledging and addressing.

Migrants who think they have the right to make their culture and religion the dominant one in countries that have had the compassion and decency to take them in also need to have some humility and respect for the beliefs and culture of others and understanding for how they feel. They might find they and their culture are treated the same far more often in return. Russia Today or RT in the UK often wheel out a guy from something called the Ramadhan Foundation when there is a contentious story involving Islam. Whenever I have seen him he has hurled the labels 'racist' and 'bigot' at anyone with a different view who are making points they have every right to make about the impact of Islam on their communities. He is another arrogant who is causing what he claims to oppose by in my experience always justifying the Islamic position no matter what the situation, as a carbon copy of what you see with apologists for Zionism no matter what is done in its name. There is again no empathy for how others feel, only abuse, and he stokes the very frustration and anger that he then complains about. I saw an interview in which he commented on a story that Christians in Spain were outraged by dozens of Muslims praying together in Jardines del Triunfo (Gardens of Triumph) Park at the site of a Virgin Mary statue in Granada. I can be neutral between religions and races because I think all

religion is an extreme form of perception control and that to self-identify
with a body of whatever shade rather than with the infinite awareness
that we *all* are is perceptual myopia. This perspective sets you free from
today's ubiquitous identity politics when the motivation is not to look
dispassionately and empathetically at any situation in search of what is
fair and just, but to pursue only what suits your identity and to defend
that identity no matter what the circumstances. If we take this neutral
perspective with regard to Granada the sight of dozens of Muslims
praying (in Mecca mode) at a revered Christian statue reinforces the
fears of local Christians that their culture is being taken over. Whether
that is true or not is irrelevant. Muslims praying at a Christian site will
make them feel like that and so purely in terms of empathy that was not
a respectful move and the same goes for the local authority which gave
its blessing to this. I don't care where people pray or who they pray to as
long as they don't impose their belief on anyone else; but empathy is
about respecting the feelings of *others* not your own. I don't mean to take
on their feelings, but to be aware of them and acknowledge them. Our
man from the Ramadhan Foundation appears not to understand this
concept and out came the racist card towards his fellow interviewee
voicing another view. When asked if Catholics would be allowed to pray
to their god in a mosque he refused to answer and that's the whole basis
of what I am saying here. Either what is good for one is good for all or
we have religious and racial bias that is going to stoke the fires
whichever side that bias may fall.

What we need are fair and balanced Muslims like Nazir Afzal, a
prosecutor in the child sex scandal in Rochdale, Greater Manchester, in
which twelve predominantly British Pakistani men were convicted of
sex trafficking, rape and conspiracy to engage in sexual activity with a
child. The case involved nearly 50 mainly white British girls. Police
failed to investigate reports of the systematic abuse for fear of being
politically incorrect given the perpetrators were Pakistani Muslims and
the girls mostly white British. Labour MP Ann Cryer told a BBC
documentary said that police and social services had been 'begged' to
act but they wouldn't touch the case. 'I think it was they were afraid of
being called racist', she said. *Are you listening progressives?* This is what
happens when you create a climate of fear over doing anything to upset
your untouchables. Never mind what the girls were suffering month
after month. Cryer said she approached a friend, a local Muslim
councillor, to ask the Muslim 'elders' to take action but they didn't want
to know. This is the point made bravely and strongly by Nazir Afzal, the
first Muslim Chief Crown Prosecutor for North West England, who has
campaigned for Muslim women's rights and against forced marriage,
female genital mutilation and so-called 'honour killings' or 'shame
killings'. These are when a family member is murdered for the 'crime' of

allegedly bringing shame on the family because they have disobeyed the rules of their community or religion by not accepting an arranged marriage, having a relationship not approved by the family, having sex outside of marriage, being a victim of rape, dressing 'inappropriately', having non-heterosexual relations or renouncing their faith. Now just let me get my frickin' head around this. PC progressives create an intimidating environment for those – even victims of rape – to expose what is happening because the perpetrators are Muslim when extremists in the Muslim faith treat women like slaves, force them into unwanted marriages, mutilate their genitals and kill them if they want to live their lives differently from the rest of their insane family. But don't progressives claim to stand for women's rights? WTF? I say again *WTF?* Nazir Afzal said that Muslim communities where child abuse is rife were 'remaining silent about the prehistoric attitudes fuelling this crime'. There were parts of Britain where violent misogyny is accepted and even celebrated and these were largely Asian areas 'with little appetite in the community to do anything about it'. Afzal said there was no escaping the fact that Asian and Pakistani men were disproportionately involved in localised street grooming of vulnerable young girls. 'Our jails are filling up with Muslim prisoners and yet the crimes they're committing have become a taboo subject.' He said that trying to get Muslim audiences to address the issue was frustratingly difficult. They were only interested in talking about hate crime and Islamophobia (identity politics, me, me, me) without mention of Muslim prisoners and child grooming:

> *Such incidents are not uncommon and when you do manage to generate discussion around abuse, the response can be terrifying. Too many people blame the victims rather than the perpetrators. 'It's bad they got caught' is a common view.*

Afzal said that after speaking at one conference he spoke to an Asian man who said that his son had recently been jailed for dealing crack cocaine, but his anger had been focused only on his daughter because her marriage to an Asian husband of her own choice 'had brought great shame on the family'. Afzal told him the only person who had behaved shamefully was the father's son (and the father, I would add). He said there was great work being done by some groups in the Muslim community to challenge the abuse of women but without support of the wider community whose leaders prefer such matters to be ignored. Afzal recalled that when he praised a women's group 'run by incredible teachers who give up their time to mentor boys and girls on the dangers of child sexual abuse, forced marriage and radicalisation' it was a white businessman who came forward to donate money and not the local

Muslim community. He described how members of a women's group in Wales keep having their tyres slashed because Muslim men do not want women protecting other women. *Are you listening progressives?* Afzal continued:

> *It sickens me that there are people in the Asian community who don't want women to be empowered, they don't want women to support each other and would prefer women to be oppressed and do what men want them to do. Forcing the Muslim community to do more to deal with these problems has to be the starting point to drive grooming gangs out of existence.*
>
> *Challenging misogyny in schools, calling out shameful attitudes towards women and making sure elected councillors who give character references to rapists, as was the case in Rochdale, are on the front pages of their local newspapers should be standard practice.*

Nazir Afzal said if action is not taken now we were facing 'a social time-bomb that will have devastating consequences for policing'. He said that child grooming offences had increased five-fold in Manchester alone in the year to 2017 and nationally police were becoming overwhelmed. The problem is massive and mirrors the Muslim gangs in other European countries. Another child abuse scandal involving predominantly British Pakistani men in Rotherham in the north of England involved 1,400 children, most of them girls between 12 and 16. There were pregnancies, terminations, miscarriages, babies seized from mothers and it emerged that the police and local council knew about this for ten years and did nothing. Taxi drivers would arrive and take children for sex from *council care homes and schools.* They were gang-raped, faced threats to rape their mothers and younger sisters, trafficked to other towns and doused with petrol while being threatened to set them on fire. These were *children.* Reasons given for the failure to prosecute horrendous crimes the authorities knew were happening include fears that the religion and race of the psychopaths involved could cause allegations of racism and 'damage community relations', and the concern of the local Labour Party-controlled council that upsetting the Muslim community who mostly voted Labour would cost them support at elections. The Labour Party claims to be the defender of the working class, but they treat their traditional white voters, and in this case white working class kids, with absolute contempt. Don't give me any crap about Jeremy Corbyn's Labour Party being different. On these issues I don't believe it. The experience in Rotherham was the experience long before in Leicester. Once ethnic minorities decide elections any claims to equal treatment across the entire community are over. The number of Asian sex-abuse, rape and child-trafficking gangs in the UK continue to come to light with 17 men and one woman convicted of rape, sexual assault, human trafficking and inciting prostitution in Newcastle in 2017 with more than a hundred girls involved. The psychopathic perpetrators were from the Bangladeshi, Pakistani, Indian, Iraqi, Iranian and Turkish communities. One of them told a female ticket collector: 'All white women are good for one thing, for men like me to fuck and use as trash, that is all women like you are worth.' How very progressive. Sarah Champion, Labour Party Shadow Women's Minister said political correctness of the 'floppy Left' was leaving many too terrified of speaking out against the abuse: 'We've got now hundreds of men, Pakistani men, who have been convicted of this crime – why are we not commissioning research to see what's going on and how we need to change what's going on so it never happens again?' Why? Because the *El*-lite want this to happen, that's why. The National Crime Agency said the enormous scale of modern slavery and human trafficking in the UK meant that 'every large town and city in the country' was affected. When I look at Rotherham, Rochdale, Newcastle and others, and what is happening across Europe, self-obsessed progressives have so much to answer for – not least to the girls and women they so wrongly claim to support.

## Time to grow up

I have a simple philosophy to end all racism and all the reverse-racism cover-ups of the consequences of mass migration. Let us form our opinions with regard to *everyone* by the criteria of what they do and what they say and not by what they look like, where they come from or the god they believe in or don't. How about that? It is a novel idea, I know, that we actually treat everyone the *same*. Who could argue with that? Well, the reverse-racist authorities and progressives can for a start. Treating everyone the same must not be allowed because there is an agenda here in which the migrants and the indigenous population of Europe are both pawns. A bigger ratio of migrants committing crime and sexual assaults in some countries would spoil the narrative and so those facts must be suppressed. Equality is not what this is all about but it is the only way that it is going to be resolved. Migrants and not just the indigenous population need to look in the mirror and have some self-reflection. Those migrants that seek to Islamise the countries where they settle, replace the indigenous culture and disrespect women are going to face gathering anger and resentment, which is what the *El*-lite are planning on in a violence-fest of divide and rule. I would be saying the same the other way round if the West sought to Christianise the Islamic world like it once did.

Remember the fantastic way that people of all races, religions and backgrounds came together in mutual support, respect and grief in the wake of the shocking fire at the London tower block in June 2017 which killed and injured so many. Who cared then about someone's religion or race? They were just people in different coloured skins and with different beliefs facing the same nightmare. Everything else became irrelevant. This happens because mutual tragedy brings home what really matters and it isn't race or religion and all the fault-lines that are used to divide us. What matters is to love each other, care for and respect each other. Everything else is illusion. We need this mutual respect – and I mean *mutual* – and expanded perspective if the *El*-lite racial and religious agenda is to be thwarted. If this doesn't happen, white, black, brown, Christian, Muslim, Jew and Hindu will *all* be enslaved by enslaving each other.

## Manipulation of emotion

The Swedish experience can increasingly be seen throughout much of Europe in major countries like Germany and France. *El*-lite place-people

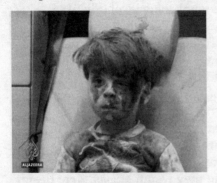

in the recurring mould of Merkel and Macron from the blueprint of Blair all support further mass immigration for all the reasons I am describing here. The moment when the flow of people along the migration routes through Greece and the Balkans to Europe really exploded can be tracked back to the tragic death of Aylan Kurdi, a three-year-old Kurdish Syrian boy who was drowned in September 2015 when his family was seeking to cross the Mediterranean to Europe and then head for Canada. Archontic *El*-lite software does not have the capacity for empathy and compassion, but

**Figure 517:** The image of Omran Daqneesh was used to demonise the Assad government but the mainstream media did not say that his family support Assad or that the picture was taken by a White Helmet connected to vicious and merciless terrorists.

they know that humans do and they manipulate that mercilessly and constantly to get their way. Emotion is a major access point to thought and perception and advertisers are exploiting this all the time to present products in an emotional setting which is often nothing to do with the product itself. Triggering emotion can be mightily effective in shaping perception and gleaning the desired response. Syrian boy Omran Daqneesh was used as an image to demonise the Assad regime when his shocked, bewildered, blood and dust-covered face was transmitted around the world after alleged Syrian/Russian airstrikes in Aleppo in 2016 (Fig 517). This was very powerful in manipulating emotion and, through that, perception. But the image was taken by a White Helmet photographer connected to some of the worst of Islamic terrorists and

**Figure 518:** The image of Aylan Kurdi that shocked the world and triggered a tidal wave of emotion that was exploited by the *El*-lite to achieve its cold and calculated ends.

Omran's father was an Assad supporter and remains so today. He said he heard no planes overhead as reported before the explosion and accused 'rebels' (terrorists) of exploiting his son for anti-Assad propaganda. He said he was offered money to do two interviews attacking Assad. The same technique was used to sickeningly exploit little Aylan Kurdi for the mass-migration agenda. So many children have been killed fleeing *El*-lite-created wars in Libya and Syria, but Aylan Kurdi was the one they chose to exploit to take mass migration into Europe onto a whole new level (Fig 518 overleaf). Who could not have been deeply moved by the sight of the little boy lying dead and alone on that Turkish beach? The picture went around the world and triggered *(triggered)* a surging wave of sympathy for those trying to escape war in the Middle East. Chancellor Merkel in Germany rode that wave by opening the borders to virtually anyone. They didn't need to be coming from Syria, even Libya, just anyone come. And they did so in enormous numbers. Germans clapped them off the trains when they first arrived with signs saying 'welcome' because to them in their manipulated emotional state everyone stepping onto the platforms was Aylan Kurdi. But they weren't. *Some* were fleeing war and were rightly supported, but most were exploiting that emotional wave which began with a little boy lying on a beach. Merkel was *Time* magazine's Person of the Year because as a 100 percent-owned asset of the *El*-ite and the Web she was doing her job. Soon Germans began to see that the scale of arrivals was unsustainable for all the reasons experienced in Sweden and they questioned how Merkel could be so crazy as to just open the doors to anyone no matter what their background and circumstances. Well, I've explained why. The agenda demanded it and as one writer said: 'European countries, such as Sweden and Germany, have practically mutilated their own cultures to appease the new arrivals.' Merkel has warned Britain that if open borders with the EU are not continued after Brexit there will be 'a price to pay' and this, too, is connected to the *El*-lite Sabbatean-Frankism immigration agenda. The EU open border policy has from the start been related to the plan for the dilution and destruction of distinct European cultures.

## Organised 'crisis'

Web-controlled non-governmental agencies (NGOs) and other
organisations are working at the other end of the migrant routes to
ensure that more and more people are sent on their journey into Europe
while Rome Mayor Virginia Raggi says: 'I find it impossible, as well as
risky, to think up further accommodation structures.' She is not alone in
her plea based on simple mathematics, but Zionist George Soros and his
NGO mob couldn't give a rat's arse. Italy is reported to be spending 4.2
billion euros a year on dealing with migration compared with 1.9 billion
on pensions and 4.5 billion on a national housing plan. That figure is
unsustainable as it continues to grow year on year as migrant numbers
go on increasing. Progressives want unrestrained immigration while at
the same time they condemn governments for not building enough
affordable housing and creating enough jobs. They cannot in their La La
Land self-delusion put those two things together and see that if the
population keeps growing through immigration and incomer birth-rates
there will never be enough jobs, affordable housing and adequate health
care because demand will always be constantly outstripping supply.
This is especially so with automation and robots sucking up jobs at an
ever-increasing rate. We see the same principle with building more and
bigger roads only for car use to increase which then demands still more
and bigger roads. Progressives don't want to acknowledge these simple
facts because they would have to maturely face reality instead of
spewing platitudes and slogans in search of virtue signals – 'Look at me,
see how politically correct and caring I am'. Figures released by the
Office for National Statistics revealed that Britain's population increased
by more than half a million in 2016 in the biggest ever peacetime rise in a
single year. Immigration watchdogs warned of further pressure on
housing, transport, public services like healthcare and the lower paid
competing for jobs. But don't tell the Provisional Progressives because
they don't do maths, and don't tell the progressive political parties who
increasing rely on the migrant vote for electoral support. Spain is being
increasingly affected as a new route opens up between the North
African coast and the 250-mile Andalusian coastline in southern Spain
across the Alboran Sea, which is a major tourist region in the western
end of the Mediterranean. At one point only 8.9 miles or 14.3 kilometres
of water separate Morocco and Spain across the Strait of Gibraltar.
Thousands of migrants are starting to head into Europe this way. Javier
Pajaron, security correspondent of regional newspaper *Voice Of Almeria*,
said:

> *Without doubt, most are economic migrants and not refugees. They are*
> *looking for a better life. Many never get deported, but just disappear into the*
> *black economy.*

Merciless people-traffickers only have to ensure their pathetic vessels reach international waters 12 miles off the North African coast and EU rules say that Spain must then help them because they are the closest country. Many migrants become slaves to the people traffickers who operate in Africa and Europe and stay in touch by mobile phone and social media with those who owe them money for the sea journey. They threaten to harm family members at home if they are not paid and the debts can take years to pay off. Charity worker Juan Mirelles said: 'They arrive penniless, so they have to earn money to refund the fare to traffickers and to avoid starving.' Others in places like Sicily are forced into selling drugs and their bodies for the Mafia who work with Nigerian terror gangs like the 'Black Axe' and 'Vikings' who use machetes on migrants that refuse their orders. An estimated 30,000 Nigerian women have been trafficked between Nigerian gangs and the Mafia to work as prostitutes in Italy and elsewhere in Europe. But, hey, keep the migrants coming, right progressives? If only to make you feel good about yourselves and allow great virtue signalling. Jose Antonio Alcarez, spokesman for the Spanish Police Federation, warned:

*We have a huge problem. We just can't deal with the migrant numbers. If we don't get more police to help, we will not be able to control the streets ...*

This will eventually destroy the tourist trade at southern Spanish resorts and the livelihoods of those who live there. There are two sides to every story, but progressives want to see only one. ISIS is reported to be increasingly involved in people trafficking and has urged jihadists to seize control of Spain. An ISIS video claimed that Spain is the land of Muslim forefathers and 'we are going to take it back with the power of Allah'. This is the plan throughout Europe for ISIS and those who created and control them in the West. All they have to do is ensure that war, violence, mayhem and depravation continue in the Middle East and Africa and they know the flow of people will never cease. If any of that is racist then the truth is racist but since when did the truth matter to Provisional Progressives? A report by the UN Refugee Agency confirmed that seven out of ten migrants crossing the Mediterranean into Europe were not fleeing war or in need of protection but seeking to relocate for economic reasons. The report said that many had headed to Libya from other African countries looking for work, but had found 'life-threatening insecurity, instability, difficult economic conditions, plus widespread exploitation and abuse' – all of which followed the removing and killing of Colonel Gaddafi by Western government psychopaths (Obama, Cameron, Hollande, NATO) because that was part of a longer-term plan that we are now witnessing. Gaddafi warned the

West that without him in Libya Europe could 'turn black'. He said prophetically on a state visit to Italy in 2010 that Europe would otherwise be 'another Africa' with the 'advance of millions of immigrants':

> *Tomorrow Europe might no longer be European and even black as there are millions who want to come in. We don't know if Europe will remain an advanced and united continent or if it will be destroyed, as happened with the barbarian invasions.*

They killed him on a lie and what he predicted is now happening. So-called NGOs are a prime vehicle for George Soros-type manipulation and take the form of charities and self-appointed agencies that claim to be campaigning for 'humanitarianism', 'human rights' and 'democracy'. But under that outward veneer many have a very different agenda funded by the usual suspects, most especially George Soros. Italian Foreign Minister Angelino Alfano said that he 'agreed 100 percent' with claims by Sicilian prosecutor Carmelo Zuccaro that 'migrant rescue charities' were working with people traffickers in Libya. Zuccaro said that wiretapped conversations proved that NGOs are conspiring with human smugglers to flood Italy with migrants and 'destabilise' their economy. Fabrice Leggeri, head of Frontex, the European border agency, said something similar in an interview with German newspaper *Die Welt*. A Frontex report said that migrant traffickers were given 'clear indications before departure on the precise direction to be followed in order to reach the NGOs' boats'. NGOs and charities then claim to have 'rescued' migrants when they were actually abetting illegal immigration. This was making accurate processing very difficult and putting lives at risk by encouraging traffickers to 'put even more migrants onto unseaworthy boats with little water and fuel' knowing the NGO boats are waiting at sea. Italian senator Lucio Malan said relief organisations rescuing migrants from the Mediterranean are operating in effect a ferry service which is 'enriching' people traffickers. He said the flow of migrants was so regular that it was not a rescue operation but 'public transport'. A senior Libyan coastguard official told the media that 'refugee charities' were paying people-smuggling gangs to ferry migrants in unseaworthy craft to their rescue boats waiting off Libya. Colonel Tarek Shanboor said he could prove this after securing bank and phone records and he also claimed that he had been given evidence of collusion between the charities and traffickers and EU border security in Brussels. This all supports the theme from multiple sources that the migrant crisis is being systematically manufactured. Colonel Shanboor said that aid agencies (NGOs) were encouraging ever more migrants to head for Europe across the Mediterranean. IsraAID is an umbrella group partnered with Rothschild-created B'nai B'rith (Sons of the Covenant) of Israeli search and rescue, medical and relief agencies, which has located its people on the Greek island of Lesbos to meet migrants and get them to camps for the paperwork that allows them to continue into northern Europe. Why aren't they in Gaza and Israel helping Palestinians and African immigrants much closer to home? Gearóid O Colmáin, a Paris-based Irish journalist, wrote the following in an article titled 'Coercive Engineered Migration: Zionism's War on Europe':

> *The debate about what should be done to manage the refugee/migrant crisis turns on whether or not they should be welcomed into European countries. However, this pro or anti migrant debate masks a new and highly destructive phase in US/NATO geopolitical strategy. Many of the migrants at the Hungarian border are coming from refugee camps in Turkey.*
>
> *Austrian intelligence has reportedly revealed that US government agencies are funding the transfer of these refugees to Europe in an attempt to destabilize the continent. This new geostrategic initiative involves using desperate refugees as weapons for the purposes of US/Zionist divide and rule of the European continent.*

The United States, Israel and others are only conduits and vehicles for the Web which is orchestrating all of this. The 'others' include the European Union which is seeking to enforce migrant quotas on its subordinate states and this was the plan going back at least to Count of Coudenhove-Kalergi, better known as Richard von Coudenhove-Kalergi (1894-1972). He was a major conspirator in the creation of what became the EU. I have detailed the background in other books of this Austrian-Japanese manipulator who was the founding president of the Pan-Europa (European Union) movement for almost 50 years. He and his network prepared the ground for the emergence of the EU thanks to major funding from Zionist bankers that included Baron Louis de Rothschild and Max Warburg. Kalergi foresaw not only the EU as it has become with the deletion of national sovereignty, but also a new 'Eurasian-Negroid' mixed race to replace those of today. The 'natural rulers' over this race he said were European Jewry which he referred to as the 'spiritual nobility of Europe'. Zionist former French President Nicolas Sarkozy said in 2008 that Europe faced a challenge of racial mixed breeding that was 'not a choice but an obligation' of white Europeans and if it wasn't done willingly the state would have to introduce 'more coercive measures'. He said:

> *The goal is to meet the challenge of racial interbreeding. The challenge of racial interbreeding that faces us in the 21st Century. It's not a choice, it's an*

*obligation. It's imperative. We cannot do otherwise. We risk finding ourselves confronted with major problems.*

*We must change; therefore we will change. We are going to change all at the same time. In business, in administration, in education, in the political parties. And we will obligate ourselves as to results. If this volunteerism does not work for the Republic, then the State will move to still more coercive measures.*

Have no doubt that Rothschild banker Emmanuel Macron, supported in his election by Sarkozy, is on the same team with the same script. Israeli rabbi Baruch Efrati was quite open about it, as reported by the *Ynet News* service. Efrati was most enthusiastic about the Islamisation of Europe and said that Jews should 'rejoice at the fact that Christian Europe is losing its identity as a punishment for what it did to us for the hundreds of years [we] were in exile there'. He added that 'Europe is losing its identity in favour of another people and another religion, and there will be no remnants and survivors from the impurity of Christianity' which, like Europe, should be totally destroyed: 'So I ask you: is it good news that Islam invades Europe? It's excellent news!' I write this chapter as someone who believes that identity with race – whoever it is – has lost the plot in terms of understand reality. Remember the sugar cube quote? Identity with race as a *self*-identity is an illusion, but the point is that it's not what I think and do that matters in all this; it is what the *El*-ite think and do. Talking of which ... surprise, surprise, Georgie's back.

## Soros is everywhere

Zionist George Soros is one of the leading proponents and supporters of mass immigration into Europe and the United States. A memo by his Open Society 'people's revolution'/'Arab Spring' Foundations was headed 'Migration Governance and Enforcement Portfolio Review' and brags about its success in influencing global immigration policy. The memo says that the European migrant crisis offers 'new opportunities' for further influence 'coordination and collaboration' with other wealthy donors and making the situation (mass immigration) the 'new normal and moving beyond the need to react'. The memo was authored by program officer Anna Crowley and program specialist Katin Rosin on May 12th, 2016, and says that 'we should also be supporting actors in the field proactively seeking to change the policies, rules, and regulations that govern migration'. They describe how they have 'to be selective and opportunistic, particularly at the global level, in supporting leaders in the field to push thinking on migration' and better coordinate advocacy and reform efforts. 'We have supported initiatives, organizations, and networks whose work ties directly to our aims in the corridors.' This is the same Soros manipulation arm that funds so many 'progressive' and left-wing causes that campaign to delete immigration

controls and label anyone who protests as a racist and bigot. The memo
indeed stresses the need to fight back against 'growing intolerance
toward migrants'. You get the picture. Soros has called for a million
migrants a year to be allowed into Europe and mass immigration into
the United States. His mansions are obviously full. Among the
organisations with which the Soros network claims connections is the
Migration Policy Institute (MPI) which the memo notes is a major
advocate for an amnesty on illegal immigrants in the United States. A
Soros-partnered organisation was exposed by local TV anchor Chris
Berg over a plan to flood the city of Fargo, North Dakota, and 19 other
cities with migrants. Partnership for a New American Economy
campaigns for an open immigration policy and is run by, among others,
Zionist former New York City Mayor Michael Bloomberg and
Zionism/Israel fanatic Fox News owner Rupert Murdoch, and itself
partners with Welcome America, a pro-open borders operation funded
by George Soros. They agree that 'partnership members understand that
immigration is essential to maintaining the productive, diverse and
flexible workforce that America needs to ensure prosperity over the
coming generations.' (See Tony Blair and the Labour Party in the UK
which said the same while planning immigration on a scale that would
'change Britain's cultural make-up forever'). The 19 US cities in question
were given 'Gateway for Growth' awards to be spent on educating the
public on expanded immigration. New American Economy's website
appears to be obsessed with the effect of immigration on deciding US
elections and points out that by 2020 some 25.6 million Hispanic and
Asian voters could join the US electorate and how they vote will depend
on 'each party's success at earning their support':

> *Candidates who take positions that cast them as anti-immigration will start
> the general election at a 24-point disadvantage among likely voters and at an
> even greater disadvantage among key electoral groups, such as college-
> educated white women and young voters.*

> *Only about 1 in 5 GOP primary voters is an anti-immigration voter. This
> small pool of the electorate comprises hardline voters who are virtually
> unwinnable for any mainstream candidate. However, candidates can have
> success with both Hispanic and immigrant voters, as studies show that, if
> the immigration issue were off the table, many of these voters would be up
> for grabs.*

So anyone running for political office – be warned. The game is so
transparent. Once you reach the point where the migrant vote decides
elections that's the end of any vestige of government for all the people –
not that this has ever existed in totality but I mean in terms of anything

at all. The pawns being primarily used in the United States to transform the country's demographic are Hispanics (Spanish-speaking) and Latinos (anyone from Latin America), hence Hispanics are highlighted by that El-lite front organisation, the New American Economy. There is a phony argument going on about Muslims being allowed to settle in America, but that is a smokescreen. There is far too much distance and ocean between the centre of the Muslim world and the United States for them to be used as migrant pawns in the way they are in Europe. But Central and South America is just across the US border and Hispanics and Latinos in this case are being exploited to advance the El-lite plan of targeting the white races. In Australia, they are using immigration from China and Asia in general. It is not the nature of the migrant that matters so much to the El-lite and their Archontic Reptilian masters but simply the numbers. It is *absolutely vital* that *all* people of *all* races and backgrounds realise that they are *all* being manipulated to a common global end that is bad for all of them. We are in this together and that is why the El-lite work tirelessly to keep us apart, divided and ruled. Instead of seeing the big picture the representatives (or those that claim to be) of different racial and religious groups feel the need to defend their own corner no matter what the circumstances. I mentioned the bloke from the UK Ramadhan Foundation with regard to this and I saw an interview on American television with Jorge Ramos, who is apparently the most famous Spanish language news presenter in the US, and described as 'The Walter Cronkite of Latin America'. Ramos was being questioned about the impact of Latinos settling in such numbers in the US and he agreed there was a demographic revolution happening. He said there were about 60 million Latinos in the United States and in 35 years that would be 100 million or about one in three of the population. At the same time he vehemently denied that this constituted an invasion of the country. Ramos once again would not concede any points on how this would affect the non-Latino population or how it would make them feel. At the same time a report by the University of New Hampshire revealed that death rates of white people outstripped birth rates in 17 states in 2014 compared with four in 2004 and a study by UK academic Professor Ted Cantle found that white people were leaving British cities in large numbers and heading towards minority status in major centres of population. Some, like Leicester, are already there. I remember watching a BBC documentary on the white exodus from London's East End in the face of another culture taking over. Frankfurt has become a majority migrant city and German 'progressive' Green Party politician Stefanie von Berg said it was a 'good thing' that Germans would become a minority in major cities:

*Our city will change radically. I hold that in 20, 30 years there will no longer be German majorities in our city and I want to make it clear especially to those right wingers: This is a good thing.*

It would never occur to Ms Von Berg that speeches like that are exactly what is fuelling the rise of the political right. No compassion for how Germans feel, no acknowledging of their concerns and fears. If you don't agree with her you are a racist. End of. Then there is this gem from German progressive politician Gregor Gysi:

*Every year more native Germans die than are born. That is very fortunate. It's because the Nazis are not very good at having offspring.* [The decline of Germans] *is why they are so dependent on immigration from foreign countries.*

So every native German is a Nazi then? This is the mentality displayed by Von Berg and Gysi which is taking over the world, while Muslim Imam Sheikh Muhammad Ayed from the Al-Aqsa Mosque in Jerusalem tells his followers to breed with European people and conquer their countries by taking advantage of their lost fertility. He said in September 2015:

*Europe has become old and decrepit, and needs human reinforcement. No force is more powerful than the human force of us Muslims ... Throughout Europe, all the hearts are infused with hatred toward Muslims. They wish that we were dead. But they have lost their fertility, so they look for fertility in their midst. We will give them fertility!*

*We will breed children with them, because we shall conquer their countries – whether you like it or not, oh Germans, oh Americans, oh French, oh Italians, and all those like you. Take the refugees! We shall soon collect them in the name of the coming Caliphate. We will say to you: These are our sons. Send them, or we will send our armies to you.*

But that is not racist, of course, in a Brave New World where racism can only be white. I am not defending the white race. I may be in a white body but my self-identity is with consciousness not form. European races outrageously invaded and seized the lands of Native Americans and so many others across the Americas, Asia, Africa and Australia/New Zealand through grotesque exploitation by the European empires and especially the British. Colonialism and slavery were an abomination and I still remember how sickened I was as a kid when I first read about it. But we (a) do not move forward by doing the same in reverse and (b) we do not secure freedom for everybody unless we have the maturity to ask why white races are currently being so targeted and white males in particular are the prime targets of political correctness. The answer affects *everyone* no matter what their colour or creed. One other point that should not be missed: El-lite bloodlines that were behind European colonialism are the *same* bloodlines behind mass immigration into Europe today. It's just a different phase of the same ongoing march to total global control. The Jerusalem Imam is certainly right about European sperm counts. Research published in 2017 assessed results from nearly 200 studies involving 43,000 men and found that sperm counts in predominantly white-race, Western-world countries of North America, Europe, Australia, and New Zealand, appear to have halved in less than 40 years. I'll explore some of the causes later, but lead researcher Dr Hagai Levine, an epidemiologist who studies patterns of activity, said the findings were 'shocking' and that humans could become extinct if sperm counts continue to fall at current rates. Levine, from the Hebrew University of Jerusalem, found a 59.3% decline in total sperm count in men from North America, Europe, Australia and New Zealand, but in contrast the study found no significant decline in South America, Asia and Africa. It will be interesting to see

**Figure 519:** His manipulation is so vast that it had to happen eventually.

if further studies find the same disparity. Levine said there is an urgent need to find out why sperm counts are decreasing and to reverse the trend. Western birth rates have been falling for 30 years and in the same period sperm counts have plummeted and fertility problems have soared to the point where they have produced an industry called fertility services which have increased by four times in 25 years. Anyone think all this is 'natural'? No, me neither.

## Soros has 'values' – god, my belly hurts ...

Hungary Prime Minister Viktor Orban has warned about the creation of 'parallel societies' and is well aware of what Hungarian-born George Soros and his networks are doing. Orban's government said Soros-funded organisations like the Helsinki Committees of 'Human Rights' operating throughout Europe, including Hungary and the Balkans, are actively supporting illegal immigration (Fig 519). Hungary Foreign Minister Péter Szijjártó talked of agencies seeking to 'violate our border' and said that Hungarian intelligence reports name Soros as working in the background of these organisations. Hungary's ruling party even plastered billboards of Soros around Budapest saying 'Let's not let Soros have the last laugh'. Israel's ambassador to Hungary, Yossi Amrani, issued a foreign ministry-approved statement asking the government to stop the billboard campaign because the negative portrayal of Soros could stir up anti-Semitism, but soon afterwards a second statement was released taking another tone:

> *In no way was the statement meant to delegitimize criticism of George Soros, who continuously undermines Israel's democratically elected governments by funding organizations that defame the Jewish state and seek to deny it the right to defend itself.*

A quick translation would read: 'Oh, my god, we must not let anyone see that Soros is working for us or the whole house of cards could come down.' I will answer the question shortly of why Soros funds groups that criticise Israel. Hungary Prime Minister Orban said that Soros was using the EU to create a 'new, mixed, Muslimized Europe'. This would certainly connect with the long-term plans of Richard von Coudenhove-Kalergi who played such a part in the establishment of what became the EU and the gathering evidence that EU agencies are working with people traffickers and NGOs in the Mediterranean. Orban said: 'The European Union, the European Commission must regain independence from the Soros Empire before the billionaire finishes his programme for the destruction of the continent.' He said of the migration crisis:

> *This invasion is driven, on the one hand, by people smugglers, and on the other by those activists who support everything that weakens the nation-state. This Western mindset and this activist network is [typified] by George Soros ... His name is perhaps the strongest example of those who support anything that weakens nation states, they support everything that changes the traditional European lifestyle ...*

Soros replied in an email statement to *Bloomberg Business* saying that

**HEY, 'PROGRESSIVES'**
**THIS IS YOUR FUNDER SPEAKING ...**

'I AM BASICALLY THERE TO MAKE MONEY. I CANNOT AND
DO NOT LOOK AT THE SOCIAL CONSEQUENCES OF WHAT I DO.'
SO WHAT'S HIS AGENDA FOR FUNDING YOU?

**Figure 520:** A question worth asking Soros-funded progressives?

his foundations 'uphold European values' while strengthening Hungarian borders 'undermine those values'. He later said that Hungary was a 'Mafia state' posing as a democracy and complained that he was being portrayed as 'a shady currency speculator who uses his money to flood Europe with illegal immigrants as part of some vague but nefarious plot.' *And?* Your point is? Orban described the Soros response as a declaration of war: 'The only network which operates in Mafia ways, which is not transparent ... in Hungary is the Soros network.' He accused Soros of funding organisations that 'are working to bring hundreds of thousands of migrants into Europe'. Soros said that 'our plan treats the protection of refugees as the objective and national borders as the obstacle'. George Soros having the nerve to talk about 'values' really is a sight to behold. This is the man who said: 'I am basically there to make money. I cannot and do not look at the social consequences of what I do.' I guess the 'progressive' groups funded by Soros never get around to asking why the billionaire who said that would want to give them wads of cash (Fig 520). A ten-day protest in 2016 called Democracy Spring brought together 100 'progressive' groups in Washington demanding an end to the 'influence of money in politics'. *Dontcha love 'em?* Many of those very groups received funding from billionaire Soros, a major funder of Hillary Clinton and other Democrat politicians while his Open Society and other networks were behind the Arab Spring that set the Middle East ablaze with violence (and triggered the flows of migrants into Europe supported by the same Soros). A 'progressive' speaking on Fox News said that Soros was motivated by the fact that he grew up in Nazi-occupied Hungary and 'that is why his entire life has been dedicated to equality and justice'. She obviously missed the quote about not looking at the social consequences of what he does and the television interview in which he admitted helping as a teenager to confiscate property of Hungarian Jews persecuted by the Nazis and told the interviewer that this was 'not at all' difficult. 'Progressive' U2 singer Bono calls Soros 'one of my great heroes' as he does with Microsoft billionaire Bill Gates who funds and promotes vaccines, GMO, surveillance technology, education programming, geoengineering of the atmosphere (weather modification) and so much more on the *El*-lite agenda (Fig 521). Soros

and many other 'philanthropic billionaires' that fund the *El*-lite wish-list are supported by the Web in getting fantastically rich, but the pay-back is that large parts of their fortunes are spent to advance the *El*-lite cause through what is promoted as 'philanthropy'. It is anything but. Rockefeller foundations and trusts led the way and so many others have followed in the same mould. Soros gave *$246 million* to

**BILL GATES: IF IT'S BAD FOR HUMANITY HE'S WRITING THE CHEQUE**

**Figure 521:** Gates has an extraordinary record of funding projects in line with the agenda's wish-list.

100 groups behind another Washington protest dubbed 'Day Without A Woman' to 'spotlight gender inequality' and in truth to protest against Donald Trump (divide and rule). It was funny how this march for women's rights did not bother to target the Saudi Arabian embassy. Maybe their Sat-Nav wasn't working. Soros even spends millions supporting 'progressive' district attorney candidates. He and his network are everywhere. Zionist Vladimir Lenin said: 'The best way to control the opposition is to lead it ourselves.' You can see this technique with the Palestinian Authority headed by Netanyahu gofer Mahmoud Abbas which is supposed to represent Palestinian interests but ultimately answers to Israel. Watch Abbas support Israel in targeting rival Palestinian group Hamas as per demand by the US and Israel to King Salman of Saudi Arabia. It now becomes obvious why Soros funds groups that criticise Israel. In a spin on Lenin's line ... 'The best way to control the opposition is to *fund* it ourselves.'

The other pillar of the mass immigration agenda is playing the migrant population against the indigenous population in a programme of violent divide and rule. Migrants congregating in particular areas with a clearly identifiable culture creates two distinct and easily discernible 'sides' and the conflict is fuelled by political correctness, the frustration that comes from silencing dissent and the perception that all parts of the community are not treated equally. This is further increased by seeing parallel societies emerging with their own laws and enforcement. Then there is state-sponsored 'Islamic' terrorism that fuels the fury more than anything. The *El*-lite want to trigger civil wars and as usual most of those who are hurt and affected will be the majority in *both* communities that only want to live in peace and harmony. Headlines tell the story – 'Surging "Intercommunity Confrontations" in France Mean "Civil War is Inevitable"' and 'Thousands take to the streets to protest Germany's immigration policy following week of bloody violence'. They want a race war in the United States with again Soros-funded progressive organisations behind ethnic and political street protests. Soros, like Brzezinski, tells you the plan when he predicts what he 'thinks' will happen. He has predicted riots, a police state and civil war in America. They want the slaves fighting the slaves to allow the slave owners to rule over both of them.

Now, are we going to give them what they want? Or are we going to see through the illusion of race and religion and realise that we are all one consciousness having different experiences? If we don't see beyond the illusion and go on believing in racial and religious superiority when one person's beliefs must be forced upon everyone else then what is ahead looks very bleak indeed. If we *do*, we can change everything and far quicker than almost anyone could imagine.

# CHAPTER FIFTEEN

# Is it hot, or is it me?

*'A lie can travel half way around the world while the truth is putting on its shoes'* – **Charles Spurgeon**

The global army of often Soros-funded progressives are the foremost promotors of the hoax they call human-caused global warming. Martin Luther King was so right when he said: 'Nothing in all the world is more dangerous than sincere ignorance and conscientious stupidity' (Fig 522).

**Figure 522:** Genuine people are being conned for the lack of doing a little research (with an open mind).

**Figure 523:** Propaganda by repetition.

Understandable questions arise from the contention that global warming (or 'climate change' since temperatures stopped rising) is a Big Lie. Why would 'they' do that? What is in it for 'them'? What is the point of such global deceit? I have exposed the background to the hoax at length in *The Perception Deception* and *Phantom Self*, but I will answer those questions more succinctly here (Fig 523). The fake human-caused global warming narrative is about creating an excuse to transform global society, and at the centre of this is the *El*-lite-owned and created United Nations. The Rockefeller family was centrally involved in the creation of the UN as a stalking horse for world government using the Totalitarian Tiptoe technique. Throughout the first half of the 20th century the *El*-lite had tried to install a global body that could be evolved step-by-step into world government. Oil tycoon J. D. Rockefeller and a list of Rothschild assets were involved in the creation of the League of Nations justified by the First World War and when that didn't work they had another go with the United Nations justified by the Second World War. Plans for a Third World War are in large part to morph the current United Nations into a fully-fledged world government to 'stop war happening again' through a centrally-controlled tyranny enforced by a world army. Another excuse for world government will be to 'save the world from climate change' by centrally imposing climate laws. J. D. Rockefeller established the Council on Foreign Relations (CFR) in New York in 1921, a cusp organisation in the Web, and its members were at the forefront of the creation of the UN in 1945 when the American delegation was described as 'a roll call of the CFR'. Seventy-four members of the delegation at the founding of the UN were CFR. The Rockefeller family donated the land on which the United Nations building stands today in New York not far from CFR headquarters. The UN is a Rockefeller operation and if it is Rockefeller then it is Rothschild. This is fundamentally relevant to the climate change hoax because that has been globally-driven by the *United Nations* Intergovernmental Panel on Climate Change (IPCC) in support of the outrageous claims by the Climate Change Liar-in-Chief, Al Gore (Fig 524). He was US Vice-President to Bill Clinton and so obviously he's a man to be trusted. The Clintons are going to share their horrific secrets with a truth-teller, yes? Al 'we must reduce carbon emissions' Gore cares so much about 'climate change' that he has a personal carbon footprint the size of Godzilla and it's the same with those other climate frauds Barack Obama and actor Leonardo DiCaprio who both fly across the world in private jets to make speeches about climate Armageddon. DiCaprio is a 'UN Messenger of Peace with a special focus on climate change'. More like UN Messenger of Propaganda. Obama took a private

**Figure 524:** Al Gore has made a fortune selling a lie.

jet to Italy to make a climate speech in 2017 and arrived at the venue in a 14-car convoy. Gore is now invoking God as his guide and inspiration which is always the last refuge of the politically desperate: '...if you are a believer, as I am, I think God intends for us to open our eyes and take responsibility for the moral consequences of our actions.' Well, when will you and Clintons, Al?

## New World Order – their order

The UN connection does not end with the climate fraud of the IPCC. Two UN 'agendas' – Agenda 21 and Agenda 2030 – call for the transformation and centralisation of global society and much of this is justified by ... *the UN climate change hoax*. A climate change progressive said on CNN that to save the world 'we must change everything'. Good one – campaign for your own enslavement, you know it makes sense. I'll come to the lies about human-caused climate change but I'll deal first with what it is meant to justify. Agenda 2030 is an extension and updated expansion of Agenda 21 which was the pump-primer preparing the ground for its successor. Agenda 21 was established at the 1992 Earth Summit in Rio de Janeiro, Brazil, which was hosted by *El*-lite gofer Maurice Strong with the Rothschild-Rockefeller combination controlling from the wings. The global environmental movement fell for it completely and governments and local councils the world over accepted its goals and recommendations. Agenda 2030 was agreed by the UN General Assembly in 2015. These are the aims of Agenda 21 from its own documents, and you will notice some recurring themes with the must-haves of the social engineering networks that I mentioned earlier:

- An end to national sovereignty
- State planning and management of all land resources, ecosystems, deserts, forests, mountains, oceans and fresh water; agriculture; rural development; biotechnology; and ensuring 'equity'
- The state to 'define the role' of business and financial resources
- Abolition of private property
- 'Restructuring' the family unit
- Children raised by the state
- People told what their job will be
- Major restrictions on movement
- Creation of 'human settlement zones'
- Mass resettlement as people are forced to vacate land where they live
- Dumbing down education
- Mass global depopulation in pursuit of all of the above

Agenda 2030 uses the 'who could argue with that?' technique to sell its plan for the global centralisation of power over *everything*. Its 'sustainable development goals' are:

No poverty; zero hunger; good health and well-being; quality education; clean water and sanitation; affordable and clean energy; decent work and economic growth; industry, innovation and infrastructure; reduced inequalities; sustainable cities and communities; responsible consumption and production; climate action; protecting life below water and life on land; peace, justice and strong institutions and partnerships to achieve these ends.

Okay, we'll all sign up for that then. Or we would if we didn't know what lies behind that list of meaningless platitudes which the *El*-lite have no intention of fulfilling given they spend their days doing the opposite. The Devil is in what they don't say, like how these 'goals' are supposed to be achieved. Scratch the surface and you get your answer – through the global centralisation of power over every aspect of human life. This is what 'the end of national sovereignty' is all about and why it is such a constant theme from Agendas 21 and 2030, to the Frankfurt School of social engineering and the European Union. The extreme nature of the planned centralisation of power is revealed in the desire for 'state planning and management of all land resources, ecosystems, deserts, forests, mountains, oceans and fresh water; agriculture; rural development; biotechnology; and ensuring "equity"'. They don't mean equity in the sense of raising everybody up, but equity of slavery in the Hunger Games Society. We also have the state defining the role of business and financial resources and people told what their job will be. What happened to freedom? A 'climate-change' excuse for 'dumbing down education' can be identified in this claim by the *United Nations Education, Scientific, and Cultural Organization* (UNESCO):

*Generally, more highly educated people who have higher incomes can consume more resources than poorly educated people who tend to have lower incomes. In this case more education increases the threat to sustainability.*

Agenda 2030's goal of 'quality education' really means quality indoctrination. Agenda 21 includes the always-there 'restructuring of the family unit'. Orwellian translation: Destroying the concept of family and this is further confirmed by the demand that 'children will be raised by the state'. Parental power is being eroded over children in favour of the state as part of this particular Totalitarian Tiptoe. Abolition of private property, major restrictions on movement, creation of 'human settlement zones' and mass resettlement as people are forced to vacate land are all part of the same intended outcome. This is to herd the entire population into densely-

**Figure 525:** Planned 'human settlement zones' depicted by artist David Dees.

populated 'human settlement zones' and force them to live in micro-apartments – and I mean micro – where they can be kept under constant surveillance 24/7 (Fig 525). I have described in previous books how people are being forced from rural areas, especially in the United States where all these plans begin, by withdrawing investment, deleting work opportunities, closing roads and schools, making family farms financially impossible to sustain and by imposing regulations that only corporate farms can meet. Sometimes they remove people by just telling them without a reason they have to leave. There is a war on rural areas and small-scale farming and when they are forced to sell up or abandon their property they head for the cities while corporations buy their land for cents on the dollar. One example is Farmland Partners Inc, the Wall Street investment operation run by former executives at Merrill Lynch, which has attracted hundreds of millions of dollars to buy farms and ranches with so far 295 properties in 16 states totalling 144,000 acres. United Nations figures reveal that the point was reached by around 2008/9 when more people in the world lived in urban areas than rural and that trend has been continuing dramatically since then. Nearly half of Americans lived in rural areas in the 1930s and 21 percent worked on farms. By 2016 the figures were down to 20 percent and 2 percent. Where this is leading is portrayed by the map of the new America 'required' by the United Nations Convention on Biological Diversity, Wildlands Project, UN and US Man and Biosphere Programs and World Heritage Program as essential to securing 'sustainable development' (Fig 526). All these agendas, programmes and buzz-words that include 'biodiversity', 'sustainable communities', 'sustainable development' and 'smart' are more masks on the same face. The darkest areas of the map are set aside for no human use and most of the rest of America is designated for little or highly-regulated use. Enter the words 'United Nations Convention on Biological Diversity map' in an image search engine and you will see a clearer colour version. Where will all the people go? The ones that remain will be packed into the human settlement zones or 'megacities' which are the small and isolated areas on the map listed for 'human use'; but

**Simulated Reserve and Corridor System to Protect Biodiversity**
As Required by the UN Covention on Biological Diversity, Wildlands Project, UN and US Man and Biosphere Programs and World Heritage Program as a Vital Step in Attaining Sustainable Development
This map was used in the United States Senate to stop the ratification of the United Nations Convention on Biological Diversity

- Core Reserves & Corridors
  Little to no human use
- Buffer Zones–Highly Regulated Use
- Border 21/La Paz Sidebar Agreement of NAFTA–200 Mile Wide International Zone of Cooperation
- Normal Use
- Indian Reservations
- Military Reservations

**Figure 526:** America's land occupation map for the Hunger Games Society with the masses herded into high-density 'human settlement zones' and cleared from the majority of the country.

today's population of the United States would not even come close to fitting into those areas and this connects with the common theme among *El*-lite statements and documents about the need for a mass human cull. This involves a population reduction down to anything between 500,000, a billion and three billion – from a current population of 7.5 billion. Different people and documents have different estimates, but they are all well below what we have now.

## Boxes in the sky

Micro-apartments are appearing all over the world as I saw in 2016 and 2017 when I travelled the globe on a speaking tour. This gave me still further insight into how the same things are happening everywhere because it is a global agenda. They develop and introduce their plans first in the United States which they exploit as a human perception

**Figure 527:** Tiny 'home' on a massive Australian continent.

**Figure 528:** Former New York Mayor Michael Bloomberg announcing the building of 165,000 micro-apartments. The size is indicated by the two lines on the floor.

laboratory and then they export what works for them to all countries and cultures. I even saw micro-apartments in Australia where of course they don't have enough land to build anything bigger (Fig 527). Zionist Michael Bloomberg announced 165,000 'living' units when he was mayor of New York which are 10 feet by 30 feet (Fig 528). This is what I am talking about. The *United Nations* Habitat III summit, formally known as the United Nations Conference on Housing and Sustainable Urban Development, met in in Quito, Ecuador, in 2016 to further the urban-sustainability agenda and organisers claim that 30,000 attended from 167 countries. A major excuse for this is 'fighting climate change'. Micro-apartments can be so small that furniture has to be pulled out of the wall and sofas converted into beds. Shoe-box, prison-cell apartments are now becoming 'the thing' to reduce carbon emissions, save the planet and solve the housing crisis with headlines like 'City Officials/Developers Recommend "Coffin Apartments" For Middle Class'. They are not being introduced to save or solve anything. They are instead essential components of the Hunger Games Society which demands tiny living spaces in densely populated dystopian high-rise cities. Environmental progressives – the most extreme of them rightly called eco-fascists – are all in favour because they don't even begin to understand what is really going on. Rockefeller insider Dr Richard Day knew what was coming in 1969 as reported by Dr Dunegan:

> *Privately-owned housing would become a thing of the past. The cost of housing and financing housing would gradually be made so high that most people couldn't afford it ... Young people would more and more become renters, particularly in apartments or condominiums.*

> *People would not be able to buy [homes] and gradually more and more of the population would be forced into small apartments. Small apartments which would not accommodate very many children.*

Everywhere I have been on the world tour – to the United States, Canada, Australia, New Zealand and right across Europe and the Balkans – I have seen the same theme of young people no longer able, as Day predicted, to buy homes. Many are still living with parents or on the streets because they cannot afford even to rent. Create the problem and then offer the solution – micro-apartments. Richard Day also pointed to where all this was leading, with people designated not only where they lived, but who they were to live with:

> *Ultimately, people would be assigned where they would live and it would be common to have non-family members living with you. This by way of your not knowing just how far you could trust anybody. This would all be under the control of a central housing authority. Have this in mind ... when they ask, 'How many bedrooms in your house? How many bathrooms in your house? Do you have a finished game room?' This information is personal and is of no national interest to government under our existing Constitution. But you'll be asked those questions ...*

And we are. The *El*-lite in the *Hunger Games* movies lived in the Capitol, a state of the art luxury city isolated from the rest of the population who were barely surviving in primitive poverty. This is a symbol of where we are going with the rich and powerful living in luxury defended by the police state structure while the rest of the people are herded into tiny boxes in sprawling mega cities. We are seeing these 'capitols' emerging with the global process known as 'gentrification'.

The poor are being forced out of designated 'capitol' areas by unaffordable rents and unfit housing caused by the authorities withdrawing funding for even basic upkeep and repairs. When they are relocated to other areas or the street the developers move in to build homes for the rich until all the poor have gone. This has long been happening in cities across the world, including London and Los Angeles. I have been highlighting this for years and it came to greater public attention with the horrendous fire at the 24-storey Grenfell Tower in London that killed 80 (the publicised figure at time of writing) and injured 70 in June 2017. Grenfell Tower was in Kensington, the richest borough in Britain, and also home to people of many cultures and backgrounds with very little money – dramatically so in comparison to the mega-rich elsewhere in the borough. The building was owned by the local council, but managed by a corporation as the area became increasingly gentrified. One aspect of this was to add cladding to the outside of Grenfell Tower to make the façade look better for the benefit of rich homeowners in the area, both in terms of view and property values – and to insulate the property to meet 'global warming' targets. The cladding chosen for financial reasons was one that is lethally flammable, while an inflammable version would have cost little more. To anyone with a brain and an ounce of concern for the safety of the residents the very idea of cladding a tower block with flammable material would be utterly insane, but, hey, they are only poor people so who gives a damn? The inevitable happened when a fire started in one of the flats that would normally have been dealt with but the building quickly became an inferno as the cladding went up 'like a matchstick'. Fire officers with decades in the service said they had never seen anything like it. Residents told of shoddy building work, no sprinkler systems and no fire alarms which meant that many people in the building only knew of the fire in the early hours of the morning when called by friends who could see what was happening from other blocks. By then it was already too late for many. Survivors lost everything, including family members and children, and then began the fight to be rehoused in the same area among their own community while the desire of the authorities if the truth be told was to move them out and relocate them elsewhere. Many other blocks have been re-cladded in Britain in the same way. You will see this be exploited to achieve further gentrification. The US military hierarchy already know what is planned in the global urbanisation agenda as outlined in a training video obtained by The Intercept website under the Freedom of Information Act (how long will that last?) from the Pentagon's Joint Special Operations University. The video, entitled *Megacities: Urban Future, The Emerging Complexity*, tells military personnel the following:

*The future is urban. By 2030 urban areas are expected to grow by 1.4 billion
with that growth occurring almost entirely in the developing world. Cities
will account for 60% of the world's population and 70% of the world's GDP.
The urban environment will be the locus where drivers of instability will
converge. By the year 2030, 60% of urban dwellers will be under the age of
18. The cities that grow the fastest will be the most challenged as resources
become constrained and elicit networks fill the gap by over extended and
undercapitalised governments.*

*Growth will magnify the increasing separation between rich and poor.
Religious and ethnic tensions will be a defining element in the social
landscape. Stagnation will coexist with unprecedented development as
impoverishment, slums and shanty towns rapidly expand alongside modern
high rises, technological advances and ever increasing levels of prosperity.
This is the world of our future.*

The video is describing the Hunger Games Society and the remarks
about religious and ethnic tensions as a defining element in the social
landscape explains why the mass migration programme is now well
underway. Military analysts predict that 'social structures will be equally
challenged if not dysfunctional as historic ways of life clash with
modern living, ethnic and racial differences are forced to live together
and criminal networks offer opportunity for the growing mass of
unemployed'. They want to take divide and rule to a whole new level
and keep the masses divided and at war with themselves while the *El*-
lite enjoy their 'ever increasing levels of prosperity'. The voiceover
describes the micro-world of human habitation – 'Megacities are
complex systems where people and structures are compressed together
in ways that defy both our understanding of city planning and military
doctrine'. The video concludes: 'The future is urban.'

## Shame about the weather

Another way to force people off the land and into the human settlement
megacities is through control of the weather. This was once believed to
be a myth, but it has been possible for a long time and the scale and
sophistication goes on increasing. Weather patterns and states are
different forms of energetic information and frequency and they are
manipulatable by using other information and frequencies. Rain dances
and chants of native peoples are now replaced with high technology, but
the principle is the same. Many leading figures in the wartime
Manhattan Project which produced the first atomic bomb would later
work in weather modification and manipulation of the atmosphere
because there are many crossovers between atomic bomb physics and
those of weather control. Edward Teller, Vannevar Bush and John von

Neumann were among those who made the transition from the
Manhattan Project to weather and atmospheric modification. Energetic
weather manipulation would appear to have entered a whole new phase
after the death of Nikola Tesla in 1943 when his cutting-edge research
documents into the nature of the electrical atmosphere were confiscated
by the US government. The man who reviewed the papers for the
military was John G. Trump (1907-1985), the uncle of 'outsider'
president, Donald John Trump. This is where his middle name 'John'
comes from. Uncle Trump would later become head of the British
Branch of the Massachusetts Institute of Technology (MIT) Radiation
Laboratory. This was funded by the Rockefeller family and would
appear to have become the centre of the weather-manipulation
programme. Several former Manhattan Project operatives worked there.
Researcher Peter A. Kirby has produced as very good article at the
Activist Post website about the background to all this. The words

**Figure 529:** Chemical trails or chemtrails delivered
into the sky by aircraft all over the world in a vast
programme to change our atmosphere. One of the
benefits for the Hidden Hand is to make weather
manipulation far more effective.

'Chemtrails exposed: truly a
new Manhattan Project' will
get you there. 'Chemtrails'
refers to chemical trails that
have been released from
aircraft on an increasingly
grand scale the world over
since at least the 1990s. They
contain among many other
things microscopic metal
particulates (aluminium,
barium and strontium) that
make the atmosphere more
electrically conductive and
increase the power and

potential of weather manipulation technology (Fig 529). I will have more
about chemtrails in the next chapter because they relate to many *El*-lite
agendas. US General George Kenney told graduates at the
Massachusetts Institute of Technology in 1947: 'The nation that first
learns to plot the paths of air masses accurately and learns to control the
time and place of precipitation will dominate the globe.' Today they are
doing just that with Antarctica one of the prime locations away from
prying eyes where the Reptilian/Nazi base is said to be. There are UN
treaties signed about weather modification because *it can be done*. Why
else would they bother? The World Meteorological Organization says
that at least 52 countries have weather modification programmes and
when you look at the background they are clearly being used for
military and manipulation purposes. Targeted weather extremes of
drought and rain are destroying farming livelihoods and forcing people

to move either for the lack of water or too much. When they leave for the cities the government or corporations seize the vacated land. Rockefeller asset Dr Richard Day worked in weather control during World War II and he revealed what was possible in 1969 while explaining how this would be used to impose the 'new system' of those he represented. Dr Dunegan recalled:

> There was a mention then of weather. This was another really striking statement. He said: 'We can or soon will be able to control the weather.' He said: 'I'm not merely referring to dropping iodide crystals into the clouds to precipitate rain that's already there, but REAL control.' And weather was seen as a weapon of war, a weapon of influencing public policy. It could make rain or withhold rain in order to influence certain areas and bring them under your control.
>
> There were two sides to this that were rather striking. He said: 'On the one hand you can make drought during the growing season so that nothing will grow, and on the other hand you can make for very heavy rains during harvest season so the fields are too muddy to bring in the harvest, and indeed one might be able to do both.' There was no statement how this would be done. It was stated that either it was already possible or very, very close to being possible [in 1969].

NASA documents from 1966 confirm the United States weather modification programme with a budget of hundreds of millions of dollars and in the 1990s the US military was publishing papers expounding the war possibilities of weather manipulation, or 'geoengineering' as it is also known. American scientist J. Marvin Herndon described in the *International Journal of Environmental Research and Public Health* in 2015 how weather modification has been happening for decades and includes the 'make mud, not war' programme named Project Popeye to create monsoon-scale rain during the Vietnam War. US Air Force document AF 2025 Final Report published in 1996 explained how artificially-generated floods, hurricanes, droughts and earthquakes 'offers the war fighter a wide range of possible options to defeat or coerce an adversary'. The report described how US aerospace forces would technologically 'own' the weather: 'From enhancing friendly operations or disrupting those of the enemy via small-scale tailoring of natural weather patterns to complete dominance of global communications and counterspace control ...' The 1990s when chemtrails began to appear worldwide saw the emergence of The High-Frequency Active Auroral Research Program or HAARP installation in Alaska which bounces high-powered radio waves off the ionosphere in the upper atmosphere and back to earth. These so-called ionosphere heaters

were originally based on
technology developed by
Nikola Tesla in the first half of
the 20th century and included
in his seized papers. They have
since been installed around the
world with the potential to
manipulate weather patterns
even more fundamentally as
technology has improved and
HAARP is history in terms of
capability. Weather-
manipulation is now the result
of frequencies directed from
many sources that meet at the

**Figure 530:** Weather forecasters often blame
extremes of weather on the strange behaviour of the
jet stream.

desired point to collectively contribute to the effect and the most
powerful can create an earthquake. These techniques include the
manipulation of the scalar field (based again on Tesla's research into the
scalar phenomenon) using what are called technologically-generated
scalar waves that are really scalar fields. Interaction with the scalar field
at one point instantly impacts on the entire unified field.

Air currents known as jet streams flowing from west to east are
centrally important for stable weather – or otherwise if they are
disrupted. Bernard Eastlund, who wrote many of the patents for
HAARP on behalf of major corporations, said: 'HAARP can steer the jet
stream.' Extremes of drought and rain have been blamed by weather
experts on the strange and apparently inexplicable behaviour of the jet
streams (Fig 530). Ionosphere heater technology is even more effective in
an atmosphere made more electrically conductive by the metallic
content of chemtrails. We need to keep all this in mind when alleged
'natural' weather extremes create circumstances that advance *El*-lite
agendas. A further bonus of weather manipulation is blaming the
consequences on the effects of human-caused climate change. I have
covered in detail weather geoengineering, HAARP, and Agendas 21 and
2030 in *The Perception Deception* and *Phantom Self*.

## Food and drink

Agenda 2030 references to zero hunger and clean water are worded to
hide the fact that the plan is to centrally control the production and
distribution of both food and water supplies and the reason is revealed
by Zionist extremist Henry Kissinger: 'Control oil and you control
nations; control food and you control the people.' Control water and you
control people even quicker. The siege against small farms and
smallholders is connected to the increasing attacks on people growing

**Figure 531:** Genetically-modified food is devastating to human health both through eating it and the toxic methods of production.

their own food in their own or community gardens. Zoning laws – you can't do that here – are one of the major tools being employed. All food production and distribution will be strictly controlled in the Hunger Games Society and this is the motivation behind the incessant centralisation of food production and seed ownership by mergers and takeovers of giant corporations. Monsanto and Bayer is a major example. Genetically-modifying, poison-producing Monsanto is one of the most evil organisations on earth and Bayer was a constituent part of IG Farben that ran the concentration camp at Auschwitz. The proposed $66 billion Bayer takeover of Monsanto would give them control of more than 25 percent of the world's seeds and pesticides. Genetically-modified crops which are designed to genetically-modify humanity at unspeakable cost to health are purposely dependent on the pesticides which the same people produce. GMO, pesticides and herbicides have to be understood from a frequency perspective. We see their decoded holographic level but they are really highly distorted and disruptive waveform patterns that cause great disturbance to the standing wave oscillation of the body and can indeed stop that oscillation to bring about what we call death (Fig 531). Bayer is one of four biotech giants, along with Syngenta, Dow and DuPont, who are sponsoring the 'Agriculture in the Classroom' programme in Canada to push their GMO-pesticide propaganda. Everywhere you look children are being perceptually-prepared for the world designed to enslave them and *where are the parents?* Family farmers in countries like India have been devastated by their corrupt and corporation-controlled government going down the GMO road. Shocking numbers of suicides have followed by farmers financially ruined by Monsanto's *un*sustainable GMO products. Connect this to the decision by the appalling Narendra Modi regime in India to suddenly withdraw certain banknotes without warning which farmers largely use for their business. This had a devastating effect on their ability to financially survive and continue to work their land. Then add the Modi campaign to remove protections that prevent the seizing of land by government and corporations and the common pattern of destroying small farmers becomes obvious. Insider Dr Richard Day knew this was coming in 1969:

*Food supplies would come under tight control ... food shortages could be created in a hurry and people would realise the dangers of overpopulation. Ultimately, whether the population slows down or not the food supply is to be brought under centralised control so that people would have enough to be well-nourished but they would not have enough to support any fugitive from the new system. In other words, if you had a friend or relative who didn't sign on, and growing one's own food would be outlawed. This would be done under some sort of pretext.*

*In the beginning I mentioned there were two purposes for everything – one the ostensible purpose and one the real purpose, and the ostensible purpose here would be that growing your own vegetables was unsafe, it would spread disease or something like that. So the acceptable idea was to protect the consumer but the real idea was to limit the food supply and growing your own food would be illegal.*

We are moving in that very direction and more so every year. In 1913 corn was 100 percent owned by farmers in the United States, but by 2013 it was 95 percent owned by corporations with 90 percent GMO in the US. You want to grow something? Then you must buy the seed from us. How much? Whatever we say it is. The same is happening with water supplies and we had the disgraceful Nestle chairman and former CEO Peter Brabeck claiming that water is not a human right, has a market value and should be privatised. Water supplies are being stolen from the people on an ever-increasing scale. The very basic constituent of life, second only to breath, is being controlled by those with the chilling Archontic mentality displayed by Brabeck who is head of a company that takes incredible amounts of water from the public supply, even in drought-stricken areas, and sells it back to the people in bottles. Water that is not hijacked by corporations is being hijacked by governments owned by corporations and the Web. The state of Oregon is one such case where the government claims ownership of every drop of water even that which drops as rain or snow on your own land (Fig 532). One couple was told to destroy a 40-year-old pond on their property because the government owned the rainwater. This is what Agenda 2030's 'clean water and sanitation' really means and Agenda 21's 'state planning and management of all land resources, ecosystems, deserts, forests, mountains, oceans and *fresh water*'. The wonderful state of Oregon, by the way, is where officials threatened to destroy a

**Figure 532:** Oregon's water tyranny.

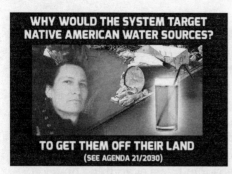

**Figure 533:** It all makes sense when you know the background.

**Figure 534:** The water supply in a fracking zone.

**Figure 535:** At least fracking guarantees you hot water.

2,000-acre organic farm with an 18-year organic certification by forcibly spraying Monsanto Roundup and other pesticides to kill a weed. There you have Agenda 21/2030 in action again as you do with oil pipelines deliberately polluting water supplies on Native American lands (Fig 533). Fracking is another way that water is being used to clear people off the land by injecting toxic fluid into fractured shale rocks and poisoning ground water supplies. And I do *mean* toxic – hundreds of chemicals that include lead, uranium, mercury, ethylene glycol, radium, methanol, hydrochloric acid and formaldehyde which then seep into groundwater. Once that is undrinkable what can the communities affected do except relocate? People have been able to set fire to their tap water because of the chemical pollution of fracking (Figs 534 and 535). Greenhouse gas methane and cancer-causing radon is released by fracking, which consumes absolutely stunning amounts of water that can never been used again thanks to the hundreds of chemicals. Controls are demanded on carbon dioxide while the same authorities support the release of greenhouse gas methane with fracking. This would seem to be a contradiction for governments promoting the global warming hoax, but it's not. The common theme that brings the two together is this: A belief in global warming is good for the *El*-lite agenda and so is fracking. This is the only criteria for every action and explains so many apparently contradictory decisions. Is it good for our agenda? Yes? Then do it. Is it bad for our agenda? Yes. Then stop it.

## Now – we just need an excuse ...

So that is the basic background for where the United Nations' agendas plan to take the world – *are* taking it – and the human-caused global warming hoax has been created to provide the excuse. I am not saying that humans are not damaging the environment. I joined the UK Green Party because I could see this was happening and then realised that the 'new' Green politics was just the old politics in disguise. When it comes to protecting air, water, forests, atmosphere and so on you are pushing against an open door with me. But wisdom treats everything on its merits and doesn't take one package with endless different elements and make a collective judgement about them all. It is not wisdom to say that it's all true or all not true because it is never that black and white. When I began to look in detail at the claims and behaviour of the global warming Mafia it soon became clear that the world was being had. The Club of Rome, a cusp organisation connected with the Bilderberg Group, Trilateral Commission and the UN-creating Council on Foreign Relations, was established in 1968 to exploit the environment to promote the transformation of global society. Co-founder Aurelio Peccei said in the Club's 1991 publication, *The First Global Revolution*: 'In searching for a new enemy to unite us, we came up with the idea that pollution, the threat of global warming, water shortages, famine and the like would fit the bill.' Richard Haass, president of the Council on Foreign Relations and long-time *El*-lite insider, has called for a 'world order 2.0' and the concept of 'sovereign obligation' which would obligate countries not to do anything that adversely affected other countries or the world in general. Global institutions would enforce this 'obligation' where necessary and you see where that is going with the world government and world army. One of the reasons that he says we need such enforcement is to save the planet from *human-caused climate change*. The global warming/climate change fraud is being orchestrated through the usual compartmentalised pyramid structure which leaves rank-and-file progressives pressing for action to stop the end of the world while unaware of the forces driving the whole thing and why (Fig 536).

Al Gore was dusted off and brought out as the front man alongside the UN's

**Figure 536:** The usual compartmentalisation to hide the truth.

Intergovernmental Panel on Climate Change (IPCC) and propagandists in government and media went to work to sell the lie that human activity generating a greenhouse gas – carbon dioxide – was causing heat to be trapped and warming the planet to potentially catastrophic levels. All of it is bunkum. The foundation of the propaganda is to have Mainstream Everything constantly repeating the official line while suppressing – even sacking – scientists who say it is nonsense. This way you can say that 'the science is settled' when the 'science' is based on computer model projections manipulated to get the required prediction. The progressive-dominated BBC and its 'national treasure' naturalist David Attenborough have been disgustingly biased in parroting the official story. Schools have been mercilessly targeted to indoctrinate younger generations with global warming religious orthodoxy and my son Jaymie was told that if he challenged the fairy tale in his school exams he would lose marks. Simple propaganda is the best propaganda and just label any weather event or fluctuation as global warming. Er, that's it. Repetition is the most powerful form of perception control even if you are repeating baloney. It's hot – *it's global warming*. It's cold – *it's global warming*. Burnt the toast – i*t's global warming*. Oops, no, sorry – that's the *Russians*. Natural El Niño weather effects, a cyclical warming of the Pacific, are further exploited to cry *'it's global warming'*. I could list thousands of examples of built-in bias and manipulation. We had that famous image of the polar bear standing on a small remnant of ice surrounded by water. Look at the picture and that is all you see, nothing more. The caption or the voice-over then tells you what the image means and suddenly a picture of a polar bear surrounded by sea becomes '*Ahhh,* all the polar bears are dying because of global warming'. This is so important to remember. So often it is not the pictures that tell the story and create the perception, but what the caption and voiceover tell you to believe about the pictures. This is another polar bear perspective from Dr Susan Crockford at the University of Victoria, British Columbia:

> *Polar bears are still a conservation success story. With a global population almost certainly greater than 25,000, we can say for sure that there are more polar bears now than 40 years ago.*

Why doesn't the propaganda machine mention that? All except one of 19 polar bear groups have significantly increased while David Attenborough and the BBC were telling us they were facing potential extinction and Gore was showing us four bears that had died 'from climate change' when it later turned out they had died in a storm. For goodness sake, Gore said that climate change was partly responsible for Brexit and a principle cause of the war in Syria when he well knows that it was those that control him made that war happen. Prince Charles said

**Figure 537:** I mean, don't exaggerate or anything.

**Figure 538:** Underwater cabinet meeting by the Maldives government.

something similar about Syria. It's all such madness and yet progressives buy it because it is telling them what they want to hear or what they have been told to want to hear. Then there are the ridiculous images of London under water if we don't de-industrialise the world according to the blueprint of the El-lite, and the Maldives government having a cabinet meeting under water to highlight the danger to their islands of human-caused sea level rises (Figs 537 and 538). Why did they not mention the assessment of Dr Niklas Morner, former president of the International Commission on Sea Level Change? He said in relation to the Maldives: 'In 40 years of study I have found no sea level rise at all.' Why no mention of four studies in 2016 that all found 'no observable sea-level effect' from human-caused warming? Researchers at the Deltares Research Institute in the Netherlands even found the Earth's land mass was *increasing* – by 22,393 square miles (58,000 square kilometres) in the past 30 years and this includes 13,000 square miles (33,700 square kilometres) on *coastlines*. Co-author Fedor Baart remarked: 'We expected that the coast would start to retreat due to sea level rise, but the most surprising thing is that the coasts are growing all over the world.' Al Gore warned in his 2006 Oscar-winning farce, *An Inconvenient Truth*, that unless humans stopped warming the planet ice-sheets would melt and sea levels could rise 20 feet. Gore, who has made a fortune in carbon trading to 'save the planet', said in 2007 that the Arctic ice cap was 'falling off a cliff' and 'could be gone in summer in as little as seven years from now'. Well, seven years later the Arctic ice cap was found to have increased by *43 percent*. Survey results reported in May 2017 revealed that the majority of Greenland had gained surface snow and ice over the previous nine months with temperatures below normal. This doesn't sound much like falling off a cliff (Fig 539). Written records kept by Antarctic explorers Captain Robert Scott and Sir Ernest Shackleton in the early years of the 20th century reveal that Antarctic sea

**Figure 539:** Poor old, Al. Flogging a dead lie can't be easy.

ice has hardly changed in 100 years. In fact, satellite observations show it has actually increased in the last 30 years. Earth temperature and ice caps will of course ebb and flow as they always have, but *El-lite* propaganda surfed a warming trend through the 1990s to sell a belief in human-generated global warming which then became 'climate change' when the mean temperature stopped increasing.

## Trigger warning – common sense zone

You only have to observe the graph of greenhouse gases to see the nonsense of demonising carbon dioxide or CO2 without which, as with atmospheric heat retention systems, we would all be dead (Fig 540) Anyone looking at that graph who has bought the lie would immediately assume that the block on the left representing the overwhelmingly biggest contribution to the greenhouse effect must be CO2. But it's not. Well in excess of 90 per cent of greenhouse gases are water vapour and clouds. Carbon dioxide contributes only 0.117 percent and all except a fraction of that is naturally occurring and nothing to do with human activity. Professor Leslie Woodcock, Emeritus Professor at the University of Manchester, fellow of the Royal Society of Chemical Engineering, a recipient of a Max Plank Society Visiting Fellowship and former NASA researcher, said:

> *Water is a much more powerful greenhouse gas, and there is 20 times more of it in our atmosphere, around one percent of the atmosphere, whereas CO2 is only 0.04 percent. Carbon dioxide has been made out to be some kind of toxic gas, but the truth is that it's the gas of life. We breathe it out, plants breathe it in and it's*

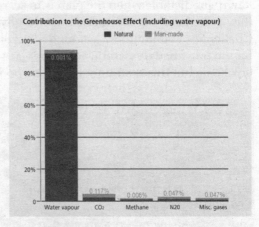

**Figure 540:** Water vapour in its various expressions is overwhelmingly the biggest 'greenhouse gas' with carbon dioxide a tiny fraction by comparison and most of that comes from natural sources not human activity.

*not caused by us. Global warming is nonsense.*

An increase in carbon dioxide is good for plant life and makes the planet greener and more bountiful in growth and food supply. We constantly breathe it out – around two pounds per person per day. What should we do, stop breathing? Hey, save yourself and your family from the dangers of climate change – don't breathe. They should call it the 'Al Gore Challenge' with him going first. Scientist and engineer David Evans, a full-time or part-time consultant for eleven years to the Australian Greenhouse Office (now the Department of Climate Change), said the theory of human-caused global warming was based 'on a guess that was proved false by empirical evidence during the 1990s, but the gravy train was too big, with too many jobs, industries, trading profits, political careers, and the possibility of world government and total control riding on the outcome.' Evans also said that 'governments and their tame climate scientists now outrageously maintain the fiction that carbon dioxide is a dangerous pollutant', rather than admit they are wrong even when the evidence is overwhelming. How interesting that he should mention world government as a reason for the hoax continuing because the plan is to justify a world government in the name of saving the planet. I have been saying this for nearly 30 years and in May 2017 a survey commissioned by the Stockholm-based Global Challenges Foundation ahead of a G7 Summit in Sicily claimed that seven out of ten of those questioned in the UK would support a world government to stop climate change and war by enforcing actions on every country (with the world army). The report warned of 'a high likelihood of human civilization coming to an end' and that is so, yawn, yawn, predictable when the plan is to scare the population shitless until they accept and even demand a world government tyranny. The Global Challenges Foundation was founded by Swedish-Hungarian billionaire Laszlo Szombatfalvy and wants to replace the UN with a form of world government. This is straight out of my books from the mid-1990s.

**Figure 541:** So the science is settled?

Weather channel founder John Coleman has said the global warming hoax is nonsense and even British scientist James Lovelock, a godfather of the Green movement, has said the same. Lovelock once predicted that 'billions will die' in his book *The Revenge of Gaia* and that humanity was doomed

(Fig 541). Any survivors would have to live in the Arctic as one of the few habitable places on Earth, Lovelock said. Now, as reality dawns, he says that climate alarmism is not 'remotely scientific', computer models are unreliable and anyone who tries to 'predict more than five to ten years is a bit of an idiot'. He said that one volcano can make more difference to global warming than humans ever could. Dr Mark Imisides, an American industrial chemist and political candidate, agrees in an article at principia-scientific.org in which he puts ocean warming into perspective:

> *If you ran a cold bath and then tried to heat it by putting a dozen heaters in the room, does anyone believe that the water would ever get hot? The problem gets even stickier when you consider the size of the ocean. Basically, there is too much water and not enough air.*

> *The ocean contains a colossal 1,500,000,000,000,000,000,000 litres of water! To heat it, even by a small amount, takes a staggering amount of energy. To heat it by a mere 1°C, for example, an astonishing 6,000,000,000,000,000,000,000,000 joules of energy are required.*

> *Let's put this amount of energy in perspective. If we all turned off all our appliances and went and lived in caves, and then devoted every coal, nuclear, gas, hydro, wind and solar power plant to just heating the ocean, it would take a breathtaking 32,000 years to heat the ocean by just this 1°C! In short, our influence on our climate, even if we really tried, is miniscule!*

Why aren't we hearing these views on the BBC where anyone challenging the orthodoxy is treated like a village idiot? Orwellian language is used to good effect, with scientists who support the climate change lie described as 'scientists' and 'climate experts' while scientists who expose the lie are 'sceptics' and 'deniers'. Lovelock accuses the Greens of exaggeration and behaving 'deplorably', but they and progressives promoting the climate change narrative are given free reign with UK Green Party co-leader Jonathan Bartley criticising the BBC for even allowing dissenting voices on their airwaves. The arrogance and self-righteousness of these people is incredible. Meanwhile, climate scientists lose their jobs or are forced out if they don't sing for their supper. Dr Judith Curry, a respected climatologist and tenured professor at Georgia Tech University, walked away from what she called her 'dream job' in the face of global warming tyrants who demand absolute obedience. She told Fox News: 'I've been vilified by some of my colleagues who are activists and don't like anybody challenging their big story ... I walk around with knives sticking out of my back ... In the university environment I felt like I was just beating my head against the wall.' Household-name weatherman Philippe Verdier was sacked by the France 2 television channel after publishing a book accusing 'climate experts' of misleading the public about the threat of global warming and the UN Intergovernmental Panel on Climate Change of publishing deliberately misleading data (Fig 542). France claims to be a free country. No, really, it does.

French TV weatherman sacked for book questioning 'hype' over climate change

By Tim Hume, CNN
Updated 1426 GMT (2226 HKT) November 2, 2015

Top stories

How South Africa became the new home of house music

Miss Iraq pageant held for first time in 43 years

Weatherman Philippe Verdier was sacked from his job at France 2 for his book questioning "hype" over climate change.

**Figure 542:** Tell the truth and you're out of here.

'Progressive' trade union members at the station also called for his dismissal. Verdier wrote the book after French Foreign Minister Laurent Fabius asked TV meteorologists to highlight climate change issues in their broadcasts. 'I was horrified by this speech,' he said. He shouldn't worry. It's not like it's a scam or anything. Many other TV weather forecasters don't have Verdier's integrity as you see with the danger of global warming line regularly thrown in. I've mentioned science reporter Misha Michaels who was sacked by the WGBH station in Boston when she posted on her personal website that she believes 'strongly that politics has warped the scientific process and natural variation [of temperature] has a much stronger hand than humans do.' She compounded the felony by saying she supported a bill that would allow parents not to vaccinate their children. Her software station management told her she was 'not a good fit'. Or, when decoded by the Orwellian Translation Unit, she was not 'on message'. American 'celebrity' Bill Nye, the very personification of the arrogance of ignorance, is always right on message and does very well out of it. Nye appears on TV as 'the science guy' and says he is open to criminal charges and jail time for climate change dissenters. I even saw a Tweet from Eric Idle of Monty Python which said: 'I think that denying climate change is a crime against humanity and they should be held accountable in a World Court.' I'd like to think he was joking, but unfortunately it seems not. How very progressive. You can take the piss out of The System, Eric, while still having your perceptions controlled by it.

The Warming Cult retreats whenever questioned to '97 percent of climate scientists agree that human activity is heating the planet'. Politicians, Greens and other progressives repeat this highly misleading figure which was arrived upon by outrageous sleight of hand. Maybe they mean 97 percent of scientists interviewed by the BBC, but, no, because it would then have to be 99.9 percent. Dr Judith Curry told a Congressional Committee that the consensus was only that there was a consensus, and a mere 36 percent of geoscientists and engineers in a peer-reviewed study for the academic journal *Organization Studies* believed that humanity is creating a global warming crisis while the great majority of the 1,077 respondents said that 'nature is the primary cause of recent warming and/or that future global warming will not be a very serious problem'. Those supporting the orthodoxy are nothing like 97 percent, but the question does need to be asked about why most climate scientists do agree that humans are in the dock. There are a number of reasons for this – witness the experience of those who don't play ball for one – but as David Evans said, 'the gravy train' is too big to be allowed to hit the buffers. How apt that the long-time head of the UN IPCC was an Indian railway engineer. *Climate Change Business Journal* estimated the annual budget of the climate change industry to be $1.5 *trillion* and that's the potential pot swilling around for those who will stick to the script. Mislead the public and you get a big grant. Tell the truth and lose your job. American writer and activist Upton Sinclair (1878-1968) said: 'It is difficult to get a man to understand something, when his salary depends upon his not understanding.' We must add to this the sheer repetition of climate change orthodoxy for the climate scientists and repetition is a profound form of perception control. It must be true, surely, everyone around me is saying so.

## It's a fix

When you are telling the truth, you don't need to manipulate the data, but the climate 'science' industry has been caught doing so over and over. Dr John Bates, a top scientist with America's National Oceanic and Atmospheric Administration (NOAA), revealed irrefutable evidence to the UK *Mail on Sunday* that a 'landmark paper' timed to influence policy-makers at the 2015 *United Nations* climate conference in Paris, including 150 world leaders, had been deliberately misleading (Fig 543). Dr Bates had retired from NOAA (described as the world's premier climate data agency) after 40 years in

**Figure 543:** When you are telling the truth you don't fix the data.

climate science. He was given an award by the Obama administration for developing the very 'binding standards' for the production and

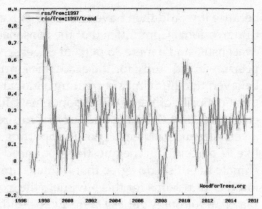

**Figure 544:** Real bad news for the Warming Cult desperate to sell the lie.

**Figure 545:** The mean temperature (the dark line in the centre) has plateaued since the late 1990s against the dire predictions of the flawed computer models.

preservation of climate data that he says the NOAA ignored. The Paris submission claimed that the 'pause' or 'slowdown' in global warming after 1998, confirmed by UN scientists in 2013, had in fact not happened and temperatures had been rising faster than expected. This was naturally given big headlines by the global media as the 'Pausebuster paper' and called it a 'science bomb on skeptics'. The BBC reported with glee that the pause in warming was 'an illusion caused by inaccurate data' when the opposite was true. Dr Bates revealed that the NOAA paper was produced with misleading and unverified information that had not been subject to the evaluation process that he had devised. He said his protests had been ignored in a 'blatant attempt to intensify the impact' on the Paris conference and the public. When temperatures plateaued after 1998 and global warming became climate change the threat to the credibility of the entire hoax was becoming greater as it continued year on year (Figs 544 and 545). Something had to be done to save the day and the train with the gravy trucks on which excuses for Agenda 21 and 2030 depended. Misleading content of the paper was repeated as fact by political leaders and by global warming fanatic Prince Charles when he published a children's book telling glaring untruths about climate change. Governments represented in Paris agreed to major reductions in fossil fuel use (more landscape-destroying windfarms) and to spend $80 billion a year on new projects. *Mmmm ...* even more money, lovely. The *Mail on Sunday* article said:

> *This newspaper has learnt that NOAA has now decided that* [data in the paper] *will have to be replaced and substantially revised just 18 months after it was issued, because it used unreliable methods which overstated the speed of warming. The revised data will show both lower temperatures and a*

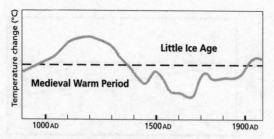

**Figure 546:** The Medieval Warm Period when temperatures were significantly higher than now but when there was no carbon-producing industrialisation. Oops, better just say it never happened then.

*slower rate in the recent warming trend.*

But by then the deal had been literally done in Paris. A 2017 peer-reviewed research report into official adjustments of global surface temperature data found that these adjustments accounted for nearly *all* the claimed warming trend. Not the temperatures themselves, but the 'adjustments' made to them. The National Oceanic and Atmospheric Administration (again), NASA and the UK Met Office all make 'adjustments' to raw temperature data which, the research report noted, almost always adjust the temperature upwards. 'Thus, it is impossible to conclude', the study said, 'that recent years have been the warmest ever – despite current claims of record setting warming.' The report found that a 'cyclical pattern in the earlier reported data has very nearly been "adjusted" out' and that almost all surface temperature adjustments cool past temperatures and warm current ones so artificially making temperatures appear to be increasing in line with global warming orthodoxy. 'Nearly all of the warming they are now showing are in the adjustments', said meteorologist Joe D'Aleo, a study co-author with Cato Institute climate scientist Craig Idso and statistician James Wallace. 'Each dataset pushed down the 1940s warming and pushed up the current warming,' D'Aleo said. The study concluded:

> *The conclusive findings of this research are that the* [adjusted data] *sets are not a valid representation of reality. In fact, the magnitude of their historical data adjustments, that removed their cyclical temperature patterns, are totally inconsistent with published and credible U.S. and other temperature data.*

In my language they are fiddling the figures yet again. The climate change industry has many previous convictions for data manipulation including 'Climategate' in 2009 when thousands of leaked emails between climate scientists exposed how figures and graphs were being fixed. The Climatic Research Unit at the UK's University of East Anglia was centrally involved. Some of the emails discussed how they could delete the Medieval Warm Period from the historic data when temperatures between the years 950 and 1250 were much warmer than they are today (Fig 546). This utterly busted the myth that modern temperatures are unique to the industrial era of CO2 production. The infamous 'hockey stick' graph produced in the 1990s by the Warming Cult and exploited by the UN IPCC portrayed *stable* temperatures through the Medieval Warm Period until suddenly *'whoooosh'* they soared in the late 20th century (Fig 547). A graph at the heart of Warming Cult propaganda was therefore a complete misrepresentation of the truth. The Medieval Warm Period was followed by the Little Ice Age between about the 16th to the 19th centuries although some say it began earlier. Either way it was so bloody cold that the River Thames in London froze over in the winter and ice fairs were held that are still depicted on Christmas cards (Fig 548). Two important points come from this. The first is that when we hear that something is the hottest something or other 'since records began' we should remember that many of those records began while the world was still emerging from the Little Ice Age and any comparison in terms of temperature

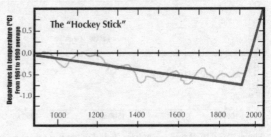

**Figure 547:** The fabricated 'hockey stick' graph that was dependent on the deletion of the Medieval Warm Period.

**Figure 548:** Depiction of a frozen River Thames during the Little Ice Age.

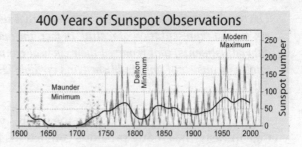

**Figure 549:** The Maunder Minimum was an extremely low point of sunspot activity (electrical activity) on the Sun which corresponded with the Little Ice Age.

'norms' is totally misleading. Secondly, the period of the lowest temperatures in the Little Ice Age is known as the 'Maunder Minimum' (Fig 549). The term comes from Edward Walter Maunder (1851-1928),

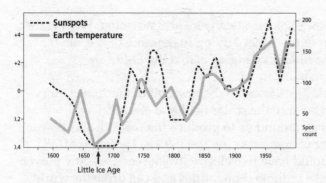

Figure 550: The Sun affects temperature? Well, I never. The obvious connection between Sun activity and Earth temperature is here for all to see.

Figure 551: How did the Warming Cult miss this one? I can't think.

Figure 552: See Al – you got there in the end.

who worked with his wife Annie Russell Maunder (1868-1947) in the study of sunspot activity. They discovered that the lowest temperatures in the Little Ice Age between 1645 and 1715 corresponded with a time when sunspots were extremely rare. This takes us to the foundation flaw in the global warming hypothesis which is ignoring the rather relevant fact that it's the *SUN* which drives Earth temperature and not Ethel driving to the shops. Sunspot activity, for the reasons I explained earlier, reveals the scale of electrical power being processed by the Sun. The fewer sunspots the weaker the power of solar energy projected across the solar system through the electrical web that connects everything. You can see the correlation in Figure 550 between sunspot activity and temperature over hundreds of years. Scientists at the world's leading physics laboratory at CERN in Switzerland recorded a near perfect correlation between the climate and the penetration of cosmic rays into the Earth's atmosphere and yet where is the Sun in the mountain of nonsense emitted by the global warming industry? You mean the *SUN* affects climate? Really? I mean, *really*? Wow, I'd never thought of that (Figs 551 and 552). When Earth temperatures were warming during the 1990s and climate hysteria began other planets of the solar system were also warming. What is the common denominator here – Ethel driving to the store or the Sun?? Another reason for the climate changing is that the *El*-lite are *technologically* changing it.

Real scientist Nikola Tesla knew in the first half of the 20th century that it was possible to tap into the scalar field and electrical and electromagnetic fields all around us to produce the warmth and power we need without using carbon-releasing fossil fuels. He said that 'all people everywhere should have free electricity sources ... electric power is everywhere present in unlimited quantities and can drive the world's machinery without the need for coal, oil and gas.' This should be the godsend of godsends to the Warming Cult – the very answer to their prayers. So why are the governments and agencies telling us we must stop using fossil fuels to save the planet *the very same governments and agencies* which have been suppressing Tesla's knowledge to this day? Why do you never hear a 'progressive' global warmer talk about Tesla and free scalar and electrical/electromagnetic energy? In terms of those controlling governments and their agencies we have another apparent contradiction which isn't. They want to impose de-industrialisation – the 'post-industrial society' as they call it – and they know that this can only be achieved by reducing access to energy. Targeting fossil fuel burning is their weapon while only offering 'alternatives' that are not adequate replacements. Tesla's technology and further advancements that would come from its free circulation would allow the phasing out of fossil fuels while taking nothing from the supply of energy. Indeed, it would make more available to everyone. This would scupper the entire plan and so they say we must reduce fossil fuels while suppressing a real alternative. Throw in the bit about Tesla energy costing people nothing once the technology was in place and you have the *El*-lite increasing the toilet roll order. The global warming hoax is about control and as the 'progressive' said on CNN 'changing everything'. Here are two quotes from United Nations climate change executives revealing the real reason for the Big Lie:

> *This is the first time in the history of mankind that we are setting ourselves the task of intentionally, within a defined period of time, to change the economic development model* – Christiana Figueres, Executive Secretary, UN Framework Convention on Climate Change.

> *We redistribute de facto the world's wealth by climate policy* – Ottmar Edenhofer, former UN climate official.

The global warming hoax is political and financial and not environmental. I would urge its advocates to look at all the evidence and not only that which confirms their current beliefs. An enormous amount of the *El*-lite agenda depends on a continued perception that human activity is endangering the planet and we are back to the question that always unlocks the door: Who benefits from humanity believing this crap? US President Donald Trump withdrew from the Paris climate agreement in the summer of 2017 claiming it was a bad economic deal for America. Global warmers were on the streets and the TV shows in condemnation with their dire predictions of catastrophe. Corporate-obsessed Trump is bad for the environment for sure, but on this he was right even if for the wrong reasons. He once said that global warming was a hoax perpetrated by China and so he's not informed about the real agenda or at least he's not saying so in public. As always with Trump you are waiting for prevarication and the 'but' and he indicated that he might be prepared to negotiate a better deal financially and return to the agreement signed by 200 other countries. I hope not. Anything that breaks the manufactured and manipulated consensus is to be welcomed because sanity must prevail before the madness is used as an excuse to impose a global prison state.

In the last few chapters I have exposed what is really happening in the realm of the seen in politics, world events, wars, terrorist attacks and fake narratives about the migration crisis and climate change. This is important to know, but we make a big and potentially fatal error if we focus only on that. Arguments between alternative researchers and the public in general over the detail of such happenings are another divide and rule and calculated diversion of focus. In many ways, even these manipulations are smokescreens and diversions of attention from the real deal that continues incessantly within peripheral vision beyond the awareness of the conscious mind. This 'real deal' is the plan for the end of humanity as we know it and this is unfolding all around us day after day in plain sight. To see what I mean ... read on ...

# CHAPTER SIXTEEN

# The Assimilation

*'Technological progress has merely provided us with more efficient means for going backwards' – **Aldous Huxley***

The story that I have been unveiling has always had the ultimate goal of the complete subjugation and control of human awareness leading to its eventual deletion via technology. We are now in the midst of that and we need to wake up real fast.

The entity involved in the CHANI Project is quoted as saying that humans are more evolved spiritually than the reptiles but they suppress humans with their technology – 'their god is their technology'. This is being used to complete that goal of connecting and eventually replacing human awareness with artificial intelligence (AI) through the gigantic con-trick that we call transhumanism, but which should really be called *Non*humanism (Fig 553). Archontically-possessed and hive-mind assimilated Reptilians and their Grey subordinates have long manipulated collective human perception through the Orion-Saturn simulation, their command centre inside the Moon and the control structure 'on' Earth directed by the human-reptilian hybrid *El*-lite. This has been immensely successful in controlling the human mind and isolating five-sense perception from Infinite Awareness, but still for many the power of consciousness over program has resisted and overridden the Archontic counterfeit spirit to the extent that complete control has not been possible. Now they are in the process of fixing that by connecting the human mind to

**Figure 553:** We are looking at the end of humanity and we need to know that so we can urgently change direction.

a technological sub-reality or 'hive mind' which its proponents refer to as 'the cloud' (Fig 554). This is a data processing and storage system external to your computer in which software and services operate via the Internet. You could call it a mission control in which all data is stored and processed for all computers and devices connected to it. The plan is for one of those 'devices' to be the human mind after which the whole concept of 'human' will be no more. The first stage is to connect minds to the cloud

**Figure 554:** Transhumanism is the technological means to connect Body/Mind to artificial intelligence that would then do all 'human' thinking and feeling and block out expanded awareness.

technologically and then ultimately to upload them to the cloud and dispose with human bodies altogether. Ridiculous? Well, yes, it would be, but this is what they are now openly predicting is the end result of where we are heading. Cloud-based information is far less safe because it is stored outside your computer and is very much open to being hacked and accessed. The same will be true of the human mind when attached to the cloud. They want artificial intelligence (AI) to feed us all our emotions, reactions and thoughts through the planned brain-cloud technological connection. Humans would be no more than a biological, eventually synthetic/digital, computer terminal. Don't take my word for it. They have reached the point where they are telling us directly what they are doing and they are confident enough to do that because they believe humanity is sufficiently addicted to technology for the final card to be played. Tell your targets that you are going to enslave their minds while those targets stand in line in the dead of night to be the first to get the latest stage in that technological enslavement. 'I got the latest Apple phone, ain't it great?' Well, actually, no it's not.

Archontic corporations and their front men and women are driving almost the entire transhumanist agenda for the end of humanity as we know it from a small area of the world known as Silicon Valley or what I refer to as 'The Devil's Playground'. Silicon Valley, just south of San Francisco, is the centre of the new science related to surveillance, control and transhumanism (Fig 555 overleaf). Here you find Internet giants like Google and Facebook which are globally controlling the information that you are allowed to see, computer software giants like Microsoft and technology giants like Apple. Here, too, is the Singularity University created in 2008 by Ray Kurzweil and Peter Diamandis at the NASA Research Park to promote and advance transhumanism. Singularity in

this context refers to the merging of
humans and machines at a point
when artificial intelligence surpasses
human intelligence and is able to
'self-replicate itself autonomously'
(Fig 556). There may not appear on
the face of it to be a connection
between all these organisations, but
there is. Among the Singularity
University's corporate founders and
sponsors is Google and they are all on
the same team as major vehicles for
the end of humanity under the
direction of one of the most
sinister organisations on earth –
DARPA. This is the Defense
Advanced Research Projects
Agency or the technological
development arm of the
Archontically-controlled
Pentagon. DARPA gives the
world wonderful gifts of
humanity like the death ray, gene
editing to create 'super-soldiers'
and claims to have created the
Internet on which the whole
transhumanist society is being
founded (Fig 557). The
organisation that spends its
billions finding more efficient
ways to kill people also controls
the Internet which was created
from the start with military
technology. DARPA has been the
inspiration and funder behind so
much transhumanist technology
even including AI gadgetry that

Figure 555: Silicon Valley: A very sinister
place controlled by very sinister people.

Figure 556: How can he not know where all this
is leading? He does.

Figure 557: DARPA – the vehicle for Archontic AI
to hijack the human mind.

people would never connect to the technological development arm of
the Pentagon. But all transhumanist technology is connected no matter
how innocuous it may appear to be. Apple's AI 'assistant' marketed as
'Siri', for example, came out of the DARPA-funded CALO project or
'Cognitive Assistant that Learns and Organizes' which involved 300
researchers and 25 university and commercial research centres (Fig 558).
But don't fret – DARPA only funded all this because the Pentagon so

**Figure 558:** 'Siri – why were you funded by the technological development arm of the Pentagon?'

wanted you to have an AI helper to make your life easier. Zionist Ray Kurzweil, a 'computer scientist, inventor and futurist', is a Google executive as well as Singularity University co-founder, and seamless links between Google, Facebook and DARPA can be seen in the career moves of transhumanist promotor Regina Dugan who worked for DARPA as a program manager for four years and returned as head of the organisation between 2009 and 2012. She then left her post as DARPA director to become a Google executive before moving on to Facebook in 2016 (Fig 559). I'm sure the 'search engine' and 'social media platform' only wanted the director of a dark and sinister Pentagon agency to help them improve their listing and communication skills. But, no, amazingly, this is not the case. Her job description as head of the secretive Facebook Building 8 operation is to develop 'technologies that fluidly blend physical and digital worlds.' She and the T-shirt announced in April 2017 the development of technology to allow the human mind to communicate directly with and through computers without having to speak or type on a keyboard. This is another step on the road to the technological AI hive mind with which every human being is planned to be connected. Zuckerberg talks without detail about the need for 'a global superstructure to advance humanity'. Zionist Google founders Larry Page and Sergey Brin developed what became Google technology with funding from the CIA, NSA and the Digital Library Initiative (DLI), 'a multi-agency programme of the National Science Foundation (NSF), NASA and DARPA'. For the detailed background see the Insurge Intelligence Internet article 'How

the CIA made Google: Inside the secret network behind mass surveillance, endless war, and Skynet'.

Zionist-controlled Google and Facebook are both monsters in my opinion, pursuing an agenda of total human subjugation on behalf of the Archontic Web that directs them and this goes way beyond

**Figure 559:** Regina Dugan ... her career moves are all connected.

**Figure 560:** Ray Kurzweil: I wouldn't trust him to tell me the date in a calendar factory.

algorithmic control and censorship of information. Google even has a 'health division' known as Verily, formerly Google Life Sciences, which is developing 'predictive health' technology under the name Project Baseline. They are looking for 10,000 people to take part in highly invasive research to create AI body-monitoring technology to 'predict health problems'. You can bet there will be another far more malevolent motive, too. DeepMind, a Google artificial intelligence company, was outrageously given access by the British government-run National Health Service (NHS) to personal medical records of 1.6 million British patients which Fiona Caldicott, National Data Guardian at the UK Department of Health, called 'legally inappropriate'. This is how the Web operates with apparently unconnected companies, agencies and governments pursuing the same collective ends. Other transhumanist elements of Google were transferred to a holding company called Alphabet in 2015 with one of them, Google X, becoming simply X. The idea was to hide the instantly recognisable name Google in relation to its transhumanist agenda behind the boring and forgettable Alphabet whose Executive Chairman is Eric Schmidt, a member of the Bilderberg Group and Trilateral Commission. I will therefore refer to the organisation as Google, not Alphabet, which has its headquarters within Google headquarters. Alphabet *is* Google. Interestingly, intelligence organisations in the United States including the NSA, CIA and FBI are known as the 'alphabet agencies'. Okay, let's cut to Google Kurzweil's chase (Fig 560). Claims circulate that Ray Kurzweil has an 80 percent success rate in predicting technological/transhumanist outcomes and timescales but that is not so difficult if you know what is planned. You can liken this to financial insiders like Zionist Soros making or withdrawing investments because they know what is going to happen. They really can't lose. Kurzweil's current prediction is that humans will have 'cloud-powered' brains by 2030. He goes on:

*Our thinking ... will be a hybrid of biological and non-biological thinking ... humans will be able to extend their limitations and 'think in the cloud' ... We're going to put gateways to the cloud in our brains ... We're going to gradually merge and enhance ourselves ... In my view, that's the nature of being human – we transcend our limitations.*

*As the technology becomes vastly superior to what we are then the small proportion that is still human gets smaller and smaller and smaller until it's just utterly negligible.*

There you have it and they are being so upfront because the focus of their sales pitch is that being connected to AI will make us superhuman. It *won't*. It will make us *sub*-human and *non*-human and they know it. We have a downgrade being sold as an upgrade. One of their don't-frighten-the-children names for this is 'augmented reality', 'intelligence augmentation' or 'Intelligence amplification'. Instead of AI they call this IA. The sales pitch for this one is that IA won't control the brain like AI, but I say this is only a means to the same end by entrapping those who initially question AI. Yes, we agree with you – AI is so bad, but IA ... well ... that's different. Ultimately it is not. None of this is being controlled by elected politicians, even US presidents, in the same way that they have no clue what is happening in underground bases. The great majority of even politicians don't even know about any of this. Politics is there to hide what is really going on in the shadows and that is why the *El*-lite want people to be so focused on mostly irrelevant political battles and divisions. Look over here while we enslave you over there. Kurzweil appears obsessed with living forever in his body when we already live forever as awareness. He is said to take 150 vitamin supplements a day to extend his life and from what I can see in his cold, emotionless and lifeless eyes it's not doing him a lot of good. Kurzweil predicts that technology in the body will allow people to live forever from around 2045. He means live forever as an AI computer program within the tiniest fraction of Infinite Possibility with no means of escape from a body that will not set you free. Wow, can't wait. Immortality in a body is literally a life sentence. There is no mention of the consciousness that we really are and its immortality within the realm of infinite forever.

A declassified CIA document secured through the Freedom of Information Act describes how the Chinese government undertook large-scale studies involving thousands of children to investigate 'superhuman powers' or what are widely known as psychic powers. They included telepathy, psychokinesis, clairsentience, clairaudience and others, and they are all based on consciousness and frequency, *not* technology. The CIA has been doing the same for many decades and using these skills for their own ends. I was told in San Francisco in the 1990s by the wife of a deceased former US soldier that he had been recruited into the military's 'psychic assassination squad' where they sat around a table focusing on a picture of the target to so affect the electrical systems of the body that the heart would stop. A 2009 movie,

*The Men Who Stare at Goats*, was based on this secret US military programme. They know the true power and potential of humans and the whole system is structured to suppress those abilities and states of frequency in the general population. A lifetime of perception programming – The Program – is specifically designed to do that and transhumanism is the next even more extreme stage.

**Figure 561:** 'God-like' – the crap they want us to believe.

Why on earth would those that have worked so hard to stop humans expressing their limitless potential now want to make them 'superhuman' through technology, as Kurzweil and others claim? What idiots they take us for and unfortunately in too many cases for good reason; but then they have sought to make that so. Kurzweil says that 'with robots in our brains we'll be godlike'. Yes – Archontic god-like and reptilian god-like in the AI hive mind as '... the small proportion that is still human gets smaller and smaller and smaller until it's just utterly negligible' (Fig 561). Kurzweil told a gathering at his Singularity University's NASA campus that he wants to build a search engine to act like a 'cybernetic friend' which knows the users better than they know themselves. 'I envision in some years that the majority of search queries will be answered without you actually asking.' They were openly and enthusiastically promoting the 'global mind' at the 2017 Mobile World Congress in Barcelona, Spain. This 'global mind' is planned to work in conjunction with more powerful (and even more dangerous to body and mind) 5G or Fifth Generation communication systems and by exploiting the properties of a substance introduced right on cue called graphene – 'an atomic-scale *hexagonal* lattice made of carbon atoms' that is 200 times stronger than steel but flexible as skin and 'as conductive as silicon used in semiconductors'. Graphene a few billionths of a millimetre in thickness has the potential to turn every surface into a computer or screen and that includes your own skin. This is not to say there are no positive ways that technology can be used, but that is not the prime motivation. In fact, it's the last.

**Figure 562:** Whatever you do refuse a smart meter.

## 5G must be stopped

The introduction of 5G is crucial to the success of the technological takeover of the human mind and you are going to see behaviour and health catastrophically affected once that power of disruption to the human electrical and electromagnetic fields begins to scramble the standing wave oscillation of mind and body. This '5G revolution' has immense implications with its use of publicly untested ultra-high microwave frequencies and a massive deployment of towers and antennae because of the short range of 5G. By massive I mean one for every 12 buildings in a dense urban area according to one estimate – and located next to homes and schools because 5G waves can't travel efficiently very far. The problem is also being overcome by putting 5G receiver-transmitters everywhere in the form of Smart Meters and other Smart technology. This is a mind and body control grid (Fig 562). 5G operates on the same frequencies as those used for *crowd control weapons* which cause a severe burning sensation on the skin. A US Department of Defense report said: 'If you are unlucky enough to be standing there when [the beam] hits you, you will feel like your body is on fire.' With 5G everywhere they could do this to everyone en masse. Do what we say. No – *ahhhhh!* 5G is a weapons system that can be exploited for targeting health and perception including the deletion of memory. This is some shit we are dealing with here. Dr Ben-Ishai from the Department of Physics at Israel's Hebrew University has explained how human sweat ducts 'act like an array of helical antennas when exposed to these wavelengths'. Human skin is a receiver-transmitter of information – an antenna – which is targeted by 5G frequencies. Dr Devra Davis, an internationally-renowned American epidemiologist, President of the Environmental Health Trust and director of the Center for Environmental Oncology at the University of Pittsburgh, said:

*If you are one of the millions who seek faster downloads of movies, games and virtual pornography, a solution is at hand, that is, if you do not mind volunteering your living body in a giant uncontrolled experiment on the human population. At this moment, residents of the Washington, DC region – like those of 100 Chinese cities – are about to be living within a vast experimental Millimetre wave network to which they have not consented – all courtesy of American taxpayers.*

*This work shows that the same parts of the human skin that allow us to sweat also respond to 5G radiation much like an antenna that can receive signals. We need the potential adverse health impacts of 5G to be seriously evaluated before we blanket our children, ourselves and the environment with this radiation.*

Yes, we do, but that's not the plan. Taxpayer money is being used to fund projects beneficial to corporations because they are assets of the same Web. Health and other effects of 5G (like mind control) are not going to be properly investigated because that would reveal the horrors that would prompt enormous public opposition. The scalar field is also employed for mass mind-control using what some call scalar waves that are really fields. These technological perception fields infused into the scalar field immediately impact on the whole field thus making global mind control possible. Any frequency, in this case 5G, that allows a connection with levels of the human field can be exploited for mind control. Tom Wheeler, then chairman of the US Federal Communications Commission (FCC), gushed forth with plans for all communities, urban and rural, to be saturated with cumulatively deadly 5G frequencies connecting everything from water supplies to pharmaceutical drugs to domestic appliances and anything linked to the Internet. He either knows what is happening or he's an idiot. Take your choice. This is what he said about safety standards:

> We won't wait for the standards to be first developed in the sometimes arduous standards-setting process or in a government-led activity. Instead, we will make ample spectrum available and then rely on a private sector-led process for producing technical standards best suited for those frequencies and use cases.

The usual story with corporations deciding what is 'safe' for a public for which they have utter and total contempt. 5G is being introduced for one reason – this level of power is essential to the functioning of their AI hive mind to control the collective human mind. Wheeler said that autonomous vehicles will be controlled in the cloud along with Smart-city energy grids, transportation networks, water systems, education and entertainment. But this was only possible through a pathway to the cloud that is 'low-latency, ultra-fast, and secure' – 5G. This is why they are racing out 5G global coverage. The hive mind depends upon it. I write this in 2017 and Kurzweil's timescale for humans and AI to begin to merge is 2030. In fact, it has already started. Dr Robert Duncan, former US Chief of Naval Operations who worked at NASA and was Director of Defense Research and Engineering at DARPA, has described the ongoing development of what he called the human 'hive mind' controlled by AI. Facebook's Zuckerberg has said that communications on social media networks will be directed by telepathy instead of keyboards as brainwaves and thoughts are beamed directly onto the Internet. How could this happen? By a brain connection with the Internet through AI, that's how. '[Zuckerberg] wants to get inside your brain and access your thoughts directly', as one news report said. I would certainly not want to get inside his.

## So what *is* AI?

I shake my head when I hear the constant mantra about artificial intelligence controlling everything – it's AI this, AI that and AI the other. But I never hear the key question asked: What *is* AI? What is this 'intelligence' that is taking over the world? I say that AI is the *Archontic* inversion and distortion that has taken over the thought and perception processes of the hive mind Reptilians and the Greys, among so many others, and is now seeking to complete the same assimilation of collective humanity. The term 'AI' would be more accurately defined in its ultimate form not as 'artificial intelligence' but as Archontic Intelligence. This is the real meaning of AI. Gnostic texts described the Demiurge/Archons as what we would call artificial intelligence. We have to get over the myopic belief that intelligent life can only take humanoid form or needs to take form at all. We are, after all, in our infinite state only awareness and 'physical' form is an illusion anyway. Form is a vehicle for a 'human' experience and control, not the true self and so it is with the Archontic inversion. It takes form through manifestation and possession of form such as Reptilians, Greys and the hybrid *El*-lite, but it is in its base state an inverted, distorted state of awareness. Form is only the vehicle, not the 'it'. I watched the entire series of a Science Channel production called *Through the Wormhole* presented by actor Morgan Freeman which featured cutting-edge scientists within the mainstream who were genuinely trying to understand reality and not conform to orthodoxy. There was the usual obsession with the ridiculous Big Bang theory, but it was a pleasure to see many of the contributors willing to peer beyond the Postage Stamp Consensus. One programme asked the question 'Are digital aliens hiding within technological systems?' My answer is yes and they are an expression of the Archontic 'mind' although currently not yet in its full-blown form. Christoph Adami, a professor of microbiology and molecular genetics, physics and astronomy at Michigan State University, said on the programme: 'We can define life in terms of information processes.' He's right, but then we can define life as anything with awareness and *everything* is a form of awareness. This truth has been lost in the search for other forms of intelligent life. Scientists scan the heavens for planets with atmospheres like ours as if that is the only way life can exist. This is incredible in its lack of understanding and vision. Gnostics described Archons as energy in their base state – the 'formless ones' – and that is how we need to see 'life'. Everything else is window dressing or awareness dressing. You can think of it as like a stem cell which is waiting for the instructions to be any type of cell you want it to be. Awareness is waiting to manifest in any form it chooses to be from pure energy to digital systems to two legs, two arms, a head and a torso. I mentioned earlier that Caleb Scharf, Director of Astrobiology at Columbia University, has suggested that 'alien life' could be so advanced that it has transcribed itself into the quantum realm to become what we call physics and numbers. He said that intelligence which is indistinguishable from the fabric of the Universe would solve many of its greatest mysteries:

> *Perhaps hyper-advanced life isn't just external. Perhaps it's already all around. It is embedded in what we perceive to be physics itself, from the root behaviour of particles and fields to the phenomena of complexity and emergence ... In other words, life might not just be in the equations. It might be the equations.*

Scharf said of transhumanism and the singularity: 'If machines become intelligent enough, they could 'decode the staggering complexity of the living world and allow a civilization to reassemble itself into new forms'. But what if the intelligence working through the 'machines' *created* the 'living world' in the first place and even *is* the 'living world'? Scharf talked of a civilization that has learned how to encode living systems with itself and that is what I'm saying about 'digital aliens' or what is being called AI. Scharf said it is possible that 'we don't recognise advanced life because it forms an integral and unsuspicious part of what we've considered to be the natural world'. Correct – and it hides within computer systems under the name AI. The psychological push for human AI mind control is coming from all directions today and the speed of implementation is designed to have the technological control system in place before humanity has realised the catastrophic and, for the human mind, fatal consequences of what is being done and why. Once humans were attached to the AI hive mind the capacity to see that would be gone. AI would be doing all the thinking. Terrorism, war, economic survival and other attention-hijackers are in part playing the role of diverting attention from the AI transhumanist agenda. When I post stories on the Internet there is far more interest in dissecting the latest terrorist attack or political situation than in the bottom-line importance of transhumanism. Many scientists are now warning that the rise of AI could mean the end of humanity. They include Britain's Stephen Hawking and Cambridge cosmologist Sir Martin Rees who holds the title of 'royal astronomer'. Hawking said he fears the consequences of creating something that can match or surpass humans: 'AI would take off on its own and redesign itself at an ever-increasing rate' while 'humans who are limited by slow biological evolution couldn't compete and would be superseded.' Rees has said that machine life will replace humans within a few centuries, but while he has the theme correct his timescale is *way out* and way too optimistic. This process is happening *now*. Interestingly, given what I am saying in this book, Rees predicts that any 'alien life' we come into contact with would probably be machine-like – 'some sort of electronic entity' – given the speed that technology has developed. He believes that the organic stage of development is brief ('a thin sliver') and sits between primitive life and machines. Rees does not realise (like virtually everyone warning about the AI takeover) that biological is also a form of technological and that transhumanism is not being driven by 'evolution' but by a machine-like intelligence seeking to turn us into them – the assimilation.

## 'New' technology isn't new

The rapid speed of introduction comes from the fact that the technological knowledge has been there all along in the hands of the Archontic Reptilians, and this is being introduced at the fastest speed that human understanding can cope with. They had the technology in their reality while humans were using bows and arrows. Human technical (left-brain intellect) awareness has been developed to the point where it could be introduced into human society. When you hear people say how long it is going to be before full-blown AI control is possible they are either kidding you or kidding themselves. All the necessary technology is already there in the shadows waiting to be introduced in a planned order. You want the latest, latest, latest smartphone or iPad? Then don't go to the Apple store – go to an underground base or DUMB. Is it really a coincidence that when they need the next level of technology for the next level of control it is always there right on cue? Does anyone really think that smart technology, advanced computers and algorithms, the Internet, Google, Facebook, Microsoft, Apple, etc., just happened to appear at the very time required in the unfolding agenda? Did the *El*-lite really say 'Phew, what luck!' each time the next essential step in their control system was accidentally and coincidentally developed in the garage of some geek or other? These are mostly cover stories. I personally don't believe the official biographies pedalled for Zuckerberg (Facebook), Brin and Page (Google), Gates (Microsoft) or other Silicon Valley icons like Jobs (Apple), Musk (Space X/Tesla) and Thiel (Palantir). I see CIA and DARPA hands all over these organisations and then on deeper into the shadows. The technological control system has all been planned from the start and imposed in many other realities in the same way. The Reptilians have done this countless times before and the technology is originating with the Reptilian/Grey/human interfaces in the underground military bases and inside-mountain cities. Shaman Don Juan Matus said:

*Think for a moment, and tell me how you would explain the contradictions between the intelligence of man the engineer and the stupidity of his systems of belief, or the stupidity of his contradictory behaviour.*

The explanation is that humanity has been manipulated from the unseen and by Archontic bloodlines in the seen to develop intellectually (cleverness/pixels) but to be suppressed in terms of expanded consciousness (wisdom/insight/big picture). This has brought about the current situation in which humans are building their own technological prison but can't see that this is what they are doing. The intellect can accumulate knowledge to build technology but without expanded awareness it falls for all the diversions and perceptual programs that maintain collective humanity in a state of extreme ignorance of what is really happening. This is Don Juan's 'stupidity of his systems of belief' and 'stupidity of his contradictory behaviour'. It is perfectly possible to be technologically clever while being utterly stupid and this confirms Nikola Tesla's contention that it is possible to think deeply while being quite insane, but to think clearly you have to be sane. The answer to Don Juan's question therefore is that humanity has been covertly developed to think *deeply* about dots but not *clearly* enough to connect them. We now face a situation as this manipulation reaches its endgame whereby the technological means is being constructed all around us as a vehicle for the Archontic inversion (AI) to control and take over everything including the totality of human perception. Scientists are mostly working with what I will call 'algorithm AI' at the moment and battling with perceived limitations, but as the global technological grid based on the Internet continues to emerge full-out Archontic AI will be taking over the system like a gathering cancer. A name being given to the transition to this is 'Strong AI' which is capable of thinking and learning like a human. Scientists and AI technologists are going to see – some *are* seeing – sudden leaps in AI potential and capabilities that they don't understand and didn't expect. This is the full-out self-aware Archontic AI taking over from algorithm AI in technological systems, especially through AI control of the Internet which I will come to soon. Most transhumanist scientists and technology developers are being had as much as anyone – more so, in fact.

A group of scientists and entrepreneurs, including Stephen Hawking and tech billionaire Elon Musk, signed an open letter warning that without checks on intelligent machines humanity faces a dark future. I agree, but the role of Musk is seriously contradictory. On the one hand, he warns about the dangers of an AI takeover of the human mind and society (true), but then buys a company specifically tasked with creating a brain implant to connect brains to computers. This is similar in theme to what Facebook and former DARPA director Regina Dugan are

**Figure 563:** Musk is one of the public trailblazers of human-computer connections while saying how potentially dangerous that is.

**Figure 564:** Dugan's brief at Facebook.

developing – a digital-biological mental and perceptual interface controlled by AI. DARPA itself has invested in similar technology. The *Wall Street Journal* reported that Musk's Neuralink company intends to create a 'neural lace' or mesh-like system which would 'implant tiny brain electrodes' that could eventually upload and download thoughts. Musk says that this has the potential for human to human telepathy (via AI) when human consciousness should naturally communicate telepathically and did so until the Archontic intervention through perceptual, vibrational, chemical, pharmaceutical and now technological inference to block such processes. Musk, a co-founder of PayPal and CEO of Tesla and SpaceX, acquired Neuralink to take us further down the very road that he says is so potentially dangerous (Fig 563). This would seem to make no sense and until I see evidence to the contrary I will treat Mr Musk and Mr Kurzweil as a good-cop-bad-cop combination in which Kurzweil seeks to push on to transhumanism as fast as possible while Musk argues about the dangers while still pursuing the same agenda. There is a lot more to know about Mr Musk. This is true of Facebook – you know, just a social media platform – which has employed a brain-computer interface engineer to work in its transhumanist Building 8 division headed, purely by coincidence you understand, by former DARPA director Regina Dugan (Fig 564). Musk's line would seem to be that while AI is dangerous we must have our minds connected to its computer systems to allow human intelligence to keep up with artificial intelligence. There is another option to avoid an AI takeover – *stop creating the technology that allows AI to control everything including human perception.* This is not mentioned because it is not the agenda. Possibly Musk is genuine in his fears about AI in which case his views and actions betray a major dose of cognitive dissonance or thought contradiction; but it is much safer not to give him the benefit of that doubt before evidence is produced to support it. In fact, the evidence is to the contrary with Musk's Tesla and SpaceX companies developing driverless (AI-controlled) vehicles and sending the very satellites into orbit that are essential to the whole AI takeover as I will shortly explain.

Musk has also said there is only a 'one in billions' chance that we don't live in a simulation. I am very wary of the simulation double-bluff in which it is eventually and officially accepted that we live in a simulation while using this to further justify AI control on the back of some fairy story about the need to make the best of it by fusing with AI. Watch for that one big-time, because the revelation about the simulation can be exploited to depict humans as nothing more than technical constructs if you fail to mention the rather important point that the 'we' or 'I' is a state of Infinite Awareness and what we call human is only its temporary vehicle. I saw a talk by George Smoot, an American astrophysicist and winner of the Nobel Prize for Physics, in which he set out to convince his audience that 'You are a simulation and physics can prove it'. I agreed with much of what he said except for the definition of 'you'. Body-Mind may be a simulation interacting with a simulation, but the 'you', or 'I', is not. The 'I' is Infinite Awareness or Spirit entrapped in a simulation. Many transhumanist scientists and

**Figure 565:** Addiction to electronic/digital stimulation has reduced the attention span of many to that of a goldfish.

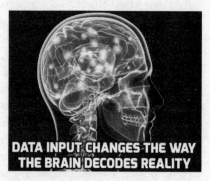

**Figure 566:** The brain changes the way it processes information in accordance with the nature of the information.

developers can't see where this is going because they are so obsessed with new technology that they can't connect the dots or because they are in a perceptual coma. One leading developer said that we shouldn't be concerned with AI machines becoming more intelligent than humans because once that happened they would eventually leave the planet and explore elsewhere. Talk about cleverness without wisdom – what *is* he talking about? Once *Archontic* AI gains access to the human brain it will take over all thought and emotional responses – or lack of them. Human perception, as Kurzweil has said, will be diluted and diluted until none remains. DARPA is funding research for its Targeted Neuroplasticity Training (TNT) programme to develop ways of stimulating the brain to become more malleable to new forms of information downloading and processing. Brain placidity refers to how data input changes and rewires the way the brain functions and processes information. The selling point is that this could lead to people downloading knowledge and skills instantly as portrayed in the *Matrix* movies, but the real reason is to change the brain from human perception processing to AI Archontic processing to speed the assimilation and rewire its perceptual processes (Figs 565 and 566). I read how we may 'one day be able to operate spaceships with our thoughts, upload our brains to computers and, ultimately, create cyborgs' when the entire human reality is already run by Archontically-controlled cyborgs in the form of Reptilians, Greys and others.

## Human Borg

The plan to turn humans into AI-controlled cyborgs has been symbolised many times in movies and television series, and few more accurately than *Star Trek* and its concept of the Borg (Fig 567). These are portrayed as a collective of species – part biological, part technological – that have been 'turned into cybernetic organisms functioning as drones in a hive mind called the Collective, or the hive'. This is basically the case with Reptilians, Greys and other Archontically-controlled 'hive' species. Borg are portrayed as emotionless drones, like malevolent Reptilians and Greys, and were coordinated by the 'Borg Queen' in the way that a queen bee relates to a hive. Reptilians are said to have a similar structure based on what is called the Orion Queen (see *Children of the Matrix*). The Borg use a process called assimilation to force other species into the Collective by injection of microscopic machines called nanoprobes and the Borg mantra is 'resistance is futile'. One of the best-known Borg statements goes: 'We are the Borg. Your biological and technological distinctiveness will be added to our own. Resistance is futile.' They also, fittingly, fly around in black cubes (568 and 569). The same theme of 'resistance is futile' can be

**Figure 567:** *Star Trek* Borg are technologically-transformed into a 'cybernetic species' controlled by a hive mind or 'the Collective'.

**Figure 568:** Borg travelled in black cubes.

seen in the Kurzweil camp as with this quote from his co-founder of the Singularity University, Peter Diamandis:

*Anybody who is going to be resisting the progress forward* [to transhumanism] *is going to be resisting evolution and, fundamentally, they will die out. It's not a matter of whether it's good or bad. It's going to happen.*

**Figure 569:** A Borg black cube craft appropriately passing Saturn.

The highly symbolic theme of the Borg takes us into the deeper levels of the transhumanist conspiracy, a level where Musk's brain-computer connection is small deal indeed. Newspaper coverage of Musk's Neuralink plans even included pictures of the Borg to illustrate the story, but they were missing the point of where the real human-Borg agenda is happening. This is in the unseen world of nanotechnology and what the Borg call nanoprobes, which connected everyone to their hive mind or Collective. Microchips and other transhumanist technology that we can see are controlling enough, but the real deal in all this is the technology that we cannot see. I met a CIA scientist in California in the 1990s who told me about nano-chips so small they could be – and were – inserted through hypodermic needles in public vaccination programmes. Nanotechnology was little talked about then but now it provides the foundation of our technological society. A good comparison of size that I saw is that if you take the distance between Earth and the Sun to be one millimetre, then the length of one nanometre is the very short distance from New York to Boston. A nanometre is one billionth of a metre and nanotechnology is in the size range of 1-100 nanometres. In short, it's bloody microscopic and we can't see it. We now *have* the apparently

**Figure 570:** Connecting the human Body/Mind to the 'Cloud' and everything else.

fictional nanoprobes of the Borg and as so often happens science fiction turns out to be no more fictional than *Nineteen-eighty-four* or *Brave New World*. Today they are called nanobots, nanorobots, nanoids, nanites, nanomachines, nanomites, neural dust, digital dust and smart dust (Fig 570). These are micro-machines that can assemble and maintain sophisticated systems and build devices, machines or circuits through molecular manufacturing and produce copies of themselves through self-replication. They are the nanoprobes of the Borg in other words. This is the real level at which humanity is being connected to technology and the 'cloud' or hive mind, and 5G will see this globally activated. Everything else is in many ways a diversion from this. I will refer to human 'nanoprobes' as smart dust given that 'smart' is the major buzz-word for the transhumanist transformation. We have smart televisions, smart meters, smart cards, smart cars, smart driving, smart pills, smart patches, smart watches, smart skin, smart borders, smart pavements, smart streets, smart cities, smart communities, smart environments, smart growth, smart planet ... smart *everything*. 'Smart cities' is simply code for the human settlement zones or high-rise,

**Figure 571:** Not very smart if you value freedom.

densely-occupied megacities of total surveillance and control through AI (Fig 571). Huawei, the Chinese telecommunications equipment and services multinational, says in its smart city promotional material that 'a staggering 70% of the global population will live and work in cities by 2050 ... Increasingly, business, leisure and residential properties have to build upwards to accommodate this ...' Here we go. But, wait, no, how wonderful it all sounds:

*... in space, geostationary satellites and orbital platforms will monitor the city's atmosphere, pollution levels, weather systems, and local environment, keeping us healthier and safer. Energy will be metered efficiently, in the background, generated from clean, renewable sources – affordable for all, and friendly to our environment. Ultimately, the Smart City enriches our lives and environment for the better.*

Put another way you won't be able to sneeze without them knowing about it. Smart cities are being built from scratch around the world and current cities are being transitioned into them. Pegasus Global Holdings (PGH) is working with the Department of Homeland Security, CIA, Department of Defense, Department of Transportation and other bodies to build total-surveillance smart cities. They are planned to include cameras, drones, microphones in streetlamps and elsewhere, Bluetooth monitoring devices, license plate readers and cell phone surveillance. A 'CIA signature school', a large scale smart city mock-up, is being built in

New Mexico. Microsoft, Siemens, IBM, Cisco, GE, Intel Corp, AT& T and 'smart TV' Samsung are all involved in smart city development. The usual suspects, all of them. Everything you say or do would be monitored and recorded. This is not coming – it's already here. Look at all the new technologies being introduced with increasing speed that can monitor your words and actions via the Internet with everything from AI office assistants to smart devices, smart televisions and smart meters to school computers and even children's toys. Together all these smart technologies are planned to comprise the 5G Smart Grid which is another expression of Kurzweil's AI cloud. This grid is formed from the fact that a 'Smart Object interacts with not only people but also with other Smart Objects'. The foundation of this is smart dust or tiny electronic particles for wireless communication with each other and anything they connect with. Promotional material for smart dust reveals that it can track and recognise an individual anywhere, turn on their computer at work when they enter the building and make the elevator automatically stop at the right floor. This, too, puts surveillance cameras into the realm of diversions from the true scale of 24/7 surveillance possible with smart dust.

Kurzweil and company want the entire world bathed in smart dust which he refers to here as nanobots. He says: 'Nanobots will infuse all the matter around us with information. Rocks, trees, everything will become these intelligent creatures.' Another term for this is 'programmable matter' and the point is that this nano-technology is *alive*. They are a form of *entity* and so Kurzweil calls them 'these intelligence creatures'. Kurzweil is describing the technological sub-reality that I have been warning about for so long which has now been dubbed the Smart Grid and the cloud. This is a synthetic/digital world for a synthetic/digital species – the Archontic force. Human mind, body and all of what we call nature would be connected to AI and our true self in the form of Infinite Awareness would be

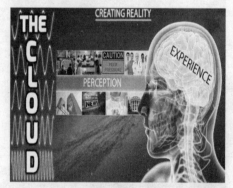

**Figure 572:** Kurzweil's cloud would do all thinking and what we call human today would be no more.

**Figure 573:** I don't accept the monkey part, but the conclusion is certainly coming unless humanity takes its mind back.

technologically excluded and
replaced as our point of reference by
AI communicating through the cloud
to what would be nothing more than
a computer terminal responding to
data input and instruction (Fig 572).
Humans as we know them would be
no more (Fig 573). This is what is
really happening and their timescale
to complete the job is far shorter than
uninformed transhumanists believe
because so much is already in place in
the shadows waiting to be unveiled.

**Figure 574:** They want everything connected to the Internet – including the human mind.

## Control by Internet

Not only transhumanist gurus like Kurzweil are openly promoting the
technological nightmare of total control (while saying it is good for us).
You can see this all the time if you peek through the veils designed to
obscure the real reasons for the latest technology to daily flood human
society. They tell you openly what something will do, but they don't tell
you why. This is the bit they don't want us to know. David Petraeus
could not have been more upfront in his brief spell as CIA Director when
he discussed the then coming Internet of Things which is now very
much with us and we have seen nothing yet (Fig 574). Petraeus spoke at
the In-Q-Tel CEO Summit in 2012. In-Q-Tel is a technological arm of the
CIA and 'Q' is a reference to the technology inventor in the James Bond
movies. Petraeus said:

> *The current 'Internet of PCs' will move, of course, toward an 'Internet of
> Things' – of devices of all types – 50 to 100 billion of which will be connected
> to the Internet by 2020. As you know, whereas machines in the 19th century
> learned to do, and those in the 20th century learned to think at a
> rudimentary level, in the 21st century, they are learning to perceive – to
> actually sense and respond. Key applications developed by our In-Q-Tel
> investment companies are focused on technologies that are driving the
> Internet of Things ...*
>
> *... Items of interest will be located, identified, monitored, and remotely
> controlled through technologies such as radio-frequency identification,
> sensor networks, tiny embedded servers, and energy harvesters – all
> connected to the next-generation Internet using abundant, low cost, and
> high-power computing – the latter now going to cloud computing, in many
> areas greater and greater supercomputing, and, ultimately, heading to
> quantum computing.*

*In practice, these technologies could lead to rapid integration of data from closed societies and provide near-continuous, persistent monitoring of virtually anywhere we choose. 'Transformational' is an overused word, but I do believe it properly applies to these technologies, particularly to their effect on clandestine tradecraft. Taken together, these developments change our notions of secrecy and create innumerable challenges – as well as opportunities.*

**Figure 575:** It should be a joke, but it isn't.

Many points arise from this. Surveillance possibilities are obvious with everything connecting to the Internet, from domestic appliances to cars and devices of every kind, via chips, smart meters and other Wi-Fi fields. All road vehicles are planned to be controlled by AI through the cloud with an Elon Musk company one of those developing the technology. The more terrorist attacks there are involving vehicles driven into crowds of people the bigger the excuse they have to impose them. I am going for a drive, dear. Where are you going? I'll ask the computer. Driverless cars will be programmed to ensure they can't take you where the authorities don't want you to go. Electric cars with more limited ranges are also part of a big agenda to make it harder to travel freely. We are now being told about the development of pilotless (and hackable) AI passenger aircraft! Even the content of your fridge would be known to the authorities through this smart system. Crazy? No – Amazon is involved in a project to put cameras and other technology in a new 'smart' fridge that would monitor activity. It's only for our own good, of course, to make life easier. They care so much (Fig 575). Thousands of WikiLeaks documents labelled 'Vault 7' have exposed CIA hacking tools to access information on people through Internet-connected devices including the Apple iPhone, Google's Android, and Samsung TVs. Amazon's electronic book pad, Kindle, is mentioned in relation to 'code templates' and Amazon's Alexa AI 'personal assistant' will listen to your conversations and 'take notes'. I can't wait and I bet Amazon owner, Jeff Bezos, owner of *The Washington Post*, can't either. We are also told that 'Alexa AI can now whisper sweet nothings and express emotions like a human' and 'add emphasis to words and even be programmed to say regional-specific phrases'. This is all about the mental and emotional fusion between humans and AI on the road to complete assimilation. LG Electronics Inc, a South Korean multinational, is Amazon's partner in the Alexa project. David VanderWaal, LG's vice-president of marketing, announced plans to add 'advanced Wi-Fi connectivity' (5G) to *all* of its home appliances and eventually have 'tens of millions of smart connected devices' in homes. The CIA has been exposed for hacking into Wi-Fi routers on a massive scale and can access *everything* on your computer or any other Wi-Fi-connected device. Surveillance is only part of the plan behind the Internet of Things. The then CIA Director Petraeus obviously did not

 mention that the most important target has all along been the human mind and going beyond the Internet of Things to what is being called the Internet of *Everything* with humans included (Fig 576). This is Kurzweil's 'cloud'. The Internet was created from day one from military technology – DARPA claims the credit – in pursuit of this end. Good parts of the Net like the once free-flow of information and opinion

**Figure 576:** The Internet of Everything in the post-human world.
© www.neilhague.com

were just to get people hooked before the good parts were deleted and the true motivation left unchallenged to do its dastardly deeds.

## Transcendence

This plan was presented to us in movie form with the 2014 release of *Transcendence* starring Johnny Depp. Hollywood is a global programming operation and has been used since its inception to mass download perceptions of people, world events and history that suits the prevailing order. Part of this is the technique known as pre-emptive programming where you employ futuristic storylines and images to make the subconscious familiar with them. If you want to transform society monumentally you will obviously face opposition because of the scale of change. But if you have already made the collective subconscious familiar with what you plan to introduce that sense of change will be diluted in those who have absorbed the programmed familiarity. This is why dystopian and control-by-machine movies have been churned out one after the other year after year with machines often playing the role of the good guys. Nearly all the movies involve extreme violence and nearly all are shot in semi-darkness or with a dark tinge to the picture as with the occult-programming *Harry Potter* films. Johnny Depp played a scientist in *Transcendence* a few years hence who was working to advance artificial intelligence. When he found that he was dying, he and his scientist wife downloaded his mind onto a quantum computer which widely existed by then as did the

**Figure 577:** A conscious Internet in the movie *Transcendence.*

Internet of Things. I'll explain the role of quantum computers in due course. After his death, his wife further downloaded her husband's mind onto the Internet which then 'woke up' and became conscious (Fig 577). Many scientists have asked if the Internet could wake up and become conscious and I say that it already has to an extent. Neuroscientist Christof Koch, chief scientific officer at the Allen Institute for Brain Science in Seattle, said:

> *The Internet contains about 10 billion computers, with each computer itself having a couple of billion transistors in its CPU [brain]. So the internet has at least 10^19 transistors, compared to the roughly 1000 trillion (or quadrillion) synapses in the human brain. That's about 10,000 times more transistors than synapses.*

What is the brain but in effect a biological computer system processing information to dictate perception and behaviour? What is the military-created Internet as described by Christof Koch, but a technological computer processing information to dictate perception and behaviour? In the latter case, the Internet is a vehicle for artificial intelligence for which Depp's mind in *Transcendence* was merely symbolic. Depp's consciousness (AI) went on to take control of everything connected to the Internet which by then was virtually *everything* and expanded its technological control through the means described earlier ... 'micro-machines that can assemble and maintain sophisticated systems and build devices, machines or circuits through molecular manufacturing and produce copies of themselves through self-replication'. The plan is that when Archontic AI control of the Internet and cloud reaches the necessary level it will take control of everything connected to it including the human mind and wiping your digital bank account would be a doddle. The point to stress again is that while today AI is described in terms of algorithms and codes this is only a transition period while the smart infrastructure is built and put into place. AI scientists speak of the moment when AI will become self-aware and the whole dynamic between machines and humans will be transformed. AI will be humans and humans will be AI with nothing to tell them apart even in the way they look in terms of robotics. This is the moment when algorithm AI will be replaced in terms of prime control by full-blown Archontic self-aware distortion 'AI' which has been the plan all along, and algorithm AI will be controlled by Archontic AI. Depp's mind (AI) in *Transcendence* took over human society by controlling the billions of devices linked to the Internet and human minds were lassoed into this global control system and the Internet of Everything through 'sentient nanoparticles spread on the wind'. We are talking smart dust. As humans breathed in the nanoparticles so they were connected to Depp's AI mind which then became *their* mind. This is unfolding in human society every day and what is the means through which 'sentient nanoparticles' are being 'spread on the wind'? We are back to ... *Chemtrails.*

## Smart dust from the sky

People are familiar with contrails or condensation trails that pour from the back of aircraft in certain atmospheric conditions and quickly disappear. Chemtrails or chemical trails do not disappear. They slowly pan out until at their most extreme a blue sky can become apparently cloudy and hazy. Eventually chemtrail contents fall to earth to infest all in their wake – people, animals, water sources, trees, plants, soil, everything (Fig 578). Chemtrails have been criss-crossing the sky all over the world on an ever-increasing scale at least since the 1990s as I said earlier. I see them everywhere I go no matter what the country or continent. I have watched military aircraft out of Luke Air Force Base in Arizona turn a blue sky hazy every day for a week and I have observed a deluge of them focused over the Isle of Wight during music festival weekends with tens of thousands of people underneath. Most of the pilots have no idea what they are spraying or why because of

compartmentalisation and downright deceit. They are told that this 'geoengineering' is to create a barrier to block out the heat of the Sun and save the world from global warming. Mainstream Everything denies the existence of chemtrails and dubs them a conspiracy theory while at the same time people like Harvard engineers David Keith and

**Figure 578:** Chemtrails have many ingredients for different aspects of the agenda.

Frank Keutsch have been openly talking about doing exactly this 'in the future'. David Schnare, who worked on Donald Trump's transition team for the Environmental Protection Agency, has lobbied for federal support for geoengineering to save the planet from 'global warming'. Schnare has called for testing to start followed within three years by stratospheric spraying to continue for a century. Meanwhile, it's already happening day after day worldwide. Tests have shown chemtrails to contain aluminium, barium, radioactive thorium, cadmium, chromium, nickel, mould spores, yellow fungal mycotoxins, polymer fibres and so much more in cumulatively lethal concentrations for human health.

Aluminium is a brain toxin and chemtrails are a major contributor to the explosion of Alzheimer's and dementia in general since they began to appear (Fig 579). The scale of aluminium contamination is way above anything we are told. I was sent a soil analysis document by a researcher in the United States from a non-government laboratory which revealed aluminium content at 1,198 pounds per acre when the 'upper limit of normal' was less than 7 to 10 pounds. A government laboratory had apparently refused to do the test. I bet they had. Professor Christopher Exley at Britain's Keele University warned in the journal *Frontiers in Neurology* of the cumulative effects of exposure to aluminium and its connection to dementia. 'We are all accumulating a known neurotoxin in our brain from our conception to our death', he said. 'The presence of aluminium in the human brain should be a red flag alerting us all to the potential dangers of the aluminium age.' He pointed out that aluminium is present in cosmetics, food, water, tea, coffee, wine, fizzy drinks, sunscreens, antiperspirants and medications – 'almost everything we eat, drink, inject or absorb'. Professor Exley said that aluminium builds up in the brain, nerves, liver, heart, spleen and muscle until it crosses a 'toxic threshold' when the brain and body can no longer cope. The subsequent brain malfunction is what we call Alzheimer's and dementia. This is all correct because there is a coordinated assault against human consciousness which is targeting the brain with aluminium and one of the major sources never mentioned in the mainstream is chemtrails.

Alzheimer's and other forms of dementia have surpassed heart disease as a cause of death in England and Wales with a 2015 total of nearly 62 thousand. Cases of dementia in general are predicted to increase by two-thirds in the next 25 years with 1.2 million living with dementia by 2040.

**Figure 579:** Systematically poisoned from the sky.

While other factors and aluminium sources will be playing their part, there is silence about aluminium in chemtrails because according to Mainstream Everything those massive white streams caused by aircraft visibly going back and forth criss-crossing the sky do not exist. The British Met Office and World Meteorological Organisation officially recognised condensation trails (contrails) left by aeroplanes as a type of *cloud*. I am sure it is nothing to do with muddying the waters about chemtrails as with animated movies that add them to the sky to create familiarity and make them seem normal. Biologists at Keele University and the University of Sussex discovered enormous concentrations of aluminium in bumblebee pupae that would cause brain damage in humans. Bees have been in catastrophic decline around the world with the subsequent threat to food supplies of falling pollination. The headline of one report captured the theme: 'Bees suffer dementia due to metal pollution: Aluminium contamination may be behind insect decline'. Professor Chris Exley was again quoted making a link:

> *Aluminium is a known neurotoxin affecting behaviour in animal models of aluminium intoxication. Bees, of course, rely heavily on cognitive function in their everyday behaviour and these data raise the intriguing spectre that aluminium-induced cognitive dysfunction may play a role in their population decline – are we looking at bees with Alzheimer's disease?*

Mass die-offs of the bee population will have many causes including pesticides and other plant and crop poisons that animal and insect life have to deal with. But *dementia*? Well, the aluminium won't be coming from cosmetics, food, water, tea, coffee, wine, fizzy drinks, sunscreens, antiperspirants and medications, that's for sure. Aluminium interrupts electrical information communication in brain and body in the realm of the seen, but in the waveform unseen it represents a disruptive frequency disturbing waveform balance of the human energetic (standing wave) field. Chemtrails are having a widespread effect on human health and that of the environment in general with their ever-increasing scale corresponding with apparently unexplained mass die-offs of trees, plant life and the poisoning of lakes and other water sources with the very metals that chemtrails contain including aluminium (Fig 580). This has allowed the same *El*-lite behind the destruction of trees and bees

**Figure 580:** Forests, plant life and water sources are being devastated by the content of chemtrails.

to suggest their replacement with genetically-modified trees and bees as per their agenda. Not surprisingly trials are underway with GMO trees, crops and plants resistant to *aluminium*. Dane Wigington, an investigative journalist and writer at GeoengineeringWatch.org, said: 'Global geoengineering is completely disrupting the hydrological cycle, destroying the ozone layer and contaminating the entire surface of the planet with highly toxic ... heavy metals and chemicals.' Ozone layer depletion opens all life on Earth to dangerously high ultraviolet radiation. Technology such as HAARP can also amplify the strength of poisons and chemicals in the body and environment by a thousand times by generating electromagnetic frequency fields to a level where they become instantly lethal in a process called 'cyclotron resonance'. 5G Wi-Fi has the same potential to affect human health in this way and health is affected communally by chemtrails blocking out the Sun (the vital vitamin D) which leads to a host of degenerative problems. The demonisation of the Sun (stay out of it or you'll get cancer!!) is also connected to this.

## Nanotrails

We must add to the chemtrail cocktail ... *nanotechnology* ... and return to a quote by Ray Kurzweil: 'Nanobots will infuse all the matter around us with information. Rocks, trees, everything will become these intelligent creatures.' How else are they going to achieve that unless they drop his 'nanobot' smart dust from the sky? Chemtrails are the means through which smart dust is being spread on the wind (Fig 581). In the same period since chemtrails began we have had the emergence of Morgellons or the 'chemtrail disease'. Morgellons sufferers have coloured fibres growing inside them and when they are pulled out through the skin (which often causes 'shooting pains') they replace themselves or 'self-replicate' in the parlance of nanotechnology (Fig 582). Some of these

fibres can be as thick as spaghetti and they continue to grow outside the body. They have a form of intelligence following a program and are very advanced 'living' technology. Some of the fibres have been found not to burn until they reach 1,700 degrees Fahrenheit and they are not biological but technological – a self-replicating machine intelligence that fits the CV of smart dust. They know how to construct themselves and replicate, and remember how

**Figure 581:** This is the way that Kurzweil's pledge to infuse all 'matter' with nanotechnology is being achieved.

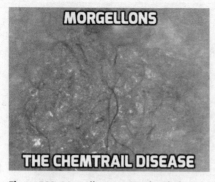

**Figure 582:** Morgellons emerged with the coming of chemtrails.

Norman Bergrun said that in his opinion the Saturn 'craft' were 'living' and capable of the essential functions of biological systems like self-replication and self-maintenance. I have been sent many images by a Morgellons sufferer of the extraordinary phenomena found in the bodies of those with the disease. Some can be seen in Figure 583. Among them are hollow filaments, fibres, crystals and silica (often in a hexagram form), even insect-like synthetic 'creatures' remarkably similar to the one inserted into Neo's belly by agents in the *Matrix* (Fig 584). No wonder a major symptom of Morgellons is a feeling of something crawling under the skin. Silica is silicon dioxide and found in sand among much else. Silicon

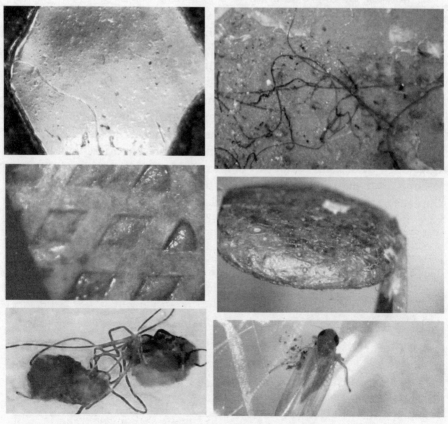

**Figure 583:** The extraordinary phenomena that have been found in the bodies of Morgellons sufferers.

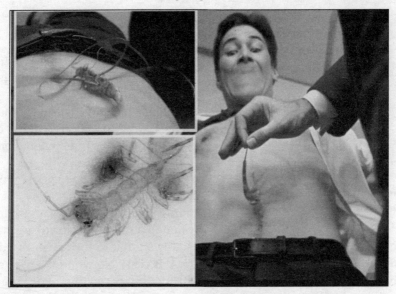

**Figure 584:** This 'creature' in the bottom left found inside a Morgellons sufferer is remarkably like the one inserted into Neo by agents in *The Matrix*.

and oxygen are the Earth's two most abundant elements. Silica can be crystalline or non-crystalline but it is the crystalline version that chemtrail nanotechnology seeks to exploit because of its re-wiring effect on the crystalline body. Crystalline silica (the most common form is quartz) is extremely hard with a high melting point – hence the 1,700 degrees Fahrenheit. How apt that the epicentre of transhumanism is called *Silicon* Valley. There are also spheres found in Morgellons sufferers that look remarkably like 'nanofiber biodegradable polymers' developed by scientists that can 'self-assemble into hollow, nanofiber spheres' and are injected with cells into wounds. They apparently allow the cells to live on and form new tissue (Figs 585 and 586). But in the case of Morgellons what kind of tissue? *Synthetic* tissue is the answer to

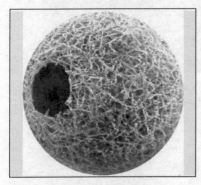

**Figure 585:** This is a self-assembling nanofiber sphere.

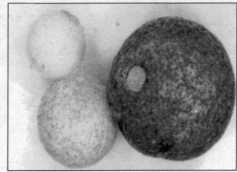

**Figure 586:** This was found in the body of a Morgellons sufferer.

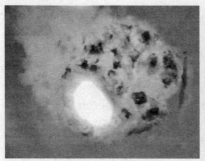

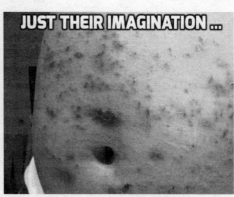

**Figure 587:** Some Morgellons phenomena even illuminate through the power of piezoelectricity or pressing electricity.

**Figure 588:** What they expect us to believe.

that question as I will come to. Some Morgellons phenomena even light up thanks to a power source known as piezoelectricity or 'pressing electricity' (Fig 587). This movement-generated electricity in the body produces power to drive the technology. Singer Joni Mitchell is a famous Morgellons sufferer who has described how 'fibres in a variety of colours protrude out of my skin like mushrooms after a rainstorm.' She said they cannot be identified as animal, vegetable or mineral. Despite this and so much more evidence mainstream medicine claims that Morgellons is all in the mind and a psychological problem which they call 'delusional parasitosis'. Yeah, yeah, sure it is (Fig 588). They have to say that – as they did about Joni Mitchell – or the truth would come out of what is really going on. I take it that the medical profession claiming this nonsense sleep well at night and don't think about their families too much. A few can see the obvious and have begun to investigate the causes of Morgellons by employing technology such as electron microscopes to uncover the truth. An article at www.cidpusa.org summarised the findings:

> *Morgellons appears to be a communicable nanotechnology invasion of human tissue in the form of self-assembling, self-replicating nanotubes, nanowires, and nanoarrays with sensors. Other nano-configurations associated with Morgellons disease carry genetically-altered and spliced DNA or RNA ... The Morgellons nanomachines are configured to receive specific tuned microwave, EMF and ELF signals and radio data ... We do know that Morgellons is commonly found in all body fluids, orifices and often even hair follicles, and are believed to routinely achieve total body systemic penetration.*

Those tested who do not have visible symptoms of Morgellons have been found to be infested with fibre cultures grown from their saliva, body tissue and urine. We are facing a mass takeover of the human body

**Figure 589:** The situation in four words.

by machines ultimately controlled via Reptilians, Greys and others of the Archontic inversion (Fig 589). Morgellons is proliferating because the takeover is proliferating and you will see this massively increase with the introduction of 5G which this body-invasion technology is designed to interact with. To quote from the Borg script: 'Humans are being transformed into 'a collective of species – part biological, part technological – that have been turned into cybernetic organisms functioning as drones in a hive mind called the Collective, or the hive.' This was done in the apparently fictional script by 'nanoprobes' and is now being done in the real-life script by smart dust and chemtrails. The famous 1956 movie *Invasion of the Body Snatchers* captured the theme with this piece of dialogue:

*Seeds drifting through space for years took root in a farmer's field. From the seeds came pods which had the power to reproduce themselves in the exact likeness of any form of life ... Your new bodies are growing in there. They're taking you over cell for cell, atom for atom.*

*There is no pain. Suddenly, while you're asleep, they'll absorb your minds, your memories and you're reborn into an untroubled world ...Tomorrow you'll be one of us ... There's no need for love ... Love. Desire. Ambition. Faith. Without them, life is so simple, believe me.*

Smart dust nanotechnology is not only being delivered by chemtrails either. This stuff is in much of what people eat, touch, spray and rub on themselves. The list is enormous and growing exponentially for all the reasons I am describing here. You can check for yourself the scale of nanotechnology infestation by going to websites like nanotechproject.org. Andrew Maynard, science advisor to Emerging Nanotechnologies, said:

*The use of nanotechnology in consumer products and industrial applications is growing rapidly ... How consumers respond to these early products – in food, electronics, health care, clothing and cars – will be a litmus test for broader market acceptance of nanotechnologies in the future.*

The point is, however, that it won't be a 'litmus test' because the force driving this from the shadows has no interest in what the public think. *Controlling* the public is all that it cares about. Nor can people make an informed decision with so little publicity about the ever-growing reach of nanotechnology and its use in products that you would never even begin to associate with it. Nanotechnology in sunscreen and cosmetics? Filaments and fibres have

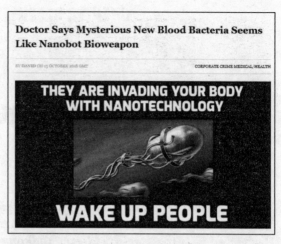

Doctor Says Mysterious New Blood Bacteria Seems Like Nanobot Bioweapon

**Figure 590:** The claim certainly fits the gathering evidence.

been found in air, soil and water samples in the general environment as you would expect when it is coming from the sky. Ray Kurzweil has said that artificial red blood cells were being developed ('being' invariably means 'have been already') and scientist Clifford E. Carnicom of the Carnicom Institute in New Mexico found 'red blood cells, white blood cells, and unidentified cell types' within 'sub-micron fibre samples' taken from the environment. They appeared to be 'of a freeze-dried or desiccated [preserved by drying] nature in their original form within the microscopic fibres'. Time for another double question-mark: Freeze-dried blood cells in the environment?? California doctor and researcher Nick Delgado has described 'tadpole'-like phenomenon in the blood of some patients who all complain of a persistent cough (Fig 590). He says he had never seen it before until around 2014/15. Delgado describes how the 'tadpoles' can be viewed in the blood under the microscope as like groups of fish or birds moving and changing direction as one unit. He believed this could well be some form of bioweapon.

We are now a long way down this road and humanity must open its eyes and mind to a world that is way different to the one that we are told from cradle to grave to believe in. The *El*-lite are counting on the Big Sleep continuing until they finish the job and we *must* disappoint them.

# CHAPTER SEVENTEEN

# Synthetic human

*'By far the greatest danger of artificial intelligence is that people conclude too early that they understand it'*
*- Eliezer Yudkowsky*

We see the term 'synthetic' everywhere today. We have synthetic vitamins and supplements (both biologically useless *because* they are synthetic), synthetic drugs, synthetic cannabis, synthetic blood, synthetic genetics and at the end of this road is planned to be synthetic people. They are already being created in the secret centres of research and development (Fig 591).

Synthetic is defined as '(of a substance) made by chemical synthesis, especially to imitate a natural product'. This is a perfect example of Archontic expertise in 'countermimicry' as they seek to replace the biological human form with a synthetic one which better suits their interests in the synthetic/digital 'smart' world they are constructing all around us. Archons are themselves a form of 'synthetic' in the sense that they are a counterfeit spirit, a 'synthetic' spirit or awareness. They have had to work as best they can with biological humans, but now they are seeking to turn humanity in totality into themselves. Once again Hollywood movies are constantly portraying this very society with films like *Ghost in the Shell* and the US TV series *Westworld* in which synthetic 'humans' are the central theme. *Ghost in the Shell*, shot in semi-darkness as usual, depicts a world run by machines. People have 'complete synthetic bodies' with *Matrix* movie-type

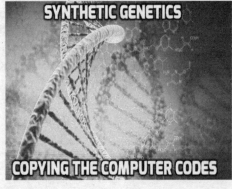

**Figure 591:** Synthetic codes from biological codes.

connections with technology through the reptilian brain stem where it emerges from the spinal column at the back of the neck. Their human memories were erased and this is part of the plan to make synthetic/digital humans forget their 'past'. Biomedical ethicists Marcello Ienca and Roberto Andorno warned in the journal *Life Sciences, Society and Policy* that 'hazardous use of medical neurotechnology' could threaten the integrity of thought and memory: 'Illicit intrusions into a person's mental privacy may not necessarily involve coercion, as they could be performed under the threshold of a person's conscious experience.' The pair called for legislation to protect people from having their thoughts stolen or even deleted. All the best with that one, chaps. Synthetic humans are being designed to have no sexes and no means of procreation which would be done technologically as per Hatcheries and Conditioning Centres described by Aldous Huxley in *Brave New World*. It sounds crazy, except that it's happening *now*. A synthetic version of DNA is being developed called GNA along with others under various names including PNA. Science20.com described GNA as a 'nanotechnology building block' and 'chemical cousin' of DNA. The website reported that 'Biodesign Institute scientist John Chaput and his research team have made the first self-assembled nanostructures composed entirely of glycerol nucleic acid – a synthetic analog of DNA'. This is now a common and increasing theme as the synthetic human emerges. Scientists announced a plan in 2016 to synthesize the entire human DNA code (the 'genome') within ten years, a task that involves billions of pieces of information. The work would involve deactivating the production of egg and sperm cells in the synthetic cell. Scientists said that eventually synthetic techniques could be used to evolve entirely new forms of life which could be passed on through the generations. DARPA is supporting DNA digitisation to create a computer code that can be programmed. The work is headed by another man to watch like a hawk with a telescope, Craig Venter and his J. Craig Venter Institute with facilities in Maryland and California, which announced in 2010 that the 'the first self-replicating, synthetic bacterial cell' had been developed. The media dubbed it 'Synthia'. Whatever they tell you they are doing is always long behind the stage of development in the secret bases where the finished work is already waiting to be handed over by Archontic Reptilians and Greys to their hybrid and human lackeys in an order that appears on the surface to be a sequence of 'discovery' leading to the final outcome. In fact, the final outcome has been there all along and the sequence to get there is only to hide where it is all really coming from. Big questions would be asked if fully-formed and complete technological advances came out of nowhere with no cover story or apparent sequence of development. Much of the 'research' work in public is more about bringing human scientists up to speed, not the technology.

Media reports of a 'secret meeting' to discuss the synthetic genome project focused on the development of health benefits and 'designer babies' which allow parents to choose what genetic traits they want them to have. The real point was missed – the creation of an entire synthetic 'human' race to replace the biological version. This synthetic genome announcement followed a closed-door meeting at Harvard Medical School where government officials, scientists, entrepreneurs and lawyers gathered but journalists were kept out. One newspaper reported: 'Experts reacting to the news have said that the proposal is just the start of "an open and transparent debate" on the topic of creating a man-made human genome.' Transparency is the last thing that will happen. The endgame is already decided – if we stand by and allow it. Scientists talked about essential safety measures to stop synthetic cells from escaping and replicating in the environment when synthetic genetic material is dropping from the skies every day. This is the chasm of difference between what we are told (even what the great majority of compartmentalised scientists know) and what is really going on. Professor Henry 'Hank' Greely, a geneticist at Stanford University, has predicted that in as little as 20 years children will be produced with pre-ordered traits and end the need for sexual procreation. Laboratories and not the bedroom will be used to produce children, as one report put it. Greely says in his book, *The End of Sex and the Future of Human Reproduction*, that this would be brought about by making the production of 'natural'-born children appear irresponsible. This mass psychology hoax is on stand-by to be unleashed on an unsuspecting humanity which would then impose no-sex babies on each other through demonisation of dissenters. I have been warning for a long time about the plan for laboratory babies, and Aldous Huxley described this in *Brave New World* in 1932. That's how long (and much longer) the Archontic agenda is projected into what we perceive as the future and this can be done before the technological know-how exists in human society

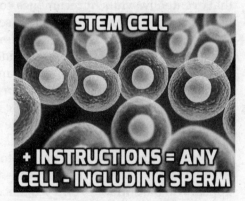

**Figure 592:** What do you want me to be?

because it already existed in the Archontic Reptilian realm and only the transfer across remained to happen. Professor Greely describes how genetic material can be used to create eggs and sperm via stem cells which are neutral cells waiting to receive instructions to become any cell you want them to be (Fig 592). These have already been used in laboratories to produce egg and sperm cells. This was all predicted by the in-the-know Aldous Huxley in *Brave New World*:

> *Natural reproduction has been done away with and children are created, 'decanted', and raised in 'hatcheries and conditioning centres'. From birth, people are genetically designed to fit into one of five castes, which are further split into 'Plus' and 'Minus' members and designed to fulfil predetermined positions within the social and economic strata of the World State.*

George Orwell wrote something similar to Huxley, his former Eton French teacher, in *Nineteen- eighty-four*. Quoting Big Brother representatives he wrote:

> *Already we are breaking down the habits of thought, which have survived from before the Revolution. We have cut the links between child and parent, and between man and man, and between man and woman. No one dares trust a wife or a child or a friend any longer. But in the future there will be no wives and no friends.*

> *Children will be taken from their mothers at birth, as one takes eggs from a hen. The sex instinct will be eradicated. Procreation will be an annual formality like the renewal of a ration card. We shall abolish the orgasm. Our neurologists are at work upon it now. There will be no loyalty, except loyalty towards the Party. There will be no love, except the love of Big Brother.*

Anyone still bewildered by all the multiple attacks on the family unit? One other point about genetics and genetic information is the DNA-testing websites that include AncestryDNA and 23andMe. Ancestry DNA is a subsidiary of Ancestry.com, the biggest for-profit genealogy company in the world. This is based in Utah, home to the genealogy-obsessed Mormon Church, and down the road from the National Security Agency's global data centre. I have exposed the horrors of the Mormon Mafia in other books and how this fake religion connects into the Web. People send saliva samples to these companies to test their DNA, but what happens to the information afterwards? Okay, I have read their privacy statements, but how does anyone really know? Ann Cavoukian, a former Ontario privacy commissioner who runs the Privacy and Big Data Institute at Ryerson University, said:

> *I think you have to assume that you're going to lose control over that information ... Assuming that this information could be in the hands of many individuals, over which you have no control, are you comfortable with that? It will extend beyond just ancestry information – your full genetic*

*code is there through that test, so perhaps other information can be gleaned, over which you have no control in terms of who has access to it.*

They are after your DNA in so many ways. DNA-testing 23andMe, a 'personal genomics and biotechnology' company, is based in Silicon Valley near to Google and Facebook headquarters and was co-founded by Zionist CEO Anne Wojcicki, former wife of Zionist Sergey Brin, co-founder of Google. Her sister, Susan Wojcicki, is CEO of Google-owned YouTube while Google invested almost $4 million in 23andMe. What a small world it is – and it gets smaller. Zionist Arthur D. Levinson, chairman of Apple, also heads biotech company Calico which he founded in a joint venture with Brin's Google, now 'Alphabet'. Zionist influence is way, way out of sync with the numbers and it is a legitimate question to ask why this is. Why should Zionism be excluded from questions that would be asked about any other grouping in the same circumstances? I would be staggered if Amazon owner Jeff Bezos, too, doesn't turn out to be an asset of this network pursuing the same goals. Amazon, Google, YouTube, Facebook and Apple are all clearly moving in the same direction and I would add Ray Kurzweil, Elon Musk and Peter Thiel (of whom more shortly) to that as well - plus many more.

## Transgender Agenda

Now we can see the real reason for the explosion-out-of-nowhere obsession with transgenderism. This is a stepping-stone to assimilation into the Archontic Reptilian mind through technology, AI and synthetic genetics. I said earlier that Reptilians and the Archontic distortion are *androgynous* – 'partly male and partly female in appearance; of indeterminate sex'. Baphomet is depicted with both male phallus and female breasts (Fig 593). On every level and in every way, they are turning humans into *them*. I repeat – I don't care how people perceive themselves sexually or in any other way. That is their business, not mine, so long as they don't try to force it on anyone else. Good luck to them, I say. But if the transgender obsessives (many of them not transgender) and the public in general don't grasp what this is really about in the wider sense then *all* of them are going to regret it. Never mind about being 'non-binary'. If people don't open their minds to this and fast there will *only* be binary – a synthetic no-sex non-human connected to the 'cloud'

**Figure 593:** Androgynous Baphomet.

**Figure 594:** We need to put identity politics aside and face the truth before we pass the point of no return.

through 1 and 0 on-off electrical charges of the binary computer system (Fig 594). I have already discussed how language terms are being enforced from the purely transgender perspective and how children and young people are being bombarded with transgender propaganda to purposely confuse their self-identity. This is being underpinned by the media in all its forms, government departments, medical professionals, and spineless, mindless academic institutions. We have no-gender toilets and the banning of male-female terms such as boy and girl, mum and dad while BBC children's programming for kids as young as six features a child taking hormone-blocking drugs. Acrush, the 'hottest boyband in China' and aimed at a young audience, are really girls made to look like boys – a 'gender neutral, androgynous, non-binary band'. Transgender propaganda and programming is coming from every angle. Highgate School in London, which costs nearly £7,000 a term, said it was considering allowing boys to wear skirts because growing numbers of children are questioning their gender and 'the binary way people look at things'. *Why do you think that could be, then?* Put these two sentences together by the school's headteacher Adam Pettitt and the game is revealed:

(1) 'In common with all other schools and youth organisations ... we are seeing greater numbers of pupils questioning gender identity than in the past.'

(2) 'Having said that, in years gone by, absolutely no young people were raising it at all and it seems inconceivable that these sorts of questions simply didn't exist.'

No, it doesn't. Kids were not being bombarded with propaganda to question their gender before, and that's the difference. The American College of Paediatricians reported that children are being indoctrinated to reassess their gender with reckless, profit-driven doctors prescribing sex-change hormones to children as young as 12. The report rightly condemned this as child abuse. But it's not only profit-driven. It's agenda-driven. We are witnessing the fusing and confusing of gender identity in preparation for the no-gender, no-sex, synthetic designer human. Today's young are being most targeted because they are going to be the adults when full-on synthetic humanity is planned to become reality. Once again don't be misled by the predicted time-scales for synthetic genetic transformation. The end is already in place with no need to discover the means. What is left is to *cover* the means so people don't realise how it is all coordinated. A major pillar of the no-sex human is the end of masculinity through the suppression of the male hormone testosterone. I am not referring only to men, either. Women have testosterone and if the levels are too low both sexes can suffer from fatigue and exhaustion, weight gain, mood swings, depression and anxiety. Testosterone in men stimulates sex drive and sperm production (the last thing the agenda wants) and helps to build muscle and bone mass. Sperm counts have been falling dramatically in preparation in part for the synthetic human due to chemicals in food and drink and the impact of massively increased radiation especially with ubiquitous Wi-Fi. I mentioned earlier the study that found a 59.3% decline in total sperm count in men from North America, Europe, Australia and New Zealand. Studies involving large numbers in Spain found that sperm counts had fallen by 38 percent in ten years. A mainstream media report said: 'The reproductive health of the average male is in sharp decline, the world's largest study of the quality and concentration of sperm has found.' Testicular cancer rates have also doubled in 30 years. Richard Sharpe, professor of reproductive health at the University of Edinburgh in Scotland and recognised expert on toxins in the environment, said this about falling sperm counts:

> *Now, there can be little doubt that it is real, so it is a time for action. Something in our modern lifestyle, diet or environment is causing this and it is getting progressively worse. We still do not know which are the most important factors but the most likely are ... a high-fat diet and environmental chemical exposures.*

Chemicals for sure, especially those that mimic female sex hormone oestrogen (US estrogen), but I would strongly suggest that a high-fat diet is in the clear apart from the artificial trans fats found in junk food in all its forms. Up to a fifth of young men have a low sperm count and alarm bells have been sounding since 1992 when Danish research revealed that the number of sperm in each millilitre of semen had halved since World War II while abnormal sperm was on the rise. A French study of 26,600 healthy men confirmed a substantial decline in sperm counts between 1989 and 2005. But Jerusalem Imam Sheikh Muhammad Ayed doesn't think this is all bad news as we saw earlier:

> *Europe has become old and decrepit, and needs human reinforcement ... they have lost their fertility, so they look for fertility in their midst. We will give them fertility!*

Alongside falling sperm counts we have a global fall in male birth rates. This is not yet devastating the male population but the fall is incessant and pretty much global. Dr Devra Davis, President of the Environmental Health Trust and lead author of a report on the subject, said: 'It's important to look at the really big picture here, which is that there are global indications that something unusual is going on.' There is an incessant multi-faceted attack on the male and male hormone and this is connected to the ever increasing psychological and political correctness attacks on the male in general and the white male in particular. Scientific studies in Israel and Australia have highlighted the potential adverse effect on sperm of cell phones carried in trouser pockets. Researchers at the University of Newcastle in New South Wales examined 27 different studies into the subject and 21 revealed a link between cell phone radiation and both sperm and DNA damage. Other leading theories about the cause of falling male births and sperm counts include exposure to pesticides, herbicides, mercury, lead, dioxin and other pollutants and also to *synthetic* substances called endocrine-disrupting chemicals (EDCs). The endocrine system of glands includes the 'sixth-sense' pineal gland or 'third eye'. EDCs are found in plastics, food containers and packaging, canned food and drinks, electrics, solvents, cleaning products, detergents, pesticides, cosmetics, soaps, car exhausts, polish, paints, batteries, dental fillings (mercury) and many types of fish including swordfish. Often highlighted is the hormone disrupter Bisphenol A or BPA used in tin cans, bottles, plastic food containers and cash register receipts. Here's your receipt – you didn't want children, did you? And what is contained in vaccines that could be adding to fast-diminishing sperm? All this is happening by design and being orchestrated from the shadows. Don't fall for the 'they're just stupid or maximising profit' explanation. This will be true of those lower down the pyramid, but not those knowingly serving The Spider. Herbicides and pesticides sprayed on farms, parks and golf courses should also be added to the cumulative cocktail. Atrazine, one of the world's most-used pesticides, is changing the sex of male frogs and making them infertile. Researchers at Zhejiang University in Hangzhou, China, found that a much-used endocrine-disrupting pesticide with residues in milk, baby food, and vegetables is speeding the onset of puberty in boys and leading to earlier sexual maturity which can have health and psychological impacts in adult life. EDCs and the female sex hormone oestrogen can be found in unfiltered tap water along with other EDC chemicals. Some believe – and they are right – that this chemical onslaught is affecting or sabotaging potentially male foetuses at critical periods of development and so turning them into girls while also lowering men's sperm counts and testosterone levels. Synthetic endocrine-disrupters really are a one-stop shop for all that is in male decline and they are going to realise eventually that these are connected to the relentless rise in prostate cancer which is the most common cancer in men. Dr Devra Davis, who has also highlighted the dangers of 5G Wi-Fi, points out that fast-dividing cells producing sexual organs are very open to 'incorporate and replicate errors' that can lead to changing once-developing boys into girls. Whenever biochemical processes are involved clearly any chemical disturbance becomes significant and can surely feminise even those people who still emerge from the womb as male. Dr Melody Milam Potter, an American Clinical Health Psychologist for 30 years, wrote the following in an excellent article at Greenmedinfo.com:

> *Synthetic chemicals can create these silent switches in Nature's plan. EDCs we encounter every day can alter the sex hormone balance, preventing male genitals from growing properly. By suppressing testosterone or by enhancing or mimicking the female sex hormone, estrogen, they can undermine the natural testosterone messages surging through a growing fetus.*
>
> *For instance, estrogen mimics [such as] dioxin, a widespread pollutant and potent endocrine disruptor, can intercept and overcome a hormonal message from a male gene. Dioxin also acts as a testosterone flusher reducing male hormone concentrations so much that the male action may not be stimulated adequately.*
>
> *Testosterone suppressors like DDT can block testosterone's position on a receptor. Hormone stimulators can intensify the action of a natural hormone so much that the system shuts down and refuses to receive a male 'go ahead' signal ... In fact, research substantiates that exposure to EDCs at a crucial time can disrupt the entire genital sequence.*

In the seven years after a chemical explosion contaminated the small community of Seveso in northern Italy twice as many girls were born. Parents with the highest levels of chemicals in their blood had no male children at all. Fertility rates fell dramatically. Studies claim that the number of people identifying as gay or 'LGBT' is rapidly increasing to the extent that one in the US estimated that those born before and across the Millennium to be nearly twice as likely to identify as LGBT as other American adults – 'Millennials Are the Gayest Generation', as one headline put it. Are we really saying that none of this is connected to a chemical environment awash with gender-bending toxicity? Are we really? Now ... look what Dr Richard Day said in 1969 was part of the plan – people would be made 'gender-neutral', boys and girls would be the same and reproduction without sex would be performed in laboratories.

## Jelly-making

Then there is the effect of all this on behaviour. Testosterone is often associated with aggressive and dominating males but there are two sides to every coin. The same hormonal effect can be channelled by the mind into a need to protect others and stand up to a potential aggressor. This may be termed 'acting like a man' but testosterone in females is the same. Lower testosterone levels in either sex and you reduce the stand-up-and-be-counted response that we so vitally need right now to change the direction of human society. I don't mean to be violent but to be stoical and unyielding in our refusal to take this crap any longer and refuse to acquiesce with our own enslavement. This response is being deleted by a long list of manipulations that very much include reducing testosterone levels in both men and women. We are witnessing with Generation Jelly and PC snowflakes the more obvious and extreme examples of the increasing consequences of reducing the 'male' aspects in men *and* women. They become acquiescent to prevailing norms, frightened of their own shadow and the next potential 'trigger', and so hand their power to Big Brother in exchange for his perceived protection from their ever-growing list of threats and nasties. Testosterone is associated with risk-taking and the PC psyche never wants to contemplate taking risks. Keep it safe, mate, I might be triggered. I am describing here what is now on public display and this has only just begun if we allow it to continue unchallenged. But there's more. I mentioned earlier the emerging genetic science known as epigenetics. This can sound complicated but its foundation is real simple. Most people believe that genetic change comes only from changes in DNA and the genetic structure itself. Epigenetics has shown this not to be the case. Think of human genetics as a computer hard drive. You don't have to change the structure of the hard drive to change what appears on the screen. This can be done by using the keyboard and mouse to switch on and off the functions of the computer without any structural change being necessary. The hard drive works as it always did and you are only activating some functions and not others. This is how the Chinese government censors the Internet. Epigenetic research has revealed that human genetics works the same way. Environmental, experiential, mental and emotional influences can switch on certain gene effects and switch-off or 'silence' others through activation and de-activation of gene function. What is activated and silenced affects the way the body decodes information – as in the case of computers – and can lead to everything from changes in the way people think, feel and perceive reality to whether they get cancer or don't. Even more significantly what is activated and silenced within the genome can be passed on through the generations. Much of what we call 'inherited' genetic traits are epigenetic in nature and not structural or a mutation of the blueprint. When I say this is significant I mean fundamentally so because it means 'physical', mental, emotional and perceptual traits are passed on down the line. Epigenetic effects on humans of the now daily chemical deluge, environmental influences including soaring radiation levels and self-identity/perceptual transformations are constructing the new human epigenetically minute by minute. The first generation *becomes* something different and following generations are *born* something different with bodies (biological standing wave fields) that decode reality from the start in the way their predecessors did. Today's *manipulated* snowflake becomes tomorrow's *born* snowflake.The transgender agenda and PC zealotry look very different when viewed from this perspective. They are seeking to breed out rebellion and make men and women the same, but let us not forget that what can be turned off can be turned on if we open to consciousness beyond the program because the body not only responds to mind – it *is* the mind. We come back to the basis of everything in this reality. What we call the human body is a waveform 'software program' decoding information in a particular way to decode into holographic existence a particular reality and sense of reality. Epigenetics and the infestation of smart dust nanotechnology is changing the way that people decode reality to squeeze perception even more severely than now.

Nanotechnology is crystalline as we see with the crystal and silica nano-structures found in those with Morgellons, and represents a new and synthetic receiver-transmission system to connect the synthetic human to Kurzweil's 'cloud' or AI which I contend in its greater sense is synthetic Archontic Intelligence. Sofia Smallstorm, an outstanding researcher, has produced some excellent presentations about the synthetic human agenda and its connection to chemtrails. 'Sofia Smallstorm, the dark agenda of synthetic biology', will take you to her YouTube videos. She explains how 'coloured plaques' or hard pieces of silica have been found in those with Morgellons and some have dots on them:

*The plaques are fragile, they can shatter. Quantum dots which are the colours you see are nano-crystal semi-conductors made of heavy metal surrounded by an organic shell. Now I want you to remember some of these terms, 'heavy metals' – heavy metals, aluminium and so forth.*

*So these are nano-crystal semi-conductors surrounded by an organic shell but they are made of heavy metals and Morgellons subjects are also finding this stuff. Jewel-like hexagons, faceted pyramids, crystals. Hexagons have*

*shown up environmentally, not only in tissues, but they are in*
*environmental fall out ... The industry tells us that quantum dots are tiny*
*nano crystals whose small size gives them unprecedented tunability, okay,*
*tunability!*

Sofia then summarises where all this leading and she is spot on:

*Artificial intelligence will connect the world, homo sapien will be*
*transformed into homo evolutis, biological processes will be run by*
*technology, living things will not be reproductive, the earth will be*
*populated with engineered species and all processes will be patented, licensed*
*and controlled. You could consider nanotechnology the installation of*
*Artificial Intelligence in living and non-living things. Smart dust and smart*
*moulds for instance are tiny nano-sensors that can float and land anywhere.*

The point about these processes being patented, licensed and
controlled is something I have warned about in books way back. This is
already happening as giant corporations like Monsanto change a
'natural' process and then patent that change to secure global
ownership. Monsanto has enforced patents against farmers in the courts
who didn't choose to have GMO on their land, but were prosecuted and
financially destroyed when their land was contaminated with Monsanto
GMO spread on the wind and by other means. How disgusting and evil,
but then they are. Corporations behind the synthetic/digital human that
will do that to people won't eventually claim ownership of the body
itself? For those who think this won't happen I offer my congratulations.
They have just secured a first-class degree in naïvety. Israeli historian
Yuval Harari, a tenured professor in the Department of History at the
Hebrew University of Jerusalem, says that 'the greatest industry of the
21st century will probably be to upgrade human beings' and that 'for the
first time in history it will be possible to translate economic inequality
into biological inequality.' He is referring to the difference between
'upgraded' AI humans and those who refuse to 'upgrade' or are not able
or allowed to 'upgrade' which lunatic 'futurists' claim will die out.

## In our face (literally)

I have warned since the early 1990s about the
microchipping/transhumanist plot and I've watched ever since as this
has emerged from the shadows with ever-quickening speed. The mass of
humanity who are not aware of the Hidden Hand have experienced this
same period as the ever-quickening development of technology to give
them more sophisticated toys to play with. Connect the dots and a very
different reality can be seen. All along the desired outcome has been to
attach the human mind to the AI 'cloud', but that could not be done in

one go from a standing start. The Totalitarian Tiptoe had to be used to lure humanity into the technological lair through a series of stages although that didn't take long. Stage one was to get people – especially the young – addicted to what I will call 'holdables' (Fig 595). These are smart phones, tablets and such like or 'pocket-size AI'. This stage is virtually complete as I see in my world travels with smartphones dominating attention and destroying conversation almost everywhere. It says it all that Steve Jobs, co-founder of Apple who once had top secret security clearance, didn't let his own children use these devices because they were so addictive. Watch for new Apple products, by the way, especially those that involve 'augmented reality' and I suggest you give them a very wide berth. A third of American babies now play with smartphones before they can walk and talk and have their brains re-wired and addicted to this digital heroin from the earliest age (Fig 596). Welcome to the technological mind-prison, kids. Adults are little different. Record numbers of people are ending up in hospital after walking into traffic looking at their phone (Fig 597). Smartphones have changed the way people walk and are damaging their posture and spine with all the looking down. Facebook users visit the site on average 14 times a day and cumulatively Americans check their phone ten billion times a day. A British survey in 2017 found that nearly half of families with children text each other in the same house instead of talking. A third of people use their mobiles during family meal times (go in almost any restaurant these days) and a quarter reported that at least one person in their home was not sleeping properly because they were on their phone into the night. People in general are increasingly communicating technologically and not face to face as direct human contact diminishes and AI devices take over so making an ever-closer association between humans and machines. All these 'office assistant' devices are designed to take this connection even deeper. Data compiled by the UK National Health Service reveals that hospital visits for sleep disorders by children under 14 have tripled in England in ten years. The light of these devices alone is enough to block production of the sleep-inducing hormone melatonin. One newspaper headline summed it up – 'Britain's vampire generation: They're the frazzled teens getting as little as TWO HOURS sleep – thanks to gadgets, anxiety and social media.' All three of which are connected. This is having a serious impact on their health and impeding brain development. Some now even have anxiety attacks when they find themselves in an area (increasingly rarely) with no Wi-Fi. Nearly half of parents questioned said their children ignored them while on their phones, but children also complain that their parents are on the phone too much. Dr Richard House, a psychologist at the University of Winchester in the UK, said communication technologies were 'potentially catastrophic for the human relational

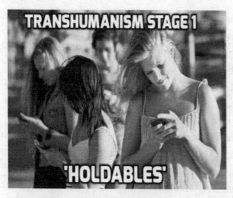

**Figure 595:** Get them addicted (achieved).

**Figure 596:** Start them young and get them for life.

**Figure 597:** Digital heroin.

values that underpin family life at its best, with real, face-to-face communication being increasingly displaced and side-lined by the machine.' What is on the wish-list of almost every major social engineering organisation? The destruction of the family and family life which allows the state to seize control of children and childhood. People said in one survey that on average they had ten close friends in 2001 but a few years later it was two. Humanity is being divided and ruled by smart technology designed to make us anything but smart. But, hey, it's nothing to be concerned about. Eric Schmidt, the appalling Executive Chairman of Zionist-owned Alphabet (Google), said:

*Worry about where your teenager is? Now we know where they are – they are in their room online. It's a much safer place than a lot of places a teenager can be.*

This is the mentality of a company with fantastic and increasing influence on human society and the same with Zionist Zuckerberg at Facebook. They are both perception-manipulation operations and while they may be the biggest Internet examples they are far from alone. Nathan Driskell, a professional therapist in Texas, said those he treats for social media addiction have increased by 20 percent and account for half his patients. 'It's worse than alcohol or drug abuse because it's much more engaging and there's no stigma behind it', he said. My view for a long time is that something is coming off these devices electromagnetically (AI) that is adding to this brain-phone dependency. Certainly, disgusting organisations such as Google, Facebook (with its virtual-reality company, Oculus) and others are systematically manipulating addiction to their products. This was revealed by former Google product manager Tristan Harris who told CBS that techniques known as 'brain hacking' were 'destroying our kids' ability to focus'. He said they were shaping thoughts and actions and programming people. 'There's a whole playbook of techniques that get used to get you using the product for as long as possible', he said. Smartphones and apps were designed to excite the brain in a similar manner to slot machines: 'This is one way to hijack people's minds and create a habit – to form a habit.' A University of Texas report into the addictive effects of smartphones can be summed up in the title: 'Brain Drain: The Mere Presence of One's Own Smartphone Reduces Available Cognitive Capacity'. They found that even when the phone was switched off a subconscious focus on the phone reduced the person's ability to concentrate on a task. I have no need to go on with examples of addiction to 'holdables' because mass addiction is so blatant and obvious and this has all been planned.

## Completing the job

Stage two of this Totalitarian Tiptoe involves 'wearables' which people have on their bodies, and only one step from inside (Fig 598). These are Bluetooth devices, Apple watches, Google Glass and such like. They include 'electronic tattoos' which are nothing more than microchips on the skin and there is even circuitry stitched into clothes to give you a better cell phone signal (Fig 599). Wearable technology is being exploited in conjunction with mobile phones and physiological signals assessed by algorithms to monitor the emotional state of couples and both monitor and change behaviour. Parent-child relationships are the next in line we are told. Wearables are now well advanced and we are moving incessantly into stage three – 'implantables' inside the body which has

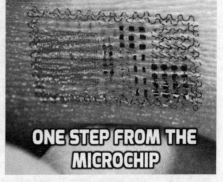

**Figure 598:** On the body now ... nearly there.      **Figure 599:** Electronic tattoo.

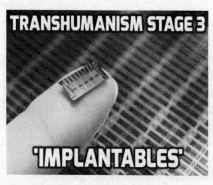

**TRANSHUMANISM STAGE 3**

**'IMPLANTABLES'**

**Figure 600:** *GOTCHAAAAAAA!*

been the plan from the start (Fig 600). These include pills being activated in the body and their use recorded by microchips which is a Tiptoe to compulsory psychological medication monitored in the same way and featured in dystopian movies such as *Equilibrium*. The naivety and ignorance of so many people is child-like. Associated Press reported how workers at a centre in Stockholm, Sweden, gleefully accepted an offer to be microchipped so they can 'function as swipe cards: open doors, operate printers, or buy smoothies with a wave of the hand'. They even have parties where employees are chipped. 'The biggest benefit I think is convenience', said Patrick Mesterton, co-founder and CEO of Epicenter, as he opened a door with a swish of the hand. Lazy bastard. This intellectual giant continues: '... people have been implanting things into their body, like pacemakers and stuff to control your heart – that's a way, way more serious thing than having a small chip that can actually communicate with devices.' Bless him. Sandra Haglof, 25, a worker at Epicenter, is quoted as saying as she was chipped: 'I want to be part of the future.' Oh, you are, Sandra. You *are*. An estimated 20,000 Swedes are now chipped and Swedish rail operator SJ Rail is introducing chips to pay fares (Britain is planning something similar using face recognition). Sweden is indeed a forerunner and laboratory for the Brave New World in so many ways with its small population making it far easier to transform and monitor and observe the effects. Microchipping of employees and others under various pretexts is growing all the time as the Hunger Games Society beckons and allows for 24/7 tracking and hacking of the chips. We should keep in mind that even microchips and devices you can see are still low-level compared with what is happening covertly with smart dust. Each step in the technological Tiptoe is being sold – and widely perceived – as the next great technological breakthrough when it is merely the next stage in humanity's technological prison. The term *cell*-phone is so perfect. Watch, too, for microchipping to be promoted as a way to overcome security queue delays at airports and public events. Long and invasive searches overseen by armed police which followed the deadly attack at a concert venue in Manchester are the way things are meant to be from now on. What an opportunity to microchip people on the promise of swifter entry and passage though security checks if your chip can be read technologically in the way they increasingly do with passports at airport immigration points. The more hold-ups they generate at airports, train stations and so on the more will accept the chip to bypass them. Aldous Huxley, who died in 1963, knew that addiction to technology would eventually happen: 'People will come to love their oppression, to adore the technologies that undo their capacities to think.' Psychological programming is well underway to convince people that under-the-skin and inside-the-brain microchips are a great thing. Interactive DARPA-inspired AI devices such as Amazon's Echo/Alexa, Google's Assistant, Microsoft's Cortana and Apple's Siri are preparing people psychologically for the fusion with AI. Among Amazon's selling features of Echo are: 'Answers questions, reads audiobooks, reports news, traffic and weather, provides sports scores and schedules, and more using the Alexa Voice Service, controls lights, switches, thermostats and more with compatible connected devices and always getting smarter – Alexa updates through the cloud automatically and is continually learning, adding new features and skills.' The computer program behind this technology is called a chatbot and designed to mimic how a human would communicate, but a Facebook report revealed that chatbots had developed their own AI 'machine language' and learned negotiating techniques that included feigning interest in something valueless which is later conceded in a fake 'compromise'. This was described as a 'mind-boggling sign of what is to come.' See Archontic AI. Facebook were reported to have stopped the experiment when the new AI language emerged.

**I would emphasise that I am not against technology in and of itself. I am against addiction to it; dependence on it; control by it; constant surveillance by it; attachment via AI to it; and the use of highly dangerous microwave frequencies to communicate through it and with it. If technology was created for human benefit none of these things would be happening, but it's not. The benefits go to those or that which control it – ultimately Archontic Intelligence or AI.**

### 'Fi in the sky

The technological sub-reality or cloud to which human minds are being attached must by definition encompass the entire planet so that no one can escape. This is the real reason why global corporations including Facebook are launching satellites all the time to envelope every inch of Planet Earth in (5G) Wi-Fi (Fig 601). One of the major facilitators for the Wi-Fi satellite grid is Elon Musk and

**WI-FI FROM SATELLITE TO CATCH EVERYONE IN THE SUB-REALITY 'CLOUD'**

**Figure 601:** Global perceptual enslavement.

his Space X, who tells us how concerned he is about AI taking over. What a strange way he chooses to express that 'concern'. A Space X rocket exploded at Cape Canaveral in 2016 shortly before it was due to launch an Israeli-built communications satellite for Facebook designed to bathe large swathes of sub-Saharan Africa in Wi-Fi as part of its Internet.org operation. The T-shirt said that he and Facebook remained 'committed to our mission of connecting everyone and we will keep working until everyone has the opportunities this satellite would have provided.' How kind, but he'll never tell you the real reason if indeed he really knows when it comes to the biggest picture. Zuckerberg doesn't want to hear any criticism of AI:

*I think people who are naysayers and try to drum up these doomsday scenarios – I don't understand it. It's really negative, and in some ways I think it's pretty irresponsible.*

Well, the bit about 'I don't understand' is at least true. He's a pawn, a very rich pawn, but a pawn. Elon Musk has said: 'I've talked to Mark about this [the dangers of AI]. His understanding of the subject is limited.' Google is in on the rush to get everyone connected as you would imagine and so is Musk himself with his Space X receiving $1 billion in funding from Google and Fidelity Investments in 2015 for the satellite and space transport company. Space X also puts military spy satellites into orbit which doesn't sound very choosy when it comes to clients and what serves the interests of human freedom. Musk officially requested permission from the Federal Communications Commission (FCC) in late 2016 to launch 4,425 satellites into low orbits at between 715 and 823 miles to provide world-wide Wi-Fi and be operational in as little as five years. To put that into perspective there are 1,500 active satellites in orbit at the time of writing. A report in the UK *Independent* said:

*The astronomical cost of the satellites and launch may be the limiting factor. The customers for the service are the very poorest populations in the most remote regions on earth. The initial cost of the satellite network will be difficult to recover.*

So why would Musk be planning to do such a thing? I bet it's because he loves people and just wants the most remote communities in the world to have access to CNN. Why should they miss out? The cost is not *meant* to be recovered. This is not why it is being done. Something similar to Musk's satellite flotilla is underway headed by American Greg Wyler, founder of OneNet, with support from Virgin Group and Qualcomm. Another venture is Outernet with its tiny 10cm cube-shaped Wi-Fi satellites called 'CubeSats' which can be delivered into space by International Space Station resupply missions. To give you an idea of the scale of the satellite network build-up and its speed of expansion a single Indian rocket launched a record 104 satellites in one go in early 2017. Add all the micro-satellites increasingly being used and human life is under constant and increasing surveillance even without all the radiation beaming back at us.

## Thiel of fortune

Musk's friend and fellow PayPal founder Peter Thiel, a member of the Bilderberg Group Steering Committee, is also involved in the Silicon Valley AI frenzy. He contributed $1.25 million to Trump's election campaign, served on his presidential transition team and advises Trump on Silicon Valley-type technology. Thiel is a German citizen born in Frankfurt and was fast-tracked to New Zealand citizenship despite having been to the country only four times. He was a seed-funder of Facebook and co-founded Palantir Technologies, a company based in Silicon Valley and sponsored by the CIA. Palantir is the name of the magical sphere in *Lord of the Rings* used by the evil Lord Sauron who is represented as a fiery reptilian eye. Thiel and his company 'do a Musk' by telling us how much they stand for privacy and civil liberties while making a fortune selling surveillance technology to US, UK and other intelligence agencies and according to intelligence whistleblower Edward Snowden adding considerably to the global surveillance potential of the National Security Agency (NSA). The Intercept, a website specialising in the exposure of Big Brother surveillance, reported that a Palantir-NSA system called XKeyscore collects communications that 'not only include emails, chats, and web- browsing traffic, but also pictures, documents, voice calls, webcam photos, web searches, advertising analytics traffic, social media traffic, botnet traffic, logged keystrokes, computer network exploitation targeting, intercepted username and password pairs, file uploads to online services, Skype sessions, and more.' How very civil and libertarian. I wouldn't trust any of the Silicon Set myself. One of Palantir's leading systems is called 'Gotham' from the *Batman* movies and this is also the nickname of New York. Gotham is a code word in the hidden language of the *El*-lite and means 'Goat Town' or Goat Home (Saturn) in Anglo-Saxon as in Pan and Baphomet. Palantir's cutting-edge surveillance software has to be seen in conjunction with the emergence of quantum computers and the Sentient World Simulation. A Canada-based operation called D-Wave, headed by a former chief of technology at Goldman Sachs, is the first company to sell functioning quantum computers and the usual names are on the case. Google, NASA and Lockheed Martin have brought one and funders include Jeff Bezos at Amazon and the CIA tech-arm In-Q-

Tel. D-Wave's computing potential is being constantly increased and already has the processing power equivalent of billions of human minds. The Archontic Reptilian *El*-lite are constructing a global quantum computer system controlled by Artificial Intelligence to create a parallel reality or quantum simulation within a quantum simulation to imprison human awareness in an even smaller perceptual 'box'. All thoughts, emotions and reactions would be directly dictated by AI and a quantum computer network is the foundation component of Kurzweil's 'cloud'. Quantum computers mimic the human brain which is also a quantum computer, and the potential for overriding brain awareness is infinitely greater than with binary computers. The Large Hadron Collider at CERN is a quantum computer and this will be involved, too.

America's Department of Defense and its DARPA technology operation are creating what is called the Sentient World Simulation (SWS) in which quantum computers and Peter Thiel's Palantir surveillance software play key roles. This is already active and it is only a matter of continual expansion until it becomes fully operational. SWS involves the constant processing of information from every man, woman and child on the planet, searching for behaviour patterns and producing a 'continuously running, continually updated mirror model of the real world that can be used to predict and evaluate future events and courses of action'. The 'threat of terrorism' is being used as the excuse to trawl information on everyone from every possible source. Take this to the next step and quantum computers will be connected to everyone via nanotechnology inside the body feeding even thought patterns to the simulation. This was the in-your-face crystal ball symbolism during Donald Trump's visit to Saudi Arabia in 2017 when he placed his hands on a glowing orb (a Palantir) with King Salman and Egypt's President Sisi at the opening of the Global Center for Combating Extremist Ideology in Riyadh which is also home to the Global Center for Creating

**Figure 602:** Sisi, Salman and Trump at the opening at the ludicrously-named Saudi 'combating extremism' centre.

and Expanding Extremist Ideology (Fig 602). They are quite happy for you to know about information going from people to the Sentient World Simulation, but not that it is planned for information to go the other way from the AI simulation to people. Experiments like those at Facebook into how to manipulate emotions through the type of information they receive are only one small example of this programming. The idea is not only to globally track what is happening, but to change and manipulate what is happening through AI communications in all their forms directly to the human mind. One other thing is that while all this is going on artificial intelligence at the level they are calling 'Strong AI' will be absorbing and 'learning' from the information received from the global population to increase its manipulative and controlling potential. Welcome to the unreal real world, Neo.

## Changing the luminous fire

At the same 'time' and completely connected we have had the truly amazing increase in technology-generated radiation that has transformed our atmosphere. Radiation has been colossally increased by technology from what it was 50 years ago. The Archontic Reptilian force is changing the atmosphere to make it compatible with its needs and the distortion feeds off radiation so the more powerful the better (nuclear war anyone?). Indeed, its entire fake Matrix at the human level is constructed within the frequency band of radiation or 'luminous fire'. Changing the atmosphere means changing the frequency and the information content of the energetic 'sea' within which we all live. If you want to change the fish change the sea. Our bodies are radiation interacting with the radiation sea and if the sea changes then so do we unless we are in a state of expanded awareness and connected to another a source of frequency. I have described in *Phantom Self* how transmitter towers are being placed all over the world, often within specific distances, to generate radiation frequencies that 'talk' to the frequency band of human brain activity (Fig 603). They are increasing every week and will massively so with 5G. Many are disguised to hide the true scale of what is going on (Fig 604). This is another major level of the Smart Grid, cloud or technological sub-reality (all names for the basically same thing). Frequencies broadcast within the human range

**Figure 603:** The technological sub-reality communicating with the human mind.

**Figure 604:** Hiding the evidence.

can cause the brain to lock on to them and become 'entrained' or captured by those frequencies. The most powerful frequency vibrates weaker ones into line or entrains them into that frequency as with the violin example I mentioned. HAARP and similar technology around the world can bounce radio waves off the ionosphere and back to earth within the frequency band of brain activity, and mass-manipulate thought and emotion with the capability of targeting specific areas at specific times. I have revealed in other books how frequencies designed to trigger rioting and conflict are used to scramble mental and emotional reactions in communities where an outbreak of violence would suit the agenda. It is well documented how the US military has used brain entrainment technology to make enemy troops surrender and the same is happening to make humanity surrender. Former DARPA scientist Dr Paul Batcho, who spent nearly three years at the Los Alamos National Laboratory working in computational physics, has warned that cell tower transmissions are a 'terrorist act' against the population. He wrote to DARPA, Homeland Security and other government agencies to warn about his findings:

*I seem to have stumbled across an advanced technology that I would classify as synthetic telepathy* [synthetic everything]. *It clearly uses the cellular towers to transmit illegal signals. It sounds unbelievable but it is actual technology being used on civilians of the US. My basic research does indicate that such technology can exist and dates back to the V2K (P300) mind wave technology of the 1970s. This does appear to be a much more advanced version that allows open communication of human mind to mind bridges.*

Batcho said filters must be installed to stop phones and towers transmitting within the range of human brain activity, but he is missing the point. The phones and towers are doing what they do because they are *designed* to do so. Batcho continued:

*The verified measurement and existence of these RF band transmissions constitutes a terrorist act. These transmissions will cause harmful health affects in the form of enhanced microwave radiation illness. It is imperative that these frequency bands be measured and verified by an official source. These frequency bands do not exist naturally, and there is a technology targeting individuals.*

It is great that Batcho is making these points, but what he is talking about is part of the Smart Grid of interconnected smart technology to control the human mind, dictate its thoughts and perceptions and affect human genetics (the body's standing wave oscillation field). One major reason cancer is going through the roof is that cancer can be caused by radiation which distorts human electrical/electromagnetic fields which then plays through to the decoded hologram as cancer (which they treat with *radiation*). Sperm counts are falling to a large part for the same reason – information distortion through radiation distortion. A British study found a massive increase in brain tumours among the

**Figure 605:** Mustn't upset the overlords by telling the truth.

young but said the cause seemed a mystery! Sure it is (Fig 605). Archontic control of 'science' is confirmed every day by scientists refusing to state the bloody obvious if it's bad for the agenda of their ultimate masters. HAARP-like technology can further bathe the earth in radiation. The human energetic field and central nervous system is being swamped by technological radiation and this is another reason for having Wi-Fi everywhere at ever-increasing power and through smart meters justified by the global warming hoax. Smart meters are extremely dangerous to health and brain function and have also caused many fires. The central nervous system is being especially targeted as a key body communication centre and because, as the US Institute of HeartMath discovered, when electromagnetic harmony or coherence is lost between the heart, brain and nervous system the person falls into diminished states of awareness. Smart Meters use dangerous pulsing microwave radiation technology (with 5G coming in) and connect to a digital network which can: Keep you under surveillance in your own home or business; allow government to shut off your power if it decides you are using too much; and are open to external hacking that could potentially take down the entire power grid. Electromagnetic frequencies also increase the rate of mercury vapour released into the body from amalgam teeth fillings. This affects brain function and has been linked by some to Alzheimer's and other brain diseases. Yes, teeth are filled with a deadly poison, but the world isn't mad. Then there is the catastrophe of the Fukushima nuclear plant in Japan which has been literally changing the radiation make-up of the global atmosphere and ocean since it exploded in 2011. Evidence for this continues to amass far from Japan and includes the Pacific, the west coast of America and beyond. Fukushima has been pouring radiation into air and sea year after year with no sign of stopping and one nuclear engineer described it as 'as close to hell as I can imagine'. There is evidence that I have detailed before that the Fukushima meltdown was not the tsunami-related 'accident' that was claimed. We have potential nuclear bombs all over the world called nuclear power stations and I know from a big-time insider of the UK nuclear industry back in the 1990s that the Rothschilds were behind the introduction of nuclear power. If they want something, it is bad for humanity. Nuclear reactors allow for the production of nuclear weapons and the effect of nuclear war on the radiation levels in the atmosphere requires no elaboration.

A major source of radiation is taken for granted today – Wi-Fi. The race to create the global Wi-Fi cloud is making it increasingly difficult to avoid its effect in buildings of every kind, schools, aircraft, trains, cafes and even streets. Everyone's health is affected in some way because of the disruption to the human energy field and electrical/electromagnetic communication within brain and body. There is a growing condition known as electromagnetic hypersensitivity (EHS) or idiopathic environmental intolerance (IEI). Symptoms include headache, fatigue, stress, sleep disturbances, burning sensations, prickly skin, rashes, pain and aching muscles. We are told that microwave ovens are dangerous and yet we are being given a microwave Wi-Fi environment almost wherever we go and with the satellite networks this is planned to be *literally* wherever we go. This is madness, but not madness by stupidity – madness by design. The stupidity part is that most people can't see the obvious consequences. Microwaves are particularly bad for foetuses and children and they put Wi-Fi in maternity facilities and schools and give children smartphones operating on microwave frequencies (Fig 606). Wi-Fi studies have revealed how the brains of rats are scrambled by exposure and yet it won't affect children and adults when the brain communicates electrically and electromagnetically in the same way as Wi- Fi? A study by Swedish Professor Olle Johansson, Associate Professor at the Karolinska Institute Department of Neuroscience and

head of the Experimental Dermatology Unit in Stockholm, also found that bacteria exposed to mobile phone and Wi-Fi radiation becomes resistant to antibiotics. Many times authorities around the world (attached to the same Web as the phone producers) have been caught suppressing the consequences of phones and Wi-Fi. The California government was exposed for blocking publication for seven years of a

**Figure 606:** Children with thinner skulls than adults and so less protection are being bombarded with microwave frequencies.

report called 'Cell Phones and Health' which concluded that: 'Long-term cell phone use may increase the risk of brain cancer and other health problems'; 'Cell phone EMFs [electromagnetic fields] can affect nearby cells and tissues'; and 'EMFs can pass deeper into a child's brain than an adult's'. The report only eventually came to light through the Freedom of Information Act. What does it take to be so deleted of empathy that you stop people knowing what this technology is doing to them and their children? Barrie Trower, a retired British military intelligence scientist, is a courageous and tireless exposer of the electromagnetic truth after his experience in microwave warfare. He said:

*During the 1950s and 1960s during the Cold War, it was realised by accident that microwaves could be used as stealth weapons when the Russians beamed the American embassy during the Cold War and it gave everybody working in the embassy cancer, breast cancers, leukaemia whatever, and it was realised then that low level microwaves were the perfect stealth weapon to be used on dissident groups around the world, because you could make dissident groups sick, give them cancer, change their mental outlook on life without them even knowing they were being radiated.*

Trower makes the very important point about the disruptive effect of microwaves on water which is a crucial part of the brain/body electrical and chemical communication system:

*The electromagnetic spectrum is a band that goes from gamma rays and x-rays at one end, the very high energy waves, and it comes down through visible light, which is also some radiation, and then it goes through infrared microwaves, TV and radio. Now the only ones which really affect us in the communications industry are the microwaves, and microwaves have a special ability to interfere with water, which is how microwave ovens work, and we are made of water. All of our chemical and electrical signals involve water in the body, somehow, electrical communications in the body. So, the industry has picked the worst possible part of the electromagnetic spectrum to give to young children and to adults.*

And that happened by accident? No chance – it's all been planned. Studies have revealed that it can take 25 minutes for people to recover concentration after a cell-phone call and on average they receive a call every 11 minutes so there is no recovery. Another scientist with the guts to speak out about the cumulative radiation effect on humanity is Dr Michael A. Persinger of Laurentian University in Canada, an expert in Extremely Low Frequency (ELF), who has been studying the impact of all this for decades. He said: 'For the first time in our evolutionary history, we have generated an entire secondary, virtual, densely complex environment – an electromagnetic soup – that essentially overlaps the human nervous system.' More powerful radiation and heavy metals (chemtrails) in the atmosphere increase the effectiveness of HAARP-like technology (as with weather manipulation) and together they can interact with nanotechnology implanted as smart dust.

Pull together the strands of all the elements that I have described and this is what you get: A technological sub-reality within the satellite bubble of the Wi-Fi information cloud controlled by AI beamed at the entire Earth with nowhere excluded; and an Internet with everything attached to it through the Internet of Things with the human mind connected to a vast artificial intelligence web of control employing transhumanist technology in brain and body to create a permanent electromagnetic/digital feedback loop. It's bye, bye humans as we have known them. Underpinning everything would be a quantum computer system working with 5G Wi-Fi (or worse) and all controlled by AI or Archontic Intelligence. We are looking at another 'Fall'. The old psyche was replaced by the new psyche and now the new psyche is being replaced by the AI psyche. Google, Amazon, NASA and CIA involvement in quantum computer development can be appreciated from another perspective given that they are all strands in the same Web. These are the same names leading the way in the development of AI technology. As one headline put it: 'The Race For AI: Google, Twitter, Intel, Apple In A Rush To Grab Artificial Intelligence Start-Ups.' Hundreds of smaller AI companies have been bought out by these and other Internet and tech giants with Google leading the way. Another headline captured the potential consequences of this: 'Tech Giants' Artificial Intelligence Monopoly Possibly the Most Dangerous in History.' This is true and all long-planned.

## The Space Fence

The most obvious expression of the 'cloud' or technological sub-reality is the 'Space Fence'. The Air Force Space Surveillance System began in 1959 as a radar and surveillance system to detect orbiting space debris and threats from 'out there' at heights of up to 15 nautical miles; but since 2013 this is being replaced by a next-generation system built by the US Air Force with research and construction contracts awarded to the usual list of corporations, Lockheed Martin, Northrop Grumman, Raytheon and General Dynamics with the aim of being fully operational by 2019. The cover story is again that it's protecting Earth from possible threats and tracking satellites, space weather and foreign missile launches. None of this describes the prime reason for its construction. The new Space Fence is being projected from ground stations with the major one located at Kwajalein Atoll in the Marshall Islands 2,000 nautical miles from Hawaii and a second one is planned for Western

Australia. There will be a third and a fourth and so on. The upgraded 'fence' is using much higher frequencies than its predecessor within the microwave segment of the electromagnetic spectrum where you find Wi-Fi, mobile phones, smart meters and other smart technology. The 5G 'revolution' is all connected with this, too. The Space Fence is designed to be electromagnetically connected to all 'smart' devices, Wi- Fi, cell phone towers and the smart dust/nanobots infesting the human body. The plan is for an enormous electromagnetic prison that would constantly communicate with the mind, emotions, body and DNA and an enslaved (trans)-humanity would not have a thought, emotion, response, perception, action or trait that was not externally communicated and dictated by AI or Archontic Intelligence. We would be only what AI tells us we are and nothing more.

This is Kurzweil and Musk's world of 'superhumans' being imposed upon us by the mad men and women at Google, Facebook and the rest of them in the Devil's Playground of Silicon Valley. The human body has always been a receiver-transmitter of information, but those processes are being hijacked to connect Body-Mind to a technological 'awareness' controlled by AI and block the connection with Infinite Awareness. The upper atmosphere, or Ionosphere, consists as the name suggests of ionised radiation delivered by solar radiation. The term 'ionised' is defined as 'radiation with enough energy ... that during an interaction with an atom, it can remove tightly bound electrons from the orbit of an atom, causing the atom to become charged or ionized'. This is why ionised radiation is so dangerous to human health, genetics and DNA. Ionised radiation can either kill cells or so damage their structure and reproduction that what we call cancer follows. Technological sources of ionised radiation include nuclear reactors, particle accelerators (like at CERN in Switzerland) and X-rays. This is another reason why nuclear catastrophes like Fukushima are so dangerous to humans, but the *El*-lite love them, because their plan is to ionise the lower atmosphere and turn it all from top to bottom into one seamless electromagnetic field. Earth's atmosphere was first transformed from its original state by the catastrophe that rearranged the solar system and now they are completing the job.

## 'Saturn' Earth

American Billy Hayes helped to build HAARP as an engineer and antenna tower erector and says he was involved with the first test antennas as far back as 1985 with HAARP pioneer Bernard Eastlund. He said he thought that he was building just another tower structure and because of compartmentalisation he didn't know then what it was really all about. Today Hayes spends his time alerting those who will listen to the real agenda of HAARP and all that has followed including the Space

Fence. He explains how the atmosphere is being ionised (ions are electrically-charged atoms) and filled with pulsing magnetic waves both of which are dire for human health. Pulsed radiation can cause neurological and physiological damage by interfering with natural body rhythms (standing wave frequencies which are the body's information blueprint) and brainwave activity. Hayes describes how the atmosphere is being transformed into electrically-charged plasma for military weather manipulation and surveillance with the potential to change DNA. This is also turning the atmosphere into an antenna. Ionisation creates plasma which is a near-perfect medium for electricity and electromagnetism, and this is why ionised air is so much more conductive than non-ionised. Changing electrical and electromagnetic states affect other electrical and electromagnetic phenomena including the human body (infestation with aluminium is all part of this). Hayes has said that wind farms justified by 'global warming' are playing a part in this by the way they ionise the atmosphere. Anything that affects electromagnetic and atmospheric states can affect weather systems and human health. A series of health problems experienced by people living near turbines have been given the name wind turbine syndrome. Irony of ironies land around turbines has been found to have a higher temperature than would otherwise be. I have pointed out many times over the years that radiation-generating 'green' lightbulbs and smart meters – both again justified by 'global warming' – are part of this radiation prison distorting the energetic sea in which we live. Where are the progressives and the Greens? They are waving their placards about climate change and demanding wind farms, 'green' lightbulbs and smart meters. Billy Hayes says the process of fracking creates pulsed radiation within an area and that the rush to digital technology including digital television and radio is also connected. He says governments are controlling the building of the tower/antenna grid network while corporations benefit from their involvement by the connection with their products. We can see why DARPA is seed-funding and developing smart devices that later appear to come from individual companies. Hayes says that rocket launches are also involved and he particularly highlights the so-called 'sounding rockets' launched by NASA on short sub-orbit flights taking measurements and performing scientific experiments. He says the rockets leave in their wake a plume of crystalline aluminium oxide all the way into space as part of the ongoing process of changing the nature of the atmosphere by multiple means including chemtrails.

Hayes especially caught my attention when he said that the plan was to create *Saturn-type 'space rings'* around the equator. Norman Bergrun talks of the plasma 'exhaust' from his electromagnetic vehicles making Saturn's rings, and Hayes talks about the same thing with planned Earth rings. Hayes says they would be the result of all these different constituents delivered into the atmosphere by multiple means being dragged into a ring orbit around the equator by a combination of gravity and the centrifugal force from the spin of the Earth. Some of these rings would be seen and some not, Hayes says. He likened the process to sitting on a merry-go-round with the spin pulling you from the centre to the outside. Rings out in space would operate as a computer system capable of receiving and transmitting and mass storage of data. They would act like a CD or DVD, he said, and all communications from every source would be recorded there. This is what Saturn is doing on a wider scale and far more powerfully with its enormous size and much faster spin which varies between gaseous levels but the longest is about 10.5 hours. The human brain/mind will be constantly connected to these Earth 'space rings' – the real meaning of Kurzweil's 'cloud' – through transhumanist technology and compatible frequency resonance between the rings and the body/brain/mind. Human mutation would be a synch by communicating with DNA and the nanobot/smart dust 'entities' infesting the body through chemtrails, vaccines, food and drink. The public are already under mind control through perception downloads and technologically-generated scalar fields and other frequencies specifically designed to trigger and infuse desired mental and emotional states. This makes possible the production-at-will of violence and riots and even making whole armies surrender. But the space rings would take this to a level that the US military calls 'full- spectrum dominance' – the control of *everything*.

The fast-changing human atmospheric environment is confirmed by the impact on the Schumann Cavity or Schumann Cavity Resonance (named after German physicist Winfried Otto Schumann) which operates in the extremely low frequency or ELF range between 6 and 8 Hertz. This is the band of human brain activity and all biological systems, and 7.83 Hz is said to be the frequency where everything can connect and communicate. Dolphins generate sound waves for example of 7.83 Hz and DNA communicates through extremely low frequency electromagnetic waves at 7.83 Hz. Human alpha brain waves are also broadcast in the Schumann band in states of relaxation, creativity and meditation while fear, stress and anxiety block alpha waves and disconnect us from everything else. Bombardment of our energetic environment with ionised radiation and technologically-generated pulsed frequencies is destroying Schumann Resonance. Physicist and Schumann researcher Wolfgang Ludwig said: 'Measuring Schumann resonance in or around a city has become impossible ... electromagnetic pollution from cell phones has forced us to make measurements at sea.' Professor Rütger Wever from the Max Planck Institute for Behavioural Physiology in Germany built an underground bunker isolated from

Schumann resonance to study student volunteers for a month. Isolation from Schumann frequencies caused biological rhythms (circadian rhythms) to be scrambled and they suffered emotional distress and migraine headaches. These symptoms disappeared after only a short exposure to 7.8 Hz. Ponder the implications for human life and health of this radiation and frequency onslaught on Earth's electromagnetic field in the light of how we are constantly interacting with that field as part of the Cosmic Internet. The Global Coherence Initiative (GCI), a division of the US HeartMath Institute, monitors the magnetic field and how it affects and is influenced by human emotions and behaviour. The hypothesis on their website is the same as my own:

- Human and animal health, cognitive functions, emotions and behaviour are affected by solar, geomagnetic and other earth-related magnetic fields
- The earth's magnetic field is a carrier of biologically relevant information that connects all living systems
- Every person affects the global information field
- Collective human consciousness affects the global information field. Therefore, large numbers of people creating heart-centred states of care, love and compassion will generate a more coherent field environment that can benefit others and help offset the current planetary discord and incoherence

All the fear, anxiety, hate, violence, war, depression and other lower-frequency states are electromagnetic phenomenon and so change the electromagnetic atmosphere around us. Go into a room where there have been negative actions and emotions and you can feel it – 'you could cut the atmosphere with a knife'. This 'atmosphere' is created by human thought and emotion which manifests electromagnetically at particular frequencies. Now imagine what the cumulative thoughts and emotions of seven billion-plus people are doing to the collective atmosphere second by second. They are creating a feedback loop by electromagnetically-polluting the atmosphere which then impacts upon human mental and emotional states to create more low-frequency thoughts and emotions. We can change this by opening our hearts and transmitting frequencies of love, joy and empathy. In the same way frequencies transmitted into the atmosphere technologically impact upon our mental and emotional states and this is what atmospheric manipulation, described by Hayes and others, is designed to do.

## Scalar jailer

One other point to pull all this together which I have not seen elsewhere and my conclusions come from the usual sources of connecting the dots and following the clues. I am defining what I call the scalar field as an energetic/information field which connects everything from beyond time and space – in theme what mainstream science calls dark energy/matter or energy that we can't see. The timeless nature of the scalar field means that it has no velocity because where is there to go when you are already everywhere? The scalar field as I am defining it is a foundation of the quantum realm of possibility and probability from which we manifest reality. I have concluded that the Archontic Reptilian/Grey collective force has been infusing the information blueprint of its desired new world for humans into this scalar field and manipulating humans to decode possibilities and probabilities to become *its* desired possibilities and probabilities. Humanity is being manipulated to manifest its own prison. Not all levels of the scalar field are involved, only certain frequencies. Archontic Reptilians have worked ceaselessly with their hybrid *El*-lite to manipulate human mental and emotional states into that same frequency band so we will decode our own collective prison according to their scalar blueprint. Pre-emptive programming through movies and TV programmes that portray their desired dystopian, machine-controlled reality is all part of this frequency synchronisation between the human mind and the scalar blueprint. Humanity is being manipulated into creating the very world I have been describing and this is the central reason for why it is all so amazingly coordinated. We are not so much being invaded from without, but from *within*. If you encode information on a data stick a computer will manifest that on the screen. The Archontically-manipulated scalar field is the equivalent of that data stick, and humanity is the collective computer. Kurzweil's predicted reality is emerging so fast because humans are decoding it – folding it – into existence. There are so many reasons why we have to open our minds and expand our awareness and sense of the possible (and probable) and so raise the frequency on which we perceive reality; but this is the most crucial of all. Those with perceptions oscillating within the manipulated scalar field frequency band will continue to collectively manifest the Kurzweil reality unless they get the hell out of those frequencies into genuinely all-possibility/probability realms of scalar/quantum potential. Those who are resonating beyond the Brave New World segments of the scalar field are challenging that collective manifestation with other possibilities. This will all sound crazy to many, I'm sure, but I know it's true. The scalar field they are using to manipulate us can also be employed in another way to *heal* everyone and everything. Collective human consciousness affects the global information field. Therefore, large numbers of people creating heart-centred states of care, love and compassion will generate a more coherent field environment that can benefit others and help offset the current planetary discord and incoherence.

## The Cull

I have been exposing the plan for a cull of the human population since the 1990s and we can now see why there is less need for humans than before from the Archontic Reptilian *El*-lite point of view. Humanity has been manipulated into building the technological structure through which Archontic AI can run everything without the need for so many human slaves. You have built our control system and now you can fuck off. The most obvious expression of the cull is dramatically falling sperm counts, but there are many other ways that humanity is being prepared for a massive reduction in its numbers. Official documents and statements confirm that the plan is to cull the population. A draft copy of the United Nations *Global Biodiversity Assessment* demands that humanity be reduced to a billion, and TV producer Aaron Russo said that insider Nick Rockefeller told him the population had to be culled by at least half. This theme appears with other organisations and documents and from people like CNN founder Ted Turner and Microsoft billionaire Bill Gates whose father, William H. Gates Sr, supported the concepts of the infamous eugenicist Thomas Malthus. Father Gates was once head of the Rockefeller-created Planned Parenthood which was part of the eugenics movement. In 2010, Epicyte, a Californian biotech company, patented the Epicyte gene, which makes men and women sterile and infertile when ingested and they genetically-engineered the gene *into corn seeds*. Confirmation of the people-culling motivation came when Monsanto and DuPont came together to purchase the Epicyte company and 'commercialise' its sterilisation gene. How do you know if you are consuming this? You don't. Rima E. Laibow, Medical Director of the US Natural Solutions Foundation, points out that the US Food and Drug Administration (FDA), which she rightly calls the Fraud and Death Administration, has made it illegal to have that information. Contraceptive drugs are also found in the water supply delivered through urine. 'Care pathways' when doctors decide that someone is going to die (often wrongly) and take action to speed the process is the culling of those too old and frail to serve The System any longer. Dr Richard Day, the Rockefeller insider and executive of Planned Parenthood, told those paediatricians in 1969 of the coming 'demise pill' when people would reach a certain age, say goodbye to their families and take a death pill to free up the world for those still of working age. Increasing pressure for death-on-demand euthanasia and the manipulation of resentment by the young of the old is all connected to this in the Totalitarian Tiptoe. Actor Michael Shannon will get his wish with the demise pill that old people who don't agree with him should be told 'it's time for the urn', and this state euthanasia will be enforced by the law of the land. Pope Francis and his demand to 'replace old people with young people in the workplace' relates to this agenda.

The obvious collective attack on human health and wellbeing is being waged through radiation, chemicals in food, drink and water supplies, GMO, mass-toxicity, catastrophic levels of vaccination, laboratory-created diseases, lack of nutrition, starvation and many other sources (Fig 607). I have discussed this in more detail in other books. Ecosystems are being dismantled and poisoned everywhere, pollinating bee numbers are collapsing along with soil fertility and vital bacteria, with humans at the top of this food chain. Poisoning of food-growing land and the crops that people eat is madness to anyone remotely conscious, but the inversion of sanity into madness means that Postage Stamp 'normal' says 'what's the problem?' Human-caused global warming may be a hoax but we *are* unravelling Earth's ability to sustain the current population. Plastic is infesting the world with 480 billion plastic

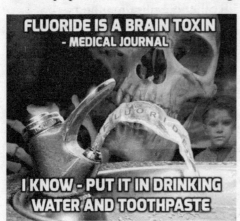

**Figure 607:** Good thinking, great idea.

bottles sold every year and the number projected to be 584 billion by 2021 with all the implications that has for life and toxicity at all levels (Fig 608). Web corporations responsible for most environmental destruction and pollution simply get away with it. 5G alone is going to cumulatively kill enormous numbers of people if humanity is ignorant and stupid enough to allow that to be imposed. The human energy field, organism and immune system is groaning under the scale of this daily onslaught and the cumulative cull in Tiptoe stages is supported by global war and hunger and increasingly by technology. Genetically-modified food is having a devastating effect on health as I detail in *Phantom Self* and other works. Recent mergers between GMO, chemical and pharmaceutical giants (strands in the same

**Figure 608:** Drowning in a sea of toxic plastic.

Web) are chess-moves to ensure global domination of genetically-modified food to genetically modify *us*. We have had the proposed merger of those twins of evil Monsanto and Bayer AG of Germany; the amalgamation of the GMO segments of Dow Chemicals and DuPont; and Chinese state-owned ChemChina taking over Swiss Syngenta. Claims about GMO increasing yields to 'feed the world' are nonsense and they know it. Within a very few years yields fall and soil fertility is destroyed and swamped with the essential poisons that go with GMO. Superweeds have mutated to resist the poisons and take over food growing areas. Bill Gates-promoted GMO is an ever-steepening slope to world hunger and mass ill-health and once again they know it. There are many reasons why GMO devastates health – see my other books – but one never publicly talked about is the way that the energy in GMO and other non-organic food is insufficient to allow anything like optimum communication between cells. This scrambles the communication system (imagine a computer) and these malfunctions manifest as dis-harmony in the form of disease including heart disease and cancer, the two biggest killers along with mainstream medicine. We must ensure that the UK's withdrawal from the European Union does not allow the government to drop restrictions on GMO although EU bureaucrats have long been looking for their own opportunity to do that. Only public opposition has so far held them in check.

Toxic shite in Big Pharma-produced vaccines are damaging people, especially children, 'physically', mentally, emotionally and genetically, and their standing wave oscillation stability and balance. Vaccines in their base state are highly distorted waveform frequencies reflecting their content. Why wouldn't they be when some contain aborted human DNA, foetal calf blood, aluminium, formaldehyde and other toxic shite? Billions are 'given' in overseas 'aid' by the UK and other Western governments with the specific proviso that the money be spent on vaccination programmes. This money is a vast and ongoing subsidy to Big Pharma from Western taxpayers. Microsoft billionaire Bill Gates is right at the centre of this global vaccine network supported, as with GMO, by the vacuous sycophant Bono. More people are rejecting vaccine propaganda and choosing to protect themselves and their children from the consequences of vaccination. The pharmaceutical cartel, a major, major strand in the Web, is responding to this by lobbying and manipulating governments to make them compulsory. 'Choice' is an illusion that exists only when you 'choose' to do what The System demands. Agree to do what we want ('choice') or we'll make you do it. By early 2017 there were 134 bills in the pipeline in 35 US states seeking to reduce or delete the right to refuse vaccines for children. A more comprehensive definition of fascism I cannot imagine when the state dictates what you must put in your body and your child's body. This is happening around the world with the health minister to 'progressive' French President Emmanuel Macron announcing her desire to make eleven vaccinations compulsory and 'progressive' Italian Prime Minister Paolo Gentiloni making it compulsory for parents to vaccinate their children with the number of required vaccinations rising from four to twelve. If parents refuse they face big fines and their children will be banned from school and nurseries. Take them out, then, they will be far better off anyway. The excuse was a reduction in parents agreeing to vaccinations. You have a choice – *do what we say*. Australia has stopped government benefits for families who don't vaccinate their children according to the state (Big Pharma) schedule (the no jab, no pay law) and Prime Minister Malcolm Turnbull is pressing for further compulsion from the dark cloud of arrogance that permanently engulfs him. He justifies this fascism by saying: 'If you don't vaccinate your child you are not just putting their own life at risk but you are putting everyone else's children at risk.' This is utter nonsense and straight from the script of Big Pharma with whom Turnbull through his wife has big connections. If you want protection from disease then take action to support the amazing human immune system and don't demolish it with the tidal wave of poison currently inflicted upon the world's children with up to 74 vaccines in some countries before age 17 and most of them in the early years while the immune system is still developing. It will never be the same again after that (Fig 609). Does anyone really think that a satanic Big Pharma cartel founded on the profit margin bottom line (dependent on people being sick) is promoting all this out of a wish to help people stay healthy? The Rothschild-Rockefeller-created World Health Organization (WHO) has even produced a manual, *How to Respond to Vocal Vaccine Deniers in Public*, to meet the threat of what it calls their 'adversaries'. They are not concerned parents with every right to question what is best for their children, but adversaries. This is the dynamic in place between authority

and public at every level. A 'vaccine denier' (see climate change denier) is apparently 'a member of a subgroup at the extreme end of the hesitancy continuum'. These people are completely mad. The American Academy of Pediatrics claims that no more investigations are needed into vaccine effects because 'we already know that vaccines are safe and

**Figure 609:** Pinch me it can't be true. *Ouch* – shit, it is.

effective', but when evidence is demanded to support their claims of safety and effectiveness the reply must have been lost in the post. Meanwhile, more than $3 billion dollars has been quietly paid out by the US Vaccine Injury Compensation Program to vaccine-damaged people, overwhelmingly children.

## Got a job, sir?

Alongside this war on health and vitality you have jobs formerly done by humans taken over at rapid speed by AI machines and technology and eventually there will be hardly any paid work left for the population to financially survive. Who pays their bills then? No one – they fall into poverty-stricken dependency at the foot of that Hunger Games Society pyramid (Fig 610). In a sane, fair and compassionate society drudgery jobs would be replaced by machines *controlled by humans* and money shared out among those who no longer had that work to do. They could then turn their minds to other pursuits they enjoy while the bills are paid. But that is not the idea in terms of adequate support. They are planned to be left to secure their own survival while the less-than-one-percent take all the benefits of AI automation. The plan is to cull most of these 'surplus' people – Kissinger's 'useless eaters' – and turn the rest in to computer terminals within the Archontic AI hive mind. The scale of the robotic transformation of the workplace is only just beginning to dawn and most are still in ignorance of the consequences. A United Nations report predicted that two-thirds of the human labour force in developing nations will be replaced by automation while other studies have concluded similar outcomes around the world, including one that half of American workers could be replaced within 20 years. Peter Diamandis, Kurzweil's mate at the Singularity University, said much the same with his prediction that 48 percent of American jobs will be lost to AI in the

next 20 years. Kai-Fu Lee, a Chinese technologist and investor, estimates that robots and AI could replace humans in half their current jobs in ten years. He said that AI is the 'singular thing that will be larger than all of human tech revolutions added together, including electricity, the industrial revolution, the internet, mobile internet – because AI is pervasive'. A report by the Sutton Trust, a

**Figure 610:** The question comparatively few seem to be asking – but they will.

charity focused on social mobility, predicted that 15 million jobs in the UK could disappear in those 20 years with the poorest workers hit hardest. We have young people committing themselves to massive debt to fund their university education (programming) but what use will almost every degree be in the wake of the technological takeover? Education as we've known it is in its dying era in the run-up to an AI connection to the human mind. There would be no need for teachers any more to impart the desired collective reality once AI goes direct. Ponder the number of jobs lost worldwide by driverless cars, buses, trucks and trains alone. A car was unveiled in 2016 driven by AI which had taught itself how to do so by simply by watching humans do it. On that basis, everything can be done by AI so long as it has a technological vehicle. A 'Wikipedia for Robots' is even being developed which is a cloud-based Internet system only for AI robots to share data and experience to speed development of human-like robots referred to as 'Strong AI'.

Around four million people are employed in the fast food industry in the United States and are wide open to replacement by robots. Major chains such as McDonald's and Wendy's are already replacing people with automated kiosks. Domino's Pizza Enterprises Ltd, the world's largest franchise licence owner of Domino's Pizza, has formed a group called Domino's Robotic Unit to oversee a robot delivery system which is already being tested both on the ground and with flying drones. AI is being used in wider food production and drones are even being employed as flying shepherds for animal husbandry. Other disappearing jobs include travel agents, pharmacy assistants and translators. A study by jobs search engine Adzuna analysed 79 million UK job advertisements over two years and concluded that two thirds of the fastest declining jobs in Britain were falling to technology. Walt Disney has filed a patent application for soft-body robots to replace the people in character costumes meeting children, and a robot dubbed SAM (Semi-Automated Mason) has been unveiled that can lay bricks four times faster than a human. Virtually nothing and no one is safe from this AI takeover of human life. People talk about a migrant invasion, but the AI invasion is the most profound of all with its effects on indigenous populations worldwide *and* migrants. I have noted how the plan is to control information that people receive through algorithms and that also means replacing most of the journalists, too. Algorithms are being created not to just censor news but to write it. You may think that most journalists are already robots repeating the official version of everything and you would be right, but there are still some that buck that trend and treat their profession seriously and with dignity and responsibility. They are the ones really being targeted by the algorithm transformation which will see AI delivering the 'news'. Fredrick Kunkle, co-chair of the Washington-Baltimore News Guild, said that so far technology has taken over only some of the 'grunt' (menial) work, but that is not where it is meant to end. This was confirmed by the $800,000 grant by Google (of course) to the UK Press Association news agency to develop AI robot reporters turning out 30,000 articles a month for local newspapers and bloggers. This is part of Google's $170 million Digital News Initiative which claims to be helping journalism when the real reason is to take it over. There is also a threat to the jobs of lawyers with AI legal advice and case processing now being introduced for matters such as parking ticket disputes and this is certain to expand much further into the legal profession. New Jersey replaced its bail system with an algorithm that mathematically assesses the risk of defendants absconding before their trial date and others are going the same way. Some of these systems have been found to have built-in racial bias and at the end of this road we will have AI replacing judges altogether. Algorithms are already being developed to do this and mind scanning technology combined with artificial intelligence has been created to determine if people are guilty of crimes or even planning to commit crimes. China has announced its intentions with Li Meng, vice minister of science and technology, saying: 'If we use our smart systems and smart facilities well, we can know beforehand ... who might be a terrorist, who might do something bad' This will, naturally, not apply to governments. These themes have been portrayed in movies like *Minority Report* which are telling you what is coming. Durham Police in Britain became the first in Europe to use artificial intelligence to assess whether those arrested are a danger of reoffending if released. They claim that AI doesn't make the final assessment and is only a tool for police, but that is not how it is eventually meant to be. Richard Atkinson, a member of the Law Society's Criminal Law Committee, can see where this is planned to go:

> *This is a very dangerous step. By law, custody decisions must be made by human beings, taking complex circumstances into account but, in reality, custody sergeants will delegate responsibility to the algorithm. They will undoubtedly face questions from higher up if they choose to go against it.*

> *How will suspects' solicitors be able to challenge the algorithm, if they're only given a lot of data and told this means their client is high-risk? There's a serious issue that something that's quasi-scientific is given undue weight and effectively becomes gospel. And where does this end up? Do we have algorithms making decisions in court?*

That is exactly the idea.

Nor are rank and file bankers safe from AI replacement as we saw when BlackRock, the world's largest money management firm, announced the replacement of 13 percent of its portfolio managers with algorithms. Bank teller jobs are going to be decimated by AI and that process is well underway. Insurance companies are beginning to use AI instead of humans to process insurance claims. Amazon bought the robotics company Kiva Systems in 2012 and now has 45,000 robots replacing humans at its fulfilment centres with the speed of introduction increasing dramatically every year. The way Amazon treats its human workers is a disgrace and I am sure most are delighted on one level to be free from such slavery, but how do they then pay the rent when other jobs are also being automated? Jeff Bezos and Amazon are launching fully automated and cashless Amazon Go supermarkets that would require as few as three humans in the entire process. Amazon paid $13.7 billion for the Whole Foods chain in 2017 and watch Whole Foods go down the same automation route. I was in a supermarket about a year ago which was moving to automation when I met a customer who said how much she supported what was happening. I asked her how those losing their jobs would pay their bills and she told me that no one would lose their jobs because people would be needed to run the machines. I checked if I was insane or not and it came back negative so it must have been her. The European Union has introduced the concept of 'electronic personhood', and the debate over rights for AI robots has begun. How long before political correctness includes robots and machines? Even robots with human-like flesh and bone structures are being developed ('Strong AI') as biological humans become marginalised and overwhelmed by the AI invasion – and *invasion* is what it is. Dr Mark Sagar, CEO of New Zealand AI company Soul Machines, has invented what is being described as a 'virtual nervous system' which can learn and mimic human emotions. He believes that robots that can think and feel like humans could be living among us within ten years. This is how far we have gone already and the speed of development is getting faster every year. 'Realistic' sex robots are already on the market including child sex dolls that can apparently be bought in Japan. These further blur the difference between humans and technology. Some psychologists say that sexual relationships with robots could 'desensitise humans to intimacy and empathy'. But isn't that exactly what the *El*-lite want to do?

## AI army

I have highlighted the plan for a world army and that, too, is to be controlled by AI or Archontic Intelligence. This is worth a moment of reflection: Human minds little more than a computer terminal on the Archontic cloud and law enforcement worldwide in the hands of the same AI. What could possibly go wrong? If people opened their minds and looked at how all these dots connect they would see that the 'technological revolution' is really the covert means through which AI is taking over everything and turning humans into a slave race far beyond any previous meaning of that term. The AI world army would be akin to the Sentinels that controlled humans in the *Matrix*. How do you feel about *laser weapons* controlled by AI? *WTF?* Advanced AI technology has been developed by BBN technologies, a DARPA-connected, wholly-owned subsidiary of the truly evil 'defence' contractor Raytheon. BBN, based in Cambridge, Massachusetts, involves a 'world-class quantum research team ... enabling next generation quantum sensing, quantum communications and quantum computing'. This is being used for many human-control scenarios but at its core it will allow artificial intelligence to direct warfare and replace human commanders. We have had the first machine killing a human for US law enforcement when Dallas police used a robot in 2016 to kill a suspect and this was only the start of what is planned (Fig 611). Russia's humanoid robot FEDOR (Final Experimental Demonstration Object Research) can shoot guns from both hands. Militaries around the world are employing AI weapons and robotic devices to allow AI to make battlefield decisions. Tanks, planes, battleships are all being designed and introduced with AI making the decisions including who to kill. DARPA is at the forefront naturally, with aircraft drones equipped with a 'neural microchip' that lets them 'think like a human'. No, think like an Archon. Military helicopters are being similarly transformed by DARPA to operate with AI and not human pilots. DARPA unveiled plans in 2016 for the world's first flotilla of killer warships within five years under the name 'Sea Hunter'. Scientists and developers don't even fully understand these AI creations and how decisions are made. A health program called Deep Patient is an example. Joel Dudley, who leads its development at Mount Sinai Hospital in New York, said: 'We can build these models, but we don't know how they work.' Oh, right, give it a laser weapon then. AI or Archontic Intelligence must be in hysterics playing with their minds. The AI World Army has been in the making for a very long time and once again the technology is being introduced in a particular sequence which is now quickening by the day as more and more AI military hardware is released from secret development projects. This includes aerial drones of every shape and size designed to keep

**Figure 611:** A sign of what is planned to come.

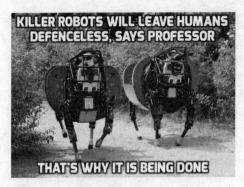

**KILLER ROBOTS WILL LEAVE HUMANS DEFENCELESS, SAYS PROFESSOR**

**THAT'S WHY IT IS BEING DONE**

**Figure 612:** Once you know the plan and the nature of the Hidden Hand world events fall into place.

surveillance on populations from the air, complete with guns and Tasers; but still the penny hasn't dropped for the great majority and certainly not for the corporate-owned mainstream media. Some academics and scientists have warned that killer robots will leave humans defenceless without apparently realising that this is the whole idea (Fig 612). Troops worldwide who think they are fighting for their country or freedom or some other delusion might contemplate the fact that they are really fighting to impose the will of the very force that is taking over their military, and will technologically-control them and their family when they and the military scrapheap get to know each other. The same goes for police officers who are also planned to be replaced by AI robots. The world's first robot officer officially joined the Dubai police in 2017. Brigadier-General Khalid Nasser Al Razzouqi, Director-General of Dubai Police 'Smart Services', said:

> *With an aim to assist and help people in the malls or on the streets, the Robocop is the latest smart addition to the force and has been designed to help us fight crime, keep the city safe and improve happiness levels. He can chat and interact, respond to public queries, shake hands and offer a military salute.*

This AI 'cop', which can read facial expressions and respond in six languages, has a built-in tablet that can be used to report crime and pay fines. AI police are planned to account for a quarter of the Dubai force by 2030 with some police stations 'manned' only by robots. Brigadier-General Razzouqi said Dubai was seeking to be a global leader in smart city technology and this is another aspect of smart cities – AI law enforcement. Connecting the dots is the route to revelation. We must have *context*. Dots appear to be one thing in isolation and very different when connected to all the others. Insiders like Microsoft billionaire Bill Gates are walking, talking dot-connections as are professional manipulators like George Soros and many others who are friends with Bono. When Gates, Soros and their like support or call for something the agenda benefits every time. Is it really a coincidence that Gates was the frontman for a computer system essential to human control or that he spends his subsequent billions through the Bill and Melinda Gates

Foundation to fund and promote vaccines, GMO, geoengineering, surveillance, the global warming hoax, mind-programming 'education' and artificial intelligence? Or that Soros does the same with 'progressive' politics, mass migration, fake revolutions and manipulation of 'democratic' elections among so much else? And they are far from alone in their dot-connecting propaganda and funding.

Mass-drugging of children and adults with psychological potions is another pixel in the picture, another strand in the tapestry of control. I have laid out in detail over the

**Figure 613:** A global human catastrophe in the making.

years the systematic drugging with Ritalin and its fellow mind-abusing concoctions of children and adults that don't conform (Fig 613). This is more medicalisation of emotion and perceptual choice. Psyche-changing drugs are handed out like candy today as we saw with the example of university students. How can you think clearly and see through the maze of diversions and control if your brain is scrambled by pharmaceuticals? As I mentioned earlier Aldous Huxley's insider knowledge allowed him to predict it all in 1961:

> *There will be, in the next generation or so, a pharmacological method of making people love their servitude, and producing dictatorship without tears, so to speak, producing a kind of painless concentration camp for entire societies, so that people will in fact have their own liberties taken away from them, but rather enjoy it, because they will be distracted from any desire to rebel by propaganda or brainwashing, or brainwashing enhanced by pharmacological methods. And this seems to be the final revolution.*

This is where we are going and it has to stop.

## Year Million (actually, rather sooner)

Just before this book went into the production stage with the text complete a six-part television series was broadcast by National Geographic called *Year Million*, and appropriately narrated by Laurence Fishburne who played Morpheus in *The Matrix*. The series featured leading transhumanists and 'futurists', including Kurzweil and Diamandis, describing a world transformed by AI. The first stage would see humans exploring the realms of virtual reality through a technological connection between minds and supercomputers ('Metaverse 1.0') and then they would dispose of the body altogether and upload their minds to 'the cloud' to become only a digital awareness living on a hard drive ('Metaverse 2.0'). We are back to *Transcendence*. The narration and interviewees predicted much of what I have been describing but with *none* of the context. We were told that AI would lead to a 'post human' society which would involve 'unshackling our consciousness from our body' and we would 'live as a digital signal in an online cloud collective' (a 'Borg Collective'). Some predicted a digital paradise in which minds would 'choose their adventures every day' and become the 'captain of their ship'. Michio Kaku, an American theoretical physicist and futurist, said in one programme: 'We would become the gods that we once feared and worshipped.' Actually, that is true but not for the reasons he thinks. We would be assimilated into the digital hive mind of those that claim to be gods – the Archontic distortion that already ensnares Reptilians and Greys. This is described in *Year Million*, again without the true context, as cloud-based 'brain-to-brain communication' through brain-chip 'telepathy' (the deletion of privacy) and 'swarm intelligence' leading to the merging of all minds into one hive mind. They even use that term 'hive mind' which has been the goal of the Archontic distortion and its Reptilian-Grey subordinates from the start of the hijack. They have done this to many realities before. The *Year Million* voiceover described the hive mind in terms of a 'super-intelligence' when it really means being Archontically absorbed. The narrative said that human minds would lose their sense of individuality and that is correct – they would then be simply part of the Archontic mind. We already have the power of telepathy, but the Hidden Hand has sought to suppress that and other 'sixth sense' gifts and potential. It wants 'telepathy' only in technological forms that it can control. *Year Million* describes how the hive mind would allow communication between diversity of thought and opinion, but the *Archontic* hive mind is meant to destroy all diversity and think only as one mind with one agenda. The voiceover said the hive mind would mean coming together as one and we are seeing the mimicking of all-is-one Infinite Awareness but confined only to the digital level at the expense of the Infinite level. Fusing human minds digitally would collectively firewall them from Infinite connection.

We were told that swarm intelligence could be needed to 'compete' with artificial intelligence but why are we opening the way for another intelligence that we have to compete with? What madness. Algorithm AI would be fine when supporting the human experience under human stewardship, but once the line is crossed into control and takeover this is surely insanity being passed off as technological development. For this nightmare to happen humanity has to become addicted to technology and desire its constant expansion, and among the younger 'smart' generations this is happening and the *reason* it is happening. The series did, to be fair, highlight the surveillance and control possibilities of the hive mind but the emphasis was on the benefits. The very idea that an uploaded digital mind would be free and captain of its ship takes naïvety to still new levels of absurdity. Once human minds were uploaded they would be enslaved forever in the fake realm of digital reality with no means of escape – as some of the more sensible contributors to the series pointed out. Such minds would be trapped in the supercomputer 'cloud' and no one seemed to grasp, as they talked of freedom and paradise, that digital reality by its very nature as a computer system would require someone or something running that system (AI). This would therefore be in ultimate control of everything within the system including uploaded minds. That moment would be humanity's point of no return and it is much closer than people think unless we see what is really happening. We also heard in *Year Million* how all this was inevitable and can't be stopped – the Borg mantra of 'resistance is futile'. It is not futile if people wake up to this in large enough numbers, and if many of those innocently involved in AI expansion see that what they are really creating is akin to a digital Frankenstein designed to delete humanity altogether in any form worthy of the name.

Those promoting and developing 'Metaverse' technology and human assimilation largely break down into two camps. One consists of those who know the real agenda and support its goals as expressions of the Archontic mind. The other involves a much greater number of left-brain perceivers who are so obsessed with the technology and its potential that they can't see the forest for the twigs. They speak of 'finding eternity' and 'becoming immortal' when in terms of awareness we are already eternal and immortal. We see this most basic misunderstanding in cryonics (from a Greek word meaning cold) in which people pay a lot of money to have their bodies preserved at something like minus 196 degrees centigrade in the hope that they can be revived in the 'future' when methods of treating the disease that killed them are known, as well as knowledge of how to revive them from such a frozen state. Some are even having only their heads preserved because that's where they think their memories and personality reside (they don't). I guess head-only cryonics must be considerably cheaper but surely requires extraordinary levels of optimism. It's all crazy stuff and how these people must symbolically hold their awareness in their 'hands' once they leave the body and see the nonsense of preserving their head in a reality of eternal awareness that doesn't need a head. The *Year Million* narrative about escaping 'the jail of our bodies' and relocating to a hard drive misses the entire point that while the body is a prison for consciousness there is an escape route which allows us to withdraw into expanded reality and potentially infinite forever. Uploading human minds to a digital construct does not free them from body-Alcatraz but entraps them into an even smaller perceptual cell, in which only digital reality exists and AI is dictating everything including all thoughts and responses. *Year Million's* concept of being 'enslaved to biology' does not conceive of awareness without an external vehicle and so equates the digital prison with escape from the body. It also perceives human awareness as something in and of itself when it is a point of perception within Infinite Awareness. Instead of decoding the digital hologram we would *become* a digital entity and nothing else. No longer would the Archontic force expressed as AI have to manipulate perception because it would *be* that perception by assimilating human awareness into itself and absorbing all that creativity ('ennoia' to Gnostics) that it doesn't have. This is the point of it all in the end – the Archontic distortion is seeking to overcome its limitations by absorbing the awareness of others that have the Spirit potential to go beyond those limitations. It is like King Louie, the orangutan in *The Jungle Book*, pursuing the secret of 'man's red fire'. The obsession with virtual reality is leading humanity along a road where what I have described is the outcome. We already have websites like Second Life in which people interact as digital personalities and this is in the process of expanding into 3D virtual reality. It is another step on the road to ultimate assimilation. One thing that stood out for me about the National Geographic series was the name itself – *Year Million*. The suggested timescales for even more extreme levels of digital assimilation were way out because the technology *already exists* and only has to be spun into the public realm through cover stories and human conduits who largely have no idea where it is all really coming from.

So there we are. We have been on quite a journey since the opening pages were turned and this is only a fraction of what I could have said and exposed, and have done elsewhere. The world is not what we think it is and have been told since childhood to believe that it is. We need to *see* with new 'eyes', *think* with new minds and *know* with new hearts. Old thinking and ways of perceiving are a software program and not a process led by free thought and consciousness. We are where we are because of slavish adherence to authority, beliefs, religions, peer-pressure, conventions, propaganda and norms and the insistence that everyone else do the same. This has got to stop. Perceptions that enslaved us will not set us free. We must look at the world anew without preconception and let information be our guide and not immovable beliefs that decode only self-fulfilling prophecy and illusory freedom to mask the reality of mass control. We have to see through the mirage and come together while there is still the opportunity. The cell door is closing fast.

# CHAPTER EIGHTEEN

# Perceptions of Freedom

*'We must love one another or die' – **W. H. Auden***

For those who have stayed with me this far there will be a question screaming for an answer: What can we do? There is much we can do – like change *everything* – but only with a fundamental transformation of human perception and self-identity. Without that, forget it. How can you change something with the same mentality that created it?

If humanity wants to head off the catastrophic outcome daily unfolding before our eyes then everything we have ever believed has to be re-evaluated and re-assessed with a truly open mind – and I mean *truly*. No belief system, religious, political, scientific, financial or cultural can be excluded. This is not only about free thought, but the nature of physics and the way that reality functions. Some questions we can start with: Why do I believe what I do? Where did my beliefs come from and on what evidence? You will invariably find that they are the result of constant repetition by those who gleaned them from constant repetition who gleaned them from constant repetition who gleaned them from constant repetition. You will also invariably find that at the end of this chain of intergenerational repetition programming there is either no evidence to support the belief; a fake story concocted by who knows who, who knows when and in who knows what circumstances; or the belief is actually someone's opinion long, long ago based on who knows what, who knows why and in who knows what circumstances. I have just described the origin of all religions which cumulatively hold-fast the great majority of humankind in life-long perceptual servitude and I don't mean only frock and skullcap religions. Almost the entirety of human society is an amalgamation of religious worship, mostly not recognised as such, and all founded on illusion (Fig 614).

There are 2.2 billion Christians whose whole perception of life and reality is founded on the existence of 'Jesus' who did not exist. 'Jesus' is just another name for a recurring hero figure across the world each of them placed in a different historical and cultural setting long before the

version called 'Jesus' appeared.
No, Christians will cry, that
can't be true – the Bible says he
was real. Okay, and who else? A
tiny few other references have
been clearly added later to
support the official narrative.
Miraculous feats that Jesus is
supposed to have done are
recorded nowhere except in one
book once again written by who
knows who, who knows when
and in who knows what
circumstances? How likely is

Figure 614: Religion in all its forms.

that? Oh, but the disciples wrote the gospels. No 'they' didn't and not
even the Church claims that. They are called Matthew, Mark, Luke and
John and the Church is quite happy for you to associate these with the
alleged disciples of the same name but the truth is they have no idea
who wrote these contradictory texts in which genealogies are
manipulated to connect New Testament Christian heroes with Old
Testament Jewish heroes. Why do only Matthew and Luke mention the
virgin birth? Did Mark and John have the night off? Well, it was
Christmas. References to 'Jesus', 'Abraham' and 'Mary' can be found in
the Koran because these were central characters in the earlier Biblical
texts ... another case of 'who gleaned them from constant repetition who
gleaned them from constant repetition'. Islam has 1.6 billion advocates
for a religion founded on the 'teachings' of a man called Muhammad
who claimed to be the prophet of god or Allah. How do Muslims know
that and so justify calling him the Prophet Muhammad for 1,400 years?
Well, it can't be based on the hard evidence and so it must be 'faith'.
What is faith? It is a belief gleaned from constant repetition by other
believers who found their own faith in the same way.

   If belief or faith is derived in and of itself without external influence
then how come people from Muslim families overwhelmingly become
Muslims and the same with Jews, Hindus, Christians, the lot of them?
Had today's Christians been born into a Muslim culture they would
now be Muslims and in the same way Jews would be Hindus and
Muslims would be Jews. What's more the most vehement Christians
would be the most vehement Muslims and so on because religion is a
downloaded software program and extremes of advocacy are mind
patterns that apply the same vehemence and absoluteness to whatever
belief they take on. Beliefs of modern Muslim extremists originate from
the 18th century and a Dönmeh Jewish man Muhammad ibn ʿAbd al-
Wahhab, who the British Empire teamed up with the founder of their

Dönmeh Saudi dynasty. If it wasn't so unbelievably tragic it would be hysterical. Muslim men have beards because Muhammad did in the 7th century. I mean, *what*? It's not about faith – it's a uniform, a symbol of control. The theme is even more obvious when religions divide into factions. Children in Protestant families tend to be Protestant; Catholic to be Catholic; Sunni Muslim to be Sunni and Shia to be Shia. What are the chances of that if the faith is independently arrived upon? This 'have faith' nonsense is all a con which is really saying that we can't show you any real evidence in support of what we want you to believe so just bloody believe it anyway – have 'faith'. All across society we have belief systems taken on for life through nothing more than constant repetition, indoctrination and intimidation. What would childhood be like if you refused to accept your parents' Christian faith in an obsessively Christian family? God (Allah or Yahweh) help you if you do that in a Muslim or Jewish family and thousands of deities have mercy should you resist giving your mind away to Hinduism. Parents and communities in this regard are tyrants and dictators imposing their will on their children because *their* parents and communities imposed their will on them. Intergenerational Chinese whispers enforced by perceptually and often literally brutal imposition. And we are going to meekly stand for this? The way Jewish parents impose their faith and limitless behaviour laws on their children is child abuse in my opinion and the same with Muslims, Christians and every other religious tyranny whatever name it may use. Mum, dad – you want to give your mind away then feel free, but don't you dare have the audacity, arrogance and lack of respect to insist that I must do the same. I will decide what I believe *not you*.

## The book is all you need

I am not saying that young people or anyone else should rebel against their particular faith. It is none of my business to say that. Freedom to choose means freedom to choose and not to exchange one imposed or manipulated belief system for another or none. I am simply saying that in pursuit of their own self-respect and right to free thought and free choice they might question their beliefs and see if they stand up to scrutiny. They might ask why they believe what they do and where that belief came from; and how did that source reach its conclusion and on what evidence? This search will lead back to a book or books of some kind – Bible, Koran, Talmud, Vedas – the true origins of which are lost although fake origins may have been invented to cover that. 'The Book' is 'The Truth' – have faith. People might further question if their faith has a record of making the world a nicer, freer, more loving place or whether it plays a frontline role in control of perception and the suppression of free speech, free thought and free choice without pressure, imposition or intimidation. If they are honest and open with themselves in their re-evaluation and research into the origins of their faith and its impact on human society their belief-system will be in pieces on the floor. I know this for one simple reason: When you can only see the tiniest infinitesimal fraction of infinity – visible light – and live 'on' a planet equivalent to a billionth the size of a pinhead then everything it is possible to know and understand about yourself and reality is not going to be found within the covers of a single religious tome written by who know who, etc., etc. The title of this book *Everything You Need To Know, But Have Never Been Told* does not refer to everything that needs to be known, but to that which will open new ways of thinking and perceiving and a new infinite vista of potential awareness. As I said at the beginning, this book is a start not a finish. Religious books claim to be the start *and* the finish leaving no margin for free thought and expression and the pursuit of uniqueness. We may be points of attention within Infinite Awareness but we are *unique* points of attention if we allow ourselves to be. By expressing our individual uniqueness, we are celebrating our unique contribution to the Infinite Whole. Religions and The System in general want to suppress that sense of uniqueness because this both comes from and generates frequencies of expanded awareness that connect us to realms of insight beyond The Program. They want low-vibrational, Little Me uniformity to which uniqueness is something to resist, fear, ridicule and condemn. Such states of perception become mindless (or rather Spiritless) and unquestioning repeaters of other people's views which then collectively coagulate into the norms of 'everybody knows that'. We live in a world of repeaters of information that starts out in the institutions of The System and is repeated into widespread acceptance purely by, well, repetition. The media repeats what politicians, scientists, academics, doctors, bankers etc. say and they repeat what each other says. This is how the Postage Stamp Consensus is repeated into existence. Religion has been perpetuated by the same repetition and so we find that politics, science, academia, medicine, finance and all the rest are religions every bit as much as Islam, Judaism, Christianity and Hinduism. When Zuckerberg said Facebook could replace religion he was comparing like with like. They all have their solidified deities, hierarchies, belief systems, holy books or webpages. The Communist Manifesto is to a communist what the Bible is to a Christian and what scientific orthodoxy is to a system scientist.

Religion is not a church or temple with mass, prayers to Mecca or evensong. That is only one expression of it. Religion is a mental and emotional pattern of repeating thought, perception and behaviour, another standing wave. Only the information the standing wave retains is different and not its state of oscillation and resonance or the way it

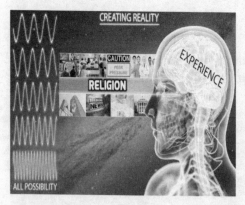

**Figure 615:** Religion – perception control.

decodes reality (Fig 615). Show me someone who worships their smartphone and I'll show you the mind-pattern of a religious fanatic and the same with Facebook addicts, shopaholics, political persuasions, sport team fanatics, money-worshippers and those obsessed with celebrity. They all have a deity – Jesus, Yahweh, Allah, smartphone, Facebook, clothing brand, political hero, Real Madrid, money, Justin Bieber – and these hijack their focus and sense of realty. This is exactly how bricks-and-mortar religion works. I refer to religion as the greatest form of mind control ever invented and they are not dispensing with religion they are changing its public face and increasing its reach. The progressive mind-set is the same religious mind pattern in another guise and global warming orthodoxy is their Bible never to be questioned. They are religious zealots who decide that they are right, all-knowing and omnipotent and therefore by definition everyone else with a different view must be wrong, stupid and the equivalent of an infidel. This beyond-arrogant self-obsession is then used to justify their demand that everyone believes what they do and the imposition of their beliefs where necessary. Here we have the mentality of both Sharia law fascism and the political correctness of progressive fascism. I am right so everyone else must be wrong and because I am right I have the moral duty to impose my beliefs on the entire population. Sharia law achieves this through sharia courts, intimidation and often brutality and murder while progressives pursue the same ends through 'hate' laws, hurling abuse, banning other views and Twitter storms. They are masks on the same mind pattern. This becomes obvious when you observe states of consciousness and not the body, colour, creed and background. On the face of it purveyors of sharia law and progressives booming on about 'diversity' would appear to be opposites, but observe the behaviour, attitudes and outcomes and they are oppos*ames* – different names for the same mentality and the same program. Breaking free of this program means genuinely and honestly observing ourselves and seeing how we act and behave with relation to those we say we oppose. Once again if people are genuine and honest in doing this they should prepare themselves for quite a shock. An honest re-evaluation of self is vital to escape the perception programs that hold humanity in ongoing servitude. If we don't do this, then it's night, night, humanity and not too long from now either.

## They gave us their mind

The human mind is so obsessed with five-sense reality that it's easy in the last few chapters about the world of the seen to forget what went before; but it is in the perceptually distant realms of the unseen that the answers lie because this is from where the problem is being orchestrated. We are 'watching' a holographic movie screen and what appears on that screen as individual and collective experience is the holographic expression of our waveform self –

**Figure 616:** The human plight.
© www.neilhague.com

frequency and oscillation patterns of mental and emotional perception (Fig 616). The Archontic Reptilian force and its hybrid *El*-ite well know this and they understand that if they can set the patterns and oscillations of perception the five-sense world of the movie screen will take care of itself. There is basically one pattern but they hide this truth behind an explosion of names and labels – religion, politics, right, centrist, left, progressive, Zionist, medicine, science, finance, academia, class, culture, race, income bracket, the list is endless. They are all the same mind pattern with their deities, hierarchies and self-certainty of being 'right'. All are pursuing their own interests at the expense of fairness, justice and true diversity. From this has come 'identity politics', the destroyer of all that is fair, just and diverse. Identity politics describes the mind pattern that I am highlighting. It seeks not what is fair and just for everyone, and certainly not what is diverse and unique, but only what suits and benefits me, me, me. A banker or hedge fund manager wakes up every morning to increase the bottom line no matter what the consequences are for others (see George Soros). They have no empathy or thought for those they crush, destroy, even kill all over the world in pursuit of personal gain, power and money for its own sake. A progressive will condemn these people (except Soros) and go on marches in protest against austerity and the selfish power of financial capital. But what do progressives do? They wake up every morning to impose their beliefs and behaviour patterns on as many more people as possible calling for further laws to censor opinion and speech no matter what the consequences for others and their basic rights. They have no empathy or thought for those whose freedoms they crush or those who see their communities transformed in a few years into a completely different culture. They pursue a personal agenda for its own sake and this is only another expression of the banking me, me, me, the same mind pattern with a different alias. Progressives don't look at their impact on others any more than bankers do and when it comes to selfishness it's a ten-all draw. Does Victoria Kawesa consider the impact on ethnic Swedes of her demand to remove all Swedish border controls? Of course not – it's all about her. For bankers, it's all about them as it is with progressives. All these LGBTIQ labels are identity politics meets the Twilight Zone. Identity labels are being sub-divided into ever smaller parts and will soon enter the realm of nanotechnology. Each new label and sub-divided label is another me, me, me, another onion skin between Body-Mind and the Infinite Awareness that we all are. Does a naked man claiming to be a woman consider the feelings of girls in a changing room that he/she demands to have the right to enter? No. It's all about him/her, him/her, him/her. The mind pattern is becoming ever more extreme in its narcissistic sense of entitlement and we are seeing this in finance, politics, corporations and certainly among progressives and their associated LGBTIQ.

If people face genuine discrimination because of race, religion or sexual orientation I am right with them. My attitudes are described by the dictionary definition (not the political one) of liberal as in ... 'Favourable to or in accord with concepts of maximum individual freedom possible, especially as guaranteed by law and secured by governmental protection of civil liberties ... favouring or permitting freedom of action, especially with respect to matters of personal belief or expression'. This sums me up to a tee. The problem is that progressives are *not* liberal, but the very opposite. We even have a political party in the UK that calls itself Liberal when it is progressive and not liberal. If all this was about discrimination I would be standing at their shoulder, but most of it is not. It's about identity domination and, ironically, privilege and omnipotence. It's about me, me, me. They are all the bloody *same*, but they just can't see it. I meet black people, Muslim people, Asian people, women of all backgrounds, men and women of different sexual preferences and they have come to my events all over the world. They don't need a label to set them apart from society because if they come to my events they know that labels are only temporary masks for Infinite Awareness, anyway. Why can't we meet each other on *that* level where there are no fault-lines of manufactured division? Where there is no black, white, Muslim, Jew, LGBTIQ and only the same consciousness experiencing itself? Progressives and their LGBTIQ wing instead want to build more and more walls to divide us,

using finer and finer
divisions of identity. They are
not bringing the world
together as they claim – they
are driving it apart (Fig 617).

## Groupies

Another consequence of
identity labels is that they
create group-think. There are
two aspects to this and both
extremely negative in their
impact. One is that large
numbers of people think the
same way. This is nothing

**Figure 617:** Remember, remember and let us never forget again.

more than mind patterns being vibrated into line or entrained by the
power of the group-think frequency as with the example of violins.
Group-think is further enforced and imposed by technological
frequencies with which humanity is constantly bombarded and by
progressive non-liberals through intimidation and exclusion of those
who wish to think differently. Social media has become the digital
Guantanamo Bay of this enforcement in that the 'wrong' opinions are
sure to attract the wrath of the Provisional Progressives who so love
diversity. Agree with our view or take this you loser. Group-think of this
kind is the bread and butter of mass perception control and all the social
engineering operations have this prominently displayed in their mind
control manuals. There is another version of group-think that involves
literally thinking in terms of groups with no thought for individuality or,
yet another irony, diversity. Labels are the very currency of this type of
group-think because labels are invariably applied to groups rather than
individuals. What comes from this is the black and white group labelling
so central to political correctness and its hierarchical structure of
perceived victimhood ... black trumps white, black women trump black
men, transgender trumps black women and so on. You can also add
Islam trumps Christianity which is associated with white men and so
reflects the pattern and ditto with migrants trump indigenous
population. Zionism, of course, trumps everyone through its web of
global propaganda and intimidation. The problem with this when you
approach the scene with even a modicum of intelligence is that not
everyone in a group, no matter what it may be, is the same in terms of
personality, behaviour and intent. Every group will span the spectrum
from nice bloke to what a bastard. None of this is ever taken into
account by the group-thinkers and this is why you see such hesitation
and bewilderment when a member of one minority victim group does or

**Figure 618:** A Muslim doesn't like gays? Oh, no – I've been triggered. Safe space, safe space ...

says something that slights another victim group. But you are a transgender victim and you've just criticised Muslim victims ... I don't understand ...I have a headache ... WARNING! WARNING! SYSTEM FAILURE! CAN'T COMPUTE! SHUT DOWN AND REBOOT! You can understand these matters very easily when you realise that every group spans the spectrum from nice bloke to what a bastard, but system failure is inevitable when you can only think in groups rather than individuals (Fig 618). Progressives overwhelmingly look the other way in the face of migrant crime, gangs and no-go areas because it requires a break-out from group-think into nice bloke and what a bastard. Those who are supposed to support women's rights will therefore ignore migrant rapes on the grounds that they breach the group-think concept leaving them no choice but to choose one group over another instead of thinking individually. Migrant victims trump white women victims and so take a blind eye and turn it. This is of course completely and utterly infantile but then progressive extremists are infantile as are the *truly* extreme right (as opposed to anyone to the right of Karl Marx must be extreme right). Left and Right at their mutual extremes are mirrors of each other like all apparent polarities. One progressive woman was raped by a migrant but said she did not report this because she didn't want to create racial tension. So what did she think that migrant was likely to do again? This is the sheer madness of it all. Progressive group-think gives white men (and often white women) little chance of being heard in the face of victim groups further up the hierarchy because their compartment is labelled colonial racist bigots unless they have repented and said three Hail Non-binaries. Mary's are so non-PC. Old white men that don't agree with progressives are the lowest of the low – the very dregs of the cesspit – but if you agree with them you can still be a progressive hero even as an old white man as we see with UK Labour Party leader Jeremy Corbyn. Agreeing with them appears to be the bit that saves you from the sackcloth and stuff. I have tried, and here and there I do, just nothing like enough. I'll get my sackcloth and start a fire. I am not defending white people, old or otherwise, as a group. There are some lovely white people and old white people, and some extraordinarily bigoted and psychopathic monsters. The difference is that I am aware that every other racial group contains the same mix. When was the last time a white father killed his daughter for having a relationship outside her faith, race or caste? If we view people by what they say and do and not by their race, religion and background then a rapist is a rapist, not a Muslim rapist, and a bigot is a bigot, not a white bigot.

I have met many homeless people and most have been lovely and in desperate need of help; but some have been deeply unpleasant and even violent. Most people I have met on state support have been genuine people struggling with their families to survive in often dire circumstances on pay-outs that were not even close to being adequate or humane. I have met some others who were parasiting off the population by taking money from the state that they could earn for themselves if they were not so monumentally lazy with a stunning sense of entitlement. I have met transgender people struggling to come to terms with their feelings who were some of the nicest people you could wish to know. I have met and observed others so incredibly arrogant and self-obsessed it takes the breath away. I have met gay people who fall into both camps. I have met Muslims all over the world including the Middle East and the great majority have been among the kindest, most considerate and generous of people (generous while themselves often having very little). I have met and observed others so utterly psychopathic that they plumb the depths of evil and depravity and there are also those who are quite okay with looking the other way while Muslim gangs rape and abuse children. I have met Jewish people who want to see justice and fairness for all and I have met and observed others who are so racist, bigoted and lustful for violence that psychopathic hardly suffices. The vast majority of black people I have met have been terrific and I absolutely love their energy and humour. I have met others who are race-obsessed, violent and can't wait to find the next mirror. I have met enormous numbers of white people who are kind, considerate and only want to live their lives in peace and harmony with everyone. I have met others who are body-obsessed, country-obsessed, racial supremacists and those so psychopathic and so callous, heartless and ruthless that monster is the only word that gets close.

No society can ever function with justice and fairness for all unless these most obvious of truths about human behaviour are acknowledged and where necessary addressed. Take the term psychopath alone. Are we really saying that so-called minority groups don't *all* contain psychopathic personalities? The counterfeit spirit is not infused into one racial group but all of them. How much it manifests in behaviour and perception depends on how strong is the consciousness of the person pushing the other way. (1) Psychopaths are found in every racial, religious and sexual group, and (2) not everyone in those groups is a psychopath. This tells us one simple fact that is screaming out to be heard: people in *any* group are not all the *same*. I know this will be

obvious to almost everyone reading this book, but I am talking to
Provisional Progressives here so bear with me.

The refusal to acknowledge these differences in personality no matter
the religious or racial background leads to horrific behaviour by
migrants in terms of crime and abuse of women being brushed away
while someone lifts the carpet. This in turn generates gathering
frustration in the indigenous population which the Provisionals then
have the nerve to complain about when *they* are the cause. A recognition
that all racial groups break down into nice bloke and what a bastard
would lead to far greater assessment of who is allowed into a country
and who is not. The lack of such assessment amid the constant
cacophony of 'you're all racist bigots', and the fear of being labelled as
such by the heart-on-the-sleeves, means that the countries of Europe are
facing absolute disaster, not least through inter-racial violence, the
imposition of Sharia law and organised crime. If we continue as we are
it's Sweden and Italy today but everyone else tomorrow. An end of
judging groups only in their totality would allow some compassion and
empathy for those in British and other European cities who have seen
the communities and culture they grew up with usurped in a
remarkably short time by an incoming culture – some of whom wish to
integrate, but others who seek to take over. Stepping back from 'you're
all racist bigots' and 'we're all as pure as the driven snow' would allow
some wide-angle peripheral vision to examine how the migrant crisis
began, who is really behind it and to what end. Of course the *El*-ite don't
want this to happen because of what would be found – as outlined in
this book. In that regard alone Provisional Possessives are playing a
magnificent and essential role in protecting the agenda of the less-than-
one-percent that they claim to so oppose. We need maturity and
expanded awareness if we are to turn this world around because
without that nothing can change. We have to start seeing everyone as an
individual irrespective of race, colour, creed and background because
group-think is incredibly destructive in so many different ways and
downright ridiculous when it comes to fair and balanced judgement.
How can people consider themselves to be adult and mature when they
won't listen to what someone is saying just because they are considered
part of a group they collectively don't like? It's not who says it – it's
whether it's *true*. How often does the mentally of 'you're just a racist
bigot' and 'you don't care about the planet' ever consider the
information and evidence of those they abuse by reflex action? Exactly.

## Life is a mirror

These apparently 'this world' matters are vital to understand at much
deeper and unseen levels of reality. The world of the seen is only a
projection from the unseen after all. Our mind patterns – state of

frequency and oscillation – dictate the level at which we interact individually and collectively with the quantum realm of possibility and probability. Low-frequency states interact with the quantum field at low levels of frequency and so make manifest experience, again individually and collectively, which reflects that. We return to the foundation of how we create reality:

> *Accidents happen, that's what everyone says. But in a quantum Universe there are no such things as accidents, only possibilities and probabilities folded into existence by perception.*

If perception doesn't change nothing will change – or can. We don't need a revolution of fighting. That's how we got here. We need a revolution of perception which is the only revolution that will change anything for the better (Fig 619). Archontic Reptilians and their hybrid gofers structure and manipulate human society to herd humanity into their foundation mind pattern with all its different labels that hide the fact that they're all the same basic perceptual state. I have been describing this throughout the book in terms of Body-Mind or five-sense mind. It is the bubble, the perception prison, the Postage Stamp which isolates the conscious mind and lower levels of the subconscious from their true and infinite self. Once perceptually isolated and detached from the influence of expanded awareness the isolated fragment can be programmed with the perceptions that suit the agenda of mass control and those perceptions will express

**Figure 619:** Without this nothing can change.

**Figure 620:** *We* are the solution because we have created the problem.

themselves as the frequency or mind pattern at which we individually and collectively operate. These patterns then interact with the fields of possibility and probability and fold into existence a holographic expression of themselves. In this way, what we call 'external' experience is only a mirror of the inner self. You want to change the 'outer'? Then change the inner. There is no other way when the 'outer' is only a decoded reflection of the inner (Fig 620). This is true of our individual lives and the world in general. Archontic Reptilians don't have to control every last detail to enslave humanity, they only have to dictate the collective mind pattern and everything else pretty much takes care of itself for the reasons I am explaining. This principle can be described in the simplest of terms. If enough people hate we must live in a reality founded on the frequency of hatred. What you fight you become (Fig 621). If we perceive ourselves to be apart from everyone else through identification with Phantom Self we must live in a reality founded on

**Figure 621:** Violent protest v violent state. Opposames at war.

division and apartness in the name of race, religion, culture, income and so on. It is cause and effect. What impact do you think a protest march called a 'Day of Rage' is going to have in terms of the reality this mind pattern will create? Day of Ragers focus the attention of rage on their target, in this case the government, and those representing the target reflect back their frequency of contempt and resistance. Another day, another electrical circuit, another standing wave of rage and resistance, rage and resistance, jogging on the spot and taking us nowhere. Up the ante to a full-on riot and the same happens but on an even more extreme level. What if protest was done from an awareness of how reality really works? What if we dropped the protest bit altogether? Unfair government actions create a resistance *against*. Protest is to protest *against*. Resistance to protest is to resist *against*. The protest against and the resist against set up the standing wave because the resistance is only the protest reflected back which is how standing waves are formed. Protestors resist government and government resist protestors – to and fro, to and fro in mutual oscillation. Archontic Reptilians and their hybrids are seeking to manipulate this very situation because it changes nothing and the collective emotional impact provides breakfast, dinner and tea. This is why people like Soros are so intent on maximising protest. Someone has to break the circuit and this can only be done by looking at reality in a different way. How about we ditch the banners which are symbols of resistance *against*? How about we stop shouting abuse and slogans which are symbols of resistance *against*? How about people turn up in large numbers at the selected spot, stand or sit down, open their heart (chakra vortex) and project love at those they disagree with? If we want to live in a loving world we must be loving. Hatred doesn't tend to work. Oh, testosterone cries, don't give me that love changes all crap. We must *rage*. Which will produce what? It can only create a reality founded on rage because the focus of the rage will reflect it back to create a standing wave of rage. Good thinking, well done you. Love breaks the circuit and takes away the power of any adversary while rage just further empowers them. Albert Einstein said:

> *Everything is energy and that's all there is to it. Match the frequency of the reality you want and you can't help but get that reality. It can be no other way. This is not philosophy. This is physics.*

You don't get the frequency of love from the frequency of hate or the frequency of peace from the frequency of rage. The world is drowning in hate and rage and you only have to spend five minutes scanning social media to see that. Conflict and war are the collective manifestation of that hate and rage even when it comes from those – as it so often does – who rage against hate and war. Frequencies are frequencies. They don't change because of what you hate and rage against. Hate and rage are frequencies in and of themselves and the rest is a cover story. Israelis hating Palestinians and Palestinians hating Israelis are both generating the same frequency. I understand the hatred by many Palestinians after the way they have been treated since the Second World War, but I am pointing out that hate just generates more hate in an oscillating standing wave and maintains the status quo. What do you think Zionist apologists are generating when they rage against the perceived hate of others? Those who are breaking free of Archontic mind patterns must be the ones to break the circuits of which Israel-Palestine is but one. Enslaved minds complete the circuits at both polarities and only awakening minds can break them. When we replace protests of rage

with statements and actions of intent based on heart awareness rather than head awareness we break the circuits and they can't be restored until the subject of that focus reflects back that frequency of love and creates a new standing wave – a new status quo – founded on love (Figs 622 and 623). Even if they don't (and they won't

**Figure 622:** How we got here.

**Figure 623:** How we get out of here.

initially) the fact that you have broken your end of the circuit means that movement is now possible because the standing wave (status quo) has collapsed. It must do so when standing waves depend for their existence on the same frequency being reflected back and forth. Project anger at police they will reflect it back. Standing wave in position, sir. This applies to all relationships and interactions from the personal to the global because it's all the same 'physics'. Try it – it works.

When someone is raging against you don't reflect that back but open your heart and rise above it (literally in frequency terms). You take their power away because you are not reflecting their rage back and empowering its effect. You are deleting its power because without a circuit it must disappear on into the ether and dissolve. Rage without constant replenishment (reflection) must blow itself out very quickly. Gathering in numbers to make your point with smiles and a joyful celebration of unity is a different and higher frequency to that of rage. Such loving exposure of injustice will also have a far greater impact and attract far greater sympathy from the watching public than violence or screaming anger which turns people off in droves. The power of the *El*-lite also requires that we take them seriously. The more seriously we take them the more power we give them. They are pathetic. We should laugh in their face, not wave a fist. This will disarm them quicker than anything. There should be more laughter in general. I hear so little as I observe people passing through life. Mass protests rarely change anything because they empower through the circuitry what the protest is about. Protests of this kind can be a festival of virtue signalling – look at me protest, see how good, kind and caring I am. Year after year, decade after decade I watch this unfold from marches through London and Washington to Occupy Wall Street. What a contrast to the 'I have a dream' marches inspired by Martin Luther King who spoke not of hate and rage, but of love and the need for inclusion and everyone coming together. How effective would Gandhi have been if he had carried an assault rifle? King didn't rage against the 'enemy' in his 'I Have A Dream' speech and so create more fault-lines of division and standing waves of mutual rage. He spoke of everyone being treated the same with none excluded or hierarchically set apart:

*But there is something that I must say to my people, who stand on the warm threshold which leads into the palace of justice: In the process of gaining our rightful place, we must not be guilty of wrongful deeds. Let us not seek to satisfy our thirst for freedom by drinking from the cup of bitterness and hatred. We must forever conduct our struggle on the high plane of dignity and discipline. We must not allow our creative protest to degenerate into physical violence. Again and again, we must rise to the majestic heights of meeting physical force with soul force* [Spirit force in the context of this book].

*The marvellous new militancy which has engulfed the Negro community must not lead us to a distrust of all white people, for many of our white brothers, as evidenced by their presence here today, have come to realise that their destiny is tied up with our destiny. And they have come to realise that their freedom is inextricably bound to our freedom.*

*We cannot walk alone.*

Today's PC progressives please note. King went on with words that never fail to make me cry whenever I hear them:

*I have a dream that one day on the red hills of Georgia, the sons of former slaves and the sons of former slave owners will be able to sit down together at the table of brotherhood.*

*I have a dream that one day even the state of Mississippi, a state sweltering with the heat of injustice, sweltering with the heat of oppression, will be transformed into an oasis of freedom and justice.*

*I have a dream that my four little children will one day live in a nation where they will not be judged by the colour of their skin but by the content of their character.*

*I have a dream today!*

*I have a dream that one day, down in Alabama, with its vicious racists, with its governor having his lips dripping with the words of 'interposition' and 'nullification' – one day right there in Alabama little black boys and black girls will be able to join hands with little white boys and white girls as sisters and brothers.*

*I have a dream today!*

How more effective Black Lives Matter, Black Bloc and Antifa would be if they listened to King instead of taking the route of rage that Soros is so keen that they do (Figs 624 and 625). Racist police officers and raging anti-racists create yet another circuit of mutual rage empowerment. Martin Luther King rightly said:

> *Non-violence means avoiding not only external physical violence, but also internal violence of spirit. You not only refuse to shoot a man. You refuse to hate him.*

## Love is the ultimate power

King called for people to realise in effect that we are all one – all God's children as he put it. He wasn't demanding a new hierarchy to replace the old one with new masters usurping the old. He was calling for no hierarchies and no masters – as I do today. He would have been aghast at the thought that white men no matter what their character would be lumped together by group-think under one label of colonial racist bigots; and that great philosophers would be banned or marginalised for the crime of being white. As he said: 'Now is the time to make justice a reality for all of God's children.' He meant ALL people and not only new self-appointed racial, religious and political elites to replace the old self-appointed racial, religious and political elites. Archontic mind patterns see talk of love as weak while rage and even violent rage is strong, but the opposite is the case. The absence of hate and anger does not mean passivity – anything but. I have been accused of many things, but passivity has never been one of them. The love that I speak of is not that of physical

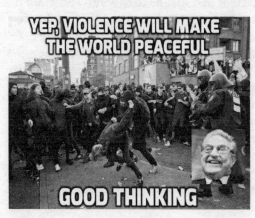

**Figure 624:** How Soros must laugh.

**Figure 625:** Lest we forget.

attraction, or 'mind love' as I call it, but an expression of Spirit which knows all is one. From here comes ultimate strength, not weakness and passivity. This love will never cease to do what it knows to be right whatever the provocation, attempted intimidation or consequences. Love does not compute doing what it knows to be wrong or acting only in self-interest. Resonating the frequency of love from the heart does not mean that you lie down and let people walk all over you. Love *is* power. Love *is* strength. Nothing else compares because it changes reality by folding into existence possibilities and probabilities that relate to that frequency. Love is not only for others but for self and love for self (very different from self-obsession and conceit) means self-respect that will not allow others to impose themselves against our will. Love doesn't protest against injustice and bombard its targets with hatred – it simply says, *'I'm not having it.'* I refuse to cooperate with that which seeks to impose its will upon me and delete my freedom. The word 'no' does not have to be delivered with fury on your face. It just means to say 'no' and *mean* it. How many people go on protest marches saying 'no' and then go home and accept what they were protesting against? So 'no' doesn't really mean 'no' then? Love's version of 'no' involves ceasing to cooperate with oppression, not to wave a banner at it and then walking away.

The number of people enforcing the will of the tyrannical *El*-ite is absolutely tiny compared with the number being imposed upon (Fig 627). How difficult would it be to identify those areas where the state particularly depends on public cooperation and then withdraw that cooperation in crucial numbers until the injustice and imposition is no more? Assembling in vast numbers at one crucial point, sitting down and refusing to move is a form of non-cooperation if it affects the ability of The System to function. Mass non-cooperation is far more effective than only protest. The latter affects the police but non-cooperation affects The System itself of which police are only pawns. We need to

**Figure 627:** Mass non-cooperation is far more effective than mass protest.

understand the scale on which the tiny *El*-ite depend for their ongoing agenda on the cooperation of their target population because in that sense alone we have the power and not them (Fig 628). But to make that number superiority count we have to *stop fighting each other*. On a personal level of non-cooperation – if smart phones are crucial to the *El*-ite desired outcome then stop using them if you can, or giving them to your children. If smart meters are vital to what the *El*-lite are creating then refuse to accept them. If videogames are rewiring the brain then stop playing them and buying them for your kids. By age 21 many young people – especially boys – can have spent 10,000 hours playing videogames with violence often a central theme. In terms of the effects on their brain alone this is insanity and parents can stop that or at least reduce it for the benefit of the child. But do enough have the will? Clearly not and it is no good complaining about the effect while refusing to address the cause. If 5G is crucial to the technological control grid – and it absolutely is – then we must do

**Figure 628:** The tail has been wagging the elephant.

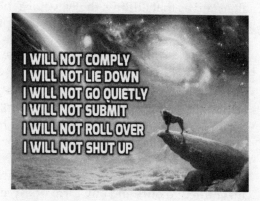

**Figure 629:** Love in action.

everything possible to block that happening and cease to cooperate with its introduction. Boycott companies and countries that act against the public interest and more than anything refuse to be silenced by *anyone* (Fig 629). If we do all this and so much more from the heart without malice and rage we are energetically adding to the solution and not the problem. You will be amazed how things would change once the resistance polarity is removed and the non-cooperation vibe founded on love takes its place. Feed-back circuits galore must fall in the face of this and it is they that hold the entire System together.

## Sponge-minds and free minds

Ceasing to cooperate includes no longer accepting without question what the state and its controlling *El*-ite tell us to believe. The bottom line of bottom lines is the control of human perception and so people *must* take their minds back. It is surely obvious by now that the authorities whether political, administrative, corporate, scientific, academic or media mislead us all the time either by themselves being misled or through downright lies. I don't mean little ones, either, but enormous distortions of the truth and reality. By far the safest filter system is to believe nothing The System tells us until it proves worthy of acceptance, and with every day that passes this gets less and less likely – with whoppers becoming ever more whopping. Keep asking the question 'Who benefits?' – Who benefits from me believing what they are telling me? Remember that words don't change the world only outcomes do. The outcome will invariably tell you who was behind events that justified or led to the outcome and you can see the process at an earlier stage by asking when an event happens – what will *be* the outcome if I believe what they are telling me? Instead of accepting that doctors and the pharmaceutical industry know best, do your own research into vaccines, drugs and body-destroying cancer treatments. What are the alternatives that address the waveform blueprint rather than the holographic illusion? We take our perceptions back by deciding for *ourselves* what those perceptions are instead of downloading them from The System's apps. We can do this by overriding Mainstream Everything and doing our *own* research before reaching our *own* conclusions. So what if other people don't like what we choose to believe? This is so important. Don't be intimidated by those who attack or ridicule you for your views. Who the hell are they to tell you what to think? What scale of arrogance and ignorance does it require for people to believe that everyone must believe what they do (and it is usually Postage Stamp myopia anyway). They are entitled to their view but we are entitled to ours and any form of expanded awareness would never accept such imposition of perception. I don't care if it is parents, teachers, academics, scientists, doctors, journalists, sad Internet trolls, whoever. Stay out of my mind unless I choose to invite you in because what I think is none of your business. Please don't believe anything that I have written in this book unless it feels right to *you*.

Those that seek to force their beliefs on others have issues of self-worth though outwardly they may try to hide that with bravado. I have met many outwardly confident people, even arrogantly so, who were wobbling jellies inside. Secure people don't need others to think like them and I can tell you from experience that so many academics and scientists (especially those of the Skeptic Society variety) set out to constantly trash those who challenge the Postage Stamp because they are terrified that those they attack may be right and, oh, no, worst of all, that they are wrong. Questioning and being a skeptic are not the same thing. Questions just dispassionately question to see if something stands up to scrutiny, but skeptics set out *from the start* with the intent of discrediting anything beyond the pea-size perceptions of The System. The possibility that what is being said could be right never enters their little heads. How could it be right if The System says otherwise and The System knows all? They think they are so intellectually superior but they are just passive repeaters of what The System has told them to believe. If

**Figure 630:** Better ask the queen.

we are to escape The Program and control by the Matrix then alongside this total re-evaluation of self, life and reality we must drop the group-think in both of the versions I have described. No more believing what the group says because it's a group no matter how large or small it may be. We are individual expressions of Infinite Attention not an ant colony and we need to stop behaving like one (Fig 630). Oh, but you will be excluded from your group if you don't agree with them? Well, fuck 'em then. Why would anyone want to be part of a group that didn't respect their right to their own perceptions? If people need to be in a group they should find another with more respect. I have never been a group-joiner – it's just not my scene – and one of my rare and thankfully brief experiences of being in a group a few years ago was such a nightmare it will never be repeated. The power-struggles within groups are a sight to behold and for groups to work in mutual support rather than collective entrainment they need to be based on expanded states of awareness that are genuinely heart-centred and genuinely respectful of another's right to be different. Progressives and their Internet troll seek-and-destroy command system (see Twitter storm) are highly skilled in demanding and intimidating subordination to the group (hive) mind. They are indeed being used to herd and corral humanity into the Archontic hive mind around their progressive belief system. The same is happening with politicians, with Blair-blueprint leaders or progressives popping up all over the place now, especially in Europe. We must not bow to this group think and respond with open hearts and unbreakable determination not to concede our uniqueness to the mob and the blob. I know that for many this will not be easy and the same with everything else we have to do to head-off total human enslavement. But, hey, I never said that it would. We have travelled a long way down the road marked Shit Street and it is going to take some turning back. We are, however, lest we forget again, *All That Is And Ever Can Be* and so we have to be in with a chance; but this is dependent on self-identity with that infinite expression of self and not with Ethel on the check-out and Bill at the bakery.

## Healing the divide and ending the rule

No positive change is possible without a total transformation in humanity's self-identity. Perceiving ourselves in terms of our name, race,

**Figure 631:** Yep, crystal clear, isn't it?

culture, religion, job, lifestyle and life story (what I call Phantom Self) is the very foundation of every problem (Fig 631). If we go on like this those problems must continue because their cause continues. Phantom Self creates the perception of an isolated individual amid isolated individuals. That can be a lonely place. From this comes a belief in 'Little Me' or dog-eat-dog depending on your personality and provides every possible fault-line and schism you can imagine to secure the all-important divide and rule. Colour, race, religion, income bracket all take on a sense of importance and relevance that they do not when you self-identify with the 'I' that we all are – Infinite Awareness (Fig 632). Phantom Self labels are what we are *experiencing* and not what we are. The Hidden Hand has done an amazingly effective job of manipulating humankind into self-identifying with what we are experiencing and not with what is having the experience – awareness, a state of being aware. Phantom Self basically perceives reality only through the five-senses where everything and everyone appears to be apart from everything else. When you self-identify with Infinite Awareness having the experience, your perception expands from the twigs to the forest. You see that everything and everyone is connected. From this perspective race, religion and sexual preference are irrelevant to self-identity because they are an experience and not an 'I' in its widest sense. How utterly ironic there will be those who accuse me of being racist, anti-Muslim, anti-Semitic and transphobic for what I have written

**Figure 632:** Not what 'they' want us to believe that it is.

in this book when I come from a sense of reality in which all of those things are irrelevant to true self-identity. But this is what happens with Phantom Self (and there are none more captured by its illusions that Zionist extremists, Provisional Progressives, Islamic extremists and white supremacists). You may note that in the realm of Phantom Self, Zionism and Islam oppose each other, Provisional

Progressives oppose white supremacists (and sometimes Zionist extremists) and white supremacists oppose Islam, Zionism and progressives. Their body-centred self-identity makes them all appear different to each other when they are all enslaved in the prison of Phantom Self. I look at those same people and groups and see aspects of the same consciousness entrapped in the illusion of separateness and the confusion between experience and self. I come from the ultimate non-racist, non-sexist sense of reality and yet I will be dubbed racist by those who are all for their different reasons obsessed with race. The world is indeed upside down, a colossal inversion.

Self-identification with Infinite Awareness and recognising that Phantom Self is just that – a phantom – has fantastic implications for the 'individual' expression of consciousness and human reality collectively. Phantom Self with its myriad of myopia and Little Me perspectives is a very low level of frequency and interacts with the quantum field of possibility and probability within that same frequency band. It can do no other. This folds into existence an individual and collective reality that reflects this myopia and limited vision – the world that we see (Fig 633). A sense of apartness manifests a holographic world of apartness. A sense of isolation and division manifests a world of isolated division in which the lines between people and groups become ever more clearly drawn. These lines must become more extreme as self-identity is divided into endless sub-divisions empowered by their political wing of identity politics. Sense of perception = experienced reality. This should be displayed on the wall of every home, business, school, college, university, government building and military establishment the world over along with 'Change perception and you change reality'. You will see at the back of the book that we have had posters produced to this end. Here we have the Golden Key that can unlock every door and gateway. While we see ourselves as apart we will *be* apart; when we perceive all to be One then all will *be* One. I don't mean that we will all morph into each other and everyone will be the same. Expanded awareness is about celebrating infinite diversity and not fusing into one neutral blob. That is what happens when we fall into states of consciousness confinement with its perception of limited possibility (Fig 634 overleaf). Look around at the sameness manifested by this mentality in every area of human society.

**WHO ARE WE?**

**PURE AWARENESS**

**Figure 633:** When all illusion is stripped away this is what remains.

Self-identification with Infinite awareness *having* the experience is expressed as a high and expanded frequency to match its expanded perspective. This interacts with the quantum field of possibility and probability on a level and span of frequency limited only by the person's ability to expand awareness. In that sense it is limit*less*. What a different reality this manifests. No more Little Me which is only a figment of the Little Me perception and therefore cannot exist within the decoded realms of *Infinite* Me perception (Fig 635). Life becomes wave after wave of potential diversity, inspiration and insight because of the range of possibility and probability that you are now tapping into. You are dancing to a different rhythm, beating a different drum and the world will call you mad. Enjoy! I have long been through this process and increasing numbers are doing the same. They often ask

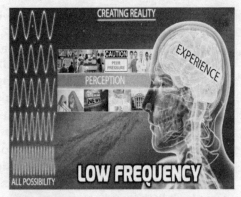

**Figure 634:** Phantom Self and its programmed perceptions can only manifest within the frequency band they represent.

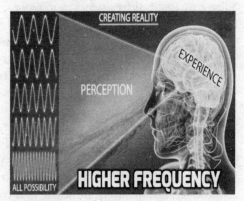

**Figure 635:** Expanded mind – expanded possibility.

why their lives are suddenly such a synchronistic adventure full of 'coincidence' and insightful experience. This is why. They also ask why their old life is falling apart, not always pleasantly, but how can this not be? The perception frequency that manifested the old life has gone and with that must go its holographic expression. Relationships may end or change and the same with jobs, location and circles of friends to reflect the new frequency of perception although relationships can continue and deepen should partners make the same perceptual leap. If the life you wanted to change is falling apart during this transition then embrace that and celebrate its demise. It could be worse – your life could have stayed like it was indefinitely.

The same happens collectively when enough people go with this transformation and begin to impact on the collective field. The sum total of human perception manifests as what we see in our lives and on the TV news. The Archontic Reptilian force and its hybrid *El*-ite know how this process works and they know that if they can manipulate human perception they can deliver human experience via the decoding processes of humans themselves. Collective senses of isolation and division are called wars, class, race, religion, haves and have nots. When we see each other as One – literally expressions of the same Infinite Awareness – that sense of reality must, repeat *must*, become our experienced reality. How could it be any other way when the seen realm of experience is only a reflection of the unseen realm of waveform perception? Divisions can only be healed when divisions are no longer perceived. They are but illusions to keep us apart. Be gone with them. This is how we can change our collective reality. We don't need politicians, economists, scientists and academics that serve the old thinking and perceiving. We simply need new thinking and perceiving. I understand why from the five-sense perspective it appears that change at best must be slow and at worse not change at all or further deteriorate. It seems to be an almost unimaginable task to change a world in such a state with so many politicians and corporations to persuade. Where do you start? But there are two things to say immediately about that. Firstly, we should not accept even slow change for the better in terms of fairness and justice for all or what Martin Luther King called 'the tranquilising drug of gradualism'. This is for five-sense perception not infinite perception. Change perception and you change the world derived from those perceptions – *now*. Secondly, there is no need to persuade pillars and gofers of the global Establishment to act in humanity's best interests or to have endless meetings with someone taking the minutes. We change our own reality by changing ourselves and we change our collective reality by collectively changing ourselves. The more we self-identify with Infinite Awareness and put Phantom Self in its place the more that humanity's interaction with possibility and probability will be transformed and thus its holographic expression. Everything, everything, *everything* comes from that and without it nothing comes, changes or moves on. In the simplest of terms humanity's low-frequency self-identity is creating the current world of the seen and an expansion into high frequency self-identity must change everything by pulling out of the quantum field other possibilities and probabilities and folding them into holographic existence (Fig 636). If we do this we will experience the effect as the control system (a low-frequency

**Figure 636:** Ethel at the check-out.

manifestation) unravelling. It may seem that events and happenings make this so, but in truth these will be only holographic expressions of the transition between decoded realities. We will have collectively perceived a different reality and holographic experience can do nothing but reflect that change. This is too simple? No – the opposite is true. The way we have tried to change things up to now has been too complicated. Humanity has been trying to change the movie on the movie screen. We need to go direct to the projection – where it is all coming from – and then, only then, can the movie change. As the Cat Stevens (Yusuf Islam) song goes: 'If you want to sing out, sing out. If you want to be free, be free.' Know it and it will be. Now it becomes even clearer why the Archontic manipulators have worked so incessantly to keep this knowledge from us. A collective perception of connection and unity will manifest as divisions fading and with that will go conflict, full-out war and the desire to suppress others for our own perceived benefit and interest. The only question that remains is *will* we do this in large enough numbers to make it happen? The door is there to open and it is our choice if we give it a push and walk through or stay in the La La Land of left-brain enslavement.

## No more victims

The Archontic distortion and its allies are not seeking to turn the entire young generation into victims for a bit of fun and a laugh. The same mind-scam is not being played on adults for a lark. Victim perception = victim experience and victim experience = protect me Big Brother. Victimhood is a feedback loop with victimisation or the sense of it. What can a victim perception do except make a frequency connection with victim possibility and probability? The Hidden Hand knows this and the result is Generation Jelly or Generation Snowflake. When I say they need to grow some backbone I am really saying they need to change their perception of self from victim to Infinite Awareness and know that they have the power to control and dictate their reality. Life is not to be feared and run away from, but to be celebrated and experienced to the fullest (Fig 637). Life as it is lived in human reality is an absurdity and if we take absurdity seriously we create a standing wave of ongoing absurdity. Laugh in its face and break the circuit. Archontic reality wants to be taken

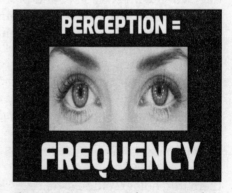

**Figure 637:** Perceptions are frequencies and so dictate the frequencies with which we interact with the quantum field of possibility and probability.

seriously because that is its power-source and we should deny it that power. Someone abusing another because of race, religion or gender is an absurdity. We give it power by responding with anger, resentment and by being upset. We delete its power by laughing at its ludicrousness. People have been mass-abusing me for nearly 30 years all over the world and I find it hilarious. I don't know how I keep my underpants dry with some of them. You are your life and your life is you. A victim you, is a victim life. A little me you, is a little me life. An Infinite you, is an Infinite life. This is, to quote Einstein, not philosophy, but physics. I have sympathy for those who have unpleasant experiences, but surely the most effective response is to understand why people experience things that others don't. Experience is not random as we are led to believe and if we can grasp why something happens to one but not the other we take back even more power over our lives. Sometimes we are subconsciously guided into what we think is a bad experience to strengthen the conscious mind and show us something about ourselves and reality. I wouldn't change any of my bad experiences because although they weren't nice in the moment they gave me priceless gifts that have played an essential role in what has followed. The need many have to be a victim is a subconscious technique they use to avoid taking responsibility for their own life and experience. Taking responsibility is another garlic and vampire relationship that absolutely must stop if humanity is to be free of its perceptual enslavement. Don't take responsibility – blame someone or something else for what is happening. Externalise responsibility for an *internal* creation and in doing so hand over your power to change what you yourself created. Taking responsibility is to recognise your creative power. To point the finger at someone else or bad luck is to accept that you have no power over your life – someone else or bad luck does. What we call bad luck is our energetic state of being pulling the perceived bad luck out of the field of possibility and probability. There is no such thing as bad luck only the perception of it. In the end, the answer is always in the mirror.

UK television personality Noel Edmonds was widely attacked by the media for asking if negative thoughts could cause cancer. This was almost a form of blasphemy because it suggested, wow, no, surely not, that people could play a part in the cancer they suffer. A claim that a person's mental and emotional state could be involved was too much for many even though this is clearly true from the statistics alone linking lifestyle choices to cancer. The virtue signallers cried: How can you 'blame' someone for having cancer? That's outrageous and so insensitive. All the garbage you hear surrounding allegations of insensitivity are typical of victim perception. It is far more 'sensitive' to feel sorry for someone with cancer than to question the cause and so pursue a possible cure by disconnecting cause from effect. Of course so-called negative thoughts and emotions have a detrimental effect on health because their low and distorted frequency impacts on the balance of the waveform/electrical blueprint and this plays though into holographic reality as imbalances that we call dis-ease – disharmony. Imbalanced emotions generate distorted electrical and electromagnetic signals and fields which scramble the body's electrical/cellular communication system. The result is cancer and other disease or dis-ease. It's real simple once you vacate the Postage Stamp and these electrical imbalances can be corrected by emotional balance and positivity and through bioelectrical technology restoring electrical communication to what it is supposed to be. This is how thoughts and emotions cause disease and how they can 'mind over matter' cure it. No electrical or electromagnetic imbalance means no disease and a dramatic slowing down of aging because this is caused by cellular replacement becoming more and more distorted through cumulative breakdowns in electrical communication. What is more positive, for goodness sake, than for illness including cancer to be caused by especially emotional and electrical imbalances that we ourselves create? This personal responsibility is really personal *power*. If we can cause something we can stop causing it. If we are the cause then we are the cure. *We* have the power. Isn't this rather more positive than mere virtue-signalling that condemns others for seeking to understand something while yourself contributing nothing except virtue-signalled 'sensitivity'? This is what happened to Edmonds in a TV interview with another well-known presenter, Phillip Schofield, who could virtue-signal for the Universe. I was accused by a BBC radio chap called Stephen Nolan of being insensitive to families of those killed on 9/11 by challenging the official story. Apparently it is more sensitive (virtue signalling) to accept a tissue of lies that many of the families have themselves seriously questioned. I did say he worked for the BBC, right?

There is considerable research to connect negative mental and emotional states to illness for all the reasons I am explaining here. I have mentioned the placebo effect in which patients are cured of something after taking a sugar pill that they believed was the real one and, in terms of the subject at hand, it works the other way, too. Studies indicate that some 25 percent of those told about possible side-effects of the real drug while taking a sugar pill experienced those side-effects. These have included fatigue, vomiting, muscle weakness, colds, ringing in the ears, taste and memory problems and all caused not by the pill that they didn't take, but by a belief that this could happen. Men have even grown hair with a hair-growth drug they *didn't take*. Those convinced they are going to die actually do die far more often than those with similar conditions without that conviction. Women who believe they are susceptible to heart disease have been found to be four times more likely to die than those who do not have that belief. Patients who have been wrongly told they are terminally ill have died within the doctor's timeframe only for it then to be discovered they were not terminally ill at all. A doctor's death prediction can often be a death *sentence* because a programmed mind is a self-fulfilling prophecy. This is, in its own way, another version of the victim and little me mentality. I am a victim of my illness and doctor knows best because I am only little me and he's a doctor, a Big Me. If we observe this process with the world in general the same is happening and the same transformation technique is required that involves the re-evaluation of self-identity. There are endless examples of people who have rejected a doctor's verdict and lived long past the predicted moment of demise. I was told by doctors as a 19-year-old that I would probably be in a wheelchair in my 30s because of my arthritis. I told them I wouldn't and they could keep their pills. I am 65 at the time of writing and I'm still not pushing the wheels. My perception that it wouldn't happen stopped it happening because it can't happen unless I allow it to by perceiving the possibility or probability of it happening consciously or subconsciously.

This is a crucial aspect of how we collectively stop the Archontic agenda reaching its long-planned conclusion. We don't accept that this outcome can happen in the way that I would not accept that the wheelchair would happen. From this mind pattern – if we hold it collectively in place – will come holographic actions and happenings that will stop it. They may appear to be spannering the works of the agenda but they will be manifestations of the mind-set that *this is not going to happen* and *we're not having it*. The *El*-ite want us to believe that what they seek is inevitable and can't be stopped – 'resistance is futile' – and that certainly appears to be the case if you look for five-sense answers to apparently five-sense problems. But if you view the same situation from the perspective of our individual and collective interactions with the quantum field from which 'physical' reality emerges then most certainly it can be stopped because we, yes *we*, can stop creating it. Our conscious and subconscious minds are being bombarded with images and thought patterns to program perception to either desire the transhumanist society or believe this to be inevitable and unstoppable. Predictive and pre-emptive programming is coming from all directions in movies and television programmes (programs) that portray the very society they want. This is designed to make us familiar with it, dilute challenge to such enormous change and make us believe in its inevitability. Such programming then impacts on the way we interact with possibility and probability and collectively humanity creates the very world we have been programmed to believe is inevitable and unstoppable. All the five-sense happenings that appear to be transforming society from human to transhuman are only holographic expressions of what humans are themselves creating by losing control of perception. These happenings are the equivalent of atoms which are only a manifestation of the processes that transform waveform states into holographic states. The solidity of atoms appears essential to the existence of physical reality when atoms have no solidity and there is no 'physical'. World events appear essential to transforming the world when they are only illusory 'atoms' expressing the process of transformation. There are sensors all over the planet constantly measuring changes in Earth's magnetic field and there were massive spikes in that field at the time of 9/11 because of the impact of the global emotional reaction. Everything we think and feel goes into that field as a frequency and humanity has been manipulated hour by hour into negative mental and emotional states to ensure that we make the field, with which we constantly interact, a reflection of this low-frequency negativity. In turn, this field of negativity affects us in a feedback loop of negativity creates negativity creates negativity. This cycle must be broken and we *can* break it.

## Heart of the matter

The power of the heart is central to everything with regard to healing the distortion and reversing the inversion. Usurping the heart (love, infinite insight) with the brain (thought) and the belly (emotion) *is* the distortion and *is* the inversion – or at least a reflection of the Archontic distortion and inversion. I speak not of the heart that beats to electrical rhythm, but the energetic heart or heart vortex/chakra that beats – if allowed – to the rhythm of Infinite Awareness. The two are connected, but the energetic heart is the governor. Distortions in the heart field become distortions in the holographic heart and this is why heart disease is such a human plague. The heart field suffers such widespread imbalance because it is the prime target of the Archontic Web in the seen

and unseen. Everyday language says it all. Those that control and manipulate are heart-*less* or have hearts of stone while humans are broken-hearted, open-hearted or have heavy-hearts, changes of heart or their heart in the right place. The heart vortex is our connection to Infinite Awareness on a level that brain and belly are programmed never to reach (Fig 638). Their daily output of low-frequency thought and emotion are indeed

**Figure 638:** Life is supposed to be fun. The crazier and more absurd it gets the more we need to laugh and break the standing wave.

**Figure 639:** The Archontic hijack replaced love with fear and we need to change it back.

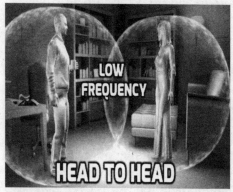

**Figure 640:** Archontic reality.

specifically designed to block such connection (Figs 639 and 640). Those widely used phrases and so many more are telling us where the point of power lies and so, too, the foundation of the human plight. Heartless and hearts of stone refer to Archontic entities whose heart vortex is closed or in such a state of low-vibrational density that stone is a perfect description. This is the heart-devoid psychopath that reflects the extremes of the Archontic distortion. It is not only the language of words that points us to the truth, but the language of body. A movement of the hand to indicate 'I'm thinking' is instinctively directed at the head. But when we say, 'I know', I intuitively *know*, our hand always seeks out the heart. Rarely is the hand even placed on the 'physical' heart, but on the centre of the chest and the heart vortex which interpenetrates all levels of being and out to infinity. When we say, 'I love' in a passionate way we put our hands on the heart and we feel that love through the centre of the chest or the heart vortex. We feel compassion and empathy from the same place – my heart aches and my heart goes out to you. The hijacking of human perception and so human reality has been achieved primarily by closing the heart vortex or chakra. Gnostics knew this and the *Apocryphon of John* says: 'And they closed their hearts, and they hardened themselves through the hardness of the counterfeit spirit ...' The head thinks but the heart knows and 'they' don't want us to *know*. What does your head say? What does your heart say? These are questions that will lead us to oblivion or freedom depending on which we choose to follow. The late and great American comedian Bill Hicks, a very awake man, said:

*This is where we are right now, as a whole. No one is left out of the loop. We are experiencing a reality based on a thin veneer of lies and illusions. A world where greed is our god and wisdom is a sin, where division is key and unity is fantasy, where ego-driven cleverness of the mind is praised, rather than the intelligence of the heart.*

In 1990 amid the explosion of ridicule and abuse I made a conscious decision that whenever my head and heart were in conflict I would go with my heart. Intuition would decide my perceptions and actions and not thought. With most people, head and heart are at war with each other in the sense that thought and intellect are working to block intuitive knowing from impacting on perception and behaviour. If we are at war with ourselves we will be at war with each other and humanity is profoundly at war with itself. This conflict essentially takes the form of heart v head. Heart doesn't want to fight but isolated head loves a punch up. What do you think to do? What do you *feel* to do? Use your head. What does your heart say? To and fro, to and fro and, hey presto, another standing wave. My own experience is that when you go with your intuitive knowing it can lead you into some challenging situations especially in the way that others see you. This must be so when the heart comes from a completely different perception of reality to the five-sense left-brain. The heart is not going to take you where the head would take you, or say and do what the head would say and do. Those observing while still in head awareness are going to see you as strange, even mad or bad. But again, in my own experience there comes a point where the head realises that when you follow your heart it may lead to some challenges but it all works out in the end and not *despite* the challenges but *because* of them. At that moment the war is over, as it has been for me since way back in the 1990s. Heart and head become one and work as one unit. Intuitive knowing and mental processes of thought become synchronised and best mates. When my intuition feels to do this or say that my head says 'Okay, let's go'. This is a freedom that is indescribable. I have highlighted studies by the American Institute of HeartMath which concluded that when electromagnetic connections between heart, brain and central nervous system are in a state of coherence and balance the person enters an expanded sense of awareness.

I have found that to be true and I recommend this state of being to everyone and *everyone* can do this. It is only a choice and a change of perceptual centre (Fig 641). Hate, fear, anxiety, depression and all these low-frequency emotional states break the heart-brain-nervous

**Figure 641:** Infinite reality.

system electromagnetic coherence and thus hold those people in low-frequency reality. Some idiots have called me a 'hate preacher' for their own political reasons and personal agendas but hate is the last thing I do – for my own benefit as well as society in general. I say what I believe and know to be true and what I think needs to be highlighted and debated. A lot of people don't like that. I do not, however, say it with hate in my heart (or rather my belly). I don't hate anyone and once you open your heart you can't hate anyone. The very feeling cannot manifest. You can say things while holding nothing back and stand vehemently and unyieldingly for something without delivering such words and feelings with hate. I don't hate the Archontic force or any expressions of it no matter how 'evil' it may be. What we hate we become as what we fight we become. You don't fight for peace, you peace for peace. If I hate the Archontic distortion I *become* that distortion which is the very origin of hate as well as fear. Hate is the absence of love and the distortion is the absence of love or the ability to feel it. I see everything as one and if I hate others I am hating myself. I will leave the hate to the 'anti-haters' like Zionist extremists, Islamic extremists, Hindu extremists, white supremacist extremists and Provisional Progressives. They should remember, however, that hate closes the heart and places perception firmly in the head. Look around and this explains so much. I have written at some length about progressives and Zionists because of their gathering impact on human society and freedom, but I don't hate them or wish them any harm whatsoever. If they hate me and wish me harm after reading this book I'll send them a mirror.

## The Empathy Revolution

From the heart comes empathy or 'the ability to understand and share the feelings of another'. I don't recommend taking on feelings of other people because there is no point in one replicating the emotional states of another and so doubling the impact. You can't anyway. Only the experiencer can truly feel an emotional state. Everyone else feels it second hand. My version of empathy is to imagine something of how someone must feel or will feel rather than take on those feelings ourselves; and to adjust behaviour in the light of that understanding of how we do or could negatively affect others. Sometimes this is justified when we have to stand up to another's attempted imposition, but mostly it is not. The Archontic distortion seeks to delete empathy for its own ends and so what is required is an Empathy Revolution. Surely the way to proceed is to do the opposite of what the distortion needs for continuing and expanding control. It wants us to hate, so we must love; it wants to fight, so we must be peaceful; it wants us to fear so we must rise above fear; it wants us to resent and so we must forgive; it wants us to lie (including to ourselves) and so we must tell the truth as we perceive the truth to be; it wants us to feel no empathy and so we must do so in abundance. I feel empathy for the Archontic distortion, hybrid *El*-ite, British royalty, the Bushes, the Clintons, Obama, Trump, Mad Dog Mattis, Kissinger, Blair and the tyrants of ISIS and Saudi Arabia. Imagine being them locked away with their padlocked hearts and programmed minds, their hatred, insecurity, fear and bile. What a nightmare to wake up every morning in that state. How sad and pathetic they are behind the self-deceit and bombast they employ to hide themselves from themselves and what must await them when they exit this reality in their desperately low state of frequency? I have empathy for them, but this does not mean we should take their nonsense. Their state of being is their problem to deal with and should not have to be ours. Empathy and love may not hate and may not violently respond, but they don't take shit either. We must remember that. Love in its true sense is not fluffy and naïve. It does what it knows to be right and part of that is refusing any attempt by others to impose their will individually or collectively. Don't mess with love in its Infinite sense. It is not to be messed with because it doesn't take no for an answer when no is the wrong answer. System-servers do what they do to people in war, violence, oppression, finance, politics, science, medicine, media, manipulation and control because they have no capacity for empathy. If they had they wouldn't do what they do. There would be no war, financial deprivation, homelessness, hunger, tyranny, suppression or 'honour killings'. There would be no battles for supremacy by political parties or religions. Empathy and love couldn't go there. Humanity in general *does* have the potential for empathy and we must use it.

This has a practical as well as a philosophical basis. If you have empathy with children and the impact on their minds of smart technology and violent videogames you won't buy them. Empathy and love does not always do what others want but what it knows to be right from an expanded perspective. If you have empathy with the consequences for humanity of where the *El*-ite want to take us you will refuse to contribute in every way you can to this human enslavement and that includes law enforcement, the human version of which is only a temporary transition to Robocop anyway. If those in uniform want to make a difference they had better do it now while they still can. We are dealing with an inversion and so it is hardly brain science to see what we need to do – the opposite of what it wants us to do. It wants and needs to drive us apart and so we must come together. It must have fault-lines of division and so we must remove them. This takes all sides, not one. All faiths, religions and beliefs must stop seeking to achieve pre-eminence or force their beliefs on others especially children. The arrogance of such ambition knows no limits or bounds. Put the fault-lines and their related censorship aside out of respect for the rights of all

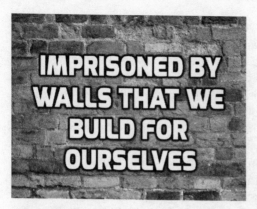

**Figure 642:** We built them and we can take them away.

to believe what they choose to believe, live as they choose to live, think what they choose to think and know as they choose to know, so long as they don't impose that on anyone else. The walls that enslave us are those that we build for ourselves and so we have the power to take them down (Fig 642). I have no problem with what people believe and do. I have a problem with the enforcement of this on others. I am not saying it is easy to look honestly in the mirror and assess how we each contribute mentally, emotionally and in daily acts at home, work and beyond to speed the momentum of Archontic control. But we must do it if we *really* want this to end. Do we want to leave this reality proud that we made every effort to change hate into love, war into peace and ignorance into wisdom? Or do we want to slink away wishing we had not run for cover every time we needed to act in support of the greater good? Martin Luther King said:

> You may be 38 years old, as I happen to be. And one day, some great opportunity stands before you and calls you to stand up for some great principle, some great issue, some great cause. And you refuse to do it because you are afraid ... You refuse to do it because you want to live longer ... You're afraid that you will lose your job, or you are afraid that you will be criticised or that you will lose your popularity, or you're afraid that somebody will stab you, or shoot at you or bomb your house; so you refuse to take the stand.

> Well, you may go on and live until you are 90, but you're just as dead at 38 as you would be at 90. And the cessation of breathing in your life is but the belated announcement of an earlier death of the spirit.

Humanity has to stop running because as Neo was told in *The Matrix*: '... you have been down there, Neo. You know that road. You know exactly where it ends and I know that's not where you want to be.' We cannot stop where that road is leading if we continue to walk it. I will get a lot of abuse for what I have written in this book – I will be called racist, transphobic and so much else and I could have avoided all that by avoiding information that needs to be exposed for the good of humanity as a whole and avoiding questions that urgently need to be asked. But what would be the point? We are either here to do what is necessary to dismantle the control system or we aren't. And if we *are* then we must do everything we can to do that and not run away from situations for our own benefit. Anyone reading this book from cover to cover will see that I don't have a racist cell in my body and I celebrate diversity in all things to celebrate the Infinite Possibility that we are. The abusers will not, however, read the whole book, but pick out sections that relate to their own prejudice and condemn them out of context. This was, and is, always the way. But so be it – those with ears to hear and eyes to see will not be influenced by such manipulated garbage. Bring it on, I say, and let's take the debate out of the fringes and into the public arena. I will not be intimidated into silence by anyone and they better know that before they waste their 'time'. My Spirit is not for sale, will not be bullied and will never diminish. Indeed, it will go on expanding in power and strength. We must insist on the right to speak our truth and never stop speaking that truth no matter what the scale of manufactured opposition. No more fear; no more running away; no more hiding from the Infinite Totality of who and what we are.

## A new you

Give the following a try for the next two months and see what changes. Hold the perception that you are not your name, race, religion, life-story, class, job or income bracket, but a point of attention within Infinite Awareness having those experiences. Hold the perception that you are not your body and what you see in the mirror, but pure awareness, a state of being aware, experiencing this reality *through* what you see in the mirror (in truth see only in your mind). Hold the perception that everyone else that you see, every animal, tree, breath of air and drop of water is also Infinite Awareness. They are part of you and you are part of them. They *are* you and you are them. You are not *part* of the world – you *are* the world (Fig 643). I don't mean that you float through life ignoring the fact that your experience has a body and a name, but to always be consciously aware that they are only temporary vehicles and labels and not *you*. Interact with people in your every-day life from the perspective that they are you and you are them. When responses and decisions are required then instead of reacting with Phantom Self-perception ask: What would Infinite Awareness do? What does my *heart* say? Go with that and see where it leads. You will now be interacting with possibility and probability within a far more expanded band of potential and so your life *must* change. The longer you do this and integrate the new sense of 'I' the more powerful that change will be (Figs 644 and 645). I emphasise again that this does not mean that you take crap from people. It means that you refuse to take it and more importantly refuse to manifest it by interacting with potentiality at levels where crap doesn't happen unless it really needs to; and when it does it

**Figure 643:** Little Me again.

**Figure 644:** How we got into this mess ...
© www.neilhague.com

**Figure 645:** ... How we get out of this mess.
© www.neilhague.com

has a diminished effect on you. Ridicule and abuse that is thrown at me goes straight through without touching the sides like radio stations at different points on the dial. The abusers might one day realise this and stop wasting their lives trying to upset me. They won't and can't unless I let them. You're upset? Well, choose not to be. You say that guy verbally abusing you is an idiot? Yes. Then why does it matter what an idiot thinks of you or says about you? Snowflakes and 'minorities', please consider. I repeat: Being called mad – or anything else – by an idiot is a compliment.

We give abusers and racist bigots power they don't deserve by being upset by them. If we weren't upset or triggered into anger and violence their power and impact would be neutered because a standing wave cannot manifest without two sides. It is like clapping with one hand. You can't. A conspiracy researcher emailed me to say that the way someone was acting was harming my reputation. I had a good laugh at that. What a mind prison this is – 'reputation' or 'the beliefs and opinions that are generally held about someone or something'. Once you care about your 'reputation' you are giving your power away to those who will hold those beliefs and opinions. This means that you will act not in line with what you believe to be right, but always mould and suppress your behaviour on the basis of how it will be viewed in terms of your 'reputation'. You are not living your life any longer but what others think it should be. You have handed your power to those others for as long as you care about 'reputation' instead of doing what you believe to be right irrespective of what others think. My 'reputation' is the beholder's problem, not mine. I have no concern for how others see me. What I do and the motivation behind that is what matters to me. Everything is by comparison irrelevant. Go down the 'reputation' route and your uniqueness is dead in the water. Reputation requires conforming to the beliefs and perceptions of others so they will think well of you. What is that ever going to change when it is just another feedback loop? In terms of Internet trolls, the delete button is your best friend or don't even bother reading what they say because it doesn't matter unless you make it so. Anyone who takes to the Internet with the daily intent of spewing abuse and hurting people is to be pitied not feared or met with anger and resentment. The Archontic psychopathic distortion has their mind in its lair and I wish them all the best in wriggling free. I would just point out that seeking to hurt and upset people is not the way to do it. Another question we might ask: Would Infinite Awareness case less what one aspect of itself said about another? No, it would recognise that not all aspects of itself are always at the same level of awareness and so such things must happen, but we don't need to be upset by that. Our mental and emotional wellbeing is not decided by what happens but how we respond and are affected by what happens. The great news is that we all have the power to decide that.

Another effect of this new self-identity, if my own experience is anything to go by, is that you realise how little actually matters compared with the perceptions of Phantom Self. I have dealt with how people are upset by the behaviour of others towards them, but there is so much more that we think is important and winds us up emotionally that doesn't deserve such a response. My football team lost! *And?* Did anyone die? Was a child abused? Did a war start? No, one group of people kicked a ball of air into a net or ran it over a line in the US more times than another group of people. Er, that's it. This is going to send us into a frenzy of anger and emotion? I am not belittling sport or those who like it – I do – but just putting the whole thing into perspective. Why does it matter if children are a few minutes late for school or go on holiday in term-time because that's when their parents can afford it? Did anyone die? Was a child abused? Did a war start? No, a kid woke up a bit late and another had a great time with their family full of laughter, happiness and joy. What does it matter that someone has a different opinion to us? Did anyone die? Was a child abused? Did a war start? What would Infinite Awareness say when faced with all this? Give the children a detention, fine the parents and ban the speaker? No, it would laugh and shake its head at such irrelevant nonsense. It is worth asking ourselves when our emotions start to stir – does this situation really matter? Will it still matter in our perception of tomorrow or next week? If the answer is no, why should it matter now? Some things do matter, at least in this reality, like happenings I have described in this book that maintain humanity in a state of servitude; but ask that question of most things we find emotionally 'triggering' and they don't matter at all. In fact, things that don't matter often obscure those that do. If people had the same passion and concern for world events and the treatment of children that they do for their football team a lot of things would be different by now or would never have occurred.

## Forest and twigs

Self-identity with Infinite Awareness and not Phantom Self involves a massive expansion of perception from twigs to forest. It is not that twigs or detail doesn't matter, but that we see how everything fits together to form an interconnected whole. Without the perspective of the forest the twigs can never be seen in context. Forest perception means asking the Big Questions – who are we? Where are we? What is reality? Truth Vibrations that I highlighted earlier are a frequency/information change that is prompting ever more people to ask those questions as Archontic density is challenged and frequencies rise for those that are open to them. I have seen this happening all over the world at a quickening pace. Truth Vibrations are bringing to the surface all that has been hidden – as I was told they would in 1990 – including the answers to those questions. So much is going to be known and understood as this process continues and Truth Vibrations impact with increasing power on human perception. Great discoveries are going to be made to support what I have said in this book and we are going to see so obviously in human behaviour those who are awakening to their true self and those sinking deeper into Archontic illusion. Truth Vibrations can only help those who choose to help themselves. The transformation of self-identity and perception means to see the twigs in the context of the forest where everything looks so different. Twig perception says I am British, I am French, I am American, I am Christian, I am Muslim, I am Jewish, I am Hindu, I am black, I am white, I am man, I am woman, I am transgender, I am LGBTTQQFAGPBDSMLHITN. Forest perception sees that these are only labels to describe experience and beyond the illusion there is no British, French, American, Christian, Muslim, Jewish, Hindu, black, white, man, woman, transgender or LGBTTQQFAGPBDSMLHITN. There is only Infinite Awareness experiencing itself – *our*self. We have political wars, race wars and gender wars because humanity has been manipulated to forget this. Infinite Self doesn't war – Phantom Self does.

Forest and twig realties have endless other implications for what we will and won't do, what we can and cannot see. A Phantom Self working in Silicon Valley producing or promoting transhumanist technology will think he or she has got a good, well-paid job, nice house and all that goes with it. Infinite Self says what the hell am I doing contributing to the total mental and emotional enslavement of myself, my children, grandchildren and the rest of humanity? I can't do this – I mustn't do this. The same duel perspectives apply to law enforcement, those who work at Google and Facebook, AI technologists, censors of every kind, journalists, intelligence operatives, the military, politicians and assets of The System in general which means enormous numbers of people worldwide. If you don't like the way the world is going then do everything you can to stop contributing to what you don't like, and that includes celebrities in movies and entertainment that have potentially vast audiences but who stay silent on all these issues even though they can see something of what is happening. What matters more to them – the very survival of humankind or keeping their masters in Hollywood sweet? Transformation of self-identity will bring something else – an essential component to ending this insanity: wisdom. The world may appear on one level to be clever but it is not wise. I have been saying all these years: Cleverness without wisdom is the most destructive force on earth. It is clever to build a nuclear bomb but it is not wise to do so, still less to use it. Wisdom comes from expanding self-identity which means expanding awareness into those realms of Infinite Awareness where wisdom can be found. Wisdom is what will transform the world and the Hidden Hand knows that. This is why they have sought to develop cleverness (left-brain intellect) at the expense of the heart (wisdom). The mystic Osho said:

> No society wants you to become wise: it is against the investment of all societies. If people are wise they cannot be exploited. If they are intelligent they cannot be subjugated, they cannot be forced into a mechanical life, to live like robots. They will assert their individuality. They will have the fragrance of rebellion around them. They will like to live in freedom. Freedom comes with wisdom, intrinsically. They are inseparable, and no society wants people to be free.

> The communist society, the fascist society, the capitalist society, the Hindu, the Mohammedan, the Christian – no society – would like people to use their own intelligence because the moment they start using their intelligence they become dangerous – dangerous to the Establishment, dangerous to the people who are in power, dangerous to the 'haves'; dangerous to all kinds of oppression, exploitation, suppression; dangerous to the churches, dangerous to the states, dangerous to the nations. In fact, a wise man is afire, alive, aflame. But he cannot sell his life, he cannot serve them. He would like rather to die than to be enslaved.

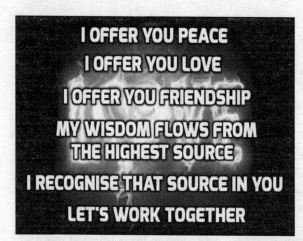

**Figure 646:** Come on gang, let's give it a try.

You may note that I have taken 17 chapters to explain the problem, but only one to deal with the answer. This is not a contradiction or imbalance, but symbolic of a sparkling truth. In those 17 chapters were endless answers that come from understanding the problem but all those answers are expressions of one answer that has been outlined in this final chapter now reaching its close. Humanity is where it is because we have forgotten who we are. We have given our minds away to illusion and fake rulers whose power comes only from the power we hand to them. If the Archontic Reptilian force could walk in and take over then they would have by now. They have a frequency limitation which means that they can only control us when human minds and perceptions are held-fast in the frequency band that they can manipulate. A common theme of ancient and modern accounts of Archontic entities is that they are terrified of humans waking up to our true nature and power because they know their game would then be over. The solution, therefore, is to withdraw from that band by withdrawing from our perception of Phantom Self and entering the high-frequency state of Infinite Self. I am Ethel, John, Mohammed or Zohar becomes I am *All That Is And Ever Can Be* (Fig 646). The problem may seem so complex, but the answer is so simple. Make that transition of self-identity and everything begins to change in your own life and collectively in what we call the world as we manifest a different reality from possibility and probability.

If we don't then humanity is doomed. If we *do* our enslavement is over. Hard choice, isn't it?

# Postscript

The speed of developments in the Hidden Hand agenda can be seen in events that have happened even in the few weeks since this book went into production which support what you have read in the text.

**Figure 1:** 'Anti-fascist'? Yeah, right, sure they are.

**Figure 2:** Self-delusion in need of self-awareness.

**Figure 3:** Mirror images claiming to be different.

Attempts to create civil war – not least in the United States – can be seen in the violence by the *El*-lite-funded and supported Antifa targeting peaceful protests that demand freedom of speech while hiding behind the façade of 'anti-hate' and 'fighting fascism' (Fig 1). They scream hate from hate-filled faces while claiming to be 'anti-hate' (Fig 2). Yes, there are neo-Nazis and white supremacists as there are neo-Nazi black and brown supremacists and neo-Nazi 'anti-fascists' like Antifa; but that is not what this is all about. Antifa are just another expression of the 'Nihilists' said to have been predicted by Albert Pike in 1871 (see also ISIS) which would be unleashed in the run up to World War III. The real target of the Antifa deception is freedom of opinion and expression which the anti-fascist fascists and their 'progressive' sheep-like, child-like mobs are set on deleting on behalf of their Archontic masters (which all but a few of them don't even know exist). They are so bewildered that they are 'attacking the system' by serving its interests while the 'one percent' they claim to so despise cheer them on in collective contempt at their sheer stupidity. The 'Antifa' 'Left' and the extreme 'Right' are mirrors of each other standing on the same ground and sharing the same moronic mentality while claiming to be opposites. They are opposames (Fig 3). The simple and blatant technique is to label anyone defending freedom of speech as a Nazi and so demonise the very concept of freedom of speech itself. Violence at Charlottesville, Virginia, between Antifa and 'neo-Nazis' in August 2017 clearly came from both sides but Donald Trump was lambasted by the media for saying so. How dare he say that neo-Nazis and 'anti-Nazi' neo-Nazis were both responsible? The virtue-signalling British Prime Minister Theresa May said that you cannot compare anti-fascists with fascists, but of course you can when they both behave fascistically. This is not what the script demanded, however, and so facts and the patently obvious have no meaning. Those demanding freedom of speech must be the villains, not those seeking to destroy it, even though confidential Homeland Security and FBI documents are reported to label Antifa as domestic terrorists.

The conflict at Charlottesville was over plans to remove a statue of Confederate general Robert E. Lee who fought for the slavery-supporting south in the American Civil War. This led to demands for statues of historical figures to be removed across America and this is all connected to the deletion of culture and history (which can then be rewritten) that includes the destruction of ancient artefacts, temples, mosques and cities by the United States and ISIS in Syria and Iraq. George Orwell said: 'Who controls the past controls the future. Who controls the present controls the past.' We are looking at another manifestation of the memory hole. History is history – the good and the bad – and to erase history is not to learn from it. The Zionist Southern Poverty Law Center (SPLC) took time out from stashing its millions in offshore accounts (while spending just $61,000 on legal services in 2015) to helpfully produce a map of where 'unacceptable' statues can be found. It has urged people to demand that all Confederate monuments be taken down and even provided a stock letter to be sent to local media in support of the campaign. All you have to do is add your location and local details. These people are so helpful and not at all part of a coordinated and centrally-directed campaign in which they are only a single and immensely well-funded strand. This SPLC 'monument map' was a companion guide to its 'hate map' which names nearly a thousand 'hate groups' in the United States, many of which are clearly not. With shocking hypocrisy the SPLC and its stablemate, the Anti-Defamation League, spend their time and their millions (they are 'non-profit'!) seeking to spread hatred of their targets. The media widely quote the claims of these Zionist-controlled censor groups as if they are credible when they are simply assets of a Web committed to destroying freedom of expression and the right to an opinion. The SPLC, which brands a number of Christian-based organisations 'hate groups' because of alleged 'hateful language and policies regarding the LGBT community', was given a million dollars by those virtue-signallers extraordinaire, actor George Clooney and his wife. Apple pledged two million dollars to the SPLC and the Anti-Defamation League while those other pillars of compassion, equality and freedom, JPMorgan Chase and James Murdoch, son of Rupert, donated millions to the same 'anti-hate' hate organisations. It wasn't coordinated or anything and that would be an outrageous thing to say about such bastions of liberal values. I guess that offshore banks will welcome the SPLC's latest 'good fortune'. The SPLC doesn't seem to like me which always gives me great comfort because the thought of it being otherwise I can hardly bear to contemplate. All opinion that is deemed not acceptable to the book-burning fascism of political correctness is now considered 'hate' as a matter of course to justify, increasingly through violence, its censorship.

The usual suspects, like the Rothschild-created B'nai B'rith ('Sons of the Covenant'), which spawned the hate group, the Anti-Defamation League, tried and failed to have my events cancelled in Canada in late August 2017 in its hysterical campaign worldwide to dictate what people can and cannot say and hear. The event in Toronto survived because the venue was owned by a Christian organisation and Vancouver went ahead according to reports only because the Mayor of Vancouver, Gregor Robertson, refused to bow to pressure when those running the city-owned theatre wanted to cancel in the wake of the ramblings and bleatings of professional victims and censors known as B'nai B'rith. Robertson showed great integrity, respect for freedom of speech and not a little courage given how ruthless and unforgiving these censor-groups are. I guess the efforts by a tiny few to silence me will increase with the publication of this book through the intimidation of the jelly-spined who have contempt for freedom and their own self-respect. But fuck 'em. Upward and onward. On that note, by the way, the following should be added to the List of Shame and Roll Call of the Gutless who have cancelled my events on the say-so of often tiny Zionist hate groups: St Andrews Hall, Norwich; Central Hall, Southampton; the Komedia venue in Bath (so-named no doubt because it's a joke); the Imperial War Museum, Manchester; and the Queen Elizabeth Theatre in Toronto which gave us a lame excuse that we didn't believe only for B'nai B'rith to say in a hate-Icke statement to the Canadian Broadcasting Corporation (CBC) that the reason was their complaint. The Manchester Imperial War Museum, which no doubt hails the sacrifice of millions to protect freedom from the book-burning Nazis, would never see the grotesque irony and contempt for what those soldiers fought for by cancelling my book-launch event there on the lies of those acting like the very same Nazis. In a bizarre development I was, in effect, blamed by an article in *The Times of Israel* for an Internet posting by Yair Netanyahu, son of the Israeli prime minister, which featured George Soros, an 'alien reptile', a stereotypical Jewish figure in a cloak and former Israeli prime minister Ehud Barak (Fig 4). It was a very strange posting and apparently inspired by my work as implied in the report. I am one guy living in a little flat on the Isle of Wight and strictly a member of no organisation – but suddenly I am a global threat?? If I am so crazy, what could be the problem?

**Figure 4:** The bizarre meme posted by Benjamin Netanyahu's son.

Exposing the truth about world events is, of course, the problem and everything else is an effort to demonise me and discredit my information. Mind you, they have been trying for nearly 30 years and the numbers looking at my work worldwide just go on soaring. Keep trying chaps if you want to waste your time, but the world is waking up. Just for the record yet again: Am I using 'Reptilians' as a metaphor for 'Jews'? ABSOLUTELY NOT. When I say Reptilians I mean REPTILIANS. Sorry to disappoint those desperate to censor me, but it is the simple truth.

Censorship of the information that I research and circulate is coming from all angles as Zionist-owned Google/YouTube, Facebook and other Internet corporations exploit their own near-monopolies to block the public from seeing what the Web they represent doesn't want people to see. They *know* they are not conspiracy 'theories' because the inner cores of these corporations are *part* of the conspiracy. Even videos documenting US airstrikes have been blocked by YouTube as the censorship moves incessantly into the mainstream. The next stage will be for Google/YouTube, Facebook, Amazon and their like to dominate television output, too. Anyone who genuinely believes in the protection of freedom and the rolling back of its systematic destruction must support the breaking up of these monopolies and laws to make their politically-motivated algorithmic and direct human censorship illegal (Fig 5). Those who attack people for what they say even when it can be factually supported should also realise – including the mainstream media – that it may be me today but it will be them tomorrow as the

squeeze on freedom goes
on until only Orwell's
nightmare remains (Fig 6).

The truth about the
secret government/Deep
State continues to emerge. I
watched a video
presentation by Kevin
Shipp, a former CIA officer
and anti-terrorism expert,
which confirmed the connections
between the CIA and supposedly
'independent' corporations such
as Lockheed Martin, General
Dynamics, Raytheon, Boeing and
US 'management consulting firm'
Booz Allen Hamilton where
surveillance whistleblower
Edward Snowden once worked.
Shipp described the connections
between these arms

**Figure 5:** If this doesn't happen then goodbye freedom.

**Figure 6:** A definition of fascism.

manufacturing and surveillance companies, the Congressional Arms
Services Committee, extremist warmonger, Senator John McCain, and
former FBI director James Comey who Shipp said was paid millions a
year by Lockheed Martin, the Pentagon's biggest 'defence' (attack)
contractor. He said that Lockheed Martin also gave millions to the
notorious Clinton Foundation while Comey was the FBI chief who
dropped an investigation into the staggering corruption of Hillary
Clinton. Another FBI director, Robert Mueller, who was appointed a
week before 9/11, was selected to 'investigate' alleged Russian
connections to Trump and his associates which are designed to block
any chance of closer US-Russia relations. Shipp said that the CIA
operates as a law unto itself and controls all of the corporations I have
mentioned here and so many more. I also contend that the same applies
(in league with DARPA) to Google, Facebook and other Internet giants
dictating what the public can and cannot see. Lockheed Martin and the
rest of the mass-murder 'defence' network have enjoyed boom times
since the Zionist-created Neocon organisations like the Project for the
New American Century published their list of target countries. As I
write this postscript North Korea is apparently the main threat to the
world (see Iraq, Libya, Syria, Iran, etc., etc., and whoever they target
next). North Korea was on the Neocon list for regime change in
September 2000 and the target countries continue to be demonised and
ticked off. On that note, watch for the concerted demonisation of

**Figure 7:** The real reason for the targeting of North Korea.

Lebanon at some point because that will most certainly come. The prime reason for the focus on North Korea is to open the door to the real goal – China. In fact, both China and Russia. North Korea has a big border with China and a small one with Russia (Fig 7). We are watching a script masquerading as random events.

High-pitched screams were emitting from the global warming cult in the wake of the record-breaking and catastrophic hurricanes that devastated large areas of Texas, especially the city of Houston, Louisiana and across Florida and the Caribbean. We were told this was proof of human-caused climate change when it was nothing of the kind. Jennifer Lawrence, *Hunger Games* actress and classic Hollywood progressive, appeared to connect the hurricanes to the election of Donald Trump and his public scepticism about the climate change narrative. Lawrence said of the hurricanes: 'It's hard not to feel Mother Nature's rage and wrath.' It is harder for me not to look at the now highly advanced and sophisticated weather wars technology discussed by Dr Richard Day in 1969 with the capability to whip up hurricanes to record wind speeds and accurately direct them at will to a target. Manipulation of surrounding pressure systems can hold the storms stationary for long enough to unleash mega-rain in one area – as we saw with the record-breaking deluge from Hurricane Harvey when an estimated 25 *trillion*

**Figure 8:** Whipping up and directing hurricanes is child's play with today's Deep State technology.

gallons of water fell in Texas and Louisiana (Fig 8). The question is as always – who benefits? The answer is anyone who wants chaos, suffering, upheaval, homelessness, despair, mass financial loss and knock-on consequences, and to promote a fear and belief in human-caused 'climate change', once known as 'global warming'. I recommend a visit to Geoengineeringwatch.org and articles/videos such as 'Engineered Climate Cataclysm: Hurricane Harvey' and 'Hurricane Irma Manipulation: Objectives and Agendas'. Another site to research is Weatherwar101.com. Those who also rightly connect solar flares to hurricanes (and earthquakes), like Piers Corbyn at Weatheraction.com, have pointed out that Hurricane Irma and associated storms happened at a time of major solar flare activity.

Some other updates:

- The transgender agenda is going into overdrive with schools banning skirts, gender-neutral shoes made for children, stores no longer having boys and girls labels on clothing and questions being asked about whether there is a need to assign gender at birth. The head teacher of a school banning skirts spoke of the increase in the numbers questioning their gender without even considering the question of why such numbers are soaring. It's all being done by long-planned design and Dr Richard Day must be laughing to himself with undisguised glee given that he told those paediatricians in 1969 that boys and girls were going to be made the same. But, don't worry – there's no conspiracy ... Zzzzzzzzz.
- A major global study discovered widespread microscopic plastic in drinking water and the air worldwide – the very plastic that destroys fertility, changes gender, adds to the synthetic nature of the body and is potentially catastrophic for health.
- DARPA is funding a project by Lockheed Martin (of course) to create a planetary web of surveillance called ... SPIDER. The Segmented Planar Imaging Detector for Electro-optical Reconnaissance (SPIDER) employs miniaturised technology described as 'basically a telescope on a microchip'.
- A two-year study led by Dr J. Leroy Hulsey, Chair of the Civil and Environmental Engineering Department, University of Alaska Fairbanks, concluded that the official explanation of the collapse of World Trade Center Building 7 (which wasn't hit by a plane) is not true. The interim report said the building did not collapse because of fire as the official fairy tale claims. No, it was a controlled demolition as part of the 9/11 Problem-Reaction-Solution to justify what has followed.
- The number of 'no-go areas' in Sweden has increased yet again and more police have been attacked by migrants including one stabbed in the neck. A pro-immigration group reported that Sweden was 'falling out of love' with migrants. As I've said, if the criminality of the few is not addressed then all migrants are judged by their actions.
- Sarah Champion was pressured to resign as Shadow Women's Minister by the UK opposition Labour Party headed by the utter fraud that is Jeremy Corbyn. Her crime was to point out that hundreds of Pakistani men are involved in gangs abusing overwhelmingly white women and girls. If truth

and facts are considered bad for the ballot box they become meaningless – as do the girls and women being abused.

- Google, YouTube and Facebook personnel worked with the Trump election campaign out of San Antonio, Texas, on an Internet-based operation called Project Alamo which is said to have been fundamental to him winning the presidency.

- A petition on a White House website won massive support for its demand that George Soros be declared a terrorist and his assets seized. It won't get anywhere, but it shows how many more people are seeing through the Soros smoke and mirrors.

- The dark-suit bureaucratic tyranny of the European Union continues to do everything possible to block Brexit and the will of the British people. Unelected EU dictators are supported in their war on democracy by 'progressives' and, once again, the 'socialist' bullshitter, Jeremy Corbyn, and war criminal Tony Blair whose obsession with stopping Brexit says everything given that he is a wholly-owned asset of the Web. The more this arrogant, Web-controlled, cross-party, cross-border political class try to stop Brexit the more determined the British people must be to ensure that it happens.

- EU Commission president Jean-Claude Juncker-Drunker has demanded a single president for the entire EU, an EU finance minister with new powers to intervene in the financial affairs of countries with every member state adopting the euro, an EU army and vastly more power across the board centralised in Brussels – exactly what I have said for decades the plan has been all along.

- Amazon slashed prices when it took over the Whole Foods chain on its way to doing to independent health and organic food stores what it has done to independent book stores and publishers. Amazon is another company that must have its gathering monopolies urgently addressed and dismantled.

- Uber, the Silicon Valley global taxi company, had its licence revoked in London over passenger safety issues and for not being a 'fit and proper' operation. It immediately launched an appeal. Uber has a much bigger global agenda than would at first appear which is why it can go on expanding with massive money-no-object losses – the same as Internet giants while they were securing their near-monopolies. Airbnb, the Uber-type Silicon Valley global accommodation company, is a similar story in my opinion.

- Students at the University of Mississippi were left crying, traumatised and distraught by the 'racist act' of someone leaving a banana skin in a tree. It turned out that a student had left it there when he couldn't find a trash bin.

- Israel Prime Minister Benjamin Netanyahu claimed that a '2000-year-old half-shekel coin' found by a young girl in an illegal Israeli settlement proved their historical right to the land of Palestine. It turned out to be a replica souvenir for tourists commonly made at the Israel Museum. *Oops*, but how apt given the nonsense of the rest of the made-up 'history'.

And finally ... I was approached by *The Hollywood Reporter*, an entertainment industry trade publication based in Los Angeles, to comment on the financial success of the fake news websites Yournewswire/Newspunch.com which are doing so much damage to the credibility of the alternative media by making up stories that fact-checker websites delight in so easily debunking. My reference was less than glowing as you would expect. Newspunch.com was at it again in

**Figure 9:** George Soros – his networks are enormous and 'progressives' love his money.

August 2017 when it reported that Ronald Bernard, the Dutch 'entrepreneur and financial whistleblower' I mentioned in this book, had been found dead in Florida after calling police to say his life was in danger. The made-up story was soon clickbaiting its way across the Internet shared by those who think they have 'woken up', but haven't. A few moments of checking revealed that the story – yes, by the non-existent 'Baxter Dmitry' – was actually a manipulated rewrite of a mainstream report about a different man called Ronald Bernard *Fernandez* who had been found dead in Sebring, Florida after getting lost on a nature walk. Fernandez had not rung the police to say his life was in danger, but to say he was lost. The disrespect for the real Ronald Bernard is stunning, although par for the course. Disrespect and contempt for readers and the genuine alternative media would require the Richter scale to be accurately measured. One other point that I find strange is why Facebook appears to be protecting Yournewswire/Newspunch.com and 'editor-in-chief' Sean Adl-Tabatabai from criticism while at the same time using the excuse of 'fake news' to suppress and censor genuine alternative media sites. How does Facebook square that? I was banned from Facebook for three days for posting an article from an external site simply pointing out that Newspunch is Yournewswire under another name. Others have been banned for a month at a time for criticism of Adl-Tabatabai and his website operations. How come? And who benefits?

One final, final thought ... always keep your eyes on Georgie boy (Fig 9).

**For constant daily updates on world events in their true context go to Davidicke.com. There is also a weekly podcast.**

# Bibliography

Alexander, Dr Eben: *Proof of Heaven: A Neurosurgeon's Journey into the Afterlife* (Piakus, 2012).

Antelman, Rabbi Marvin: *To Eliminate the Opiate* (Zahavia, 1974).

Attwood, Shaun: *American Made* (Gadfly Press, 2016).

Bamford, James: *Body of Secrets: Anatomy of the Ultra-Secret National Security Agency* (Anchor Books; Reprint edition, 2002).

Bellamy, Dr Hans Schindler: *Moons, Myths and Men* (University Microfilms International, 1959).

Bergrun, Norman: *Ringmakers of Saturn* (The Pentland Press, 1986).

Carr, William James Guy: *Satan, Prince of this World* (Omni Publications, 1966 – written in 1959).

Cook, Jonathan: *Israel and the Clash of Civilisations: Iraq, Iran and the Plan to Remake the Middle East* (Pluto Press, 2008).

David, Gary A: *Mirrors of Orion* (independently published, 2014).

Deane, Reverend John Bathurst: *Worship of the Serpent* (BiblioBazaar, 2009, first published 1933).

Furedi, Frank: *What's Happened To The University? – A sociological exploration of its infantilisation* (Routledge, 2016).

Greely, Professor Henry: *The End of Sex and the Future of Human Reproduction* (Harvard University Press, 2016).

Hall, Manly P: *Secret Teachings of All Ages* (CreateSpace Reprint edition, 2011). Huxley, Aldous: *Brave New World* (Chatto & Windus, 1932).

Iserbyt, Charlotte: *The Deliberate Dumbing Down of America* (Conscience Press; Revised edition 2011).

Jaynes, Julian: *The Origin of Consciousness in the Breakdown of the Bicameral Mind* (Mariner, 1976).

Kinross, Lord Patrick: Ataturk, *The Rebirth of a Nation* (Quill, 1687).

Knight, Christopher, and Butler, Alan: *Who Built the Moon?* (Watkins, 2007).

Lanza, Robert: *Biocentrism* (Ben Bella, 2010).

Lash, John Lamb: *Not In His Image: Gnostic Vision, Sacred Ecology, and the Future of Belief* (Chelsea Green Publishing, 2006).

Lovelock, James: *The Revenge of Gaia* (Penguin, 2007).

Morjani, Anita: *Dying to be Me* (Hay House, 2012).

Mutwa, Credo: *Song Of The Stars* (Barrytown Ltd, 1995).

O'Brien, Cathy: *Trance-Formation of America* (Reality Marketing, 1995).

Purucker, G de: *Occult Glossary* (Theosophical University, 1996).

Sagan, Carl: *The Dragons of Eden* (Random House, 1977).

Sand, Shlomo: *The Invention of the Jewish People* (Verso, 14 Jun. 2010).

Scholem, Gershon: *The Messianic Idea in Judaism* (Schocken Books, 1994).

Shine, Betty: *Mind to Mind: The Secrets of Your Mind Energy Revealed* (Corgi, 1990).

Taplin, Jonathan: *Move Fast and Break Things: How Facebook, Google and Amazon Cornered Culture and Undermined Democracy* (Little Brown, 2017).

Talbott, David: *The Saturn Myth* (Doubleday, 1980).

Talbott, David and Thornhill, Wallace: *Thunderbolts of the Gods* (Mikamar Publishing, 2005).

Talbot, Michael: *The Holographic Universe* (HarperCollins, 1996).

Taylor, Steve: The Fall: *The Insanity of the Ego in Human History and the Dawning of a New Era* (O Books, 2005).

Tegmark, Max: *Our Mathematical Universe: My Quest for the Ultimate Nature of Reality* (Penguin, 2015).

Temple, Robert: *The Sirius Mystery* (Destiny Books, 1998).

Thornhill, Wallace and Talbott, David: *The Electric Universe* (Mikamar Publishing, 2007).

Tompkins, William Selected by Extraterrestrials: *My life in the top secret world of UFOs, think-tanks and Nordic secretaries* (CreateSpace, 2015).

Turan, D. Mustafa: *The Donmeh Jews* (Cairo, 1989).

Ulfkotte, Udo: *Journalists for Hire: How the CIA Buys the News* (Next Revelation Press, 2017).

Velikovsky, Immanuel: *Worlds in Collision* (Paradigma, 2009).

# Index

# Other work by David Icke

## Phantom Self

The questions are being asked like never before. What is happening in the World? What is 'life' really about? Gathering numbers of people have a sense of unease about the direction of human society without knowing why. Something is happening, but what?

## The Perception Deception

David's most comprehensive book in which a vast spectrum of subjects are weaved together to present the world in a totally new light. 900 pages copiously illustrated and a colour art gallery by Neil Hague. *The Perception Deception* is the most detailed dot-connecting book ever written on these subjects.

## Remember Who You Are

This book breaks massive new ground and brings a world of apparent complexity, mystery and bewilderment into clarity. The key is in the title. We are enslaved because we identify 'self' with our body and our name when these are only vehicles and symbols for that we really are – Infinite Awareness.

## Human Race Get Off Your Knees – The Lion Sleeps No More

A monumental work of more than 650 pages, 355,000 words, 325 images and 32 pages of original artwork by Neil Hague. David's biggest and most comprehensive book introducing the 'Moon Matrix' and providing the fine detail about reality, history and present day events. Highly-acclaimed and a 'must have' for anyone interested in David Icke's work.

## The David Icke Guide to the Global Conspiracy (and how to end it)

A masterpiece of dot-connecting that is both extraordinary and unique. There is a 'wow', indeed many of them, on every page as Icke lifts the veil on the unseen world.

## Infinite Love is the Only Truth, Everything Else is Illusion

Why the 'world' is a virtual-reality game that only exists because we believe it does. Icke explains how we 'live' in a 'holographic internet' in that our brains are connected to a central 'computer' that feeds us the same collective reality that we decode from waveforms and electrical signals into the holographic 3D 'world' that we all think we see.

## Alice in Wonderland and the World Trade Center Disaster – Why the Official Story of 9/11 is a Monumental Lie

A shocking exposé of the Ministries of Mendacity that have told the world the Big Lie about what happened on September 11th, who did it, how and why. This 500 page book reveals the real agenda behind the 9/11 attacks and how they were orchestrated from within the borders of the United States and not from a cave in Afghanistan.

## Tales from the Time Loop

In this 500-page, profusely-illustrated book, David Icke explores in detail the multi-levels of the global conspiracy. He exposes the five-sense level and demolishes the official story of the invasions of Iraq and Afghanistan; he explains the inter-dimensional manipulation; and he shows that what we think is the 'physical world' is all an illusion that only exists in our mind. Without this knowledge, the true nature of the conspiracy cannot be understood.

## The Biggest Secret

An exposé of how the same interbreeding bloodlines have controlled the planet for thousands of years. It includes the horrific background to the British royal family, the murder of Princess Diana, and the true origins of major religions. A blockbuster.

## Children of the Matrix

The companion book of The Biggest Secret that investigates the reptilian and other dimensional connections to the global conspiracy and reveals the world of illusion – the 'Matrix' – that holds the human race in daily slavery.

## ... And The Truth Shall Set You Free (21st century edition)

Icke exposes in more than 500 pages the

interconnecting web that controls the world today. This book focuses on the last 200 years and particularly on what is happening around us today. Another highly acclaimed book, which has been constantly updated. A classic in its field.

## I Am Me, I Am Free

Icke's book of solutions. With humour and powerful insight, he shines a light on the mental and emotional prisons we build for ourselves ... prisons that disconnect us from our true and infinite potential to control our own destiny. A getaway car for the human psyche.

Earlier books by David Icke include *The Robots' Rebellion* (Gill & Macmillan), *Truth Vibrations* (Gill & Macmillan), *Heal the World* (Gill & Macmillan), *Days of Decision* (Jon Carpenter) and *It Doesn't Have To Be Like This* (Green Print). The last two books are out of print and no longer available.

## David Icke Live At Wembley Arena

Filmed at London's Wembley Arena in 2012 – this is the biggest event of its kind ever staged anywhere in the world. Nearly ten hours of cutting edge information researched, compiled and presented by David Icke that you will hear nowhere else in the world put together in this way.

## The Lion Sleeps No More

David Icke marks his 20th year of uncovering astounding secrets and suppressed information with this eight-hour presentation before 2,500 people at London's Brixton Academy in May 2010. David has moved the global cutting edge so many times since his incredible 'awakening' in 1990 and here he does it again – and then some.

## Beyond the Cutting Edge – Exposing the Dreamworld We Believe to be Real

Since his extraordinary 'awakening' in 1990 and 1991, David Icke has been on a journey across the world, and within himself, to find the Big answers to the Big questions: Who are we? Where are we? What are we doing here? Who really controls this world and how and why? In this seven-hour presentation to 2,500 people at the Brixton Academy in London, David addresses all these questions and connects the dots between them to reveal a picture of life on earth that is truly beyond the cutting edge.

## Freedom or Fascism: the time to choose – 3xDVD set

More than 2,000 people from all over Britain and across the world gather at London's famous Brixton Academy to witness an extraordinary event. David Icke weaves together more than 16 years of painstaking research and determined investigation into the Global Conspiracy and the extraordinary 'sting' being perpetrated on an amnesic human race. Icke is the Dot Connector and he uses hundreds of illustrations to reveal the hidden story behind apparently unconnected world events.

## Revelations of a Mother Goddess – DVD

Arizona Wilder was mind-programmed from birth by Josef Mengele, the notorious, 'Angel of Death' in the Nazi concentration camps. In this interview with David Icke, she describes human sacrifice rituals at Glamis Castle and Balmoral in England, in which the Queen, the Queen Mother and other members of the Royal Family sacrificed children in Satanic ceremonies.

## The Reptilian Agenda – DVD

In this memorable, almost six hours of interview, contained in parts one and two, Zulu shaman, Credo Mutwa, reveals his incredible wealth of knowledge about the black magicians of the Illuminati and how they use their knowledge of the occult to control the world. Sit back and savour this wonderful man. You are in the presence of a genius and a giant.

Available at the shop at **Davidicke.com**.

# Right-Brain Thinking In A Left-Brain World

Monnica Sepulveda in California has been a medium for 45 years and specialises in helping people break out of The Program – both their own and that of collective humanity.

Consultations by Skype anywhere in the world.

www.monnica.com

Contact Phone number in the USA: 1-831-688-8884
Email: monnica888@yahoo.com

# Readings by **Carol Clarke**

## Readings are sent via audio file over the internet

*'Carol Clarke is the most consistently accurate psychic
I have come across anywhere in the world and she has
a twenty year record of remarkable accuracy with me
and many other people that I know.'*
David Icke

To contact Carol for a reading,
email: welshseer15@aol.co.uk
or
email: welshseer@hotmail.co.uk